Cultural Anthropology: The Human Challenge

Boston University

Haviland

CENGAGE
Learning

Australia • Brazil • Japan • Korea • Mexico • Singapore • Spain • United Kingdom • United States

Cultural Anthropology:
The Human Challenge

Boston University

Haviland

Executive Editors:
Michele Baird

Maureen Staudt

Michael Stranz

Project Development Manager:
Linda deStefano

Senior Marketing Coordinators:
Sara Mercurio

Lindsay Shapiro

Production/Manufacturing Manager:
Donna M. Brown

PreMedia Services Supervisor:
Rebecca A. Walker

Rights & Permissions Specialist:
Kalina Hintz

Cover Image:
Getty Images*

* Unless otherwise noted, all cover images used by Custom Solutions, a part of Cengage Learning, have been supplied courtesy of Getty Images with the exception of the Earthview cover image, which has been supplied by the National Aeronautics and Space Administration (NASA).

For product information and technology assistance, contact us at
Cengage Learning Customer & Sales Support, 1-800-354-9706

For permission to use material from this text or product,
submit all requests online at **cengage.com/permissions**
Further permissions questions can be emailed to
permissionrequest@cengage.com

ISBN-13: 978-0-495-49333-4

ISBN-10: 0-495-49333-3

Cengage Learning
5191 Natorp Boulevard
Mason, Ohio 45040
USA

Cengage Learning is a leading provider of customized learning solutions with office locations around the globe, including Singapore, the United Kingdom, Australia, Mexico, Brazil, and Japan. Locate your local office at:
international.cengage.com/region

Cengage Learning products are represented in Canada by Nelson Education, Ltd.

For your lifelong learning solutions, visit **custom.cengage.com**

Visit our corporate website at **cengage.com**

Printed in the United States of America

Dedicated to
the World's Indigenous Peoples
in Their Quest for Human Rights

Putting the World in Perspective

Although all humans that we know about are capable of producing accurate sketches of localities and regions with which they are familiar, *cartography* (the craft of mapmaking as we know it today) had its beginnings in 13th century Europe, and its subsequent development is related to the expansion of Europeans to all parts of the globe. From the beginning, there have been two problems with maps: the technical one of how to depict on a two-dimensional, flat surface a three-dimensional spherical object, and the cultural one of whose world-view they reflect. In fact, the two issues are inseparable, for the particular projection one uses inevitably makes a statement about how one views one's own people and their place in the world. Indeed, maps often shape our perception of reality as much as they reflect it.

In cartography, a *projection* refers to the system of intersecting lines (of longitude and latitude) by which part or all of the globe is represented on a flat surface. There are more than 100 different projections in use today, ranging from polar perspectives to interrupted "butterflies" to rectangles to heart shapes. Each projection causes distortion in size, shape, or distance in some way or another. A map that shows the shape of land masses correctly will of necessity misrepresent the size. A map that is accurate along the equator will be deceptive at the poles.

Perhaps no projection has had more influence on the way we see the world than that of Gerhardus Mercator, who devised his map in 1569 as a navigational aid for mariners. So well suited was Mercator's map for this purpose that it continues to be used for navigational charts today. At the same time, the Mercator projection became a standard for depicting land masses, something for which it was never intended. Although an accurate navigational tool, the Mercator projection greatly exaggerates the size of land masses in higher latitudes, giving about two-thirds of the map's surface to the northern hemisphere. Thus, the lands occupied by Europeans and European descendants appear far larger than those of other people. For example, North America (19 million square kilometers) appears almost twice the size of Africa (30 million square kilometers), while Europe is shown as equal in size to South America, which actually has nearly twice the land mass of Europe.

A map developed in 1805 by Karl B. Mollweide was one of the earlier equal-area projections of the world. Equal-area projections portray land masses in correct relative size, but, as a result, distort the shape of continents more than other projections. They most often compress

MERCATOR

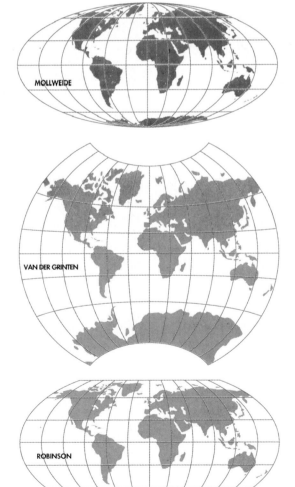

MOLLWEIDE

VAN DER GRINTEN

ROBINSON

and warp lands in the higher latitudes and vertically stretch land masses close to the equator. Other equal-area projections include the Lambert Cylindrical Equal-Area Projection (1772), the Hammer Equal-Area Projection (1892), and the Eckert Equal-Area Projection (1906).

The Van der Grinten Projection (1904) was a compromise aimed at minimizing both the distortions of size in the Mercator and the distortion of shape in equal-area maps such as the Mollweide. Allthough an improvement, the lands of the northern hemisphere are still emphasized at the expense of the southern. For example, in the Van der Grinten, the Commonwealth of Independent States (the former Soviet Union) and Canada are shown at more than twice their relative size.

The Robinson Projection, which was adopted by the National Geographic Society in 1988 to replace the Van der Grinten, is one of the best compromises to date between the distortion of size and shape. Although an improvement over the Van der Grinten, the Robinson projection still depicts lands in the northern latitudes as proportionally larger at the same time that it depicts lands in the lower latitudes (representing most third-world nations) as proportionally smaller. Like European maps before it, the Robinson projection places Europe at the center of the map with the Atlantic Ocean and the Americas to the left, emphasizing the cultural connection between Europe and North America, while neglecting the geographical closeness of northwestern North America to northeast Asia.

The following pages show four maps that each convey quite different "cultural messages." Included among them is the Peters Projection, an equal-area map that has been adopted as the official map of UNESCO (the United Nations Educational, Scientific, and Cultural Organization), and a map made in Japan, showing us how the world looks from the other side.

The Robinson Projection

The map above is based on the Robinson Projection, which is used today by the National Geographic Society and Rand McNally. Although the Robinson Projection distorts the relative size of land masses, it does so to a much lesser degree than most other projections. Still, it places Europe at the center of the map. This particular view of the world has been used to identify the location of many of the cultures discussed in this text.

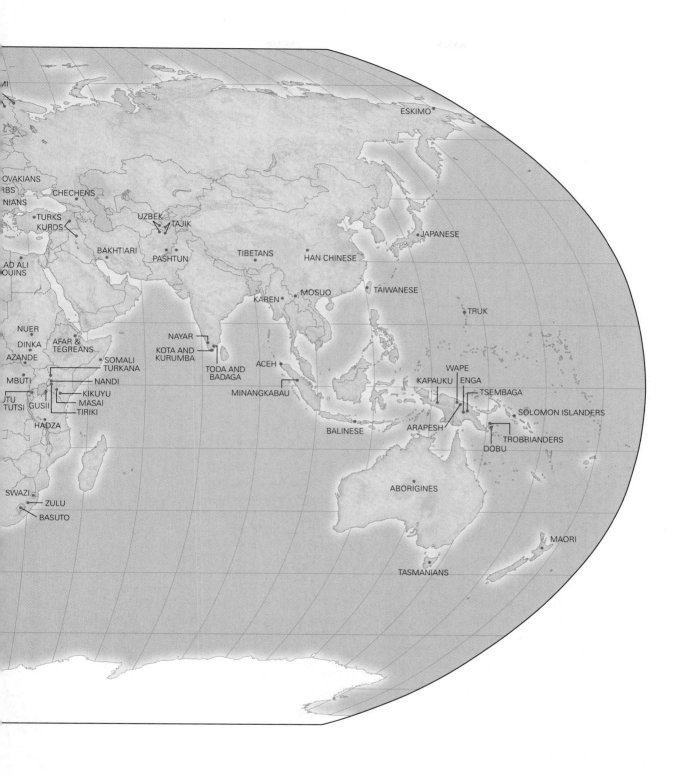

ESKIMO

OVAKIANS
RBS
NIANS
CHECHENS
TURKS
KURDS
UZBEK
TAJIK
JAPANESE
BAKHTIARI
PASHTUN
TIBETANS
HAN CHINESE
AD ALI
OUINS
TAIWANESE
MOSUO
TRUK
NUER
KAREN
NAYAR
AFAR &
TEGREANS
DINKA
KOTA AND
KURUMBA
SOMALI
WAPE
AZANDE
TURKANA
ACEH
KAPAUKU
ENGA
TODA AND
BADAGA
TSEMBAGA
MBUTI
NANDI
MINANGKABAU
SOLOMON ISLANDERS
KIKUYU
JTU
MASAI
ARAPESH
TUTSI
GUSII
TROBRIANDERS
TIRIKI
BALINESE
DOBU
HADZA

SWAZI
ZULU
ABORIGINES
BASUTO

MAORI

TASMANIANS

vii

The Peters Projection

The map above is based on the Peters Projection, which has been adopted as the official map of UNESCO. While it distorts the shape of continents (countries near the equator are vertically elongated by a ratio of two to one), the Peters Projection does show all continents according to their correct relative size. Though Europe is still at the center, it is not shown as larger and more extensive than the third world.

Japanese Map

Not all maps place Europe at the center of the world, as this Japanese map illustrates. Besides reflecting the importance the Japanese attach to themselves in the world, this map has the virtue of showing the geographic proximity of North America to Asia, a fact easily overlooked when maps place Europe at their center.

GREENLAND

UNITED
STATES

CANADA

UNITED STATES

MEXICO

THE
BAHAMAS

CUBA

HAITI
DOMINICAN REPUBLIC

JAMAICA

BELIZE
GUATEMALA
EL SALVADOR
HONDURAS
COSTA RICA
PANAMA
ECUADOR

NICARAGUA

VENEZUELA

FRENCH GUIANA

COLOMBIA

GUYANA
SURINAM

BRAZIL

PERU

BOLIVIA

PARAGUAY

CHILE

ARGENTINA

URUGUAY

NEW ZEALAND

ANTARCTICA

A NEW WORLD of Understanding

Ever since maps were first drawn, certain countries have been located at the top, others below. Since "on top," "over," and "above" are equated with superiority, while "down there," "beneath," and "below" imply the reverse, these wholly arbitrary placements, over the years, have led to misconceptions and misjudgments.

This Turnabout Map of the Americas serves to correct the imbalance. It focuses attention in new directions toward areas of exploding populations, energies and potentialities. It is geographically correct. Only the perspective has been changed.

The Turnabout Map

The way maps may reflect (and influence) our thinking is exemplified by the "Turnabout Map," which places the South Pole at the top and the North Pole at the bottom. Words and phrases such as "on top," "over," and "above" tend to be equated by some people with superiority. Turning things upside down may cause us to rethink the way North Americans regard themselves in relation to the people of Central America. © 1982 by Jesse Levine Turnabout Map™—Dist. by Laguna Sales, Inc., 7040 Via Valverde, San Jose, CA 95135

Brief Contents

Contents

CHAPTER 4   Becoming Human: The Origin and Diversity of Our Species   68

CHAPTER 5   Language and Communication   98

Features Contents

Preface

It is common for students to enter an introductory cultural anthropology class intrigued by the general subject but with little more than a vague sense of what it is all about. Thus, the first and most obvious task of our text is to provide a thorough introduction to the discipline—its foundations as a domain of knowledge and its major insights into the rich diversity of humans as a culture-making species. In doing this, we draw from the research and ideas of a number of traditions of anthropological thought, exposing students to a mix of theoretical perspectives and methodologies. Such inclusiveness reflects our conviction that different approaches offer distinctly important insights about human biology, behavior, and beliefs.

If most students start out with only a vague sense of what anthropology is, they often have less clear—and potentially more problematic—views of the superiority of their own culture and its place in the world. A secondary task for this text, then, is to prod students to appreciate the rich complexity and breadth of human behavior. Along with this is the task of helping them understand why there are so many differences and similarities in the human condition, past and present. Debates regarding globalization and notions of progress, the "naturalness" of the mother/father/child(ren) nuclear family, new genetic technologies, and how gender roles relate to biological variation all benefit greatly from the fresh and often fascinating insights gained through anthropology. This probing aspect of our discipline is perhaps the most valuable gift we can pass on to those who take our classes. If we, as teachers (and textbook authors), do our jobs well, students will gain a wider and more open-minded outlook on the world and a critical but constructive perspective on their own cultures. To paraphrase the poet T. S. Eliot: After all our explorations, they will come home and know the place for the first time.

More than ever before, students need anthropological tools to step out of culture-bound ways of thinking and acting so that they can gain tolerance and respect for other ways of life. Thus, we have written this text, in large part, as a tool to help students make sense of our increasingly complex world and to navigate through its interrelated biological and cultural networks with knowledge and skill, whatever professional path they take. We see it as a guide for people entering the often bewildering maze of global crossroads in the 21st century.

ORGANIZATION OF THE BOOK
Unifying Themes

In our own teaching, we have come to recognize the value of marking out themes that help students see the big picture as they grapple with the great array of concepts and information encountered in the study of human beings. In *Cultural Anthropology* we employ a trio of unifying themes that tie the book together to prevent students from feeling lost.

1. We present anthropology as a study of humankind's responses through time to the fundamental **challenges of survival.** Each chapter is framed by this theme, opening with a Challenge Issue paragraph and photograph and ending with Questions for Reflection tied to that particular challenge.

2. We emphasize the integration of human culture and biology in the steps humans take to meet these challenges. This **Biocultural Connection** theme appears throughout the text—as a thread in the main narrative and in a boxed feature that highlights this connection with a topical example for each chapter.

3. We track the emergence of **globalization and its disparate impact on various peoples and cultures around the world.** While European colonization was a global force for centuries, leaving a significant, often devastating, footprint on the affected peoples in Asia, Africa, and the Americas, decolonization began about 200 years ago and became a worldwide wave in the mid-1900s. Since the 1960s, however, political-economic hegemony has taken a new and fast-paced form, namely globalization (in many ways a concept that expands or builds on imperialism). Attention to both forms of global domination—colonialism and globalization—runs through *Cultural Anthropology,* culminating in the final chapter where we apply the concept of structural power to globalization, discussing it in terms of hard and soft power and linking it to structural violence.

PEDAGOGY

Cultural Anthropology features a range of learning aids, in addition to the three unifying themes described above. Each pedagogical piece plays an important role in the learning process—from clarifying and enlivening the material to revealing relevancy and aiding recall.

Accessible Language and a Cross-Cultural Voice

What could be more basic to pedagogy than clear communication? In addition to our standing as professional anthropologists, all four coauthors have made a specialty of speaking to audiences outside of our profession. Using that experience in the writing of this text, we consciously cut through a lot of unnecessary jargon to speak directly to students. Manuscript reviewers recognized this, noting that even the most difficult concepts are presented in prose that is straightforward and easy for today's first- and second- year college students to understand, without feeling they are being "spoken down to." Where technical terms are necessary, they appear in bold-faced type, are carefully defined in the narrative, and are defined again in the running glossary in simple, clear language, as well as appearing in the glossary at the end of the book.

Accessibility involves not only clear writing but also an engaging voice or style. The voice of *Cultural Anthropology* is distinct among introductory texts in the discipline, for it has been written from a cross-cultural perspective. This means we strove to avoid the typical Western "we–they" voice in favor of a more inclusive one that will resonate with both Western and non-Western students and professors. Moreover, the book highlights the theories and work of anthropologists from all over the world. Finally, its cultural examples come from industrial and postindustrial societies as well as nonindustral ones.

Challenge Issues and Questions for Reflection

Each chapter opens with a Challenge Issue and accompanying photograph, which together carry forward the book's theme of humankind's responses through time to the fundamental challenges of survival within the context of the particular chapter. And each chapter closes with Questions for Reflection relating back to the Challenge Issue presented on the chapter's opening page. These questions are designed to stimulate and deepen thought, trigger class discussion, and link the material to the students' own lives.

Chapter Preview

In every chapter the page facing the opening Challenge Issue and photo presents three or four preview questions that mark out the key issues covered in the chapter. Beyond orienting students to the chapter contents, these questions provide study points useful when preparing for exams.

Barrel Model of Culture

Every culture, past and present, is an integrated and dynamic system of adaptation that responds to a combination of internal and external factors. This is illustrated by a pedagogical device we refer to as the "barrel model" of culture. Depicted in a simple, but telling, drawing (Figure 2.2), the barrel model shows the interrelatedness of social, ideological, and economic factors within a cultural system along with outside influences of environment, climate, and other societies. Throughout the book examples are linked back to this point.

Visuals

Maintaining a key pedagogical tradition of the Haviland et al. textbooks, *Cultural Anthropology is* richly illustrated with a notable array of maps, photographs, and figures. This is important since humans—like all primates—are visually oriented, and a well-chosen image may serve to "fix" key information in a student's mind. Unlike some competing texts, all of our visuals are in color, enhancing their appeal and impact.

Photographs

This edition features a hard-sought collection of new and truly compelling photographs—with a greater number of them sized larger to increase their effectiveness. With some of the images, we provide longer-than-usual captions, tying concepts directly to visuals in a way that helps students to see the rich photographic content and then hang on to the information. We have retained our popular "Visual Counterpoint" feature—side-by-side photos to compare and contrast cultures from around the world.

Maps

In addition to our various map features—"Putting the World in Perspective" map series, locator maps, and distribution maps providing overviews of key issues such as pollution and energy consumption—this edition introduces a new and highly engaging map feature: Globalscape. Appearing in six chapters, the Globalscape feature charts the global flow of people, goods, and services, as well as pollutants and pathogens. Showing how the world is interconnected through human activity, they contribute to the text's globalization theme with topics geared toward student interests. Each one ends with a "Global Twister"—a question that prods students to think critically about globalization.

The Globalscape features in this edition are as follows: "A Global Body Shop?," which investigates human organ trafficking around the world; "Operator, Where Are You?," which offers a short story on how outsourcing impacts travelers; "How Much for a Red Delicious?," which follows Jamaican migrant laborers working in Maine and Florida; "Soccer Diplomacy?," which traces the life of an Ivory Coast soccer star and the numerous countries in which he has trained and played; "Do Coffins Fly?," which highlights the work of a Ghanaian custom coffin maker gaining global recognition as art; and *"Probo Koala's* Dirty Secrets," which investigates the dumping of First World toxic waste in Third World countries.

Integrated Gender Coverage

In contrast to many introductory texts, *Cultural Anthropology* integrates rather than separates gender coverage. Thus, material on gender-related issues is included in *every* chapter. The result of this approach is a measure of gender-related material that far exceeds the single chapter that most books contain.

Why is the gender-related material integrated? Because concepts and issues surrounding gender are almost always too complicated to remove from their context. Moreover, spreading this material through all of the chapters has a pedagogical purpose, for it emphasizes how considerations of gender enter into virtually everything people do. Further, integration of gender into the book's "biological" chapter allows students to grasp the analytic distinction between sex and gender, illustrating the subtle influence of gender norms on biological theories about sex difference. Gender-related material ranges from discussions of gender roles in evolutionary discourse and studies of nonhuman primates, to intersexuality, homosexual identity, same-sex marriage, and female genital mutilation. Through a steady drumbeat of such coverage, this edition avoids ghettoizing gender to a single chapter that is preceded and followed by resounding silence.

Glossary

The running glossary is designed to catch the student's eye, reinforcing the meaning of each newly introduced term. It is also useful for chapter review, as the student may readily isolate the new terms from those introduced in earlier chapters. A complete alphabetical glossary is also included at the back of the book. In the glossaries each term is defined in clear, understandable language. As a result, less class time is required for going over terms, leaving instructors free to pursue other matters of interest.

Special Boxed Features

Our text includes four types of special boxed features: Biocultural Connections, Original Studies, Anthropology Applied, and Anthropologists of Note. Every chapter contains three of the features: a Biocultural Connection, along with two of the others. These are carefully placed and introduced within the main narrative to alert students to their importance and relevance—and to ensure that they will be read.

Biocultural Connections

Now appearing in every chapter, this signature feature of the Haviland et al. textbooks illustrates how cultural and biological processes interact to shape human biology, beliefs, and behavior. It reflects the integrated biocultural approach central to the field of anthropology today. The sixteen Biocultural Connection titles hint at the intriguing array of topics covered by this feature: "The Anthropology of Organ Transplantation"; "Adult Human Stature and the Effects of Culture: An Archaeological Example"; "Pig Lovers and Pig Haters" by Marvin Harris; "Paleolithic Prescriptions for the Diseases of Civilization"; "The Biology of Human Speech"; "A Cross-Cultural Perspective on Psychosomatic Symptoms and Mental Health"; "Surviving in the Andes: Aymara Adaptation to High Altitude"; "Cacao: The Love Bean in the Money Tree"; "Marriage Prohibitions in the United States" by Martin Ottenheimer; "Maori Origins: Ancestral Genes and Mythical Canoes"; "African Burial Ground Project" by Michael Blakey; "Sex, Gender, and Human Violence"; "Change Your Karma and Change Your Sex?" by Hillary Crane; "Peyote Art: Divine Visions among the Huichol"; "Studying the Emergence of New Diseases"; and "Toxic Breast Milk Threatens Arctic Culture."

Original Studies

Written expressly for this text, or selected from ethnographies and other original works by anthropologists, these studies present concrete examples that bring specific concepts to life and convey the passion of the authors. Each study sheds additional light on an important anthropological concept or subject area found in the chapter where it appears. Notably, these boxes are carefully integrated within the flow of the chapter narrative, signaling students that their content is not extraneous or supplemental. Appearing in twelve chapters, Original Studies cover a wide range of topics, evident from their titles: "Fighting HIV/AIDS in Africa: Traditional Healers on the Front Line" by Suzanne Leclerc-Madlala; "The Importance of Trobriand Women" by Annette B. Weiner; "Reconciliation and Its Cultural Modification in Primates" by Frans B. M. de Waal; "Language and the Intellectual Abilities of Orangutans" by H. Lyn White Miles; "The Blessed Curse" by R. K. Williamson; "Gardens of the Mekranoti Kayapo" by Dennis Werner; "Arranging Marriage in India" by Serena Nanda; "Honor Killings in the Netherlands" by Clementine van Eck; "The Jewish *Eruv*: Symbolic Place in Public Space" by Susan Lees; "Healing among the Ju/'hoansi of the Kalahari" by Marjorie Shostak; "The Modern Tattoo Community" by Margo DeMello; and "Standardizing the Body: The Question of Choice" by Laura Nader.

Anthropology Applied

These succinct and compelling profiles illustrate anthropology's wide-ranging relevance in today's world and give students a glimpse into a variety of the careers anthropologists enjoy. Featured in ten chapters, they include: "Forensic Anthropology: Voices for the Dead"; "New Houses for Apache Indians" by George S. Esber; "Language Renewal among the Northern Ute" by William Leap; "Agricultural Development and the Anthropologist"; "Anthropology in the Corporate Jungle" by Karen Stephenson; "Resolving a Native American Tribal Membership Dispute"; "Anthropologists and Social Impact Assessment"; "Dispute Resolution and the Anthropologist"; "Reconciling Modern Medicine with Traditional Beliefs in Swaziland" by Edward C. Green; and "Development Anthropology and Dams."

Anthropologists of Note

Profiling pioneering and contemporary anthropologists from many corners of the world, this feature puts the work of noted anthropologists in historical perspective and draws attention to the international nature of the discipline in terms of both subject matter and practitioners. This edition highlights fourteen distinct anthropologists from all four fields of the discipline: Arjun Appadurai, Gregory Bateson, Ruth Fulton Benedict, Franz Boas, Jane Goodall, Kinji Imanishi, Jomo Kenyatta, Frederica de Laguna, Claude Lévi-Strauss, Bronislaw Malinowski, Margaret Mead, Laura Nader, Matilda Coxe Stevenson, and Eric R. Wolf.

TWELFTH EDITION CHANGES AND CHAPTER HIGHLIGHTS

The pedagogical features described above strengthen each of the sixteen chapters in *Cultural Anthropology*, serving as threads that tie the text together and help students feel the holistic nature of the discipline. In addition, the engagingly presented concepts themselves provide students with a solid foundation in the principles and practices of anthropology today.

The text in hand has a significantly different feel to it than previous editions. Although still rich and varied in content, it is less "busy," for the narrative has been streamlined, the boxed features are more fluidly incorporated, and the photographs are fewer in number but greater in size and quality.

All chapters have been revised extensively—with the word count streamlined by about 15 percent, the data and examples updated, and the chapter openers refreshed with new, up-to-date Challenge Issues and related photographs. In addition to these overall changes, each chapter has undergone specific modifications and additions. The inventory presented below provides brief previews of the chapter contents and changes in this edition.

Chapter 1: The Essence of Anthropology

The book's opening chapter introduces students to the holistic discipline of anthropology, the unique focus of each of its four fields, and the common philosophical and methodological approaches they share. Touching briefly on fieldwork and the comparative method, along with ethical issues and examples of applied anthropology in all four fields, this chapter provides a foundation for an entirely new field methods chapter that looks at the history, methods, and theory of doing ethnographic fieldwork. An Anthropology Applied box on forensic anthropology and archaeology illustrates the importance of forensics in the investigations of international human rights abuses. Two boxed features help illustrate the interconnection of biology and culture in the human experience: Suzanne Leclerc-Madlala's compelling Original Study, "Fighting HIV/AIDS in Africa: Traditional Healers on the Front Line," and a Biocultural Connection highlighting Margaret Lock's cross-cultural research on human organ transplantation. The impact of the Biocultural Connection is strengthened by a new Globalscape, which profiles a particular organ donor. The chapter closes with a section titled "Anthropology and Globalization," in which we show the relevance of anthropology to several of today's most significant social and political issues.

Chapter 2: Characteristics of Culture

Here we address anthropology's core concept of culture, exploring the term and its significance for human individuals and societies. Elaborating on culture as the medium through which humans handle the problems of existence, we mark out its characteristics as something that is learned, shared, based on symbols, integrated, and dynamic. This chapter includes a new and more elaborate treatment of ethnocentrism and cultural relativism, as well as discussions on culture and adaptation; the functions of culture; culture, society, and the individual; and culture and change. Our ethnographic narrative on the Amish has been significantly revised, brought forward to the present. The "Functions of Culture" section has also undergone a thorough reworking and now includes a new ethnographic sketch of cremation rituals in Bali. Special boxes include a new Biocultural Connection on "Adult Human Stature and the Effects of Culture," George Esber's revised Anthropology Applied box, "New Houses for Apache Indians," and an Anthropologists of Note box on Bronislaw Malinowski. Also in this chapter is an original illustration we call the "barrel model," which conveys the integrative and dynamic nature of culture and introduces the concepts of infrastructure/social structure/superstructure.

Theory material that appeared in the last edition has been moved to the new chapter on ethnographic fieldwork.

Chapter 3: Ethnographic Fieldwork: Its History, Methods, and Theories

This entirely new chapter takes a unique approach to discussing ethnographic research. It begins with an historical overview on the subject—from the colonial era and salvage ethnography to acculturation studies, advocacy anthropology, and multi-sited ethnography in the era of globalization. The work of numerous anthropologists, past and present, are used to illustrate this historical journey. The chapter continues with an overview of research methods—marking out what is involved in choosing a research site and question and how one goes about doing preparatory research and participant observation. This section also covers ethnographic tools and aids, data gathering methods, fieldwork challenges, issues of subjectivity, and the creation of an ethnography in written, film, or digital formats. The third section of this chapter offers an overview of anthropology's theoretical perspectives, contrasts doctrine and theory, discusses the comparative method and the Human Relations Area Files, and explores the moral dilemmas and ethical responsibilities encountered in anthropological research. Special features include a new Biocultural Connection, "Pig Lovers and Pig Haters," adapted from Marvin Harris' work, Annette Weiner's Original Study, "The Importance of Trobriand Women," and an Anthropologists of Note box that profiles the pioneering visual anthropology work of Gregory Bateson and Margaret Mead

Chapter 4: Becoming Human: The Origin and Diversity of Our Species

This chapter plays a key role in our effort to convey biology's role in culture, establishing mammalian primate biology as a vital part of being human and presenting it as a continuum rather than humans versus animals. The chapter bypasses the terms *hominid* and *hominin* so that students will not get lost in the disputes where scientists employ alternate taxonomies. Under the heading "Human Biological Variation and the Problem of Race," we discuss why the concept of race is not useful for studying human biological variation, presenting a historical overview on the creation of false racial categories and marking out the role of anthropology in criticizing the notion of biological race. Subheads in this section explore "Race as a Social Construct" and "Skin Color: A Case Study in Adaptation." Special features include a Biocultural Connection, "Paleolithic Prescriptions for the Diseases of Civilization"; Frans de Waal's Original Study, "Reconciliation and Its Cultural Modification in Primates"; and Anthropologists of Note profiles on Jane Goodall and Kinji Imanishi.

Chapter 5: Language and Communication

This chapter, trimmed and rearranged to flow more smoothly, investigates the nature of language and the three branches of linguistic anthropology—descriptive linguistics, historical linguistics, and the study of language in its social and cultural settings (ethnolinguistics and sociolinguistics). The latter features new discussions of linguistic relativity and linguistic determinism. Also found here are sections on paralanguage and tonal languages, as well as language and gender and body language (proxemics and kinesics)—including new material on the impact of electronic media on language and communication worldwide. The historical sketch about writing takes readers from traditional speech performatives and memory devices to Egyptian hieroglyphics to the conception and spread of the alphabet to the 2003 to 2012 Literacy Decade established by the United Nations. An overhauled section on language loss and revival includes the latest data on the digital divide and its impact on ethnic minority languages—plus a new chart showing Internet language populations. Special features include a revised Biocultural Connection box, "The Biology of Human Speech," a lively new abridged version of H. Lyn White Miles' Original Study, "Language and the Intellectual Abilities of Orangutans," and William Leap's updated telling of his applied anthropology project, "Language Renewal among the Northern Ute." Finally, the chapter includes a new Globalscape on outsourcing.

Chapter 6: Social Identity, Personality, and Gender

Looking at individual identity within a sociocultural context, this chapter surveys a range of issues: the concept of "self," enculturation and the behavioral environment, social identity through personal naming, the development of personality, the concepts of group and modal personality, and the idea of national character. New ethnographic examples include a Navajo naming and First Laugh Ceremony in the section on naming, and a description of *sadhus* (ascetic Hindu monks) in the section "Normal and Abnormal Personality in Social Context." A substantial section titled "Alternative Gender Models from a Cross-Cultural Perspective" provides a thought-provoking historical overview of intersexuality, transsexuality, and transgendering, including current statistics on the incidence of intersexuality worldwide. Boxed features include the Biocultural Connection "A Cross-Cultural Perspective on Psychosomatic Symptoms and Mental Health," a shortened version of R. K. Williamson's stirring Original Study on intersexuality, "The Blessed Curse," and an Anthropologists of Note on Margaret Mead and Ruth Fulton Benedict.

Chapter 7: Patterns of Subsistence

Here we investigate the various ways humans meet their basic needs and how societies adapt through culture to the environment. We begin with a discussion of adaptation, followed by profiles on modes of subsistence in which we look at food-foraging and food-producing societies—pastoralism, crop cultivation, and industrialization. The chapter's boxed features include a new Biocultural Connection on "Surviving in the Andes: Aymara Adaptation to High Altitude," along with a trimmed version of Dennis Werner's Original Study "Gardens of the Mekranoti Kayapo" (which analyzes the productivity of a slash-and-burn gardening community in the central Amazon basin in Brazil), and an Anthropology Applied piece "Agricultural Development and the Anthropologist" (about a rural development organization that revives ancient farming practices). Also in this chapter is a new Globalscape, "How Much for a Red Delicious," profiling migrant laborers from Jamaica.

Chapter 8: Economic Systems

In this chapter covering the production, distribution, and consumption of goods, we delve into such matters as the control of resources (natural, technological, labor) and types of labor division (gender, age, cooperative labor, craft specialization). A section on distribution and exchange defines various forms of reciprocity (with a detailed and illustrated description of the Kula ring and a new discussion of silent trade), along with redistribution and market exchange. The discussion on leveling mechanisms has been revised and expanded, with new narratives on cargos and the potlatch (including a rare and remarkable contemporary potlatch photograph). The section on market exchange includes a new narrative on the invention and spread of money, including a new Biocultural Connection titled "Cacao: The Love Bean in the Money Tree." Other boxed features are Karen Stephenson's "Anthropology in the Corporate Jungle" and an Anthropologist of Note about independent Kenya's first president, Jomo Kenyatta, who was academically trained in anthropology and took the concept of cooperation from the local level to the state.

Chapter 9: Sex, Marriage, and Family

Exploring the close interconnection among sexual reproductive practices, marriage, family, and household, we discuss the household as the basic building block in a culture's social structure, the center where child rearing, as well as shelter, economic production, consumption, and inheritance are commonly organized. Particulars addressed in this chapter include the incest taboo, endogamy and exogamy, dowry and bride-price, cousin marriage, same-sex marriage, divorce, residence patterns, and non-family households. Updated definitions of marriage, family, nuclear family, and extended family encompass current real-life situations around the world, as does a discussion of how new reproductive technologies (NRTs) are impacting the ways humans think about and form families. Boxed features include a shortened version of Serena Nanda's engaging Original Study, "Arranging Marriage in India"; Martin Ottenheimer's Biocultural Connection, "Marriage Prohibitions in the United States"; and an Anthropologist of Note box on Claude Lévi-Strauss.

Chapter 10: Kinship and Descent

This chapter marks out the various forms of descent groups and the roles descent plays as an integrated feature in a cultural system. Details and examples are presented concerning lineages, clans, phratries, and moieties (highlighting Hopi Indian matriclans and Scottish highland patriclans, among others), followed by illustrated examples of a representative range of kinship systems and their kinship terminologies.

There is a new discussion on diasporic communities in today's globalized world. New ethnographic examples include the Han Chinese, Maori of New Zealand, and Canela Indians of Brazil. In addition to the revised Anthropology Applied box that relays the role descent played in "Resolving a Native American Tribal Membership Dispute," this chapter includes two new boxed features: Clementine van Eck's compelling Original Study about Turkish immigrants, "Honor Killings in the Netherlands," and a Biocultural Connection, "Maori Origins: Ancestral Genes and Mythical Canoes," which shows how Maori oral traditions about their origins fit quite well with recent genetic research.

Chapter 11: Grouping by Gender, Age, Common Interest, and Class

This much refined chapter includes discussions of grouping by gender, age, common interest, and class or social rank. The section on age grouping features revised and new ethnographic material from the Mundurucu of Brazil, and the Tiriki and Maasai of East Africa. Common-interest group examples range from the Shriners to the

Crips to the Jewish diaspora. A revised narrative on caste explores its historical context and role in India's Hindu culture and also presents examples of castelike situations from other parts of the world. A new "wealth inequality" chart provides a clear visual of wealth distribution in the United States. Boxed features include a Biocultural Connection box, "African Burial Ground Project" (the archaeological dig in New York City that revealed the physical wear and tear of an entire community brought on by the social institution of slavery); a fully reworked Applied Anthropology piece "Anthropologists and Social Impact Assessment"; and Susan Lees' new Original Study, "The Jewish *Eruv*: Symbolic Place in Public Space." Also new to this chapter is a Globalscape tracing the life of an Ivory Coast soccer star and the numerous countries in which he has trained and played.

Chapter 12: Politics, Power, and Violence

Looking at a range of uncentralized and centralized political systems—from kin-ordered bands and tribes, to chiefdoms and states—this chapter explores the question of power, the intersection of politics and religion, and issues of political leadership and gender. Discussing the maintenance of order, we look at internalized and externalized controls (including a new discussion on gossip's role in curbing socially unacceptable behavior), along with social control through witchcraft and through law. We mark the functions of law and the ways different societies deal with crime, including new sentencing laws in Canada based on traditional Native American restorative justice techniques such as the Talking Circle. Then, shifting our focus from maintaining order *within* a society to political organization and *external* affairs, we discuss warfare and present a 5,000-year overview of armed conflicts among humans right up to today. Special features in this chapter include a Biocultural Connection box, "Sex, Gender, and Human Violence," an Anthropology Applied box, "Dispute Resolution and the Anthropologist," and an Anthropologist of Note box profiling Laura Nader.

Chapter 13: Spirituality, Religion, and the Supernatural

Opening with a description of the anthropological approach to religion and noting current distinctions between religion and spirituality, this chapter goes on to discuss beliefs concerning supernatural beings and forces (gods and goddesses, ancestral spirits, animism, and animatism), religious specialists (priests and priestesses, as well as shamans), and rituals and ceremonies (rites of passage and rites of intensification). A section on shamanism explores the origins of the term and presents our "shamanic complex" model of how shamanic healings take place. A section on religion, magic, and witchcraft high-

lights Ibibio witchcraft, while another section marks out religion's psychological and social functions, including efforts to heal physical, emotional, and social ills. Touching on religion and cultural change, this chapter looks at revitalization movements and new material on indigenous Christian churches in Africa. Also new to the chapter are discussions on sacred places and women's roles in religious leadership. Of special note are the many new and evocative photographs. Boxed features include Hillary Crane's new and arresting Biocultural Connection about Taiwanese Buddhist nuns, "Change Your Karma and Change Your Sex?," along with Marjorie Shostak's Original Study, "Healing among the Ju/'hoansi," and an Anthropology Applied piece on "Reconciling Modern Medicine with Traditional Beliefs in Swaziland."

Chapter 14: The Arts

This chapter explores in detail three key categories of art—visual, verbal, and musical—illustrating what they reveal about and what functions they play in societies. A long and detailed discussion about aesthetic and interpretive approaches to analyzing art, as applied to rock art in southern Africa has been shortened and reworked to make it more lively and engaging. Among numerous high points in the section "Functions of Art" is a new and remarkable photograph of a sand painting healing ceremony. Of particular note in this chapter is the section on "Art, Globalization, and Cultural Survival," which investigates how threatened indigenous groups use aesthetic traditions as part of a cultural survival strategy. Boxed features include a new Biocultural Connection, "Peyote Art: Divine Visions among the Huichol," a newly illustrated Original Study on "The Modern Tattoo Community" by Margo DeMello, and an Anthropologist of Note profile about Frederica de Laguna's work among the Tlingit of Yakutat, Alaska.

Also new in this chapter is the Globalscape highlighting the work of a Ghanaian custom coffin maker that is gaining global recognition as art.

Chapter 15: Processes of Change

The themes and terminology of globalization are woven through this chapter, which includes definitions that distinguish *progress* from *modernization,* *rebellion* from *revolution,* and *acculturation* from *enculturation.* Here, we discuss mechanisms of change—innovation, diffusion, and cultural loss, as well as repressive change. Our exploration of the latter covers acculturation, ethnocide, and genocide, citing a range of the all-too-many repressive-change examples from around the world—including a new discussion of ethnocide in Tibet. This chapter also looks at reactions to such change, including revitalization movements, rebellions, and revolutions. A discussion on modernization touches on the issue of self-determination among indigenous peoples and high-lights two contrasting cases: Skolt Lapp reindeer herders in Finland, and Shuar Indians of Ecuador. Also featured are the historical profile of applied or practical anthropology and the emergence of action or advocacy anthropology in collaboration with indigenous societies, ethnic minorities, and other besieged or repressed groups. The chapter's last pages discuss globalization as a worldwide process of accelerated modernization in which all parts of the earth are becoming interconnected in one vast, in-terrelated, and all-encompassing system. Boxed features include a Biocultural Connection on the Emergence of new diseases, an Anthropology Applied piece titled "De-velopment Anthropology and Dams," and an Anthropol-ogist of Note box on Eric Wolf.

Chapter 16: Global Challenges, Local Responses, and the Role of Anthropology

Our final chapter zeroes in on numerous global chal-lenges confronting the human species today—and prods students to use the anthropological tools they have learned to think critically about these issues and take in-formed steps to help bring about a future in which hu-mans live in harmony with each other and the nature that sustains us all. Sections on global culture and ethnic resurgence look at Westernization and its counterforce of growing nationalism and the breakup of multi-eth-nic states. We present examples of resistance to global-ization, and discuss pluralism and multiculturalism. A substantial section about the rise of global corporations places this phenomenon in historical context and high-lights the largest corporations (making particular note of media corporations and the emergence of the "global mediascape").

Under the heading "Structural Power in the Age of Globalization," we recount the ever-widening gap between those who have wealth and power and those who do not. We define and illustrate the term *structural power* and its two branches—hard power (military and economic might) and soft power (media might that gains control through ideological influence). We then address "Problems of Structural Violence"—from pollution to epidemics of hunger and obesity. We also touch on "the culture of discontent," including the psychological prob-lems born of powerful marketing messages that shape cultural standards concerning the ideal human body. Tied to this is Laura Nader's Original Study "Standardiz-ing the Body: The Question of Choice." Also featured is a new Biocultural Connection, "Toxic Breast Milk Threat-ens Arctic Culture," an Anthropologist of Note box on Arjun Appadurai, and a new Globalscape on the deadly results of toxins being shipped to the Third World. The chapter closes with a stirring photo and commentary on indigenous peoples, noting anthropology's potential for helping to solve problems of inequity on local and global levels.

SUPPLEMENTS

Cultural Anthropology comes with a strong supplements program to help instructors create an effective learning environment both inside and outside the classroom and to aid students in mastering the material.

Supplements for Instructors

Online Instructor's Manual and Print Test Bank

The Instructor's Manual offers detailed chapter outlines, lecture suggestions, key terms, and student activities such as *InfoTrac College Edition* exercises and Internet ex-ercises. A print test bank contains over seventy-five chap-ter test questions including multiple choice, true/false, fill-in-the-blank, short answer, and essay.

ExamView Computerized Test Bank

Create, deliver, and customize tests and study guides (both print and online) in minutes with this easy to use assessment and tutorial system. ExamView offers both a Quick Test Wizard and an Online Test Wizard that guide you step-by-step throughout the process of creat-ing tests, while its unique "WYSWYG" capability allows you to see the test you are creating on screen exactly as it will print or display online. You can build tests of up to 250 questions using up to twelve question types. Using ExamView's complete word processing capabilities, you can enter an unlimited number of new questions or edit existing questions.

Multimedia Manager for Anthropology: A Microsoft PowerPoint Link Tool

This new CD-ROM contains digital media and Microsoft PowerPoint presentations for all of Wadsworth's 2008 in-troductory anthropology texts, placing images, lectures and video clips at your fingertips. This CD-ROM includes preassembled Microsoft PowerPoint presentations, and charts, graphs, maps, line art, and images with a NEW zoom feature from all Wadsworth © 2008 anthropology texts. You can add your own lecture notes and images to create a customized lecture presentation.

JoinIn on TurningPoint

The anthropology discipline at Thomson Wadsworth is pleased to offer **JoinIn**™ (clicker) content for Audience Response Systems tailored to this text. Use the program by posing your own questions and display students' an-swers instantly within the Microsoft® PowerPoint® slides of your existing lecture. Or, utilize any or all of the following content that will be included with your Anthropology JoinIn product:

- **Opinion polls** on issues important to each anthropology chapter (five questions per chapter). Students may feel uncomfortable talking about sensitive subjects such as sexuality or religion. JoinIn gives students complete anonymity and helps students feel connected to the issues.
- **Conceptual quiz questions** for each chapter. Give students a quick quiz during or after the chapter lecture and determine if they have understood the material.
- Plus, **pre-assembled PowerPoint lecture slides** for each chapter of your book are included with the material above integrated into the slides. All of the work integrating clicker questions into the chapter lecture slides has been done for you!

The program can be used to simply take role, or it can assess your students' progress and opinions with in-class questions. Enhance how your students interact with you, your lecture, and each other. For college and university adopters only. *Contact your local Thomson representative to learn more.*

Wadsworth Anthropology Video Library

Qualified adopters may select full-length videos from an extensive library of offerings drawn from such excellent educational video sources as *Films for the Humanities and Sciences.*

ABC Anthropology Video Series

This exclusive video series was created jointly by Wadsworth and ABC for the anthropology course. Each video contains approximately 60 minutes of footage originally broadcast on ABC within the past several years. The videos are broken into short 2- to 7-minute segments, perfect for classroom use as lecture launchers or to illustrate key anthropological concepts. An annotated table of contents accompanies each video, providing descriptions of the segments and suggestions for their possible use within the course.

A Guide to Visual Anthropology

Prepared by Jayasinhji Jhala of Temple University, this guide provides a compendium of fifty of the most outstanding classic and contemporary anthropological films. The guide describes the films, tells why they are important, and gives suggestions for their use in the classroom.

AIDS in Africa DVD

Southern Africa has been overcome by a pandemic of unparalleled proportions. This documentary series focuses on the new democracy of Namibia and the many actions that are being taken to control HIV/AIDS. Included in this series are four documentary films created by the Periclean Scholars at Elon University: (1) *Young Struggles, Eternal Faith,* which focuses on caregivers in the faith community; (2) *The Shining Lights of Opuwo,* which shows how young people share their messages of hope through song and dance; (3) *A Measure of Our Humanity,* which describes HIV/AIDS as an issue related to gender, poverty, stigma, education, and justice; and (4) *You Wake Me Up,* a story of two HIV-positive women and their acts of courage helping other women learn to survive. Thomson/Wadsworth is excited to offer these award-winning films to instructors for use in class. When presenting topics such as gender, faith, culture, poverty, and so on, the films will be enlightening for students and will expand their global perspective of HIV/AIDS.

Online Resources for Instructors and Students

Anthropology Resource Center

This online center offers a wealth of information and useful tools for both instructors and students in all four fields of anthropology. It includes interactive maps, learning modules, video exercises, breaking news in anthropology, and a case study forum with short synopses of case studies and critical thinking questions written by the authors. For instructors, the Resource Center includes a gateway to time-saving teaching tools, such as an image bank, sample syllabi, and more. To get started with the Anthropology Resource Center, students and instructors are directed to www.thomsonedu.com where they can create an account through 1Pass.

Book Premium Companion Website

Access to this text-specific website is available free when bundled with the text or for purchase at a nominal fee. This site includes: learning modules on key cultural anthropology concepts, animations, interactive exercises, map exercises, video exercises with questions, tutorial quizzes with feedback, and essay questions, all of which can be e-mailed to professors.

Thomson InSite for Writing and Research with Turnitin Originality Checker

InSite features a full suite of writing, peer review, online grading, and e-portfolio applications. It is an all-in-one tool that helps instructors manage the flow of papers electronically and allows students to submit papers and peer reviews online. Also included in the suite is Turnitin, an originality check that offers a simple solution for instructors who want a strong deterrent against plagiarism, as well as encouragement for students to employ proper research techniques. Access is available for packaging with each copy of this book. For more information, visit http://insite.thomson.com.

InfoTrac College Edition

InfoTrac College Edition is an online library that offers full-length articles from thousands of scholarly and popular publications. Among the journals available are *American Anthropologist, Current Anthropology,* and *Canadian Review of Sociology and Anthropology.* To get started with InfoTrac College Edition, students are directed to www.thomsonedu.com where they can create an account through 1Pass.

Supplements for Students

Thomson Audio Study Products

Thomson Audio Study Products provide audio reinforcement of key concepts students can listen to from their personal computer or MP3 player. Created specifically for this edition of Haviland et al.'s *Cultural Anthropology,* **Thomson Audio Study Products** provide approximately 10 minutes of up-beat audio content, giving students a quick and convenient way to master key concepts, test their knowledge with quiz questions, and listen to a brief overview on the major themes of each chapter. Students may purchase access to **Thomson Audio Study Products** for this text online at www.thomsonedu.com.

Study Guide and Workbook

The Study Guide includes learning objectives, detailed chapter outlines and key terms to aid in student study; activities such as InfoTrac College Edition exercises and Internet exercises help students apply their knowledge, and over fifty practice test questions are provided per chapter including multiple choice, true/false, fill-in-the-blank, short answer, and essay questions.

Telecourse Study Guide

A new telecourse, **Cultural Anthropology: Our Diverse World,** available in the fall of 2007 provides online and print companion study guide options that include study aids, interactive exercises, videos, and more.

Globalization and Change in Fifteen Cultures: Born in One World, Living in Another, edited by George Spindler and Janice E. Stockard

In this anthology, fifteen case study authors write about culture change in today's diverse settings around the world. Each original article provides insight into the ef-
fects of globalization at the local level, and the dynamics and meanings of change in four key areas, including challenges to identity and power; changing gender hierarchies; new patterns of migration and mobility; and the effects of economic change and modernization.

Case Studies in Cultural Anthropology, edited by George Spindler and Janice E. Stockard

Select from more than sixty classic and contemporary ethnographies representing geographic and topical diversity. Newer case studies focus on culture change and culture continuity, reflecting the globalization of the world.

Case Studies on Contemporary Social Issues, edited by John A. Young

Framed around social issues, these new contemporary case studies are globally comparative and represent the cutting-edge work of anthropologists today.

Additional Student Resources

Modules in Physical and Cultural Anthropology

Each free-standing module is actually a complete text chapter, featuring the same quality of pedagogy and illustration that are contained in Thomson Wadsworth's anthropology texts.

Coming Fall of 2007, Medical Anthropology!

Coming Fall of 2007, Evolution of the Brain: Neoroanatomy, Development, and Paleontology!

Human Environment Interactions by Cathy Galvin

Cathy Galvin provides students with an introduction to the basic concepts in human ecology, before discussing cultural ecology, human adaptation studies, human behavioral ecology—including material on systems approaches and cognitive and critical approaches—and political ecology. She concludes the module with a discussion of resilience and global change as a result of human–environment interactions today, and the tools used.

Acknowledgments

In this day and age, no textbook comes to fruition without extensive collaboration. Beyond the shared endeavors of our author team, this book owes its completion to a wide range of individuals, from colleagues in the discipline to those involved in the production process. We are particularly grateful for the remarkable group of manuscript reviewers listed below. They provided unusually detailed and thoughtful feedback that helped us to hone and re-hone our narrative.

Barbara Bonnekessen, University of Missouri at Kansas City

Rebecca Cramer, Johnson County Community College

Matthea Cremers, University of California at Santa Barbara

Terri Castaneda, California State University, Sacramento

Lynn Gamble, San Diego State University

Stevan R. Jackson, Radford University

Susan Kirkpatrick Smith, Kennesaw State University

Susan Krook, Normandale Community College

Monica Rothschild-Boros, Orange Coast College

Orit Tamir, New Mexico Highlands University

Melody Yeager, Butte College

Ellen Zimmerman, Framingham State College

We carefully considered and made use of the wide range of comments provided by these individuals. Our decisions on how to utilize their suggestions were influenced by our own perspectives on anthropology and teaching, combined with the priorities and page limits of this text. Thus, neither our reviewers, nor any of the other anthropologists mentioned here, should be held responsible for any shortcomings in this book. They should, however, be credited as contributors to many of the book's strengths.

Thanks, too, go to colleagues who provided material for some of the Original Study, Biocultural Connection, and Anthropology Applied boxes in this text: Mary Jo Arnoldi, Michael Blakey, Hillary Crane, Margo DeMello, Clementine van Eck, George Esber, Edward C. Green, Marvin Harris, Michael M. Horowitz, Susan Lees, William Leap, Suzanne LeClerc-Madlala, H. Lyn White Miles, Laura Nader, Serena Nanda, Martin Ottenheimer, Marjorie Shostak, Clyde C. Snow, Karen Stephenson, William Ury, Frans B. M. de Waal, Annette B. Weiner, Dennis Werner, and R. K. Williamson. Among these individuals we particularly want to acknowledge our admiration, affection, and appreciation for our mutual friend and colleague Jim Petersen, whose life came to an abrupt and tragic end while returning from fieldwork in the Brazilian Amazon.

We have debts of gratitude to office workers in our departments for their cheerful help in clerical matters: Debbie Hedrick, Karen Rundquist, Emira Smailagic, Gretchen Gross, and Sheri Youngberg. And to research librarian extraordinaire Nancy Bianchi and colleagues Yvette Pigeon, John Fogarty, Lewis First, Martin Ottenheimer, Harriet Ottenheimer, and Michael Wesch for engaging in lively discussions of anthropological and pedagogical approaches. Also worthy of note here are the introductory anthropology teaching assistants who, through the years, have shed light for us on effective ways to reach new generations of students.

Our thanksgiving inventory would be incomplete without mentioning individuals at Wadsworth Publishing who helped conceive this text and bring it to fruition. Special gratitude goes to Senior Acquisitions Editor Lin Marshall for her vision, vigor, and anthropological knowledge and to Developmental Editor Julie Cheng for her calming influence and attention to detail. Our thanks also go out to Wadsworth's skilled and enthusiastic editorial, marketing, design, and production team: Eve Howard (Vice President and Editor-in-Chief), Dave Lionetti (Technology Project Manager), Jessica Jang (Editorial Assistant); Caroline Concilla (Executive Marketing Manager), as well as Jerilyn Emori (Content Project Manager) and Maria Epes (Executive Art Director).

In addition to all of the above, we have had the invaluable aid of several most able freelancers, including Christine Davis of Two Chicks Advertising & Marketing, and our expert and enthusiastic photo researcher Billie Porter, who was always willing to go the extra mile to find the most telling and compelling photographs, and our skilled graphic designer Carol Zuber-Mallison of ZM Graphics who can always be relied upon to deliver fine work and great humor. We are especially thankful to have had the opportunity to work once again with copyeditor Jennifer Gordon and production coordinator Robin Hood, who bring calm efficiency and grace to the demands of meeting difficult deadlines.

And finally, all of us are indebted to family members who have not only put up with our textbook preoccupation, but cheered us on in the endeavor. Dana had the tireless support and keen eye of husband Peter Bingham—along with the varied contributions of their three sons Nishan, Tavid, and Aram Bingham. As co-author spouses under the same roof, Harald and Bunny have picked up slack for each other on every front to help this project move along smoothly. But the biggest debt of gratitude may be in Bill's corner: For more than three decades he has had invaluable input and support in his textbook tasks from his spouse Anita de Laguna Haviland.

About the Authors

While distinct from one another, all four members of this author team share overlapping research interests and a similar vision of what anthropology is (and should be) about. For example, all are "true believers" in the four-field approach to anthropology and all have some involvement in applied work.

WILLIAM A. HAVILAND is Professor Emeritus at the University of Vermont, where he founded the Department of Anthropology and taught for thirty-two years. He holds a Ph.D. in Anthropology from the University of Pennsylvania.

He has carried out original research in archaeology in Guatemala and Vermont; ethnography in Maine and Vermont; and physical anthropology in Guatemala. This work has been the basis of numerous publications in various national and international books and journals, as well as in media intended for the general public. His books include The Original Vermonters, coauthored with Marjorie Power, and a technical monograph on ancient Maya settlement. He also served as technical consultant for the award-winning telecourse, *Faces of Culture,* and is coeditor of the series *Tikal Reports,* published by the University of Pennsylvania Museum of Archaeology and Anthropology.

Besides his teaching and writing, Dr. Haviland has lectured to numerous professional, as well as, nonprofessional audiences in Canada, Mexico, Lesotho, South Africa, and Spain, as well as in the United States. A staunch supporter of indigenous rights, he served as expert witness for the Missisquoi Abenakis of Vermont in an important court case over aboriginal fishing rights.

Awards received by Dr. Haviland include being named University Scholar by the Graduate School of the University of Vermont in 1990, a Certificate of Appreciation from the Sovereign Republic of the Abenaki Nation of Missisquoi, St. Francis/Sokoki Band in 1996, and a Lifetime Achievement Award from the Center for Research on Vermont in 2006. Now retired from teaching, he continues his research, writing, and lecturing from the coast of Maine.

HARALD E. L. PRINS (Ph.D., New School 1988) is a University Distinguished Professor of Anthropology at Kansas State University and guest curator at the National Museum of Natural History, Smithsonian Institution. Born in The Netherlands, he studied at universities in Europe and the United States. He has done extensive fieldwork among indigenous peoples in South and North America, published dozens of articles in five languages,

Authors Bunny McBride, Dana Walrath, Harald Prins, and William Haviland

co-edited some books, and authored "The Mi'kmaq: Resistance, Accommodation, and Cultural Survival" (1996). He also made award-winning documentaries and served as president of the Society for Visual Anthropology and visual anthropology editor of the "American Anthropologist." Dr. Prins has won his university's most prestigious undergraduate teaching awards and held the Coffman Chair for University Distinguished Teaching Scholars (2004–05). Most recently, Dr. Prins was selected as Professor of the Year for the State of Kansas by the Carnegie Foundation for the Advancement of Teaching. Active in human rights, he served as expert witness in Native rights cases in the U.S. Senate and various Canadian courts, and was instrumental in the successful federal recognition and land claims of the Aroostook Band of Micmacs (1991).

DANA WALRATH is Assistant Professor of Family Medicine at the University of Vermont and a Women's Studies affiliated faculty member. She earned her Ph.D. in Anthropology from the University of Pennsylvania and is a medical and biological anthropologist with principal interests in biocultural aspects of reproduction, the cultural context of biomedicine, genetics, and evolutionary medicine. She directs an innovative educational program at the University of Vermont's College of Medicine that brings anthropological theory and practice to first-year medical students. Before joining the faculty at the University of Vermont in 2000, she taught at the University of Pennsylvania and Temple University. Her research has been supported by the National Science Foundation, Health Resources and Services Administration, the Centers for Disease Control and the Templeton Foundation. Dr. Walrath's publications have appeared in *Current Anthropology, American Anthropologist,* and *American*

Journal of Physical Anthropology. An active member of the Council on the Anthropology of Reproduction, she has also served on a national committee to develop women's health-care learning objectives for medical education and works locally to improve health care for refugees and immigrants.

BUNNY MCBRIDE (M.A. Columbia University, 1980) is an award-winning author specializing in cultural anthropology, indigenous peoples, international tourism, and nature conservation issues. Published in dozens of national and international print media, she has reported from Africa, Europe, China, and the Indian Ocean. Highly rated as a teacher, she served as visiting anthropology faculty at Principia College, the Salt Institute for Documentary Field Studies, and since 1996 as adjunct lecturer of anthropology at Kansas State University. McBride's many publications include *Women of the Dawn* (1999) and *Molly Spotted Elk: A Penobscot in Paris* (1995). Collaborating with Native communities in Maine, she curated various museum exhibits based on her books. The Maine state legislature awarded her a special commendation for significant contributions to Native women's history (1999). A community activist and researcher for the Aroostook Band of Micmacs (1981–91), she assisted this Maine Indian community in its successful efforts to reclaim lands, gain tribal status, and revitalize cultural traditions. Currently, McBride serves as co-principal investigator for a National Park Service ethnography project, guest curator for an exhibition on the Rockefeller Southwest Indian Art Collection, oral history advisor for the Kansas Humanities Council, and board member of the Women's World Summit Foundation, based in Geneva, Switzerland.

1 The Essence of Anthropology

CHALLENGE ISSUE

It is a challenge to make sense of who we are. Where did we come from? Why are we so radically different from other animals and so surprisingly similar to others? Why do our bodies look the way they do? How do we explain so many different beliefs, languages, and customs? What makes us tick? As just one of 10 million species, including 4,000 fellow mammals, we humans are the only creatures on earth with the mental capacity to ask such questions about ourselves and the world around us. We do this not only because we are curious but also because knowledge has enabled us to adapt to radically contrasting environments all across the earth and helps us create and improve our material and social living conditions. Adaptations based on knowledge are essential in every culture, and culture is our species' ticket to survival. Understanding humanity in all its biological and cultural variety, past and present, is the fundamental contribution of anthropology. This contribution has become all the more important in the era of globalization, when appreciating our common humanity and respecting cultural differences are essential to human survival.

What Is Anthropology?

Anthropology, the study of humankind everywhere, throughout time, produces knowledge about what makes people different from one another and what they all share in common. Anthropologists work within four fields of the discipline. While physical anthropologists focus on humans as biological organisms (tracing evolutionary development and looking at biological variations), cultural anthropologists investigate the contrasting ways groups of humans think, feel, and behave. Archaeologists try to recover information about human cultures—usually from the past—by studying material objects, skeletal remains, and settlements. Meanwhile, linguists study languages—communication systems by which cultures are maintained and passed on to succeeding generations. Practitioners in all four fields are informed by one another's findings and united by a common anthropological perspective on the human condition.

How Do Anthropologists Do What They Do?

Anthropologists, like other scholars, are concerned with the description and explanation of reality. They formulate and test hypotheses—tentative explanations of observed phenomena—concerning humankind. Their aim is to develop reliable theories— interpretations or explanations supported by bodies of data—about our species. These data are usually collected through fieldwork—a particular kind of hands-on research that makes anthropologists so familiar with a situation that they can begin to recognize patterns, regularities, and exceptions. It is also through careful observation (combined with comparison) that anthropologists test their theories.

How Does Anthropology Compare to Other Disciplines?

In studying humankind, early anthropologists came to the conclusion that to fully understand the complexities of human thought, feelings, behavior, and biology, it was necessary to study and compare all humans, wherever and whenever. More than any other feature, this unique cross-cultural, long-term perspective distinguishes anthropology from other social sciences. Anthropologists are not the only scholars who study people, but they are uniquely holistic in their approach, focusing on the interconnections and interdependence of all aspects of the human experience, past and present. It is this holistic and integrative perspective that equips anthropologists to grapple with an issue of overriding importance for all of us today: globalization.

For as long as they have been on earth, people have sought answers to questions about who they are, where they come from, and why they act as they do. Throughout most of human history, though, people relied on myth and folklore for answers, rather than on the systematic testing of data obtained through careful observation. Anthropology, over the last 150 years, has emerged as a tradition of scientific inquiry with its own approaches to answering these questions. Simply stated, **anthropology** is the study of humankind in all times and places. While focusing primarily on *Homo sapiens*—the human species—anthropologists also study our ancestors and close animal relatives for clues about what it means to be human.

THE DEVELOPMENT OF ANTHROPOLOGY

Although works of anthropological significance have a considerable antiquity—two examples being cross-cultural accounts of people written by the Greek historian Herodotus about 2,500 years ago and the North African Arab scholar Ibn Khaldun nearly 700 years ago—anthropology as a distinct field of inquiry is a relatively recent product of Western civilization. In the United States, for example, the first course in general anthropology to carry credit in a college or university (at the University of Rochester in New York) was not offered until 1879. If people have always been concerned about themselves and their origins, and those of other people, then why did it take such a long time for a systematic discipline of anthropology to appear?

The answer to this is as complex as human history. In part, it relates to the limits of human technology. Throughout most of history, people have been restricted in their geographic horizons. Without the means of traveling to distant parts of the world, observation of cultures and peoples far from one's own was a difficult—if not impossible—undertaking. Extensive travel was usually the exclusive privilege of a few; the study of foreign peoples and cultures was not likely to flourish until improved modes of transportation and communication could be developed.

anthropology The study of humankind in all times and places.

This is not to say that people have been unaware of the existence of others in the world who look and act differently from themselves. The Bible's Old and New Testaments, for example, are full of references to diverse ancient peoples, among them Babylonians, Egyptians, Greeks, Jews, and Syrians. However, the differences among these people pale by comparison to those among any of the more recent European nations and (for example) traditional indigenous peoples of the Pacific islands, the Amazon rainforest, or Siberia.

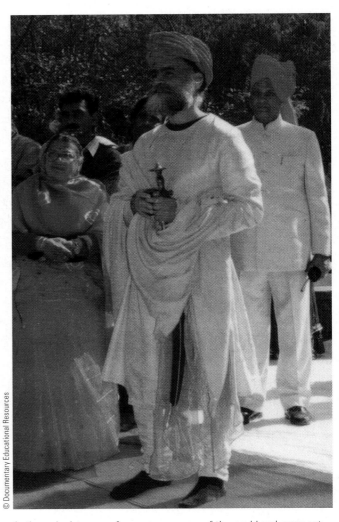

© Documentary Educational Resources

Anthropologists come from many corners of the world and carry out research in a huge variety of cultures all around the globe. Dr. Jayasinhji Jhala, pictured here, hails from the old city of Dhrangadhra in Gujarat, northwest India. A member of the Jhala clan of Rajputs, an aristocratic caste of warriors, he grew up in the royal palace of his father, the maharaja. After earning a bachelor of arts degree in India, he came to the United States and earned a master's in visual studies from MIT, followed by a doctorate in anthropology from Harvard. Currently a professor and director of the programs of Visual Anthropology and the Visual Anthropology Media Laboratory at Temple University, he returns regularly to India with students to film cultural traditions in his own caste-stratified society.

With the invention of the magnetic compass for use aboard better-equipped sailing ships, it became easier to determine geographic direction and travel to truly far-away places and meet for the first time such radically different groups. It was the massive encounter with hitherto unknown peoples—which began 500 years ago as Europeans sought to extend their trade and political domination to all parts of the world—that focused attention on human differences in all their amazing variety.

Another significant element that contributed to the emergence of anthropology was that Europeans gradually came to recognize that despite all the differences, they might share a basic humanity with people everywhere. Initially, Europeans labeled societies that did not share their fundamental cultural values as "savage" or "barbarian." Over time, however, Europeans came to recognize such highly diverse groups as fellow members of one species and therefore relevant to an understanding of what it is to be human. This growing interest in human diversity, coming at a time when there were increasing efforts to explain things in scientific terms, cast doubts on the traditional explanations based on religious texts such as the Torah, Bible, or Koran and helped set the stage for the birth of anthropology.

Although anthropology originated within the historical context of European culture, it has long since gone global. Today, it is an exciting, transnational discipline whose practitioners come from a wide array of societies all around the world. Societies that have long been studied by European and North American anthropologists—several African and Native American societies, for example—have produced anthropologists who have made and continue to make a mark on the discipline. Their distinct perspectives shed new light not only on their own cultures but also on those of others. It is noteworthy that in one regard diversity has long been a hallmark of the discipline: From its earliest days both women and men have entered the field. Throughout this text, we will be spotlighting individual anthropologists, illustrating the diversity of these practitioners and their work.

THE ANTHROPOLOGICAL PERSPECTIVE

Many academic disciplines are concerned in one way or another with our species. For example, biology focuses on the genetic, anatomical, and physiological aspects of organisms. Psychology is concerned primarily with cognitive, mental, and emotional issues, while economics examines the production, distribution, and management of material resources. And various disciplines in the humanities look into the artistic and philosophical achievements of human cultures. But anthropology is distinct because of its focus on the interconnections and interdependence of all aspects of the human experience in all places and times—both biological and cultural, past and present. It is this **holistic perspective** that best equips anthropologists to broadly address that elusive phenomenon we call human nature.

Anthropologists welcome the contributions of researchers from other disciplines and in return offer their own findings for the benefit of these other disciplines. Anthropologists do not expect, for example, to know as much about the structure of the human eye as anatomists or as much about the perception of color as psychologists. As synthesizers, however, anthropologists are prepared to understand how these bodies of knowledge relate to color-naming practices in different human societies. Because they look for the broad basis of human ideas and practices without limiting themselves to any single social or biological aspect, anthropologists can acquire an especially expansive and inclusive overview of the complex biological and cultural organism that is the human being.

The holistic perspective also helps anthropologists stay keenly aware of ways that their own culture's perspective and social values may influence their research. As the old saying goes, people often see what they believe, rather than what appears before their eyes. By maintaining a critical awareness of their own assumptions about human nature—checking and rechecking the ways their beliefs and actions might be shaping their research—anthropologists strive to gain objective knowledge about people. Equipped with this awareness, anthropologists have contributed uniquely to our understanding of diversity in human thought, biology, and behavior, as well as our understanding of the many things humans have in common.

While other social sciences have concentrated predominantly on contemporary peoples living in North American and European (Western) societies, anthropologists have traditionally focused on non-Western peoples and cultures. Anthropologists believe that to fully understand the complexities of human ideas, behavior, and biology, all humans, wherever and whenever, must be studied. A cross-cultural and long-term evolutionary perspective not only distinguishes anthropology from other social sciences, but also guards against the danger that theories of human behavior will be **culture-bound:**

---

holistic perspective A fundamental principle of anthropology: that the various parts of human culture and biology must be viewed in the broadest possible context in order to understand their interconnections and interdependence.
culture-bound Theories about the world and reality based on the assumptions and values of one's own culture.

VISUAL COUNTERPOINT

Although infants in the United States typically sleep apart from their parents, cross-cultural research shows that co-sleeping, of mother and baby in particular, is the rule. The photo on the right shows a Nenet family sleeping together in their *chum* (reindeer-skin tent). Nenet people are arctic reindeer pastoralists living in Siberia.

that is, based on assumptions about the world and reality that come from the researcher's own particular culture.

As a case in point, consider the fact that infants in the United States typically sleep apart from their parents. To most North Americans, this may seem normal, but cross-cultural research shows that co-sleeping, of mother and baby in particular, is the rule. Only in the past 200 years, generally in Western industrial societies, has it been considered proper for parents to sleep apart from their infants. In a way, this practice amounts to a cultural experiment in child rearing.

Recent studies have shown that separation of mother and infant in Western societies has important biological and cultural consequences. For one thing, it increases the length of the child's crying bouts. Some mothers incorrectly interpret the cause as a deficiency in breast milk and switch to less healthy bottle formulas; and in extreme cases the crying may provoke physical abuse. But the benefits of co-sleeping go beyond significant reductions in crying: Infants also nurse more often and three times as long per feeding; they receive more stimulation (important for brain development); and they are apparently less susceptible to sudden infant death syndrome (SIDS or "crib death"). There are benefits to the mother as well: Frequent nursing prevents early ovulation after childbirth, and she gets at least as much sleep as mothers who sleep without their infants.[1]

These benefits may lead us to ask, Why do so many mothers continue to sleep apart from their infants? In North America the cultural values of independence and consumerism come into play. To begin building individual identities, babies are provided with rooms (or at least space) of their own. This room of one's own also provides parents with a place for the toys, furniture, and other paraphernalia associated with good parenting in North America.

Anthropology's early emphasis on studying traditional, non-Western peoples has often led to findings that run counter to generally accepted opinions derived from Western studies. Thus, anthropologists were the first to demonstrate

that the world does not divide into the pious and the superstitious; that there are sculptures in jungles and paintings in deserts; that political order is possible without centralized power and principled justice without codified rules; that the norms of reason were not fixed in Greece, the evolution of morality not consummated in England. . . . We have, with no little success, sought to keep the world off balance; pulling out rugs, upsetting tea tables, setting off firecrackers. It has been the office of others to reassure; ours to unsettle.[2]

Although the findings of anthropologists have often challenged the conclusions of sociologists, psychologists, and economists, anthropology is absolutely indispensable to them, as it is the only consistent check against

[1]Barr, R. G. (1997, October). The crying game. *Natural History, 47.* Also, McKenna, J. J. (2002, September-October). Breastfeeding and bedsharing. *Mothering,* 28–37; and McKenna, J. J., & McDade, T. (2005, June). Why babies should never sleep alone: A review of the co-sleeping controversy in relation to SIDS, bedsharing, and breast feeding. *Pediatric Respiratory Reviews* 6(2), 134–152.

[2]Geertz, C. (1984). Distinguished lecture: Anti anti-relativism. *American Anthropologist 86,* 275.

culture-bound assertions. In a sense, anthropology is to these disciplines what the laboratory is to physics and chemistry: an essential testing ground for their theories.

ANTHROPOLOGY AND ITS FIELDS

Individual anthropologists tend to specialize in one of four fields or subdisciplines: physical anthropology, archaeology, linguistic anthropology, or cultural anthropology (Figure 1.1). Some anthropologists consider archaeology and linguistics as part of the broader study of human cultures, but, archaeology and linguistics also have close ties to biological anthropology. For example, while linguistic anthropology focuses on the cultural aspects of language, it has deep connections to the evolution of human language and the biological basis of speech and language studied within physical anthropology. Each of anthropology's fields may take a distinct approach to the study of humans, but all gather and analyze data that are essential to explaining similarities and differences among humans, across time and space. Moreover, all of them generate knowledge that has numerous practical applications.

Within the four fields are individuals who practice **applied anthropology,** which entails using anthropological knowledge and methods to solve practical problems, often for a specific client. Applied anthropologists do not offer their perspectives from the sidelines. Instead, they actively collaborate with the communities in which they work—setting goals, solving problems, and

Figure 1.1

The four fields of anthropology. Note that the divisions among them are not sharp, indicating that their boundaries overlap. Moreover, each operates on the basis of a common body of knowledge. All four are involved in theory building, developing their own research methodologies, and solving practical problems through applied anthropology.

conducting research together. In this book, examples of how anthropology contributes to solving a wide range of the challenges humans face appear in Anthropology Applied features.

One of the earliest contexts in which anthropological knowledge was applied to a practical problem was

applied anthropology The use of anthropological knowledge and methods to solve practical problems, often for a specific client.

Biocultural
Connection
The Anthropology of Organ Transplantation

In 1954, the first organ transplant occurred in Boston when surgeons removed a kidney from one identical twin to place it inside his sick brother. Though some transplants rely upon living donors, routine organ transplantation depends largely upon the availability of organs obtained from individuals who have died.

From an anthropological perspective, the meanings of death and the body vary cross-culturally. While death could be said to represent a particular biological state, social agreement about this state's significance is of paramount importance. Anthropologist Margaret Lock has explored differences between Japanese and North American acceptance of the biological state of "brain death" and how it affects the practice of organ transplants.

Brain death relies upon the absence of measurable electrical currents in the brain and the inability to breathe without technological assistance. The brain-dead individual, though attached to machines, still seems alive with a beating heart and pink cheeks. North Americans find brain death acceptable, in part, because personhood and individuality are culturally located in the brain. North American comfort with brain death has allowed for the "gift of life" through organ donation and subsequent transplantation.

By contrast, in Japan, the concept of brain death is hotly contested and organ transplants are rarely performed. The Japanese do not incorporate a mind–body split into their models of themselves and locate personhood throughout the

body rather than in the brain. They resist accepting a warm pink body as a corpse from which organs can be harvested. Further, organs cannot be transformed into "gifts" because anonymous donation is not compatible with Japanese social patterns of reciprocal exchange.

Organ transplantation carries far greater social meaning than the purely biological movement of an organ from one individual to another. Cultural and biological processes are tightly woven into every aspect of this new social practice.

(Based on M. Lock (2001). Twice dead: Organ transplants and the reinvention of death. Berkeley: University of California Press.)

the international public health movement that began in the 1920s, marking the beginning of *medical anthropology*—a specialization that brings theoretical and applied approaches from the fields of cultural and biological anthropology to the study of human health and disease. The work of medical anthropologists sheds light on the connections between human health and political and economic forces, both globally and locally. Examples from this specialization appear in some of the Biocultural Connections featured in this text, including the one presented in this chapter, "The Anthropology of Organ Transplantation."

Physical Anthropology

Physical anthropology, also called *biological anthropology,* is the systematic study of humans as biological organisms. Traditionally, biological anthropologists concentrated on human evolution, primatology, growth and development, human adaptation, and forensics. Today, **molecular anthropology,** or the anthropological study of genes and genetic relationships, is another vital component of biological anthropology. Comparisons among groups separated by time, geography, or the frequency of a particular gene can reveal how humans have adapted and where they have migrated. As experts in the anatomy of human bones and tissues, physical anthropologists lend their knowledge about the body to applied areas such as gross anatomy laboratories, public health, and criminal investigations.

Paleoanthropology

Human evolutionary studies (known as **paleoanthropology**) investigate the origins and predecessors of the present human species, focusing on biological changes through time to understand how, when, and why we became the kind of organisms we are today. In biological terms, we humans are primates, one of the many kinds of mammal. Because we share a common ancestry with other primates, most specifically apes, paleoanthropologists look back to the earliest primates (65 or so million years ago) or even the earliest mammals (225 million years ago) to reconstruct the complex path of human evolution. Paleoanthropology unlike other evolutionary studies, takes a **biocultural** approach, focusing on the interaction of biology and culture.

physical anthropology Also known as biological anthropology. The systematic study of humans as biological organisms.
molecular anthropology A branch of biological anthropology that uses genetic and biochemical techniques to test hypotheses about human evolution, adaptation, and variation.
paleoanthropology The study of the origins and predecessors of the present human species.
biocultural Focusing on the interaction of biology and culture.

The fossilized skeletons of our ancestors allow paleoanthropologists to reconstruct the course of human evolutionary history. They compare the size and shape of these fossils to one another and to the bones of living species. With each new fossil discovery, paleoanthropologists have another piece to add to human evolutionary history. Biochemical and genetic studies add considerably to the fossil evidence. As we will see in later chapters, genetic evidence establishes the close relationship between humans and ape species—chimpanzees, bonobos, and gorillas. Genetic analyses indicate that the human line originated 5 to 8 million years ago. Physical anthropology therefore deals with much greater time spans than archaeology or other fields of anthropology.

Human Growth, Adaptation, and Variation

Another specialty of physical anthropologists is the study of human growth and development. Anthropologists examine biological mechanisms of growth as well as the impact of the environment on the growth process. Franz Boas (see Anthropologists of Note box, page 15), a pioneer of anthropology of the early 20th century, compared the heights of European immigrants who spent their childhood in "the old country" to the increased heights obtained by their children who grew up in the United States. Today, physical anthropologists study the impacts of disease, pollution, and poverty on growth. Comparisons between human and nonhuman primate growth patterns can provide clues to the evolutionary history of humans. Detailed anthropological studies of the hormonal, genetic, and physiological basis of healthy growth in living humans also contribute significantly to the health of children today.

Studies of human adaptation focus on the capacity of humans to adapt or adjust to their material environment—biologically and culturally. This branch of physical anthropology takes a comparative approach to humans living today in a variety of environments. Humans are remarkable among the primates in that they now inhabit the entire earth. Though cultural adaptations make it possible for our species to live in some environmental extremes, biological adaptations also contribute to survival in extreme cold, heat, and high altitude.

Some of these biological adaptations are built into the genetic makeup of populations. The long period of human growth and development provides ample opportunity for the environment to shape the human body. These *developmental adaptations* are responsible for some features of human variation such as the enlargement of the right ventricle of the heart to help push blood to the lungs among the Quechua Indians of highland Peru. *Physiological adaptations* are short-term changes in response to a particular environmental stimulus. For example, a person who normally lives at sea level will undergo a series of physiological responses if she suddenly moves to a high altitude. All of these kinds of biological adaptation contribute to present-day human variation.

Variation in visible traits such as height, body build, and skin color, as well as biochemical factors such as blood type and susceptibility to certain diseases, contribute to human biological diversity. Still, we remain members of a single species. Physical anthropology applies all the techniques of modern biology to achieve fuller understanding of human variation and its relationship to the different environments in which people have lived. Research in physical anthropology on human variation has debunked false notions of biologically defined races—a notion based on widespread misinterpretation of human variation.

Forensic Anthropology

One of the many practical applications of physical anthropology is **forensic anthropology:** the identification of human skeletal remains for legal purposes. Although they are called upon by law enforcement authorities to identify murder victims, forensic anthropologists also investigate human rights abuses such as systematic genocides, terrorism, and war crimes. These specialists use details of skeletal anatomy to establish the age, sex, and stature of the deceased; forensic anthropologists can also determine whether the person was right- or left-handed, exhibited any physical abnormalities, or experienced trauma. While forensics relies upon differing frequencies of certain skeletal characteristics to establish population affiliation, it is nevertheless false to say that all people from a given population have a particular type of skeleton. (See the Anthropology Applied feature to read about the work of several forensic anthropologists and forensic archaeologists.)

Primatology

Studying the anatomy and behavior of the other primates helps us understand what we share with our closest living relatives and what makes humans unique. Therefore, **primatology,** or the study of living and fossil primates, is a vital part of physical anthropology. Primates include the Asian and African apes, as well as monkeys, lemurs, lorises, and tarsiers. Biologically, humans are apes—large-bodied, broad-shouldered primates with no tail. Detailed studies of ape behavior in the wild indicate that the sharing of learned behavior is a significant part of their social life. Increasingly, primatologists designate the shared, learned behavior of nonhuman apes as culture. For example, tool use and communication systems indicate the elementary basis of language in some ape societies.

Primate studies offer scientifically grounded perspectives on the behavior of our ancestors, as well as greater appreciation and respect for the abilities of our closest living relatives. As human activity encroaches on all parts of the world, many primate species are endangered. Primatologists often advocate for the preservation of primate habitats so that these remarkable animals will continue to inhabit the earth with us.

Cultural Anthropology

Cultural anthropology (also called *social* or *sociocultural anthropology*) is the study of customary patterns in human behavior, thought, and feelings. It focuses on humans as culture-producing and culture-reproducing creatures. Thus, in order to understand the work of the cultural anthropologist, we must clarify what we mean by **culture**—a society's shared and socially transmitted ideas, values, and perceptions, which are used to make sense of experience and which generate behavior and are reflected in that behavior. These standards are socially learned, rather than acquired through biological inheritance. Because they determine, or at least guide, normal day-to-day behavior, thought, and emotional patterns of the members of a society, human activities, ideas, and feelings are above all culturally acquired and influenced. The manifestations of culture may vary considerably from place to place, but no person is "more cultured" in the anthropological sense than any other.

Cultural anthropology has two main components: ethnography and ethnology. An **ethnography** is a detailed description of a particular culture primarily based on **fieldwork,** which is the term anthropologists use for on-location research. Because the hallmark of ethnographic fieldwork is a combination of social participation and personal observation within the community being studied, as well as interviews and discussions with individual members of a group, the ethnographic method is commonly referred to as **participant observation.**

---

forensic anthropology Applied subfield of physical anthropology that specializes in the identification of human skeletal remains for legal purposes.

primatology The study of living and fossil primates.

cultural anthropology Also known as social or sociocultural anthropology. The study of customary patterns in human behavior, thought, and feelings. It focuses on humans as culture-producing and culture-reproducing creatures.

culture A society's shared and socially transmitted ideas, values, and perceptions, which are used to make sense of experience and which generate behavior and are reflected in that behavior.

ethnography A detailed description of a particular culture primarily based on fieldwork.

fieldwork The term anthropologists use for on-location research.

participant observation In ethnography, the technique of learning a people's culture through social participation and personal observation within the community being studied, as well as interviews and discussion with individual members of the group over an extended period of time.

Anthropology Applied

Forensic Anthropology: Voices for the Dead ▪ Clyde C. Snow, Karen Burns, Amy Zelson Mundorff, and Michael Blakey

Forensic anthropology is the analysis of skeletal remains for legal purposes. Law enforcement authorities call upon forensic anthropologists to use skeletal remains to identify murder victims, missing persons, or people who have died in disasters, such as plane crashes. Forensic anthropologists have also contributed substantially to the investigation of human rights abuses in all parts of the world by identifying victims and documenting the cause of their death.

Among the best-known forensic anthropologists is Clyde C. Snow. He has been practicing in this field forty years, first for the Federal Aviation Administration and more recently as a freelance consultant. In addition to the usual police work, Snow has studied the remains of General George Armstrong Custer and his men from the 1876 battlefield at Little Big Horn, and in 1985 he went to Brazil, where he identified the remains of the notorious Nazi war criminal Josef Mengele.

He was also instrumental in establishing the first forensic team devoted to documenting cases of human rights abuses around the world. This began in 1984 when he went to Argentina at the request of a newly elected civilian gov-

ernment to help with the identification of remains of the *desaparecidos*, or "disappeared ones," the 9,000 or more people who were eliminated by government death squads during seven years of military rule. A year later, he returned to give expert testimony at the trial of nine junta members and to teach Argentineans how to recover, clean, repair, preserve, photograph, x-ray, and analyze bones. Besides providing factual accounts of the fate of victims to their surviving kin and refuting the assertions of revisionists that the massacres never happened, the work of Snow and his Argentinean associates was crucial in convicting several military officers of kidnapping, torture, and murder.

Since Snow's pioneering work, forensic anthropologists have become increasingly involved in the investigation of human rights abuses in all parts of the world, from Chile to Guatemala, Haiti, the Philippines, Rwanda, Iraq, Bosnia, and Kosovo. Meanwhile, they continue to do important work for more typical clients. In the United States these clients include the Federal Bureau of Investigation and city, state, and county medical examiners' offices.

Forensic anthropologists specializing in skeletal remains commonly work closely with forensic archaeologists.

© Susan Meiselas/Magnum Photos

Physical anthropologists do not just study fossil skulls. Here Clyde Snow holds the skull of a Kurd who was executed by Iraqi security forces. Snow specializes in forensic anthropology and is best known for his work identifying victims of state-sponsored terrorism.

Ethnographies provide the information used to make systematic comparisons among cultures all across the world. Known as **ethnology,** such cross-cultural research allows anthropologists to develop anthropological theories that help explain why certain important differences or similarities occur among groups.

Ethnography

Through participant observation—eating a people's food, sleeping under their roof, learning how to speak and behave acceptably, and personally experiencing their habits

© Bruce Broce

Sociologists conduct structured interviews and administer questionnaires to *respondents*, while psychologists experiment with *subjects*. Anthropologists, by contrast, learn from and often collaborate with *informants*. The researcher here is Dutch anthropologist Harald Prins, a coauthor of this book. Doing fieldwork among the Plains Apache Indians in Oklahoma, he is using a camera to document part of the community's oral history project with tribal chief Alfred Chalepah.

ethnology The study and analysis of different cultures from a comparative or historical point of view, utilizing ethnographic accounts and developing anthropological theories that help explain why certain important differences or similarities occur among groups.

The relation between them is rather like that between a forensic pathologist, who examines a corpse to establish time and manner of death, and a crime scene investigator, who searches the site for clues. While the forensic anthropologist deals with the human remains—often only bones and teeth—the forensic archaeologist controls the site, recording the position of all relevant finds and recovering any clues associated with the remains. In Rwanda, for example, a team assembled in 1995 to investigate a mass atrocity for the United Nations included archaeologists from the U.S. National Park Service's Midwest Archaeological Center. They performed the standard archaeological procedures of mapping the site, determining its boundaries, photographing and recording all surface finds, and excavating, photographing, and recording buried skeletons and associated materials in mass graves.[a]

In another example, Karen Burns of the University of Georgia was part of a team sent to northern Iraq after the 1991 Gulf War to investigate alleged atrocities. On a military base where there had

been many executions, she excavated the remains of a man's body found lying on its side facing Mecca, conforming to Islamic practice. Although there was no intact clothing, two threads of polyester used to sew clothing were found along the sides of both legs. Although the threads survived, the clothing, because it was made of natural fiber, had decayed. "Those two threads at each side of the leg just shouted that his family didn't bury him," says Burns.[b] Proper though his position was, no Islamic family would bury their own in a garment sewn with polyester thread; proper ritual would require a simple shroud.

In recent years two major anthropological analyses of skeletal remains have occurred in New York City dealing with both past and present atrocities. Amy Zelson Mundorff, a forensic anthropologist for New York City's Office of the Chief Medical Examiner, was injured in the September 11, 2001, terrorist attack on the World Trade Center. Two days later she returned to work to supervise and coordinate the management, treatment, and cataloguing of people who lost their lives in the attack.

Just a short walk away, construction workers in lower Manhattan discovered a 17th- and 18th-century African burial ground in 1991. Archaeological investigation of the burial ground revealed the horror of slavery in North America, showing that even young children were worked so far beyond their ability to endure that their spines were fractured. Biological archaeologist Michael Blakey, who led the research team, notes:

Although bioarchaeology and forensics are often confused, when skeletal biologists use the population as the unit of analysis (rather than the individual), and incorporate cultural and historical context (rather than simply ascribing biological characteristics), and report on the lifeways of a past community (rather than on a crime for the police and courts), it is bioarchaeology rather than forensics.[c]

Thus, several kinds of anthropologists analyze human remains for a variety of purposes, contributing to the documentation and correction of atrocities committed by humans of the past and present.

[a]Conner, M. (1996). The archaeology of contemporary mass graves. *SAA Bulletin 14*(4), 6, 31.

[b]Cornwell, T. (1995, November 10). Skeleton staff. *Times Higher Education*, 20.

[c]Blakey, M. Personal communication, October 29, 2003.

and customs—the ethnographer seeks to understand a particular way of life to a far greater extent than any non-participant researcher ever could. Being a participant observer does not mean that the anthropologist must join in a people's battles in order to study a culture in which warfare is prominent; but by living among a warlike people, the ethnographer should be able to understand how warfare fits into the overall cultural framework. She or he must observe carefully to gain an overview without placing too much emphasis on one part at the expense of another. Only by discovering how *all* aspects of a culture—its social, political, economic, and religious practices and institutions—relate to one another can the ethnographer begin to understand the cultural system. This is the holistic perspective so basic to the discipline.

The popular image of ethnographic fieldwork is that it occurs among people who live in far-off, isolated places. To be sure, much ethnographic work has been done in the remote villages of Africa or South America,

the islands of the Pacific Ocean, the Indian reservations of North America, the deserts of Australia, and so on. However, as the discipline of anthropology developed in response to the end of colonialism since the mid-20th century, peoples and cultures in industrialized nations, including Europe and the United States, also became a legitimate focus of anthropological study. Some of this shift occurred as scholars from non-Western nations became anthropologists. An even more significant factor is *globalization*, a worldwide process that rapidly transforms cultures—shifting, blurring, and even breaking long-established boundaries between different peoples.

Ethnographic fieldwork has changed from anthropological experts observing, documenting, and analyzing people from distant "other places" to collaborative efforts among anthropologists and the communities in which they work, producing knowledge that is valuable not only in the academic realm but also to the people being studied. Today, anthropologists from all parts of the globe employ research techniques similar to those developed in the study of traditional non-Western peoples to investigate a wide range of cultural niches, including those in industrial and postindustrial societies—from religious movements to conflict resolution, street gangs, schools, corporate bureaucracies, and health-care systems.

Ethnology

Although ethnographic fieldwork is basic to cultural anthropology, it is not the sole occupation of the cultural anthropologist. Largely descriptive in nature, ethnography provides the raw data needed for ethnology—the branch of cultural anthropology that involves cross-cultural comparisons and theories that explain differences or similarities among groups.

Intriguing insights into one's own beliefs and practices may come from cross-cultural comparisons. Consider, for example, the amount of time spent on domestic chores by industrialized peoples and traditional food foragers (people who rely on wild plant and animal resources for subsistence). Anthropological research among food foragers has shown that they work far less at domestic tasks, and indeed less at all subsistence pursuits, than do people in industrialized societies. Urban women in the United States who were not working for wages outside their homes put 55 hours a week into their housework—this despite all the "labor-saving" dishwashers, washing machines, clothes dryers, vacuum cleaners, food processors, and microwave ovens; in contrast, aboriginal women in Australia devoted 20 hours a week to their chores.[3]

Considering such cross-cultural comparisons, one may think of ethnology as the study of alternative ways of doing things. But more than that, by making systematic comparisons, ethnologists seek to arrive at scientific conclusions concerning the function and operation of cultural practices in all times and places. Today many cultural anthropologists apply such insights in a variety of contexts ranging from business to education to governmental interventions to humanitarian aid.

Archaeology

Archaeology is the field of anthropology that studies human cultures through the recovery and analysis of material remains and environmental data. Material products scrutinized by archaeologists include tools, pottery, hearths, and enclosures that remain as traces of cultural

---

[3]Bodley, J. H. (1985). *Anthropology and contemporary human problems* (2nd ed., p. 69). Palo Alto, CA: Mayfield.

archaeology The study of human cultures through the recovery and analysis of material remains and environmental data.

practices in the past, as well as human, plant, and animal remains, some of which date back 2.5 million years. The details of exactly how these traces were arranged when they were found reflect specific human ideas and behavior. For example, shallow, restricted concentrations of charcoal that include oxidized earth, bone fragments, and charred plant remains, located near pieces of fire-cracked rock, pottery, and tools suitable for food preparation, indicate cooking and food processing. Such remains can reveal much about a people's diet and subsistence practices. Together with skeletal remains, these material remains help archaeologists reconstruct the biocultural context of human life in the past.

Archaeologists can reach back for clues to human behavior far beyond the mere 5,000 years to which historians are confined by their reliance on written records. Calling this time period "prehistoric" does not mean that these societies were less interested in their history or that they did not have ways of recording and transmitting history. It simply means that written records do not now exist. That said, archaeologists are not limited to the study of societies without written records; they may also study those for which historic documents are available to supplement the material remains. In most literate societies, written records are associated with governing elites rather than with farmers, fishers, laborers, or slaves. Although written records can tell archaeologists much that might not be known from archaeological evidence alone, it is equally true that material remains can tell historians much about a society that is not apparent from its written documents.

Although most archaeologists concentrate on the human past, some of them study material objects in contemporary settings. One example is the Garbage Project, founded by William Rathje at the University of Arizona in 1973. This carefully controlled study of household waste continues to produce thought-provoking information about contemporary social issues. Among its accomplishments, the project has tested the validity of survey techniques, upon which sociologists, economists, and other social scientists and policymakers rely heavily.

For example, in 1973 conventional techniques were used to construct and administer a questionnaire to find out about the rate of alcohol consumption in Tucson. In one part of town, 15 percent of respondent households affirmed consumption of beer, but no household reported consumption of more than eight cans a week. Analysis of garbage from the same area, however, demonstrated that some beer was consumed in over 80 percent of households, and 50 percent discarded more than eight empty cans a week. Another interesting finding of the Garbage Project is that when beef prices reached an all-time high in 1973, so did the amount of beef wasted by households (not just in Tucson but in other parts of the country as well). Although common sense would lead us to suppose

Few places have caused as much speculation as Rapa Nui, a tiny volcanic island in the middle of the southern Pacific Ocean. Better known as Easter Island, it is one of the most remote and remarkable places on earth. The landscape is punctuated by nearly 900 colossal stone "heads," some towering to 65 feet. The islanders call them *moai,* and they have puzzled visitors ever since Dutch seafarers first discovered the island on Easter Day, 1722. By then, it was a barren land with a few thousand people for whom the *moai* were already ancient relics. Since the 1930s, anthropologists have used evidence from many subfields, especially oral traditions and archaeological excavations, to reconstruct a fascinating but troubling island history of environmental destruction and internal warfare.[4]

just the opposite, high prices and scarcity correlate with more, rather than less, waste. Such findings are important for they demonstrate that ideas about human behavior based on conventional interview-survey techniques alone can be seriously in error. Likewise, they show that what people actually do does not always match what they think they do.

In 1987, the Garbage Project began a program of excavating landfills in different parts of the United States and Canada. From this work came the first reliable data on what materials actually go into landfills and what happens to them there. And once again, common beliefs turned out to be at odds with the actual situation. For example, biodegradable materials such as newspapers take far longer to decay when buried in deep compost landfills than anyone had previously expected. This kind of information is a vital step toward solving waste disposal problems.[5]

Cultural Resource Management

While archaeology may conjure up images of ancient pyramids and the like, much archaeological research is carried out as **cultural resource management.** This branch of archaeology is tied to government policies for the protection of cultural resources and involves surveying and/or excavating archaeological and historical remains threatened by construction or development. For example, in the United States, if the transportation department of a state government plans to replace an inadequate highway bridge, steps have to be taken to identify and protect any significant prehistoric or historic resources that might be affected by this new construction. Federal legislation passed since the mid-1960s now requires cultural resource management for any building project that is partially funded or licensed by the U.S. government. As a result, the practice of cultural resource management has flourished. Many archaeologists are employed by such agencies as the U.S. Army Corps of Engineers, the National Park Service, the U.S. Forest Service, and the U.S. Soil and Conservation Service to assist in the preservation, restoration, and salvage of archaeological resources.

Archaeologists are also employed by state historic preservation agencies. Moreover, they consult for engineering firms to help them prepare environmental impact statements. Some of these archaeologists operate out of universities and colleges, while others are on the staffs of independent consulting firms. Finally, some archaeologists now also work for American Indian nations involved in cultural resource management on reservation lands.

---

[4]For more information, see the following: Anderson, A. (2002). Faunal collapse, landscape change, and settlement history in Remote Oceania. *World Archaeology 33*(3),375–390; Van Tilburg, J. A. (1994). *Easter Island: Archaeology, ecology, and culture.* London: British Museum Press.

[5]Details about the Garbage Project's past and present work can be seen on its website:http://info-center.ccit.arizona.edu/~bara/report.htm.

cultural resource management A branch of archaeology tied to government policies for the protection of cultural resources and involving surveying and/or excavating archaeological and historical remains threatened by construction or development.

Linguistic Anthropology

Perhaps the most distinctive feature of the human species is language. Although the sounds and gestures made by some other animals—especially by apes—may serve functions comparable to those of human language, no other animal has developed a system of symbolic communication as complex as that of humans. Language allows people to preserve and transmit countless details of their culture from generation to generation.

The field of anthropology that studies human languages is called **linguistic anthropology.** Linguists may deal with the description of a language (such as the way a sentence is formed or a verb conjugated), the history of languages (the way languages develop and change with the passage of time), or with language in relation to social and cultural contexts. All three approaches yield valuable information about how people communicate and how they understand the world around them. The everyday language of English-speaking North Americans, for example, includes a number of slang words, such as *dough, greenback, dust, loot, bucks, change,* and *bread,* to identify what an indigenous inhabitant of Papua New Guinea would recognize only as "money." The profusion of names helps to identify a thing of special importance to a culture.

Anthropological linguists also make a significant contribution to our understanding of the human past. By working out relationships among languages and examining their spatial distributions, they may estimate how long the speakers of those languages have lived where they do. By identifying those words in related languages that have survived from an ancient ancestral tongue, they can also suggest not only where, but how, the speakers of the ancestral language lived. Such work shows linguistic ties between geographically distant groups such as the people of Finland and Turkey.

Linguistic anthropology is practiced in a number of applied settings. For example, linguistic anthropologists have collaborated with indigenous communities and ethnic minorities in the preservation or revival of languages lost during periods of oppression by dominant societies. Anthropologists have helped to create written forms of some languages that previously existed only by word of mouth. These examples of applied linguistic anthropology represent the kind of true collaboration that is characteristic of much anthropological fieldwork today.

---

linguistic anthropology The study of human languages, looking at their structure, history, and/or relation to social and cultural contexts.
empirical Based on observations of the world rather than on intuition or faith.
hypothesis A tentative explanation of the relation between certain phenomena.

ANTHROPOLOGY, SCIENCE, AND THE HUMANITIES

Anthropology has been called the most humane of the sciences and the most scientific of the humanities—a designation that most anthropologists accept with pride. Given their intense involvement with people of all times and places, it should come as no surprise that anthropologists have amassed considerable information about human failure and success, weakness and greatness—the real stuff of the humanities. While anthropologists steer clear of an impersonal scientific approach that reduces people and the things they do and think to mere numbers, their quantitative studies have contributed substantially to the scientific study of the human condition. But even the most scientific anthropologists always keep in mind that human societies are made up of individuals with rich assortments of emotions and aspirations that demand respect.

Beyond this, anthropologists remain committed to the proposition that one cannot fully understand another culture by simply observing it; as the term *participant observation* implies, one must *experience* it as well. This same commitment to fieldwork and to the systematic collection of data, whether it is qualitative or quantitative, is also evidence of the scientific side of anthropology. Anthropology is an **empirical** social science based in observations about humans. But what distinguishes anthropology from other sciences are the diverse ways in which scientific research is conducted within anthropology.

Science, a carefully honed way of producing knowledge, aims to reveal and explain the underlying logic, the structural processes that make the world "tick." It is a creative endeavor that seeks testable explanations for observed phenomena, ideally in terms of the workings of hidden but unchanging principles, or laws. Two basic ingredients are essential for this: imagination and skepticism. Imagination, though capable of leading us astray, is required to help us recognize unexpected ways phenomena might be ordered and to think of old things in new ways. Without it, there can be no science. Skepticism is what allows us to distinguish fact (an observation verified by others) from fancy, to test our speculations, and to prevent our imaginations from running away with us.

In their search for explanations, scientists do not assume that things are always as they appear on the surface. After all, what could be more obvious than that the earth is a stable entity, around which the sun travels every day? And yet, it isn't so.

Like other scientists, anthropologists often begin their research with a **hypothesis** (a tentative explanation or hunch) about the possible relationships between certain observed facts or events. By gathering various kinds of data that seem to ground such suggested explanations on evidence, anthropologists come up with a

Anthropologists of Note

Franz Boas (1858–1942) ■ Matilda Coxe Stevenson (1849–1915)

Franz Boas was not the first to teach anthropology in the United States, but it was he and his students, with their insistence on scientific rigor, who made anthropology courses a common part of college and university curricula. Born and raised in Germany, where he studied physics, mathematics, and geography, Boas did his first ethnographic research among the Inuit (Eskimos) in Arctic Canada in 1883–1884. After a brief academic career in Berlin, he came to the United States. There, after work in museums interspersed with ethnographic research among Kwakiutl Indians in the Canadian Pacific, he became a professor at Columbia University in New York City in 1896. He authored an incredible number of publications, founded professional organizations and journals, and taught

© Bettmann/Corbis

two generations of great anthropologists, including numerous women and ethnic minorities.

As a Jewish immigrant, Boas recognized the dangers of ethnocentrism and especially racism. Through ethnographic fieldwork and comparative analysis, he demonstrated that white supremacy theories and other schemes ranking non-European peoples and cultures as inferior were biased, ill-informed, and unscientific. Throughout his long and illustrious academic career, he not only promoted anthropology as a human science but also as an instrument to combat racism and prejudice in the world.

Among the founders of North American anthropology were a number of women who were highly influential among women's rights advocates in the late 1800s. One such pioneering anthropologist was **Matilda Coxe Stevenson**, who did fieldwork among the Zuni Indians of Arizona. In 1885, she founded the Women's Anthropological Society in Washington, D.C., the first professional association for women scientists. Three years later, hired by the Smithsonian's Bureau of American Ethnology, she became one of the first women in the world to receive a full-time official position in science.

The tradition of women being active in anthropology continues. In fact,

© Smithsonian Institution Photo # 56196

since World War II more than half the presidents of the now 12,000-member American Anthropological Association have been women.

Recording observations on film as well as in notebooks, Stevenson and Boas were also pioneers in visual anthropology. Stevenson used an early box camera to document Pueblo Indian religious ceremonies and material culture, while Boas photographed Inuit (Eskimos) in northern Canada in 1883 and Kwakiutl Indians from the early 1890s for cultural as well as physical anthropological documentation. Today, these old photographs are greatly valued not only by anthropologists and historians, but also by indigenous peoples themselves.

---

theory—an explanation supported by a reliable body of data. In their effort to demonstrate linkages between known facts or events, anthropologists may discover unexpected facts, events, or relationships. An important function of theory is that it guides us in our explorations and may result in new knowledge. Equally important, the newly discovered facts may provide evidence that certain explanations, however popular or firmly believed to be true, are unfounded. When the evidence is lacking or fails to support the suggested explanations, anthropologists are forced to drop promising hypotheses or attractive hunches. In other words, anthropology relies on empirical evidence. Moreover, no scientific theory, no matter how widely accepted by the international community of scholars, is beyond challenge.

Straightforward though the scientific approach may seem, its application is not always easy. For instance, once a hypothesis has been proposed, the person who

suggested it is strongly motivated to verify it, and this can cause one to unwittingly overlook negative evidence and unanticipated findings. This is a familiar problem in all science as noted by paleontologist Stephen Jay Gould: "The greatest impediment to scientific innovation is usually a conceptual lock, not a factual lock."[6] Because culture provides humans with their concepts and shapes our very thoughts, it can be challenging to frame hypotheses or develop interpretations that are not culture-bound. By encompassing both humanism and science, the discipline of anthropology can draw on its internal diversity to overcome conceptual locks.

---

[6]Gould, S. J. (1989). *Wonderful life* (p. 226). New York: Norton.

theory In science, an explanation of natural phenomena, supported by a reliable body of data.

Fieldwork

All anthropologists are aware that personal and cultural background may shape their research questions and, more importantly, modify or even distort their actual observations. Engaging in such critical self-reflection, they rely on a technique that also has proved successful in other disciplines: They immerse themselves in the data to the fullest extent possible. In the process, anthropologists become so thoroughly familiar with even the smallest details that they may begin to identify possible relationships and underlying patterns in the data. Recognition of such suspected relationships and patterns enables anthropologists to frame meaningful hypotheses, which then may be subjected to further testing on location or "in the field." Within anthropology, such fieldwork brings additional rigor to the concept of total immersion in the data.

Touched upon above in our discussion of cultural anthropology, fieldwork is also characteristic of the other anthropological subdisciplines. Archaeologists and paleoanthropologists excavate sites in the field. A biological anthropologist interested in the effects of globalization on nutrition and human growth will reside in the particular community of people selected for study. A primatologist might live among a group of chimpanzees or baboons just as a linguist will study the language of a people by living among them and sharing their daily life. Fieldwork, being on location and fully immersed in another way of life, challenges the anthropologist to be constantly aware of the possible ways that otherwise unsuspected cultural factors may influence the research questions, observations, and explanations.

Fieldwork requires researchers to step out of their cultural comfort zone into a world that is unfamiliar and sometimes unsettling. Anthropologists in the field are likely to face a host of challenges—physical, social, mental, political, and ethical. They may have to deal with the physical challenge of adjusting to unfamiliar food, climate, and hygiene conditions. Typically, anthropologists in the field struggle with such mental challenges as loneliness, feeling like a perpetual outsider, being socially clumsy and clueless in their new cultural setting, and having to be alert around the clock because anything that is happening or being said may be significant to their research. Political challenges include the possibility of unwittingly letting oneself be used by factions within the community or being viewed with hostility by government authorities who may suspect the anthropologist is a spy. And there are ethical dilemmas: what to do if faced with a cultural practice one finds troubling, such as female circumcision; how to deal with demands for food supplies and/or medicine; how to handle the temptation to use deception to gain vital information; and so on.

At the same time, fieldwork often leads to tangible and meaningful personal, professional, and social rewards, ranging from lasting friendships to vital knowledge and insights concerning the human condition that make positive contributions to people's lives. Something of the meaning of anthropological fieldwork—its usefulness and its impact on researcher and subject—is conveyed in the following Original Study by Suzanne Leclerc-Madlala, an anthropologist who left her familiar New England surroundings two decades ago to do AIDS research among Zulu-speaking people in South Africa. Her research interest has changed the course of her own life, not to mention the lives of individuals who have HIV/AIDS and the type of treatment they receive.

Original Study ▪ By Suzanne Leclerc-Madlala

Fighting HIV/AIDS in Africa: Traditional Healers on the Front Line

In the 1980s, as a North American anthropology graduate student at George Washington University, I met and married a Zulu-speaking student from South Africa. It was the height of apartheid, and upon moving to that country I was classified as "honorary black" and forced to live in a segregated township with my husband. The AIDS epidemic was in its infancy, but it was clear from the start that an anthropological understanding of how people perceive and engage with this disease would be crucial for developing interventions. I wanted to learn all

that I could to make a difference, and this culminated in earning a Ph.D. from the University of Natal on the cultural construction of AIDS among the Zulu. The HIV/AIDS pandemic in Africa became my professional passion.

Faced with overwhelming global health-care needs, the World Health Organization passed a series of resolutions in the 1970s promoting collaboration between traditional and modern medicine. Such moves held a special relevance for Africa where traditional healers typically outnumber practitioners

of modern medicine by a ratio of 100 to 1 or more. Given Africa's disproportionate burden of disease, supporting partnership efforts with traditional healers makes sense. But what sounds sensible today was once considered absurd, even heretical. For centuries Westerners generally viewed traditional healing as a whole lot of primitive mumbo jumbo practiced by witchdoctors with demonic powers who perpetuated superstition. Yet, its practice survived. Today, as the African continent grapples with an HIV/AIDS epidemic of crisis proportion, millions of sick people who are either too poor or too distant to access modern health care are proving that traditional healers are an invaluable resource in the fight against AIDS.

Of the world's estimated 40 million people currently infected by HIV, 70 percent live in sub-Saharan Africa, and the vast majority of children left orphaned by AIDS are African. From the 1980s onward, as Africa became synonymous with the rapid spread of HIV/AIDS, a number of prevention programs involved traditional healers. My initial research in South Africa's KwaZulu-Natal province—where it is estimated that 36 percent of the population is HIV infected—revealed that traditional Zulu healers were regularly consulted for the treatment of sexually transmitted disease (STD). I found that such diseases, along with HIV/AIDS, were usually attributed to transgressions of taboos related to birth, pregnancy, marriage, and death. Moreover, these diseases were often understood within a framework of pollution and contagion, and like most serious illnesses, ultimately believed to have their causal roots in witchcraft.

In the course of my research, I investigated a pioneer program in STD and HIV education for traditional healers in the province. The program aimed to provide basic biomedical knowledge about the various modes of disease transmission, the means available for prevention, the diagnosing of symptoms, the keeping of records, and the making of patient referrals to local clinics and hospitals. Interviews with the healers showed that many maintained a deep suspicion of modern medicine. They perceived AIDS education as a one-way street intended to press them into formal health struc-

tures and convince them of the superiority of modern medicine. Yet, today, few of the 6,000-plus KwaZulu-Natal healers who have been trained in AIDS education say they would opt for less collaboration; most want to have more.

Treatments by Zulu healers for HIV/AIDS often take the form of infusions of bitter herbs to "cleanse" the body, strengthen the blood, and remove misfortune and "pollution." Some treatments provide effective relief from common ailments associated with AIDS such as itchy skin rashes, oral thrush, persistent diarrhea, and general debility. Indigenous plants such as *unwele (Sutherlandia*

Medical anthropologist Suzanne Leclerc-Madlala visits with "Doctor" Koloko in KwaZulu-Natal, South Africa. This Zulu traditional healer proudly displays her official AIDS training certificate.

© Kerry Cullinan

frutescens) and African potato *(Hypoxis hemerocallidea)* are well-known traditional medicines that have proven immuno-boosting properties.

Both have recently become available in modern pharmacies packaged in tablet form. With modern anti-retroviral treatments still well beyond the reach of most South Africans, indigenous medicines that can delay or alleviate some of the suffering caused by AIDS are proving to be valuable and popular treatments.

Knowledge about potentially infectious bodily fluids has led healers to change some of their practices. Where porcupine quills were once used to give a type of indigenous injection, patients are now advised to bring their own sewing needles to consultations. Patients provide their own individual razor blades for making incisions on their skin, where

previously healers reused the same razor on many clients. Some healers claim they have given up the practice of biting clients' skin to remove foreign objects from the body. It is not uncommon today, especially in urban centers like Durban, to find healers proudly displaying AIDS training certificates in their inner-city "surgeries" where they don white jackets and wear protective latex gloves.

Politics and controversy have dogged South Africa's official response to HIV/AIDS. But back home in the waddle-and-daub, animal-skin-draped herbariums and divining huts of traditional healers, the politics of AIDS holds little relevance. Here the sick and dying are coming in droves to be treated by healers who have been part and parcel of community life (and death) since time immemorial. In many cases traditional healers have transformed their homes into hospices for AIDS patients. Because of the strong stigma that still plagues the disease, those with AIDS symptoms are often abandoned or sometimes chased away from their homes by family members. They seek refuge with healers who provide them with comfort in their final days. Healers' homes are also becoming orphanages as healers respond to what has been called the "third wave" of AIDS destruction: the growing legions of orphaned children.

The practice of traditional healing in Africa is adapting to the changing face of health and illness in the context of HIV/AIDS. But those who are suffering go to traditional healers not only in search of relief for physical symptoms. They go to learn about the ultimate cause of their disease—something other than the immediate cause of a sexually transmitted "germ" or "virus." They go to find answers to the "why me and not him" questions, the "why now" and "why this." As with most traditional healing systems worldwide, healing among the Zulu and most all African ethnic groups cannot be separated from the spiritual concerns of the individual and the cosmological beliefs of the community at large. Traditional heal-

CONTINUED

CONTINUED

ers help to restore a sense of balance between the individual and the community, on one hand, and between the individual and the cosmos, or ancestors, on the other hand. They provide health care that is personalized, culturally appropriate, holistic, and tailored to meet the needs and expectations of the patient. In many ways it is a far more satisfactory form

of healing than that offered by modern medicine.

Traditional healing in Africa is flourishing in the era of AIDS, and understanding why this is so requires a shift in the conceptual framework by which we understand, explain, and interpret health. Anthropological methods and its comparative and holistic perspective

can facilitate, like no other discipline, the type of understanding that is urgently needed to address the AIDS crisis.
(By Suzanne Leclerc-Madlala. Adapted in part from S. Leclerc-Madlala (2002). Bodies and politics: Healing rituals in the democratic South Africa. In V. Faure (Ed.), Les cahiers de 'I'IFAS, No. 2. Johannesburg: The French Institute.) ■

ANTHROPOLOGY'S COMPARATIVE METHOD

The end product of anthropological research, if properly carried out, is a coherent statement about a people that provides an explanatory framework for understanding the beliefs, behavior, or biology of those who have been studied. And this, in turn, is what permits the anthropologist to frame broader hypotheses about human beliefs, behavior, and biology. A single instance of any phenomenon is generally insufficient for supporting a plausible hypothesis. Without some basis for comparison, the hypothesis grounded in a single case may be no more than a particular historical coincidence. On the other hand, a single case may be enough to cast doubt on, if not refute, a theory that had previously been held to be valid. For example, the discovery in 1948 that aborigines living in Australia's northern Arnhem Land put in an average workday of less than 6 hours, while living well above a level of bare sufficiency, was enough to call into question the widely accepted notion that food-foraging peoples are so preoccupied with finding scarce food that they lack time for any of life's more pleasurable activities. The observations made in the Arnhem Land study have since been confirmed many times over in various parts of the world.

Hypothetical explanations of cultural and biological phenomena may be tested through comparison of archaeological, biological, linguistic, historical, and/or ethnographic data for several societies found in a particular region. Carefully controlled comparison provides a broader basis for drawing general conclusions about humans than does the study of a single culture or population. The anthropologist who undertakes such a comparison may be more confident that events or features believed to be related really are related, at least within the area under investigation; however, an explanation that is valid in one area is not necessarily so in another.

Ideally, theories in anthropology are generated from worldwide comparisons or comparisons across species or

through time. Anthropologists examine a global sample of societies in order to discover whether or not hypotheses proposed to explain cultural phenomena or biological variation are universally applicable. However, cross-cultural researchers depend upon data gathered by other scholars as well as their own. Similarly, archaeologists and biological anthropologists rely on artifacts and skeletal collections housed in museums, as well as published descriptions of these collections.

QUESTIONS OF ETHICS

The kinds of research carried out by anthropologists, and the settings within which they work, raise a number of important moral questions about the potential uses and abuses of our knowledge. Who will utilize our findings and for what purposes? Who decides what research questions are asked? Who, if anyone, will profit from the research? For example, in the case of research on an ethnic or religious minority whose values may be at odds with dominant mainstream society, will governmental or corporate interests use anthropological data to suppress that group? And what of traditional communities around the world? Who is to decide what changes should, or should not, be introduced for community "betterment"? And who defines what constitutes betterment—the community, a national government, or an international agency like the World Health Organization? What are the limits of cultural relativism when a traditional practice is considered a human rights abuse globally?

Then there is the problem of privacy. Anthropologists deal with matters that are private and sensitive, including things that individuals would prefer not to have generally known about them. How does one write about such important but delicate issues and at the same time protect the privacy of the individuals who have shared their stories? The American Anthropological Association (AAA) maintains a Statement of Ethics, which is regularly examined and modified to reflect the practice of anthropology in a changing world. This educational document lays out the rules and ideals applicable to anthropologists in all the subdisciplines. While the AAA has no legal authority, it does issue policy statements on research ethics questions as they come up. For example, recently the AAA recommended that field notes from medical settings should be protected and not subject to subpoena in malpractice lawsuits. This honors the ethical imperative to protect the privacy of individuals who have shared their stories with anthropologists.

Anthropologists recognize that they have special obligations to three sets of people: those whom they study, those who fund the research, and those in the profession who expect us to publish our findings so that they may be used to further our collective knowledge. Because fieldwork requires a relationship of trust between fieldworkers and the community in which they work, the anthropologist's first responsibility clearly is to the individuals who have shared their stories and the greater community. Everything possible must be done to protect their physical, social, and psychological welfare and to honor their dignity and privacy. This task is frequently complex. For example, telling the story of a group of people gives information both to relief agencies who might help them and to others who might take advantage of them.

While anthropologists regard as basic a people's right to maintain their own culture, any connections with outsiders can endanger the cultural identity of the community being studied. To overcome these obstacles, anthropologists frequently collaborate with and contribute to the communities in which they are working, allowing the people being studied to have some say about how their stories are told.

ANTHROPOLOGY AND GLOBALIZATION

A holistic perspective and a long-term commitment to understanding the human species in all its variety is the essence of anthropology. Thus, anthropology is well equipped to grapple with an issue that has overriding importance for all of us at the beginning of the 21st century: **globalization.** This term refers to worldwide interconnectedness, evidenced in global movements of natural resources, human labor, finance capital, information, infectious diseases, and trade goods (including human organs as described in this chapter's Globalscape). Although worldwide travel, trade relations, and information flow have existed for several centuries, the pace and magnitude of these long-distance exchanges has picked up enormously in recent decades; the Internet, in particular, has greatly expanded information exchange capacities.

The powerful forces driving globalization are technological innovations, lower transportation and commu-

nication costs, faster knowledge transfers, and increased trade and financial integration among countries. Touching almost everybody's life on the planet, globalization is about economics as much as politics, and it changes human relations and ideas as well as our natural environments. Even geographically remote communities are quickly becoming more interdependent through globalization.

Doing research in all corners of the world, anthropologists are confronted with the impact of globalization on human communities wherever they are located. As participant observers, they describe and try to explain how individuals and organizations respond to the massive changes confronting them. Anthropologists may also find out how local responses sometimes change the global flows directed at them.

Dramatically increasing every year, globalization can be a two-edged sword. It may generate economic growth and prosperity, but it also undermines long-established institutions. Generally, globalization has brought significant gains to higher-educated groups in wealthier countries, while doing little to boost developing countries and actually contributing to the erosion of traditional cultures. Upheavals born of globalization are key causes for rising levels of ethnic and religious conflict throughout the world.

Since all of us now live in a global village, we can no longer afford the luxury of ignoring our neighbors, no matter how distant they may seem. In this age of globalization, anthropology may not only provide humanity with useful insights concerning diversity, but it may also assist us in avoiding or overcoming significant problems born of that diversity. In countless social arenas, from schools to businesses to hospitals to emergency centers, anthropologists have done cross-cultural research that makes it possible for educators, businesspeople, doctors, and humanitarians to do their work more effectively.

The wide-ranging relevance of anthropological knowledge in today's world may be illustrated by three quite different examples. In the United States today, discrimination based on notions of race continues to be a serious issue affecting economic, political, and social relations. Far from being a biological reality, anthropologists have shown that the concept of race emerged in the 18th century as a device for justifying European dominance over Africans and American Indians. In fact, differences of skin color are simply surface adaptations to different climatic zones and have nothing to do with physical or mental capabilities. Indeed, geneticists find

globalization Worldwide interconnectedness, evidenced in global movements of natural resources, trade goods, human labor, finance capital, information, and infectious diseases.

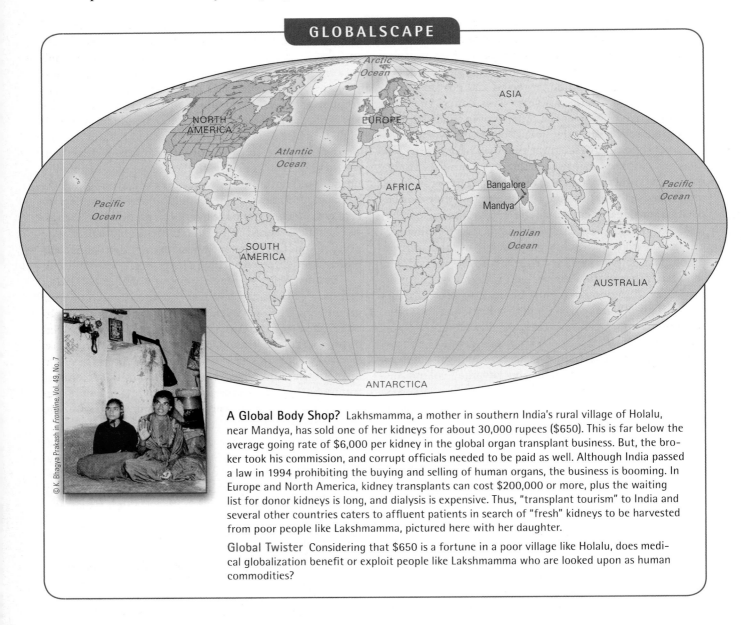

GLOBALSCAPE

A Global Body Shop? Lakhsmamma, a mother in southern India's rural village of Holalu, near Mandya, has sold one of her kidneys for about 30,000 rupees ($650). This is far below the average going rate of $6,000 per kidney in the global organ transplant business. But, the broker took his commission, and corrupt officials needed to be paid as well. Although India passed a law in 1994 prohibiting the buying and selling of human organs, the business is booming. In Europe and North America, kidney transplants can cost $200,000 or more, plus the waiting list for donor kidneys is long, and dialysis is expensive. Thus, "transplant tourism" to India and several other countries caters to affluent patients in search of "fresh" kidneys to be harvested from poor people like Lakshmamma, pictured here with her daughter.

Global Twister Considering that $650 is a fortune in a poor village like Holalu, does medical globalization benefit or exploit people like Lakshmamma who are looked upon as human commodities?

far more biological variation *within* any given human population than *among* them. In short, human "races" are divisive categories based on prejudice, false ideas of differences, and erroneous notions of the superiority of one's own group. Given the importance of this issue, race and other aspects of biological variation will be discussed further in upcoming sections of the text.

A second example involves the issue of same-sex marriage. In 1989, Denmark became the first country to enact a comprehensive set of legal protections for same-sex couples, known as the Registered Partnership Act. At this writing, more than a half-dozen other countries and some individual states within the United States have passed similar laws, variously named, and numerous countries around the world are considering or have passed legislation providing people in homo-

sexual unions the benefits and protections afforded by marriage.[7] In some societies—including Spain, Canada, Belgium, and the Netherlands—same-sex marriages are considered socially acceptable and allowed by law, even though opposite-sex marriages are far more common.

As individuals, countries, and states struggle to define the boundaries of legal protections they will grant to same-sex couples, the anthropological perspective on

[7]Merin, Y. (2002). *Equality for same-sex couples: The legal recognition of gay partnerships in Europe and the United States.* Chicago: University of Chicago Press; "Court says same-sex marriage is a right" (2004, February 5), *San Francisco Chronicle;* current overviews and updates on the global status of same-sex marriage are posted on the Internet by the Partners Task Force for Gay & Lesbian Couples at www .buddybuddy.com.

marriage is useful. Anthropologists have documented same-sex marriages in many human societies in various parts of the world, where they are regarded as acceptable under appropriate circumstances. Homosexual behavior occurs in the animal world just as it does among humans.[8] The key difference between people and other animals is that human societies entertain beliefs regarding homosexual behavior, just as they do for heterosexual behavior—beliefs that specify when, where, how, and with whom sexual relations are appropriate or "normal." An understanding of global variation in marriage patterns and sexual behavior does not dictate that one pattern is more right than another. It simply illustrates that all human societies define the boundaries for social relationships.

A final example relates to the common confusion of *nation* with *state*. Anthropology makes an important distinction between these two: States are politically organized territories that are internationally recognized, whereas nations are socially organized bodies of people, who putatively share ethnicity—a common origin, language, and cultural heritage. For example, the Kurds constitute a nation, but their homeland (Kurdistan) is di-

---

[8]Kirkpatrick, R. C. (2000). The evolution of human homosexual behavior. *Current Anthropology 41*, 384.

vided among several states, primarily Turkey, Iraq, and Iran. The modern boundaries of these states were drawn up after World War I, with little regard for the region's ethnic groups or nations. Similar processes have taken place throughout the world, especially in Asia and Africa, often making political conditions in these countries inherently unstable.

As we will see in later chapters, states and nations rarely coincide, nations being split among different states, and states typically being controlled by members of one nation who commonly use their control to gain access to the land, resources, and labor of other nationalities within the state. Most of the armed conflicts in the world today, such as the many-layered conflicts among the peoples of the former Yugoslavia, are of this sort and are not mere acts of tribalism or terrorism, as commonly asserted.

As these examples show, ignorance about other peoples and their ways causes serious problems throughout the world, especially now that we have developed a global system of fast information exchange and mass transportation that greatly increase our interaction and interdependence. Anthropology offers a way of looking at and understanding the world's peoples—insights that are nothing less than basic skills for survival in this age of globalization.

Questions for Reflection

1. Anthropology uses a holistic approach to explain all aspects of human beliefs, behavior, and biology. How might anthropology challenge your personal perspective on the following questions: Where did we come from? Why do we act in certain ways? What makes us tick?

2. From the holistic anthropological perspective, humans have one leg in culture and the other in nature. Are there examples from your life that illustrate the interconnectedness of human biology and culture?

3. Globalization can be described as a two-edged sword. How does it foster growth and destruction simultaneously?

4. The textbook definitions of *state* and *nation* are based on scientific distinctions between both organizational types. However, this distinction is commonly lost in everyday language. Consider, for instance, the names *United States of America* and the *United Nations*. How does confusing the terms contribute to political conflict?

5. The Biocultural Connection in this chapter contrasts different cultural perspectives on brain death, while the Original Study features a discussion about traditional Zulu healers and their role in dealing with AIDS victims. What do these two accounts suggest about the role of applied anthropology in dealing with cross-cultural health issues around the world?

Suggested Readings

Bonvillain, N. (2000). *Language, culture, and communication: The meaning of messages* (3rd ed.). Upper Saddle River, NJ: Prentice-Hall.

An up-to-date text on language and communication in a cultural context.

Fagan, B. M. (1999). *Archeology: A brief introduction* (7th ed.). New York: Longman.

This primer offers an overview of archaeological theory and methodology, from field survey techniques to excavation to analysis of materials.

Jones, S., Martin R., & Pilbeam, D. (Eds.). (1992). *Cambridge encyclopedia of human evolution*. New York: Cambridge University Press.

This comprehensive introduction to the human species covers the gamut of biological anthropology, from genetics, primatology, and the fossil evidence to a detailed exploration of contemporary human ecology, demography, and disease. Contributions by over seventy scholars.

Kedia, S., & Van Willigen, J. (2005). *Applied anthropology: Domains of application*. New York: Praeger.

Compelling essays by prominent scholars on the potential, accomplishments, and methods of applied anthropology in domains including development, agriculture, environment, health and medicine, nutrition, population displacement and resettlement, business and industry, education, and aging. The contributors show how anthropology can be used to address today's social, economic, health, and technical challenges.

Peacock, J. L. (2002). *The anthropological lens: Harsh light, soft focus* (2nd ed.). New York: Cambridge University Press.

This lively and innovative book gives the reader a good understanding of the diversity of activities undertaken by cultural anthropologists, while at the same time identifying the unifying themes that hold the discipline together. Additions to the second edition include such topics as globalization, gender, and postmodernism.

Thomson Audio Study Products

 Enjoy the MP3-ready Audio Lecture Overviews for each chapter and a comprehensive audio glossary of key terms for quick study and review. Whether walking to class, doing laundry, or studying at your desk, you now have the freedom to choose when, where, and how you interact with your audio-based educational media. See the preface for information on how to access this on-the-go study and review tool.

The Anthropology Resource Center

www.thomsonedu.com/anthropology

The Anthropology Resource Center provides extended learning materials to reinforce your understanding of key concepts in the four subfields of anthropology. For each of the four subdisciplines, the Resource Center includes dynamic exercises including video exercises, map exercises, simulations, and "Meet the Scientists" interviews, as well as critical thinking questions that can be assigned and e-mailed to instructors. The Resource Center also provides breaking news in anthropology and interesting material on applied anthropology to help you link what you are learning to the world around you.

2 Characteristics of Culture

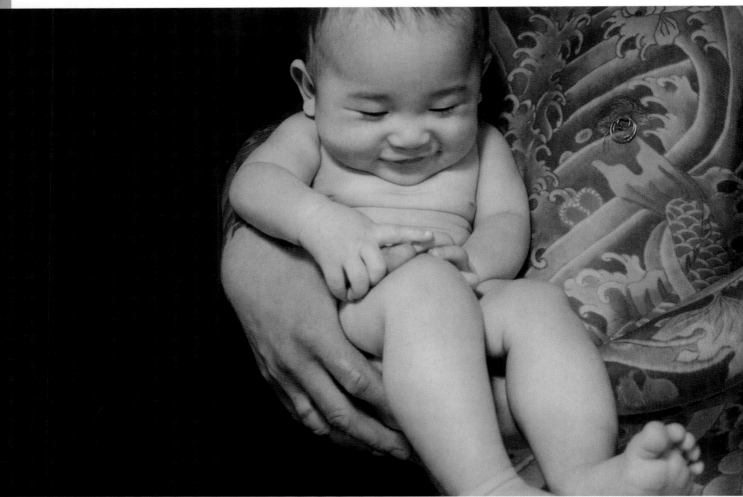

© Sandi Fellman, 1984

CHALLENGE ISSUE

Born naked and speechless, we are naturally incapable of surviving alone. As humans, we rely on culture, a shared way of living, to meet the physical, social, economic, and ideological challenges of human survival. In fact, it is through culture that we become fully human. Culture is manifested in countless ways, but one of its most visible expressions is self-adornment—the distinctive ways groups of people dress, style their hair, and otherwise decorate their bodies. We may enter the world in a natural state with a biological profile, but over time we acquire a cultural identity, etched into our minds and sometimes into our very skin—as shown in this photograph of Japanese tattoo artist Horiyoshi II, holding his unmarked newborn son.

What Is Culture?

Culture consists of the abstract ideas, values, and perceptions of the world that inform and are reflected in people's behavior. Culture is shared by members of a society and produces behavior that is intelligible to other members of that society. Cultures are learned rather than inherited biologically, and all the different parts of a culture function as an integrated whole.

Why Do Cultures Exist?

Every culture provides a design for thought and action that helps people survive and deal with all the challenges of existence. To endure, a culture must satisfy the basic needs of those who live by its rules, and it must provide an orderly existence for the members of a society. In doing so, a culture must strike a balance between the self-interests of individuals and the needs of society as a whole. Moreover, it must have the capacity to change in order to adapt to new circumstances or to altered perceptions of existing circumstances.

Ethnocentrism: Are Some Cultures Better than Others?

Humans are born into families forming part of wider communities. Raised by relatives and other members of these groups, we learn to behave, speak, and think like others in our society. Because each of us is reared to regard the world from the vantage point of our own social group, the human perspective is typically "ethnocentric"—believing that the ways of one's own culture are the only proper ones. Crossing cultural boundaries, we discover that people in our own society are not unique in being ethnocentric. Anthropologists challenge ethnocentrism by striving to understand each culture in its own right.

Students of anthropology are bound to find themselves studying a seemingly endless variety of human societies, each with its own distinctive environment and system of economics, politics, and religion. Yet for all this variety, these societies have one thing in common: Each is a group of people cooperating to ensure their collective survival and well-being. Group living and cooperation are impossible unless individuals know how others are likely to behave in any given situation. Thus, some degree of predictable behavior is required of each person within the society. In humans, it is culture that sets the limits of behavior and guides it along predictable paths that are generally acceptable to those who fall within the culture.

THE CONCEPT OF CULTURE

Anthropologists conceived the modern concept of culture toward the end of the 19th century. The first really clear and comprehensive definition came from the British anthropologist Sir Edward Tylor. Writing in 1871, he defined culture as "that complex whole which includes knowledge, belief, art, law, morals, custom, and any other capabilities and habits acquired by man as a member of society."

Since Tylor's time, definitions of culture have proliferated, so that by the early 1950s, North American anthropologists A. L. Kroeber and Clyde Kluckhohn were able to collect over a hundred of them from the academic literature. Recent definitions tend to distinguish more clearly between actual behavior and the abstract ideas, values, and perceptions of the world that inform that behavior. To put it another way, **culture** goes deeper than observable behavior; it is a society's shared and socially transmitted ideas, values, and perceptions, which are used to make sense of experience and generate behavior and are reflected in behavior.

THOMSON AUDIO STUDY PRODUCTS Take advantage of the MP3-ready Audio Lecture Overviews and comprehensive audio glossary of key terms for each chapter. See the preface for information on how to access this on-the-go study and review tool.

culture A society's shared and socially transmitted ideas, values, and perceptions, which are used to make sense of experience and which generate behavior and are reflected in that behavior.

enculturation The process by which a society's culture is transmitted from one generation to the next and individuals become members of their society.

CHARACTERISTICS OF CULTURE

Through the comparative study of many human cultures, past and present, anthropologists have gained an understanding of the basic characteristics evident in all of them: Every culture is learned, shared, based on symbols, integrated, and dynamic. A careful study of these characteristics helps us to see the importance and the function of culture itself.

Culture Is Learned

All culture is learned rather than biologically inherited, prompting U.S. anthropologist Ralph Linton to refer to it as humanity's "social heredity." One learns one's culture by growing up with it, and the process whereby culture is transmitted from one generation to the next is called **enculturation.**

Most animals eat and drink whenever the urge arises. Humans, however, are enculturated to do most of their eating and drinking at certain culturally prescribed times and feel hungry as those times approach. These eating times vary from culture to culture, as does what is eaten, how it is prepared, how it is eaten, and where. To add complexity, food is used to do more than merely satisfy nutritional requirements. When used to celebrate rituals and religious activities, as it often is, food "establishes relationships of give and take, of cooperation, of sharing, of an emotional bond that is universal."[1]

Through enculturation every person learns socially appropriate ways of satisfying the basic biologically determined needs of all humans: food, sleep, shelter, companionship, self-defense, and sexual gratification. It is important to distinguish between the needs themselves, which are not learned, and the learned ways in which they are satisfied—for each culture determines in its own way how these needs will be met. For instance, a North American's idea of a comfortable way to sleep may vary greatly from that of a Japanese person.

Learned behavior is exhibited in some degree by most, if not all, mammals. Several species may even be said to have elementary culture, in that local populations share patterns of behavior that, just like humans, each generation learns from the one before and that differ from one population to another. Elizabeth Marshall Thomas, for example, has described a distinctive pattern of behavior among lions of southern Africa's Kalahari Desert—behavior that fostered nonaggressive interaction with the region's indigenous hunters and gatherers and that each generation of lions passed on

---

[1]Caroulis, J. (1996). Food for thought. *Pennsylvania Gazette 95* (3), 16.

VISUAL COUNTERPOINT

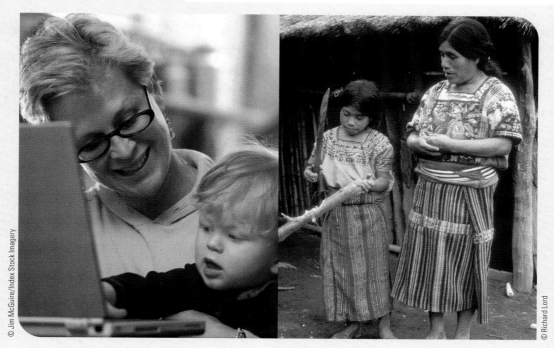

In all human societies adults teach social roles and pass on cultural skills to the next generation. Here a North American mother introduces her child to the computer, and a Maya Indian mother in Guatemala shows her daughter how to handle a machete—useful for a multitude of tasks, from gardening to chopping food to cutting wood for fire and buildings.

to the next.[2] She has shown as well how Kalahari lion culture changed over a thirty-year period in response to new circumstances. That said, it is important to note that not all learned behavior is cultural. For instance, a pigeon may learn tricks, but this behavior is reflexive, the result of conditioning by repeated training, not the product of enculturation.

Beyond our species, examples of cultural behavior are particularly evident among other primates. A chimpanzee, for example, will take a twig, strip it of all leaves, and smooth it down to fashion a tool for extracting termites from their nest. Such tool making, which juveniles learn from their elders, is unquestionably a form of cultural behavior once thought to be exclusively human. In Japan, macaques that learned the advantages of washing sweet potatoes before eating them passed the practice on to the next generation. Within any given primate species, the culture of one population often differs from that of others, just as it does among humans. We have discovered both in captivity and in the wild that primates in general and apes in particular "possess a near-human intelligence generally, including the use of sounds in representational ways, a rich awareness of the aims and objec-

tives of others, the ability to engage in tactical deception, and the ability to use symbols in communication with humans and each other."[3]

Given the remarkable degree of biological similarity between apes and humans, it should come as no surprise that they are like us in other ways as well. In fact, in many respects the differences between apes and humans are differences of degree rather than kind (although the degree *does* make a major difference). Growing knowledge of ape/human similarities contradicts a belief that is deeply embedded in Western cultures: the idea that there is a vast and unbridgeable gap between people and animals. It has not been easy to overcome this bias, and indeed we still have not come to grips fully with the moral implications with respect to the way humans treat fellow primates in research laboratories.

Culture Is Shared

As a shared set of ideas, values, perceptions, and standards of behavior, culture is the common denominator that makes the actions of individuals intelligible to other members of their society. It enables them to predict how

---

[2]Thomas, E. M. (1994). *The tribe of the tiger: Cats and their culture* (pp. 109–186). New York: Simon & Schuster.

[3]Reynolds, V. (1994). Primates in the field, primates in the lab. *Anthropology Today 10* (2), 4.

others are most likely to behave in a given circumstance, and it tells them how to react accordingly. A group of people from different cultures, stranded for a time on a desert island, may become a society of sorts. They would have a common interest—survival—and would develop techniques for living and working together. However, each person would retain his or her own cultural identity and the group would disintegrate once everyone was rescued from the island and returned home. It would have been merely an aggregate in time and not a cultural entity. **Society** may be defined as an organized group or groups of interdependent people who generally share a common territory, language, and culture and who act together for collective survival and well-being. The ways in which these people depend upon one another can be seen in such features as their economic, communication, and defense systems. They are also bound together by a general sense of common identity.

Because culture and society are such closely related concepts, anthropologists study both. Obviously, there can be no culture without a society. Conversely, there are no known human societies that do not exhibit culture. This cannot be said for all other animal species. Ants and bees, for example, instinctively cooperate in a manner that clearly indicates a remarkable degree of social organization, yet this instinctual behavior is not a culture. Whether or not animals other than humans exhibit cultural behavior is a question that we will deal with shortly.

Although a culture is shared by members of a society, it is important to realize that all is not uniform. For one thing, no two people share the exact same version of their culture. And there are bound to be other variations. At the very least, there is some difference between the roles of men and women. This stems from the fact that women give birth but men do not and that there are obvious differences between male and female reproductive anatomy and physiology. Every society gives cultural meaning to biological sexual differences by explaining them in a particular way and specifying what their significance is in terms of social roles and expected patterns of behavior.

Because each culture does this in its own way, there can be tremendous variation from one society to another. Anthropologists use the term **gender** to refer to the cultural elaborations and meanings assigned to the biological differentiation between the sexes. So, although one's sex is biologically determined, one's gender is so-

Newborn girls (under pink blankets) and boys (under blue blankets) in hospital nursery. Euramerican culture requires that newborn infants be assigned a gender identity of either male or female. Yet, significant numbers of infants are born each year whose genitalia do not conform to cultural expectations. Because only two genders are recognized, the usual reaction is to make the young bodies conform to cultural requirements through gender assignment surgery that involves constructing male or female genitalia. This is in contrast to many Native American cultures in which more than two genders are recognized.[4]

cially constructed within the context of one's particular culture.

The distinction between sex, which is biological, and gender, which is cultural, is an important one. Presumably, gender differences are at least as old as human culture—about 2.5 million years—and arose from the biological differences between early human males and females. As in chimps and gorillas today, the species most closely related to humans, early human males were on average substantially larger than females (although size contrasts were not as great as among gorillas). Average male–female size difference in modern humans appears to be significantly less than among our remote ancestors. Moreover, technological advancements in the home and workplace over the last century or two have greatly diminished the cultural significance of many remaining male–female biological differences in many societies all across the world.

Thus, apart from sexual differences directly related to reproduction, any biological basis for contrasting gender roles has largely disappeared in modern industrialized and postindustrial societies. (For example, hydraulic lifts used to move heavy automobile engines in an assembly line eliminate the need for muscular strength in

---

society An organized group or groups of interdependent people who generally share a common territory, language, and culture and who act together for collective survival and well-being.
gender The cultural elaborations and meanings assigned to the biological differentiation between the sexes.

---

[4]For statistics on this, see Blackless, M., et al. (2000). How sexually dimorphic are we? Review and synthesis. *American Journal of Human Biology 12*, 151–166.

that task.) Nevertheless, all cultures exhibit at least some role differentiation related to biology—some far more so than others.

In addition to cultural variation associated with gender, there is also variation related to age. In any society, children are not expected to behave as adults, and the reverse is equally true. But then, who is a child and who is an adult? Again, although age differences are "natural," cultures give their own meaning and timetable to the human life cycle. In North America, for example, individuals are generally not regarded as adults until the age of 18; in many others, adulthood begins earlier—often around age 12. That said, the status of adulthood often has less to do with age than with passage through certain prescribed rituals.

Subcultures: Groups Within a Larger Society

Besides age and gender variation, there may be cultural variation between subgroups in societies that share an overarching culture. These may be occupational groups in societies where there is a complex division of labor, or social classes in a stratified society, or ethnic groups in some other societies. When such groups exist within a society, each functioning by its own distinctive standards of behavior while still sharing some common standards, we speak of **subcultures.** The word *subculture* carries no suggestion of lesser status relative to the word *culture*.

Amish communities comprise one example of a subculture in North America. Specifically, they are an **ethnic group**—people who collectively and publicly identify themselves as a distinct group based on various cultural features such as shared ancestry and common origin, language, customs, and traditional beliefs. The Amish originated in western Europe during the Protestant revolutions that swept through Europe in the 16th century. Today members of this group number about 100,000 and live mainly in Pennsylvania, Ohio, Illinois, and Indiana in the United States, and in Ontario, Canada.

These pacifist, rural people base their lives on their traditional Anabaptist beliefs, which hold that only adult baptism is valid and that "true Christians" as they define them should not hold government office, bear arms, or use force. They prohibit marriage outside their faith, which calls for obedience to radical Christian teachings, including social separation from what they see as the wider "evil world" and rejection of material wealth as "vainglorious." Among themselves they usually speak a German dialect known as Pennsylvania Dutch (from *Deutsch,* meaning "German"). They use High German for religious purposes, and children learn English in school. Valuing simplicity, hard work, and a high degree of neighborly cooperation, they dress in a distinctive plain garb and even today rely on the horse for transpor-

subculture A distinctive set of standards and behavior patterns by which a group within a larger society operates, while still sharing common standards with that larger society.
ethnic group People who collectively and publicly identify themselves as a distinct group based on various cultural features such as shared ancestry and common origin, language, customs, and traditional beliefs.

© Andre Jenny/Alamy

The Amish people have held on to their traditional agrarian way of life in the midst of industrialized North American society. By maintaining their own schools to instill Amish values in their children, prohibiting mechanized vehicles and equipment, and dressing in their distinctive plain clothing, the Amish proclaim their own special identity.

tation as well as agricultural work.[5] In short, they share the same **ethnicity.** This term, rooted in the Greek word *ethnikos* ("nation") and related to *ethnos* ("custom") is the expression of the set of cultural ideas held by an ethnic group.

The goal of Amish education is to teach youngsters reading, writing, and arithmetic, as well as Amish values. Adults in the community reject what they regard as "worldly" knowledge and the idea of schools producing good citizens for the state. Resisting all attempts to force their children to attend regular public schools, they insist that education take place near home and that teachers be committed to Amish ideals.

Their nonconformity to many standards of mainstream culture has caused frequent conflict with state authorities, as well as legal and personal harassment. Pressed to compromise, they have introduced "vocational training" beyond junior high to fulfill state requirements, but they have managed to retain control of their schools, and maintain their way of life.

Confronted with economic challenges that make it impossible for most Amish groups to subsist solely on farming, some work outside their communities. Many more have established cottage industries and actively market homemade goods to tourists and other outsiders. Yet, while their economic separation from mainstream society has declined over the past four decades, their cultural separation has not.[6] They remain a reclusive community, more distrustful than ever of the dominant North American culture surrounding them and mingling as little as possible with non-Amish people.

The Amish are but one example of the way a subculture may develop and be dealt with by the larger culture within which it functions. Different as they are, the Amish actually put into practice many values that other North Americans primarily respect in the abstract: thrift, hard work, independence, a close family life. The degree of tolerance accorded to them, in contrast to some other ethnic groups, is also due in part to the fact that the Amish are "white" Europeans; they are defined as being of the same "race" as those who comprise dominant mainstream society. Although the concept of race has been shown to have no biological validity when applied

to humans, it still persists as a powerful social classification. This can be seen in the general lack of tolerance shown toward American Indians, typically viewed as racially different by members of the dominant society.

Implicit in the discussion thus far is that subcultures may develop in different ways. On the one hand, Amish subculture in the United States emerged as the product of the way these European immigrants have communicated and interacted in pursuit of their common goals within the wider society. On the other hand, North American Indian subcultures are formerly independent cultural groups that underwent colonization by European settlers and were forcibly brought under the control of federal governments in the United States and Canada.

Although all American Indian groups have experienced enormous changes due to colonization, many have held on to traditions significantly different from those of the dominant Euramerican culture surrounding them, so that it is sometimes difficult to decide whether they remain as distinct cultures as opposed to subcultures. In this sense, *culture* and *subculture* represent opposite ends of a continuum, with no clear dividing line in the gray area between. The Anthropology Applied feature examines the intersection of culture and subculture with an example concerning Apache Indian housing.

This raises the issue of the multi-ethnic or **pluralistic society** in which two or more ethnic groups or nationalities are politically organized into one territorial state but maintain their cultural differences. Pluralistic societies could not have existed before the first politically centralized states arose a mere 5,000 years ago. With the rise of the state, it became possible to bring about the political unification of two or more formerly independent societies, each with its own culture, thereby creating what amounts to a more complex order that transcends the theoretical one culture–one society linkage.

Pluralistic societies, which are common in the world today (Figure 2.1), all face the same challenge: They are comprised of groups that, by virtue of their high degree of cultural variation, are all essentially operating by different sets of rules. Since social living requires predictable behavior, it may be difficult for the members of any one subgroup to accurately interpret and follow the different standards by which the others operate. This can lead to significant misunderstandings, such as the following case reported in the *Wall Street Journal* of May 13, 1983:

> Salt Lake City—Police called it a cross-cultural misunderstanding. When the man showed up to buy the Shetland pony advertised for sale, the owner asked what he intended to do with the animal. "For my son's birthday," he replied, and the deal was closed.

---

[5]Hostetler, J., & Huntington, G. (1971). *Children in Amish society.* New York: Holt, Rinehart & Winston.

[6]Kraybill, D. B. (2001). *The riddle of Amish culture* (pp. 1–6, 244, 268–269). Baltimore: Johns Hopkins University Press.

ethnicity This term, rooted in the Greek word *ethnikos* ("nation") and related to *ethnos* ("custom"), is the expression of the set of cultural ideas held by an ethnic group.

pluralistic society A society in which two or more ethnic groups or nationalities are politically organized into one territorial state but maintain their cultural differences.

Anthropology Applied

New Houses for Apache Indians ▪ George S. Esber

The United States, in common with other industrialized countries of the world, contains a number of more or less separate subcultures. Those who live by the standards of one particular subculture have their closest relationships with one another, receiving constant reassurance that their perceptions of the world are the only correct ones and coming to take it for granted that the whole culture is as they see it. As a consequence, members of one subculture frequently have trouble understanding the needs and aspirations of other such groups. For this reason anthropologists, with their special understanding of cultural differences, are frequently employed as go-betweens in situations requiring interaction between peoples of differing cultural traditions.

As an example, while I was still a graduate student in anthropology, one of my professors asked me to work with architects and a community of Tonto Apache Indians to research housing needs for a new Apache community.[a] Although

the architects knew of the cross-cultural differences in the use of space, they had no idea of how to get relevant information from the Indian people. For their part, the Apaches had no explicit awareness of their needs, for these were based on unconscious patterns of behavior. For that matter, few people are consciously aware of the space needs for their own social patterns of behavior.

My task was to persuade the architects to hold back on their planning long enough for me to gather, through participant observation and a review of written records, the data from which Apache housing needs could be abstracted. At the same time, I had to overcome Apache anxieties over an outsider coming into their midst to learn about matters as personal as their daily lives as they are acted out, in and around their homes. With these hurdles overcome, I was able to identify and successfully communicate to the architects those features of Apache life having importance for home and community design. At the same

time, discussions of my findings with the Apaches enhanced their own awareness of their unique needs.

As a result of my work, the Apaches moved into houses that had been designed with *their* participation, for *their* specific needs. Among my findings was the realization that the Apaches preferred to ease into social interactions rather than to shake hands and begin interacting immediately, as is more typical of the Anglo pattern. Apache etiquette requires that people be in full view of one another so each can assess the behavior of others from a distance prior to engaging in social interaction with them. This requires a large, open living space. At the same time, hosts feel compelled to offer food to guests as a prelude to further social interaction. Thus, cooking and dining areas cannot be separated from living space. Nor is standard middle-class Anglo kitchen equipment suitable, since the need for handling large quantities among extended families requires large pots and pans, which in turn calls for extra-large sinks and cupboards. Built with such ideas in mind, the new houses accommodated long-standing native traditions.

[a]Adapted from Esber, G. (1987). Designing Apache houses with Apaches. In R. M. Wulff & S. J. Fiske (Eds.), *Anthropological praxis:*

Translating knowledge into action. Boulder, CO: Westview Press.

The buyer thereupon clubbed the pony to death with a two-by-four, dumped the carcass in his pickup truck and drove away. The horrified seller called the police, who tracked down the buyer. At his house they found a birthday party in progress. The pony was trussed and roasting in a *luau pit*. "We don't ride horses, we eat them," explained the buyer, a recent immigrant from Tonga [an island in the Pacific Ocean].

Unfortunately, the difficulty members of one subgroup within a pluralistic society may have making sense of the standards by which members of other groups operate can go far beyond mere misunderstanding. It can intensify to the point of anger and violence. Among many examples of this is the pluralistic society of Guatemala, where a central government distrustful of the country's largely rural Maya Indian majority unleashed a deadly reign of terror against them.

Every culture includes individuals who behave in abnormal ways that earn them such labels as "oddball," "eccentric," or "crazy." Typically, because they differ too much from the acceptable standard, they are looked upon with disapproval by their society. And if their behavior becomes too peculiar, they are sooner or later excluded from participating in the activities of the group. Such exclusion acts to keep what is defined as deviant behavior outside the group.

Interestingly, behavior viewed as deviant in one society may not be in another. In many American Indian societies, for example, a few exceptional individuals were permitted to assume for life the role normally associated with people of the opposite sex. Thus, a man could dress as a woman and engage in what were conventionally defined as female activities; conversely, women could achieve renown in activities normally in the masculine domain. In effect, four different gender identities were available: masculine men, feminine men, feminine women, and masculine women. Furthermore,

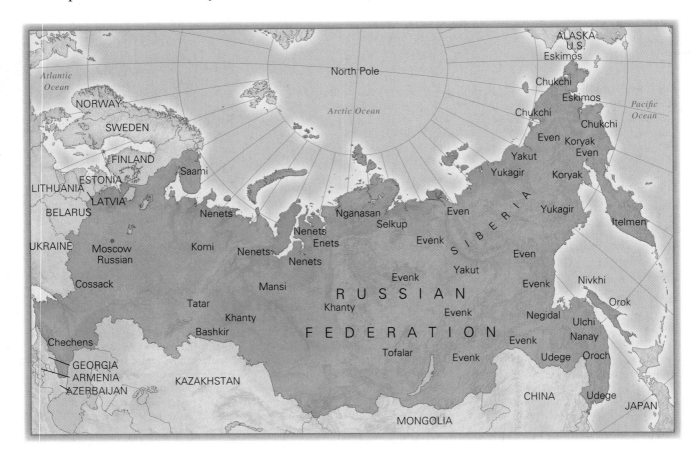

Figure 2.1
Shown here are some of the ethnic groups of the Russian Federation, the dominant and by far the largest
part of the former Union of Soviet Socialist Republics.

masculine women and feminine men were not merely
accepted, but were highly respected.

Culture Is Based on Symbols

Much of human behavior involves **symbols**—signs,
sounds, emblems, and other things that are linked to
something else and represent them in a meaningful way.
Because often there is no inherent or necessary relationship between a thing and its representation, symbols are
commonly arbitrary, acquiring specific meanings when
people agree on usage in their communications.

In fact, symbols—ranging from national flags to
wedding rings to money—enter into every aspect of culture, from social life and religion to politics and economics. We're all familiar with the fervor and devotion that
a religious symbol can elicit from a believer. An Islamic
crescent, Christian cross, or a Jewish Star of David, as

symbol A sign, sound, emblem, or other thing that is arbitrarily
linked to something else and represents it in a meaningful way.

well as the sun among the Inca, a cow among the Hindu,
a white buffalo calf among Plains Indians, or any other
object of worship, may bring to mind years of struggle
and persecution or may stand for a whole philosophy or
creed.

The most important symbolic aspect of culture is
language—using words to represent objects and ideas.
Through language humans are able to transmit culture
from one generation to another. In particular, language
makes it possible to learn from cumulative, shared experience. Without it, one could not inform others about
events, emotions, and other experiences to which they
were not a party. Language is so important that an entire
chapter in this book is devoted to the subject.

Culture Is Integrated

For purposes of comparison and analysis, anthropologists customarily imagine a culture as a well-structured
system made up of distinctive parts that function together as an organized whole. While they may sharply
distinguish each part as a clearly defined unit with its

own characteristic features and special place within the larger system, anthropologists recognize that reality is a more complex intertwining, and divisions between cultural units are often blurry. However, because all aspects of a culture must be reasonably well integrated in order to function properly, anthropologists seldom focus on an individual feature in isolation. Instead, they view each in terms of its larger context and carefully examine its connections to related cultural features.

Broadly speaking, a society's cultural features fall within three categories: social structure, infrastructure, and superstructure. **Social structure** concerns rule-governed relationships—with all their rights and obligations—that hold members of a society together. Households, families, associations, and power relations, including politics, are all part of social structure. It establishes group cohesion and enables people to consistently satisfy their basic needs, including food and shelter for themselves and their dependents, by means of work. So, there is a direct relationship between a group's social structure and its economic foundation, which includes subsistence practices and the tools and other material equipment used to make a living.

Because subsistence practices involve tapping into available resources to satisfy a society's basic needs, this aspect of culture is known as **infrastructure.** Supported by this economic foundation, a society is also held together by a shared sense of identity and worldview. This collective body of ideas, beliefs, and values by which a group of people makes sense of the world—its shape, challenges, and opportunities—and their place in it is known as ideology or **superstructure.** Including religion and national ideology, it structures the overarching ideas that people in a society have about themselves and everything else that exists around them—and it gives meaning and direction to their lives. Influencing and reinforcing one another, these three interdependent structures together form part of a cultural system (Figure 2.2).

The integration of economic, social, and ideological aspects of a culture can be illustrated by the Kapauku Papuans, a mountain people of Western New Guinea, studied in 1955 by the North American anthropologist Leopold Pospisil.[7] The Kapauku economy relies on plant cultivation, along with pig breeding, hunting, and fishing. Although plant cultivation provides most of the people's food, it is through pig breeding that men achieve political power and positions of legal authority.

Among the Kapauku, pig breeding is a complex business. Raising a lot of pigs requires a lot of food to feed them. The primary fodder is sweet potatoes, grown in garden plots. According to Kapauku culture, certain garden activities and the caring of pigs are tasks that fall

[7]Pospisil, L. (1963). *The Kapauku Papuans of west New Guinea.* New York: Holt, Rinehart & Winston.

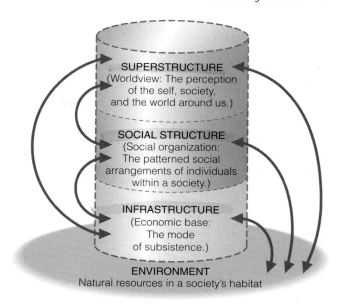

Figure 2.2

The barrel model of culture. Every culture is an integrated and dynamic system of adaptation that responds to a combination of internal factors (economic, social, ideological) and external factors (environmental, climatic). Within a cultural system, there are functional relationships among the economic base (infrastructure), the social organization (social structure), and the ideology (superstructure). A change in one leads to a change in the others.

exclusively in the domain of women's work. So, to raise many pigs, a man needs numerous women in the household. Thus, in Kapauku society, multiple wives (polygyny) are not only permitted, they are highly desired. For each wife, however, a man must pay a bride price, and this can be expensive. Furthermore, wives have to be compensated for their care of the pigs. Put simply, it takes pigs, by which wealth is measured, to get wives, without whom pigs cannot be raised in the first place. Needless to say, this requires considerable entrepreneurship. It is this ability that produces leaders in Kapauku society.

The interrelatedness of the various parts of Kapauku culture is even more complicated. For example, one condition that encourages polygyny is a surplus of adult fe-

social structure The rule-governed relationships—with all their rights and obligations—that hold members of a society together. This includes households, families, associations, and power relations, including politics.

infrastructure The economic foundation of a society, including its subsistence practices and the tools and other material equipment used to make a living.

superstructure A society's shared sense of identity and worldview. The collective body of ideas, beliefs, and values by which a group of people makes sense of the world—its shape, challenges, and opportunities—and their place in it. This includes religion and national ideology.

Biocultural Connection

Adult Human Stature and the Effects of Culture: An Archaeological Example

Among human beings, each of us is genetically programmed at conception to achieve a certain stature as an adult. Whether or not we actually wind up as tall as our genes would allow, however, is influenced by experiences during our period of growth and development.

For example, if an individual becomes severely ill, this may arrest growth temporarily, a setback that will not be made up when growth resumes. Critically important as well is the quality of diet. Without adequate nutrition, a person will not grow up to be as tall as

would otherwise be possible. Thus, in class-structured societies, individuals of upper-class standing have tended to be the tallest individuals, as they generally have access to the best diets and are shielded from many of life's harsher realities. Conversely, individuals of lower class standing have tended to be shorter, owing to poor diets and generally harsher lives.

At the ancient Maya city of Tikal, in the Central American country of Guatemala, analysis of human skeletons from burials reveal stature differences

characteristic of stratified societies. On average, males interred in rich "tombs" were taller than those in simple graves associated with relatively small houses. Those buried near intermediate-sized houses are generally taller than those from simple graves, but not as tall as those from "tombs."

Thus, the analysis provides strong support for a reconstruction of Tikal society into three strata: lower class commoners, higher class commoners, and (at the top) the ruling elite.

males, sometimes caused by loss of males through warfare. Among the Kapauku, recurring warfare has long been viewed as a necessary evil. By the rules of Kapauku warfare, men may be killed but women may not. This system works to promote the sort of imbalanced sex ratio that fosters polygyny. Polygyny tends to work best if a man's wives all come to live in his village, and so it is among the Kapauku. With this arrangement, the men of a village are typically "blood" relatives of one another, which enhances their ability to cooperate in warfare. Considering all of this, it makes sense that Kapauku typically trace descent (ancestry) through men.

Descent reckoning through men, coupled with near-constant warfare, tends to promote male dominance. So it is not surprising to find that positions of leadership in Kapauku society are held exclusively by men, who appropriate the products of women's labor in order to play their political "games." Such male dominance is by no means characteristic of all human societies. Rather, as in the Kapauku case, it arises only under particular sets

of circumstances that, if changed, will alter the way in which men and women relate to each other.

In sum, for a culture to function properly, its various parts must be consistent with one another. But consistency is not the same as harmony. In fact, there is often friction and potential for conflict within every culture—among individuals, factions, and competing institutions. Even on the most basic level of a society, individuals rarely experience the enculturation process in precisely the same way, nor do they perceive their reality in precisely identical fashion. Moreover, conditions may change, brought on by inside or outside forces.

A society will function reasonably well as long as its culture is capable of handling the daily strains and tensions. However, when a culture no longer provides adequate solutions or when its component parts are no longer consistent, a situation of cultural crisis ensues. Also, as this chapter's Biocultural Connection illustrates, the cultural system in stratified societies generally favors the ruling elite, while the groups scraping by on the bottom benefit the least. The difference may be measured in terms of material wealth as well as physical health.

Culture Is Dynamic

Cultures are dynamic systems that respond to motions and actions within and around them. When one element within the system shifts or changes, the entire system strives to adjust, just as it does when an outside force applies pressure. To function adequately, a culture must be flexible enough to allow such adjustments in the face of unstable or changing circumstances.

All cultures are, of necessity, dynamic, but some are far less so than others. When a culture is too rigid or static and fails to provide its members with the means required for long-term survival under changing conditions, it is not likely to endure. On the other hand, some cultures are so fluid and open to change that they may lose their distinctive character. The Amish mentioned earlier in this chapter typically resist change as much as possible but are constantly making balanced decisions to adjust when absolutely necessary. North Americans in general, however, have created a culture in which change has become a positive ideal.

CULTURE AND ADAPTATION

In the course of their evolution, humans, like all animals, have continually faced the challenge of adapting to their environment. The term *adaptation* refers to a gradual process by which organisms adjust to the conditions of the locality in which they live. Organisms have generally adapted biologically as the frequency of advantageous anatomical and physiological features increase in a population through a process known as natural selection. For example, body hair coupled with certain other physiological traits protects mammals from extremes of temperature; specialized teeth help them to procure the kinds of food they need; and so on.

Humans, however, have increasingly come to depend on cultural adaptation, using a unique combination of brain power and physical skills to alter their circumstances. Biology has not provided them with built-in fur coats to protect them in cold climates, but it has given them the ability to make their own coats, build fires, and construct shelters to shield themselves against the cold. They may not be able to run as fast as a cheetah, but they are able to invent and build vehicles that can carry them faster and further than any other creature. Through culture and its many constructions, the human species has secured not just its survival but its expansion as well. By manipulating environments through cultural means, people have been able to move into a vast range of environments, from the icy Arctic to the Sahara Desert. They have even set foot on the moon.

This is not to say that everything that humans do they do *because* it is adaptive to a particular environment. For one thing, people do not just react to an environment as given; rather, they react to it as they perceive it, and different groups of people may perceive the same environment in radically different ways. They also react to things other than the environment: their own biological natures; their beliefs and attitudes; and the short- and long-term consequences of their behavior for themselves and other life forms that share their habitats. Although people maintain cultures to deal with problems, some cultural practices have proved to be maladaptive and have actually created new problems—such as toxic water and air caused by certain industrial practices, or North America's obesity epidemic brought on by the culture of cars, fast food, television, and personal computers.

A further complication is the relativity of any given adaptation: What is adaptive in one context may be seriously maladaptive in another. For example, the sanitation practices of food-foraging peoples—their toilet habits and methods of garbage disposal—are appropriate to contexts of low population densities and some degree of residential mobility. But these same practices become serious health hazards in the context of large, fully sedentary populations. Similarly, behavior that is adaptive in the short run may be maladaptive over the long run. Thus, the development of irrigation in ancient Mesopotamia (modern-day Iraq) made it possible over the short run to increase food production, but over time it favored the gradual accumulation of salts in the soils. This, in turn, contributed to the collapse of civilization there about 4,000 years ago.

Likewise, today, the development of prime farmland in places like the eastern United States for purposes other than food production makes us increasingly dependent on food raised in marginal environments. High yields on marginal lands are presently possible through the application of expensive technology, but continuing loss of topsoil, increasing salinity of soils through evaporation of irrigation waters, and silting of irrigation works, not to mention impending shortages of water and fossil fuels, make continuing high yields over the long term unlikely. All of this said, it should be clear that for a culture to sur-

© Alec Duncan

What is adaptive at one time may not be at another. In the United States, the principal source of fruits, vegetables, and fiber is the Central Valley of California, where irrigation works have made the desert bloom. As happened in ancient Mesopotamia, evaporation concentrates salts in the water, but here pollution is made even worse by chemical fertilizers. These poisons are now accumulating in the soil and threaten to make the valley a desert again, but this time a true wasteland.

Anthropologists of Note

Bronislaw Malinowski (1884–1942)

Courtesy Phoebe Apperson Hearst Museum of Anthropology

Polish-born Bronislaw Malinowski argued that people everywhere share certain biological and psychological needs and that the ultimate function of all cultural institutions is to fulfill those needs. Everyone, for example, needs to feel secure in relation to the physical universe. Therefore, when science and technology are inadequate to explain certain natural phenomena—such as eclipses or earthquakes—people develop religion and magic to account for those phenomena and to establish a feeling of security. The nature of the institution, according to Malinowski, is determined by its function.

Malinowski outlined three fundamental levels of needs that he claimed had to be resolved by all cultures:

1. A culture must provide for biological needs, such as the need for food and procreation.
2. A culture must provide for instrumental needs, such as the need for law and education.
3. A culture must provide for integrative needs, such as religion and art.

If anthropologists could analyze the ways in which a culture fills these needs for its members, Malinowski believed that they could also deduce the origin of cultural traits.

Although this belief was never justified, the quality of data called for by Malinowski's approach set new standards for anthropological fieldwork. He was the first to insist that it was necessary to settle into the community being studied for an extended period of time in order to really understand it. He himself showed the way with his work in the Trobriand Islands between 1915 and 1918. Never before had such in-depth work been done, nor had such insights been gained into the workings of another culture. Such was the quality of Malinowski's Trobriand research that, with it, ethnography (the detailed description of a particular culture based primarily on fieldwork) can be said to have come of age as a scientific enterprise.

vive, it must produce behavior that is generally adaptive to the natural environment.

Functions of Culture

Polish-born anthropologist Bronislaw Malinowski argued that people everywhere share certain biological and psychological needs and that the ultimate function of all cultural institutions is to fulfill these needs (see Anthropologist of Note). Others have marked out different criteria and categories, but the idea is basically the same: A culture cannot endure if it does not deal effectively with basic challenges. It must include strategies for the production and distribution of goods and services considered necessary for life. To ensure the biological continuity of its members, it must also provide a social structure for reproduction and mutual support. It must offer ways to pass on knowledge and enculturate new members so they can assist one another and contribute to their community as well-functioning adults. It must facilitate social interaction and provide ways to avoid or resolve conflicts within their group as well as with outsiders.

Since a culture must support all aspects of life, as indicated in our barrel model, it must also meet the psychological and emotional needs of its members. This last function is met, in part, simply by the measure of predictability that each culture, as a shared design for thought and action, brings to everyday life. Of course it involves much more than that, including a worldview that helps individuals understand their place in the world and face major changes. For example, every culture provides its members with certain customary ideas and rituals that enable them to think creatively about the meaning of life and death. Many cultures even make it possible for people to imagine an afterworld that no one has actually been to and returned from to tell about. Invited to suspend disbelief and engage in such imaginings, people find the means to deal with the grief of losing a loved one.

In Bali, for instance, Hindu worshipers stage spectacular cremation rituals at special places where they burn the physical remains of their dead. After a colorful procession with musicians, the corpse is carried to the cremation site in a large cremation tower, or *wadah,* representing the three-layered cosmos. It is then transferred into a large and beautifully decorated sarcophagus, made of wood and cloth artfully shaped in the form of an animal—a bull when the deceased belonged to the highest caste of priests (*brahman*), a winged lion for the second highest caste of warriors and administrators (*satria*), and a half-fish/half-elephant for the next caste of merchants (*wesia*). After relatives and friends place their last offerings atop or inside the sarcophagus, a Hindu priest sets the structure on fire. Soon, the body burns, and according to Balinese Hindu belief the animal sarcophagus symbolically guides the soul of the deceased to Bali's "mother" mountain Gunung Angung. This is the sacred dwelling place of the island's gods and ancestors, the place many Balinese believe they return to when they die. Freed from the flesh, the soul may later transmigrate and return in the flesh. This belief in reincarnation of the soul allows the Balinese to cope with death as a celebration of life.

In addition to meeting such emotional needs and all of the other functions noted above, a culture must be able to change if it is to remain adaptive under shifting conditions.

Culture and Change

Cultures have always changed over time, although rarely as rapidly or as massively as many are doing today. Changes take place in response to such events as population growth, technological innovation, environmental crisis, the intrusion of outsiders, or modification of behavior and values within the culture.

Changes are often signified by apparel. For example, in North America, where swift change is driven by capitalism and the need for incessant market growth, clothing fashions change quickly. Over the past half century or so, as advertisers increasingly utilized sexuality to promote sales, it became culturally permissible

for men and women alike to wear clothing that revealed more and more of their bodies. Along with this has come greater permissiveness about body exposure in photographs, movies, and television, as well as less restrictive sexual attitudes and practices among many. In our current age of globalization we are witnessing a much accelerated pace of widespread and radical cultural change, discussed in detail in the last two chapters of this book.

Although cultures must have some flexibility to remain adaptive, culture change can also bring unexpected and often disastrous results. For example, consider the relationship between culture and the droughts that periodically afflict so many people living in African countries just south of the Sahara Desert. The lives of some 14 million pastoral nomadic people native to this region are centered on cattle and other livestock, herded from place to place as required for pasturage and water. For thousands of years these people have been able to go about their business, efficiently utilizing vast areas of arid lands in ways that allowed them to survive severe droughts many times in the past. Unfortunately, their way of life is frowned upon by the central governments of modern states in the region because it involves moving back and forth across relatively new international boundaries, making the nomads difficult to track for purposes of taxation and other governmental controls.

Seeing nomads as a challenge to their authority, these governments have gone all out to stop them from ranging through their traditional grazing territories and to convert them into sedentary villagers. Imposed loss of mobility has resulted in overgrazing; moreover, the problem has been compounded by government efforts to press pastoralists into a market economy by giving them

© Tony Karumba/AFP/Getty Images

Pastoralists herd their grazing animals, moving slowly across vast territories in search of food. As nomadic peoples who depend on their mobility for survival, they may cross unmarked international borders. Difficult to control by central governments trying to impose taxes on them, these nomads face major obstacles in pursuing their customary way of life. No longer able to range through their traditional grazing territories due to government restrictions on land use, these African herders and their cattle are hit all the harder when droughts occur. So it is in this photo taken in Kenya, where the combination of limited grazing lands and severe drought resulted in the death of many animals and turned others into "bones on hoofs."

incentives to raise many more animals than required for their own needs in order to have a surplus to sell and thus add to the tax base. The resulting devastation, where there had previously been no significant overgrazing or erosion, now makes droughts far more disastrous than they would otherwise be. In fact, it places the very existence of the nomads' traditional way of life in jeopardy.

CULTURE, SOCIETY, AND THE INDIVIDUAL

Ultimately, a society is no more than a union of individuals, all of whom have their own special needs and interests. To survive, it must succeed in balancing the immediate self-interest of its individual members against the needs and demands of the collective well-being of society as a whole. To accomplish this, a society offers rewards for adherence to its culturally prescribed standards. In most cases, these rewards assume the form of social approval. For example, in contemporary North American society a person who holds a good job, takes care of family, pays taxes, and does volunteer work in the neighborhood may be spoken of as a "model citizen" in the community. To ensure the survival of the group, each person must learn to postpone certain immediate personal satisfactions. Yet the needs of the individual cannot be suppressed too far or the result may be a degree of emotional stress and growing resentment that results in protest, disruption, and sometimes even violence.

Consider, for example, the matter of sexual expression, which, like anything that people do, is shaped by culture. Sexuality is important in any society, for it helps to strengthen cooperative bonds among members of society, ensuring the perpetuation of society itself. Yet sex can be disruptive to social living. If the issue of who has sexual access to whom is not clearly spelled out, competition for sexual privileges can destroy the cooperative bonds on which human survival depends. Uncontrolled sexual activity, too, can result in reproductive rates that cause a society's population to outstrip its resources. Hence, as it shapes sexual behavior, every culture must balance the needs of society against the individual's sexual needs and desires so that frustration does not build up to the point of being disruptive in itself.

Of course, cultures vary widely in the way they go about this. On one end of the spectrum, societies such as the Amish in North America or the Muslim Brotherhood in Egypt have taken an extremely restrictive approach, specifying no sex outside of marriage. On the other end are such societies as the Norwegians in northern Europe who generally accept premarital sex and often choose to have children outside marriage, or even more extreme, the Canela Indians in Brazil, whose social codes guar-

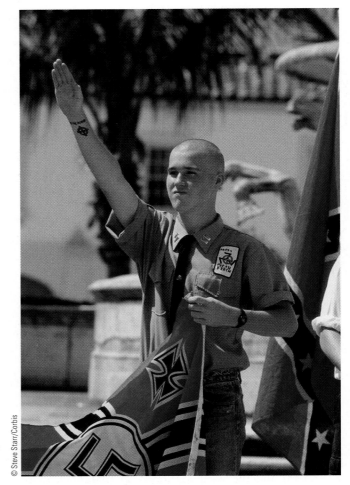

Some people whose needs are not readily met by society direct their frustrations against scapegoats, usually minorities. In Australia, Europe, and North America, such resentment fueled the rise of "skinheads" who express their hatred with Nazi symbols such as swastikas.

antee that, sooner or later, everyone in a given village has had sex with just about everyone of the opposite sex. Yet, even as permissive as the latter situation may sound, there are nonetheless strict rules as to how the system operates.[8]

Not just in sexual matters, but in all life issues, cultures must strike a balance between the needs and desires of individuals and those of society as a whole. When those of society take precedence, people experience excessive stress. Symptomatic of this are increased levels of mental illness and behavior regarded as antisocial: violence, crime, abuse of alcohol and other drugs, depression, suicide, or simply alienation. If not corrected, the situation can result in cultural breakdown. But just as problems develop if the needs of society take precedence

---

[8]Crocker, W. A., & Crocker, J. (1994). *The Canela, bonding through kinship, ritual and sex* (pp. 143–171). Fort Worth: Harcourt Brace.

over those of the individual, so too do they develop if the balance is upset in the other direction.

EVALUATION OF CULTURE

We have knowledge of numerous highly diverse cultural solutions to the challenges of human existence. The question often arises, Which is best? Anthropologists have been intrigued to find that all cultures tend to see themselves as the best of all possible worlds. This is reflected in the way individual societies refer to themselves: Typically, a society's traditional name for itself translates roughly into "true human beings." In contrast, their names for outsiders commonly translate into

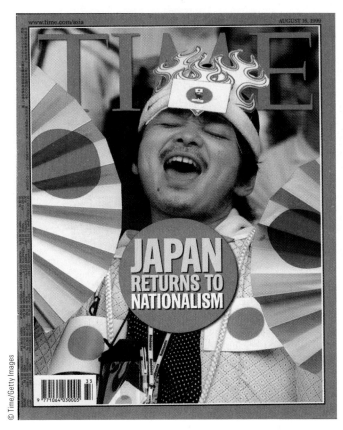

Japanese traditionally referred to their own people as a "divine nation," governed by the *mikado* (emperor) who was revered as a god. Today, a revival of Japanese nationalism is expressed by the restoration of controversial symbols in public places. These include singing (at public events and in some schools) the *kimigayo*, a hymn of praise to the divine emperor that served as Imperial Japan's national anthem. And the *hinomaru* (the rising sun flag), once raised by Japanese soldiers in conquered territories, can increasingly be seen flying in public places and private homes. Historically associated with militant Japanese imperialism, these nationalist symbols reflect a tradition of ethnocentrism not unlike those of other nations claiming a divine association, as in "One Nation under God," "God's Own Country," "God's Chosen People," and "God's Promised Land."

various versions of "subhumans," including "monkeys," "dogs," "weird-looking people," "funny talkers," and so forth. We now know that any adequately functioning culture regards its own ways as the only proper ones, a view known as **ethnocentrism.**

Anthropologists have been actively engaged in the fight against ethnocentrism ever since they started to study and actually live among traditional peoples with radically different cultures—thus learning by personal experience that they were no less human than anyone else. Resisting the common urge to rank cultures, anthropologists have instead aimed to understand individual cultures and the general concept of culture. To do so, they have examined each culture on its own terms, aiming to discern whether or not the culture satisfies the needs and expectations of the people themselves. If a people practiced human sacrifice or capital punishment, for example, anthropologists asked about the circumstances that made the taking of human life acceptable according to that particular group's values.

The idea that one must suspend judgment on other peoples' practices in order to understand them in their own cultural terms is called **cultural relativism.** Only through such an approach can one gain a meaningful view of the values and beliefs that underlie the behaviors and institutions of other peoples and societies as well as clearer insights into the underlying beliefs and practices of one's own society.

Take, for example, the 16th-century Aztec practice of sacrificing humans for religious purposes. Few (if any) North Americans today would condone such practices, but by suspending judgment one can get beneath the surface and discern how it functioned to reassure the populace that the Aztec state was healthy and that the sun would remain in the heavens.

Moreover, an impartial and open-minded exploration of Aztec sacrifice rituals may offer a valuable comparative perspective on the death penalty in countries such as the United States today. Numerous studies by social scientists have clearly shown that the death penalty does not deter violent crime, any more than Aztec sacrifice really provided sustenance for the sun. In fact, cross-cultural studies show that homicide rates mostly decline after its abolition.[9] Similar to Aztec human sacrifice, capital punishment may be seen as an institutionalized

---

[9]Ember, C. R., & Ember, M. (1996). What have we learned from cross-cultural research? *General Anthropology 2* (2), 5.

ethnocentrism The belief that the ways of one's own culture are the only proper ones.
cultural relativism The idea that one must suspend judgment of other people's practices in order to understand them in their own cultural terms.

magical response to perceived disorder. As U.S. anthropologists Anthony Paredes and Elizabeth D. Purdum point out, it "reassures many that society is not out of control after all, that the majesty of the law reigns, and that God is indeed in his heaven."[10]

Clearly, cultural relativism is essential as a research tool. However, employing it as a tool does not mean suspending judgment forever, nor does it require the anthropologist to defend a people's right to engage in any cultural practice, no matter how destructive. All that is necessary is that we avoid *premature* judgments until we have a full understanding of the culture in which we are interested. Then, and only then, may the anthropologist adopt a critical stance and in an informed way consider the advantages and disadvantages particular beliefs and behaviors have for a society and its members. As British anthropologist David Maybury-Lewis emphasizes, "one does not avoid making judgments, but rather postpones them in order to make informed judgments later."[11]

Forty years ago U.S. anthropologist Walter Goldschmidt devised a still-useful formula to help colleagues avoid the pitfalls of ethnocentrism without ending up in the "anything goes" position of cultural relativism pushed to absurdity.[12] In his view the important question to ask is, How well does a given culture satisfy the physical and psychological needs of those whose behavior it guides?

Specific indicators are to be found in the nutritional status and general physical and mental health of its population; the incidence of violence, crime, and delinquency; the demographic structure, stability, and tranquility of domestic life; and the group's relationship to its resource base. The culture of a people who experience high rates of malnutrition, violence, crime, delinquency, suicide, emotional disorders and despair, and environmental degradation may be said to be operating less well than that of another people who exhibit few such problems. In a well-working culture, people "can be proud, jealous, and pugnacious, and live a very satisfactory life without feeling '*angst*,' 'alienation,' 'anomie,' 'depression,' or any of the other pervasive ills of our own inhuman and civilized way of living."[13] When traditional ways of coping no longer seem to work, and people feel helpless to shape

© Clay McLachlan/Reuters/Corbis

San Quentin Prison cell block. One sign that a culture is not adequately satisfying a people's needs and expectations is a high incidence of crime and delinquency. It is sobering to note that 25 percent of all imprisoned people in the world are incarcerated in the United States. In the past ten years the country's jail and prison population jumped by more than 600,000—from 1.6 to 2.2 million. Ironically, people in the United States think of their country as "the land of the free," yet it has the highest incarceration rate in the world (724 per 100,000 inhabitants).

their own lives in their own societies, symptoms of cultural breakdown become prominent.

In short, a culture is essentially a maintenance system to ensure the continued well-being of a group of people. Therefore, it may be deemed successful as long as it secures the survival of a society in a way that its members find to be reasonably fulfilling. What complicates matters is that any society is made up of groups with different interests, raising the possibility that some people's interests may be served better than those of others. Therefore, a culture that is quite fulfilling for one group within a society may be less so for another.

[10]Paredes, J. A., & Purdum, E. D. (1990). "Bye, bye Ted . . ." *Anthropology Today 6* (2), 9.

[11]Maybury-Lewis, D. H. P. (1993). A special sort of pleading. In W. A. Haviland & R. J. Gordon (Eds.), *Talking about people* (2nd ed., p. 17). Mountain View, CA: Mayfield.

[12]Bodley, J. H. (1990). *Victims of progress* (3rd ed., p. 138). Mountain View, CA: Mayfield.

[13]Fox, R. (1968). *Encounter with anthropology* (p. 290). New York: Dell.

For this reason, the anthropologist must always ask, *Whose* needs and *whose* survival are best served by the culture in question? Only by looking at the overall situation can a reasonably objective judgment be made as to how well a culture is working. But anthropologists today recognize that few peoples still exist in total or near-total isolation and understand that globalization affects the dynamics of culture change in almost every corner of our global village. Accordingly, as will be detailed in many of the following chapters, we must widen our scope and develop a truly worldwide perspective that enables us to appreciate cultures as increasingly open and interactive (and sometimes reactive) systems.

Questions for Reflection

1. Like everyone else in the world, you are meeting daily challenges of survival through your culture. And since you are made "fully human" by your own culture, how do you express your individual identity in your own community? What do your hairstyle, clothes, shoes, jewelry, and perhaps tattoos communicate about who you are? How do you think people from a different cultural background might interpret your choices of self-adornment?

2. Many large modern societies are pluralistic. Are you familiar with any subcultures in your own society? How different are these subcultures from one another? Could you make friends or even marry someone from another subculture? What kind of problems would you be likely to encounter?

3. Although all cultures across the world display some degree of ethnocentrism, some are more ethnocentric than others. In what ways is your own society ethnocentric? Considering the modern fact of globalization (as described in Chapter 1), do you think ethnocentrism poses more of a problem in today's world than in the past?

4. The barrel model offers you a simple framework to imagine what a culture looks like from an analytical point of view. How would you apply that model to your own community?

5. If culture is a maintenance system to continue the well-being of a group of people, how do you think an anthropologist would explain why, in some societies, many members end up in jail or prison? What does a society's incarceration rate tell you about its cultural system?

Suggested Readings

Brown, D. E. (1991). *Human universals*. New York: McGraw-Hill.

Fascination with cultural diversity should not eclipse the study of human universals, which have relevance for our understanding of the nature of all humanity and raise issues transcending boundaries of biological and social science, as well as the humanities.

Gamst, F. C., & Norbeck, E. (1976). *Ideas of culture: Sources and uses*. New York: Holt, Rinehart & Winston.

Selected writings (with editorial comments) on the culture concept, illustrating how the concept has grown and given rise to narrow specializations within the field of anthropology.

Hatch, E. (1983). *Culture and morality: The relativity of values in anthropology*. New York: Columbia University Press.

Traces anthropological grapplings with the concept of cultural relativity—looking at it in relation to relativity of knowledge, historical relativism, and ethical relativism.

Lewellen, T. C. (2002). *The anthropology of globalization: Cultural anthropology enters the 21st century*. Westport, CT: Greenwood Publishing.

A useful and digestible undergraduate textbook on the anthropology of globalization—looking at theory, migration, and local–global relationships.

Urban, G. (2001). *Metaculture: How cultures move through the modern world*. Westport, CT: Greenwood Press.

Examines the dynamics and implications of the rapid circulation of contemporary capitalist culture with its constant striving for "newness."

Thomson Audio Study Products

 Enjoy the MP3-ready Audio Lecture Overviews for each chapter and a comprehensive audio glossary of key terms for quick study and review. Whether walking to class, doing laundry, or studying at your desk, you now have the freedom to choose when, where, and how you interact with your audio-based educational media. See the preface for information on how to access this on-the-go study and review tool.

The Anthropology Resource Center

www.thomsonedu.com/anthropology
The Anthropology Resource Center provides extended learning materials to reinforce your understanding of key concepts in the four fields of anthropology. For each of the four fields, the Resource Center includes dynamic exercises including video exercises, map exercises, simulations, and "Meet the Scientists" interviews, as well as critical thinking questions that can be assigned and e-mailed to instructors. The Resource Center also provides breaking news in anthropology and interesting material on applied anthropology to help you link what you are learning to the world around you.

3 Ethnographic Research: Its History, Methods, and Theories

© Julia Jean

Anthropologists take on the challenge of studying and describing cultures around the world and finding scientific explanations for their differences and similarities. Why do people think, feel, and act in certain ways—and find it wrong or impossible to do otherwise? Answers must come from fact-based knowledge about cultural diversity—knowledge that is not culture-bound and is widely recognized as significant. Over the years, anthropology has generated such knowledge through various theories and research methods. In particular, anthropologists obtain information through long-term, full-immersion fieldwork based on participant observation—illustrated by this photo of anthropologist Julia Jean (in the orange blouse), who is both observing *and* participating in a Hindu ritual at a temple for the Goddess Kamakhya in northeastern India.

How and Why Did Ethnographic Research Evolve?

In the early years of the discipline, many anthropologists documented traditional cultures they assumed would disappear due to disease, warfare, or acculturation imposed by colonialism, growing state power, or international market expansion. Some worked as government anthropologists, gathering data used to formulate policies concerning indigenous peoples or to help predict the behavior of enemies during wartime. After the colonial era ended in the 1960s, anthropologists established a code of ethics to ensure their research does not harm the groups they study. Today it is common for anthropologists to collaborate with minority groups and communities under siege and to assist in cultural revitalization efforts. Anthropological methods and knowledge are also applied to a range of globalization challenges, including economic development, conflict resolution, business, and politics. Finally, anthropologists do research to better understand what makes us tick and to explain cross-cultural differences and similarities.

What Are Ethnographic Research Methods?

Although anthropology relies on various research methods, its hallmark is extended fieldwork in a particular community or cultural group. This fieldwork features participant observation in which the researcher not only observes and documents the daily life of the community being studied, but also participates in that life. Typically, an anthropologist's initial fieldwork is carried out solo and lasts a full year. However, some anthropologists work in teams, and some field stays may be briefer or longer. It is not uncommon for anthropologists to return to their field sites periodically over the course of several decades.

How Is Research Related to Theory?

Data resulting from research, whether collected through fieldwork or another method, provide anthropologists with material needed to produce a comprehensive written (or filmed) *ethnography,* or description, of a culture. Moreover, it supplies details that are fundamental to *ethnology*—cross-cultural comparisons and theories that explain different cultural beliefs and behaviors. Beyond offering explanations, theories help us frame new questions that deepen our understanding of cultural phenomena. Anthropologists have come up with a wide variety of theories, some of which have been replaced or improved through the discovery of new information or better explanations. Gradually, much of what was puzzling or unknown about our complex species and its fascinating social and cultural diversity is exposed, revealed, or made clearer through theoretically informed research.

As briefly discussed in Chapter 1, cultural anthropology has two main scholarly components: *ethnography* (a detailed description of a particular culture primarily based on fieldwork) and *ethnology* (the study and analysis of different cultures from a comparative or historical point of view, utilizing ethnographic accounts and developing anthropological theories that help explain why certain important differences or similarities occur among groups).

Historically, anthropology focused on non-Western traditional peoples whose languages were not recorded in writing—people whose communication is often direct and face-to-face, and whose knowledge about the past is based primarily on oral tradition. Even in societies where writing exists, most of what is of interest to anthropologists is not documented. Thus, anthropologists have made a point of going to these places in person to see and experience people and their culture firsthand. This is called *fieldwork.*

Today, anthropological fieldwork takes place not only in small-scale communities in distant corners of the world, but also in modern urban neighborhoods in industrial or postindustrial societies. Anthropologists can be found doing fieldwork in a wide range of places and within a host of diverse groups, including transnational corporations, international migrant workers, and peoples scattered and dispersed because of wars, famines, poverty, or persecution.

In our unsettled and globalizing world, where long-standing boundaries between cultures are being erased, new social networks and cultural constructs are emerging, made possible by long-distance mass transportation and communication technology—including electronic media such as radio, television, cell phones, and the Internet. Anthropologists today are adjusting their research methods to better describe, explain, and understand these complex but fascinating dynamics in the rapidly changing human condition of the 21st century.

HISTORY OF ETHNOGRAPHIC RESEARCH AND ITS USES

Cultural anthropology emerged as a formal discipline during the heyday of colonialism (1870s–1950s) when many European anthropologists focused on the study of traditional peoples and their cultures in the colonies overseas. For instance, French anthropologists did most of their research in North and West Africa and Southeast Asia; British anthropologists in southern and East Africa;

urgent anthropology Ethnographic research that documents endangered cultures; also known as salvage ethnography.

Dutch anthropologists in what has become Indonesia, Western New Guinea, and Suriname; and Belgian anthropologists in the Congo of Africa.

Meanwhile, anthropologists in Canada and the United States focused primarily on their own countries' American Indian and Eskimo communities—usually residing on tracts of land known as reservations, or in remote Arctic villages. Because these indigenous groups are surrounded by a more dominant society that has settled on what used to be exclusively native lands, and they are no longer completely independent from that larger and more complex society's national government, their reservations are sometimes described as *internal colonies.*

At one time it was common practice to compare peoples still pursuing traditional lifeways, based on hunting, fishing, gathering, and/or small-scale farming or herding, with the ancient prehistoric ancestors of Europeans and to categorize the cultures of these traditional peoples as "primitive." Although anthropologists have long abandoned such ethnocentric terminology, many others continue to think and speak of these traditional cultures in terms of being "underdeveloped" or even "undeveloped." This misconception helped state societies, commercial enterprises, and other powerful outside groups justify expanding their activities and even invading the lands belonging to these peoples, often exerting overwhelming pressure on them to change their ancestral ways.

THOMSON AUDIO STUDY PRODUCTS Take advantage of the MP3-ready Audio Lecture Overviews and comprehensive audio glossary of key terms for each chapter. See the preface for information on how to access this on-the-go study and review tool.

Salvage Ethnography or Urgent Anthropology

In the disturbing and often violent historical context of expansion and domination by European and other powerful political states and commercial enterprises, the survival of thousands of traditional communities worldwide has been at stake. In fact, many of these threatened peoples have become physically extinct. Others survived but could not hold onto their territories or were forced to give up their way of life. Although anthropologists have seldom been able to prevent such tragic events, they did try to make a record of these cultural groups. This important early anthropological practice of documenting endangered cultures was called *salvage ethnography* and is now also known as **urgent anthropology.**

By the late 1800s, many European and North American museums were sponsoring anthropological expeditions to collect cultural artifacts and other material remains (including skulls, bones, utensils, weapons, clothing, and ceremonial objects), as well as vocabularies, myths, and other relevant cultural data. Some early anthropologists also began taking ethnographic photographs, and by the 1890s some began shooting documentary films or recording speech, songs, and music of these so-called vanishing peoples.

Although the first generation of anthropologists often began their careers working for museums, increasingly those coming later were academically trained in the emerging discipline and became active in newly founded anthropology departments. In North America, most of the latter did their fieldwork on tribal reservations where indigenous communities were falling apart in the face of disease, poverty, and despair brought on by pressures of forced culture change. These anthropologists interviewed American Indian elders still able to recall the ancestral way of life prior to their reservation confinement. They also collected oral histories, traditions, myths, legends, and other information, as well as old artifacts for research, preservation, and public display.

Beyond documenting social practices, beliefs, artifacts, and other disappearing cultural features, anthropologists also sought to reconstruct traditional ways of life that had already been abandoned and that were often only remembered by surviving elders. Although anthropological theories have come and gone during the past

hundred years, the plight of indigenous peoples struggling for cultural survival endures. Anthropologists can and still do contribute to that effort, assisting in cultural preservation efforts. In that work, utilizing a variety of new methods, they can tap into and continue to build on a professional legacy of salvage ethnography.

Acculturation Studies

Since the 1930s, anthropologists have been aware that the number of traditional cultures is quickly diminishing. In response, some began studying asymmetrical (sharply uneven) culture contact, or *acculturation*—the often disruptive process of culture change occurring in traditional societies coming in contact with more powerful state societies, in particular industrialized or capitalist societies.

Typically, as the dominant (often foreign) power establishes its superiority, local indigenous cultures are made to appear inferior, ridiculous, or otherwise not worth preserving—and are often forced to adopt the ways of the dominant society pressing in on them. Government-sponsored programs designed to force indigenous groups to abandon their traditional languages, religious beliefs, and social practices for those of mainstream society have ripped apart the unique cultural fabric of one group after another. These programs left

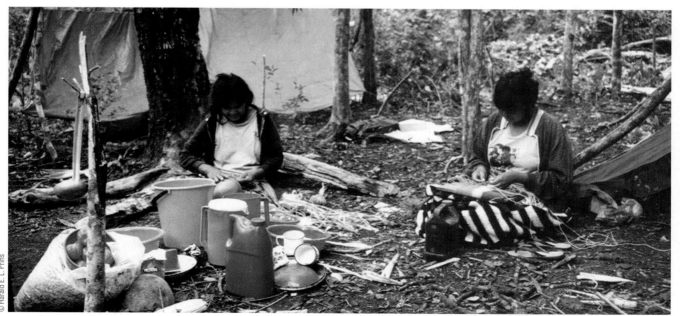

© Harald E. L. Prins

Until recently, Ayoreo Indian bands lived largely isolated in the Gran Chaco, a vast wilderness in South America's heartland. One by one, these migratory foragers have been forced to "come out" due to outside encroachment on their habitat. Today, most dispossessed Ayoreo Indians find themselves in different stages of acculturation. This photo shows Ayoreo women of Zapocó in Bolivia's forest. Dressed in Western hand-me-downs and surrounded by plastic from the modern society that is pressing in on them, they weave natural plant fibers into traditionally patterned bags to sell for cash, while the men make money by cutting trees for logging companies.

many indigenous families impoverished, demoralized, and desperate.

One of the first U.S. anthropologists to study acculturation was Margaret Mead in her 1932 fieldwork among the Omaha Indians of Nebraska. In that research, she focused on community breakdown and cultural disintegration of this traditional American Indian tribe. In the course of the 20th century, numerous other anthropologists carried out acculturation studies in Asia, Africa, Australia, Oceania, the Americas, and even in parts of Europe itself, thereby greatly contributing to our knowledge of complex and often disturbing processes of culture change.

Applied Anthropology

In identifying the disintegrating effects of asymmetrical culture contact, acculturation studies gave birth to *applied anthropology*—the use of anthropological knowledge and methods to solve practical problems in communities confronting new challenges. For societies in colonized territories or on reservations, government officials began looking at how anthropological research might help these traditional groups struggling with imposed economic, social, and political changes. Voicing the need for an applied anthropology to address the negative effects of colonial policies, British anthropologist Bronislaw Malinowski (born in Poland) commented: "The anthropologist who is unable to . . . register the tragic errors committed at times with the best intentions . . . remains an antiquarian covered with academic dust and in fool's paradise."[1]

In 1937 the British government set up an anthropological research institute in what is now Zambia to study the impact of international markets on Central Africa's traditional societies. In the next decade, anthropologists worked on a number of problem-oriented studies throughout Africa, including the disruptive effects of the mining industry and labor migration on domestic economies and cultures.

Facing similar problems in North America, the U.S. Bureau of Indian Affairs (BIA), which oversees federally recognized tribes on Indian reservations, established an applied anthropology branch in the mid-1930s. Beyond studying the problems of acculturation, the handful of applied anthropologists hired by the BIA were to identify practical culturally appropriate ways for the U.S. government to introduce social and economic development programs to reduce poverty, promote literacy, and solve a host of other problems on the reservations.

In 1941, the now international Society for Applied Anthropology was founded at Harvard University to promote scientific investigation of the principles controlling the relations of human beings to one another and the encouragement of their wide application. Today, a large number of professionally trained anthropologists specialize in applied research, working for a variety of local, regional, national, and international institutions, in particular nongovernmental organizations (NGOs), and are active on numerous fronts in every corner of the world.

Studying Cultures at a Distance

During World War II (1939–1945) and the early years of the Cold War (between capitalist countries led by the United States and communist countries led by Russia), some anthropologists shifted their attention from small-scale traditional communities to modern state societies. Aiming to discover basic personality traits, or psychological profiles, shared by the majority of the people in modern state societies, several U.S. and British anthropologists became involved in a wartime government program of "national character" studies. Such studies were believed to be significant in order to better understand and deal with the newly declared enemy states of Japan and Germany (in World War II) and later Russia and others.

Since on-location ethnographic fieldwork in enemy societies during wartime was impossible, and in most other foreign countries difficult if not prohibitive, Mead, Ruth Benedict, and other anthropologists developed innovative techniques for studying "culture at a distance"—through the analysis of newspapers, literature, photographs, and popular films. They also collected information through structured interviews with immigrants and refugees from the enemy nations, as well as foreigners from other countries.[2]

For instance, by investigating child-rearing practices, cultural beliefs, and attitudes, and by examining any documented material for the appearance of recurrent themes and values, these anthropologists tried to portray the national character of the peoples inhabiting these distant countries. This cultural information and anthropological understanding of foreign societies was also used for propaganda and psychological warfare. After the war, some of the information and insights based on such long-distance anthropological studies were found useful in temporarily governing the occupied territories and dealing with newly liberated populations in other parts of the world.

---

[1] In Mair, L. (1957). *An introduction to social anthropology* (p. 4). London: Oxford University Press. See also Malinowski, B. (1945). *The dynamics of culture change: An inquiry into race relations in Africa* (pp. 1–13). New Haven and London: Yale University Press.

[2] Mead, M., & Métraux, R. (Eds.). (1953). *The study of culture at a distance*. Chicago: University of Chicago Press.

Studying Contemporary State Societies

Although there were theoretical flaws in the national character studies and methodological problems in studying cultures at a distance, anthropological research on contemporary state societies was more than just a war-related endeavor. Even in the early decades of the discipline, when anthropologists devoted themselves primarily to researching non-Western small-scale communities, they recognized that a generalized understanding of human ideas and behavior depends upon knowledge of *all* cultures and peoples, including those in complex, large-scale industrial societies organized in political states, such as modern France or the United States. Thus, already during the years of the Great Depression (1930s), several anthropologists worked in their own countries in settings ranging from factories to farming communities and suburban neighborhoods.

One interesting example of an early anthropologist doing research on the home front is Hortense Powdermaker. After studying anthropology in London, this U.S. anthropologist did her first major ethnographic fieldwork among Melanesians in the southern Pacific. Then, returning to the United States, she researched a racially segregated town in Mississippi in the 1930s.[3] During the next decade, she focused on combating dominant society's racism against African Americans and other ethnic minorities.

While in the South, Powdermaker became keenly aware of the importance of the mass media in shaping people's worldviews.[4] To further explore this ideological force in modern culture, she cast her critical eye on the domestic film industry and did a year of fieldwork in Hollywood (1946–1947).

As Powdermaker was wrapping up her Hollywood research, several other anthropologists were launching other kinds of studies in large-scale societies. For instance, Benedict and Mead, convinced that governments and colonial administrations, as well as new global institutions such as the United Nations (founded in 1945), could and should benefit from anthropological insights, initiated a team project in comparative research on contemporary cultures based at Columbia University in New York (1947–1952).

In 1950, Swiss anthropologist Alfred Métraux put together an international team of U.S., French, and Brazilian researchers to study contemporary race relations in the South American country, Brazil. The project, sponsored by UNESCO (the United Nations Education, Science, and Culture Organization), was part of the UN's global campaign against racial prejudice and discrimination. Headquartered in Paris, Métraux selected Brazil as a research site primarily for comparative purposes. Like the United States, it was a former European colony with a large multi-ethnic population and a long history of black slavery. Brazil had abolished slavery twenty-five years later than the United States but had made much more progress in terms of its race relations. In contrast to the racially segregated United States, Brazil was believed to be an ideal international example of harmonious, tolerant, and overall positive cross-racial relations. The research findings yielded unexpected results, showing that dark-skinned Brazilians of African descent did face systemic social and economic discrimination—albeit not in the political and legal form of racial segregation as was the case in the United States at the time.[5]

In 1956 and 1957, U.S. anthropologist Julian Steward supervised an anthropological research team in developing countries such as Kenya, Nigeria, Peru, Mexico, Japan, Burma, Malaya, and Indonesia—to study the comparative impact of industrialization and urbanization upon these different populations. Other anthropologists launched similar projects in other parts of the world.

Peasant Studies

As anthropologists widened their scope to consider more fully the complex state societies that were impacting traditional small-scale indigenous communities central to early anthropological study, some zeroed in on peasant communities. Peasants represent an important category, standing midway between modern industrial society and traditional subsistence foragers, herders, farmers, and fishers. Forming part of larger, more complex societies, peasant communities exist worldwide, and peasants number in the many hundreds of millions.

Peasantry represents the largest social category of our species so far. Because peasant unrest over economic and social problems fuels political instability in many "developing countries," anthropological studies of these rural populations in Latin America, Africa, Asia, and elsewhere are considered significant and practical.[6] In addition to improving policies aimed at social and economic development in rural communities, anthropological peasant studies may offer insights into how to deal with peasants resisting challenges to their traditional way of life. Such anthropological research may be useful

---

[3]Powdermaker, H. (1939). *After freedom: A cultural study in the Deep South*. New York: Viking.

[4]Wolf, E. R., & Trager, G. L. (1971). Hortense Powdermaker 1900–1970. *American Anthropologist 73* (3), 784.

---

[5]Prins, H. E. L., & Krebs, E. (2006). Toward a land without evil: Alfred Métraux as UNESCO anthropologist 1948–1962. In *60 years of UNESCO history. Proceedings of the international symposium in Paris, 16–18 November 2005*. Paris: UNESCO.

[6]Redfield, R. (1953). *The primitive world and its transformations* (pp. 40–41). Ithaca, NY: Cornell University Press; Wolf, E. R. (1966). *Peasants* (p. 1). Englewood Cliffs, NJ: Prentice-Hall.

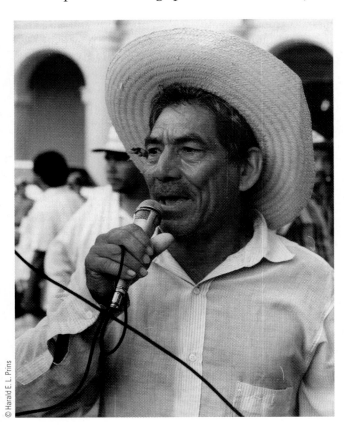

© Harald E. L. Prins

A peasant leader addresses a crowd in front of the presidential palace in Paraguay's capital city Asunción at a massive protest rally against land dispossession.

in promoting social justice by helping to solve, manage, or avoid social conflicts and political violence, including rebellions and guerrilla warfare or insurgencies.[7]

Advocacy Anthropology

By the 1960s, European colonial powers had lost almost all of their overseas territorial possessions. Many anthropologists turned their attention to the newly independent countries in Africa and Asia, while others focused on South and Central America. However, as political unrest made fieldwork increasingly difficult in many parts of the world, significant numbers of anthropologists investigated important issues of culture change and conflict inside Europe and North America. Many of these issues, which remain focal points to this day, involve immigrants and refugees who come from places where anthropologists have conducted research.

Some anthropologists have gone beyond studying such groups to playing a role in helping them adjust to their new circumstances—an example of applied anthropology. Others have become *advocates* for peasant communities, ethnic or religious minorities, or indigenous groups struggling to hold onto their ancestral lands, natural resources, and customary ways of life.

Although anthropologists have privately long championed the rights of indigenous peoples and other culture groups under siege, one of the first anthropological research projects explicitly and publicly addressing the quest for social justice and cultural survival took place among the Meskwaki, or Fox Indians, on their reservation in the state of Iowa (1948–1959). Based on long-term fieldwork with this North American Indian community, U.S. anthropologist Sol Tax challenged government-sponsored applied anthropological research projects and proposed instead that researchers work directly with "disadvantaged, exploited, and oppressed communities [to help *them*] identify and solve their [*own*] problems."[8]

Especially over the past few decades, anthropologists committed to social justice and human rights have become actively involved in efforts to assist indigenous groups, peasant communities, and ethnic minorities. Today, most anthropologists committed to community-based and politically involved research refer to their work as **advocacy anthropology.**

U.S. anthropologist Robert Hitchcock has practiced advocacy anthropology for over three decades. Specializing in development issues, he has focused primarily on land rights, as well as the social, economic, and cultural rights, of indigenous peoples in southern Africa—especially Bushmen (San, Basarwa) groups in Botswana. Hitchcock's work has involved helping Bushmen to ensure their rights to land—for foraging, pasturing, farming, and income-generation purposes—in the face of development projects aimed at setting aside land for the ranching, mining, or conservation interests of others. He helped draw up legislation on subsistence hunting in Botswana, making it the only country in Africa that allows broad-based hunting rights for indigenous peoples who forage for part of their livelihoods.[9]

[7]Firth, R. (1946). *Malay fishermen: Their peasant economy* (pp. ix–x). London: Kegan Paul, Trench, Trubner & Co., Ltd.; see also Wolf, E. R. (1969). *Peasant wars of the twentieth century* (pp. ix–xiii, 276–302). New York: Harper & Row.

advocacy anthropology Research that is community-based and politically involved.

[8]Field, L. W. (2004). Beyond "applied" anthropology. In T. Biolsi (Ed.), *A companion to the anthropology of American Indians* (pp. 472–489). Oxford: Blackwell Publishing. See also Lurie, N. O. (1973). Action anthropology and the American Indian. In *Anthropology and the American Indian: A symposium* (p. 6). San Francisco: Indian Historical Press.

[9]Hitchcock, R. K., & Enghoff, M. (2004). *Capacity-building of first people of the Kalahari, Botswana: An evaluation.* Copenhagen: International Work Group for Indigenous Affairs.

Today's most wide ranging advocacy anthropologist is Rodolfo Stavenhagen, special rapporteur on indigenous rights for the United Nations High Commission on Human Rights. A research professor at the Colegio de Mexico since 1965, he is founder and first president of the Mexican Academy of Human Rights. Dr. Stavenhagen leads investigations on the human rights situation and fundamental freedoms of indigenous peoples, discusses claims of injustice with government officials, and seeks solutions. Here he greets indigenous leader Lourdes Tiban after reporting on the situation of Ecuador's indigenous peoples at a 2006 conference in Quito.

AP Photo/Dolores Ochoa R.

Studying Up

Especially since the 1960s, growing numbers of anthropologists have been doing ethnographic research in their own countries. Largely because of a well-established tradition of participant observation in small-scale communities, most still prefer to do fieldwork in rural villages and urban neighborhoods among culturally distinctive groups such as immigrants or ethnic and religious minorities.

Nevertheless, because of anthropology's mission to gain a more comprehensive understanding of the human condition in its full cross-cultural range and complexity, not just in distant places or at the margins of our own societies, some scholars have urged ethnographic research in the centers of political and economic power in the world's dominant societies. Of particular note is U.S. anthropologist Laura Nader. Coining the term "study up," she has called upon anthropologists to focus on Western elites, government bureaucracies, global corporations, philanthropic foundations, media empires, business clubs, and so on.

Of course, studying up is easier said than done, because it is a formidable challenge to do participant observation in such well-guarded circles. And when these elites are confronted with research projects or findings not of their liking, they have the capacity and political power to stop or seriously obstruct the research or the dissemination of its results.

Globalization and Multi-Sited Ethnography

As noted in Chapter 1, the impact of globalization is everywhere. Of relevance to anthropologists is the fact that distant localities are becoming linked in such a way that local events and situations are shaped by forces and activities occurring thousands of miles away, and vice versa. Connected by modern transportation, world trade, finance capital, transnational labor pools, and information superhighways, even the most geographically remote communities are becoming increasingly interdependent. Indeed, all of humanity now lives in what we refer to in this text as a "globalscape"—a worldwide interconnected landscape with multiple intertwining and overlapping peoples and cultures on the move.

One of the many consequences of globalization is the formation of *diasporic* populations (*diaspora* is a Greek word, originally meaning "scattering"), living and working far from their original homelands. While this has left some people feeling displaced and fragmented, others are transcending vast distances and staying in touch with family and friends from home with the aid of modern transportation and communication technologies. Through e-mail, Internet forums, and World Wide Web access to local news, geographically dispersed individuals spend part of their lives in cyberspace, dubbed "ethnoscapes" by anthropologist Arjun Appadurai from

India.[10] This electronically mediated environment enables people who are far from home to remain informed, to maintain their social networks, and even to hold onto a shared sense of ethnic identity that distinguishes them from the collectivity of individuals with whom they share their daily routines in actual geographic space.

Globalization has given rise to a new trend in anthropological research and analysis known as **multi-sited ethnography**—the investigation and documentation of peoples and cultures embedded in the larger structures of a globalizing world, utilizing a range of methods in various locations of time and space. Engaged in such mobile ethnography, researchers seek to capture the emerging dimension of the global by following individual actors, organizations, objects, images, stories, conflicts, and even pathogens as they move about in various interrelated transnational situations and locations.[11]

An example of multi-sited ethnographic research on a diasporic ethnic group is a recent study on transnational Chinese identities by Chinese American anthropologist Andrea Louie. Louie's fieldwork carried her to an array of locations in San Francisco, Hong Kong, and southern China—including her ancestral home in the Cantonese village Tiegang in Guangdong Province. Her paternal great grandfather left the village in the 1840s, crossing the Pacific Ocean to work on railroad construction during the California Gold Rush. But other family members remained in the area. Investigating Chinese identities from different and changing perspectives, Louie described her research like this:

> My fieldwork on Chinese identities employed a
> type of mobile [ethnography] aimed at examining various parts of a "relationship" being forged
> anew across national boundaries that draws on
> metaphors of shared heritage and place. In my
> investigation of "Chineseness" I conducted
> participant observation and interviews in San
> Francisco with Chinese American participants of
> the In Search of Roots program,[12] as well as later

Courtesy of Andrea Louie

In her explorations on the construction of Chinese identities in the context of U.S. and Chinese racial and multicultural politics, anthropologist Andrea Louie (center) has done multi-sited research in St. Louis, San Francisco, Hong Kong, and China. Here she sits with a couple and the daughter they adopted from China in 1995, who have been part of her research. (The child on Louie's lap is her own.)

> in China when they visited their ancestral villages and participated in government-sponsored
> Youth Festivals. In China, I researched from a
> number of bases the shifting attitudes of Chinese
> living in the Pearl River Delta region of Guangdong, including a village in the emigrant region
> of Zhongshan County, the Taishan region, and a
> middle school in the Special Economic Zone of
> Shenzhen. I interviewed people in their homes,
> and apartments; in cafes, culture centers, and
> MacDonald's restaurants; and in rural Chinese
> villages and on jet planes, focusing on various
> moments and contexts of interaction within
> which multiple and often discrepant discourses
> of Chineseness are brought together. . . .[13]

Also emerging in multi-sited ethnography are greater interdisciplinary approaches to fieldwork, bringing in theoretical ideas and research methods from cul-

---

[10]Appadurai, A. (1996). *Modernity at large: Cultural dimensions of globalization.* Minneapolis: University of Minnesota Press.

[11]Marcus, G. (1995). Ethnography in/of the world system: The emergence of multi-sited ethnography. *Annual review of anthropology 24,* 95–117; Robben, A. C. G. M., & Sluka, J. A. (Eds.). (2007). *Ethnographic fieldwork: An anthropological reader* (Part VII). Malden, MA: Blackwell Publishers.

[12]This program, run by organizations in Guangzhou and San Francisco, provides an opportunity for young adults (ages 17 to 25) of Cantonese descent to visit their ancestral villages in China.

multi-sited ethnography   The investigation and documentation of peoples and cultures embedded in the larger structures of a globalizing world, utilizing a range of methods in various locations of time and space.

---

[13]Louie, A. (2004). *Chineseness across borders: Renegotiating Chinese identities in China and the United States* (pp. 8–9). Durham and London: Duke University Press.

tural studies, media studies, and mass communication, among others. One example is the emergence of ethnographic studies of online "imagined communities" or *cyberethnography.*

Even in the fast-changing, globalizing world of the 21st century, core ethnographic research methods developed about a century ago continue to be relevant and revealing. New technologies have been added to the anthropologist's toolkit, but the hallmarks of our discipline—holistic research through fieldwork with participant observation—is still a valued and productive tradition. Having presented a sweeping historical overview of shifting anthropological research challenges and strategies, we turn now to the topic of research methods.

DOING ETHNOGRAPHY: CULTURAL ANTHROPOLOGY RESEARCH METHODS

Every culture comprises underlying rules or standards that are rarely obvious. A major challenge to the anthropologist is to identify and analyze those rules. Fundamental to the effort is **ethnographic fieldwork**—extended on-location research to gather detailed and in-depth information on a society's customary ideas, values, and practices through participation in its collective social life.

While it is true that early anthropologists worked primarily in small-scale societies and that the scope of social-cultural anthropology has since expanded to include urban life in complex industrial and postindustrial societies, ethnographic fieldwork methods developed in the early stage of the discipline continue to be central to anthropological research in all types of communities. For instance, they still feature personal observation of and participation in the everyday activities of the community, along with interviews, mapping, collection of genealogical data, and recording of sounds and visual images—all toward the gathering and analysis of data. However, it all begins with selecting a research site and a research problem or question.

Site Selection and Research Question

Anthropologists usually work outside their own culture, society, or ethnic group, most often in a foreign country. Although it has much to offer, anthropological study within one's own society may present special problems, as described by noted British anthropologist Sir Edmund Leach:

> Surprising though it may seem, fieldwork in a cultural context of which you already have intimate first hand experience seems to be

much more difficult than fieldwork which is approached from the naïve viewpoint of a total stranger. When anthropologists study facets of their own society their vision seems to become distorted by prejudices which derive from private rather than public experience.[14]

For this reason, most successful anthropological studies of societies to which the researchers themselves belong are done by individuals who first worked in some other culture. The more one learns of other cultures, the more one gains a fresh and more revealing perspective on one's own.

But wherever the site, the research requires advance planning. This includes finding funding and securing permission from the community to be studied (and, where mandated, from government officials as well). If possible, researchers make a preliminary trip to the field site to make these and other arrangements before moving there for more extended research. After spending time exploring the local conditions and circumstances, they have the opportunity to better define their specific research question or problem. For instance, what is the psychological impact of a new highway on members of a traditionally isolated farming community? Or how does the introduction of new electronic media such as cell phones influence long-established gender relations in cultures with religious restrictions on social contact between men and women?

Preparatory Research

Before heading into the field, anthropologists do preparatory research. This includes delving into any existing written, visual, or sound information available about the people and place one has chosen to study. It may involve contacting and interviewing others who have some knowledge about or experience with the community, region, or country.

Because anthropologists must be able to communicate with the people they have chosen to study, they will also have to learn the language used in the community selected for fieldwork. Because many of the more than 6,000 languages currently spoken in the world have already been recorded and written down, especially during the past 100 years or so, it is possible to learn some foreign languages prior to fieldwork. However, as in the

---

[14]Leach, E. (1982). *Social anthropology* (p. 124). Glasgow: Fontana Paperbacks.

ethnographic fieldwork Extended on-location research to gather detailed and in-depth information on a society's customary ideas, values, and practices through participation in its collective social life.

early days of the discipline, some of today's anthropologists do research among peoples whose native languages have not yet been written down. In such a case, they may find bilingual or multilingual individuals to help them gain some basic linguistic proficiency. Another possibility is to first learn an already recorded and closely related language, which may provide the researcher with some elementary communication skills during the first phase of the actual fieldwork.

Finally, anthropologists prepare for fieldwork by studying theoretical, historical, ethnographic, and other literature relevant to the research problem to be investigated. For instance, anthropologists interested in the problem of human violence, both between and within groups, will read studies describing and theoretically explaining conflicts such as wars, feuds, vengeance killing, and so on. Having delved into the existing literature, they may then formulate a theoretical framework and research question to guide them in their fieldwork. Such was the case when U.S. anthropologist Napoleon Chagnon applied natural selection theory to his study of violence within Yanomami Indian communities in South America's tropical rainforest, suggesting that males with

an aggressive reputation as killers are reproductively more successful than those without such a status.[15]

Christopher Boehm took a different theoretical approach in his research on blood revenge among Slavic mountain people in Montenegro. He framed his research question in terms of the ecological function of this violent tradition, as it regulated relations between groups competing for survival in a harsh environment with scarce natural resources.[16]

Participant Observation

Once in the field, anthropologists are anything but passive onlookers. They rely on *participant observation*—a research method in which one learns about a group's beliefs and behaviors through social participation and personal observation within the community, as well as interviews and discussion with individual members of

---

[15]Chagnon, N. A. (1988). Life histories, blood revenge, and warfare in a tribal population. *Science 239*, 935–992.

[16]Boehm, C. (1984). *Blood revenge.* Lawrence: University of Kansas Press.

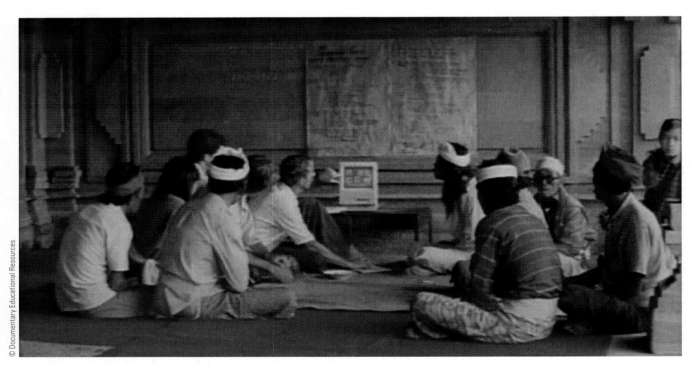

© Documentary Educational Resources

During fieldwork, anthropologists use computers not only for recording and processing data, but as a means of communicating with the peoples being studied. Here we see ecologist James Kremer and anthropologist Stephen Lansing (behind Kremer) who have researched the traditional rituals and network of water temples linked to the irrigation management of rice fields on the island of Bali in Indonesia. They are explaining a computer simulation of this system to the high priest of the supreme water temple, as other temple priests look on. Located on the crater rim above the caldera and lake of Mount Batur, this temple is associated with the Goddess of the Crater Lake. Every year people from hundreds of villages bring offerings here, expressing gratitude to this deity for the gift of water.

the group over an extended stay in the community. Although researchers may focus on a particular cultural aspect or issue, they will consider the culture as a whole for the sake of context. This requires being tuned in to nearly countless details of daily life—both the ordinary and the extraordinary. By taking part in community life anthropologists learn why and how events are organized and carried out. Through alert and sustained participation—carefully watching, questioning, listening, and analyzing over a period of time—they can usually identify, explain, and often predict a group's behavior.

Ethnographic Tools and Aids

An anthropologist's most essential ethnographic tools in the field are notebooks, pen/pencil, camera, sound recorder, and, increasingly, a laptop computer sometimes equipped with a variety of specific data processing programs. Beyond such tools of the trade, he or she needs to be able to socially and psychologically adapt to a strange community with a different way of life. Keen personal observation skills are also essential. One must cultivate the ability to perceive collective life in the other culture with *all* the senses—sight, touch, smell, taste, and hearing.

When participating in an unfamiliar culture, anthropologists are often helped by one or more generous individuals in the village or neighborhood. They may also be taken in by a family and through participation in the daily routine of a household, they will soon become familiar with the community's basic shared cultural features.

Anthropologists may also formally enlist the assistance of **key consultants**—members of the society being studied, who provide information that helps researchers understand the meaning of what they observe. (Early anthropologists referred to such individuals as *informants*.) Just as parents guide a child toward proper behavior, so do these insiders help researchers unravel the mysteries of what at first is a strange world full of puzzles. To compensate local individuals for their help in making anthropologists feel welcome in the community and gain access to the treasure troves of inside information, fieldworkers may thank them for their time and expertise with goods, services, or cash.

Data Gathering:
The Ethnographer's Approach

Information collected by ethnographers falls in two main categories: quantitative and qualitative data. **Quantitative data** consist of statistical or measurable information, such as: population density, demographic composition of people and animals, and the number and size of houses; the hours worked per day; the types and quantities of crops grown; the amount of carbohydrates or animal protein consumed per individual; the quantity of wood, dung, or other material for fuel used to cook food or heat dwellings; the number of children born out of wedlock; the ratio of spouses born and raised within or outside the community, and so on.

Qualitative data concern nonstatistical information about such features as settlement patterns, natural resources, social networks of kinship relations, customary beliefs and practices, personal life histories, and so on. Often, these nonquantifiable data are the most important part of ethnographic research because they capture the essence of a culture and provide us with deeper insights into the unique lives of different peoples, making us truly understand what, why, and how they feel, think, and act in their own distinctive ways.

Beyond the generalities of participant observation, how exactly do ethnographers gather data? Field methods include formal and informal interviewing, mapping, collection of genealogical data, and recording sounds and images. Cultural anthropologists may also use surveys, but not in the way you might think. Below we touch on several key methods for collecting information.

Taking Surveys

Unlike many other social scientists, anthropologists do not usually go into the field equipped with prefigured surveys or questionnaires; rather, they recognize that there are many things that can be discovered only by keeping an open mind while thoughtfully watching, listening, participating, and asking questions. As fieldwork proceeds, anthropologists sort their complex impressions and observations into a meaningful whole, sometimes by formulating and testing limited or low-level hypotheses, but just as often by making use of imagination or intuition and following up on hunches. What is important is that the results are constantly checked for accuracy and consistency, for if the parts fail to fit together in a way that is internally coherent, it may be that a mistake has been made, and further inquiry is necessary.

This is not to say that anthropologists do not conduct surveys. Some do. But these are just one part of a much larger research strategy that includes a considerable amount of qualitative data as well as quantitative.

key consultant A member of the society being studied, who provides information that helps researchers understand the meaning of what they observe; early anthropologists referred to such individuals as informants.
quantitative data Statistical or measurable information, such as demographic composition, the types and quantities of crops grown, or the ratio of spouses born and raised within or outside the community.
qualitative data Nonstatistical information such as personal life stories and customary beliefs and practices.

Also, in ethnographic fieldwork, surveys are usually carried out after one has spent enough time on location to have gained the community's confidence and to know how to compose a questionnaire with categories that are culturally relevant.

Two studies of a village in Peru illustrate the contrast between anthropological and other social science approaches. One was carried out by a sociologist who, after conducting a survey by questionnaire, concluded that people in the village invariably worked together on one another's privately owned plots of land. By contrast, a cultural anthropologist who lived in the village for over a year (including the brief period when the sociologist did his study) witnessed that particular practice only once. The anthropologist's long-term participant observation revealed that although the idea of labor exchange relations was important to the people's sense of themselves, it was not a common economic practice.[17]

The point here is *not* that all sociological research is flawed, and all anthropological research is solid. It is that relying exclusively or even primarily on questionnaire surveys is a risky business, no matter who does it. That is because questionnaires all too easily embody the concepts and categories of the researcher, who is an outsider, rather than those of the people being studied. Even where this is not a problem, questionnaire surveys alone are not good ways of identifying causal relationships. They tend to concentrate on what is measurable, answerable, and acceptable as a question, rather than probing the less obvious and more complex qualitative aspects of society or culture.

Moreover, for a host of reasons—fear, caution, wishful thinking, ignorance, exhaustion, hostility, hope of benefit—people may give partial, false, or self-serving information.[18] Keeping culture-bound ideas out of research methods, as illustrated through the example of standardized questionnaires, is an important point in all ethnographic research.

Interviewing

Asking questions is fundamental to ethnographic fieldwork and takes place in **informal interviews** (unstructured, open-ended conversations in everyday life) and **formal interviews** (structured question/answer sessions

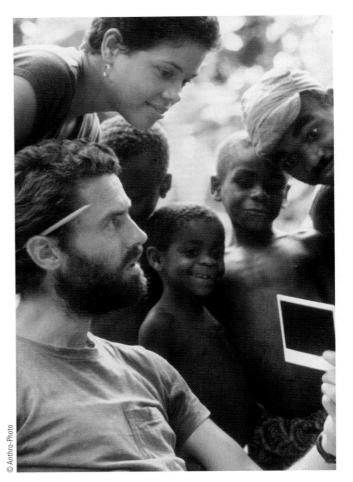

© Anthro-Photo

In addition to using photographs for cultural documentation, anthropologists sometimes use them during fieldwork as eliciting devices, sharing pictures of cultural objects or activities for example, to encourage locals to talk about and explain what they see. Here anthropologists Nadine Peacock and Bob Bailey show photos to Efe people in the Ituri Forest in Congo, Africa.

carefully notated as they occur and based on prepared questions). Informal interviews may be carried out anytime and anywhere—on horseback, in a canoe, by a cooking fire, during ritual events, while walking through the community with a local inhabitant, and the list goes on. Such casual exchanges are essential, for it is often in these conversations that people share most freely. Moreover, questions put forth in formal interviews typically grow out of cultural knowledge and insights gained during informal ones.

Getting people to open up is an art born of a genuine interest in both the information and the person who is sharing it. It requires dropping all assumptions and cultivating the ability to *really* listen. It may even require a willingness to be the village idiot by asking simple questions to which the answers may seem obvious. Also, effective interviewers learn early on that numerous followup questions are vital since first answers may mask truth rather than reveal it. Questions generally fall into

---

[17]Chambers, R. (1983). *Rural development: Putting the last first* (p. 51). New York: Longman.

[18]Sanjek, R. (1990). On ethnographic validity. In R. Sanjek (Ed.), *Field notes* (p. 395). Ithaca, NY: Cornell University Press.

informal interview An unstructured, open-ended conversation in everyday life.
formal interview A structured question/answer session carefully notated as it occurs and based on prepared questions.

one of two categories: broad, *open-ended questions,* such as, Can you tell me about your childhood?, and *closed questions* seeking specific pieces of information, such as, Where and when were you born?

In ethnographic fieldwork, interviews are used to collect a vast range of cultural information, from life histories, genealogies, and myths to craft techniques and midwife procedures, to beliefs concerning everything from illness to food taboos. Genealogical data can be especially useful, as it provides information about a range of social practices (such as cousin marriage), worldview (such as ancestor worship), political relations (such as alliances), and economic arrangements (such as hunting or harvesting on clan-owned lands).

Researchers employ numerous **eliciting devices**—activities and objects used to draw out individuals and encourage them to recall and share information. There are countless examples of this: taking a walk with a local and asking about a legend, inviting the person to comment on it or to offer another; sharing details about one's own family and neighborhood and inviting a telling in return; joining in a community activity and asking a local to explain the practice and why they are doing it; taking and sharing photographs of cultural objects or activities and asking locals to explain what they see in the pictures.

Mapping

Because many anthropologists still do fieldwork among traditional peoples in all corners of the earth, they may find themselves in distant places about which there is little detailed geographic knowledge. Although cartographers may already have mapped the region, standard maps seldom show geographic and spatial features that are culturally significant to the people living there. People inhabiting areas that form part of their ancestral homeland have a particular understanding of the area and their own names for local places. These native names may convey essential geographic information, describing the distinctive features of a locality such as its physical appearance, its specific dangers, or its precious resources.

Some place names may derive from certain political realities such as headquarters, territorial boundaries, and so on. Others may make sense only in the cultural context of a local people's worldview as recounted in their myths, legends, songs, or other narrative traditions. Thus, to truly understand the lay of the land, anthropologists may have to make their own detailed geographic maps documenting culturally relevant geographic features in the landscape inhabited by the people they study.

Especially since the early 1970s, anthropologists have become involved in indigenous land use and occupancy studies for various reasons, including the documenta-

tion of traditional land claims. Information based on a combination of local oral histories, early written descriptions of explorers, traders, missionaries, and other visitors, combined with data obtained from archaeological excavations may be collected as general background for individual map biographies.

One such ethnogeographic research project took place in northwestern Canada, during the planning stage of the building of the Alaska Highway natural gas pipeline. Since the line would cut directly though Native lands, local indigenous community leaders and federal officials insisted that a study be done to determine how the new construction would affect indigenous inhabitants. Canadian anthropologist Hugh Brody, one of the researchers in this ethnogeographic study, explained: "These maps are the key to the studies and their greatest contribution. Hunters, trappers, fishermen, and berry-pickers mapped out all the land they had ever used in their lifetimes, encircling hunting areas species by species, marking gathering location and camping sites—everything their life on the land had entailed that could be marked on a map."[19]

In addition to mapping the local place names and geographic features, anthropologists may also map out information relevant to the local subsistence such as animal migration routes, favorite fishing areas, places where medicinal plants can be harvested or firewood cut, and so on.

Today, by means of the technology known as global positioning system (GPS), researchers can measure precise distances by triangulating the travel time of radio signals from various orbiting satellites. They can create maps that pinpoint human settlement locations and the layout of dwellings, gardens, public spaces, water holes, pastures, surrounding mountains, rivers, lakes, seashores, islands, swamps, forests, deserts, and any other relevant feature in the regional environment.

To store, edit, analyze, integrate, and display this geographically referenced spatial information, some anthropologists use cartographic digital technology, known as geographic information systems (GIS). GIS makes it possible to map the geographic features and natural resources in a certain environment—and to link these data to ethnographic information about population density and distribution, social networks of kinship relations, seasonal patterns of land use, private or collective claims of ownership, travel routes, sources of water, and so on. With GIS researchers can also integrate infor-

---

[19]Brody, H. (1981). *Maps and dreams* (p. 147). New York: Pantheon Books.

eliciting device An activity or object used to draw out individuals and encourage them to recall and share information.

Anthropologists of Note

Gregory Bateson (1904–1980) ▪ Margaret Mead (1901–1978)

From 1936 to 1938 Margaret Mead and Gregory Bateson did collaborative ethnographic fieldwork in Bali. Bateson, Mead's husband at the time, was a British anthropologist trained by Alfred C. Haddon, who led the 1898 Torres Strait expedition and is credited with making the first ethnographic film in the field. During their stay in Bali, Bateson took about 25,000 photographs and shot 22,000 feet of motion picture film. Afterward, the couple co-authored the photographic ethnography *Balinese Character: A Photographic Analysis* (1942).

That same year, Bateson worked as an anthropological film analyst studying German motion pictures. Soon Mead and a few other anthropologists became involved in thematic analysis of foreign fictional films. She later compiled a number of such visual anthropology studies in a co-edited volume titled *The Study of Culture at a Distance* (1953).

Mead became a tireless promoter of the scholarly use of ethnographic

In 1938, after two years of fieldwork in Bali, Margaret Mead and Gregory Bateson began research in Papua New Guinea, where they staged this photograph of themselves to highlight the importance of cameras as part of the ethnographic toolkit. (Note camera on tripod behind Mead and other cameras atop the desk.)

photography and film. In 1960, the year the portable sync-sound film camera was invented, Mead was serving as president of the American Anthropology Association. In her presidential address at the association's annual gathering, she pointed out what she saw as shortcomings in the discipline and urged anthropologists to use cameras more effectively.[a] Chiding her colleagues for not fully utilizing new technological developments, she complained that anthropology had come "to depend on words, and words, and words."

Mead's legacy is commemorated in numerous venues, including the Margaret Mead Film Festival hosted annually since 1977 by the American Museum of Natural History in New York City. Thus it was fitting that during the Margaret Mead Centennial celebrations in 2001 the American Anthropological Association endorsed a landmark visual media policy statement urging academic committees to consider ethnographic visuals—and not just ethnographic writing—when evaluating scholarly output of academics up for hiring, promotion, and tenure.

[a]Mead, M. (1960). Anthropology among the sciences. *American Anthropologist 63*, 475–482.

Library of Congress

mation about beliefs, myths, legends, songs, and other culturally relevant data associated with distinct locations. Moreover, they can create interactive inquiries for analysis of research data as well as natural and cultural resource management.[20]

Photographing and Filming

Most anthropologists use cameras for fieldwork, as well as notepads, computers, or sound recording devices to record their observations. In fact, photography has been instrumental in anthropological research for more than a century. For instance, German-born U.S. anthropologist Franz Boas already took photographs during his first fieldwork among the Inuit in the Canadian Arctic in the early 1880s. And just a few years after the invention of the moving picture camera in 1894, anthropologists began filming traditional dances by indigenous Australians and other ethnographic subjects of interest.

Especially following the invention of the portable synchronous-sound camera in 1960, ethnographic filmmaking took off. New technological developments were making it increasingly obvious that visual media could serve a wide range of cross-cultural research purposes. Some anthropologists employed still photography in community surveys and elicitation techniques. Others turned to film to document and research traditional patterns of nonverbal communication such as body language and social space use. Cameras have also been (and continue to be) instrumental in documenting the disappearing world of traditional foragers, herders, and farmers surviving in remote places. The Anthropologists of Note feature details the long history of such equipment in anthropology.

[20]Schoepfle, M. (2001). Ethnographic resource inventory and the National Park Service. *Cultural Resource Management 5*, 1–7.

Challenges of Ethnographic Fieldwork

While ethnographic fieldwork offers a range of opportunities to gain better and deeper insight into the community being studied, it comes with a Pandora's box of challenges. Certainly it involves at least a measure of strain and pain, for it usually requires researchers to step out of their cultural comfort zone into an unknown world that is sometimes unsettling. As touched upon in Chapter 1, anthropologists in the field are likely to face a wide array of challenges—physical, social, mental, political, and ethical.

Among the numerous mental challenges anthropologists commonly face are culture shock, loneliness, feeling like an ignorant outsider, and being socially awkward in a new cultural setting. Physical challenges typically include adjusting to unfamiliar food, climate, and hygiene conditions, along with needing to be constantly alert because anything that is happening or being said may be significant to one's research. In addition to engaging fully in work and social activities with the community, ethnographers must spend considerable time doing a host of other things, such as interviewing, making copious notes, and analyzing data.

In the following paragraphs we offer details on some of the most common personal struggles anthropologists face in the field.

Gaining Social Acceptance in the Community

Having decided where to do ethnographic research and what to focus on, anthropologists embark on the journey to their field site. Because few choose to do research in their own home communities, fieldwork almost always involves making new social contacts with strangers who do not know who you are, why you have come, or what you want from them. In short, a visiting anthropologist is as much a mystery to those she or he intends to study as the group is to the researcher.

Although there is no sure way of predicting how one will be received, it is certain that success in ethnographic fieldwork depends on mutual goodwill and the ability to develop friendships and other meaningful social relations. As New Zealand anthropologist Jeffrey Sluka noted, "The classic image of successful rapport and good fieldwork relations in cultural anthropology is that of the ethnographer who has been 'adopted' or named by the tribe or people he or she studies."[21]

Among the numerous ethnographic examples of anthropologists being adopted by a family, lineage, or clan is the case of Canadian anthropologist Richard Lee, adopted by a group of Ju/'hoansi (Bushmen) foragers in the Kalahari Desert. He describes the informal way in which this took place:

> One day in March 1964, I was visiting a !Xabe village, when Hwan//a, a woman about my age who was married to one of the Tswana Headman Isak's three sons, playfully began to call me, "Uncle, uncle, /Tontah, come see me."
>
> Puzzled, I drew closer; until that time the Ju had referred to me simply as the White Man (/*Ton*) or the bearded one. . . . Hwan//a smiled and said, "You are all alone here and I have no children, so I will name you /Tontah after my *tsu* /Tontah who is dead, and, as I have named you, you shall call me mother."
>
> Pleased, I asked Hwan//a to tell me how she decided on the name /Tontah. She explained that I was a European, a "/*ton*," and the traditional Ju name /Tontah sounds like it. Since her late *tsu* had no namesake, she decided to name me /Tontah to do honor to him and to my exotic status. [This] was the famous name relationship—the Ju/'hoan custom of naming everyone after an older person according to a repertoire of personal names [and] I was excited to be named in this way. The name stuck. Soon people all over the Dobe area were calling me /Tontah.[22]

Anthropologists adopted into networks of kinship relations not only gain social access and certain rights but also assume a range of social obligations associated with their new kinship status. These relationships can be deep and enduring—as illustrated by Smithsonian anthropologist William Crocker's description of his 1991 return to the Canela community after a twelve-year absence. He had lived among these Amazonian Indians in Brazil for a total of 66 months from the 1950s through the 1970s. When he stepped out of the single-motor missionary plane that had brought him back, he was quickly surrounded by Canela:

> Once on the ground, I groped for names and terms of address while shaking many hands. Soon my Canela mother Tutkhwey (dove-woman), pulled me over to the shade of a plane's wing and pushed me down to a mat on the ground. She put both hands on my shoulders and, kneeling beside me, her head by mine, cried out words of mourning in a loud yodeling manner. Tears and phlegm dripped onto my shoulder and knees. According to a custom now abandoned by the younger women, she was cry-

---

[21]Sluka, J. A. (2007). Fieldwork relations and rapport: Introduction. In A. C. G. M. Robben & J. A. Sluka (Eds.), *Ethnographic fieldwork: An anthropological reader* (p. 122). Malden, MA: Blackwell Publishers.

[22]Lee, R. B. (1993). *The Dobe Ju/'hoansi* (p. 61). Ft. Worth: Harcourt Brace.

U.S. anthropologist William Crocker did fieldwork among Canela Indians in Brazil over several decades. He still visits the community regularly. In this 1964 photograph, a Canela woman (M~i~i- kw'ej, or Alligator Woman) gives him a traditional haircut while other members of the community look on. She is the wife of his adoptive Canela "brother" and therefore a "wife" to Crocker in Canela kinship terms. Among the Canela, it was improper for a mother, sister, or daughter to cut a man's hair.

ing for the loss of a grown daughter, Tsep-khwey (bat-woman), as well as for my return.[23]

Since that 1991 reunion, Crocker has visited the Canela community every other year—always receiving a warm welcome and staying with locals. Although many anthropologists are successful in gaining social acceptance and even adoption status in communities where they do participant observation, they rarely go completely native and abandon their own homeland. For even after long stays in a community, after learning to behave appropriately and communicate well, few fieldworkers become true insiders.

Political Challenges

Political challenges during fieldwork include the possibility of being caught in rivalries and used unwittingly by factions within the community; the anthropologist may be viewed with suspicion by government authorities who may suspect the anthropologist is a foreign spy.

U.S. anthropologist June Nash, for instance, has faced serious political and personal challenges doing fieldwork in various Latin American communities experiencing violent changes. As an outsider, Nash tried to avoid becoming embroiled in local conflicts but could not maintain her position as an impartial observer while researching a tin mining community in the Bolivian highlands. When the conflict between local miners and bosses controlling the armed forces became violent, Nash found herself in a revolutionary setting in which miners viewed her tape recorder as an instrument of espionage and suspected her of being a CIA agent.[24]

All anthropologists face the overriding challenge of winning the trust that allows people to be themselves and share an unmasked version of their culture with a newcomer. Some do not succeed in meeting this challenge. So it was with U.S. anthropologist Lincoln Keiser in his difficult fieldwork in the remote town of Thull, situated in the Hindu Kush Mountains of northwestern Pakistan. Keiser ventured there to explore customary blood feuding among a Kohistani tribal community of 6,000 Muslims making their living by a mix of farming and herding in the rugged region. However, many of the people he had traveled so far to study did not appreciate his presence. As Keiser recounted, many of the fiercely independent tribesmen in this area, "where the AK-47 [sub-machine gun] symbolizes the violent quality of male social relations," treated him as a foreign "infidel" and with great disdain and suspicion:

> Throughout my stay in Thull, many people remained convinced I was a creature sent by the devil to harm the community. The stories of my alleged evil doings always amazed me, both in their number and detail. [Doing fieldwork in Thull] was a test I failed, for a *jirga* [political council] of my most vocal opponents ultimately forced me to leave Thull three months before I had planned. . . . Obviously, I have difficulty claiming the people of Thull as "my people"

[23]Crocker, W. H., & Crocker, J. G. (2004). *The Canela: Kinship, ritual, and sex in an Amazonian tribe* (p. 1). Belmont, CA: Wadsworth.

[24]Nash, J. (1976). Ethnology in a revolutionary setting. In M. A. Rynkiewich & J. P. Spradley (Eds.), *Ethics and anthropology: Dilemmas in fieldwork* (pp. 148–166). New York: Wiley.

because so many of them never ceased to despise me. . . . Still, I learned from being hated.[25]

Challenges Linked to Gender, Age, Ideology, Ethnicity, and Skin Color

Keiser's fieldwork challenges stemmed in part from his non-Muslim religious identity, marking him as an outsider in the local community of the faithful. Gender, age, ethnicity, and skin color can also impact a researcher's access to a community. For instance, African American anthropologist Norris Brock-Johnson encountered social obstacles while doing fieldwork in the American Midwest, but his dark skin color helped him gain "admission to the world of black Caribbean shipwrights" on the island of Bequia where he studied traditional boatmaking.[26]

In earlier days, when anthropologist Hortense Powdermaker did fieldwork in a Mississippi town during the early 1930s, she became sharply aware of her own status as a white person in what was then a racially segregated state in the Christian conservative center of the southern Bible Belt. Although she could not change her skin color, she did conceal her Jewish identity to avoid problems.[27]

With respect to gender, male ethnographers may face prohibitions or severe restrictions in interviewing women or observing certain women's activities. Similarly, a female researcher may not find ready reception among males in communities with gender-segregation traditions.

And there are other political, personal, and ethical dilemmas facing anthropologists doing fieldwork: What does the researcher do if faced with a troubling or even reprehensible cultural practice? How does the researcher deal with demands for food supplies and/or Western medicines? What about the temptation to use deception to gain vital information? Finally, all ethnographers must grapple with the very real challenge of subjectivity—his or her own and that of members in the community being studied.

The Problem of Subjectivity: Things Are Not as They Seem

Whether working near home or abroad, when endeavoring to identify the rules that underlie each culture, ethnographers must contend with bias or subjectivity—with the fact that perceptions of reality vary. Consider, for example, the following discussion of exogamy (marriage outside one's own group) among the Trobriand Islanders in Melanesia, as described by Polish anthropologist Bronislaw Malinowski:

> If you were to inquire into the matter among the Trobrianders, you would find that . . . the natives show horror at the idea of violating the rules of exogamy and that they believe that sores, diseases, even death might follow clan incest. [But] from the viewpoint of the native libertine, *suvasova* (the breach of exogamy) is indeed a specially interesting and spicy form of erotic experience.[28]

Malinowski himself determined that although such breaches did occur, they were much less frequent than gossip would have it. Had he relied solely on what the Trobrianders told him, his description of their culture would have been flawed. The same sort of discrepancy between cultural ideals and the way people actually behave can be found in any culture, as illustrated in our Chapter 1 discussion of William Rathje's Garbage Project, which revealed that people consumed notably more alcohol than they said they did. Because of this, an anthropologist must be extremely careful in describing a culture. To do so accurately, he or she needs to seek out and consider three kinds of data:

1. The people's own understanding of their culture and the general rules they share—that is, their ideal sense of the way their own society ought to be.

2. The extent to which people believe they are observing those rules—that is, how they think they really behave.

3. The behavior that can be directly observed—that is, what the anthropologist actually sees happening. (In the example of the Trobrianders, one would watch to see whether or not the rule of exogamy is actually violated.)

Clearly, the way people think they *should* behave, the way in which they think they *do* behave, and the way in which they *actually* behave may be distinctly different. By carefully examining and comparing these elements, anthropologists can draw up a set of rules that may explain the acceptable range of behavior within a culture.

Beyond the possibility of drawing false conclusions based on a group's ideal sense of itself, anthropologists run the risk of misinterpretation due to personal feelings and biases shaped by their own culture, as well as gender and age. It is important to recognize this challenge and make every effort to overcome it, for otherwise one may seriously misconstrue what one sees.

---

[25]Keiser, L. (1991). *Friend by day, enemy by night: Organized vengeance in a Kohistani community* (p. 103). Fort Worth: Holt, Rinehart & Winston.

[26]Robben, A. C. G. M. (2007). Fieldwork identity: Introduction. In A. C. G. M. Robben & J. A. Sluka (Eds.), *Ethnographic fieldwork: An anthropological reader* (p. 61). Malden, MA: Blackwell Publishers; Johnson, N. B. (1984). Sex, color, and rites of passage in ethnographic research. *Human Organization 43* (2), 108–120.

[27]Powdermaker, H. (1976). *Stranger and friend: The way of an anthropologist*. London: Secker and Warburg.

[28]Malinowski, B. (1922). *Argonauts of the western Pacific*. London: Routledge & Kegan Paul.

A case in point is the story of how male bias in the Polish culture that Malinowski grew up in caused him to ignore or miss significant factors in his pioneering study of the Trobrianders. Unlike today, when anthropologists receive special training before going into the field, Malinowski set out to do fieldwork early in the 20th century with little formal preparation. The follow-ing Original Study, written by anthropologist Annette Weiner who ventured to the same islands sixty years after Malinowski, illustrates how gender can impact one's research findings—both in terms of the bias that may affect a researcher's outlook and in terms of what key consultants may feel comfortable sharing with a particular researcher.

Original Study • By Annette B. Weiner

The Importance of Trobriand Women

Walking into a village at the beginning of fieldwork is entering a world without cultural guideposts. The task of learning values that others live by is never easy. The rigors of fieldwork involve listening and watching, learning a new language of speech and actions, and most of all, letting go of one's own cultural assumptions in order to understand the meanings others give to work, power, death, family, and friends. During my fieldwork in the Trobriand Islands of Papua New Guinea, I wrestled doggedly with each of these problems—and with the added challenge that I was working in the footsteps of a celebrated anthropological ancestor, Bronislaw Kasper Malinowski. . . .

In 1971, before my first trip to the Trobriands, I thought I understood many things about Trobriand customs and beliefs from having read Malinowski's exhaustive writings. Once there, however, I found that I had much more to discover about what I thought I already knew. For many months I worked with these discordant realities, always conscious of Malinowski's shadow, his words, his explanations. Although I found significant differences in areas of importance, I gradually came to understand how he reached certain conclusions. The answers we both received from informants were not so dissimilar, and I could actually trace how Malinowski had analyzed what his informants told him in a way that made sense and was scientifically signifi-cant—given what anthropologists gener-ally then recognized about such societies. Sixty years separate our fieldwork, and any comparison of our studies illustrates not so much Malinowski's mistaken interpretations but the developments in anthropological knowledge and inquiry from his time to mine. . . .

My most significant point of depar-ture from Malinowski's analyses was the attention I gave to women's produc-tive work. In my original research plans, women were not the central focus of study, but on the first day I took up residence in a village I was taken by them to watch a distribution of their own wealth—bundles of banana leaves and ba-nana fiber skirts—which they exchanged with other women in commemoration of someone who had recently died. Watch-ing that event forced me to take women's economic roles more seriously than I would have from reading Malinowski's studies. Although Malinowski noted the high status of Trobriand women, he attributed their importance to the fact that Trobrianders reckon descent through women, thereby giving them genealogical significance in a matrilineal society. Yet he never considered that this signifi-cance was underwritten by women's own wealth because he did not systemati-cally investigate the women's productive activities. Although in his field notes he mentions Trobriand women making these seemingly useless banana bundles to be exchanged at a death, his published work only deals with men's wealth.

My taking seriously the importance of women's wealth not only brought women as the neglected half of society clearly into the ethnographic picture but also forced me to revise many of Malinowski's assumptions about Trobriand men. For

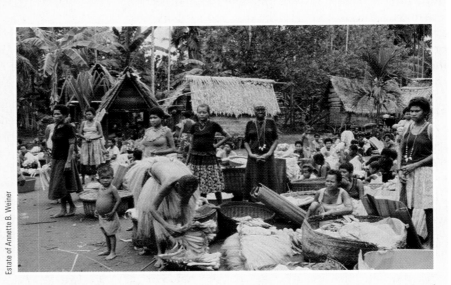

In the Trobriand Islands, women's wealth consists of skirts and banana leaves, large quantities of which must be given away on the death of a relative.

example, Trobriand kinship as described by Malinowski has always been a subject of debate among anthropologists. For Malinowski, the basic relationships within a Trobriand family were guided by the matrilineal principle of "mother-right" and "father-love." A father was called "stranger" and had little authority over his own children. A woman's brother was the commanding figure and exercised control over his sister's sons because they were members of his matrilineage rather than their father's matrilineage. . . .

In my study of Trobriand women and men, a different configuration of matrilineal descent emerged. A Trobriand father is not a "stranger" in Malinowski's definition, nor is he a powerless figure as the third party to the relationship between a woman and her brother. The father is one of the most important

persons in his child's life, and remains so even after his child grows up and marries. Even his procreative importance is incorporated into his child's growth and development. He gives his child many opportunities to gain things from his matrilineage, thereby adding to the available resources that he or she can draw upon.

At the same time, this giving creates obligations on the part of a man's children toward him that last even beyond his death. Thus, the roles that men and their children play in each other's lives are worked out through extensive cycles of exchanges, which define the strength of their relationships to each other and eventually benefit the other members of both their matrilineages. Central to these exchanges are women and their wealth.

That Malinowski never gave equal time to the women's side of things, given the deep significance of their role in societal and political life, is not surprising. Only recently have anthropologists begun to understand the importance of taking women's work seriously. . . . In the past, both women and men ethnographers generally analyzed the societies they studied from a male perspective. The "women's point of view" was largely ignored in the study of gender roles, since anthropologists generally perceived women as living in the shadows of men—occupying the private rather than the public sectors of society, rearing children rather than engaging in economic or political pursuits.

(Excerpted from A. B. Weiner (1988). The Trobrianders of Papua New Guinea (pp. 4–7). New York: Holt, Rinehart & Winston.) ■

Ethnographic Reflexivity: Acknowledging the Researcher as Subject

As the Original Study makes clear, validation of anthropological research is uniquely challenging. In the natural sciences, replication of observations and/or experiments is a major means of establishing the reliability of a researcher's conclusions. Thus, one can see for oneself if one's colleague has "gotten it right."

Validation in ethnographic research is uniquely challenging because observational access is often limited. Access to sites previously researched may be constrained by a number of factors: insufficient funding, logistical difficulties in reaching the site, problems in obtaining permits, and the fact that cultural and environmental conditions often change. Factors such as these mean that what could be observed in a certain context at one particular time cannot be at others. Thus, one researcher cannot easily confirm the reliability or completeness of another's account. For this reason, anthropologists bear a heavy responsibility for accurate reporting, including disclosing key issues related to their research: Why was a particular location selected as a research site and for which research objectives? What were the local conditions during fieldwork? Who provided the key information and major insights? How were data collected and recorded? Without such background information, it is difficult to judge the validity of the account and the soundness of the researcher's conclusions.

In anthropology, researchers are expected to self-monitor through constantly checking their own per-

sonal or cultural biases and assumptions as they work and presenting these self-reflections along with their observations, a practice known as *reflexivity*. Commenting on the development of this reflexive ethnography since the 1970s, Dutch anthropologist Antonius Robben recently noted that this:

> conscious self-examination of the ethnographer's interpretive presuppositions [has] enriched fieldwork by making anthropologists pay much closer attention to the interactional processes through which they acquired, shared, and transmitted knowledge. . . . Reflexivity also prompted an interest in narrative styles, because if ethnography was all about intercultural and intersubjective translation and construction, then form, style, and rhetoric were of central importance.[29]

Putting It All Together: Completing an Ethnography

After collecting ethnographic information, the next challenge is to piece together all that has been gathered into a coherent whole that accurately describes the culture. Traditionally, ethnographies are detailed written descriptions comprised of chapters on topics such as the circumstances and place of fieldwork itself; historical background; the community or group today; its natural

---

[29]Robben, A. C. G. M. (2007). Reflexive ethnography: Introduction. In A. C. G. M. Robben & J. A. Sluka (Eds.), *Ethnographic fieldwork: An anthropological reader* (pp. 443–446). Malden, MA: Blackwell Publishers.

environment; settlement patterns; subsistence practices; networks of kinship relations and other forms of social organization; marriage and sexuality; economic exchanges; political institutions; myths, sacred beliefs, and ceremonies; and current developments. These may be illustrated with photographs and accompanied by maps, kinship diagrams, and figures showing social and political organizational structures, settlement layout, floor plans of dwellings, seasonal cycles, and so on.

Sometimes ethnographic research is documented not only in writing but also with sound recordings and on film. Visual records may be used for documentation and illustration as well as for analysis or as a means of gathering additional information in interviews. Moreover, footage shot for the sake of documentation and research may also be edited into a documentary film. Not unlike a written ethnography, such a film is a structured whole composed of numerous selected sequences, visual montage, juxtaposition of sound and visual image, and narrative sequencing, all coherently edited into an accurate visual representation of the ethnographic subject.[30]

In recent years some anthropologists have been experimenting with digital media. Today, anthropology's potential in research, interpretation, and presentation appears to be greater than ever with the emergence of digital ethnography. Sometimes called *hypermedia ethnography,* **digital ethnography** is the use of digital technologies (audio and visual) for the collection, analysis, and representation of ethnographic data. Digital recording devices provide ethnographers with a wealth of material to analyze and utilize toward building hypotheses. They also open the door to sharing findings in new, varied, and interactive ways in the far-reaching digitalized realm of the Internet.[31] Digital ethnographers, having amassed a wealth of digital material while researching, are able to share their findings through DVDs, CD-ROMs, photo essays, podcasts, or blogs.

---

[30]See Collier, J., & Collier, M. (1986). *Visual anthropology: Photography as a research method.* Albuquerque: University of New Mexico Press; el Guindi, F. (2004). *Visual anthropology: Essential method and theory.* Walnut Creek, CA: Altamira Press.

[31]Michael Wesch, personal communication.

digital ethnography The use of digital technologies (audio and visual) for the collection, analysis, and representation of ethnographic data.

ethnohistory A study of cultures of the recent past through oral histories, accounts of explorers, missionaries, and traders, and through analysis of records such as land titles, birth and death records, and other archival materials.

theory In science an explanation of natural phenomena, supported by a reliable body of data.

doctrine An assertion of opinion or belief formally handed down by an authority as true and indisputable. Also known as dogma.

Ethnohistory

Ethnohistory is a kind of historical ethnography that studies cultures of the recent past through oral histories, the accounts of explorers, missionaries, and traders, and through analysis of such records as land titles, birth and death records, and other archival materials. The ethnohistorical analysis of cultures is a valuable approach to understanding change and plays an important role in theory building.

ETHNOLOGY: FROM DESCRIPTION TO INTERPRETATION AND THEORY

Largely descriptive in nature, ethnography provides the basic data needed for *ethnology*—the branch of cultural anthropology that makes cross-cultural comparisons and develops theories that explain why certain important differences or similarities occur between groups. As noted in Chapter 1, the end product of anthropological research, if properly carried out, is a theory or coherent statement about culture or human nature that provides an explanatory framework for understanding the ideas and actions of the people who have been studied. In short, a **theory** is an explanation or interpretation supported by a reliable body of data.

Anthropologists do not claim any theory about culture to be the only and final word or absolute truth. Rather they judge or measure a theory's validity and soundness by varying degrees of probability; what is considered to be "true" is what is most probable. But while anthropologists are reluctant about making absolute statements about complex issues such as exactly how cultures function or change, they can and do provide fact-based evidence about whether assumptions have support or are unfounded and thus not true. Thus, a theory, contrary to widespread misuse of the term, is much more than mere speculation; it is a critically examined explanation of observed reality.

In this respect, it is important to distinguish between scientific theories—which are always open to future challenges born of new evidence or insights—and doctrine. A **doctrine,** or dogma, is an assertion of opinion or belief formally handed down by an authority as true and indisputable.

For instance, those who accept a creationist doctrine on the origin of the human species as recounted in sacred texts or myths passed down the generations do so on the basis of religious authority, conceding that such views may be contrary to genetic, geological, biological, or other scientific explanations. Such doctrines cannot be tested or proved one way or another: They are basically accepted as matters of faith.

In contrast to religious doctrine, however, scientific theory depends on demonstrable, fact-based evidence and repeated testing. So it is that, as our cross-cultural knowledge expands, the odds favor some anthropological theories over others; old explanations or interpretations must sometimes be discarded as new theories based on better or more complete evidence are shown to be more effective or probable.

Ethnology and the Comparative Method

A single instance of any phenomenon is generally insufficient for supporting a plausible hypothesis. Without some basis for comparison, the hypothesis grounded in a single case may be no more than a hunch born of a unique happenstance or particular historical coincidence. Theories in anthropology may be generated from worldwide cross-cultural or historical comparisons or even comparisons with other species. For instance, anthropologists may examine a global sample of societies in order to discover whether a hypothesis proposed to explain certain phenomena is supported by fact-based evidence. Of necessity, the cross-cultural researcher depends upon evidence gathered by other scholars as well as his or her own.

A key resource that makes this possible is the **Human Relations Area Files (HRAF),** a vast collection of cross-indexed ethnographic and archaeological data catalogued by cultural characteristics and geographic location. Initiated at Yale University in the mid-1900s, this ever-growing data bank classifies more than 700 cultural characteristics and includes nearly 400 societies, past and present, from all around the world. Archived in about 300 libraries (on microfiche and/or online) and approaching a million pages of information, the HRAF facilitates comparative research on almost any cultural feature imaginable—warfare, subsistence practices, settlement patterns, marriage, rituals, and so on.

Among other things, anthropologists interested in finding explanations for certain social or cultural beliefs and practices can use HRAF to test their hypotheses. For example, Peggy Reeves Sanday examined a sample of 156 societies drawn from HRAF in an attempt to answer such questions as: Why do women play a more dominant role in some societies than others? Why, and under what circumstances, do men dominate women? Her study, published in 1981 (*Female Power and Male Dominance*), disproves the common misperception that women are universally subordinate to men, sheds light on the way men and women relate to each other, and ranks as a major landmark in the study of gender.

Although HRAF is a valuable research tool, it should be used with caution. For instance, the files only allow us to establish correlations between cultural features; they do not permit conclusions about cause and effect. In other words, while HRAF makes it possible to develop functional explanations (how things work), it does not provide us with causal explanations. For that, anthropologists may have to engage in more in-depth historical analysis of particular cultural practices.

Cultural comparisons are not restricted to contemporary ethnographic data. Indeed, anthropologists frequently turn to archaeological or historical data to test

Human Relations Area Files (HRAF) A vast collection of cross-indexed ethnographic and archaeological data catalogued by cultural characteristics and geographic locations. Archived in about 300 libraries (on microfiche and/or online).

Anthropologist David Maybury-Lewis interviews Xavante Indians in the Brazilian savannah where he has made numerous fieldwork visits since the 1950s. Maybury-Lewis is founder of the indigenous advocacy organization Cultural Survival, based in Cambridge, Massachusetts. He, like other anthropologists around the world, reaches beyond the "do no harm" clause of the AAA ethics code to actually work on behalf of indigenous groups.

hypotheses about culture change. Cultural characteristics thought to be caused by certain specified conditions can be tested archaeologically by investigating similar situations where such conditions actually occurred. Also useful are data provided in ethnohistories.

Anthropology's Theoretical Perspectives: A Brief Overview

Entire books have been written about each of anthropology's numerous theoretical perspectives. Here we offer a general overview to convey the scope of anthropological theory and its role in explaining and interpreting cultures.

In the previous chapter, we presented the barrel model of culture as a dynamic system of adaptation in which infrastructure, social structure, and superstructure are intricately interactive. Helping us to imagine culture as an integrated whole, this model allows us to think about something very complex by reducing it to a simplified scheme or basic design. Anthropologists refer to such a perspective on culture as holistic and integrative.

Although most anthropologists generally agree with a perspective on culture as holistic and integrative, they may have very different takes on the relative significance of different elements comprising the whole and exactly how they relate to one another. When analyzing a culture, some anthropologists argue that humans act primarily on the basis of their ideas, concepts, or symbolic representations. In their research and analysis, these anthropologists usually emphasize that to understand or explain why humans behave as they do, one must first get into other people's heads and try to understand how they imagine, think, feel, and speak about the world in which they live. Because of the primacy of the superstructure (ideas, values), this is known as an **idealistic perspective** (not to be confused with idealism in the sense of fantasy or hopeful imagination).

Examples of idealist perspectives include psychological and cognitive anthropology (culture and personality), ethnoscience, structuralism, and postmodernism, as well as symbolic and interpretive anthropology. The latter approach is most famously associated with U.S. anthropologist Clifford Geertz, who viewed humans primarily as "symbolizing, conceptualizing, and meaning-seeking" creatures. Drawing on words from German historical sociologist Max Weber, he wrote: "Man is an animal suspended in webs of significance he himself has spun. I take culture to be those webs, and the analysis of it to be therefore not an experimental science in search of law but an interpretive one in search of meaning."[32] Geertz developed an artful ethnographic research strategy in which a culturally significant event or social drama (for instance, a Balinese cockfight) is chosen for observation and analysis as a form of "deep play" that may provide essential cultural insights. Peeling back layer upon layer of socially constructed meanings, the anthropologist offers what Geertz called a "thick description" of the event in a detailed ethnographic narrative.

Many other anthropologists hold a theoretical perspective in which they stress explaining culture by first analyzing the material conditions that they see as determining people's lives. They may begin their research with an inventory of available natural resources for food and shelter, the number of mouths to feed and bodies to keep warm, the tools used in making a living, and so on. Anthropologists who highlight such environmental or economic factors as primary in shaping cultures basically share a **materialist perspective.**

Examples of materialist theoretical approaches include Marxism, cultural ecology, neo-evolutionism, and cultural materialism. In cultural ecology, anthropologists focus primarily on the subsistence mechanisms in a culture that enable a group to successfully adapt to its natural environment. Building on cultural ecology, some anthropologists include considerations of political economy such as industrial production, capitalist markets, wage labor, and finance capital. A political economy perspective is closely associated with Marxist theory, which essentially explains major change in society as the result of growing conflicts between opposing social classes, namely those who possess property and those who do not.

One result of widening the scope—combining cultural ecology and political economy to take into account the emerging world systems of international production and trade relations—is known as political ecology. Closely related is cultural materialism, a theoretical research strategy identified with Marvin Harris.[33] Placing primary emphasis on the role of environment, demography, technology, and economy in determining a culture's mental and social conditions, he argued that anthropologists can best explain ideas, values, and beliefs as adaptations to economic and environmental conditions (see Biocultural Connection).

idealist perspective A theoretical approach stressing the primacy of superstructure in cultural research and analysis.
materialist perspective A theoretical approach stressing the primacy of infrastructure (material conditions) in cultural research and analysis.

[32]Geertz, C. (1973). *The interpretation of culture*. London: Hutchinson.

[33]Harris, M. (1979). *Cultural materialism: The struggle for a science of culture*. New York: Random House.

Biocultural Connection

Pig Lovers and Pig Haters ▪ By Marvin Harris

In the Old Testament of the Bible, the Israelite's God (Yahweh) denounced the pig as an unclean beast that pollutes if tasted or touched. Later, Allah conveyed the same basic message to his prophet Muhammad. Among millions of Jews and Muslims today, the pig remains an abomination, even though it can convert grains and tubers into high-grade fats and protein more efficiently than any other animal.

What prompted condemnation of an animal whose meat is relished by the greater part of humanity? For centuries, the most popular explanation was that the pig wallows in its own urine and eats excrement. But linking this to religious abhorrence leads to inconsistencies. Cows kept in a confined space also splash about in their own urine and feces.

These inconsistencies were recognized in the 12th century by Maimonides, a widely respected Jewish philosopher and physician in Egypt, who said God condemned swine as a public health measure because pork had "a bad and damaging effect upon the body." The mid-1800s discovery that eating undercooked pork caused trichinosis appeared to verify Maimonides's reasoning. Reform-minded Jews then renounced the taboo, convinced that if well-cooked pork did not endanger public health, eating it would not offend God.

Scholars have suggested this taboo stemmed from the idea that the animal was once considered divine—but this explanation falls short since sheep, goats, and cows were also once worshiped in the Middle East, and their meat is enjoyed by all religious groups in the region.

I think the real explanation for this religious condemnation lies in the fact that pig farming threatened the integrity of the basic cultural and natural ecosystems of the Middle East. Until their conquest of the Jordan Valley in Palestine over 3,000 years ago, the Israelites were nomadic herders, living almost entirely from sheep, goats, and cattle. Like all pastoralists, they maintained close relationships with sedentary farmers who held the oases and the great rivers. With this mixed farming and pastoral complex, the pork prohibition constituted a sound ecological strategy. The pastoralists could not raise pigs in their arid habitats, and among the semi-sedentary farming populations pigs were more of a threat than an asset.

The basic reason for this is that the world zones of pastoral nomadism correspond to unforested plains and hills that are too arid for rainfall agriculture and that cannot easily be irrigated. The domestic animals best adapted to these zones are ruminants (including cattle, sheep, and goats), which can digest grass, leaves, and other cellulose foods more effectively than other mammals.

The pig, however, is primarily a creature of forests and shaded riverbanks. Although it is omnivorous, its best weight gain is from foods low in cellulose (nuts, fruits, tubers, and especially grains), making it a direct competitor of man. It cannot subsist on grass alone and is ill-adapted to the hot, dry climate of the grasslands, mountains, and deserts in the Middle East. To compensate for its lack of protective hair and an inability to sweat, the pig must dampen its skin with external moisture. It prefers to do

this by wallowing in fresh clean mud, but will cover its skin with its own urine and feces if nothing else if available. So there is some truth to the theory that the religious uncleanliness of the pig rests upon actual physical dirtiness.

Among the ancient mixed farming and pastoralist communities of the Middle East, domestic animals were valued primarily as sources of milk, cheese, hides, dung, fiber, and traction for plowing. Goats, sheep, and cattle provided all of this, plus an occasional supplement of lean meat. From the beginning, therefore, pork must have been a luxury food, esteemed for its succulent, tender, and fatty qualities.

Between 4,000 and 9,000 years ago, the human population in the Middle East increased sixty-fold. Extensive deforestation accompanied this rise, largely due to damage caused by sheep and goat herds. Shade and water, the natural conditions appropriate for raising pigs, became ever more scarce, and pork became even more of a luxury.

The Middle East is the wrong place to raise pigs, but pork remains a luscious treat. People find it difficult to resist such temptations on their own. Hence Yahweh and Allah were heard to say that swine were unclean—unfit to eat or touch. In short, it was ecologically maladaptive to try to raise pigs in substantial numbers, and small-scale production would only increase the temptation. Better then, to prohibit the consumption of pork entirely.

(Excerpted from M. Harris (1989). Cows, pigs, wars, and witches: The riddles of culture *(pp. 35–60). New York: Vintage Books/Random House.)*

Not all anthropologists can be easily grouped in idealist or materialist camps. Giving primacy to social structure, many analyze a cultural group by first and foremost focusing on this middle layer in our barrel model. Although it is difficult to neatly pigeonhole various perspectives in this group, theoretical explanations worked out by pioneering French social thinkers like Émile Durkheim and his student Marcel Mauss influenced the development of structural-functionalism. Primarily associated with British anthropologists in the mid-1900s, this approach focuses on the underlying patterns or structures of social relationships, attributing functions to cultural institutions in terms of the contributions they make toward maintaining a group's social order.

Beyond these three general groups, there exist various other anthropological approaches. Some stress the importance of identifying general patterns or even discovering laws. Early anthropologists believed that they could discover such laws by means of the theory of *unilinear cultural evolution* of universal human progress, beginning with what was then called "savagery," followed by "barbarism," and gradually making progress toward a condition of human perfection known as "high civilization."[34]

Although anthropologists have long abandoned such sweeping generalizations as unscientific and ethnocentric, some continued to search for universal laws in the general development of human cultures by focusing on technological development as measured in the growing capacity for energy capture per capita of the population. This theoretical perspective is sometimes called *neo-evolutionism.* Others seek to explain recurring patterns in human social behavior in terms of laws of natural selection by focusing on possible relationships with human genetics, a theoretical perspective identified with sociobiology. Yet others stress that broad generalizations are impossible because each culture is distinct and can only be understood as resulting from unique historical processes and circumstances. Some even go a step further and focus on in-depth description and analysis of personal life histories of individual members in a group in order to reveal the work of a culture.

Beyond these cultural historical approaches, there are other theoretical perspectives that do not aim for laws or generalizations to explain culture. Theoretical perspectives that reject measuring and evaluating different cultures by means of some sort of universal standard, and stress that they can only be explained or interpreted in their own unique terms, are associated with the important anthropological principle known as *cultural relativism,* discussed in the previous chapter.

---

[34]Carneiro, R. L. (2003). *Evolutionism in cultural anthropology: A critical history.* Boulder, CO: Westview Press.

---

informed consent Formal, recorded agreement to participate in research.

MORAL DILEMMAS AND ETHICAL RESPONSIBILITIES IN ANTHROPOLOGICAL RESEARCH

Today, universities require that anthropologists, like other researchers, communicate in advance the nature, purpose, and potential impact of the planned study to individuals who provide information—and obtain their **informed consent** or formal recorded agreement to participate in the research. Of course, this requirement is easier to fulfill in some societies or cultures than in others, as most anthropologists recognize. When it is a challenge to obtain informed consent, or even impossible to precisely explain the meaning and purpose of this concept and its actual consequences, anthropologists may protect the identities of individuals, families, or even entire communities by altering their names and locations. For example, when anthropologists study violent secret groups such as the Sicilian mafia, they may find it difficult or even unwise to obtain informed consent and instead opt not to disclose their real identities.

The dilemma facing anthropologists is also recognized in the preamble of the American Anthropological Association's Code of Ethics (discussed in Chapter 1), first formalized in 1971 and modified in its current form in 1998. This document outlines the various ethical responsibilities and moral obligations of anthropologists, including this central maxim: "Anthropological researchers must do everything in their power to ensure that their research does not harm the safety, dignity, or privacy of the people with whom they work, conduct research, or perform other professional activities."

Questions for Reflection

1. In describing and interpreting human cultures, anthropologists have long relied on ethnographic fieldwork, including participant observation. What makes this research method uniquely challenging and effective—and of what use might the findings be for meeting the unique challenges of our globalizing world?

2. Early anthropologists engaged in salvage ethnography to create a reliable record of indigenous cultures once widely expected to vanish. Although many indigenous communities did lose customary practices due to acculturation, descendants of those cultures can now turn to anthropological records to re-vitalize their ancestral ways of life. Do you think this is a good thing or not?

3. In our globalizing world, a growing number of anthropologists carry out multi-sited ethnography rather than conduct research in a single community. If you would do such a multi-sited research project, what would you focus on, and where would you conduct your actual participant observations and interviews?

4. If you were invited to "study up," on which cultural group would you focus? How would you go about getting access to that group for participant observation, and what are some of the serious obstacles you might expect to run into?

5. Although many people talk about the importance of ethics in research, how can anthropologists get informed consent from nonliterate members of a closed traditional community?

Suggested Readings

Angrosino, M. V. (2004). *Projects in ethnographic research.* Long Grove, IL: Waveland Press.

Presenting a related set of three very doable research projects with clear instructions and guidelines, this compact volume is a useful introduction to some important field techniques. Rich with examples, it lays out relevant concepts and the how-to details of ethnographic research—from methods, principles, and site selection, to observation and interviewing, to analysis and presentation.

Bernard, H. R. (2002). *Research methods in anthropology: Qualitative and quantitative approaches* (3rd ed.). Walnut Creek, CA: Altamira Press.

Written in a conversational style and rich with examples, this extremely useful and accessible book has twenty chapters divided into three sections: preparing for fieldwork, data collection, and data analysis. It touches on all the basics, from literature search and research design to interviewing, field note management, multivariate analysis, ethics, and more.

Dicks, B., et al (2005). *Qualitative research and hypermedia: Ethnography for the digital age (New technologies for social research).* Thousand Oaks, CA: Sage Publications.

Introducing emerging ethnographic research methods that utilize new technologies, the authors explain how to conduct data collection, analysis, and representation using new technologies and hypermedia—and discuss how digital technologies may transform ethnographic research.

Erickson, P. A., & Murphy, L. D. (2003). *A history of anthropological theory.* (2nd ed.). Peterborough, Ontario: Broadview Press.

A clear and concise survey that spans from antiquity to the modern era, effectively drawing the lines between the old and new. This edition features several new and expanded sections on topics including feminist anthropology, globalization, and medical anthropology.

Pink, S. (2001). *Doing visual ethnography: Images, media and representation in research.* Thousand Oaks, CA: Sage Publications.

Exploring the use and potential of photography, video, and hypermedia in ethnographic and social research, this text offers a reflexive approach to the practical, theoretical, methodological, and ethical issues of using these media. Following each step of research, from planning to fieldwork to analysis and representation, the author suggests how visual images and technologies can be combined to form an integrated process from start to finish.

Robben, A. C. G. M., & Sluka, J. A. (Eds.). (2007). *Ethnographic fieldwork: An anthropology reader.* Malden, MA: Blackwell Publishers.

This up-to-date text provides a comprehensive selection of classic and contemporary reflections, examining the tensions between self and other, the relationships between anthropologists and key consultants, conflicts and ethical challenges, various types of ethnographic research (including multi-sited fieldwork), and different styles of writing about fieldwork.

Thomson Audio Study Products

 Enjoy the MP3-ready Audio Lecture Overviews for each chapter and a comprehensive audio glossary of key terms for quick study and review. Whether walking to class, doing laundry, or studying at your desk, you now have the freedom to choose when, where, and how you interact with your audio-based educational media. See the preface for information on how to access this on-the-go study and review tool.

The Anthropology Resource Center

www.thomsonedu.com/anthropology
The Anthropology Resource Center provides extended learning materials to reinforce your understanding of key concepts in the four fields of anthropology. For each of the four fields, the Resource Center includes dynamic exercises including video exercises, map exercises, simulations, and "Meet the Scientists" interviews, as well as critical thinking questions that can be assigned and e-mailed to instructors. The Resource Center also provides breaking news in anthropology and interesting material on applied anthropology to help you link what you are learning to the world around you.

4

Becoming Human: The Origin and Diversity of Our Species

CHALLENGE ISSUE

These 31,000-year-old images, painted on a wall in the multichambered Chauvet Cave in the Ardèche region of southern France, provide spectacular evidence of early artistic creativity among our ancestors. They suggest that humans, as a thoughtful and self-reflecting species, have always faced the challenge of understanding where and how we fit in the larger natural system of all life forms, past and present. In addition to the Ice Age animals depicted here—horses, wild ox, rhino, and bison—the chambers of Chauvet feature renderings of ten other species: bear, lion, mammoth, mountain goat, giant deer, owl, panther, red deer, and reindeer, as well as human hand prints. Why were they painted and what do they mean? Anthropologists play a key role in unlocking the answers to such fascinating questions.

To What Group of Animals Do Humans Belong?

Biologists classify humans as *Homo sapiens,* members of the primates—a subgroup of mammals. Biological species are defined by reproductive isolation and designated by a two-part name including genus (*Homo*) and species (*sapiens*). Other primates include lemurs, lorises, tarsiers, monkeys, and apes. Because human culture is rooted in our mammalian primate biology, studying the anatomy and behavior of other primates, particularly our closest living ape relatives, helps us understand how and why early humans developed as they did.

When and How Did Humans Evolve?

Present evidence suggests that humans evolved from small African apes between 5 and 8 million years ago. Bipedalism, or walking on two feet, was the first change to distinguish the human evolutionary line. The behavior of these early bipeds was comparable to that of modern-day chimpanzees. Several million years after the evolution of bipedalism, brain size began to expand, along with the development of cultural activities such as making stone tools. The earliest stone tools date to between 2.5 and 2.6 million years ago, coinciding with the appearance of the first members of the genus *Homo* in the fossil record. From then on, shared, learned behavior—culture—played an increasingly important role in human survival.

Is the Biological Concept of Race Useful for Studying Physical Variation in Humans?

No. Biologically defined, *race* refers to subspecies, and no subspecies exist within modern *Homo sapiens*. The vast majority of biological variation within our species occurs *within* populations rather than among them. Furthermore, the differences that do exist among populations occur in gradations from one neighboring population to another, without sharp breaks. For these and other reasons, anthropologists have actively worked to expose the fallacy of race as a biological concept while recognizing the significance of race as a social category.

Anthropologists gather information from a variety of sources to piece together an understanding of evolutionary history and humankind's place in the animal kingdom. Studies of living primates (our closest mammal relatives), ancient fossils, and even molecular biology contribute to the story of how humans evolved. On one level, human evolutionary studies are wholly scientific, formulating and testing hypotheses about biological and behavioral processes in the past. At the same time, like all scientists, anthropologists are influenced by changing cultural values. Thus, **paleoanthropologists,** who study human evolutionary history, and **primatologists,** who study living primates, as well as the physical or biological anthropologists who study contemporary biological diversity, must be critically aware of their personal beliefs and cultural assumptions as they construct their theories.

THOMSON AUDIO STUDY PRODUCTS Take advantage of the MP3-ready Audio Lecture Overviews and comprehensive audio glossary of key terms for each chapter. See the preface for information on how to access this on-the-go study and review tool.

EVOLUTION THROUGH ADAPTATION

In a general sense, **evolution** (from the Latin word *evolutio,* literally meaning "unrolling" or "rolling forth") refers to change through time. Biologically, it refers to changes in the genetic makeup of a population over generations. (Passed from parents to offspring, **genes** are basic physical units of heredity that specify the biological traits and characteristics of each organism.) While some evolution takes place through a process known as **adaptation**—a series of beneficial adjustments of organisms to their environment—random forces also contribute critically to evolutionary change.

Adaptation is the cornerstone of the theory of evolution by **natural selection,** originally formulated by English naturalist Charles Darwin in 1859. In this theory, individuals having biological characteristics best suited to a particular environment survive and reproduce with greater frequency than do individuals without those characteristics. Today, scientists understand that random genetic mutation is the source of variation that gives organisms this reproductive edge.

In this chapter, we will discuss the evolutionary history of our species. Looking at the biology and behavior of our closest living relatives, the other primates, will complement the examination of our past. We will also explore some aspects of human biological variation and the cultural meanings given to this variation.

Unique among humans is the biological capacity to produce a rich array of *cultural adaptations,* a complex of ideas, activities, and technologies that enable people to survive and even thrive in their environment. Early humans, like all other creatures, greatly depended on physical attributes for survival. But in the course of time, humans came to rely increasingly on culture as an effective way of adapting to the environment. They figured out how to manufacture and utilize tools; they organized into social units that made food-foraging more successful; and they learned to preserve and share their traditions and knowledge through the use of symbols that ultimately included spoken language.

The ability to solve a vast array of challenges through culture has made our species unusual among creatures on this planet. Humans do not merely adapt to the environment through biological change; we shape the environment to suit human needs and desires. Today, computer technology enables us to organize and manipulate an ever-increasing amount of information to keep pace with the environmental changes we have wrought. Space technology may enable us to propagate our species in extraterrestrial environments. If we manage to avoid self-destruction through misuse of our sophisticated tools, biomedical technology may eventually enable us to control genetic inheritance and thus the future course of our biological evolution.

The fundamental elements of human culture came into existence about 2.5 million years ago. Using scientific know-how to reach far back in time, we can trace the roots of our species and reconstruct the origins of human culture.

paleoanthropologist An anthropologist specializing in the study of human evolutionary history.
primatologist A specialist in the behavior and biology of living primates and their evolutionary history.
evolution Changes in the genetic makeup of a population over generations.
genes The basic physical units of heredity that specify the biological traits and characteristics of each organism.
adaptation A series of beneficial adjustments of organisms to their environment.
natural selection The principle or mechanism by which individuals having biological characteristics best suited to a particular environment survive and reproduce with greater frequency than individuals without those characteristics.

HUMANS AND OTHER PRIMATES

As noted in the beginning of this book, humans are one of 10 million species on earth, 4,000 of which are fellow mammals. **Species** are populations or groups of populations having common attributes and the ability to interbreed and produce live, fertile offspring. Different species are reproductively isolated from one another. Biologists organize or classify species into larger groups of biologically related organisms. The human species is one kind of **primate,** a subgroup of mammals that also includes lemurs, lorises, tarsiers, monkeys, and apes. Among fellow primates, humans are most closely related to apes—chimpanzees, bonobos, gorillas, orangutans, and gibbons—all of particular interest to primatologists.

European scientists have argued long and hard over issues of species classification, especially since the start of the Age of Exploration about 500 years ago that brought them to distant lands inhabited by life forms they had never before seen, including apes. Most vexing was the question concerning the difference between these apes and humans. In 1698, after dissecting a young male chimpanzee captured in West Africa and brought to Europe, an English physician concluded the creature was almost human and classified it as *Homo sylvestris* ("man of the forest").

A few decades later, Swedish naturalist Carolus Linnaeus (1707–1778) published the first edition of his famous *System of Nature* (1735). In it he classified humans with sloths and monkeys in the same order: Anthropomorpha ("human-shaped"). By the time Linnaeus published the tenth edition of his famous book in 1758, he had replaced the name "Anthropomorpha" with "Primate" and included bats, lemurs, monkeys, and humans in that category. Moreover, he now recognized not just one human species but two: *Homo sapiens* or *Homo diurnus* ("active during daylight") and an apelike human he called *Homo nocturnus* ("active during night"). He also referred to the latter as *Homo troglodytes* ("human cave-dweller"). Linnaeus' shifting categories typify the struggle of early scientists to classify humans within the natural system.

Perhaps the best illustration of the perplexity involved is a comment made by an 18th-century French bishop upon seeing an orangutan in a menagerie. Uncertain whether the creature before him was human or beast, he proclaimed: "Speak and I shall baptize thee!"[1]

In the course of the 18th century, European scientists continued to debate the proper classification of the

---

[1]Corbey, R. (1995). Introduction: Missing links, or the ape's place in nature (p. 1). In R. Corbey & B. Theunissen (Eds.), *Ape, man, apeman: Changing views since 1600.* Leiden: Department of Prehistory, Leiden University.

© Hulton-Deutsch Collection/Corbis

Early scientific struggles to classify great apes, and to identify and weigh the significance of the similarities and differences between them and humans, is reflected in early European renderings of apes, including this 18th-century image of a chimpanzee portrayed as a biped equipped with a walking stick.

great apes (as well as human "savages" encountered overseas) and placed chimpanzees and orangutans (gorillas were not recognized as a separate species until 1847) squarely between humans and the other animals. Perhaps going further than any other reputable scholar in Europe at the time, the famous Scottish judge Lord Monboddo argued in several widely read scholarly publications in the 1770s and 1780s that orangutans should

---

species A population or group of populations having common attributes and the ability to interbreed and produce live, fertile offspring. Different species are reproductively isolated from one another.
primate The subgroup of mammals that includes lemurs, lorises, tarsiers, monkeys, apes, and humans.

be considered part of the human species. He pointed out that they could walk erect and construct shelters and that they used sticks to defend themselves. He even suggested that at least in principle these "savages" were capable of speech.[2] Still, most Europeans clung to the notion of a marked divide between humans on the one hand and animals on the other. Debates about the exact relationship between humans and other animals continue to this day. These debates include biological data on ancient fossils and genetics, as well as philosophical stances on the "humane" treatment of our closest ape relatives.

One could question the value of including non-human primates in this textbook when the distinctive cultural capacities of humans are our major concern. However, humans have a long evolutionary history as mammals and primates that set the stage for the cultural beings we are today. By studying our evolutionary history as well as the biology and behavior of our closest living relatives, we gain a better understanding of how and why humans developed as they did.

Evidence from ancient skeletons indicates the first mammals appeared over 200 million years ago as small nocturnal (night-active) creatures. The earliest primate-like creatures came into being about 65 million years ago when a new, mild climate favored the spread of dense tropical and subtropical forests over much of the earth. The change in climate and habitat, combined with the sudden extinction of dinosaurs, favored mammal diversification, including the evolutionary development of arboreal (tree-living) mammals from which primates evolved.

The ancestral primates possessed biological characteristics that allowed them to adapt to life in the forests. Their relatively small size enabled them to use tree branches not accessible to larger competitors and predators. Arboreal life opened up an abundant new food supply. The primates were able to gather leaves, flowers, fruits, insects, bird eggs, and even nesting birds, rather than having to wait for them to fall to the ground. Natural selection favored those who judged depth correctly and gripped the branches tightly. Those individuals who survived life in the trees passed on their genes to the succeeding generations.

Although the earliest primates were nocturnal, today most primate species are diurnal (active in the day). The transition to diurnal life in the trees required important biological adjustments that helped shape the biology and behavior of humans today.

---

[2]Barnard, A. (1995). Monboddo's *Orang Outang* and the definition of man (pp. 71–85). In R. Corbey & B. Theunissen (Eds.), *Ape, man, apeman: Changing views since 1600.* Leiden: Department of Prehistory, Leiden University.

Anatomical Adaptation

Ancient and modern primate groups possess a number of anatomical characteristics described below. However, compared to other mammals, primates have only a few anatomical specializations while their behavior patterns are very diverse and flexible.

Primate Dentition

The varied diet available to arboreal primates—shoots, leaves, insects, and fruits—required relatively unspecialized teeth, compared to those found in other mammals. Comparative anatomy and the fossil record reveal that mammals ancestral to primates possessed three incisors, one canine, four premolars, and three molars on each side of the jaw, top and bottom, for a total of forty-four teeth. The incisors (in the front of the mouth) were used for gripping and cutting, canines (behind the incisors) for tearing and shredding, and molars and premolars (the "cheek teeth") for grinding and chewing food.

The evolutionary trend for primate dentition has been toward a reduction in the number and size of the teeth (Figure 4.1). Over the millennia, the first and second premolars became smaller and eventually disappeared altogether; the third and fourth premolars grew larger and gained a second pointed projection, or cusp, thus becoming "bicuspid." The molars also evolved from a three-cusp to a four- and even five-cusp pattern.

Figure 4.1

As seen in all reptiles, the crocodile jaw pictured above contains a series of identically shaped teeth. If a tooth breaks or falls out, a new tooth will emerge in its place. By contrast, primates, like all mammals, have only two sets of teeth; "baby" and adult teeth. Apes and humans possess precise numbers of specialized teeth, each with a particular shape, as indicated on this chimpanzee jaw: Incisors in front are shown in blue, canines behind in red, followed by two premolars and three molars in yellow (the last being the wisdom teeth in humans).

Sensory Organs

The primates' adaptation to arboreal life involved changes in the form and function of their sensory organs. The sense of smell was vital for the earliest ground-dwelling, night-active mammals. It enabled them to operate in the dark, to sniff out their food, and to detect hidden predators. However, for active tree life during daylight, good vision is a better guide than smell in judging the location of the next branch or tasty morsel. Accordingly, the sense of smell declined in primates, while vision became highly developed.

Traveling through trees demands judgments concerning depth, direction, distance, and the relationships of objects hanging in space, such as vines or branches. Monkeys and apes achieved this through binocular stereoscopic color vision (Figure 4.2), the ability to see the world in the three dimensions of height, width, and depth.

Tree-living primates also possess an acute sense of touch. An effective feeling and grasping mechanism helps keep them from falling and tumbling while speeding through the trees. The early mammals from which primates evolved possessed tiny touch-sensitive hairs at the tips of their hands and feet. In primates, sensitive pads backed up by nails on the tips of the animals'

Figure 4.2

Anthropoid primates possess binocular stereoscopic vision. Binocular vision refers to overlapping visual fields due to forward-facing eyes. Three-dimensional or stereoscopic vision comes from binocular vision and the transmission of information from each eye to both sides of the brain.

Primary receiving area
for visual information

fingers and toes replaced these hairs. In some monkeys from Central and South America, this feeling and grasping ability extends to the tail.

The Primate Brain

An increase in brain size, particularly in the cerebral hemispheres—the areas supporting conscious thought—occurred in the course of primate evolution. In monkeys, apes, and humans the cerebral hemispheres completely cover the cerebellum, the part of the brain that coordinates the muscles and maintains body balance. One of the most significant outcomes of this is the flexibility seen in primate behavior. Rather than relying on reflexes controlled by the cerebellum, primates constantly react to a variety of features in the environment.

The Primate Skeleton

The skeleton gives vertebrates—animals with internal backbones—their basic shape or silhouette, supports the soft tissues, and helps protect vital internal organs. Some evolutionary trends are evident in the primate skeleton. For example, as primates relied increasingly on vision rather than smell, the eyes rotated forward to become enclosed in a protective layer of bone. Simultaneously, the snout reduced in size. The opening at the base of the skull for the spinal cord to pass assumed a more forward position, reflecting some degree of upright posture rather than a constant four-footed stance.

The limbs of the primate skeleton follow the same basic ancestral plan seen in the earliest vertebrates. The upper portion of each arm or leg has a single long bone, the lower portion has two bones, and then hands or feet with five radiating digits. Other animals possess limbs specialized to optimize a particular behavior, such as speed. In nearly all of the primates, the big toe and thumb are *opposable*, making it possible to grasp and manipulate objects such as sticks and stones with their feet as well as their hands. Humans and their direct ancestors are the only exceptions, having lost the opposable big toe. The generalized limb pattern allows for flexible movements by primates.

In the apes, a sturdy collarbone (clavicle) orients the arms at the side rather than the front of the body, allowing for heightened flexibility. With their broad flexible shoulder joints, apes can hang suspended from tree branches and swing from tree to tree.

The retention of the flexible vertebrate limb pattern in primates was a valuable asset to evolving humans. It was, in part, having hands capable of grasping that enabled our own ancestors to manufacture and use tools and thus alter the course of their evolution.

Behavioral Adaptation

Primates adapt to their environments not only anatomically but also through a wide variety of behaviors. Young apes spend more time reaching adulthood than do most other mammals. During their lengthy growth and development, they learn the behaviors of their social group. While biological factors play a role in the duration of primate dependency, many of the specific behaviors learned during childhood derive solely from the traditions of the group. The behavior of primates, particularly apes, provides anthropologists with clues about the earliest development of human cultural behavior.

Many studies of the behavior of apes in their natural habitat have been undertaken to provide models to reconstruct the behavior of evolving humans. While no living primate lives exactly as our ancestors did, these studies have revealed remarkable variation and sophistication in ape behavior. Primatologists increasingly interpret these variations as cultural because they are learned rather than genetically programmed or instinctive. We shall look at the behavior of two closely related African species of chimpanzee: common chimpanzees and bonobos.

Chimpanzee and Bonobo Behavior

Like nearly all primates, chimpanzees and bonobos are highly social animals. Among chimps, the largest social organizational unit is the community, usually composed of fifty or more individuals who collectively inhabit a large geographic area. Rarely, however, are all of these animals together at one time. Instead, they are usually found ranging singly or in small subgroups consisting of adult males, or females with their young, or males and females together with young. In the course of their travels, subgroups may join forces and forage together, but sooner or later these will break up again into smaller units. Typically, when some individuals split off others join, so the composition of subunits shifts frequently.

Relationships among individuals within the ape communities are relatively harmonious. In the past, primatologists believed that male dominance hierarchies, in which some animals outrank and can dominate others,

formed the basis of primate social structures. They noted that physical strength and size play a role in determining an animal's rank. By this measure males generally outrank females. However, the male-biased cultures of many early primatologists may have contributed to this theoretical perspective with its emphasis on domination through superior size and strength. With the benefit of detailed field studies over the last forty years, including cutting-edge research by female primatologists such as Jane Goodall (see Anthropologists of Note), the nuances of primate social behavior and the importance of female primates has been documented.

High-ranking female chimpanzees may dominate low-ranking males. And among bonobos, female rank determines the social order of the group far more than male rank. While greater strength and size do contribute to an animal's higher rank, several other factors also come into play in determining its social position. These include the rank of its mother, which is largely determined through her cooperative social behavior and how effective each individual animal is at creating alliances with others.

On the whole, bonobo females form stronger bonds with one another than do chimpanzee females. Moreover, the strength of the bond between mother and son interferes with bonds among males. Not only do bonobo males defer to females in feeding, but *alpha* (high-ranking) females have been observed chasing alpha males; such males may even yield to low-ranking females, particularly when groups of females form alliances.[3]

Widening his gaze beyond social ranking and attack behavior among great apes, Japanese primatologist Kinji Imanishi (see Anthropologists of Note) initiated field studies of bonobos, investigating and demonstrating the importance of social cooperation rather than competition. Likewise, Dutch primatologist Frans de Waal's research, highlighted in the following Original Study, shows that reconciliation after an attack may be even more important from an evolutionary perspective than the actual attacks.

---

[3]de Waal, F., Kano, T., & Parish, A. R. (1998). Comments. *Current Anthropology 39*, 408, 410, 413.

Original Study ▪ By Frans B. M. de Waal

Reconciliation and Its Cultural Modification in Primates

Despite the continuing popularity of the struggle-for-life metaphor, it is increasingly recognized that there are drawbacks to open competition, hence that there are sound evolutionary reasons

for curbing it. The dependency of social animals on group life and cooperation makes aggression a socially costly strategy. The basic dilemma facing many animals, including humans, is that they

sometimes cannot win a fight without losing a friend.

This photo shows what may happen after a conflict—in this case between two female bonobos. About 10 minutes after

Two adult female bonobos engage in so-called GG-rubbing, a sexual form of reconciliation typical of this species.

their fight, the two females approach each other, with one clinging to the other and both rubbing their clitorises and genital swellings together in a pattern known as genito-genital rubbing, or GG-rubbing. This sexual contact, typical of bonobos, constitutes a so-called reconciliation. Chimpanzees, which are closely related to bonobos (and to us: bonobos and chimpanzees are our closest animal relatives), usually reconcile in a less sexual fashion, with an embrace and mouth-to-mouth kiss.

There is now evidence for reconciliation in more than twenty-five different primate species, not just in apes but also in many monkeys. The same sorts of studies have been conducted on human children in the schoolyard, and of course children show reconciliation as well. Researchers have even found reconciliation in dolphins, spotted hyenas, and some other nonprimates. Reconciliation seems widespread: a common mechanism found whenever relationships need to be maintained despite occasional conflict.[a,b]

The definition of reconciliation used in animal research is a friendly reunion between former opponents not long after a conflict. This is somewhat different from definitions in the dictionary, primarily because we look for an empirical definition that is useful in observational studies—in our case, the stipulation that the reunion happen not long after the conflict. There is no intrinsic reason that a reconciliation could not occur after hours or days, or, in the case of humans, generations.

Let me describe two interesting elaborations on the mechanism of reconciliation. One is *mediation*. Chimpanzees are the only animals to use mediators in conflict resolution. In order to be able to mediate conflict, one needs to understand relationships outside of oneself, which may be the reason why other animals fail to show this aspect of conflict resolution. For example, if two male chimpanzees have been involved in a fight, even on a very large island as where I did my studies, they can easily avoid each other, but instead they will sit opposite from each other, not too far apart, and avoid eye contact. They can sit like this for a long time. In this situation, a third party, such as an older female, may move in and try to solve the issue. The female will approach one of the males and groom him for a brief while. She then gets up and walks slowly to the other male, and the first male walks right behind her.

We have seen situations in which, if the first male failed to follow, the female turned around to grab his arm and make him follow. So the process of getting the two males in proximity seems intentional on the part of the female. She then begins grooming the other male, and the first male grooms her. Before long, the female disappears from the scene, and the males continue grooming: She has in effect brought the two parties together.

There exists a limited anthropological literature on the role of conflict resolution, a process absolutely crucial for the maintenance of the human social fabric in the same way that it is crucial for our primate relatives. In human society, mediation is often done by high-ranking or senior members of the community, sometimes culminating in feasts in which the restoration of harmony is celebrated.[c]

The second elaboration on the reconciliation concept is that it is not purely instinctive, not even in our animal relatives. It is a learned social skill subject to what primatologists now increasingly call "culture" (meaning that the behavior is subject to learning from others as opposed to genetic transmission).[d] To test the learnability of reconciliation, I conducted an experiment with young rhesus and stumptail monkeys. Not nearly as conciliatory as stumptail monkeys, rhesus monkeys have the reputation of being rather aggressive and despotic. Stumptails are considered more laid-back and tolerant. We housed members of the two species together for 5 months. By the end of this period, they were a fully integrated group: They slept, played and groomed together.

After 5 months, we separated them again, and measured the effect of their time together on conciliatory behavior.

The research controls—rhesus monkeys who had lived with one another, without any stumptails—showed absolutely no change in the tendency to reconcile. Stumptails showed a high rate of reconciliation, which was also expected, because they also do so if living together. The most interesting group was the experimental rhesus monkeys, those who had lived with stumptails. These monkeys started out at the same

[a]de Waal, F. B. M. (2000). Primates—A natural heritage of conflict resolution. *Science 28*, 586–590.
[b]Aureli, F., & de Waal, F. B. M. (2000). *Natural conflict resolution.* Berkeley: University of California Press.

[c]Reviewed by Frye, D. P. (2000). Conflict management in cross-cultural perspective. In F. Aureli & F. B. M. de Waal, *Natural conflict resolution* (pp. 334–351). Berkeley: University of California Press.
[d]See de Waal, F. B. M. (2001). *The ape and the sushi master.* New York: Basic Books, for a discussion of the animal culture concept.

CONTINUED

CONTINUED

low level of reconciliation as the rhesus controls, but after they had lived with the stumptails, and after we had segregated them again so that they were now housed only with other rhesus monkeys who had gone through the same experience, these rhesus monkeys reconciled as much as stumptails do. This means that we created a "new and improved" rhesus monkey, one that made up with its

opponents far more easily than a regular rhesus monkey.[c]

This was in effect an experiment on social culture: We changed the culture of

a group of rhesus monkeys and made it more similar to that of stumptail monkeys by exposing them to the practices of this other species. This experiment also shows that there exists a great deal of flexibility in primate behavior. We humans come from a long lineage of primates with great social sophistication and a well-developed potential for behavioral modification and learning from others. ■

[c]de Waal, F. B. M., & Johanowicz, D. L. (1993). Modification of reconciliation behavior through social experience: An experiment with two macaque species. *Child Development 64*, 897–908.

Prior to the 1980s primates other than humans were thought to be vegetarians. However, ground-breaking research by Jane Goodall, among others, showed otherwise. This British researcher's fieldwork among chimpanzees in their forest habitat at Gombe, a wildlife reserve on the eastern shores of Lake Tanganyika in Tanzania, revealed that these apes supplement their primary diet of fruits and other plant foods with insects and also meat. Even more surprising, she found that in addition to killing small invertebrate animals for food, they also hunted and ate monkeys, usually flailing them to death.

Chimpanzee females sometimes hunt, but males do so far more frequently and may spend up to 2 hours watching, following, and chasing intended prey. Moreover, in contrast to the usual primate practice of each animal finding its own food, hunting frequently involves teamwork, particularly when the prey is a baboon. Once a potential victim has been isolated from its troop, three or more adult chimps will carefully position themselves so as to block off escape routes while another pursues the prey. Following the kill, most who are present get a share of the meat, either by grabbing a piece as chance affords or by begging for it.

Whatever the nutritional value of meat, hunting is not done purely for dietary purposes, but for social and sexual reasons as well. U.S. anthropologist Craig Stanford, who has done fieldwork among the chimpanzees of Gombe since the early 1990s, found that these sizable apes (100-pound males are common) frequently kill animals weighing up to 25 pounds and eat much more meat than previously believed. Hunts usually take place during the dry season when plant foods are less readily available and female chimps display genital swelling, which signals that they are ready to mate. Moreover, fertile females are more successful than others at begging for meat, and males often share the meat after copulation.[4]

For female chimps ready for pregnancy, a supply of protein-rich food benefits her physical condition during

a period of increased nutritional requirements. Beyond sharing meat to attract sexual partners, males use their catch to reward friends and allies, gaining status in the process. In other words, although Stanford links male hunting and food-sharing behavior with female reproductive biology, these behaviors are part of a complex social system that may be rooted more in the cultural traditions and history of Gombe than in chimpanzee biology.

Somewhat different chimpanzee hunting practices have been observed in West Africa. At Tai National Park in the Ivory Coast, for instance, chimpanzees engage in highly coordinated team efforts to chase monkeys hiding in very tall trees in the dense tropical forest. Individuals who have especially distinguished themselves in a successful hunt see their contributions rewarded with more meat. Recent research shows that bonobos in Congo's rainforest also supplement their diet with meat obtained by means of hunting. Although their behavior resembles that of the chimpanzees, there are crucial differences. Among bonobos hunting is primarily a female activity. Also, female hunters regularly share carcasses with other females, but less often with males. Even when the most dominant male throws a tantrum nearby, he may still be denied a share of meat.[5] Such discriminatory sharing among female bonobos is also evident when it comes to other foods such as fruits.

Chimpanzees and bonobos have not only developed different hunting strategies, but also different sexual practices. For chimps, sexual activity—initiated by either the male or the female—occurs only during the periods when females signal their fertility through genital swelling. By most human standards, chimp sexual behavior is promiscuous. A dozen or so males have been observed to have as many as fifty copulations in one day with a single female. Dominant males try to monopolize females when the latter are most receptive sexually, although cooperation from the female is usually required for this to succeed. In addition, an individual female and a lower-

[4]Stanford, C. B. (2001). *Chimpanzee and red colobus: The ecology of predator and prey.* Cambridge, MA: Harvard University Press.

[5]Ingmanson, E. J. (1998). Comment. *Current Anthropology 39,* 409.

Female chimpanzees display their fertility through swelling of the genitalia at the time of ovulation. In contrast to humans and bonobos, animals with time limited displays are sexually receptive only during these times of fertility.

© Bromhall/Animals Animals

ranking male sometimes form a temporary bond, leaving the group together for a few private days during the female's fertile period. Thus, dominant males do not necessarily father all (or even most) of the offspring in a social group. Social success, achieving alpha male status, does not translate neatly into the evolutionary currency of reproductive success.

In contrast to chimpanzees, bonobos (like humans) do not limit their sexual behavior to times of female fertility. Whereas the genitals of chimpanzee females are swollen only at times of fertility, bonobo female genitals are perpetually swollen. The constant swelling, in effect, conceals the females' ovulation, or moment when an egg released into the womb is receptive for fertilization. As among humans, concealed ovulation in bonobos may play a role in the separation of sexual activity for social reasons and pleasure from the purely biological task of reproduction.

In fact, among bonobos (as among humans) sexuality goes far beyond male–female mating for purposes of biological reproduction. Primatologists have observed virtually every possible combination of ages and sexes engaging in a remarkable array of sexual activities, including oral sex, tongue-kissing, and massaging each other's genitals. Male bonobos may mount each other, or one may rub his scrotum against that of the other. They have also been observed "penis fencing"—hanging face to face from a branch and rubbing their erect penises together as if crossing swords. Among females, genital rubbing is particularly common. As described in this chapter's Original Study, the primary function of most of this sex, both hetero- and homosexual, is to reduce tensions and resolve social conflicts. Notably, although forced

copulation among chimpanzees is known to occur, such rape has never been observed among bonobos.[6]

Chimpanzee and Bonobo Childhood Development

Chimpanzee and bonobo dependence on learned social behavior is related to their extended period of childhood development. Born without built-in responses dictating specific behavior in complex situations, the young chimp or bonobo, like the young human, learns by observation, imitation, and practice how to strategically interact with others and even manipulate them for his or her own benefit. Making mistakes along the way, young primates modify their behavior based on the reactions of other members of the group. They learn to match their interactive behaviors according to each individual's social position and temperament. Anatomical features such as a free upper lip (unlike lemurs or cats, for example) allow monkeys and apes varied facial expression, contributing to greater communication among individuals.

Young chimpanzees also learn other functional behaviors from adults, such as how to make and use tools. Beyond deliberately modifying objects to make them suitable for particular purposes, chimps can to some extent modify them to regular patterns and may even prepare objects at one location in anticipation of future use at another place. For example, they commonly select a long, slender branch, strip off its leaves, and carry it on a "fishing" expedition to a termite nest. Reaching their destination, they insert the stick into the nest, wait a few minutes, and then pull it out to eat the insects clinging to it. Bonobos in the wild have not been observed mak-

---

[6]de Waal, F. (1998). Comment. *Current Anthropology 39*, 407.

Anthropologists of Note

Jane Goodall (b. 1934) ▪ Kinji Imanishi (1902–1992)

In July 1960, **Jane Goodall** arrived with her mother at the Gombe Chimpanzee Reserve on the shores of Lake Tanganyika in Tanzania. Goodall was the first of three women Kenyan anthropologist Louis Leakey sent out to study great apes in the wild (the others were Dian Fossey and Birute Galdikas, who were to study gorillas and orangutans, respectively); her task was to begin a long-term study of chimpanzees. Little did she realize that, more than forty years later, she would still be at it.

Born in London, Goodall grew up and was schooled in Bournemouth, England. As a child, she dreamed of going to live in Africa, so when an invitation arrived to visit a friend in Kenya, she jumped at the opportunity. While in Kenya, she met Leakey, who gave her a job as an assistant secretary. Before long, she was on her way to Gombe. Within a year, the outside world began to hear the most extraordinary things about this pioneering woman: tales of tool-making apes, cooperative hunts by chimpanzees, and what seemed like exotic chimpanzee rain dances. By the mid-1960s, her work had earned her a doctorate from Cambridge University, and Gombe was on its way to becoming one of the most dynamic field

stations for the study of animal behavior anywhere in the world.

Although Goodall is still very much involved with her chimpanzees, she spends a good deal of time these days lecturing, writing, and overseeing the work of others. She also is heavily committed to primate conservation, and no one is more dedicated to efforts to halt the illegal trafficking in chimps nor a more eloquent champion of humane treatment of captive chimpanzees.

Kinji Imanishi, a naturalist, explorer, and mountain climber, profoundly influenced primatology in Japan and throughout the world. Like all Japanese scholars, he was fully aware of Western methods and theories but developed a radically different approach to the scientific study of the natural world.

He dates his transformation to a youthful encounter with a grasshopper: "I was walking along a path in a valley, and there was a grasshopper on a leaf in a shrubbery. Until that moment I had happily caught insects, killed them with chloroform, impaled them on pins, and looked up their names, but I realized I knew nothing at all about how this grasshopper lived in the wild."[a] In his most important work, *The World of Living Things*, first published in 1941, Imanishi developed a comprehensive theory about the natural world rooted in Japanese cultural beliefs and practices.

Imanishi's work challenged Western evo-

© Bunataro Imanishi

lutionary theory in several ways. First, Imanishi's theory, like Japanese culture, does not emphasize differences between humans and other animals. Second, rather than focusing on the biology of individual organisms, Imanishi suggested that naturalists examine "specia" (a species society) to which individuals belong as the unit of analysis. Rather than focusing on time, Imanishi emphasized space in his approach to the natural world. He highlighted the harmony of all living things rather than conflict and competition among individual organisms.

Imanishi's research techniques, now standard worldwide, developed directly from his theories: long-term field study of primates in their natural societies using methods from ethnography.

Imanishi and his students conducted pioneering field studies of African apes, and Japanese and Tibetan macaques, long before Louis Leakey sent the first Western primatologists into the field. Japanese primatologists were the first to document the importance of kinship, the complexity of primate societies, patterns of social learning, and the unique character of each primate social group. Because of the work by Imanishi and his students, we now think about the distinct cultures of primate societies.

© Michael Nichols/National Geographic Image Collection

[a]Heita, K. (1999). Imanishi's world view. *Journal of Japanese Trade and Industry 18* (2), 15.

ing and using tools to the extent that chimpanzees do. But tool-making capabilities have been shown by a captive bonobo who independently made stone tools remarkably similar to the earliest tools made by our own ancestors.

Building on the research of leading primatologists like Imanishi and Goodall, researchers are uncovering increasing evidence of the remarkable behavioral sophistication and intelligence of chimpanzees and other apes—including a capacity for conceptual thought previously unsuspected by most scientists. The widespread practice of caging our primate "cousins" and exploiting them for entertainment or medical experimentation becomes increasingly controversial.

HUMAN ANCESTORS

Classifying humans within the animal kingdom is as controversial and challenging in the 21st century as it was in the 18th when Linnaeus was working on his *System of Nature*. Today, paleoanthropologists working out taxonomic or classification schemes for humans and their ancestors reach beyond Linnaeas' focus on shared morphology or physical characteristics to consider genetic makeup. Humans are classified as **hominoids,** the broad-shouldered tailless group of primates that includes all living and extinct apes and humans. Humans and their ancestors are distinct among the hominoids for **bipedalism**—a special form of locomotion in which an organism walks upright on two feet.

In the past thirty years, genetic and biochemical studies have confirmed that the African apes—chimpanzees, bonobos, and gorillas—are our closest living relatives (Figure 4.3). By comparing genes and proteins among all the apes, scientists have estimated that gibbons, followed by orangutans, were the first to diverge from a very ancient common ancestral line. At some time between 5 and 8 million years ago, humans, chimpanzees, and gorillas began to follow separate evolutionary courses. Chimpanzees later diverged into two separate species: the common chimpanzee and the bonobo. Early human evolutionary development followed a path that produced, eventually, only one surviving bipedal species: *Homo sapiens*.

Larger brains and bipedal locomotion constitute the most striking differences between humans and our closest primate relatives. Although we might like to think that it is our larger brains that make us special among fellow primates, it is now clear that bipedalism appeared at the beginning of the ancestral line leading to humans and played a pivotal role in setting us apart from the apes. Brain expansion came later.

The First Bipeds

Between 5 and 15 million years ago, various kinds of hominoids lived throughout Africa, Asia, and Europe. One of these apes living in Africa between 5 and 8 million years ago was a direct ancestor to the human line. Each new fossil from this critical time period (such as the 6 million-year-old *Orrorin* fossils discovered in Kenya in 2001[7] or the 6 to 7 million-year-old skull discovered in Chad, Central Africa[8]) is proposed as the latest missing link in the evolutionary chain leading to humans.

For a hominoid fossil to be definitively classified as part of the human evolutionary line, certain evidence of bipedalism is required. However, all early bipeds are not necessarily direct ancestors to the humans. Nevertheless, new discoveries of ancient humanlike fossils, especially in East Africa, repeatedly stir the scientific and popular imagination that a "missing link" has been identified in "the great chain" between the earliest bipeds and the human species today.

Between 4 and 5 million years ago, the environment of eastern and southern Africa was mostly a mosaic of open country with pockets of closed woodland. Some early bipeds seem to have lived in one of the woodland pockets. Later human ancestors inhabited more open country known as savannah—grasslands with scattered trees and groves—and are assigned to one or another species of the genus ***Australopithecus*** (from Latin *austra-*

---

[7]Senut, B., et al. (2001). First hominid from the Miocene (Lukeino formation, Kenya). *C. R. Academy of Science, Paris 332,*137–144.

[8]Brunet, M., et al. (2002). A new hominid from the Upper Miocene of Chad, Central Africa. *Nature 418,* 145–151.

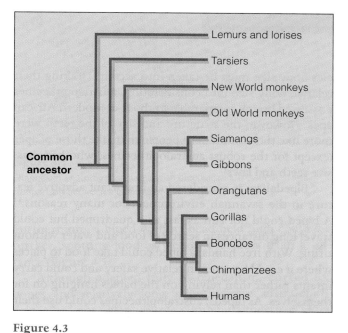

Figure 4.3
The relationship among monkeys, apes, and humans can be established by molecular similarities and differences. Molecular evidence indicates that the split between the human and African ape lines took place between 5 and 8 million years ago. Several important fossil finds dating from between 5 to 7 million years ago have been discovered over the last few years.

hominoid The broad-shouldered tailless group of primates that includes all living and extinct apes and humans.
bipedalism A special form of locomotion in which an organism walks upright on two feet—characteristic of humans and their ancestors.
Australopithecus The genus including several species of early bipeds from southern, eastern, and central Africa (Chad) living between about 1.1 and 4.3 million years ago, one of whom was directly ancestral to humans.

---

day, but rather the fatty marrow and whatever other edible leftover flesh remained in and on the bones of dead animals.

Early *Homo*

Increased meat consumption by our early ancestors was important for human evolution. On the savannah, it is hard for a primate with a humanlike digestive system

Paleolithic tools are part of the **Oldowan** tool tradition, a name first given to the tools found at Olduvai Gorge in the 1960s.

Lower Paleolithic The first part of the Old Stone Age spanning from about 200,000 or 250,000 to 2.6 million years ago.
Oldowan The first stone tool industry, beginning between 2.5 and 2.6 million years ago at the start of the Lower Paleolithic.

Figure 4.4
Australopithecine fossils have been found in South Africa, Malawi, Tanzania, Kenya, Ethiopia, and Chad. Among recent important finds is the 3.3 million-year-old skull and partial skeleton of a 3-year-old *Australopithecus afarensis* unearthed by Ethiopian paleoanthropologist Zeresenay Alemseged in his home country.

Biocultural Connection

Paleolithic Prescriptions for the Diseases of Civilization

Though increased life expectancy is often hailed as one of modern civilization's greatest accomplishments, in some ways we in the developed world lead far less healthy lifestyles than our ancestors. Throughout most of our evolutionary history, humans led more physically active lives and ate a more varied low-fat diet than we do now. They did not drink or smoke. They spent their days scavenging or hunting for animal protein while gathering vegetable foods with some insects thrown in for good measure. They stayed fit through traveling great distances each day over the savannah and beyond.

Today we may survive longer but in old age are beset by chronic disease. Heart disease, diabetes, high blood pressure, and cancer shape the experience of old age in wealthy industrialized nations. The prevalence of these "diseases of civilization" has increased rapidly over the past sixty years. Anthropologists Melvin Konner and Marjorie Shostak and physician Boyd Eaton have suggested that

our Paleolithic ancestors have provided a prescription for a cure. They propose that as "stone-agers in a fast lane," people's health will improve by returning to the lifestyle to which their bodies are adapted. Such Paleolithic prescriptions are an example of evolutionary medicine—a branch of medical anthropology that uses evolutionary principles to contribute to human health.

Evolutionary medicine bases its prescriptions on the idea that rates of cultural change exceed the rates of biological change. Our food-forager physiology was shaped over millions of years, while the cultural changes leading to contemporary lifestyles have occurred rapidly.

Anthropologist George Armelagos suggests that the downward trajectory for human health began with the earliest human village settlements some 10,000 years ago. When humans began farming rather than gathering, they often switched to single-crop diets. In addition, settlement into villages led directly to the

increase in infectious disease. While the cultural invention of antibiotics has cured many infectious diseases, it also led to the increase in chronic diseases.

In many cases, alternative treatments for these conditions stem from evolutionary medicine.

Prior to the Lower Paleolithic, australopithecines probably used tools such as heavy sticks to dig up roots or ward off animals, unmodified stones to hurl as weapons or to crack open nuts and bones, and simple carrying devices made of hollow gourds or knotted plant fibers. These tools, however, are not traceable in the long-term archaeological record.

Since the late 1960s, a number of sites in southern and eastern Africa have been discovered with fossil remains of a lightly built biped with a body all but indistinguishable from that of the earlier australopithecines, except that the teeth are smaller and the brain is significantly larger relative to body size.[12] Furthermore, the

inside of the skull shows a pattern in the left cerebral hemisphere that, in contemporary people, is associated with a language area. While this does not prove that these bipeds could speak, it suggests a marked advance in information-processing capacity over that of australopithecines. Since major brain-size increase and tooth-size reduction are important trends in the evolution of the genus *Homo*, paleoanthropologists designated these fossils as a new species: ***Homo habilis*** ("handy human").[13] Significantly, the earliest fossils to exhibit these trends appeared around 2.5 to 2.6 million years ago, about the same time as the earliest evidence of stone tool making.

Tools, Food, and Brain Expansion

Evolutionary transformations often occur suddenly as large random mutations produce novel organisms that, by chance, are well adapted to a particular environment.

---

[12]Conroy, G. C. (1997). *Reconstructing human origins: A modern synthesis* (pp. 264–265, 269–270). New York: Norton.

Homo habilis "Handy human." The first fossil members of the genus *Homo* appearing 2.5 to 2.6 million years ago, with larger brains and smaller faces than australopithecines.

[13]Some have argued that *H. habilis* was not the only species of early *Homo*.

Michael Rogers, Southern Connecticut State University

© Michael Rogers, Southern Connecticut State University

The earliest stone tools dated to the beginning of the Lower Paleolithic or Old Stone Age between 2.5 and 2.6 million years ago were discovered by Ethiopian paleoanthropologist Sileshi Semaw (pictured here) at Gona, located in the west-central Afar region of Ethiopia. The 2.6 million-year-old Gona flake on the right is a well-struck cutting tool with sharp edges.

Sometimes natural selection produces change more gradually. This appears to have taken place following the arrival of *Homo habilis,* the first species in the genus *Homo;* with the demonstrated use of tools, our human ancestors began a course of gradual brain expansion that continued until some 200,000 years ago. By then, brain size had approximately tripled and reached the levels of today's humans.

Many scenarios proposed for the adaptation of early *Homo,* such as the relationship among tools, food, and brain expansion, rely upon a feedback loop between brain size and behavior. The behaviors made possible by larger brains confer advantages to large-brained individuals, contributing to their increased reproductive success. Over time, their genetic variance becomes more common in successive generations, and the population gradually evolves to acquiring a larger-brained form. In the case of tool making, the archaeological record provides us with tangible data concerning our ancestors' cultural abilities fitting with the simultaneous biological expansion of the brain. Tool making itself puts a premium on manual dexterity as opposed to hand use emphasizing power. In addition, the patterns of stone tools and fossilized animal bones at Oldowan sites in Africa suggest improved organization of the nervous system.

The sources for stone used to make cutting and chopping tools were often far from the sites where tools were used to process parts of animal carcasses. Also, the high density of fossil bones at some Oldowan sites and patterns of seasonal weathering indicate such sites were used repeatedly over a period of years. It appears that the Oldowan sites were places where tools and the raw materials for making them were stockpiled for later use in butchering. This implies advanced preparation for meat processing and thereby attests to the growing importance of foresight and the ability to plan ahead. Beginning with *Homo habilis* in Africa about 2.5 to 2.6 million years ago, human evolution began a sure course of increasing brain size relative to body size and increasing cultural development, each acting upon and thereby promoting the other.

Homo erectus and the Spread of the Genus *Homo*

Shortly after 2 million years ago, at a time that *Homo habilis* and Oldowan tools had become widespread in Africa, a new species, **Homo erectus** ("upright human"), appeared on that continent. Unlike *H. habilis,* however, *H. erectus* did not remain confined to Africa. In fact, evidence of *H. erectus* fossils almost as old as those discovered in Africa have been found in the Caucasus Mountains of Georgia (between Turkey and Russia), South Asia, China, the island of Java (Indonesia), and western Europe.

Because the fossil evidence also suggests some differences within and among populations of *H. erectus* inhabiting discrete regions of Africa, Asia, and Europe, some paleoanthropologists prefer to split *H. erectus* into several distinct groups. Nonetheless, regardless of species designation, it is clear that beginning 1.8 million

Homo erectus "Upright human." A species within the genus *Homo* first appearing just after 2 million years ago in Africa and ultimately spreading throughout the Old World.

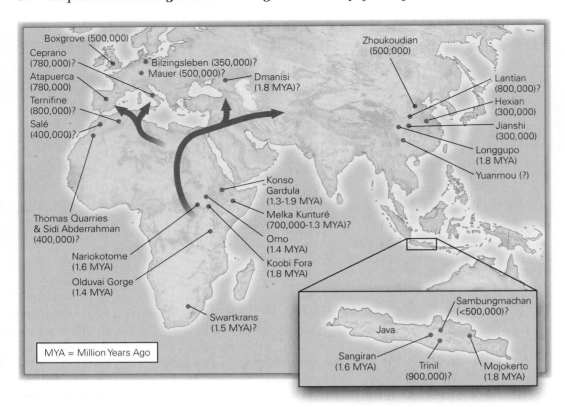

Figure 4.6

Paleoanthropological sites, with dates, at which *Homo erectus* remains have been found. The arrows indicate the proposed routes by which *Homo* spread from Africa to Eurasia.

years ago, these larger-brained members of the genus *Homo* lived not only in Africa but also had spread to Eurasia (Figure 4.6).

The emergence of *H. erectus* as a new species in the long course of human evolution coincided with the beginning of the Pleistocene epoch or Ice Age, which spanned from 10,000 to almost 2 million years ago. During this period of global cooling, Arctic cold conditions and abundant snowfall in the earth's northern hemisphere created vast ice sheets that temporarily covered much of Eurasia and North America. These fluctuating but major glacial periods often lasted tens of thousands of years, separated by intervening warm periods. During interglacial periods the world warmed up to the point that the ice sheets melted and sea levels rose, but during much of this time sea levels were much lower than today, exposing large surfaces of low-lying lands now under water.[14]

Of all the epochs in the earth's 4.6 *billion*-year history, the Pleistocene is particularly significant for our species, for this era of dramatic climatic shifts is the period in which humans—from *H. erectus* to *H. sapiens*—evolved and spread all across the globe. Confronted by environmental changes due to climatic fluctuations or movements into different geographic areas, our early human ancestors were constantly challenged to make bio-

logical and, especially, cultural adaptations in order to survive and successfully reproduce.

In the course of this long evolutionary process, random mutations introduced new characteristics into evolving populations in different regions of the world. The principle of natural selection was at work on humans as it was on all forms of life, favoring the perpetuation of certain characteristics within particular environmental conditions. At the same time, other characteristics that conferred no particular advantage or disadvantage also appeared by random mutation in geographically removed populations. The end result was a gradually growing physical variation in the human species. In this context, it is not surprising that *H. erectus* fossils found in Africa, Asia, and Europe reveal levels of physical variation not unlike those seen in modern human populations living across the globe today.

Available fossil evidence indicates that *H. erectus* had a body size and proportions similar to modern humans, though with heavier musculature. Differences in body size between the sexes diminished considerably compared to earlier bipeds, perhaps to facilitate successful childbirth. Based on fossil skull evidence, *H. erectus'* average brain size fell within the higher range of *H. habilis* and within the lower range of modern human brain size. The dentition was fully human, though relatively large by modern standards.

As one might expect, given its larger brain, *H. erectus* outstripped its predecessors in cultural development. In

[14]Fagan, B. M. (2000). *Ancient lives: An introduction to archaeology.* (pp. 125–133). Englewood Cliffs, NJ: Prentice-Hall.

One of the oldest—at 1.6 million years—and most complete fossils of *Homo erectus* is the "strapping youth" from Lake Turkana, Kenya: a tall and muscular boy who was already 5 feet 3 inches tall when he died at about the age of 13.

can remain reasonably comfortable down to 50 degrees Fahrenheit (10 degrees Celsius) with minimal clothing as long as they keep active. Below that temperature, hands and feet cool to the point of pain. Without controlled use of fire, it is unlikely that early humans could have moved successfully into regions where winter temperatures regularly dropped below that point—as they must have in northern China and most of Europe, where *H. erectus* spread some 780,000 years ago.

Fire gave our human ancestors more control over their environment. It permitted them to continue activities after dark and provided a means to frighten away predators. It supplied them with the warmth and light needed for cave dwelling, and it enabled them to cook food.

The ability to modify food culturally through cooking may have contributed to the eventual reduction in the tooth size and jaws of later fossil groups since cooked food requires less chewing. However, cooking does more than tenderize food. It detoxifies a number of otherwise poisonous plants. In addition, it alters substances in plants, allowing important vitamins, minerals, and proteins to be absorbed from the gut rather than passing unused through the intestines. And, finally, it makes high-energy complex carbohydrates, such as starch, digestible. In short, when our human ancestors learned to employ fire to warm and protect themselves and to cook their food, they dramatically increased their geographic range and nutritional options.

With *H. erectus* we also have evidence of organized hunting as the means for procuring meat, animal hides, horn, bone, and sinew. Early evidence demonstrating the hunting technology of these ancestors includes 400,000-year-old wooden spears discovered in a peat bog (what was originally marsh or swamp land) in northern Germany, although it is likely that evolving humans had begun to hunt before then. Increased organizational ability is also indicated in prehistoric sites such as Ambrona and Torralba in Spain where group hunting techniques were used to drive a variety of large animals (including elephants) into a swamp for killing.[15]

With *H. erectus,* then, we find a clearer manifestation than ever before of the complex interplay among biological, cultural, and ecological factors. Social organization and technology developed along with an increase in brain size and complexity and a reduction in tooth and jaw size. The appearance of cultural adaptations such as controlled use of fire, cooking, and more complex tool kits may have facilitated language development. (See Chapter 5 for more on language origins.) Improvements in communication and social organization brought about

Africa and Eurasia, the Oldowan chopper was replaced by the more sophisticated hand axe. At first, the hand axes—shaped by regular blows giving them a larger and finer cutting edge than chopper tools—were probably all-purpose implements for food procurement and processing, and defense. But *H. erectus* also developed cleavers (like hand axes but without points) and various scrapers to process animal hides for bedding and clothing. In addition, this human ancestor relied on flake tools used "as is" to cut meat and process vegetables, or refined by "retouching" into points and borers for drilling or punching holes in materials. Improved technological efficiency is also evident in *H. erectus'* use of raw materials. Instead of making a few large tools out of big pieces of stone, these ancestors placed a new emphasis on smaller tools, thus economizing their raw materials.

Remains found in southern Africa suggest that *H. erectus* may have learned to use fire by 1 million years ago. Although there exists considerable variation in physiological conditioning among different human groups and even among individuals within each group, studies of modern humans indicate that most people

[15]Freeman, L. G. (1992). *Ambrona and Torralba: New evidence and interpretation.* Paper presented at the 91st Annual Meeting, American Anthropological Association.

by language undoubtedly contributed to better methods for food gathering and hunting, to a population increase, and to territorial expansion. Continuous biological and cultural change through natural selection in the course of hundreds of thousands of years gradually transformed *H. erectus* into the next emerging species: *Homo sapiens*.

The Beginnings of *Homo sapiens*

At various sites in Africa, Asia, and Europe, a number of fossils have been found that date between roughly 200,000 and 400,000 years ago. The best population sample, bones of about thirty individuals of both sexes and all ages (but none older than about 40) comes from Atapuerca, a 400,000-year-old site in Spain. Overall, these bones show a mixture of characteristics of *Homo erectus* with those of early *Homo sapiens*, exactly what one would expect of fossil remains transitional between the two. For example, brain size overlaps the upper end of the *H. erectus* range and the lower end of the range for *H. sapiens*.

Whether one chooses to call these or any other contemporary fossils early *H. sapiens*, late *H. erectus*, or *Homo antecessor*, as did the Spanish anthropologists who discovered them, is more than a name game. Fossil names indicate researchers' perspectives about evolutionary relationships among groups. When specimens are given separate species names, it signifies that they form part of a reproductively isolated group.

Some paleoanthropologists approach the fossil record with the perspective that making such detailed biological determinations is arbitrary and that variability exists in any group. Arguing that it is impossible to prove whether or not a collection of ancient bones and teeth represents a distinctive species, they tend to be "lumpers," placing more or less similar-looking fossil specimens together in more inclusive groups. "Splitters," by contrast, focus on the variation in the fossil record and may interpret even minor differences in the shape of skeletons or skulls as evidence of distinctive biological species with corresponding cultural capacities. Referring to the variable shape of the boney ridge above ancient

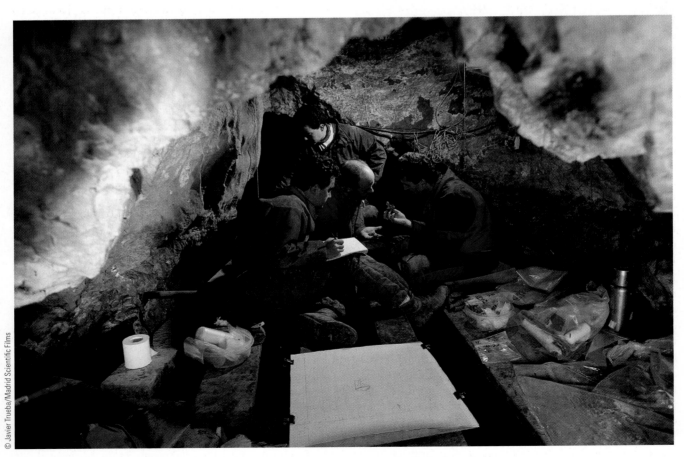

© Javier Trueba/Madrid Scientific Films

In a cave beneath a hillside in Atapuerca, Spain, lies one of the most remarkable sites in all of paleoanthropology: the Sima de los Huesos ("Pit of the Bones"). The bottom of the pit is crammed with animal bones, including cave bears, lions, foxes, and wolves. Even more remarkable, thousands of early human fossils dating back 400,000 years have been found here. The well-preserved remains come from at least twenty-eight individuals and comprise the greatest single cache of ancient *Homo erectus* fossils in the world.

eyebrows, South African paleoanthropologist Philip Tobias has quipped, "Splitters will create a new species at the drop of a brow ridge."[16]

The Neandertal Debate

As we proceed along the human evolutionary trajectory, the fossil record provides us with many more human specimens compared to earlier periods. The record is particularly rich when it comes to the Neandertals, a distinct and certainly controversial ancient member of the genus *Homo*. Typically, they are represented as the classic "cave men," stereotyped in Western popular media and even in natural history museum displays as wild and hairy club-wielding brutes.

Based on abundant fossil evidence, we know that **Neandertals** were a distinct and extremely muscular group within the genus *Homo* inhabiting Europe and Southwest Asia from about 30,000 to 125,000 years ago. While having brains on average somewhat larger than modern humans, they often possessed faces and skulls quite different from those of later fossilized remains referred to as anatomically modern humans. Their large noses and teeth projected forward more than is the case with modern people. They generally had a sloping forehead and prominent boney brow ridges over their eyes, and on the back of the skull, a bony mass provided for attachment of powerful neck muscles. These features, while not exactly in line with modern ideals of European beauty, are common in Norwegian and Danish skulls dating to about 1,000 years ago—the time of the Vikings.[17] Nevertheless, these characteristics do little to negate the popular image of Neandertals as cave-dwelling brutes.

The rude reputation of Neandertals may also derive from the time of their discovery, as the first widely publicized Neandertal skull was found in 1856, well before scientific theories to account for human origins had gained acceptance. This odd-looking old skull, happened upon near Düsseldorf in Germany's Neander "Valley" (*Tal* in German), took German scientists by surprise. Initially, they explained its extraordinary features as evidence of some disfiguring disease in an invading "barbarian" from the east who had crawled into a deep cave to die. Although it became evident that the skull belonged to an ancient human fossil, Neandertals are still a perplexing group surrounded by controversy.

All of this said, we now understand that many aspects of the Neandertal's unique skull shape and body form represent its biological adaptation to an extremely cold climate. We also know that its intellectual capacity for cultural adaptation was noticeably superior to that of earlier members of the genus *Homo*.

One of the most hotly debated arguments in paleoanthropology has been the genetic relationship of Neandertals to anatomically modern humans. Were they a separate species that became extinct less than 30,000 years ago? Or were they a subspecies of *Homo sapiens*? And if they were not a dead-end and inferior side branch in human evolution, did they actually contribute to our modern human gene pool? In that case, so the argument goes, their direct descendants walk the earth today.[18]

Meanwhile, other parts of the world were inhabited by variants of archaic *H. sapiens,* lacking the mid-facial projection and massive muscle attachments on the back of the skull common among the Neandertals. Human fossil skulls found near the Solo River in Java are a prime example. Dates for these specimens range anywhere between about 27,000 and 200,000 years ago. The fossils, with their modern-sized brains, display certain features of *H. erectus* combined with those of archaic as well as more modern *H. sapiens*. Human fossils from various parts of Africa, the most famous being a skull from Kabwe in Zambia, also show a combination of ancient and modern traits. Finally, similar remains have been found at several places in China.

Adaptations to a wide range of different natural environments by archaic *Homo sapiens* were, of course, both biological and cultural, but their capacity for cultural adaptation was predictably superior to what it had been in earlier members of the genus *Homo*. Neandertals' extensive use of fire, for example, was essential to survival in a cold climate like that of Europe during the various glacial periods. They lived in small bands or single-family units, both in the open and in caves, probably communicating through language (see Chapter 5). Evidence of deliberate burials of the deceased among Neandertals reflects a measure of ritual behavior in their communities. Moreover, the fossil remains of an amputee discovered in Iraq and an arthritic man excavated in France imply that Neandertals took care of the disabled, something not seen previously in the human fossil record.

The tool-making tradition of all but the latest Neandertals is called the **Mousterian** tradition after a site (Le

---

[16]Personal communication.

[17]Ferrie, H. (1997). An interview with C. Loring Brace. *Current Anthropology* 38, 861.

---

[18]See Orlando, L.., et al. (6 June 2006). Correspondence: Revisiting Neandertal diversity with a 100,000 year old mtDNA sequence. *Current Biology* 16, 400–402; and Hawks, J. (21 July 2006). Neandertal Genome Project. http://johnhawks.net/weblog.

Neandertals A distinct group within the genus *Homo* inhabiting Europe and Southwest Asia from approximately 30,000 to 125,000 years ago.

Mousterian The tool industry found among Neandertals in Europe and Southwest Asia, and their human contemporaries in northern Africa, during the Middle Paleolithic, generally dating from about 40,000 to 125,000 years ago.

Paul Jaronski, UM Photo Services

As this face-off between U.S. paleoanthropologist Milford Wolpoff and his reconstruction of a Neandertal shows, the latter did not differ all that much from modern humans of European descent.

Moustier) in the Dordogne region of southern France. We see this tradition among Neandertals in Europe and Southwest Asia and among their human contemporaries in northern Africa during the Middle Paleolithic, generally dating from about 40,000 to 125,000 years ago. Although considerable variability exists, Mousterian tools are generally lighter and smaller than those of earlier traditions. Whereas previously only two or three flakes could be obtained from the entire stone core, Mousterian toolmakers obtained many smaller flakes, which they skillfully retouched and sharpened. Their tool kits also contained a greater variety of types than the earlier ones: hand axes, flakes, scrapers, borers, notched flakes for shaving wood, and many types of points that could be attached to wooden shafts to make spears. This variety of tools facilitated more effective use of food resources and enhanced the quality of clothing and shelter. These types of stone tools were used by *all* people, Neandertals and their contemporaries elsewhere, including North Africa and Southwest Asia during this time period.

For archaic *H. sapiens,* improved cultural adaptive abilities relate to the fact that the brain had achieved

modern size. Such a brain made possible not only sophisticated technology but also conceptual thought of considerable intellectual complexity. Decorative pendants and objects with carved and engraved markings also appear in the archaeological record from this period. Objects were also commonly colored with pigments such as manganese dioxide and red or yellow ocher. The ceremonial burial of the dead and nonutilitarian, decorative objects provide additional evidence supporting theoretical arguments in favor of symbolic thinking and language use in these ancient populations.

In the course of the Middle Paleolithic, individuals with a somewhat more anatomically modern human appearance began to appear in Africa and Southwest Asia. Like the genetically closely related Neandertals, these early *Homo sapiens* used Mousterian tools. In Europe, the transition to the tools of the Upper Paleolithic occurred between 35,000 and 40,000 years ago. By this time, Neandertal technology was also comparable to the industries used by these anatomically modern *H. sapiens.*[19]

---

[19]Mellars, P. (1989). Major issues in the emergence of modern humans. *Current Anthropology 30,* 356–357.

Anatomically Modern Peoples and the Upper Paleolithic

A veritable explosion of tool types and other forms of cultural expression beginning about 40,000 years ago constitutes what is known as the **Upper Paleolithic** transition. Upper Paleolithic tool kits include increased prominence of "blade" tools: long, thin, precisely shaped pieces of stone demonstrating the considerable skill of their creators. The Upper Paleolithic, lasting until about 10,000 years ago, is best known from archaeological evidence found in Europe where numerous distinctive tool industries from successive time periods have been documented. In addition, the European archaeological record is rich with cave wall paintings, engravings, and bas-relief sculptures as well as many portable nonutilitarian artifacts from this period.

In Upper Paleolithic times, humans began to manufacture tools for more effective hunting and fishing, as well as gathering. Cultural adaptation also became more highly specific and regional, thus enhancing human chances for survival under a wide variety of environmental conditions. Instead of manufacturing all-purpose tools, Upper Paleolithic populations inhabiting a wide range of environments—mountains, marshlands, tundra, forests, lake regions, river valleys, and seashores—all developed specialized devices suited to the resources of their particular habitat and to the different seasons. This versatility also permitted humans to spread out by crossing open water and Arctic regions to places never previously inhabited by humans, most notably Australia (between 40,000 and 60,000 years ago) and the Americas (about 15,000 to 30,000 years ago).

This degree of specialization required improved manufacturing techniques. The blade method of manufacture (Figure 4.7), invented by archaic *H. sapiens* and later used widely in Europe and western Asia, required less raw material than before and resulted in smaller and lighter tools with a better ratio between weight of flint and length of cutting edge (Figure 4.8).

Invented by Mousterian toolmakers, the *burin* (a stone tool with chisel-like edges) came into common use in the Upper Paleolithic. The burin provided an excellent means of working bone and antler used for tools such as fishhooks and harpoons. The spear-thrower, or *atlatl* (a Nahuatl word used by Aztec Indians in Mexico, referring to a wooden device, 1 to 2 feet long, with a hook on the end for throwing a spear), also appeared at this time. By effectively elongating the arm, the atlatl gave hunters increased force behind the spear throw (Figure 4.9).

Art was an important aspect of Upper Paleolithic culture. As far as we know, humans had not produced representational artwork before. In some regions, tools and weapons were engraved with beautiful animal figures; pendants were made of bone and ivory, as were fe-

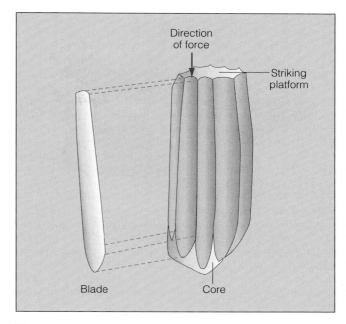

Figure 4.7
During the Upper Paleolithic, this new, more refined technique of manufacturing stone tools became common. The stone was broken to create a striking platform. Then, with another hard object, long, almost parallel-sided flakes were struck from the sides, resulting in sharp-edged blades to be used for a variety of cutting purposes.

male figurines; and small sculptures were carved out of stone or modeled out of clay. Spectacular paintings and engravings depicting humans and animals of this period have been found on the walls of caves and rock shelters in Spain, France, Australia, and Africa. Because the southern African rock art tradition spanned 27,000 years and lasted into historic times, documented accounts tell us that much of it depicts visions artists have when in altered states of consciousness related to spiritual practices. Along with the animals, the art also includes a variety of geometric motifs based on mental images spontaneously generated by the human nervous system when in trance.

Australian cave art, some of it older than European cave art and also associated with trancing, includes similar motifs. The occurrence of the same geometric designs in the cave art of Europe suggests trancing was a part of these prehistoric foraging cultures as well. The geometric motifs in Paleolithic art have also been interpreted as stylized human figures and patterns of descent. Given the great importance of kinship in all historically

Upper Paleolithic The last part (10,000–40,000 years ago) of the Old Stone Age, featuring tool industries characterized by long slim blades and an explosion of creative symbolic forms.

Figure 4.8
Pressure flaking—in which a bone, antler, or wooden tool is used to press rather than strike off small flakes—is another technique of tool manufacture that became widespread during the Upper Paleolithic. Here we see two pressure flaking methods.

© Reunion des Musees Nationaux/Art Resource, NY

The techniques of the Upper Paleolithic allowed for the manufacture of a variety of tool types. The finely wrought Solutrean bifaces of Europe, made using a pressure flaking method as illustrated in Figure 4.8, are shaped like plant leaves.

known communities of hunters, fishers, and gatherers, this should not be surprising.

Whether or not a new kind of human, anatomically modern with correspondingly superior intellectual abilities, is responsible for this cultural explosion is hotly debated within paleoanthropology.

Hypotheses on the Origins of Modern Humans

On a biological level the great debate can be distilled to a question of whether one, some, or all populations of the archaic groups played a role in the evolution of modern *H. sapiens*. Those supporting the **multiregional hypothesis** argue that the fossil evidence suggests a simultaneous local transition from *H. erectus* to modern *H. sapiens* throughout the parts of the world inhabited by early members of the genus *Homo*. By contrast, those supporting the **recent African origins hypothesis** (also known as the *Eve* or *Out of Africa* hypothesis) use genetic and other evidence to argue that all anatomically modern humans living today descend directly from one single population of archaic *H. sapiens* in Africa. Improved cultural capabilities then allowed members of this group to replace other archaic human forms as they began to

multiregional hypothesis The hypothesis that modern humans originated through a process of simultaneous local transition from *Homo erectus* to *Homo sapiens* throughout the inhabited world.
recent African origins hypothesis The hypothesis that all modern people are derived from one single population of archaic *H. sapiens* from Africa who migrated out of Africa after 100,000 years ago, replacing all other archaic forms due to their superior cultural capabilities. Also called the "Eve" or "Out of Africa" hypothesis.

spread out of Africa some time after 100,000 years ago. So while both models place human origins firmly in Africa, the first argues that our human ancestors began moving into Asia and Europe as early as 1.8 million years ago, whereas the second maintains that anatomically modern *H. sapiens* evolved only in Africa, completely replacing other members of the genus *Homo* as they spread throughout the world.

Though the recent African origins hypothesis is accepted by many paleoanthropologists, not every scholar supports it. Among those with opposing views, Chinese paleoanthropologists generally favor the multiregional hypothesis in part because it fits better with the fossil discoveries from Australia and Asia. The claim of ancient human roots in eastern Asia also resonates well with the region's traditional ethnocentric ideas about China as the place of human origins and the world's most ancient civilization—the center of humanity on earth, China is traditionally imagined as "the Middle Kingdom."

By contrast, the recent African origins hypothesis depends more upon the interpretation of genetic evidence, fossils, and cultural remains from Europe, Africa, and Southwest Asia. However, this model can be critiqued on several grounds. For example, the molecular evidence upon which it is based has been strongly criticized as more recent genetic studies indicate that Africa

Figure 4.9

Invented by early humans in the late Ice Age about 15,000 years ago, the atlatl or spear-thrower continued to be used by hunting peoples in many parts of the world until quite recently. Devised many thousands of years before the bow and arrow, this remarkable tool enhanced a hunter's success, making it possible to throw light spears much further and with great force and accuracy. The entire atlatl would have been a foot or two long, with a handle on one end and a hook on the other that fitted into the blunt end of the spear. The hook was sometimes made of beautifully carved antler, bone or stone.

was not the sole source of DNA in modern humans.[20] Recent African origins proponents argue that anatomically modern people co-existed for a time with other archaic populations until the superior cultural capacities of the moderns resulted in extinction of the archaic peoples.

That said, by 30,000 years ago, many of the distinctive anatomical features seen in archaic groups like Neandertals seem to disappear from the fossil record in Europe. Instead, individuals with generally higher foreheads, smoother brow ridges, and more distinct chins seemed to have Europe to themselves. However, a comparative examination of skulls representing the full range of individual human variation found in every part of the world today reveals now living people with skulls not meeting the anatomical definition of modernity proposed in the recent African origins model.[21]

HUMAN BIOLOGICAL VARIATION AND THE PROBLEM OF RACE

The Neandertal debate raises fundamental questions about the complex relationship between biological and cultural human variation. As we reviewed the human fossil record throughout this chapter, inferences were made about the cultural capabilities of our ancestors partially based on biological features.

Such questions are deeply embedded within a discipline that has a long history of studying cultural and biological variation within the human species and how it relates to the concept of **race** as a subspecies or discrete biological division within a species. Today, anthropologists agree that no subspecies exist within currently surviving *Homo sapiens*. Consequently, as far as contemporary humanity is concerned, race is not a valid biological category. In fact, anthropologists work actively to expose the concept of race as scientifically inapplicable to humans. At the same time, they recognize the powerful symbolic significance of race as a socio-political category in many countries, including the United States, Germany, Brazil, and South Africa.

Race as a Social Construct

To deal with the politically divisive aspects of racial symbolism, we must begin by understanding how the notion of distinct human races came to be. Earlier in this chapter, we discussed how European scholars struggled to make sense of the massive amounts of new informa-

---

[20]Gibbons, A. (1997). Ideas on human origins evolve at anthropology gathering. *Science 276*, 535–536; Pennisi, E. (1999). Genetic study shakes up out of Africa theory. Science 283, 1,828.

[21]Wolpoff, M., & Caspari, R. (1997). *Race and human evolution* (pp. 344–345, 393). New York: Simon & Schuster.

race In biology, a subgroup within a species, not scientifically applicable to humans because there exist no subspecies within modern *Homo sapiens*.

Some living people, such as this indigenous Australian, do not all meet the problematic definition of anatomical modernity according to skull shape proposed in the recent African origins model. Therefore, some paleoanthropologists suggest that this narrow definition of anatomical modernity is flawed, perhaps even ethnocentric, because all living people are clearly full-fledged members of the species *Homo sapiens.*

© Michael Coyne/Getty Images

tion generated since the Age of Exploration, beginning about 500 years ago. Coming to them from the most remote corners of the world, this information forced them to critically rethink deeply rooted ideas about humanity and its relationship to other forms of life. In the quest for understanding, they reasoned not only on the basis of scientific facts but also from the perspective of their particular religious beliefs and cultural traditions. Looking back on their writings, we are now painfully aware of how ethnocentrism and other prejudices clouded their findings.

Among the most telling examples of this is the racial categorizing done by German anatomist Johann Blumenbach (1752–1840), sometimes called the father of physical anthropology. Initially, Blumenbach adopted the classification system devised by the Swedish naturalist Linnaeus in 1758, which divided the human species into four major groups according to geographic area and classified all Europeans as "white," Africans as "black," American Indians as "red," and Asians as "yellow."

Later, in the 1795 edition of his book *On the Natural Variety of Mankind,* Blumenbach introduced some significant changes to this four-race scheme. Based on a comparative examination of his human skull collection, he judged as most beautiful the skull of a woman from the Caucasus Mountains between Russia and Turkey. It was more symmetrical than the others, and he thought it reflected nature's ideal form: the circle. Surely, Blumenbach reasoned, this perfect specimen resembled God's original creation. Moreover, he thought that the living inhabitants of the Caucasus region were the most beautiful in the world. Based on these criteria, he concluded that this

high mountain range not far from the lands mentioned in the Bible was near the place of human origins.

Building on his idea that the southeastern Europeans inhabiting the Caucasus looked most like the first humans, Blumenbach decided that all light-skinned peoples in Europe and adjacent parts of western Asia and northern Africa belonged to the same race. On this basis, he dropped the European race label and replaced it with "Caucasian." Although he continued to distinguish American Indians as a separate race, he regrouped dark-skinned Africans as "Ethiopian" and split those Asians not considered Caucasian into two separate races: "Mongolian" (referring to most inhabitants of Asia, including China and Japan) and "Malay" (indigenous Australians, Pacific Islanders, and others).

But, Blumenbach did more than change labels: He also introduced a formal hierarchical ordering of the races he delineated. Convinced that Caucasians were closest to the original ideal humans created in God's image, he ranked them as superior. The other races, he argued, were the result of "degeneration"; moving away from their place of origin and adapting to different environments and climates, they had degenerated physically and morally into what many Europeans came to think of as inferior races.[22]

Critically reviewing this and other early historical efforts in classifying humanity in higher and lower forms, we now clearly recognize their factual errors and ethnocentric biases with respect to the concept of race. Especially disastrous is the notion of superior and infe-

_____

[22]Gould, S. J. (1994). The geometer of race. *Discover 15* (11), 65–69.

rior races, as this has been used as justification for brutalities ranging from repression to slavery to mass murder or genocide. It has also been employed to justify stunning levels of mockery, as painfully illustrated in the following tragic story of Ota Benga, an African pygmy man who in the early 1900s was caged in a New York zoo with an orangutan.

Captured in a raid in the Congo, Ota Benga somehow came into the possession of a North American missionary-explorer looking for exotic "savages" for exhibition in the United States. In 1904, Ota and a group of fellow pygmies were shipped across the Atlantic and exhibited at a World's Fair in Saint Louis, Missouri. About 23 years old at the time, Ota was 4 feet 11 inches in height and weighed 103 pounds. Throngs of visitors came to see displays of dozens of indigenous peoples from around the globe, shown in their traditional dress and living in replica villages doing their customary things. The fair was a success for the organizers, and all the pygmies survived to be shipped back to their homeland.

The enterprising missionary also returned to Congo and with Ota's help collected artifacts to be sold to the American Museum of Natural History in New York City. In the summer of 1906 he returned to the United States, along with Ota. Soon thereafter, the missionary went bankrupt and lost his entire collection to the bank. Left stranded in the big city, Ota was placed in the care of the museum and then taken to the Bronx Zoo where he was put on exhibit in the monkey house, with an orangutan as company. Ota's sharpened teeth (a cultural practice among his own people) were seen as evidence of his supposedly cannibal nature. After intensive protest, zoo officials released the unfortunate pygmy from his cage and during the day let him roam free in the park, where he was often harassed by teasing visitors. Ota (usually referred to as a "boy") was then turned over to an orphanage for African American children. In 1916, upon hearing that he would never return to his homeland, he took a revolver and shot himself through the heart.[23]

The racist display at the Bronx Zoo a century ago was by no means unique. Just a tip of the ethnocentric iceberg, it was the manifestation of a powerful ideology in which one small part of humanity sought to demonstrate and justify its claims of biological and cultural superiority. This had particular resonance in North America, where people of European descent were thrown together in a society with Native Americans, African slaves, and (later) Asians imported as a source of cheap labor. Indeed, such claims, based on false notions of race, have resulted in the oppression and genocide of millions of humans because of the color of their skin or the shape of their skulls.

---

[23]Bradford, P. V., & Blume, H. (1992). *Ota Benga: The pygmy in the zoo.* New York: St. Martin's Press.

Fortunately, by the early 20th century, some scholars began to challenge the concept of racial superiority. Among the strongest critics was Franz Boas (1858–1942), a Jewish scientist who immigrated to the United States because of rising anti-Semitism in his German homeland and went on to become the founder of North America's academic anthropology. As president of the American Association for the Advancement of Science, Boas criticized hierarchical notions of race in an important speech titled "Race and Progress," published in the prestigious journal *Science* in 1909.

Ashley Montagu (1905–1999), a British student of Boas and one of the best-known anthropologists of his time, devoted much of his career to combating scientific racism. Like Boas, he was born into a Jewish family and personally felt the sting of anti-Semitism. Originally named Israel Ehrenberg, he changed his name in the 1920s and emigrated from England to the United States, where he fought racism in his writing and in academic and public lectures. Of all his works, none is more important than his book *Man's Most Dangerous Myth: The Fallacy of Race.* Published in 1942, it took the lead in exposing, on purely scientific grounds, the fallacy of human races as clearly bounded biological categories. The book has since gone through six editions, the last in 1999. Although Montagu's once controversial ideas have now become mainstream, his text remains the most comprehensive treatment of its subject.

Race as a Biological Construct

Social constructions of race are often tied up in the false but tenacious idea that there really is a biological foundation to the concept of human races. As already mentioned, in biology a race is defined as a subspecies: a population within a species that differs in terms of genetic variance from other populations of the same species. Simple and straightforward though such a definition may seem, there are three very important things to note about it. First, it is arbitrary; there is no agreement on how many differences it takes to make a race. For some who are interested in the topic, different frequencies in the variants of one gene are sufficient; for others, different frequencies involving several genes are necessary. Ultimately, it proved impossible to reach agreement not just on the number of genes, but also on precisely which ones are the most important for defining races.

After arbitrariness, the second important thing to note about the biological definition of race is that it does not mean that any one so-called race has exclusive possession of any particular variant of any gene or genes. In human terms, the frequency of a trait like type O blood, for example, may be high in one "race" population and low in another, but it is present in both. In other words, populations are genetically "open," meaning that genes

Many people have become accustomed to viewing so-called racial groups as natural and separate divisions within our species based on visible physical differences. However, these groups differ from one another in only 6 percent of their genes. For many thousands of years, individuals belonging to different human social groups have been in sexual contact. Exchanging their genes, they maintained the human species in all its colorful variety and prevented the development of distinctive subspecies (biologically defined races). This continued genetic mixing is effectively illustrated by the above photo of distant relatives, all of whom are descendents of Sally Hemings, an African American slave, and Thomas Jefferson, the Euramerican gentleman-farmer who had 150 slaves working for him at his Virginia plantation and served as the third U.S. president (1801–1809).

flow between them. Because human populations are genetically open, no fixed racial groups have developed within our modern species.

The third important thing to note about the scientifically inappropriate use of the term *race* with respect to humans is that the differences among individuals within a particular population are generally greater than the differences among populations. As the science writer James Shreeve puts it, "most of what separates me genetically from a typical African or Eskimo also separates me from another average American of European ancestry."[24]

In sum, the biological concept of race does not apply to *Homo sapiens*. That said, to dismiss race as a biologically invalid category is not to deny the reality of human biological diversity. The task for anthropologists is to explain that diversity and the social meanings given to it rather than to try to falsely split our species into discrete categories called races.

Skin Color: A Case Study in Adaptation

The popular idea of race is commonly linked to skin color, a complex biological trait. Skin color is subject to great variation and is attributed to several key factors: the transparency or thickness of the skin; a copper-

colored pigment called carotene; reflected color from the blood vessels (responsible for the rosy color of lightly pigmented people); and, most significantly, the amount of melanin (from *melas,* a Greek word meaning "black")—a dark pigment in the skin's outer layer. People with dark skin have more melanin-producing cells than those with light skin, but everyone (except albinos) has a measure of melanin.

Exposure to sunlight increases melanin production, causing skin color to deepen. Melanin is known to protect skin against damaging ultraviolet solar radiation;[25] consequently, dark-skinned peoples are less susceptible to skin cancers and sunburn than are those with less melanin. Because the highest concentrations of dark-skinned people tend to be found in the tropical regions of the world, it appears that natural selection has favored heavily pigmented skin as a protection against exposure where ultraviolet radiation is most constant.[26]

In northern latitudes light skin has an adaptive advantage related to the skin's important biological func-

[24]Shreeve, J. (1994) Terms of estrangement. *Discover 15* (11), 60.

[25]Neer, R. M. (1975). The evolutionary significance of vitamin D, skin pigment, and ultraviolet light. *American Journal of Physical Anthropology 43,* 409–416.

[26]Branda, R. F., & Eatoil, J. W. (1978). Skin color and photolysis: An evolutionary hypothesis. *Science 201,* 625–626.

tion as the manufacturer of vitamin D through a chemical reaction dependent upon sunlight. Vitamin D is vital for maintaining the balance of calcium in the body. In northern climates with little sunshine, light skin allows enough sunlight to penetrate the skin and stimulate the formation of vitamin D, essential for healthy bones. Dark pigmentation interferes with this process. The severe consequences of vitamin D deficiency can be avoided through culture. Until recently, children in northern Europe and North America were regularly fed a spoonful of cod liver oil during the dark winter months. Today, pasteurized milk is often fortified with vitamin D.

Given what we know about the adaptive significance of human skin color, and the fact that, until 800,000 years ago, members of the genus *Homo* were exclusively creatures of the tropics, it is likely that lightly pigmented skins are a recent development in human history. Conversely, and consistent with humanity's African origins, darkly pigmented skins likely are quite ancient. The enzyme tyrosinase, which converts the amino acid tyrosine into the compound that forms melanin, is present in lightly pigmented peoples in sufficient quantity to make them very "black." The reason it does not is that they have genes that inactivate or inhibit it.[27]

Human skin, more liberally endowed with sweat glands and lacking heavy body hair compared to other primates, effectively eliminates excess body heat in a hot climate. This would have been especially advantageous to our ancestors on the savannah, who could have avoided confrontations with large carnivorous animals by carrying out most of their activities in the heat of the day. For the most part, tropical predators rest during this period, hunting primarily from dusk until early morning. Without much hair to cover their bodies, selection would have favored dark skin in our human ancestors. In short, based on available scientific evidence, all humans appear to have a "black" ancestry, no matter how "white" some of them may appear to be today.

Obviously, one should not conclude that, because it may be a more recent development, lightly pigmented skin is better, or more highly evolved, than heavily pigmented skin. The latter is clearly better evolved to the conditions of life in the tropics or at high altitudes where exposure to ultraviolet light increases, although with cultural adaptations like protective clothing, hats, and more recently invented sunscreen lotions, lightly pigmented peoples can survive there. Conversely, the availability of supplementary sources of vitamin D allows more heavily pigmented peoples to do quite well far away from the tropics. In both cases, culture has rendered skin color differences largely irrelevant from a purely biological perspective. With time and with the efforts we see being made in many cultures today, skin color may lose its social significance as well.

Over the course of our long evolutionary history, we have become an amazingly diverse and yet still unified single species inhabiting the entire earth. Biological adaptation to a wide geographic range of natural environments is responsible for some aspects of human variation. However, while biological evolution continues into the present, our different cultures shape both the expression and the interpretation of human biological variation at every step. Human bipeds do indeed stand with one foot in nature and another in culture.

---

[27]Wills, C. (1994). The skin we're in. *Discover 15* (11), 79.

Questions for Reflection

1. Over the course of their evolutionary history, humans increasingly used the medium of culture to face the challenges of existence. How does studying the biological basis of human culture through living primates and human evolution help address the challenge of knowing ourselves?

2. Given your understanding of the concept of culture, do you think that chimps and bonobos possess culture?

3. How might you relate the Neandertal debates to stereotyping or racism in contemporary society?

4. Some aspects of human variation derive clearly from biological adaptations to the environment. As humans came to rely more upon cultural adaptations, what were the effects on our biology? How has culture shaped our interpretations of our biology?

5. Early U.S. presidents kept African Americans as slaves, and an African pygmy was exhibited in the monkey house at the Bronx Zoo in the early 1900s. Considering the historical context of slavery and racist behavior, do you think "Caucasian" as an ethnocentric label of superiority played a role in how Europeans and their descendents in America and elsewhere justified white supremacy as normal? Why are racial categories such as "Caucasian" still used?

Suggested Readings

De Waal, F. (2001). *The ape and the sushi master.* New York: Basic Books.

In an accessible style, one of the world's foremost experts on bonobos demonstrates ape culture and challenges theories that exclude animals from the "culture club." His discussion takes the concept of ape culture beyond anthropocentrism and ties it to communication and social organization.

Goodall, J. (2000). *Reason for hope: A spiritual journey.* New York: Warner Books.

A personal memoir linking this famous primatologist's lifework with chimpanzees in Tanzania's Gombe wildlife preserve to her spiritual convictions. Exploring difficult topics such as environmental destruction, animal abuse, and genocide, Goodall expands the concept of humanity and advocates basic human rights for chimpanzees.

Jones, S., Martin, R., & Pilbeam, D. (1992). *Cambridge encyclopedia of human evolution* New York: Cambridge University Press.

Over seventy scholars contributed to this comprehensive introduction to the human species, covering the gamut—from genetics, primatology, and the fossil evidence to contemporary human ecology, demography, and disease.

Klein, R. G., & Edgar, B. (2002). *The dawn of human culture*. New York: Wiley.

Reexamining the archaeological evidence and bringing in new discoveries in the study of the human brain, the authors detail the changes that enabled humans to think and behave in far more sophisticated ways than before, resulting in the incredibly rapid evolution of new skills.

Marks, J. (2002). *What it means to be 98 percent chimpanzee: Apes, people, and their genes*. Berkeley: University of California Press.

This provocative book places the ongoing study of the relationship between genes and behavior in historical and cultural contexts. Marks uses the close genetic relationship of chimps and humans to demonstrate the limits of genetics for explaining differences in complex traits such as behavior or appearance. His discussion of the absence of a genetic basis for race is particularly good.

Wolpoff, M., & Caspari, R. (1997). *Race and human evolution: A fatal attraction*. New York: Simon & Schuster.

A historical account of efforts to develop a scientific theory of race in Western societies is joined with an analysis of the fossil evidence for modern human origins in this fascinating book. Its authors, champions of the multiregional hypothesis, document the social processes leading to the division of contemporary humans into racial groups suggesting that the division of fossil groups into separate species represents a similar application of the false concept of biological race.

Thomson Audio Study Products

 Enjoy the MP3-ready Audio Lecture Overviews for each chapter and a comprehensive audio glossary of key terms for quick study and review. Whether walking to class, doing laundry, or studying at your desk, you now have the freedom to choose when, where, and how you interact with your audio-based educational media. See the preface for information on how to access this on-the-go study and review tool.

The Anthropology Resource Center

www.thomsonedu.com/anthropology
The Anthropology Resource Center provides extended learning materials to reinforce your understanding of key concepts in the four fields of anthropology. For each of the four fields, the Resource Center includes dynamic exercises including video exercises, map exercises, simulations, and "Meet the Scientists" interviews, as well as critical thinking questions that can be assigned and e-mailed to instructors. The Resource Center also provides breaking news in anthropology and interesting material on applied anthropology to help you link what you are learning to the world around you.

5 Language and Communication

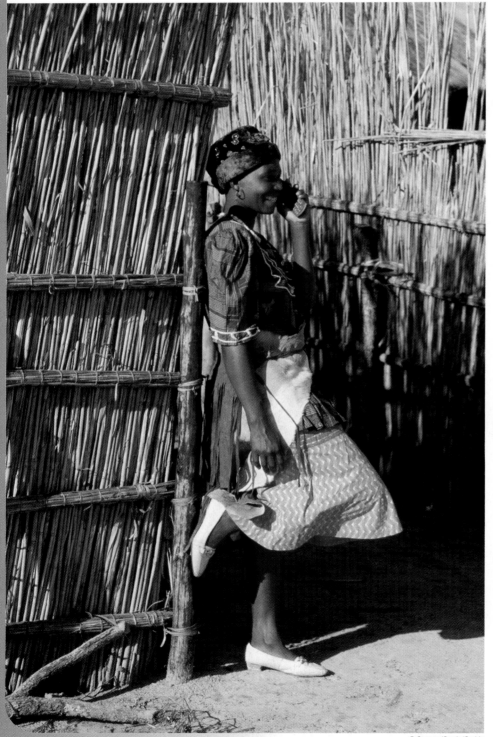

© Strauss/Curtis/Corbis

What Is Language?

A language is a system of symbolic communication using sounds and/ or gestures that are put together according to rules resulting in meanings that are based on agreement by a society and intelligible to all who share that language. Although humans rely heavily on spoken language, or speech, to communicate with one another, it is not their sole means of communication. Human language is embedded in an age-old gesture-call system in which body motions and facial expressions, along with vocal features such as tone and volume, play vital roles in conveying messages.

How Is Language Related to Culture?

Without our capacity for complex language, human culture as we know it could not exist. Languages are shared by people who belong to societies that have their own distinctive cultures. Social variables, such as age, gender, and economic status, may influence how people use language. Moreover, people communicate what is meaningful to them, and that is largely defined by their particular culture. In fact, our use of language has an effect on, and is influenced by, our culture.

How Do Languages Change?

All languages are constantly transforming—new words are adopted or coined, others are dropped, and some shift in meaning. Languages change for various reasons, ranging from selective borrowing by one language from another, or the need for new vocabulary to deal with technological innovations or altered social realities. On one hand, domination of one society by another may result in erosion or loss of a particular language. On the other, cultural revitalization may result in the resurgence or revival of a threatened or even extinct language.

All normal humans are born with the ability to communicate through language and may spend a considerable part of each day doing so. Indeed, language is so much a part of our lives that it involves everything we do, and everything we do involves language.

There is no doubt that our ability to communicate, whether through sounds or gestures (sign languages, such as the American Sign Language (ASL) used by the hearing impaired, are fully developed languages in their own right), rests squarely upon our biological makeup. We are "programmed" for language, although only in a general sort of way. Beyond the cries of babies, which are not learned but which do communicate, humans must learn their language. So it is that any normal child from anywhere in the world readily learns the language of his or her culture.

We define **language** as a system of communication using sounds and/or gestures that are put together according to certain rules, resulting in meanings that are intelligible to all who share that language. These sounds and gestures fall into the category of a *symbol* (defined as a sign, sound, gesture, or other thing that is arbitrarily linked to something else and represents it in a meaningful way). For example, the word *crying* is a symbol, a combination of sounds to which we assign the meaning of a particular action and which we can use to communicate that meaning, whether or not anyone around us is actually crying. **Signals,** unlike culturally learned symbols, are instinctive sounds and gestures that have a natural or self-evident meaning. Screams, signs, or coughs, for example, are signals that convey some kind of emotional or physical state.

THOMSON AUDIO STUDY PRODUCTS Take advantage of the MP3-ready Audio Lecture Overviews and comprehensive audio glossary of key terms for each chapter. See the preface for information on how to access this on-the-go study and review tool.

language A system of communication using sounds or gestures that are put together in meaningful ways according to a set of rules.
signal An instinctive sound or gesture that has a natural or self-evident meaning.

Today's language experts are not certain how much credit to give to animals, such as dolphins or chimpanzees, for the ability to use symbols as well as signals. But it has become evident that these animals and many others communicate in remarkable ways. Apes have demonstrated an ability to understand language quite well, even using rudimentary grammar. Several chimpanzees, gorillas, and orangutans have been taught American Sign Language. Researchers have discovered that even vervet monkeys utilize distinct calls for communication. These calls go beyond merely signaling levels of fear or arousal. Among other things, these small African monkeys have specific calls to signify the type of predator threatening the group. According to primatologist Allison Jolly,

> [The calls] include which direction to look in or where to run. There is an audience effect: calls are given when there is someone appropriate to listen . . . monkey calls are far more than involuntary expressions of emotion.[1]

What are the implications of this for our understanding of the nature and evolution of language? No final answer will be evident until we gain more knowledge about the various systems of animal communication. Meanwhile, even as debate continues over how human and animal communication relate to each other, we cannot dismiss communication among nonhuman species as a set of simple instinctive reflexes or fixed action patterns.[2]

A remarkable example of the many scientific efforts underway on this subject is the story of an orangutan named Chantek, featured in the following Original Study. Among other things, it illustrates the creative process of language development and the capacity of a nonhuman primate to recognize symbols.

---

[1]Jolly, A. (1991). Thinking like a vervet. *Science 251,* 574. See also Seyfarth, R. M., et al. (1980). Monkey responses to three different alarm calls: Evidence for predator classification and semantic communication. *Science 210,* 801–803.

[2]Armstrong, D. F., Stokoe, W. C., & Wilcox, S. E. (1993). Signs of the origin of syntax. *Current Anthropology 34,* 349–368; Burling, R. (1993). Primate calls, human language, and nonverbal communication. *Current Anthropology 34,* 25–53.

Language and the Intellectual Abilities of Orangutans

In 1978, after researchers began to use American Sign Language for the deaf to communicate with chimpanzees and gorillas, I began the first long-term study of the language ability of an orangutan named Chantek. There was criticism that symbol-using apes might just be imitating their human caregivers, but there is now growing agreement that orangutans, gorillas, and both chimpanzee species can develop language skills at the level of a 2- to 3-year-old human child.

The goal of Project Chantek was to investigate the mind of an orangutan through a developmental study of his cognitive and linguistic skills. It was a great ethical and emotional responsibility to engage an orangutan in what anthropologists call "enculturation," since I would not only be teaching a form of communication, I would be teaching aspects of the culture upon which that language was based. If my project succeeded, I would create a symbol-using creature that would be somewhere between an ape living under natural conditions and an adult human. This threatened to raise as many questions as I sought to answer.

A small group of caregivers at the University of Tennessee, Chattanooga, began raising Chantek when he was 9 months old. They communicated with him by using gestural signs based on the American Sign Language for the deaf. After a month, Chantek produced his own first sign and eventually learned to use approximately 150 different signs, forming a vocabulary similar to that of a very young child. Chantek learned names for people (LYN, JOHN), places (YARD, BROCK-HALL), things to eat (YOGURT, CHOCOLATE), actions (WORK, HUG), objects (SCREWDRIVER, MONEY), animals (DOG, APE), colors (RED, BLACK), pronouns (YOU, ME), location (UP, POINT), attributes (GOOD, HURT), and emphasis (MORE, TIME-TO-DO).

© H. Lyn Miles

Though the orangutans diverged from humans, chimps, and gorillas about 12 million years ago, all of these ape species share a number of qualities. Orangutans have an insightful, humanlike thinking style characterized by longer attention spans and quiet deliberate action. Orangutans make shelters, tie knots, recognize themselves in mirrors, use one tool to make another, and are the most skilled of the apes in manipulating objects. In this photo, Chantek begins the sign for "tomato."

We found that Chantek's signing was spontaneous and nonrepetitious. He did not merely imitate his caregivers, but rather he actively used signs to initiate communications and meet his needs. Almost immediately, he began using signs in combinations and modulated their meanings with slight changes in how he articulated and arranged his signs. He commented "COKE DRINK" after drinking his coke, "PULL BEARD" while pulling a caregiver's hair through a fence, and "TIME HUG" while locked in his cage as his caregiver looked at her watch. But, beyond using signs in this way, could he use them as symbols, that is, more abstractly to represent a person, thing, action, or idea, even apart from its context or when it was not present?

One indication of the capacity of both deaf and hearing children to use symbolic language is the ability to point, which some researchers argued that apes could not do spontaneously. Chantek began to point to objects when he was 2 years old, somewhat later than human children. First, he showed and gave us objects, and then he began pointing where he wanted to be tickled and to where he wanted to be carried. Finally, he could answer questions like WHERE HAT? WHICH DIF-FERENT? and WHAT WANT? by pointing to the correct object.

As Chantek's vocabulary increased, the ideas that he was expressing became more complex, such as when he signed BAD BIRD at noisy birds giving alarm calls, and WHITE CHEESE FOODEAT for cottage cheese. He understood that things had characteristics or attributes that could be described. He also created combinations of signs that we had never used before.

In the way that a child learns language, Chantek began to over- or under-extend the meaning of his signs, which gave us insight into his emotions and how he was beginning to classify his world. For example, he used the sign DOG for actual dogs, as well as for a picture of a dog in his Viewmaster, orangutans on television, barking noises on the radio, birds, horses, a tiger at the circus, a herd of cows, a picture of a cheetah, and a noisy helicopter that presumably sounded like it was barking. For Chantek, the sign BUG included crickets, cockroaches, a picture of a cockroach, beetles, slugs, small moths, spiders, worms, flies, a picture of a graph shaped like a butterfly, tiny brown pieces of cat food, and small bits of feces. He signed BREAK before he broke and shared pieces of crackers, and after he broke his toilet. He signed BAD to himself before he grabbed a cat, when he bit into a radish, and for a dead bird.

We also discovered that Chantek could comprehend our spoken English (after the first couple of years we used speech as well as signing). When he was 2 years old, Chantek began to sign for things that were not present. He frequently asked to go to places in his yard to look for animals, such as his pet squirrel and cat, who served as playmates. He also made requests for ICE CREAM, signing CAR RIDE and pulling us toward the parking lot for a trip to a local ice-cream shop.

CONTINUED

CONTINUED

We learned that an orangutan can tell lies. Deception is an important indicator of language abilities since it requires a deliberate and intentional misrepresentation of reality. In order to deceive, you must be able to see events from the other person's perspective and negate his or her perception. Chantek began to deceive from a relatively early age, and we caught him in lies about three times a week. He learned that he could sign DIRTY to get into the bathroom to play with the washing machine, dryer, soap, and so on, instead of using the toilet. He also used his signs deceptively to gain social advantage in games, to divert attention in social interactions, and to avoid testing situations and coming home after walks on campus.

On one occasion, Chantek stole food from my pocket while he simultaneously pulled my hand away in the opposite direction. On another occasion, he stole a pencil eraser, pretended to swallow it, and "supported" his case by opening his mouth and signing FOOD-EAT, as if to say that he had swallowed it. However, he really held the eraser in his cheek, and later it was found in his bedroom where he commonly hid objects.

We carried out tests of Chantek's mental ability using measures developed for human children. Chantek reached a mental age equivalent to that of a 2- to 3-year-old child, with some skills of even older children. On some tasks done readily by children, such as using one object

to represent another and pretend play, Chantek performed as well as children, but less frequently. He engaged in chase games in which he would look over his shoulder as he darted about, although no one was chasing him. He also signed to his toys and offered them food and drink.

By 4½ years of age, Chantek showed evidence of planning, creative simulation, and the use of objects in novel relations to one another to invent new meanings. For example, he simulated the context for food preparation by giving his caregiver two objects needed to prepare his milk formula and staring at the location of the remaining ingredient. A further indication that Chantek had mental images is found in his ability to respond to his caregiver's request that he improve the articulation of a sign. When his articulation became careless, we would ask him to SIGN BETTER. Looking closely at us, he would sign slowly and emphatically, taking one hand to put the other into the proper shape.

Chantek was extremely curious and inventive. When he wanted to know the name of something, he offered his hands to be molded into the shape of the proper sign. But language is a creative process, so we were pleased to see that Chantek began to invent his own signs. He invented: NO-TEETH (to show us that he would not use his teeth during rough play); EYE-DRINK (for contact lens solution used by his caregivers); and DAVE-MISSING-FINGER (a name for a favorite university employee who had a

hand injury). Like our ancestors, Chantek had become a creator of language. *(See H. L. W. Miles. (1993). Language and the orangutan: The old "person" of the forest. In P. Cavalieri & P. Singer (Eds.), The great ape project (pp. 45–50). New York: St. Martin's Press.)*

2004 update: My relationship and research with Chantek continues, through the Chantek Foundation in Atlanta, Georgia. Chantek now uses several hundred signs and has invented new signs for CAR WATER (bottled water that I bring in my car), KATSUP, and ANNOYED. He makes stone tools, arts and crafts, necklaces, and other jewelry, and small percussion instruments used in my rock band Animal Nation. He even co-composes songs with the band.

Plans are in the making for Chantek and other enculturated apes to live in culture-based preserves where they have more range of choices and learning opportunities than zoos or research centers. An exciting new project under the auspices of ApeNet will give Chantek an opportunity to communicate with other apes via the Internet. It is of special note that based on great ape language skills, efforts will be underway in the next decade to obtain greater legal rights for these primates, as well as greater recognition of them as another type of "person." (For more information, see www.chantek.org.) ■

While language studies such as the one involving Chantek are fascinating and reveal much about primate cognition, the fact remains that human culture is ultimately dependent on an elaborate system of communication far more complex than that of any other species—including our fellow primates. The reason for this is the sheer amount of what must be learned by each person from other individuals in order to control the knowledge and rules for behavior necessary for full participation in society. Of course, a significant amount of learning can and does take place in the absence of language by way of observation and imitation, guided by a limited number of meaningful signs or symbols. However, all known human cultures are so rich in content that they require communication systems that not only can give precise labels to various classes of phenomena but also permit

people to think and talk about their own and others' experiences and expectations—past, present, and future.

The central and most highly developed human system of communication is language. Knowledge of the workings of language, then, is essential to a full understanding of what culture is about and how it operates.

LINGUISTIC RESEARCH AND THE NATURE OF LANGUAGE

Any human language—Chinese, English, Swahili, or whatever—is obviously a means of transmitting information and sharing with others both collective and individual experiences. Because we tend to take language

For linguists studying language in the field, laptops and recording devices are indispensable tools. Here Tiffany Kershner of Kansas State University works with native Sukwa speakers in northern Malawi, Africa.

for granted, it is perhaps not so obvious that language is also a system that enables us to translate our concerns, beliefs, and perceptions into symbols that can be understood and interpreted by others.

In spoken language, this is done by taking a few sounds—no language uses more than about fifty—and developing rules for putting them together in meaningful ways. Sign languages, such as American Sign Language, do the same thing but with gestures rather than sounds. The vast array of languages in the world—some 6,500 or so different ones—may well astound and mystify us by their great variety and complexity, yet language experts have found that all languages, as far back as we can trace them, are organized in the same basic way.

The roots of **linguistics**—the systematic study of all aspects of language—go back a long way, to the works of ancient language specialists in India more than 2,000 years ago. The European age of exploration from the 16th through the 18th centuries set the stage for a great leap forward in the scientific study of language. Explorers, invaders, and missionaries accumulated information about a huge diversity of languages from all around the world. An estimated 10,000 languages still existed when they began their inquiries.

Linguists in the 19th century, including anthropologists, made a significant contribution in discovering system, regularity, and relationships in the data and tentatively formulating laws and regular principles concerning language. In the 20th century, while still collecting data, they made considerable progress in unraveling the reasoning process behind language construction, testing and working from new and improved theories.

Insofar as theories and facts of language are verifiable by independent researchers looking at the same materials, there may now be said to be a science of linguistics. This science has three main branches: descriptive linguistics, historical linguistics, and a third branch that focuses on language in relation to social and cultural settings.

DESCRIPTIVE LINGUISTICS

How can an anthropologist, a trader, a missionary, a diplomat, or anyone else approach and make sense of a language that has not yet been described and analyzed, or for which there are no readily available written materials? There are hundreds of such undocumented languages in the world; fortunately, effective methods have been developed to help with the task. Descriptive linguistics involves unraveling a language by recording, describing, and analyzing all of its features. It is a painstaking process, but it is ultimately rewarding in that it provides deeper understanding of a language—its structure, its unique linguistic repertoire (figures of speech, word plays, and so on), and its relationship to other languages.

The process of unlocking the underlying rules of a spoken language requires a trained ear and a thorough understanding of the way multiple different speech

linguistics The modern scientific study of all aspects of language.

sounds are produced. Without such know-how, it is extremely difficult to write out or make intelligent use of any data concerning a particular language. To satisfy this preliminary requirement, most people need special training in phonetics, discussed below. As for the biology that makes human speech possible, that is explained in this chapter's Biocultural Connection.

Phonology

Rooted in the Greek word *phone* (meaning "sound"), **phonetics** is defined as the systematic identification and description of the distinctive sounds of a language. Phonetics is basic to **phonology,** the study of language sounds. In order to analyze and describe any language, one needs first an inventory of all its distinctive sounds.

While some of the sounds used in other languages may seem very much like those of the researcher's own speech pattern, others may be unfamiliar. For example, the *th* sound common in English does not exist in the Dutch language and is difficult for most Dutch speakers to pronounce, just as the *r* sound used in numerous languages is tough for Japanese speakers. And the unique "click" sounds used in Bushman languages in southern Africa are difficult for speakers of just about every other language. Sometimes words that feature sounds notoriously difficult for outsiders to pronounce are used as passwords to identify foreigners. For instance, because Germans find it hard to pronounce the sound *sch* the way their Dutch neighbors do, resistance fighters in the Netherlands during World War II chose the place name *Scheveningen* as a test word to identify Dutch-speaking German spies trying to infiltrate their groups. Such a password is known as a *shibboleth*.

While collecting speech sounds or utterances, the linguist works to isolate the **phonemes**—the smallest units of sound that make a difference in meaning. This isolation and analysis may be done by a process called the minimal-pair test. The researcher tries to find two short words that appear to be exactly alike except for one sound, such as *bit* and *pit* in English. If the substitution of *b* for *p* in this minimal pair makes a difference in meaning, as it does in English, then those two sounds have been identified as distinct phonemes of the language and will require two different symbols to record. If, however, the linguist finds two different pronunciations (as when "butter" is pronounced "budder") and then finds that there is no difference in their meaning for a native speaker, the sounds represented will be considered variants of the same phoneme. In such cases, for economy of representation only one of the two symbols will be used to record that sound wherever it is found.

Morphology

While making and studying an inventory of distinctive sounds, linguists also look into **morphology,** the study of the patterns or rules of word formation in a language (including such things as rules concerning verb tense, pluralization, and compound words). They do this by marking out specific sounds and sound combinations that seem to have meaning. These are called **morphemes**—the smallest units of sound that carry a meaning in a language.

Morphemes are distinct from phonemes, which can alter meaning but have no meaning by themselves. For example, a linguist studying English in a North American farming community would soon learn that *cow* is a morpheme—a meaningful combination of the phonemes *c, o,* and *w*. Pointing to two of these animals, the linguist would elicit the word *cows* from local speakers. This would reveal yet another morpheme—the *s*—which can be added to the original morpheme to indicate "plural."

Syntax and Grammar

The next step in unraveling a language is to identify its **syntax**—the patterns or rules by which morphemes are arranged into phrases and sentences. The **grammar** of the language will ultimately consist of all observations about its morphemes and syntax. An important component of syntax is the identification of *form classes*—the parts of speech or categories of words that function the same way in a sentence. This can be done by using *substitution frames*. For example, there exists a category we call "nouns," defined as any word that will fit the substitution frame "I see a ___." The linguist simply makes the frame, tries out a number of words in it, and has a native speaker indicate yes or no for whether the words work. In English, the words *house* and *cat* will fit this frame and will be said to belong to the same form class, but the word *think* will not.

---

phonetics The systematic identification and description of distinctive speech sounds in a language.

phonology The study of language sounds.

phoneme The smallest unit of sound that makes a difference in meaning in a language.

morphology The study of the patterns or rules of word formation in a language (including such things as rules concerning verb tense, pluralization, and compound words).

morpheme The smallest unit of sound that carries a meaning in language. It is distinct from a phoneme, which can alter meaning but has no meaning by itself.

syntax The patterns or rules by which morphemes are arranged into phrases and sentences.

grammar The entire formal structure of a language, including morphology and syntax.

Biocultural Connection

The Biology of Human Speech

While other primates have shown some capacity for language (a socially agreed upon code of communication), actual speech is unique to humans. It comes at a price, for the anatomical organization of the human throat and mouth that make speech possible also increase the risk of choking.

Of particular importance are the positions of the human larynx (voice box) and the epiglottis. The larynx, situated in the respiratory tract between the pharynx (throat) and trachea (wind pipe), contains the vocal chords. The epiglottis is the structure that separates the esophagus or food pipe from the wind pipe as food passes from the mouth to the stomach. (See Figure 5.1 for comparative diagrams of the anatomy of this region in chimps and humans.)

The overlapping routes of passage for food and air can be seen as a legacy of our evolutionary history. Fish, the earliest vertebrates (animals with backbones), obtained both food and oxygen from water entering through their mouths. As land vertebrates evolved, separate means for obtaining food and air developed out of the preexisting combined system. As a result, the pathways for air and food overlap. In most mammals, including human infants and apes of all ages, choking on food is not a problem because the larynx is relatively high in the throat so that the epiglottis seals the windpipe from food with every swallow. The position of the larynx and trachea make it easy for babies to coordinate breathing with eating.

However, as humans mature and develop the neurological and muscular coordination for speech, the larynx and epiglottis shift to a downward position. The human tongue bends at the back of the throat and is attached to the pharynx, the region of the throat where the food and airways share a common path. Sound occurs as air exhaled from the lungs passes over the vocal cords and causes them to vibrate.

Through continuous interactive movements of the tongue, pharynx, lips, and teeth, as well as nasal passages, the sounds are alternately modified to produce speech—the uniquely patterned sounds of a particular language. Based on long-standing socially learned patterns of speech, different languages stress certain distinctive types of sounds as significant and ignore others. For instance, languages belonging to the Iroquoian family, such as Mohawk, Seneca, and Cherokee, are among the few in the world that have no bilabial stops (*b* and *p* sounds). They also lack the labio-dental spirants (*f* and *v* sounds), leaving the bilabial nasal *m* sound as the only consonant requiring lip articulation.

It takes many years of practice for people to master the muscular movements needed to produce the precise sounds of any particular language. But no human could produce the finely controlled speech sounds without a lowered position of the larynx and epiglottis.

Nasal cavity
Palate
Tongue
Epiglottis
Larynx
Pharynx
Trachea

Figure 5.1

One of the strengths of modern descriptive linguistics is the objectivity of its methods. For example, an English-speaking anthropologist who specializes in this will not approach a language with the idea that it must have nouns, verbs, prepositions, or any other of the form classes identifiable in English. She or he instead sees what turns up in the language and makes an attempt to describe it in terms of its own inner workings. This allows for unanticipated discoveries. For instance, unlike many other languages, English does not distinguish between feminine and masculine nouns. So it is that English speakers use the definite article *the* in front of any noun, while French requires two types of such definite articles: *la* for feminine nouns and *le* for masculine—as in *la lune* (the moon) and *le soleil* (the sun). German speakers go one step further, utilizing three types of articles: *der* in front of masculine nouns, *die* for feminine, and *das* for neutral. It is also interesting to note that in contrast to their French neighbors, Germans consider the moon as masculine, so they say *der Mon,* and the sun as feminine, which makes it *die Sonne.* In another corner of the world, the highlands of Peru and Bolivia in South America, indigenous peoples who speak Quechua are not concerned about such gendered nouns, for there are no definite articles in their language.

HISTORICAL LINGUISTICS

While descriptive linguistics focuses on all features of a particular language as it is at any one moment in time, historical linguistics deals with the fact that languages change. In addition to deciphering "dead" languages that are no longer spoken, specialists in this field investigate relationships between earlier and later forms of the same language, study older languages for developments in modern ones, and examine interrelationships among older languages. For example, they attempt to sort out the development of Latin (spoken almost 1,500 years ago in southern Europe) into Italian, Spanish, Portuguese, French, and Romanian by identifying natural shifts in the original language, as well as modifications brought on by direct contact during the next few centuries with Germanic-speaking invaders from northern Europe.

That said, historical linguists are not limited to the faraway past, for even modern languages are constantly transforming—adding new words, dropping others, or changing meaning. Over the last decade or so, Internet use has widened the meaning of a host of already existing English words—from *hacking* and *surfing* to *spam.* Entirely new words, such as *blogging,* have been coined.

Especially when focusing on long-term processes of change, historical linguists depend on written records of languages. They have achieved considerable success in working out the relationships among different languages, and these are reflected in schemes of classification. For example, English is one of approximately 140 languages classified in the larger Indo-European language family (Figure 5.2). A **language family** is a group of languages descended from a single ancestral language. This family is subdivided into some eleven subgroups, which reflects the fact that there has been a long period (6,000 years or so) of **linguistic divergence** from an ancient unified language (reconstructed as Proto-Indo-European) into separate "daughter" languages. English is one of several languages in the Germanic subgroup (Figure 5.3), all of which are more closely related to one another than they are to the languages of any other subgroup of the Indo-European family.

So it is that, despite the differences between them, the languages of one subgroup share certain features when compared to those of another. As an illustration, the word for "father" in the Germanic languages always starts with an *f* or closely related *v* sound (Dutch *vader,* German *Vater,* Gothic *Fadar*). Among the Romance languages, by contrast, the comparable word always starts with a *p:* French *père,* Spanish and Italian *padre*—all derived from the Latin *pater.* The original Indo-European word for "father" was *p'tēr,* so in this case, the Romance languages have retained the earlier pronunciation, whereas the Germanic languages have diverged. Thus, many words that begin with *p* in the Romance languages, like Latin *piscis* and *pes,* become words like English *fish* and *foot* in the Germanic languages.

language family A group of languages descended from a single ancestral language.
linguistic divergence The development of different languages from a single ancestral language.

Figure 5.2
The Indo-European languages.

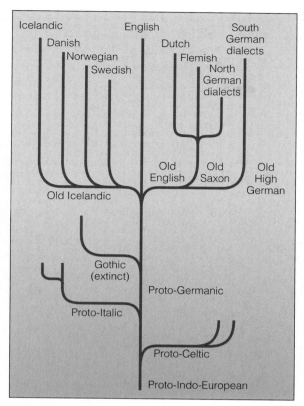

Figure 5.3

English is one of a group of languages in the Germanic subgroup of the Indo-European family. This diagram shows its relationship to other languages in the same subgroup. The root was Proto-Indo-European, an ancestral language originally spoken by early farmers and herders who spread north and west over Europe, bringing with them both their customs and their language.

In addition to describing the changes that have taken place as languages have diverged from ancient parent languages, historical linguists have also developed methods to estimate when such divergences occurred. One such technique is known as **glottochronology,** a term derived from the Greek word *glottis,* which means "tongue" or "language." This method compares the **core vocabularies** of languages—pronouns, lower numerals, and names for body parts and natural objects. It is based on the assumption that these basic vocabularies change more slowly than other words and at a more or less constant rate of 14 to 19 percent per 1,000 years. (Linguists determined this rate by calculating changes documented in thirteen historic written languages.) By applying a mathematical formula to two related core vocabularies, one can roughly determine the approximate number of years since the languages separated. Although not as precise as we might like, glottochronology, in conjunction with other chronological dating methods such as those based on archaeological and genetic data, can help determine the time of linguistic divergence.

Processes of Linguistic Divergence

Studying modern languages in their specific cultural contexts can help us understand the processes of change that may have led to linguistic divergence. Clearly, one force for change is selective borrowing by one language from another. This is evident in the many French words present in the English language—and in the growing number of English words cropping up in languages all around the world due to globalization. Technological breakthroughs resulting in new equipment and products also prompt linguistic shifts. For instance, the electronic revolution that brought us radio, television, and computers has created entirely new vocabularies.

Increasing professional specialization is another driving force. We see one of many examples in the field of biomedicine where today's students must learn the specialized vocabulary and idioms of the profession—over 6,000 new words in the first year of medical school. There is also a tendency for any group within a larger society to create its own unique vocabulary, whether it is a street gang, sorority, religious group, prison inmates, or platoon of soldiers. By changing the meaning of existing words or inventing new ones, members of the "in-group" can communicate with fellow members while effectively excluding outsiders who may be within hearing range. Finally, there seems to be a human tendency to admire the person who comes up with a new and clever idiom, a useful word, or a particularly stylish pronunciation, as long as these do not seriously interfere with communication. All of this means that no language stands still.

Phonological differences among groups may be regarded in the same light as vocabulary differences. In a class-structured society, for example, members of the upper class may try to keep their pronunciation distinct from that of lower classes, or vice versa, as a means of reinforcing social boundaries.

Language Loss and Revival

Perhaps the most powerful force for linguistic change is the domination of one society over another, as demonstrated during 500 years of European colonialism. Such dominations persist in many parts of the world to the present time, such as Taiwan's aboriginal peoples being governed by Mandarin-speaking Chinese, Tarascan Indians by Spanish-speaking Mexicans, or Bushmen by English-speaking Namibians.

glottochronology In linguistics, a method for identifying the approximate time that languages branched off from a common ancestor. It is based on analyzing core vocabularies.
core vocabularies The most basic and long-lasting words in any language—pronouns, lower numerals, and names for body parts and natural objects.

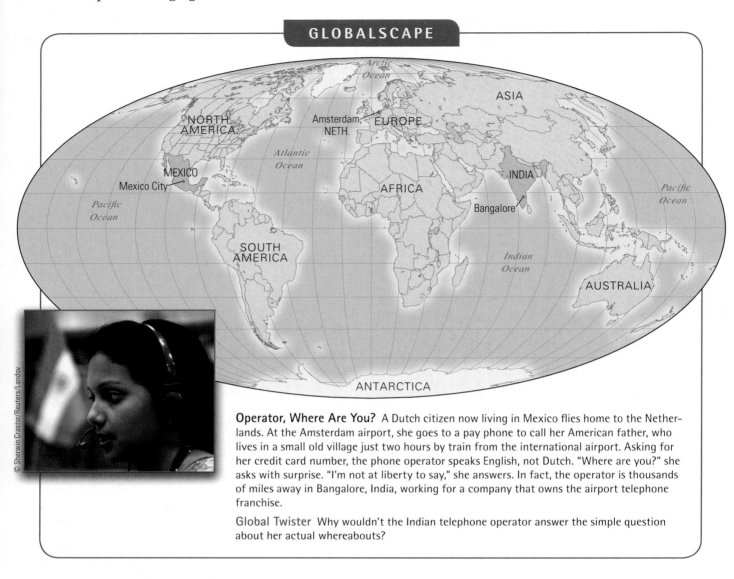

GLOBALSCAPE

Operator, Where Are You? A Dutch citizen now living in Mexico flies home to the Netherlands. At the Amsterdam airport, she goes to a pay phone to call her American father, who lives in a small old village just two hours by train from the international airport. Asking for her credit card number, the phone operator speaks English, not Dutch. "Where are you?" she asks with surprise. "I'm not at liberty to say," she answers. In fact, the operator is thousands of miles away in Bangalore, India, working for a company that owns the airport telephone franchise.

Global Twister Why wouldn't the Indian telephone operator answer the simple question about her actual whereabouts?

In many cases, foreign political control has resulted in linguistic erosion or even complete disappearance, sometimes leaving only a faint trace in old, indigenous names for geographic features such as hills and rivers. In fact, over the last 500 years about 3,500 of the world's 10,000 or so languages have become extinct as a direct result of warfare, epidemics, and forced assimilation brought on by colonial powers and other aggressive outsiders. Most of the remaining 6,500 languages are spoken by very few people, and many of them are losing speakers rapidly due to globalization. In fact, half have fewer than 10,000 speakers each, and a quarter have fewer than 1,000. In North America, for instance, only 150 of the original 300 indigenous languages still exist, and many of these surviving tongues are seriously endangered and moving toward extinction at an alarming rate.

Anthropologists predict that the number of languages still spoken in the world today will be cut in half by the year 2100, in large part because children born in ethnic minority groups no longer use the ancestral language when they go to school, migrate to cities, join the larger workforce, and are exposed to printed and electronic media. The printing press, radio, satellite television, Internet, and text messaging on cell phones are driving the need for a shared language that many understand, and increasingly that is English. In the past 500 years, this language—originally spoken by about 2.5 million people living only in part of the British Isles in northwestern Europe—has spread around the world. Today some 375 million people (6 percent of the global population) claim English as their native tongue. Close to a billion others (about 15 percent) speak it as a second or foreign language.

While a common language allows people from different ethnic backgrounds to communicate, there is the risk that a global spread of one language may contribute to the disappearance of others. And with the extinction of each language, a measure of humankind's richly varied cultural heritage, including countless insights on life, is lost.

The United Nations Educational, Scientific, and Cultural Organization (UNESCO) recently marked out key factors used to assess the endangerment status of a language.[3] Beyond obvious points—such as declining numbers of speakers, discriminatory governmental policies, non-literacy, and insufficient means for language education—a key issue is the impact electronic media such as the Internet have on language groups. Today, Internet content exists in only a handful of languages, and 80 percent of Internet users are native speakers of just ten of the world's 6,500 languages. On one hand, there is the serious risk that such overwhelming presence of a handful of already dominant languages on the Internet further threatens endangered languages. On the other hand, the Internet offers a powerful tool for maintaining and revitalizing disappearing languages and the cultures they are tied to—as indicated in the ever-growing number of indigenous groups developing computer programs to help teach their native tongues.

Ensuring digital access to local content is a new and important component in language preservation efforts. In 2001, UNESCO established Initiative B@bel, which uses information and communication technologies to support linguistic and cultural diversity. Promoting multilingualism on the Internet, this initiative aims to bridge the digital divide—to make access to Internet content and services more equitable for users worldwide (Figure 5.4).

Sometimes, in reaction to a real or perceived threat of cultural dominance by powerful foreign societies, ethnic groups and even entire countries may seek to maintain or reclaim their unique identity by purging their vocabularies of "foreign" terms. Emerging as a significant force for linguistic change, such **linguistic nationalism** is particularly characteristic of the former colonial countries of Africa and Asia today. It is by no means limited to those countries, however, as one can see by periodic French attempts to purge their language of such Americanisms as *le hamburger*. A recent example of this is France's decision to substitute the word *e-mail* with the newly minted government-approved term *couriel*.

Also in the category of linguistic nationalism are revivals of languages long out of daily use by ethnic minorities and sometimes even whole nations. Examples include efforts among American Indian groups to restore their language and Greece's successful revival of Greek after many centuries of Turkish domination. Perhaps the most remarkable example is the revival of ancient He-

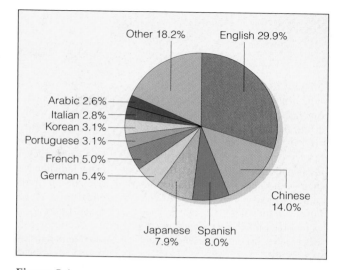

Figure 5.4

Although the world's digital divide is diminishing, it is still dramatic. As illustrated here, over 80 percent of today's Internet users are native speakers of just ten of the world's 6,500 languages.
Source: www.internetworldstats.com, 2006.

brew (after it had not been spoken as a daily language for almost 2,000 years) as the basis for the national language of Jews in the modern state of Israel.

For many ethnic minorities, efforts to counter the threat of linguistic extinction or to resurrect already extinct languages form part of their struggle to maintain a sense of cultural identity and dignity. A prime means by which powerful groups try to assert their dominance over minorities living within their borders is to actively suppress their languages.

A dramatic illustration of this is an old government-sanctioned effort to repress Native American cultures in Canada and the United States and fully absorb these cultures into the main body of North American society. Government polices included taking Indian children away from their parents and putting them in boarding schools where only English was allowed, and students were often punished for speaking their traditional languages. Upon returning to their homes, many could no longer communicate with their own close relatives and neighbors.

While now abolished, these institutions and the historical policies that shaped them did lasting damage to American Indian groups striving to maintain their cultural heritage. Especially over the past three decades many of these besieged indigenous communities have

linguistic nationalism The attempt by ethnic minorities and even countries to proclaim independence by purging their language of foreign terms.

[3] www.unesco.org/webworld/babel.

Anthropology Applied

Language Renewal among the Northern Ute ■ By William Leap

On April 10, 1984, the Northern Ute tribe became the first community of American Indians in the United States to affirm the right of its members to regain and maintain fluency in their ancestral language, as well as their right to use it as a means of communication throughout their lives. Like many other Native Americans, they had experienced a decline in fluency in their native tongue, as they were forced to interact more and more intensively with outsiders who spoke only English.

Once the on-reservation boarding school was closed in 1953, Ute children had to attend schools where teachers and most other students were ignorant of the Ute language. Outside the classroom as well, children and adults alike were increasingly bombarded by English as they sought employment off reservation, traded in non-Indian communities, or were exposed to television and other popular media. By the late 1960s, although Ute language fluency was still highly valued, many members of the community could no longer speak it.

Alarmed by this situation, a group of Ute parents decided that action needed to be taken, lest their native language be lost altogether. With the help of other community leaders and educators, they organized meetings to discuss how to remedy the situation. Aware of my work on language education with other tribes, they invited me to participate in the discussions, and subsequently the Utes

asked me to assist with their linguistic renewal efforts.

The first thing I did when I began working with the Utes in 1978 was to conduct a first-ever, reservation-wide language survey. The survey revealed that many individuals had retained a "passive fluency" in the language and could understand it, even though they couldn't speak it.[a] It also showed that children who were still able to speak Ute had fewer problems with English in school than did nonspeakers.

Over the next few years, I helped set up a Ute language renewal program within the tribe's Division of Education, helped secure funding, led staff training workshops in linguistic transcription and grammatical analysis, provided assistance in designing a practical writing system for the language, and supervised data-gathering sessions with already fluent speakers of the language.

In 1980, the local public school established an in-school program to provide instruction in English and Ute for Indian and other interested children. I helped train the language teachers (all of whom were Ute and none of whom had degrees in education) and did research

[a]See Leap, W. L. (1987). Tribally controlled culture change: The Northern Ute language renewal project. In R. M. Wulff & S. J. Fiske (Eds.), *Anthropological praxis: Translating knowledge into action.* Boulder, CO: Westview Press.

that resulted in numerous technical reports, publications, and workshops. I also helped prepare a Ute language handbook for home use so that parents and grandparents might enrich the children's language learning experience, and I put together a preliminary text for the tribe's statement of policy on language. By 1984, this policy was official, and several language development projects were in place on the reservation, all monitored and coordinated by a tribally approved language and culture committee. Although writing in Ute was not a goal, practical needs resulted in development of writing systems, and a number of people in fact became literate in the language.

I feel that these successes were possible only because the Ute themselves were actively involved in all stages of the process, from identifying the need to designing and carrying out the program. Today, Ute language and culture instruction is part of the curriculum in a tribally operated high school, and community programs have been established to build language awareness and literacy. My involvement with this effort has continued, including working with a Ute language staff to develop a dictionary and complete a grammar of sentence and paragraph structures. Most recently, the Ute's Audiovisual Department has partnered in the effort, helping design materials for Ute language instruction in electronic format.

been actively involved in language reclamation efforts, often with the aid of anthropologists specializing in linguistics—as described in this chapter's Anthropology Applied.

LANGUAGE IN ITS SOCIAL AND CULTURAL SETTINGS

As discussed in the section on descriptive linguistics, language is not simply a matter of combining sounds according to certain rules to come up with meaningful utterances. It is important to remember that languages are

spoken by people who are members of distinct societies. In addition to the fact that most societies have their own unique cultures, individuals within each society tend to vary in the ways they use language based on social factors such as gender, age, class, and ethnicity.

We choose words and sentences to communicate meaning, and what is meaningful in one community or culture may not be in another. Our use of language reflects, and is reflected by, the rest of our culture. For that reason, linguistic anthropologists also research language in relation to its various distinctive social and cultural contexts. This third branch of linguistic study falls into two categories: sociolinguistics and ethnolinguistics.

Sociolinguistics

Sociolinguistics, the study of the relationship between language and society, examines how social categories (such as age, gender, ethnicity, religion, occupation, and class) influence the use and significance of distinctive styles of speech.

Language and Gender

As a major factor in personal and social identity, gender is often reflected in language use, so it is not surprising that numerous thought-provoking sociolinguistic topics fall under the category of language and gender. These include research on **gendered speech**—distinct male and female speech patterns, which vary across social and cultural settings.

One of the first in-depth studies in this vein, done in the early 1970s, asserted that neither language nor gender can be studied independently of the socially constructed communities in which we live. Exploring the relationship of gender and power, it addressed specific issues including social factors said to contribute to North American women exhibiting less decisive speech styles than men. This study and a subsequent wave of related scholarly works have produced new insights about language as a social speech "performance" in both private and public settings.[4]

Gendered speech research also includes the study of distinct male and female syntax exhibited in various languages around the world, such as the Lakota language, still spoken at the Pine Ridge and Rosebud Indian reservations in South Dakota. When a Lakota woman asks someone, "How are you?" she says, *"Tonikthkahe?"* But when her brother poses the same question, he says, *"Toniktukahwo?"* As explained by Michael Two Horses, "Our language is gender-specific in the area of commands, queries, and a couple of other things."[5]

Learning these nuances of language is not difficult for a child growing up surrounded by Lakota speakers, but it can be hard for newcomers. So it was for U.S. film director/actor Kevin Costner and other actors in the 1990 film *Dances with Wolves,* which tells the fictional story of a white soldier's relationship with a Lakota Indian community in the 1800s. Since Costner (who plays the soldier) and several of the American Indian actors did not speak Lakota, the producers hired a Lakota woman to coach them, aiming to make the feature film as culturally authentic as possible.

Upon release, the film won critical acclaim and drew crowds to cinemas all across the country. When it showed in a theater in Rapid City, South Dakota, Lakota people

Orion Pictures Corporation/Everett Collection

Makers of the 1990 feature film *Dances with Wolves* aimed for cultural authenticity by casting Native American actors and hiring a language coach to teach Lakota to those who did not know how to speak it. However, the lessons did not include the "gendered speech" aspect of Lakota—the fact that females and males follow different rules of syntax. Consequently, when native speakers of the language later saw the finished film, they were amused to hear the actors who portrayed the Lakota warriors speaking like women.

from the nearby reservations arrived on the scene eager to see this movie about their ancestors. But when they heard Costner and his on-screen warrior friends speak, they began to snicker. As the dramatic scenes unfolded, their laughter grew. What was so hilarious? While it was true that Lakota in the audience were generally pleased to hear their own language in a major Hollywood film, they thought it very funny to hear the white hero, along with some non-Lakota Indian actors dressed as warriors, speak Lakota like women. Because the language coach had had to teach both male and female actors, and because they found the language difficult to learn, she had decided not to bother them with the complexities of gendered speech.

Social Dialects

Sociolinguists are also interested in **dialects**—varying forms of a language that reflect particular regions, occupations, or social classes and that are similar enough to be mutually intelligible.

Distinguishing dialects from languages and revealing the relationship between power and language, the

sociolinguistics The study of the relationship between language and society through examining how social categories (such as age, gender, ethnicity, religion, occupation, and class) influence the use and significance of distinctive styles of speech.

gendered speech Distinct male and female speech patterns, which vary across social and cultural settings.

dialects Varying forms of a language that reflect particular regions, occupations, or social classes and that are similar enough to be mutually intelligible.

---

[4]See Lakoff, R.T. (2004). *Language and woman's place.* M. Bucholtz (Ed.). New York: Oxford University Press.

[5]Personal communication, April 2003.

noted linguist/political activist Noam Chomsky often quoted the saying that a dialect is a language without an army.[6] Technically, all dialects are languages—there is nothing partial or sublinguistic about them—and the point at which two different dialects become distinctly different languages is roughly the point at which speakers of one are almost totally unable to communicate with speakers of the other.

Boundaries may be psychological, geographical, social, or economic, and they are not always very sharp. In the case of regional dialects, there is frequently a transitional territory, or perhaps a buffer zone, where features of both are found and understood, as between central and southern China. The fact is that if you learn the Chinese of Beijing, you will find that a Chinese person from Canton or Hong Kong will understand almost nothing of what you say, although both languages—or dialects—are usually lumped together as Chinese.

A classic example of the kind of dialect that may set one group apart from others within a single society is one spoken by many inner-city African Americans. Technically known as African American Vernacular English (AAVE), it has often been referred to as "black English" and "Ebonics." Unfortunately, there is a widespread misperception among non-AAVE speakers that this dialect is somehow substandard or defective. A basic principle of linguistics is that the selection of a so-called prestige dialect—in this case, what we may call "Standard English" as opposed to AAVE—is determined by social historical forces such as wealth and power and is not dependent on virtues or shortcomings of the dialects themselves. In fact, AAVE is a highly structured mode of speech with patterned rules of sounds and sequences like any other language or dialect. Many of its distinctive features stem from the retention of sound patterns, grammatical rules concerning verbs, and even words of the West African languages spoken by the ancestors of present-day African Americans.[7]

---

[6]See biographical entry for Chomsky in Shook, J. R., et al. (Eds.). (2004). *Dictionary of modern American philosophers, 1860–1960.* Bristol, England: Theommes Press. The saying is attributed to Yiddish linguist Max Weinreich.

[7]Monaghan, L., Hinton, L., & Kephart, R. (1997). Can't teach a dog to be a cat? The dialogue on ebonics. *Anthropology Newsletter 38* (3), 1, 8, 9.

code switching Changing from one level of language to another as the situation demands, whether from one language to another or from one dialect of a language to another.
ethnolinguistics A branch of linguistics that studies the relationships between language and culture and how they mutually influence and inform each other.
linguistic relativity The idea that distinctions encoded in one language are unique to that language.

Because the AAVE dialect differs so much from Standard English and has been discredited by mainstream society, those who speak it frequently find themselves at a disadvantage outside of their own communities. Schoolteachers, for example, often view African American children as deficient in verbal skills and have even misdiagnosed some of them as "learning impaired." The great challenge for the schools is to find ways of teaching these children how to use Standard English in those situations where it is to their advantage to do so, without detracting from their ability to use the dialect of their own community.

This has been achieved with considerable success in several other countries that have similar challenges. In Scotland, for example, Scots English is now recognized in the schools as a valid and valued way of speaking and is utilized in the teaching of Standard English. As a consequence, individuals become skilled at switching back and forth between the two dialects, depending on the situation in which one is speaking.

Without being conscious of it, we all do the same sort of thing when we switch from formality to informality in our speech, depending upon where we are and to whom we are talking. The process of changing from one language mode to another as the situation demands, whether from one language to another or from one dialect of a language to another, is known as **code switching,** and it has been the subject of a number of sociolinguistic studies.

Ethnolinguistics

The study of the relationships between language and culture, and how they mutually influence and inform each other, is the domain of **ethnolinguistics.**

In this type of research, anthropologists may investigate how a language reflects the culturally significant aspects of a people's traditional natural environment. Among the Inuit in the Canadian Arctic, for instance, we find numerous words for different types of snow, whereas Americans in a city like Detroit most likely possess a rich vocabulary allowing them to precisely distinguish between many different types of cars, categorized by model, year, and manufacturer. This is an example of **linguistic relativity**—the idea that distinctions encoded in one language are unique to that language. Another example concerns cultural categories of color. Languages have different ways of dividing and naming elements of the color spectrum, which is actually a continuum of multiple hues with no clear-cut boundaries between them. In English we speak of red, orange, yellow, green, blue, indigo, and violet, but other languages mark out different groupings. For instance, Indians in Mexico's northwestern mountains speaking Tarahumara have just one word for both "green" and "blue"—*siyoname.*

Linguistic Determinism

Related to linguistic relativity is the principle of **linguistic determinism,** the idea that language to some extent shapes the way in which people view and think about the world around them. An extreme version of this principle holds that language actually determines thought and thereby shapes behavior and culture itself. A more widely accepted view holds that thought is merely influenced by language.

Linguistic determinism is associated with the pioneering ethnolinguistic research of anthropologist Edward Sapir and his student Benjamin Lee Whorf during the 1930s and 1940s. Their research resulted in what is now known as the *Sapir-Whorf hypothesis:* that each language provides particular grooves of linguistic expression that predispose speakers of that language to perceive the world in a certain way. In Whorf's own words, "The structure of the language one habitually uses influences the manner in which one understands his environment. The picture of the universe shifts from tongue to tongue."[8]

Whorf gained many of these insights while translating English into Hopi, a North American Indian language still spoken in Arizona. Doing this work, he discovered that Hopi differs from English not only in vocabulary but also in terms of its grammatical categories such as nouns and verbs. For instance, Hopi use numbers for counting and measuring things that have physical existence, but they do not apply numbers in the same way to abstractions like time. They would have no problem translating an English sentence such as, "I see fifteen sheep grazing on three acres of grassland," but an equally simple sentence such as, "Three weeks ago, I enjoyed my fifteen minutes of fame" would require a much more complex translation into Hopi.

It is also of note that Hopi verbs express tenses differently than English verbs do. Rather than marking past, present, and future, with *-ed, -ing,* or *will,* Hopi requires additional words to indicate if an event is completed, still ongoing, or is expected to take place. So instead of saying, "Three strangers stayed for fifteen days in our village," a Hopi would say something like, "We remember three strangers stay in our village until the sixteenth day." In addition, Hopi verbs do not express tense by their forms. Unlike English verbs that change form to indicate past, present, and future, Hopi verbs distinguish between a statement of fact (if the speaker actually witnesses a certain event), a statement of expectation, and a statement that expresses regularity. For instance, when you ask an English-speaking athlete, "Do you run?" he may answer, "Yes," when in fact he may at that moment be sitting in an armchair watching TV. A Hopi athlete

asked the same question in his own language might respond, "No," because in Hopi the statement of fact "he runs" translates as *wari* ("running occurs"), whereas the statement that expresses regularity—"he runs" (on the track team) translates as *warikngwe* (running occurs characteristically).

Considering such linguistic distinctions between Hopi and English, Whorf concluded that the Hopi language structures thinking and behavior with a focus on the present—on getting ready and carrying out what needs to be done right now. He summed it up like this: "A characteristic of Hopi behavior is the emphasis on preparation. This includes announcing and getting ready for events well beforehand, elaborate precautions to insure persistence of desired conditions, and stress on good will as the preparer of good results."[9]

In the 1990s linguistic anthropologists devised new research strategies to actually test Sapir and Whorf's original hypothesis.[10] One study found that speakers of Swedish and Finnish (neighboring peoples who speak radically different languages) working at similar jobs in similar regions under similar laws and regulations show significantly different rates of on-the-job accidents. The rates are substantially lower among the Swedish speakers. What emerges from comparison of the two languages is that Swedish (one of the Indo-European languages) emphasizes information about movement in three-dimensional space. Finnish (a Ural-Altaic language unrelated to Indo-European languages) emphasizes more static relations among coherent temporal entities. As a consequence, it seems that Finns organize the workplace in a way that favors the individual person over the temporal organization in the overall production process. This in turn leads to frequent production disruptions, haste, and (ultimately) accidents. Intriguing as such studies may be, they are not sufficient by themselves for a full understanding of the relation between language and thought. Supplementary approaches are being developed.

A more obvious ethnolinguistic observation is that language mirrors or reflects, rather than determines, cultural reality. Aymara Indians living in the Bolivian highlands, for example, depend on the potato (or *luki*) as their major source of food. Their language has over

---

[8]Quoted in Hoebel, E. A. (1958). *Man in the primitive world: An introduction to anthropology* (p. 571). New York: McGraw-Hill.

[9]Carroll, J. B. (Ed.). (1956). *Language, thought and reality: Selected writings of Benjamin Lee Whorf* (p. 148). Cambridge, MA: MIT Press.

[10]Lucy, J. A. (1997). Linguistic relativity. *Annual Review of Anthropology 26,* 291–312.

---

linguistic determinism The idea that language to some extent shapes the way in which we view and think about the world around us; sometimes called the Sapir-Whorf hypothesis after its originators Edward Sapir and his student Benjamin Lee Whorf.

Kazuyoshi Namachi/Corbis

Aymara Indians living in the high-lands of Bolivia and Peru in South America depend on the potato as their major source of food. Their language has over 200 words for this vegetable, reflecting the many varieties they traditionally grow and the many different ways that they preserve and prepare it.

200 words for potatoes, reflecting the many varieties they traditionally grow and the many different ways that they preserve and prepare this food. Similarly, anthropologists have noted that the language of the Nuer, a nomadic African people of southern Sudan, is rich in words and expressions having to do with cattle; not only are more than 400 words used to describe cattle, but Nuer boys actually take their names from them. Thus, by studying the language we can determine the significance of cattle in Nuer culture and the whole etiquette of human and cattle relationships.

If language does mirror cultural reality, it would follow that changes in a culture will sooner or later be reflected in changes in the language. We see this happening all around the world today, including in the English language.

Consider, for example, the cultural practice of marriage. Historically, English-speaking North Americans have defined marriage as a legally binding union between one man and one woman. However, a growing tolerance toward homosexuals over the past two decades or so, coupled with legislation prohibiting sexual discrimination, resulted in a ruling by Canada's Supreme Court in summer 2003 that it is illegal to exclude same-sex unions from the definition of marriage. Consequently, the meaning of the word *marriage* is now being stretched. It is no longer possible to automatically assume that the term refers to the union of one man and one woman—or that a woman who mentions her spouse is speaking of a man. Such changes in the English language reflect the wider process of change in North America's cultural reality.

Linguists have found that although language is generally flexible and adaptable, established terminologies do tend to perpetuate themselves, reflecting and revealing the social structure and worldview of groups and people. For example, American English has a wide array of words having to do with conflict and warfare. It also features an abundance of militaristic metaphors, such as "conquering" space, "fighting" the "battle" of the bulge, carrying out a "war" against drugs, making a "killing" on the stock market, "shooting down" an argument, "torpedoing" a plan, "spearheading" a movement, "decapitating" a foreign government, or "bombing" on an exam, to mention just a few. An observer from an entirely different and perhaps less aggressive culture, such as the Hopi in Arizona or the Jain in India, could gain considerable insight into the importance of open competition, winning, and military might in the U.S.A. simply by tuning into such commonly used phrases.

Kinship Terms

Ethnolinguists are also interested in the kinship terms people use when referring to their relatives, for these words can reveal much about a culture. By looking at the names people in a particular society use for their relatives, an anthropologist can glean how families are structured, what relationships are considered especially important, and sometimes what the prevailing attitudes are concerning various relationships.

Kinship terminology varies considerably across cultures. For instance, a number of languages use the same word to denote a brother and a cousin, and others have a single word for cousin, niece, and nephew. Some cultures find it useful to distinguish an oldest brother from his younger brothers and have different words for these brothers. And unlike English, many languages distinguish between an aunt who is mother's sister and one who is father's sister. In an upcoming chapter on kinship, we will discuss in detail the meanings behind these and other contrasting kinship terminologies.

LANGUAGE VERSATILITY

In many societies throughout the world, it is not unusual for individuals to be fluent in two, three, or more different languages. They succeed in this in large part because they experience training in multiple languages as children—not as high school or college students, which is the educational norm in the United States.

In some regions where groups speaking different languages co-exist and interact, people often understand one another but may choose not to speak the other's language. Such is the case in the borderlands of northern Bolivia and southern Peru where Quechua-speaking and Aymara-speaking Indians are neighbors. When an Aymara farmer speaks to a Quechua herder in Aymara, the Quechua will reply in Quechua, and vice versa, each knowing that the other understands both languages even if speaking just one. The ability to comprehend two languages but express oneself in only one is known as *receptive* or *passive bilingualism.*

In the United States, perhaps reflecting the country's enormous size and power, many citizens are not interested in learning a second or foreign language. This is especially significant—and troubling—since the United States is not only one of the world's most ethnically diverse countries, but it is also the world's largest economy and heavily dependent on international trade relations. Moreover, in our globalized world, being bilingual or multilingual may open doors of communication not only for trade but for work, diplomacy, art, and friendship.

BEYOND WORDS: THE GESTURE–CALL SYSTEM

Efficient though languages are at naming and talking about ideas, actions, and things, all are insufficient to some degree in communicating certain kinds of information that people need to know in order to fully understand what is being said. For this reason, human speech is always embedded within a gesture-call system of a type that we share with nonhuman primates.

The various sounds and gestures of this system serve to "key" speech, providing listeners with the appropriate frame for interpreting what a speaker is say-

ing. Messages about human emotions and intentions are effectively communicated by this gesture-call system: Is the speaker happy, sad, mad, enthusiastic, tired, or in some other emotional state? Is he or she requesting information, denying something, reporting factually, or lying? Very little of this information is conveyed by spoken language alone. In English, for example, at least 90 percent of emotional information is transmitted not by the words spoken but by body language and tone of voice.

Body Language

The **gesture** component of the gesture-call system consists of facial expressions and bodily postures and motions that convey intended as well as subconscious messages. The method for notating and analyzing this body language is known as **kinesics.**

Humankind's repertoire of body language is enormous. This is evident if you consider just one aspect of it: the fact that a human being has eighty facial muscles and is thereby capable of making more than 7,000 facial expressions! Thus, it should not be surprising to hear that at least 60 percent of our total communication takes place nonverbally. Often, gestural messages complement spoken messages—for instance, nodding the head while af-

gesture Facial expressions and bodily postures and motions that convey intended as well as subconscious messages.
kinesics A system of notating and analyzing postures, facial expressions, and bodily motions that convey messages.

Learned gestures to which different cultures assign different meanings are known as conventional gestures. The "Hook 'em, horns" salute flashed by U.S. President Bush and his family during his 2005 inauguration shocked many Europeans who interpreted it as a salute to Satan. Known as the "devil's hand" in some parts of the world, in Bush's home state of Texas the gesture is a sign of love for the University of Texas Longhorns, whose fans shout out "Hook 'em, horns!" at sporting events. Here, Bush's daughter Jenna gives the sign.

VISUAL COUNTERPOINT

Cultures around the world have noticeably different attitudes concerning proxemics or personal space—how far apart people should position themselves in nonintimate social encounters. How does the gap between the shirt-and-tie U.S. businessmen pictured here compare with that of the robed men of Saudi Arabia?

firming something verbally, raising eyebrows when asking a question, or using hands to illustrate or emphasize what is being talked about. However, nonverbal signals are sometimes at odds with verbal ones, and they have the power to override or undercut them. For example, a person may say the words "I love you" a thousand times to someone, but if it's not true, the nonverbal signals will likely communicate that falseness.

Little scientific notice was taken of body language prior to the 1950s, but since then a great deal of research has been devoted to this intriguing subject. Cross-cultural studies in this field have shown that there are many similarities around the world in such basic facial expressions as smiling, laughing, crying, and displaying shock or anger. The smirks, frowns, and gasps that we have inherited from our primate ancestry require little learning and are harder to "fake" than conventional or socially obtained gestures that are shared by members of a group, albeit not always consciously so.

Routine greetings are also similar around the world. Europeans, Balinese, Papuans, Samoans, Bushmen, and at least some South American Indians all smile and nod, and if the individuals are especially friendly, they will raise their eyebrows with a rapid movement, keeping them raised for a fraction of a second. By doing so, they signal a readiness for contact. The Japanese, however, suppress the eyebrow flash, regarding it as indecent, showing that there are important differences, as well as similarities, cross-culturally. This can be seen in gestural expressions for yes and no. In North America, one nods

the head down then up for yes or shakes it left and right for no. The people of Sri Lanka also nod to answer yes to a factual question, but if asked to do something, a slow sideways movement of the head means yes. In Greece, the nodded head means yes, but no is indicated by jerking the head back so as to lift the face, usually with the eyes closed and the eyebrows raised.

Another aspect of body language has to do with social space: how people position themselves physically in relation to others. **Proxemics,** the cross-cultural study of humankind's perception and use of space, came to the fore through the work of anthropologist Edward Hall, who coined the term. Growing up in the culturally diverse southwestern United States, Hall glimpsed the complexities of intercultural relations early on in life. As a young man in the 1930s, he worked with construction crews of Hopi and Navajo Indians, building roads and dams. In 1942 he earned his doctorate in anthropology under the famous Franz Boas, who stressed the point that "communication constitutes the core of culture."

This idea was driven home for Hall during World War II when he commanded an African American regiment in Europe and the Philippines and again when he worked with the U.S. State Department to develop the new field of intercultural communication at the Foreign Service Institute (FSI). It was during his years at FSI (1950–1955), while training some 2,000 Foreign Service workers, that Hall's ideas about proxemics began to crystallize. He articulated them and other aspects of nonverbal communication in his 1959 book, *The Silent Language,* now recognized as the founding document for the field of intercultural communication.

His work showed that people from different cultures have different frameworks for defining and organizing

proxemics The cross-cultural study of humankind's perception and use of space.

The Origins of Language 117

space—the personal space they establish around their bodies, as well as the macrolevel sensibilities that shape cultural expectations about how streets, neighborhoods, and cities should be arranged. Among other things, his investigation of personal space revealed that every culture has distinctive norms for closeness. (You can see this for yourself if you are watching a foreign film, visiting a foreign country, or find yourself in a multicultural group. How close to one another do the people you are observing stand when talking in the street or riding in a subway or elevator? Does the pattern match the one you are accustomed to in your own cultural corner?)

Hall identified four categories of proxemically relevant spaces or body distances: intimate (0–18 inches), personal-casual (1½ – 4 feet), social-consultive (4–12 feet), and public distance (12 feet and beyond). Hall warned that different cultural definitions of socially accepted use of space within these categories can lead to serious miscommunication and misunderstanding in cross-cultural settings. His research has been a foundation stone for the present-day training of international businesspeople, diplomats, and others involved in intercultural work.

Paralanguage

The second component of the gesture-call system is **paralanguage**—specific voice effects that accompany speech and contribute to communication. These include vocalizations such as giggling, groaning, or sighing, as well as voice qualities such as pitch and tempo.

The importance of paralanguage is suggested by the comment, "It's not so much *what* was said as *how* it was said." Recent studies have shown, for example, that subliminal messages communicated below the threshold of conscious perception by seemingly minor differences in phrasing, tempo, length of answers, and the like are far more important in courtroom proceedings than even the most perceptive trial lawyer may have realized. Among other things, how a witness gives testimony alters the reception it gets from jurors and influences the witness' credibility.[11]

Communication took a radical turn in the 1990s when the use of e-mail and Internet chat rooms became widespread. Both resemble the spontaneity and speed of face-to-face communication but lack the body signals and voice qualifiers that nuance what is being said (and hint how it is being received). According to a recent study, the intended tone of e-mail messages is perceived correctly only 56 percent of the time. A misunderstood message can quickly escalate into a "flame war" with hostile and insulting messages. Because the risk of miscommunica-

tion on the Internet abounds, even with the use of interpretation signals such as LOL (laugh out loud) or the smiley face (☺), certain sensitive exchanges are usually better made in person.[12]

TONAL LANGUAGES

There is an enormous diversity in the ways languages are spoken. In addition to hundreds of vowels and consonants, sounds can be divided into tones—rises and falls in pitch that play a key role in distinguishing one word from another. About 70 percent of the world's languages are **tonal languages** in which the various distinctive sound pitches of spoken words are not only an essential part of their pronunciation but are also key to their meaning; worldwide, at least one-third of the population speaks a tonal language.

Many languages in Africa, Central America, and East Asia are tonal. For instance, Mandarin Chinese, the most common language in China, has four contrasting tones: flat, rising, falling, and falling then rising. These tones are used to distinguish among normally stressed syllables that are otherwise identical. Thus, depending on intonation, *ba* can mean "to uproot," "eight," "to hold," or "a harrow" (farm tool).[13] Cantonese, the primary language in southern China and Hong Kong, uses six contrasting tones, and some Chinese dialects have as many as nine. In nontonal languages such as English, tone can be used to convey an attitude or to change a statement into a question, but tone alone does not change the meaning of individual words as it does in Mandarin, where careless use of tones with the syllable *ma* could cause one to call someone's mother a horse!

THE ORIGINS OF LANGUAGE

Cultures all around the world have sacred stories or myths addressing the age-old question of the origin of human languages. Anthropologists collecting these stories have often found that cultural groups tend to locate the place of origin in their own ancestral homelands and believe that the first humans also spoke their language.

---

[11]O'Barr, W. M., & Conley, J. M. (1993). When a juror watches a lawyer. In W. A. Haviland & R. J. Gordon (Eds.), *Talking about people* (2nd. ed., pp. 42–45). Mountain View, CA: Mayfield.

[12]Kruger, J., et al. (2005, December). Egocentrism over e-mail: Can people communicate as well as they think? *Journal of Personality and Social Psychology* 89 (6), 925–936.

[13]Catford, J. C. (1988). *A practical introduction to phonetics* (p. 183). Oxford, England: Clarendon Press.

---

paralanguage Voice effects that accompany language and convey meaning. These include vocalizations such as giggling, groaning, or sighing, as well as voice qualities such as pitch and tempo.
tonal language A language in which the sound pitch of a spoken word is an essential part of its pronunciation and meaning.

The unfinished Tower of Babel, described in the first book of the Bible, symbolizes an ancient West Asian myth about the origins of language diversity.

© Archivo Iconographico, S. A./Corbis

For example, the Incas of Peru tell the story of Pachamacac, the divine creator, who came to the valley of Tiwanaku in the Andean highlands in ancient times. As the story goes, Pachamacac drew people up from the earth, making out of clay a person of each nation, painting each with particular clothing, and giving to each a language to be spoken and songs to be sung. On the other side of the globe, ancient Israelites believed that it was Yahweh, the divine creator and one true god, who had given them Hebrew, the original tongue spoken in paradise. Later, when humans began building the massive Tower of Babel to signify their own power and to link earth and heaven, Yahweh intervened. He created a confusion of tongues so that people could no longer understand one another, and he scattered them all across the face of the earth, leaving the tower unfinished.

The question of the origin of language has also been a fascinating subject among scientists, who have put forth some reasonable and some not so reasonable ideas on the subject: Exclamations became words, sounds in nature were imitated, or people simply got together and assigned sounds to objects and actions.

The main trouble with early efforts to explain the origin of language was that so little data were available. Today, there is more scientific evidence, including genetic data, to work with—better knowledge of primate brains, new studies of primate communication, more information on the development of linguistic competence in children, more human fossils that can be used to tentatively reconstruct what ancient brains and vocal tracts were like, and a better understanding of the lifeways of early human ancestors. We still cannot conclusively prove how, when, and where human language first developed, but we can now theorize reasonably on the basis of more and better information.

The archaeological record shows that archaic humans known as Neandertals (living from 30,000 to 125,000 years ago in Europe and Southwestern Asia) had the neural development and anatomical features necessary for speech. Recently, scientists at the Max Planck Institute for Evolutionary Anthropology in Leipzig, Germany, reported the discovery of a so-called language gene in humans, named the FOXP2 gene. Differing from versions of the gene found in other primates, it may control the ability to make fine movements of the mouth and larynx necessary for spoken language.[14]

Some noted scientists dismiss the idea of a single language gene.[15] Leading evolutionary theorist Philip Lieberman argues that the human language ability is the confluence of a succession of separate evolutionary developments rigged together by natural selection for an evolutionarily unique ability.[16]

[14]Enard, W., et al. (2002). Molecular evolution of FOXP2, a gene involved in speech and language. *Nature 418*, 869–872.

[15]For example, Robbins Burling, professor emeritus of anthropology and linguistics at the University of Michigan, commented, "It's more likely a *symphony* of genes" (personal communication). See also Burling, R. (2005). *The talking ape: How language evolved.* Oxford: Oxford University Press.

[16]Lieberman, P. (2006). *Toward an evolutionary biology of language.* Cambridge, MA: Belknap Press.

As human language is embedded within a gesture-call system of a type that we share with nonhuman primates, anthropologists have gained considerable insight on human language by observing the communication systems of fellow primates (especially apes)—comparing their anatomy with that of humans past and present and testing their ability to learn and use forms of human language such as American Sign Language (ASL). Attempts to teach other primates to actually speak like humans have not been successful. In one famous experiment in communication that went on for seven years, for example, the chimpanzee Viki learned to voice only a very few words, such as *up, mama,* and *papa*. This inability to speak is not the result of any obvious sensory or perceptual deficit, and apes can in fact produce many of the sounds used in speech. Evidently, their failure to speak has to do with either a lack of motor control mechanisms to articulate speech or to the virtually complete preoccupation of the throat and mouth for expressing emotional states, such as anger, fear, or joy.

Better results have been achieved through nonvocal methods. Recognizing the importance of gestural communication to apes, psychologists Allen and Beatrice Gardner began teaching ASL to their young chimpanzee Washoe, the first of several who have since learned to sign. With vocabularies of over 400 signs, chimps have shown themselves able to transfer each sign from its original referent to other appropriate objects and even to pictures of objects. Their vocabularies include verbs, adjectives, and such words as *sorry* and *please*; furthermore, they can string signs together properly to produce original sentences, even inflecting their signs to indicate person, place, and instrument. More impressive still, Washoe was observed spontaneously teaching her adopted son Loulis how to sign by deliberately manipulating his hand. For five years, humans had refrained from signing when in sight of Loulis, over which time he learned no fewer than fifty signs.

Chimps have not been the only subjects of ape language experiments. Gorillas and orangutans have also been taught ASL with results that replicate those obtained with chimps. As a consequence, there is now a growing agreement among researchers that all of the great apes can develop language skills at least to the level of a 2- to 3-year-old human. Not only are comprehension skills similar, but so is acquisition order: *What* and *where, what-to-do* and *who,* as well as *how* questions are acquired in that order by both apes and humans. Like humans, apes are capable of referring to events removed in time and space, a phenomenon known as **displacement** and one of the distinctive features of human language.

One of the most difficult problems for students dealing with the origin of language is the origin of syntax, which was necessary to enable our ancestors to articulate and communicate more complex ideas. Another problem involves the relationship between manual gestures and spoken language. Because continuity exists between gestural and spoken language, the latter could have emerged from the former through increasing emphasis on finely controlled movements of the mouth and throat—a scenario consistent with the appearance of neurological structures underlying language in the earliest representatives of the genus *Homo* and steady en-

displacement Referring to things and events removed in time and space.

Several species of apes have been taught to use American Sign Language. Some chimpanzees have acquired signing vocabularies surpassing 400 words, and a lowland gorilla named Koko has a working vocabulary of more than 1,000 words.

© Susan Kuklin/Photo Researchers, Inc.

largement of the human brain *before* the alteration of the vocal tract began that allows us to speak the way we do.

The advantage of spoken over gestural language to a species increasingly dependent on tool use for survival is obvious. To talk with your hands, you must stop whatever else you are doing with them; speech does not interfere with that. Other benefits include being able to talk in the dark, past opaque objects, or among speakers whose attention is diverted. Just when the changeover to spoken language took place is not known, although all would agree that spoken languages are at least as old as the species *Homo sapiens.*

Early anthropologists searched for a truly "primitive" language spoken by a living people that might show the processes of language just beginning or developing. That search has now been abandoned, for anthropologists have come to realize that there is no such thing as a "primitive" language in the world today, or even in the recent past. So far, all human languages that have been described and studied, even among people with something approximating a Stone Age technology, are highly developed, complex, and capable of expressing infinite meanings. Every language or dialect now known has a long history and has developed its own particular subtleties and complexities that reflect its speakers' way of life and what they want or need to communicate with others. Thus, anthropologists recognize that all languages are more or less equally effective as systems of communication within their own particular cultural contexts.

FROM SPEECH TO WRITING

When anthropology developed as an academic discipline over a century ago, it concentrated its attention on small traditional communities that relied primarily on personal interaction and oral communication for survival. Cultures that depend on talking and listening often have rich traditions of storytelling and speechmaking. For them, oration (from the Latin *orare,* "to speak") plays a central role in education, conflict resolution, political decision making, spiritual or supernatural practices, and many other aspects of life. Consequently, people capable of making expressive and informed speeches usually enjoy great prestige in such societies.

Today as in the past, traditional orators are typically trained from childhood in memorizing genealogies, ritual prayers, customary laws, and diplomatic agreements. In ceremonies that can last many hours, even days, they eloquently recite the oral traditions by heart. Their extraordinary memories are often enhanced by oral devices such as rhyme, rhythm, and melody. Orators may also employ special objects to help them remember proper sequences and points to be made—memory devices such as notched sticks, knotted strings, bands embroidered with shells, and so forth. Traditional Iroquois Indian orators, for example, often performed their formal speeches with wampum belts made of hemp string and purple-blue and white shell beads (quahog and whelk shells) woven into distinctive patterns. More than artful motifs, wampum designs were used to symbolize any of a variety of important messages or agreements, including treaties with other nations.

Such symbolic designs are found all over the world, some dating back more than 30,000 years. When ancient artifacts of bone, antler, stone, or some other material have been etched or painted, anthropologists try to determine if these markings were created to symbolize specific ideas such as seasonal calendars, kinship relations, trade records, and so forth. From basic visual signs such as these emerged a few writing systems, including the alphabet.

Thousands of languages, past and present, have existed only in spoken form, but many others have been documented in graphic symbols of some sort. Over time, visual representations in the form of simplified pictures of things (pictographs) evolved into more stylized symbolic forms.

Although different peoples invented a variety of graphic styles, anthropologists distinguish an actual **writing system** as a set of visible or tactile signs used to represent units of language in a systematic way. Recently discovered symbols carved into 8,600-year-old tortoise shells found in western China may represent the earliest evidence of elementary writing found anywhere.[17]

A fully developed early writing system is Egyptian hieroglyphics, developed some 5,000 years ago and in use for about 3,500 years. One of the other oldest systems in the world is cuneiform, an arrangement of wedge-shaped imprints developed primarily in Mesopotamia (present-day Iraq), which lasted nearly as long. Cuneiform writing stands out among other early forms in that it led to the first and only phonetic writing system (that is, an alphabet), ultimately spawning a wide array of alphabetic writing systems. About two millennia after these systems were established, others began to appear, developing independently in distant locations around the world. These include the oldest known hieroglyphics in the Americas, used as early as 2,900 years ago by Olmec Indians inhabiting what is now Vera Cruz, Mexico.[18]

---

writing system A set of visible or tactile signs used to represent units of language in a systematic way.

[17]Li, X. et al. (2003). The earliest writing? Sign use in the seventh millennium BC at Jiahu, Henan Province, China. *Antiquity 77,* 31–44.

[18]del Carmen Rodríguez Martínez, M., et al. (2006). Oldest writing in the New World. *Science 313* (5793), 1,610–1,614.

Tee Yee Neen Ho Ga Row, Mohawk chief of the Iroquois Confederacy, holding a wampum belt made of hemp string and shell beads (quahog and whelk shells). Wampum designs were used to symbolize a variety of important messages or agreements, including treaties with other nations. (By Dutch painter Johannes Verelst in 1710. National Archives of Canada collections.)

Tac Yee Neen Ho Gar Ton (Red Indian) Emperor of the Six Nations 1710, Verelst, Johannes or Jan (b. 1648-fl 1719)/Private Collection/The Bridgeman Art Library

Inscriptions recently discovered in Egypt's western desert suggest that our **alphabet** (a series of symbols representing the *sounds* of a language) was invented almost 4,000 years ago by Semitic-speaking peoples in that region. Analysis of the Semitic inscriptions, which were carved into a natural limestone wall alongside hundreds of Egyptian hieroglyphs, reveals that these early Semites adopted a limited number of Egyptian hieroglyphs as symbols for sounds in their own language. For instance, they took the Egyptian glyph for "ox" and determined that it would stand for the sound at the start of the Semitic word for "ox," which is *aleph*. (This symbol looks like the horned head of an ox—and like the letter *A* upside-down). Likewise, they chose the Egyptian glyph for "house" to stand for the opening sound of the Semitic word for "house," which is *beth*. (This symbol looks like a two-room house—and like the letter *B* tipped back.) The result was a writing system with characters based on a selection of Egyptian glyphs but used to represent sounds in an early Semitic language. Over the next 1,000 years, Semitic-speaking peoples inhabiting the eastern Mediterranean (including Canaanites, Hebrews, and Phoenicians) adopted this system and developed the script into a more linear form.[19]

Most of the alphabets used today descended from the Phoenician one. The Greeks adopted it about 2,800 years ago, modifying the characters to suit sounds in their own language. The word *alphabet* comes from the first two letters in the Greek writing system, *alpha* and *beta* (otherwise meaningless words in Greek.). From Greek colonies in southern Italy, the writing system spread north to Rome. Then, when Latin-speaking Romans expanded their empire throughout much of Europe, northern Africa, and western Asia, small groups of formally educated people from dozens of different nations in the realm communicated in the Latin language and used its associated alphabet. The Roman alphabet, slightly modified from Greek, spread even further from the 15th century onward as European nations expanded their trade networks and built colonial empires overseas. The 15th-century invention of the printing press fueled worldwide diffusion of the alphabet, making it possible to mechanically reproduce writings in any human language.

Although other writing systems, such as Chinese, are very widely used by millions of people, North American inventions such as the Internet in the late 20th century help solidify the use of the alphabet as a global writing system.

Literacy in Our Globalizing World

Thousands of years have passed since literacy first emerged, yet today more than 860 million adults worldwide cannot read and write. Illiteracy condemns already disadvantaged people to ongoing poverty—migrant rural workers, refugees, ethnic minorities, and those living in rural backlands and urban slums throughout the world. For example, a third of India's 1 billion inhabitants cannot read and write, and some 113 million children around the world are not enrolled in school.

Declaring literacy a human right, the United Nations established September 8 as International Literacy Day and proclaimed the period 2003 to 2012 as the Literacy Decade with the objective of extending literacy to all humanity. Every September 8 during this decade the UNESCO awards prizes to individuals or groups making particularly effective contributions to the fight against illiteracy.

[19]Himmelfarb, E. J. (2000, January/February). First alphabet found in Egypt. Newsbrief. *Archaeology 53* (1).

alphabet A series of symbols representing the sounds of a language arranged in a traditional order.

Questions for Reflection

1. In what ways do you feel prepared or unprepared to meet the challenge of communicating effectively in our increasingly globalized world?

2. Up to 4,000 languages have disappeared over the last 500 years, most of them vanishing without a trace. Only 6,500 languages remain. If the same rate of extinction continues, and just one or two languages exist in the year 2500, would that be a loss or a gain? How so?

3. Applying the principle of linguistic determinism to your own language, consider how your perceptions of objective reality might have been shaped by your language. How might your sense of reality be different if you grew up speaking Hopi?

4. Think about the gestures commonly used in your own family. Are they more or less powerful than the words expressed?

5. From its earliest days writing was linked to political power. How does that apply to modern media and globalization?

Suggested Readings

Duranti, A. (2001). Linguistic anthropology: History, ideas, and issues. In A. Duranti (Ed.), *Linguistic anthropology: A reader* (pp. 1–38). Oxford, England: Blackwell.

Good summary of the development of the field of linguistic anthropology.

Gladdol, D. (2006). *English next*. London: British Council.

A fascinating overview of the rise of English as a global language—and the socioeconomic problems this spread presents to monolingual English-speaking people. (PDF available online, free)

Lakoff, R. T. (2004). *Language and woman's place*. M. Bucholtz (Ed.). New York: Oxford University Press.

A new edition of Lakoff's 1975 seminal book on gender and language, featuring annotations by Lakoff and twenty-five essays by scholars whose own language and gender research grew out of positive and negative reactions to her original work.

Lieberman, P. (2006) *Toward an evolutionary biology of language*. Cambridge, MA: Belknap Press.

A leading evolutionary theorist of language draws on evidence from evolutionary biology, genetics, physical anthropology, anatomy, and neuroscience.

Morse, D., et al. (1979). *Gestures: Their origins and distribution*. New York: Stein & Day.

This well-illustrated text explores the derivations and distributions of dozens of gestures, as well as the varied meanings they have in different parts of the world.

Yip, M. (2002). *Tone*. New York: Cambridge University Press.

A comprehensive and clearly organized introduction to tone and tonal phonology, covering the main types of tonal systems found in Africa, the Americas, and Asia.

Thomson Audio Study Products

 Enjoy the MP3-ready Audio Lecture Overviews for each chapter and a comprehensive audio glossary of key terms for quick study and review. Whether walking to class, doing laundry, or studying at your desk, you now have the freedom to choose when, where, and how you interact with your audio-based educational media. See the preface for information on how to access this on-the-go study and review tool.

The Anthropology Resource Center

www.thomsonedu.com/anthropology
The Anthropology Resource Center provides extended learning materials to reinforce your understanding of key concepts in the four fields of anthropology. For each of the four fields, the Resource Center includes dynamic exercises including video exercises, map exercises, simulations, and "Meet the Scientists" interviews, as well as critical thinking questions that can be assigned and e-mailed to instructors. The Resource Center also provides breaking news in anthropology and interesting material on applied anthropology to help you link what you are learning to the world around you.

6 Social Identity, Personality, and Gender

© Richard Lord

CHALLENGE ISSUE

Every society faces the challenge of humanizing its children, teaching them the values and social codes that will enable them to be functioning and contributing members in the community. This is essential, for it helps ensure that the society will perpetuate itself culturally as well as biologically. Ethnographic research has revealed a wide range of approaches to raising children in order to meet this goal. These different child-rearing methods and their possible effects on adult personalities have long been of interest to anthropologists. Here, three Afghani mothers hold their daughters, whose growing up years in their traditional gender-segregated society are likely to be quite distinct from those in many other corners of the world.

What Is Enculturation?

As noted in the previous chapter, enculturation is the process by which culture is passed from one generation to the next and through which individuals become members of their society. In this chapter we investigate the details of this process, which begins soon after birth with the development of self-awareness—the ability to perceive oneself as a unique phenomenon in time and space and to judge one's own actions. For self-awareness to function, the individual must be provided with a behavioral environment. The way a person perceives and gets oriented to surrounding objects is specified by the culture in which he or she grows up. Along with object orientation, a behavioral environment includes spatial, temporal, and normative orientations.

How Does Enculturation Influence Personality?

Studies have shown that there is some kind of structural relationship between enculturation and personality development. It is also clear that each individual begins with certain broad potentials and limitations that are genetically inherited. In some cultures, "particular child-rearing practices seem to promote the development of compliant personalities, while in others different practices seem to promote more independent, self-reliant personalities.

Are Different Personalities Characteristic of Different Cultures?

Every culture emphasizes certain personality traits as good and others as bad—and has distinct ways of encouraging or discouraging those traits accordingly. Nonetheless, it is difficult to characterize cultures in terms of particular personalities. Of the several attempts made, the concept of modal personality is the most satisfactory. This recognizes that any human society has a range of individual personalities, but some will be more typical than others. Those that approximate the modal personality of a particular culture are thought of as normal. Since modal personalities may differ from one culture to another and since cultures may differ in the range of variation they will accept, it is clear that abnormal personality is a relative concept.

In 1690 English philosopher John Locke presented his *tabula rasa* theory in his book *An Essay Concerning Human Understanding*. This notion held that a newborn human was like a blank slate used as a tablet or blackboard for writing on with chalk. And what the individual became in life was written on the slate by his or her life experiences. The implication is that at birth all individuals are basically the same in their potential for personality development and that their adult personalities are exclusively the products of their postbirth experiences, which differ from culture to culture.

Locke's idea offered high hopes for the all-embracing impact of intellectual and moral instruction on a child's character formation, but it missed the mark, for it did not take into consideration what we now know: Based on recent breakthroughs in human genetic research, most anthropologists now recognize that a substantial portion of our behavior is influenced by genetic factors.[1] What scientific research has not determined, however, is which genes or gene combinations are linked to human social behavior, and to what degree social, cultural, environmental, or a variety of other factors play a formative role in determining adult personality. Indeed, even though genetic coding is tied to aspects of personality, cultural factors play a vital role as they shape how biological variations are interpreted and valued. In other words, while this genetic inheritance sets certain broad potentials and limitations, an individual's cultural identity and unique life experiences, particularly in the early years, also play a significant role in this formation.

Since different cultures handle the raising and instruction or education of the young in different ways, child-rearing practices and their effects on adult personalities are important subjects of anthropological inquiry. Such cross-cultural studies gave rise to the specialization of psychological anthropology and are the subjects of this chapter.

ENCULTURATION: THE HUMAN SELF AND SOCIAL IDENTITY

From the moment of birth, a person faces multiple survival challenges. Obviously, newborns cannot take care of their own biological needs. Only in myths and romantic fantasies do we encounter stories about children successfully coming of age alone in the wilderness or accomplishing this feat having been raised by animals in the wild. For example, Italians in Rome still celebrate the mythological founders of their city, the twin broth-

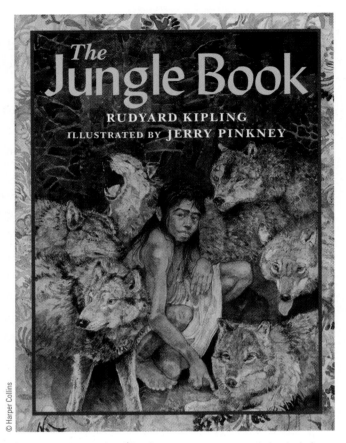

© Harper Collins

In 1916 the international Boy Scout movement expanded to include younger boys in a "cub scout" program inspired by Rudyard Kipling's *The Jungle Book* (1894). Born in former British India (1865), Kipling wrote this story about a young boy in India named Mowgli being raised by a wolf as one of her own cubs. Translated into some forty languages, including Hindi, Swahili, and Chinese, the book has been the subject of many cartoons and movies. Despite happy wild-child legends, human infants are biologically ill-equipped to survive successfully without culture.

ers Romulus and Remus, who according to legend were suckled as infants by a she-wolf. Also, millions of children around the world have been fascinated by stories about Tarzan and the apes or the jungle boy Mowgli and the wolves. Moreover, young and old alike have been captivated by newspaper hoaxes about "wild" children, such as a 10-year-old boy reported to have been found running among gazelles in the Syrian desert in 1946.

Fanciful imaginations aside, human children are biologically ill-equipped to survive without culture. This point has been driven home by several documented cases about feral children (feral comes from *fera,* which is Latin for "wild animal") who grew up deprived of human contact. None of them had a happy ending. For instance, there was nothing romantic about the girl Kamala, supposedly rescued from a wolf den in India in 1920: She moved about on all fours and could not feed herself. And everyone in Paris considered the naked "wild boy" captured in the woods outside Aveyron village in 1800 an

---

[1]http://www.healthanddna.com/behavioralgenetics.html.

incurable idiot. Clearly, the biological capacity for what we think of as human, which entails culture, must be nurtured to be realized.

Because culture is socially constructed and learned rather than biologically inherited, all societies must somehow ensure that culture is adequately transmitted from one generation to the next—a process we have already defined as *enculturation*. Since each group lives by a particular set of cultural rules, a child will have to learn the rules of his or her society in order to survive. Most of that learning takes place in the first few years when a child learns how to feel, think, speak, and, ultimately, act like an adult who embodies being Japanese, Kikuyu, Lakota, Norwegian, or whatever ethnic or national group into which it is born.

The first agents of enculturation in all societies are the members of the household into which a person is born. Initially, the most important member of this household is the newborn's mother. (In fact, cultural factors are at work even before a child is born, through what a pregnant mother eats, drinks, and inhales, as well as the sound, rhythm, and activity patterns of her daily life.) Soon thereafter, other household members come to play roles in the enculturation process. Just who these others are depends on how households are structured in the particular society.

THOMSON AUDIO STUDY PRODUCTS Take advantage of the MP3-ready Audio Lecture Overviews and comprehensive audio glossary of key terms for each chapter. See the preface for information on how to access this on-the-go study and review tool.

As the young person matures, individuals outside the household are brought into the enculturation process. These usually include other relatives and certainly the individual's peers. The latter may be included informally in the form of playgroups or formally in age associations, where children actually teach other children. In some societies, and the United States is a good example, professionals are brought into the process to provide formal instruction. In many societies, however, children are pretty much allowed to learn through observation and participation, at their own speed.

Self-Awareness

Enculturation begins with the development of **self-awareness**—the ability to identify oneself as an individual creature, to reflect on oneself, and to evaluate oneself. Humans do not have this ability at birth, even though it is essential for their successful social functioning. It is self-awareness that permits one to assume responsibility for one's conduct, to learn how to react to others, and to assume a variety of roles in society. An important aspect of self-awareness is the attachment of positive value to one's self. Without this, individuals cannot be motivated to act to their advantage rather than disadvantage.

Self-awareness does not come all at once. In modern industrial and postindustrial societies, for example, self and non-self are not clearly distinguished until a child is about 2 years of age. This development of self-awareness in children growing up in such large-scale societies, however, may lag somewhat behind other cultures. Self-awareness develops in concert with neuromotor development, which is known to proceed at a slower rate in infants from industrial societies than in infants in many, perhaps even most, small-scale farming or foraging communities. The reasons for this slower rate are not yet clear, although the amount of human contact and stimulation that infants receive seems to play an important role. In the United States, for example, infants generally do not sleep with their parents, most often being put in rooms of their own. This is seen as an important step in making them into individuals, "owners" of themselves and their capacities, rather than part of some social whole. As a consequence, they do not experience the steady stream of personal stimuli, including smell, movement, and warmth, that they would if co-sleeping. Private sleeping also takes away the opportunity for frequent nursing through the night.

In traditional societies, infants routinely sleep with their parents, or at least their mothers. Also, they are carried or held most other times, usually in an upright position. The mother typically responds to a cry or "fuss" literally within seconds, usually offering the infant her breast. So it is among traditional Ju/'hoansi (pronounced "zhutwasi") people of southern Africa's Kalahari Desert, whose infants breastfeed on demand in short frequent bouts—commonly nursing about four times an hour, for 1 or 2 minutes at a time. Overall, a 15-week-old Ju/'hoansi infant is in close contact with its mother about 70 percent of the time, as compared with 20 percent for home-reared infants in the United States. Moreover, they usually have contact with numerous other adults and children of virtually all ages.

Overall, infants in traditional societies are usually exposed to a steady stream of various stimuli far more than most babies in contemporary North America and most other industrial and postindustrial societies. This is significant, for recent studies show that stimulation plays a key role in the "hard wiring" of the brain—it is necessary for development of the neural circuitry. Looking at breastfeeding in particular, studies show that the longer a child is breastfed, the higher he or she will score on cognitive tests and the lower the risk of attention deficit

self-awareness The ability to identify oneself as an individual, to reflect on oneself, and to evaluate oneself.

VISUAL COUNTERPOINT

Self-awareness is not restricted to humans. This chimpanzee knows that the individual in the mirror is himself and not some other chimp, just as the girl recognizes herself.

hyperactivity disorder. Furthermore, breastfed children have fewer allergies, fewer ear infections, less diarrhea, and are at less risk of sudden infant death syndrome. Nonetheless breastfeeding tends to be relatively short-lived at best in the industrialized world, in part due to workplace conditions that rarely facilitate it.[2]

Social Identity Through Personal Naming

Personal names are important devices for self-definition in all cultures. It is through naming that a social group acknowledges a child's birthright and establishes its social identity. Without a name, an individual has no identity, no self. For this reason, many cultures consider name selection to be an important issue and mark the naming of a child with a special event or ritual known as a **naming ceremony.**

For instance, Aymara Indians in the Bolivian highland village of Laymi do not consider an infant truly human until they have given it a name. And naming does not happen until the child begins to speak the Aymara language, typically around the age of 2. Once the child shows the ability to speak like a human, he or she is considered fit to be recognized as such with a proper name. The naming ceremony marks their social transition from a state of "nature" to "culture" and consequently to full acceptance into the Laymi community.

There are countless contrasting approaches to naming. Icelanders name babies at birth and still follow an ancient custom in which children use their father's personal given name as their last name. A son adds the suffix *sen* to the name and a daughter adds *dottir*. Thus, a brother and sister whose father is named Sven Olafsen would have the last names Svensen and Svendottir. Among the Netsilik Inuit in Arctic Canada, women experiencing a difficult delivery would call out the names of deceased people of admirable character. The name being called at the moment of birth was thought to enter the infant's body and help the delivery, and the child would bear that name thereafter. Inuit parents may also name their children for deceased relatives in the belief that the spiritual identification will help shape their character.[3]

In many cultures, a person receives a name soon after birth but may acquire new names during subsequent life phases. A Hopi child, for instance, is born into its mother's clan. Cared for by the elder women, the new-

[2]Dettwyler, K. A. (1997, October). When to wean. *Natural History,* 49; Stuart-MacAdam, P., & Dettwyler, K. A. (Eds.). (1995). *Breastfeeding: Biocultural perspectives.* New York: Aldine de Gruyter.

naming ceremony A special event or ritual to mark the naming of a child.

[3]Balikci, A. (1970). *The Netsilik Eskimo.* Garden City, NY: Natural History Press.

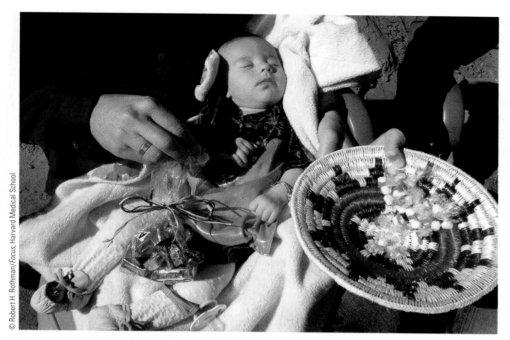

Navajo babies begin to learn the importance of community at a special First Laugh Ceremony (Chi Dlo Dil). At this event, the person who prompted an infant's first laugh teaches the little child (and reminds the community) about the joy of generosity by helping the baby give symbolic gifts of sweets and rock salt to each guest. Pictured here is the baby daughter of a pediatrician working at a remote clinic on the reservation. She celebrates her first laugh wearing a Navajo dress and jewelry given to her by her mother's Navajo patients.

born spends the first nineteen days of its life wrapped in a blanket and secluded indoors. Placed next to the infant are two perfectly shaped ears of corn, referred to as Mother Corn. On the twentieth day, the father's sister gives the baby its name in a sunrise ceremony. At age 6, the child receives another name in a religious ceremony. Reaching adulthood, the person gets yet another name and keeps that one till the end of her or his life. Yet one more name is bestowed upon a Hopi at death, a name that is not to be mentioned after it is given.

Navajo Indians from the southwestern United States name children at birth, but traditionalists often give the baby an additional ancestral clan name soon after the child laughs for the first time. Among the Navajo, the laugh represents an infant's first expression of human language. It signals the beginning of life as a social being and is therefore an occasion for celebration. The person who prompted that very first laugh invites family and close friends to a First Laugh Ceremony (Chi Dlo Dil). At the gathering, the party sponsor holds and helps the child through an important social ritual: Placing rock salt in the baby's hand, he or she helps brush the salt all over the little one's body. Representing tears—of both laughter and crying—the salt is said to provide strength and protection, leading to a long, happy life. Then the ancestral name is given. Next, because a central purpose of the occasion is to ensure that the child will become a generous and selfless adult, the sponsor helps the baby give sweets and a piece of salt to each and every guest as they step forward to greet and welcome the child into the embrace of the community. By accepting these symbolic gifts, guests also receive strength and protection.

And by participating in this laughing ceremony, young and old alike are pleasantly reminded of the importance of generosity and sharing as traditional values in their community. After the ritual, everyone enjoys a great meal together.[4]

Among the many cultural rules that exist in each society, those having to do with naming are unique because they individualize a person while at the same time identify one as part of a group and even connect the person to the spirit world. In short, name-giving customs play an important role in a person's life journey as a socially accepted member of a culture.

The Self and the Behavioral Environment

The development of self-awareness requires basic orientations that structure the psychological field in which the self acts. These include object orientation, spatial orientation, temporal orientation, and normative orientation.

First, each individual must learn about a world of objects other than the self. Through this *object orientation*, each culture singles out for attention certain environmental features, while ignoring others or lumping them together into broad categories. A culture also *explains* the perceived environment. This is important, for a cultural explanation of one's surroundings imposes a measure of

---

[4]Authors' participant observation at traditional Navajo First Laugh ceremony of Wesley Bitsie-Baldwin; personal communication LaVerne Bitsie-Baldwin and Anjanette Bitsie.

order and provides the individual with a sense of direction needed to act meaningfully and effectively.

Behind this lies a powerful psychological drive to reduce uncertainty—part of the common human need for a balanced and integrated perspective on the relevant universe. When confronted with ambiguity and uncertainty, people invariably strive to clarify and give structure to the situation; they do this, of course, in ways that their particular culture deems appropriate. Thus, we should not be surprised to find that observations and explanations of the universe are largely culturally constructed and mediated symbolically through language. In fact, everything in the physical environment varies in the way it is perceived and experienced by humans. In short, we might say that the world around us is perceived through a cultural lens.

The behavioral environment in which the self acts also involves *spatial orientation,* or the ability to get from one object or place to another. In all societies, the names and significant features of places are important references for spatial orientation. Traditionally, geographic place names often contain references to significant features in the landscape. For instance, the name of the Mississippi in North America means literally "big river"; the English coastal city of Plymouth is located at the mouth of the river Plym; and the riverside city of Bamako, Mali, in West Africa translates as "crocodile river." Finding your way to class, remembering where you left your car keys, directing someone to the nearest bus stop, or traveling through deep underground networks in subway tunnels are examples of highly complex cognitive tasks based on spatial orientation and memory. So is a desert nomad's ability to travel long distances from one remote oasis to another—determining the route by means of a mental map of the vast open landscape and gauging his location by the position of the sun in daytime, the stars at night, and even by the winds and smell of the air. Without these spatial orientations, navigating through daily life would be impossible.

Temporal orientation, which gives people a sense of their place in time, is also part of the behavioral environment. Connecting past actions with those of the present and future provides a sense of self-continuity. This is the function of calendars, for example. Derived from the Latin word *kalendae,* which originally referred to a public announcement at the first day of a new month, or moon, such a chart gives people a sense of where they are in the earth's annual cycle. Just as the perceived environment of objects is organized in cultural terms, so too are time and space.

A final aspect of the behavioral environment is the *normative orientation.* Moral values, ideals, and principles, which are purely cultural in origin, are as much a part of the individual's behavioral environment as

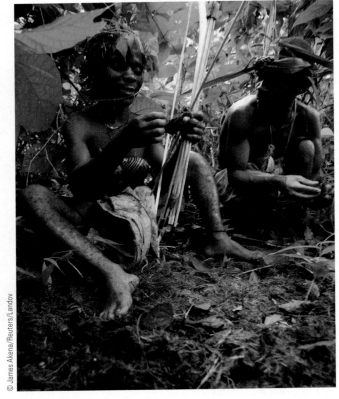

Dark and foreboding to outsiders, the Ituri forest in the tropical heart of Africa is viewed with affection by the Mbuti foragers who live there. In their eyes, it is like a benevolent parent, providing them with all they ask for: sustenance, protection, and security.

are trees, rivers, and mountains. Without them people would have nothing by which to gauge their own actions or those of others. In short, the self-evaluation aspect of self-awareness could not be made functional. Normative orientation includes standards that indicate what ranges of behavior are acceptable for males and females in a particular society. Such behavior is embedded in biology but modified by culture, so it should not be surprising that they vary cross-culturally.

PERSONALITY

In the process of enculturation, we have seen that each individual is introduced to the ideas of self and the behavioral environment characteristic of his or her culture. The result is the creation of a kind of mental map of the world in which the individual will think and act. It is his or her particular map of how to run the maze of life. When we speak of someone's personality, we are generalizing about that person's cognitive map over time. Hence, personalities are products of enculturation, as experienced by individuals, each with his or her distinctive genetic makeup.

Personality does not lend itself to a formal definition, but for our purposes we may take it as the distinctive way a person thinks, feels, and behaves. Derived from the Latin word *persōna,* meaning "mask," the term relates to the idea of learning to play one's role on the stage of daily life. Gradually, the "mask," as it is "placed" on the face of a child, begins to shape that person until there is little sense of the mask as a superimposed alien force. Instead it feels natural, as if one were born with it. The individual has successfully internalized the culture.

The Development of Personality

Although *what* one learns is important to personality development, most anthropologists assume that *how* one learns is no less important. Along with psychological theorists, anthropologists view childhood experiences as strongly influencing adult personality. Indeed, many anthropologists have been attracted to Freudian psychoanalytic theory, but with a critical eye.

Psychological literature tends to be long on speculative concepts, clinical data, and studies that are culture-bound. Anthropologists, for their part, are most interested in studies that seek to prove, modify, or at least shed light on the cultural differences in shaping personality. For example, the traditional ideal in Western societies has been for men to be tough, aggressive, assertive, dominant, and self-reliant, whereas women have been expected to be gentle, passive, obedient, and caring. To many, these personality contrasts between the sexes seem so natural that they are thought to be biologically grounded and therefore fundamental, unchangeable, and universal. But are they? Have anthropologists identified any psychological or personality characteristics that universally differentiate men and women?

North American anthropologist Margaret Mead is well known as a pioneer in the cross-cultural study of both personality and gender (see Anthropologists of Note, p. 389). In the early 1930s she studied three ethnic groups in Papua New Guinea—the Arapesh, the Mundugamor, and the Tchambuli. This comparative research suggested that whatever biological differences exist between men and women, they are extremely malleable. In short, she concluded, biology is not destiny. Mead found that among the Arapesh, relations between men and women were expected to be equal, with both genders exhibiting what most North Americans traditionally consider feminine traits (cooperative, nurturing, and gentle).[5] She also discovered gender equality among the Mundugamor (now generally called Biwat); however, in that community both genders displayed supposedly masculine traits (individualistic, assertive, volatile, aggressive). Among the Tchambuli (now called Chambri), however, Mead found that women dominated men.

Recent anthropological research suggests that some of Mead's interpretations of gender roles were incorrect—for instance, Chambri women neither dominate Chambri men, nor vice versa. Yet, overall her research generated new insights into the human condition, showing that male dominance is a cultural construct and, consequently, that alternative gender arrangements can be created. Although biological influence in male–female behavior cannot be ruled out (in fact, debate continues about the genetic and hormonal factors at play), it has nonetheless become clear that each culture provides different opportunities and has different expectations for ideal or acceptable behavior.[6]

To understand the importance of child-rearing practices for the development of gender-related personality characteristics, we may take another brief look at the already mentioned Ju/'hoansi, people native to the Kalahari Desert of Namibia and Botswana in southern Africa. The Ju/'hoansi are one of a number of groups traditionally referred to as Bushmen, who were once widespread through much of southern Africa. Traditionally subsisting as nomadic hunter–gatherers (foragers), in the past three decades many Ju/'hoansi have been forced to settle down—tending small herds of goats, planting gardens for their livelihood, and engaging in occasional wage labor.[7]

Among those who traditionally forage for a living, equality is stressed, and dominance and aggressiveness are not tolerated in either gender. Ju/'hoansi men are as mild-mannered as the women, and women are as energetic and self-reliant as the men. By contrast, among the Ju/'hoansi who have recently settled in permanent villages, men and women exhibit personality characteristics resembling those traditionally thought of as typically masculine and feminine in North America and other industrial societies.

Among the food foragers, each newborn child receives lengthy, intensive care from its mother during the first few years of life, for the space between births is typically four to five years. This is not to say that mothers are constantly with their children. For instance, when

---

[5]Mead, M. (1950). *Sex and temperament in three primitive societies.* New York: New American Library. (orig. 1935).

[6]Errington, F. K., & Gewertz, D. B. (2001). *Cultural alternatives and a feminist anthropology: An analysis of culturally constructed gender interests in Papua New Guinea.* Cambridge, England, and New York: Cambridge University Press.

[7]Draper, P. (1975). !Kung women: Contrasts in sexual egalitarianism in foraging and sedentary contexts. In R. Reiter (Ed.), *Toward an anthropology of women* (pp. 77–109). New York: Monthly Review Press.

personality The distinctive way a person thinks, feels, and behaves.

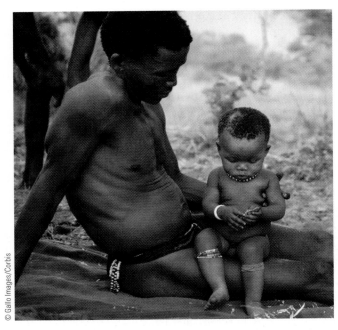

In traditional Ju/'hoansi society, fathers as well as mothers show great indulgence to children, who do not fear or respect men more than women.

women go to collect wild plant foods in the bush, they do not always take their offspring along. At such times, the children are supervised by their fathers or other community adults, one-third to one-half of whom are always found in camp on any given day. Because these include men as well as women, children are as much habituated to the male as to the female presence.

Traditional Ju/'hoansi fathers spend much time with their offspring, interacting with them in nonauthoritarian ways. Although they may correct their children's behavior, so may women who neither defer to male authority nor use the threat of paternal punishment. Thus, among Ju/'hoansi foragers, no one grows up to respect or fear male authority any more than female authority. In fact, instead of being punished, a child who misbehaves will simply be carried away and introduced to some other more agreeable activity.

Neither boys nor girls are assigned chores. Children of both sexes do equally little work. Instead, they spend much of their time in playgroups that include members of both sexes of widely different ages. And when it comes to older children keeping an eye out for the younger ones, this is done spontaneously rather than as an assigned task, and the burden does not fall more heavily on girls than boys. In short, Ju/'hoansi children in traditional foraging groups have few experiences that set one gender apart from the other.

The situation is different among Ju/'hoansi who have been forced to abandon their traditional life as foragers and now reside in permanent settlements: Women spend much of their time in and around the home preparing food, attending to other domestic chores, and tending the children. Men, meanwhile, spend many hours outside the household growing crops, raising animals, or doing wage labor. As a result, children are less habituated to their presence. This remoteness of the men, coupled with their more extensive knowledge of the outside world and their cash, tends to strengthen male influence within the household.

Within village households, gender typecasting begins early. As soon as girls are old enough, they are expected to attend to many of the needs of their younger siblings, thereby allowing their mothers more time to deal with other domestic tasks. This not only shapes but also limits the behavior of girls, who cannot range as widely or explore as freely and independently as they could without little brothers and sisters in tow. Indeed, they must stay close to home and be more careful, more obedient, and more sensitive to the wishes of others than they otherwise might be. Boys, by contrast, have little to do with the handling of infants, and when they are assigned work, it generally takes them away from the household. Thus, the space that village girls occupy becomes restricted, and they are trained in behaviors that promote passivity and nurturance, whereas village boys begin to learn the distant, controlling roles they will later play as adult men.

From this comparison, we may begin to understand how a society's economy helps structure the way a child is brought up, and how this, in turn, influences the adult personality. It also shows that alternatives exist to the way that children are raised—which means that changing the societal conditions in which one's children grow up can alter significantly the way men and women act and interact.

Dependence Training

Some years after Margaret Mead's pioneering comparative research on gender in three Papua communities, psychological anthropologists carried out a significant and more wide-ranging series of cross-cultural studies on the effects of child rearing on personality. Among other things, their work showed that it is possible to distinguish between two general patterns of child rearing. These patterns stem from a number of practices that, regardless of the reason for their existence, have the effect of emphasizing dependence on the one hand and independence on the other. Thus, for convenience, we may speak of "dependence training" and "independence training."[8]

Dependence training socializes people to think of themselves in terms of the larger whole. Its effect is to create community members whose idea of selfhood transcends individualism, promoting compliance in the performance of assigned tasks and keeping individuals within the group. This pattern is typically associated with extended families, which consist of several husband-wife-children units within the same household. It is most likely to be found in societies with an economy based on subsistence farming but also in foraging groups where several family groups may live together for at least part of the year. Big extended families are important, for they provide the labor force necessary to till the soil, tend whatever flocks are kept, and carry out other part-time economic pursuits considered necessary for existence. These large families, however, have built into them certain potentially disruptive tensions. For example, important family decisions must be collectively accepted and followed. In addition, the in-marrying spouses—husbands and/or wives who come from other groups—must conform themselves to the group's will, something that may not be easy for them.

Dependence training helps to keep these potential problems under control and involves both supportive and corrective aspects. On the supportive side, indulgence is shown to young children, particularly in the form of breastfeeding, which is provided on demand and continues for several years. This may be interpreted as rewarding the child for seeking support within the family, the main agent in meeting the child's needs. Also on the supportive side, children at a relatively early age are assigned a number of child-care and domestic tasks, all of which make significant and obvious contributions to the family's welfare. Thus, family members all actively work to help and support one another.

On the corrective side, behavior the adults interpret as aggressive or selfish is likely to be actively discouraged. Moreover, the adults tend to be insistent on overall obedience, which commonly inclines the individual toward being subordinate to the group. This combination of encouragement and discouragement in the socialization process teaches individuals to put the group's needs above their own—to be obedient, supportive, noncompetitive, and generally responsible, to stay within the fold and not do anything potentially disruptive. Indeed, a person's very definition of self comes from the individual being a part of a larger social whole rather than from his or her mere individual existence.

Independence Training

By contrast, **independence training** fosters individual independence, self-reliance, and personal achievement. It is typically associated with societies in which a basic social unit consisting of parent(s) and offspring fends for itself. Independence training is particularly characteristic of mercantile (trading), industrial, and postindustrial societies where self-sufficiency and personal achievement are important traits for success, if not survival—especially for men, and increasingly for women.

Again, this pattern of training involves both encouragement and discouragement. On the negative side, infant feeding is prompted more by schedule than demand. In North America, as noted above, babies are rarely nursed for more than a year, if that. Many parents resort to an artificial nipple or teething ring (pacifier) to satisfy the baby's sucking instincts—typically doing so to calm the child rather than out of an awareness that infants need sucking to strengthen and train coordination in the muscles used for feeding and speech.

In addition, North American parents are comparatively quick to start feeding infants baby food and even try to get them to feed themselves. Many are delighted if they can prop their infants up in the crib or playpen so that they can hold their own bottles. Moreover, as soon after birth as possible, children are commonly given their own private space, away from their parents. As already noted, infants do not receive the amount of attention they so often do in nonindustrial societies. In the United States a mother may be very affectionate with her 15-week-old infant during the 20 percent of the time she is in contact with it, but typically for the other 80 percent of the time the baby is more or less on its own, usually within hearing range of the mother or caretaker(s).

Collective responsibility is not pushed in children; they are not usually given responsible tasks to perform until later in childhood; and these are often carried out for personal benefit (such as to earn an allowance to spend as they wish) rather than as contributions to the family's welfare.

---

[8]Whiting, J. W. M., & Child, I. L. (1953). *Child training and personality: A cross-cultural study.* New Haven, CT: Yale University Press.

---

dependence training Child-rearing practices that foster compliance in the performance of assigned tasks and dependence on the domestic group, rather than reliance on oneself.
independence training Child-rearing practices that foster independence, self-reliance, and personal achievement.

Displays of individual will, assertiveness, and even aggression are encouraged, or at least tolerated to a greater degree than where dependence training is the rule. In schools, and even in the family, competition and winning are emphasized. Schools in the United States, for example, devote considerable resources to competitive sports. Competition is fostered within the classroom as well: overtly through such devices as spelling bees and awards, covertly through such devices as grading on a curve. In addition, there are various popularity contests, such as crowning a prom queen and king or holding an election to choose the classmate who is "best looking" or "most likely to succeed."

Thus, by the time individuals have grown up in U.S. society, they have received a clear message: Life is about winning or losing, and losing is equal to failure. Often, success is viewed as something that comes at someone else's expense. As anthropologist Colin Turnbull observed, "Even the team spirit, so loudly touted" in U.S. school athletics (or out of school in Little League baseball and the like), "is merely a more efficient way, through limited cooperation, to 'beat' a greater number of people more efficiently."[9]

In sum, independence training generally encourages individuals to seek help and attention rather than to give it and to try to exert individual dominance. Such qualities are useful in societies with hierarchical social structures that emphasize personal achievement and where individuals are expected to look out for their own interests. Its socialization patterns match cultural values and expectations increasingly prevalent in the spread of global capitalism.

Combined Dependence/Independence Training

In actuality, dependence and independence training represent extremes along a continuum, and particular situations may include elements of both. This is the case in child-rearing practices in food-foraging societies, for example. "Share and share alike" is the order of the day, so competitive behavior, which can interfere with the cooperation on which all else depends, is discouraged. Thus, infants receive much in the way of positive, affectionate attention from adults, including extended breastfeeding from the mother. This, as well as low pressure for compliance and a lack of emphasis on competition, encourages individuals to be more supportive of one another than is often the case in modern industrial and postindustrial societies. At the same time, personal achievement and independence are encouraged, for those individuals most capable of self-reliance are apt to be the most successful in the food quest.

---

[9]Turnbull, C. M. (1983). *The human cycle* (p. 74). New York: Simon & Schuster.

In North America the argument is sometimes made that "permissive" child rearing produces irresponsible adults. Yet the practices of food foragers seem to be about as "permissive" as they can get, and socially responsible adults are produced. The fact is that none of these child-rearing systems is inherently better or worse than any other; what matters is whether the system is functional or dysfunctional in the context of a particular society. If compliant adults who are accepting of authority are required, then independence training will not work well in that society. Nor will dependence training serve very well a society whose adults are expected to be self-reliant, questioning of authority, and ready to explore and embrace new ways of doing things.

Group Personality

From studies such as those reviewed here, it is clear that personality, child-rearing practices, and other aspects of culture are systemically interrelated. The existence of a close, if not causal, relationship between child-rearing practices and personality development, coupled with variation in child-rearing practices from one society to another, have led to a number of attempts to characterize whole societies in terms of particular kinds of personalities. Indeed, common sense suggests that personalities appropriate for one culture may be less appropriate for others. For example, an egocentric, aggressive personality would be out of place where cooperation and sharing are the keys to success.

Unfortunately, common sense, like conventional wisdom in general, is not always the truth. A question worth asking is: Can we describe a group personality without falling into stereotyping? The answer appears to be a qualified yes; in an abstract way, we may speak of a generalized "cultural personality" for a society, as long as we do not expect to find a uniformity of personalities within that society. Put another way, each individual develops certain personality characteristics that, from common experience, resemble those of other people. Yet, each human being also acquires distinct personality traits because every individual is exposed to unique sets of experiences and may react to shared experiences in novel ways. Moreover, each person brings to these experiences a one-of-a-kind genetic potential (except in the case of identical twins) that plays a role in determining personality.

This is evident, if not obvious, in every society—including even the most traditional ones. Consider for example the Yanomami Indians, who subsist on foraging and horticulture in the tropical forests of northern Brazil and southern Venezuela. Commonly, Yanomami men strive to achieve a reputation for fierceness and aggressiveness, and they defend that reputation at the risk

Anthropologists of Note

Margaret Mead (1901–1978) ▪ Ruth Fulton Benedict (1887–1947)

© AP Images

Although all of the academic sciences are able to look back and honor certain "founding fathers," anthropologists take pride in the fact that they have a number of "founding mothers" whose pioneering work they celebrate. One is **Margaret Mead,** who was encouraged by her professor Franz Boas to pursue a career in anthropology when few other professions accepted women into their ranks.

As a 24-year-old doctoral candidate, she set out for the Pacific Ocean island of Samoa to test the theory (then widely accepted) that the biological changes of adolescence were always fraught with social, psychological, and emotional stress. Based on her fieldwork there, she later wrote the book *Coming of Age in Samoa: A Psychological Study of Primitive Youth for Western Civilization,* explaining that adolescence does not have to be a time of stress and strain, but cultural conditions may make it so. Published in 1928, this book is generally credited as marking the beginning of psychological anthropology (culture and personality).

Pioneering works, however, are rarely without their faults, and *Coming of Age* is no exception. For one, Mead's time in the field (nine months) was not enough to understand fully the nuances of native speech and body language necessary to comprehend the innermost feelings of her informants. Furthermore, her sample of Samoan adolescents was a mere fifty, half of whom had not yet passed puberty. That she exaggerated her findings is suggested by her dismissal as "deviant" those girls who did not fit her ideal and by inconsistencies with data collected elsewhere in Polynesia.

Despite its faults, Mead's book stands as a landmark for several reasons: Not only was it a deliberate test of a Euramerican psychological hypothesis, but it also showed psychologists the value of modifying intelligence tests to make them appropriate for the population under study. Furthermore, by emphasizing the lesson to be drawn for Mead's own society, it laid the groundwork for the popularization of anthropology and advanced the cause of applied anthropology.

Ruth Benedict came late to anthropology; after her graduation from Vassar College, she taught high school English, published poetry, and tried her hand at social work. At age 31, she began studying anthropology, first at the New School for Social Research in New York City, and then at Columbia University. Having earned her doctorate under Boas, she joined his department. One of her own first students was Margaret Mead.

As Benedict herself once said, the main purpose of anthropology is "to make the world safe for human differences." In anthropology, she developed the idea that culture was a collective projection of the personality of those who created it. In her most famous book *Patterns of Culture* (1934), she compared the cultures of three peoples—the Kwakiutl Indians of the Pacific Northwest

© The Granger Collection, New York

coast in Canada, the Zuni Indians of the Arizona desert in the United States, and the Melanesians of Dobu Island off the southern shore of Papua New Guinea. She held that each was comparable to a great work of art, with an internal coherence and consistency of its own.

Seeing the Kwakiutl as egocentric, individualistic, and ecstatic in their rituals, she labeled their cultural configuration "Dionysian" (named after the Greek God of wine and noisy feasting). The Zuni, whom she saw as living by the golden mean, wanting no part of excess or disruptive psychological states and distrusting of individualism, she characterized as "Apollonian" (named after the Greek God of poetry who exemplified beauty). The Dobuans, whose culture seemed to her magic-ridden, with everyone fearing and hating everyone else, she characterized as "paranoid."

Another theme of *Patterns of Culture* is that deviance should be understood as a conflict between an individual's personality and the norms of the culture to which the person belongs. Still in print today, *Patterns* has sold close to 2 million copies in a dozen languages. It had great influence on Mead during her cross-cultural gender studies among the Papuans in New Guinea.

Although *Patterns of Culture* still enjoys popularity in some nonanthropological circles, anthropologists have long since abandoned its approach as impressionistic and not susceptible to replication. To compound the problem, Benedict's characterizations of cultures are misleading (the supposedly "Apollonian" Zunis, for example, indulge in such seemingly "Dionysian" practices as sword swallowing and walking over hot coals), and the use of such value-laden terms as "paranoid" prejudices others against the culture so labeled. Nonetheless, the book did have an enormous and valuable influence by focusing attention on the problem of the interrelation between culture and personality and by popularizing the reality of cultural variation.

of serious personal injury and death. Yet, among the Ya-nomami there are men who have quiet and somewhat retiring personalities. It is all too easy for an outsider to overlook these individuals when other, more "typical" Yanomami are in the front row, pushing and demanding attention.

Modal Personality

Obviously, any productive approach to the problem of group personality must recognize that each individual is unique to a degree in both genetic inheritance and life experiences, and it must leave room for a range of different personality types in any society. In addition, personality traits that may be regarded as appropriate in men may not be so regarded in women, and vice versa. Given all this, we may focus our attention on the **modal personality** of a group, defined as the body of character traits that occur with the highest frequency in a culturally bounded population.

Modal personality is a statistical concept rather than the personality of an average person in a particular society. As such, it opens up for investigation the questions of how societies organize diversity and how diversity relates to culture change. Such questions are easily missed if one associates a certain type of personality with one particular culture, as did some earlier anthropologists (see Ruth Benedict in Anthropologists of Note). At the same time, modal personalities of different groups can be compared.

Data on modal personality are best gathered by means of psychological tests administered to a sample of the population in question. Known as projective personality tests, those most often used by anthropologists include the Rorschach "inkblot" test and the Thematic Apperception Test (TAT). Such tests require individuals to look at an indeterminate visual image or meaningless object and tell the researcher what they see. In their description or interpretation of selected standard images or objects, individuals are assumed to project their conscious and unconscious ideas, values, and feelings.

The Rorschach test, named after a Swiss psychiatrist who first published it in the 1920s, contains ten inkblots (five in different colors and five printed in black and white). This test became especially significant for psychological anthropologists interested in modal personality studies in cultures where writing does not exist or is not widely used. The TAT, which was developed in the early 1940s, consists of a series of twenty visual images depicting one or more individuals in nonspecific or ambiguous everyday scenes or situations. Showing these pictures to different individuals in the study group, the researcher asks them to make up a story about what they are seeing and explain what the people portrayed in each picture are doing, thinking, or feeling.

These and other sorts of projective tests have in common a purposeful ambiguity that forces the individual being tested to structure the situation before responding. The idea is that one's personality is reflected in the sort of structure or definition that he or she projects into the ambiguous situation. Along with such projective tests, recording the frequency of certain behaviors, collecting and analyzing life histories and dreams, and analyzing popular tales, jokes, legends, and traditional myths can yield useful data on modal personality.

While having much to recommend it, the concept of modal personality as a means of dealing with group personality nevertheless presents certain difficulties. One is the complexity of the measurement techniques, which may be difficult to do in the field. For instance, an adequate representative sample of subjects is necessary. The problem here is twofold: making sure the sample is really representative and having the time and personnel necessary to administer the tests, conduct interviews, and so on, all of which can be lengthy proceedings.

In addition to questions about the reliability and validity of the methodology, the projective tests themselves constitute a problem, for those devised in one cultural setting may not be relevant, applicable, or inappropriate in another. (This is more of a problem with the TAT than with some other tests, although different pictures have been devised for other cultures.) To minimize any cultural bias, it is best not to rely on projective tests alone. In addition to all this, language differences or conflicting cultural values between the researcher and the individuals being studied may inhibit communication and/or lead to misinterpretation. Finally, what is being measured must be questioned. Just what, for example, is aggression? Does everyone define it the same way? Is it a legitimate entity, or does it involve other variables?

National Character

In summer 2003, Italy's tourism minister publicly commented on "typical characteristics" of Germans, referring to them as "hyper-nationalistic blondes" and "beer drinking slobs" holding "noisy burping contests" on his country's beaches.[10] Outraged (and proud of his country's excellent beer), Germany's prime minister canceled his planned vacation to Italy and demanded an official apology. Of course, many Germans think of Italians as

---

modal personality The body of character traits that occur with the highest frequency in a culturally bounded population.

[10]Italy-Germany verbal war hots up. (2003, July 9). *Deccan Herald* (Bangalore India).

dark-eyed, hot-blooded spaghetti eaters. To say so in public, however, might cause an uproar.

Unflattering stereotypes about foreigners are deeply rooted in cultural traditions everywhere. Many Japanese believe Koreans are stingy, crude, and aggressive, while many Koreans see the Japanese as cold and arrogant. Similarly, we all have in mind some image, perhaps not well defined, of the typical citizen of Russia or Mexico or England. Essentially, these are simply stereotypes. We might well ask, however, if these stereotypes have any basis in fact. In reality, does such a thing as *national character* exist?

Some anthropologists once thought that the answer might be yes. Accordingly, they embarked upon national character studies in the 1930s and 1940s, aiming to discover basic personality traits shared by the majority of the people of modern state societies. In what came to be known as the *culture and personality* movement, their research emphasized child-rearing practices and education as the factors theoretically responsible for such characteristics.

Objections to National Character Studies

The national character studies, as was recognized early on, were flawed, mainly because they made overgeneralized conclusions based on limited data, relatively small samples of informants, and questionable assumptions about developmental psychology. For instance, the concept of modal personality has a certain statistical validity, they argue, but to generalize the qualities of a complex country on the basis of such limited data is to lend insufficient recognition to the countless individuals who vary from the generalization.

Further, such studies tend to be highly subjective; for example, the tendency during the late 1930s and 1940s for anthropologists to characterize the German people as aggressive paranoids was obviously a reflection of wartime hostility rather than scientific objectivity. Finally, it has been pointed out that occupation and social status tend to cut across national boundaries. A French farmer may have less in common with a French lawyer than he does with a German farmer.

These flaws notwithstanding, national character studies were important in that they helped change the anthropological focus from traditional small-scale communities of foragers, herders, and farmers in exotic places to large-scale contemporary state societies. Moreover, they prompted new theoretical and methodological approaches to serious interdisciplinary group research.[11]

© Simon Kwong/Corbis

The collectively shared core values of Chinese culture promote the integration of the individual into a larger group, as we see in this large gathering of Hong Kong residents doing Tai Chi together.

Core Values

An alternative approach to national character—one that allows for the fact that not all personalities will conform to cultural ideals—is that of anthropologist Francis Hsu. His approach was to study **core values** (values especially promoted by a particular culture) and related personality traits. The Chinese, he suggested, value kin ties and cooperation above all else. To them, mutual dependence is the very essence of personal relationships and has been for thousands of years. Compliance and subordination of one's will to that of family and kin transcend all else, while self-reliance is neither promoted nor a source of pride.

Perhaps the core value held in highest esteem by North Americans of European descent is rugged individ-

---

[11]See Beeman, W. O. (2000). Introduction: Margaret Mead, cultural studies, and international understanding. In M. Mead & R. Métraux (Eds.), *The study of culture at a distance* (pp. xiv–xxxi). New York and Oxford: Berghahn Books.

core values Those values especially promoted by a particular culture.

ualism—traditionally for men but in recent decades for women as well. Each individual is supposed to be able to achieve anything he or she likes, given a willingness to work hard enough. From their earliest years, individuals are subjected to relentless pressures to excel, and as we have already noted, competition and winning are seen as crucial to this. Undoubtedly, this contributes to the restlessness and drive seen as characteristic for much of North American society today.

Also, to the degree that it motivates individuals to work hard and to go where the jobs are, it fits well with the demands of a modern economy. Thus, while individuals in Chinese traditional society are firmly bound into a larger group to which they have lifelong obligations, most urban North Americans are isolated from relatives other than their young children and spouse—and even the commitment to marriage has lessened. This is evident in the growing number of North American couples cohabiting without being married or having plans for marriage (Figure 6.1). Increasingly, when couples do marry, prenuptial agreements are made to protect individual assets in case of divorce—and close to 50 percent of marriages do end in divorce. Even parents and children have no legal obligations to one another once the latter have reached the age of majority.[12]

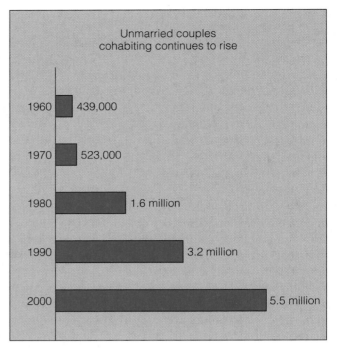

Figure 6.1

Number of unmarried couples cohabiting in the United States, by year. According to the most recent national census, in the year 2000, 8.5 percent of all cohabiting couples in the United States were unmarried. That number continues to rise.

ALTERNATIVE GENDER MODELS FROM A CROSS-CULTURAL PERSPECTIVE

As we have already discussed, the gender roles assigned to each sex vary from culture to culture and have an impact on personality formation. But what if the sex of an individual is not self-evident, as revealed in the following Original Study? Written when its author was an undergraduate student of philosophy at Bryn Mawr College in Pennsylvania, this narrative offers a compelling personal account of the emotional difficulties associated with intersexuality and gender ambiguity, while making the important point that attitudes toward gender vary cross-culturally. However, some of the cultural information is overly generalized and therefore not quite accurate, including the idea that all or most Native American spiritual-religious worldviews were and are nonhierarchical.[13]

---

[12]Observations on North American culture in this section are drawn primarily from Natadecha-Sponsal, P. (1993). The young, the rich and the famous: Individualism as an American cultural value. In P. R. DeVita & J. D. Armstrong (Eds.), *Distant mirrors: America as a foreign culture* (pp. 46–53). Belmont, CA: Wadsworth. See also Whitehead, B. D., & Popenoe, D. (2004). *The state of our unions: The social health of marriage in America 2004*. Rutgers, NJ: Rutgers University National Marriage Project.

---

[13]For scholarly accounts of the issues presented here, readers may turn to several excellent books, including the one mentioned in the Original Study: Roscoe, W. (1991). *Zuni man-woman*. Albuquerque: University of New Mexico Press.

Original Study ▪ R. K. Williamson

The Blessed Curse

One morning not so long ago, a child was born. This birth, however, was no occasion for the customary celebration. Something was wrong: something very grave, very serious, very sinister. This child was born between sexes, an "intersexed" child. From the day of its birth, this child would be caught in a series of struggles involving virtually every aspect of its life. Things that required little thought under "ordinary" circumstances were, in this instance, extraordinarily difficult. Simple questions now had an air of complexity: "What is it, a girl or a boy?" "What do we name it?" "How shall we raise it?" "Who (or what) is to blame for this?"

A Foot in Both Worlds

The child referred to in the introductory paragraph is myself. As the great-granddaughter of a Cherokee woman, I was exposed to the Native American view of people who were born intersexed, and those who exhibited transgendered characteristics. This view, unlike the Euramerican one, sees such individuals in a very positive and affirming light. Yet my immediate family (mother, father, and brothers) were firmly fixed in a negative Christian Euramerican point of view. As a result, from a very early age I was presented with two different and conflicting views of myself. This resulted in a lot of confusion within me about what I was, how I came to be born the way I was, and what my intersexuality meant in terms of my spirituality as well as my place in society.

I remember, even as a small child, getting mixed messages about my worth as a human being. My grandmother, in keeping with Native American ways, would tell me stories about my birth. She would tell me how she knew when I was born that I had a special place in life, given to me by God, the Great Spirit, and that I had been given "a great strength that girls never have, yet a gentle tenderness that boys never know" and that I was "too pretty and beautiful to be a boy only and too strong to be a girl only." She rejoiced at this "special gift" and taught me that it meant that the Great Spirit had "something important for me to do in this life." I remember how good I felt inside when she told me these things and how I soberly contemplated, even at the young age of 5, that I must be diligent and try to learn and carry out the purpose designed just for me by the Great Spirit.

My parents, however, were so repulsed by my intersexuality that they would never speak of it directly. They would just refer to it as "the work of Satan." To them, I was not at all blessed with a "special gift" from some "Great Spirit," but was "cursed and given over to the Devil" by God. My father treated me with contempt, and my mother wavered between contempt and distant indifference.

I was taken from one charismatic church to another in order to have the "demon of mixed sex" cast out of me. At some of these "deliverance" services I was even given a napkin to cough out the demon into!

In the end, no demon ever popped out of me. Still I grew up believing that there was something inherent within me that caused God to hate me, that my intersexuality was a punishment for this something, a mark of condemnation.

Whenever I stayed at my grandmother's house, my fears would be allayed, for she would once again remind me that I was fortunate to have been given this special gift. She was distraught that my parents were treating me cruelly and pleaded with them to let me live with her, but they would not let me stay at her home permanently. Nevertheless, they did let me spend a significant portion of my childhood with her. Had it not been for that, I might not have been able to survive the tremendous trials that awaited me in my walk through life.

Blessed Gift:
The Native American View

It is now known that most, if not all, Native American societies had certain individuals that fell between the categories of "man" and "woman." The various nations had different names for such people, but a term broadly used and recognized is *berdache*, a word of French origin that designated a male, passive homosexual. [The preferred term today is *two-spirit*.] Some of these individuals were born physically intersexed. Others appeared to be anatomically normal males, but exhibited the character and the manners of women—or vice versa. The way native people treated such individuals reveals some interesting insights into Native American belief systems.

The Spirit

The extent to which Native Americans see spirituality is reflected in their belief that all things have a spirit: "Every object—plants, rocks, water, air, the moon, animals, humans, the earth itself—has a spirit. The spirit of one thing (including a human) is not superior to the spirit of any other. . . . The function of religion is not to try to condemn or to change what exists, but to accept the realities of the world and to appreciate their contribu-

tions to life. Everything that exists has a purpose."

This paradigm is the core of Native American thought and action. Because everything has a spirit, and no spirit is superior to that of another, there is no "above" or "below," no "superior" or "inferior," no "dominant" and "subordinate." These are only illusions that arise from unclear thinking. Thus, an intersexed child is not derided or viewed as a "freak of nature" in many traditional Native American cultures. Intersexuality (as well as masculinity in a female or effeminacy in a male) is seen as the manifestation of the spirit of the child, so an intersexed child is respected as much as a girl child or a boy child. It is the spirit of the child that determines what the gender of the child will ultimately be. According to a Lakota, Lame Deer, "the Great Spirit made them *winktes* [two-spirit], and we accepted them as such." In this sense, the child has no control over what her or his gender will be. It follows that where there is no choice, there can be no accountability on the part of the child. Indeed, the child who is given the spirit of a *winkte* is unable to resist becoming one.

"When an Omaha boy sees the Moon Being [a feminine Spirit] on his vision quest, the spirit holds in one hand a man's bow and arrow and in the other a woman's pack strap. . . . 'When the youth tried to grasp the bow and arrows, the Moon Being crossed hands very quickly, and if the youth was not very careful he seized the pack strap instead of the bow and arrows, thereby fixing his lot in later life. In such a case he could not help acting [like a] woman, speaking, dressing, and working just as . . . women . . . do.'"

The Curse: The Euramerican View

In contrast to the view of respect and admiration of physical intersexuality and transgendered behavior traditionally held by Native Americans, the Europeans who came to "Turtle Island" (the Cherokee name for North America) brought with them their worldview, shaped by their Judaeo-Christian beliefs. According to this religious perspective, there had to be, by mandate of God, a complete dichotomy of the sexes. . .

Will Roscoe, in his book *The Zuni Man-Woman*, reports (pp. 172–73): "Spanish oppression of 'homosexual' practices in the New World took brutal

CONTINUED

CONTINUED

forms. In 1513, the explorer Balboa had some forty berdaches thrown to his dogs [to be eaten alive]—'a fine action by an honorable and Catholic Spaniard,' as one Spanish historian commented. In Peru, the Spaniards burned 'sodomites, . . . and in this way they frightened them in such a manner that they left this great sin.'"

It is abundantly clear that Christian Euramericans exerted every effort to destroy Native American culture: "In 1883, the U.S. Office of Indian Affairs issued a set of regulations that came to be known as the Code of Religious Offenses, or Religious Crimes Code. . . . Indians who refused to adopt the habits of industry, or to engage in 'civilized pursuits or employments' were subject to arrest and punishment. . . . By interfering with

native sexuality [and culture], the agents of assimilation effectively undermined the social fabric of entire tribes" (Roscoe, p. 176).

A Personal Resolution
For me, the resolution to the dual message I was receiving was slow in coming, largely due to the fear and self-hatred instilled in me by Christianity. Eventually, though, the spirit wins out. I came to adopt my Grandmother's teaching about my intersexuality. Through therapy, and a new, loving home environment, I was able to shed the constant fear of eternal punishment I felt for something I had no control over. After all, I did not create myself.

Because of my own experience, and drawing on the teaching of my grand-

mother, I am now able to see myself as a wondrous creation of the Great Spirit— but not only me. All creation is wondrous. There is a purpose for everyone in the gender spectrum. Each person's spirit is unique in her or his or her-his own way. It is only by living true to the nature that was bestowed upon us by the Great Spirit, in my view, that we are able to be at peace with ourselves and be in harmony with our neighbor. This, to me, is the Great Meaning and the Great Purpose . . .
(Adapted from R. K. Williamson (1995). The blessed curse: Spirituality and sexual difference as viewed by Euramerican and Native American cultures. The College News, 18*(4).) Reprinted with permission of the author.)* ∎

The biological facts of human nature are not always as clear-cut as most people assume. At the level of chromosomes, biological sex is determined according to whether a person's 23rd chromosomal set is XX (female) or XY (male). Some of the genes on these chromosomes control sexual development. This standard biological package does not apply to all humans, for a considerable number are **intersexuals**—people who are born with reproductive organs, genitalia, and/or sex chromosomes that are not exclusively male or female. These individuals do not fit neatly into a binary gender standard.[14]

For example, some people are born with a genetic disorder that gives biological females only one X chromosome instead of the usual two. A person with this chromosomal complex, known as Turner syndrome, develops female external genitalia but has nonfunctional ovaries and is therefore infertile. Other individuals are born with the XY sex chromosomes of a male but have an abnormality on the X chromosome that affects the

body's sensitivity to androgens (male hormones). This is known as androgen insensitivity syndrome (AIS). An adult XY person with complete AIS appears fully female with a normal clitoris, labia, and breasts. Internally, these individuals possess testes (up in the abdomen, rather than in their usual descended position in the scrotal sac), but they are otherwise born without a complete set of either male or female internal genital organs. They generally possess a short, blind-ended vagina.

"Hermaphrodites" comprise a distinct category of intersexuality—although the terms "male pseudohermaphrodite" and "female pseudohermaphrodite" are often used to refer to a range of intersex conditions. The name, objected to by many, comes from a figure in Greek mythology: Hermaphroditus (son of Hermes, messenger of the gods, and Aphrodite, goddess of beauty and love) who became half-male and half-female when he fell in love with a nymph and his body fused with hers.

True hermaphrodites have both testicular and ovarian tissue. They may have a separate ovary and testis, but more commonly they have an ovotestis—a gonad containing both sorts of tissue. About 60 percent of hermaphrodites possess XX (female) sex chromosomes, and the remainder may have XY or a mosaic (a mixture). Their external genitalia may be ambiguous or female, and they may have a uterus or (more commonly) a hemi-uterus (half uterus).

U.S. biologist Anne Fausto-Sterling, a specialist in this area, notes that the concept of intersexuality is "rooted in the very ideas of male and female" in an idealized biological world in which:

---

[14]This section is based on several sources: Chase, C. (1998). Hermaphrodites with attitude. *Gay and Lesbian Quarterly* 4 (2), 189–211; Dumurat-Dreger, A. (1998, May/June). "Ambiguous sex" or ambivalent medicine? *The Hastings Center Report* 28 (3), 2,435 (posted on the Intersex Society of North America website: www.isna.org); Fausto-Sterling, A. (1993). The five sexes: Why male and female are not enough. *The Sciences 33* (2), 20–24; the Mayo Clinic website.

intersexual A person born with reproductive organs, genitalia, and/or sex chromosomes that are not exclusively male or female.

human beings are divided into two kinds: a perfectly dimorphic species. Males have an X and a Y chromosome, testes, a penis and all of the appropriate internal plumbing for delivering urine and semen to the outside world. They also have well-known secondary sexual characteristics, including a muscular build and facial hair. Women have two X chromosomes, ovaries, all of the internal plumbing to transport urine and ova to the outside world, a system to support pregnancy and fetal development, as well as a variety of recognizable secondary sexual characteristics.

That idealized story papers over many obvious caveats: some women have facial hair, some men have none; some women speak with deep voices, some men veritably squeak. Less well known is the fact that on close inspection, absolute dimorphism disintegrates even at the level of basic biology. Chromosomes, hormones, the internal sex structures, the gonads and external genitalia all vary more than most people realize. Those born outside of the . . . dimorphic mold are called intersexuals.[15]

Intersexuality may be unusual but is not uncommon. In fact, about 1 percent of all humans are intersexed in some (not necessarily visible) way—in other words, over 60 million people worldwide.[16] Until recently, it was rarely discussed publicly in many societies. Since the mid-20th century, individuals with financial means in technologically advanced parts of the world have had the option of reconstructive surgery and hormonal treatments to alter such conditions, and many parents faced with raising a visibly intersexed child in a culture intolerant of such minorities have chosen this option for their baby. However, there is a growing movement to put off such irreversible procedures indefinitely or until the child becomes old enough to be the one to make the choice. Obviously, a society's attitude toward these individuals can impact their personality—their fundamental sense of self and how they express it.

In addition to people who are biologically intersexed, throughout history some individuals have been subjected to a surgical removal of some of their sexual organs. In many cultures, male prisoners or war captives have undergone forced castration, crushing or cutting the testicles. While castration of adult males does not eliminate the sex drive or the possibility of having an

erection, it does put an end to the production of sperm necessary for reproduction.

Archaeological evidence from ancient Egypt, Iraq, Iran, and China suggests that the cultural practice of castrating war captives may have begun several thousand years ago. Young boys captured during war or slave-raiding expeditions were often castrated before being sold and shipped off to serve in foreign households, including royal courts. In the Ottoman Empire of the Turks, where they could occupy a variety of important functions in the sultan's household from the mid-15th century onward, they became known as *eunuchs*. As suggested by the original meaning of the word, which is Greek for "guardian of the bed," castrated men were often put in charge of a ruler's harem, the women's quarters in a household. Eunuchs could also rise to high status as priests and administrators and were even appointed to serve as army commanders. Some powerful lords, kings, and emperors kept hundreds of eunuchs in their castles and palaces.

In addition to forced castration, there were also men who engaged in self-castration or underwent voluntary castration. For example, early Christian monks in Egypt and neighboring regions voluntarily abstained from sexual relationships and sometimes castrated themselves for the sake of the kingdom of heaven. Such genital mutilation was also practiced among Coptic monks in Egypt and Ethiopia, until the early 20th century.[17]

In the late 15th century, Europe saw the emergence of a category of musical eunuchs known as *castrati*. These eunuchs sang female parts in church choirs after Roman Catholic authorities banned women singers on the basis of Saint Paul's instruction, "Let your women keep silence in the churches." Simultaneously, castrati began performing female roles in operas. Castrated before they reached puberty so as to retain their high voices, these selected boys were often orphaned or came from poor families. Without a functioning testis to produce male sex hormones, physical development into manhood is aborted, so deeper voices, as well as body hair, semen production, and other usual male attributes, were not part of a castrati's biology.

During the 1700s, at the height of castrati popularity, an estimated 4,000 boys a year were castrated in Italy alone. Some became celebrated performers, drawing huge fees, adopting fantastic stage names, and gaining notoriety for their eccentricity on and off stage. Not necessarily homosexual, castrati were "gender benders" who could engage in sexual relations with men or women, or both. The phenomenon of castrati continued until about 1900, when Roman Catholic authorities in the Vatican banned their role in church music. By then, the eunuch

[15]Fausto-Sterling, A. (2000, July). The five sexes revisited. *The Sciences*, 20–24.

[16]Fausto-Sterling, A. (2003, August 2). Personal e-mail communication from this recognized expert on the subject. For published statistics, see her article co-authored with Blackless, M., et al. (2000). How sexually dimorphic are we? Review and synthesis. *American Journal of Human Biology* 12, 151–166.

[17]Abbot, E. (2001). *A history of celibacy*. Cambridge, MA: Da Capo Press.

systems in the Chinese and Ottoman empires were also about to be abolished.[18]

Although human castration was not practiced among North American Indians, many indigenous communities in the Great Plains and Southwest created alternative social space for intersexed or transgendered individuals. **Transgenders** are people who cross over or occupy a culturally accepted position in the binary male–female gender construction.) For example, the Lakota of the northern Plains had an intermediate category of culturally accepted transgendered males who dressed as women and were thought to possess both male and female spirits. They called (and still call) these third-gender individuals *winkte,* applying the term to a male "who wants to be a woman." Thought to have special curing powers, *winktes* traditionally enjoyed considerable prestige in their communities. Among the neighboring Cheyenne, such a person was called *hemanah,* literally meaning "half-man, half-woman."[19]

French traders who came to the Great Plains in the 1600s eventually encountered cross-dressing Native American men, whom they called *berdache* (also spelled *burdash*). The name derived from the Persian word *bardah,* which referred to eunuchs or slaves. The French term *berdache* had acquired obvious contemptuous applications for effeminacy and celibacy, as well as cowardice, and it was broadly used for eunuchs, castrati, cross-dressers, and homosexuals alike. Although early anthropological literature adopted the word, the preferred term among North American Indians today is "two-spirits," which avoids the negative connotations associated with the term *berdache.*[20]

Mapping the sexual landscape, anthropologists have come to realize that gender bending exists in many cultures all around the world, playing a significant role in shaping behaviors and personalities. For instance, third-gender individuals are well known in Samoa, where males who take on the identity of females are referred to as *fa'afafines* ("the female way"). Becoming a *fa'afafine* is an accepted option for boys who prefer to dance, cook, clean house, and care for children and the elderly. In large families, it is not unusual to find two or three boys

Transgendering occurs in many cultures, but is not always publicly tolerated. Among Polynesians inhabiting Pacific Ocean islands such as Tonga and Samoa, however, such male transvestites are culturally accepted. Samoans refer to these third genders as *fa'afafines* ("the female way").

being raised as girls to take on domestic roles in their households. As North American anthropologist Lowell Holmes recently reported,

> In fact, they tend to be highly valued because they can do the heavy kinds of labor that most women find difficult. A Samoan nun once told me how fortunate it is to have a fa'afafine in the family to help with the household chores. [There] is also the claim made that fa'afafines never have sexual relations with each other but, rather, consider themselves to be "sisters." [They] are religious and go to church regularly dressed as women and . . . some are even Sunday school teachers. Fa'afafines often belong to women's athletic teams, and some even serve as coaches.[21]

Among many other third genders, the best known may be the *hijra* (or *hijadas*) in India. *Hijra* is an Urdu term that covers transgendered men, castrated males, and her-

---

[18]Taylor, G. (2000). *Castration: Abbreviated history of western manhood* (pp. 38–44, 252–259). New York: Routledge.

[19]Medicine, B. (1994). Gender. In M. B. Davis (Ed.), *Native America in the twentieth century.* New York: Garland.

[20]Jacobs, S. E. (1994). Native American two-spirits. *Anthropology Newsletter 35* (8), 7.

transgender A person who crosses over or occupies a culturally accepted position in the binary male–female gender construction.

---

[21]Holmes, L. D. (2000). Paradise bent (film review). *American Anthropologist 102* (3), 604–605.

maphrodites who dress and behave like women in an ex-aggerated way. As Hindu devotees of the Mother Goddess Bahuchara Mata, their cultural role is to perform blessings for young married couples and male babies. Beyond small earnings for those rituals, they survive by begging, chanting, running bathhouses, and sometimes prostitution.[22]

None of these transgendered cultural types can be simply lumped together as homosexuals. For example, the Tagalog-speaking people in the Philippines use the word *bakla* to refer to a man who views himself "as a male with a female heart." These individuals cross-dress on a daily basis, often becoming more female than females in their use of heavy makeup, in the clothing they wear, and in the way they walk. Like the Samoan *fa'afafines,* they are generally not sexually attracted to other *bakla* but are drawn to heterosexual men instead.

Since some people are gender variants, permanent or incidental transvestites without being homosexuals, it is obvious that the cross-cultural sex and gender scheme is complex. Indeed, the late 19th-century "homosexuality" label is quite inadequate to cover the full range of sex and gender diversity.

In sum, human cultures in the course of thousands of years have creatively dealt with a wide range of inherited and artificially imposed sexual features. The importance of studying complex categories involving intersexuality and transgendering is that doing so enables us to recognize the existing range of gender alternatives and to debunk false stereotypes. It is one more piece of the human puzzle—an important one that prods us to rethink social codes and the range of forces that shape personality as well as each society's definition of normal.

NORMAL AND ABNORMAL PERSONALITY IN SOCIAL CONTEXT

The cultural standards that define normal behavior for any society are determined by that society itself. So it is that in mainstream European and North American societies, in contrast to those just noted, transgender behavior has traditionally been regarded as culturally abnormal. If a male in those societies dresses as a woman, he is still widely viewed as emotionally troubled, or even mentally ill, and his abnormal behavior may lead to psychiatric intervention. There are countless such examples of the fact that what is considered normal and acceptable (if not always popular) in one society is abnormal and

unacceptable (ridiculous, shameful, and sometimes even criminal) in another.

Not only are the boundaries that distinguish the normal from the abnormal culturally variable (and thus neither absolute nor fixed), but so are the standards of what is socially acceptable. In other words, there are individuals in each society who deviate in appearance or behavior from general social standards or norms but are not considered "abnormal" in the strict sense of the word—and are not socially rejected, ridiculed, censured, condemned, jailed, or otherwise penalized. Quite to the contrary, some cultures tolerate or accept a much wider range of diversity than others and may even accord special status to the deviant or eccentric as unique, extraordinary, even sacred.

A fascinating ethnographic example of a culture in which abnormal individuals are socially accepted and even honored is provided by religious mystics in India and Nepal. This example also illustrates the degree to which one's social identity and sense of personal self are cultural constructs.

Sadhus: Holy Men in Hindu Culture

When a young Hindu man in India or Nepal decides to become an ascetic monk, or *sadhu,* he must transform his personal identity, change his sense of self, and leave his place in the social order. Detaching himself from the pursuit of earthly pleasures (*kama*), power and wealth (*artha*), he makes a radical break with his family and friends and abandons the moral principles and rules of code of conduct prescribed for his caste (*dharma*). Symbolically expressing his "death" as a normal Hindu person, he participates in his own funeral ceremony, followed by a ritual rebirth. As a born-again, he acquires a new identity as a *sadhu* and is initiated into a particular ascetic order or sect.

---

[22]Nanda, S. (1990). *Neither man nor woman: The hijras of India.* Belmont, CA: Wadsworth.

Shaivite *sadhu* of the Aghori sub-sect drinks from human skull bowl. He is a strict follower of the Hindu god Shiva, whose picture can be seen behind him. The practice of eating and drinking from a human skull is a daily reminder of human mortality. These ascetics remain naked and often wear a rosary made of bones around their neck. To become a *sadhu*, one must transform his personal identity, leave his place in the social order, and surrender all attachments to normal human pleasures.

Having surrendered all social, material, and even sexual attachments to normal human pleasures and delights, the *sadhu* dedicates himself to achieving spiritual union with the divine or universal Soul. This is done through intense meditation (chanting sacred hymns or mystical prayer texts—*mantras*) and yoga (an ascetic and mystic discipline involving prescribed postures and controlled breathing). The goal is to become a fully enlightened soul, liberated from the physical limits of the individual mortal self, including the cycle of life and death.

The *sadhu* path to this divine state of pure consciousness and total inner freedom (*mokshe*) is acutely challenging. It demands extraordinary concentration and near superhuman effort, as can be seen in the most extreme yoga postures. This chosen life of suffering may even include self-torture as a form of extreme penance. For instance, some *sadhus* pierce their tongue or cheeks with a long iron rod, stab a long knife through their arm or leg, or stick their head into a small hole in the ground for

hours on end. Among the more extreme examples, one *sadhu* is known to have kept his right arm continuously stretched up into the air for twenty-five years (transforming his hand into a useless stump).

Most Hindus revere and sometimes even fear *sadhus*. When they encounter one—by a temple or cemetery, or perhaps near a forest, riverbank, or mountain cave, they typically offer him food or other alms. Sightings are not uncommon since an estimated 5 million *sadhus* live in India and Nepal. They belong to different sub-sects of ascetic orders, each with its own characteristics and ritual practices. Some *sadhus* are believed to have succeeded in achieving divine status as *jivan mukta* ("a soul liberated while still alive") and are devoutly honored as great saints or even as gods on earth.

Perhaps the most remarkable *sadhus* belong to a very small sub-sect of the Shaivite Order, devoted to worshiping Shiva, the Hindu god of destruction and reproduction. Known as *aghoris* (meaning "not terrible," one of

Shiva's names), these extremely ascetic monks challenge the cosmic order itself and turn normal rules of Hindu conduct upside-down. Naked or near naked ("sky-clad"), they spend most of their time around cremation grounds. On a regular basis they apply ashes to their body, face, and long matted hair. They also drink and eat from human skull bowls, occasionally challenging themselves in their devotion to Shiva by eating their own excrement and decomposed human flesh torn from a body awaiting cremation.[23]

Of course, if one of these bearded, long-haired, Hindu monks, especially an aghori, decided to practice his extreme yoga exercises and other sacred devotions as a Shiva worshiper in western Europe or North America, such a holy man would be viewed as severely mentally disturbed. And if this *sadhu* was seen walking around naked and drinking from his human skull bowl in a place like Kansas City, he would no doubt face arrest for disorderly and even criminal conduct. In all likelihood, he would be declared insane and forced to spend the rest of his life doing penance of another kind.

A Cross-Cultural Perspective on Mental Disorders

No matter how eccentric or even bizarre certain behaviors might seem in a particular place and time, it is possible for the "abnormal" to become socially accepted in cultures that are changing. In this vein, anthropologist Emily Martin cites recent new attitudes toward manic depression (now more properly called *bipolar disorder*) and attention deficit hyperactivity disorder (ADHD), previously regarded as dreaded liabilities.[24]

She suggests that, in North America, the manic and hyperactivity aspects are gradually becoming viewed as assets in the quest for success. More and more, they are interpreted as indicative of "finely wired, exquisitely alert nervous systems" that make one highly sensitive to signs of change, able to fly from one thing to another while pushing the limits of everything, and doing it all with an intense level of energy focused totally in the future. These are extolled as high virtues in the corporate world, and to be called "hyper" or "manic" is increasingly an expression of approval.

Not only do social attitudes concerning a wide range of both psychological and physical differences

change over time within a society, they also vary across cultures—as evident in this chapter's Biocultural Connection.

Is all of this to suggest that "normalcy" is a meaningless concept when applied to personality? Within the context of a particular culture, the concept of normal personality is quite meaningful. Irving Hallowell, a major figure in the development of psychological anthropology, somewhat ironically observed that it is normal to share the delusions traditionally accepted by one's society. Abnormality involves the development of a delusional system of which the culture does not approve. The individual who is disturbed because he or she cannot adequately measure up to the norms of society and be happy may be termed "neurotic." When a person's delusional system is so different that it in no way reflects his or her society's norms, the individual may be termed "psychotic."

If severe enough, culturally induced conflicts can produce psychosis and also determine the form of the psychosis. In a culture that encourages aggressiveness and suspicion, the insane person may be one who is passive and trusting. In a culture that encourages passivity and trust, the insane person may be the one who is aggressive and suspicious. Just as each society establishes its own norms, each individual is unique in his or her perceptions.

Many anthropologists see the only meaningful criterion for personality evaluation as the correlation between personality and social conformity. From their point of view, insanity is a culturally constructed mental illness, and people are considered insane when they fail to conform to a culturally defined range of normal behavior. This is not to say that psychosis is simply a matter of an especially bad fit between an individual and his or her particular culture.

Although it is true that each particular culture defines what is and is not normal behavior, the situation is complicated by findings suggesting that major categories of mental disorders may be universal types of human affliction. Take, for example, schizophrenia—probably the most common of all psychoses and one that may be found in any culture, no matter how it may manifest itself. Individuals afflicted by schizophrenia experience distortions of reality that impair their ability to function adequately, so they often withdraw from the social world into their own psychological shell. Although environmental factors play a role, evidence suggests that schizophrenia is caused by a biochemical disorder for which there is an inheritable tendency. One of its more severe forms is paranoid schizophrenia. Those suffering from it fear and mistrust nearly everyone. They hear voices that whisper dreadful things to them, and they are convinced that someone is "out to get them." Acting on this con-

---

[23]See Kelly, T. L. (2006). Sadhus, the great renouncers. Photography exhibit, Indigo Gallery, Naxal, Kathmandu, Nepal. Posted online at www.asianart.com/exhibitions/sadhus/index.html. See also Heitzman, J., & R. L. Wordem, R. L. (Eds.). (2006). *India: A country study* (sect. 2, 5th ed.). Washington, D.C.: Federal Research Division, Library of Congress.

[24]Martin, E. (1999). Flexible survivors. *Anthropology News 40* (6), 5–7.

Biocultural Connection

A Cross-Cultural Perspective on Psychosomatic Symptoms and Mental Health

Biomedicine, the dominant medical system of Euramerican cultures, sometimes identifies physical ailments experienced by individuals as "psychosomatic"—a term derived from *psyche* ("mind") and *soma* ("body"). These ailments can be serious and painful, but because a precise physiological cause cannot be identified through scientific methods, the illness is viewed as something rooted in mental or emotional causes—and thus on some level not quite "real."

Each culture possesses its own historically developed ideas about health, illness, and associated healing practices. While biomedicine is based in modern Western traditions of science, it is also steeped in the cultural beliefs and practices of societies within which it operates. Fundamentally informed by a dualistic mind–body model, biomedicine represents the human body as a complex machine with parts that can be manipulated by experts. This approach has resulted in spectacular treatments, such as antibiotics that have eradicated certain infectious diseases.

Today, the remarkable breakthroughs of biomedicine are spreading rapidly throughout the world, and people from cultures with different healing systems are moving into countries where

biomedicine dominates. This makes treating illnesses defined by biomedicine as psychosomatic disorders all the more difficult.

Indicative of our biocultural complexity, psychological factors such as emotional stress, worry, and anxiety may stem from cultural contexts and result in increased physiological agitation like irregular heart pounding or palpitations, heightened blood pressure, headaches, stomach and intestinal problems, muscle pains and tensions, rashes, appetite loss, insomnia, fatigue, and a range of other troubles. Indeed, when individuals are unable to deal successfully with stressful situations in daily life and do not get the opportunity for adequate mental rest and relaxation, even their natural immune systems may weaken, increasing their chances of getting a cold or some other infection. For people forced to adapt to a quickly changing way of life in their own country or immigrants adjusting to a foreign culture, these pressures may result in a range of disorders that are difficult to explain from the perspective of biomedicine.

Medical and psychological approaches developed in European and North American societies are often unsuccessful in dealing with these problems,

for a number of reasons. For one, the various immigrant ethnic groups have different concepts of mind and body than do medical practitioners trained in Western (Euramerican) medicine. Among many Caribbean peoples, for example, a widely held belief is that spiritual forces are active in the world and that they influence human identity and behavior. Thus, for someone with a psychosomatic problem, it is normal to seek help from a local *curandero* or *curandera* (folk healer), *santiguadora* (herbalist), or even a *santéro* (a Santéria priest) rather than a medical doctor or psychiatrist. Not only does the client not understand the symbols of Western psychiatry, but to go to a psychiatrist is often too expensive and may imply that he or she is *loco* (crazy).

During the past few decades, however, anthropologists have become increasingly involved in cross-cultural medical mediation, challenging negative biases and correcting misinformation about non-Western indigenous perceptions of mind–body connections. The inclusion of culturally appropriate healing approaches has gained growing acceptance among the Western medical and psychological establishment in Europe, North America, and many other parts of the world.

viction, they engage in bizarre sorts of behaviors, which lead to their removal from society.

Ethnic Psychoses

Ethnic psychoses are mental disorders specific to particular cultural groups (Table 6.1). Among these is Windigo psychosis, limited to northern Algonquian Indian groups such as the Cree and Ojibwa. In their traditional belief systems, these northern Indians recognized the existence of cannibalistic monsters called Windigos. In-

ethnic psychosis A mental disorder specific to a particular ethnic group.

dividuals afflicted by the psychosis developed the delusion that, falling under the control of these monsters, they were themselves transformed into Windigos, with a craving for human flesh. As this happened, the psychotic individuals saw people around them turning into various edible animals—fat, juicy beavers, for instance. Although there are no known instances where sufferers of Windigo psychosis actually ate another human being, they were acutely afraid of doing so, and people around them were genuinely fearful that they might.

Windigo psychosis may seem different from clinical cases of paranoid schizophrenia found in Euramerican cultures, but a closer look suggests otherwise. The disorder was merely being expressed in ways compatible with traditional northern Algonquian cultures. Ideas of perse-

TABLE 6.1	ETHNIC PSYCHOSES AND OTHER CULTURE-BOUND SYNDROMES	
Name of Disorder	**Culture**	**Description**
Amok	Malaysia (also observed in Java, Philippines, Africa, and Tierra del Fuego)	A disorder characterized by sudden, wild outbursts of homicidal aggression in which the afflicted person may kill or injure others. The rage disorder is usually found in males who are rather withdrawn, quiet, and inoffensive prior to the onset of the disorder. Stress, sleep deprivation, extreme heat, and alcohol are among the conditions thought to precipitate the disorder. Several stages have been observed: Typically in the first stage the person becomes more withdrawn; then a period of brooding follows in which a loss of reality contact is evident. Ideas of persecution and anger predominate. Finally, a phase of automatism, or *amok,* occurs, in which the person jumps up, yells, grabs a knife, and stabs people or objects within reach. Exhaustion and depression usually follow, with amnesia for the rage.
Anorexia nervosa	Western countries	A disorder occurring most frequently among young women in which a preoccupation with thinness produces a refusal to eat. This condition can result in death.
Latah	Malaysia	A fear reaction often occurring in middle-aged women of low intelligence who are subservient and self-effacing. The disorder is precipitated by the word *snake* or by tickling. It is characterized by echolalia (repetition of the words and sentences of others). The disturbed individual may also react with negativism and the compulsive use of obscene language.
Koro	Southeast Asia (particularly Malaysia)	A fear reaction or anxiety in which the person fears that his penis will withdraw into his abdomen and he will die. This reaction may appear after sexual overindulgence or excessive masturbation. The anxiety is typically very intense and of sudden onset. The condition is "treated" by having the penis held firmly by the patient or by family members or friends. Often the penis is clamped to a wooden box.
Windigo	Algonquian Indians of Canada and northern United States	A fear reaction in which a hunter becomes anxious and agitated, convinced that he is bewitched. Fears center on his being turned into a cannibal by the power of a monster with an insatiable craving for human flesh.
Kitsunetsuki	Japan	A disorder in which victims believe that they are possessed by foxes and are said to change their facial expressions to resemble foxes. Entire families are often possessed and banned by the community.
Pibloktoq and other Arctic hysterias	Circumpolar peoples from Lapland eastward across Siberia, northern Alaska, and Canada to Greenland	A disorder brought on by fright, which is followed by a short period of bizarre behavior; victim may tear clothes off, jump in water or fire, roll in snow, try to walk on the ceiling, throw things, thrash about, and "speak in tongues." Outburst followed by return to normal behavior.

SOURCE: Based on Carson, R. C., Butcher, J. N., & Coleman, J. C. (1990). *Abnormal psychology and modern life* (8th ed., p. 85). Glenview, IL: Scott Foresman.

cution, instead of being directed toward other humans, were directed toward supernatural beings (the Windigo monsters); cannibalistic panic replaced panic expressed in other forms. Northern Algonquian Indians, like Euramericans, expressed their problems in terms compatible with the appropriate view of the self and its behavioral environment. However, the Algonquians protected their families from such seriously deranged individuals

by killing them—for in their small-scale communities, there existed nothing resembling what we would recognize as a mental institution.

Windigo behavior has seemed exotic and dramatic to Euramericans, but psychotic individuals draw upon whatever imagery and symbolism their culture has to offer, and in northern Algonquian culture, these include myths featuring cannibal giants. By contrast, the delusions of Irish schizophrenics draw upon the images and symbols of Irish Catholicism and feature virgin and savior motifs. Euramericans, on the other hand, tend toward secular or electromagnetic persecution delusions. The underlying structure of the mental disorder is the same in all cases, but its expression is culturally specific.

Anthropologists view all mental health issues in their cultural context, in recognition of the fact that each individual's social identity, unique personality, and overall sense of mental health is molded by the particular culture within which the person is born and raised to function as a valued member of the community.

Questions for Reflection

1. Every society faces the challenge of humanizing its children, teaching them the values and social codes that will enable them to be functioning and contributing members in the community. What child-rearing practices did you experience that embody the values and social codes of your society?

2. Considering the cultural significance of naming ceremonies in so many societies, what do you think motivated your parents when they named you? Does that have any influence on your sense of self?

3. Margaret Mead's cross-cultural research on gender relations suggests that male dominance is a cultural construct and, consequently, that alternative gender arrangements can be created. Looking at your grandparents, parents, and siblings, do you see any changes in your own family? What about your own community? Do you think such changes are positive?

4. Do you fit within the acceptable range of your society's modal personality? How so?

5. Given that over 60 million people in today's world are intersexed, and in light of the fact that a very small fraction of these people have access to reconstructive sexual surgery, what do you think of societies that have created cultural space for a third-gender option?

Suggested Readings

Barnouw, V. (1985). *Culture and personality* (4th ed.). Homewood, IL: Dorsey Press.

This is a revision of a well-respected text designed to introduce students to psychological anthropology.

Brettell, C. B., & Sargent, C. F. (Eds.). (2000). *Gender in cross-cultural perspective* (3rd. ed.). Upper Saddle River, NJ: Prentice-Hall.

Classic and contemporary gender readings on a range of topics, including the cultural construction of femininity and masculinity and the impact of globalization on gender issues.

LaFont, S. (Ed.). (2003). *Constructing sexualities: Readings in sexuality, gender, and culture.* Upper Saddle River, NJ: Prentice-Hall.

A broad yet detailed look at sexuality and gender behavior. Statistics, ethnographic examples, and theoretical insights on numerous themes—from the biological basics and sex categories to sexual orientation and transsexuality.

Shore, B. (1996). *Culture in mind: Meaning, construction, and cultural cognition.* New York: Oxford University Press.

A readable exploration of developmental and cognitive psychology and the cultural context of individual psychology.

Suárez-Orozoco, M. M., Spindler, G., & Spindler, L. (1994). *The making of psychological anthropology, II.* Fort Worth, TX: Harcourt Brace.

This collection of articles consists of firsthand accounts of the objectives, accomplishments, and failures of well-known specialists in psychological anthropology.

Whiting, J. W. M., & Child, I. (1953). *Child training and personality: A cross-cultural study.* New Haven, CT: Yale University Press.

Exploring the relationship between culture and personality, this classic text is oriented toward testing general hypotheses about human behavior in any and all societies.

Thomson Audio Study Products

 Enjoy the MP3-ready Audio Lecture Overviews for each chapter and a comprehensive audio glossary of key terms for quick study and review. Whether walking to class, doing laundry, or studying at your desk, you now have the freedom to choose when, where, and how you interact with your audio-based educational media. See the preface for information on how to access this on-the-go study and review tool.

The Anthropology Resource Center

www.thomsonedu.com/anthropology
The Anthropology Resource Center provides extended learning materials to reinforce your understanding of key concepts in the four fields of anthropology. For each of the four fields, the Resource Center includes dynamic exercises including video exercises, map exercises, simulations, and "Meet the Scientists" interviews, as well as critical thinking questions that can be assigned and e-mailed to instructors. The Resource Center also provides breaking news in anthropology and interesting material on applied anthropology to help you link what you are learning to the world around you.

7 Patterns of Subsistence

© Jeremy Horner/Corbis

CHALLENGE ISSUE

Facing the challenge of getting food, fuel, shelter, and other necessities, humans must gather, produce, or buy the means to satisfy such needs. During the span of human existence, this has been accomplished in a range of highly contrasting natural environments by different biological and cultural adaptations. Inventing and applying various technologies, humans have developed a great variety of distinctive subsistence arrangements to harness energy and process required resources. Thus we may find hunters in Namibia's desert, fishers on Norway's coasts, manioc planters in Brazil's rainforest, goat herders in Iran's mountains, automakers in Korea, and Jamaican apple pickers in the United States. While all human activities impact their environments, some are more invasive than others—as we see in this photo of the Andean mountains reshaped with terracing by generations of traditional Indian farmers aiming to capture rainwater and prevent erosion while cultivating the soil.

What Is Adaptation?

Adaptation refers to beneficial adjustments of organisms to their environment, a process that not only leads to changes in the organisms but also impacts their environment. Such dynamic interaction is necessary for the survival of all life forms, including human beings. The human species adapts not only biologically but culturally. In fact, in the course of evolution, humans came to rely increasingly on culture rather than biological change as a means of effectively adapting to different and changing environments.

How Do Humans Adapt Culturally?

Through cultural adaptation, humans develop ways of doing things that are compatible with the resources they have available to them and within the limitations of the various habitats in which they live. In a particular region, people living in similar environments tend to borrow from one another customs that work well in those settings. Once achieved, adaptations may be remarkably stable for long periods of time, even thousands of years. Humankind's unique creative capacity to adapt by means of culture has enabled our species to inhabit an extraordinary variety of environments.

What Sorts of Cultural Adaptations Have Humans Achieved Through the Ages?

Food foraging is the oldest and most universal type of human adaptation and typically involves geographic mobility. Other adaptations, involving domestication of plants and animals, began to develop in some parts of the world about 10,000 years ago. Horticulture (cultivating plants with hand tools) led to more permanent settlements (villages and towns) while pastoralism (herding grazing animals) required mobility to seek out pasture and water. Cities began to develop as early as 5,000 years ago in some world regions, as intensive agriculture and long-distance trading produced sufficient resources to support larger populations and various full-time specialists. These changes led to increasingly complex and large-scale social organizations—but did not necessarily improve the overall conditions of human existence.

All living beings must satisfy certain basic needs to stay alive—including food, water, and shelter. Moreover, because these needs must be met on a regular basis, no creature could long survive if its relations with its environment were random and chaotic. All require regular access to a supply of food and water and a reliable means of obtaining and using it. A lion might die if all its prey disappeared, if its teeth and claws grew soft, or if its digestive system failed.

Although people face similar sorts of problems, they have an overwhelming advantage over other creatures: People have culture. If the rains do not come, and the hot sun turns grassland into desert, we may pump water from deep wells, quenching our thirst, irrigating the pastures, and feeding our grazing animals. Conversely, if the rains do not end, and our pastures turn into marshlands, we may choose to build earth mounds for our villages or dig canals to drain flooded fields. And to keep our food supplies from rotting, we can preserve them by drying or roasting and keep them in safe storage places for protection and future use. When our tools fail or are inadequate, we may choose to replace them or invent better ones. And if our stomachs are incapable of digesting a particular food, we can prepare it by cooking.

THOMSON AUDIO STUDY PRODUCTS Take advantage of the MP3-ready Audio Lecture Overviews and comprehensive audio glossary of key terms for each chapter. See the preface for information on how to access this on-the-go study and review tool.

We are, nonetheless, subject to similar basic needs and pressures as all other living creatures, and it is important to understand human survival from this point of view. The crucial concept that underlies such a perspective is adaptation or how humans adjust to and act upon the burdens and opportunities presented in daily life.

ADAPTATION

As discussed earlier in this book, adaptation is the process organisms undergo to achieve a beneficial adjustment to a particular environment. What makes human adaptation unique among all other species is our capacity to produce and reproduce culture, enabling us to creatively adapt to an extraordinary range of radically different environments. The biological underpinnings of this capacity include large brains and a long period of growth and development. How humans adjust to the burdens and opportunities presented in daily life is the basic concern of all cultures. A people's **cultural adaptation** consists of a complex of ideas, activities, and technologies that enable them to survive and even thrive and that, in turn, impact their environment.

The process of adaptation establishes an ever-shifting balance between the needs of a population and the potential of its environment. This process can be illustrated by the Tsembaga people of Papua New Guinea, one of about twenty local groups of Maring speakers who support themselves chiefly through cultivating crops using simple hand tools such as digging sticks or hoes.[1] Although the Tsembaga also raise pigs, they eat them only under conditions of illness, injury, warfare, or celebration. At such times the pigs are sacrificed to ancestral spirits, and their flesh is ritually consumed. (This guarantees a supply of high-quality protein when it is most needed.)

Traditionally, the Tsembaga and their neighbors are bound together in a unique cycle of pig sacrifices that serves to mark the end of hostilities between groups. Hostilities are periodically fueled by ecological pressures in which pigs play a significant role. Pigs are rarely slaughtered because they fulfill important roles: omnivorous eaters, they keep the village free of garbage and even human feces; moreover, they serve as status symbols for their owners who reserve them for significant rituals. But keeping them alive and allowing them to multiply comes at a cost since their numbers grow quickly. Invading the village gardens, the hungry pigs eat the sweet potatoes and other crops, leaving almost nothing for their human owners. In short, they become a problem.

The need to expand food cultivation in order to feed the prestigious but pesky pigs puts a strain on the land

---

cultural adaptation A complex of ideas, activities, and technologies that enable people to survive and even thrive.

[1]Rappaport, R. A. (1969). Ritual regulation of environmental relations among a New Guinea people. In A. P. Vayda (Ed.), *Environment and cultural behavior* (pp. 181–201). Garden City, NY: Natural History Press.

best suited for farming. Sooner or later, fighting breaks out between the Tsembaga and their neighbors. Hostilities usually end after several weeks, followed by a pig feast ritual. For this event, the Tsembaga butcher and roast almost all of their pigs and feast heartily on them with invited allies. By means of this feast, the Tsembaga not only pay their debts to their allies and gain prestige, but also eliminate a major source of irritation and complaint between neighbors. Moreover, the feast leaves everyone well fed and physically strengthened as a result of the animal protein intake. Even without hostilities over scarce land, such large pig feasts have been held whenever the pig population has become unmanageable—every five to ten years, depending on the groups' success in growing crops and raising animals. Thus, the cycle of fighting and feasting keeps the ecological balance among humans, land, and animals.

Through their distinctive cultures, different human groups have managed to adapt to a very diverse range of natural environments—from Arctic snowfields to Polynesian coral islands, from the Sahara Desert to the Amazon rainforest. In all these different environments, cultural adaptation is fundamental to human survival. Adaptation occurs not only when humans make all kinds of changes in their natural environment, but also when they are biologically changed by their natural environment. The Biocultural Connection provides an example of such a biocultural interaction, found in the central Andean highlands of Bolivia.

The Unit of Adaptation

The unit of adaptation includes both organisms and their environment. Organisms, including human beings, exist as members of a population; populations, in turn, must have the flexibility to cope with variability and change within the natural environment that sustains them. In biological terms, this flexibility means that different organisms within the population have somewhat differing genetic endowments. In cultural terms, it means that variation occurs among individual skills, knowledge, and personalities. Indeed, organisms and environments form dynamic interacting systems. And although environments do not determine culture, they do present certain possibilities and limitations: People might just as easily farm as fish, but we do not expect to find farmers in Siberia's frozen tundra or fishermen in the middle of North Africa's Sahara Desert.

Some anthropologists have adopted the ecologists' concept of **ecosystem,** defined as a system composed of both the natural environment and all the organisms living within it. The system is bound by the activities of the organisms, as well as by such physical processes as erosion and evaporation.

Adaptation in Cultural Evolution

Human groups adapt to their environments by means of their cultures. However, cultures may change over the course of time; they evolve. This is called **cultural evolution.** The process is sometimes confused with the idea of **progress**—the notion that humans are moving forward to a better, more advanced stage in their development toward perfection. Yet, not all changes turn out to be positive in the long run, nor do they improve conditions for every member of a society even in the short run. Complex, urban societies are not more "highly evolved" than those of food foragers. Rather, both are "highly evolved," but in quite different ways.

Cultural adaptation must also be understood from a historical point of view. To fit into an ecosystem, humans (like all organisms) must have the potential to adjust to or become a part of it. A good example of this is the Comanche, whose history begins in the highlands of southern Idaho.[2] Living in that harsh, arid region, these North American Indians traditionally subsisted on wild plants, small animals, and occasionally larger game. Their material equipment was simple and limited to what they (and their dogs) could carry or pull. The size of their groups was restricted, and what little social power could develop was in the hands of the shaman, who was a combination of healer and spiritual guide.

At some point in their nomadic history, the Comanche moved east onto the Great Plains, where bison were abundant and they could hunt. As larger groups could be supported by the new and plentiful food supply, the Comanche needed a more complex political organization.

Eventually the Comanche acquired horses and guns from European settlers, which enhanced their hunting capabilities significantly and led to the emergence of powerful hunting chiefs. The Comanche became raiders in order to get horses (which they did not breed for themselves), and their hunting chiefs evolved into war chiefs. The once materially poor and peaceful hunter–gatherers of the dry highlands became wealthy, and raiding became a way of life.

In the late 18th and early 19th centuries, they dominated the southern plains (now primarily Texas and Oklahoma). In moving from one regional environment

---

[2]Wallace, E., & Hoebel, E. A. (1952). *The Comanches.* Norman: University of Oklahoma Press.

---

ecosystem A system, or a functioning whole, composed of both the natural environment and all the organisms living within it.
cultural evolution Culture change over time (not to be confused with progress).
progress The notion that humans are moving forward to a better, more advanced stage in their cultural development toward perfection.

Biocultural Connection

Surviving in the Andes: Aymara Adaptation to High Altitude

However adaptable we are as a species through our diverse cultures, some natural environments pose such extreme climatic challenges that the human body must make physical adaptations to successfully survive. The central Andean highlands of Bolivia offer an interesting example of complex biocultural interaction, where a biologically adapted human body type has emerged due to natural selection.

Known as the *altiplano,* this high plateau has an average elevation of 4,000 meters (13,000 feet). Many thousands of years ago, small groups of human foragers in the warm lowlands climbed up the mountain slopes in search of game and other food. The higher they moved, the harder it became to breathe due to decreasing molecular concentration, or partial pressure, of oxygen in the inspired air. However, upon reaching the cold and treeless highlands, they found herds of llamas and hardy food plants, including potatoes—reasons to stay. Eventually (about 4,000 years ago) their descendants domesticated both the llamas and the potatoes and developed a new way of life as high-altitude agropastoralists.

The llamas provided meat and hides, as well as milk and wool. And the potatoes, a rich source of carbohydrates, became their staple food. In the course of many centuries, the Aymara selectively cultivated more than 200 varieties of these tubers on small family-owned tracts of land. They boiled them fresh for immediate consumption and also freeze-dried and preserved them as *chuño,* which is the Aymara's major source of nutrition to this day.

Still surviving as highland subsistence farmers and herders, these Aymara Indians have adapted culturally and biologically to the cold and harsh conditions of Bolivia's altiplano. They live and go about their work at extremely high altitudes (up to 4,800 meters/15,600 feet), where partial pressure of oxygen in the air is far lower than most humans are biologically accustomed to.

Experiencing a marked hypoxeamia (insufficient oxygenation of the blood), a person's normal physiological response to being active at such heights is quick and heavy breathing. Most outsiders visiting the altiplano typically need several days to acclimatize to these conditions. Going too high too quickly can cause *soroche* (mountain sickness), with physiological problems such as pulmonary hypertension, increased heart rates, shortness of breath, headaches, fever, lethargy, and nausea. These symptoms usually disappear when one becomes fully acclimated, but most people will still be quickly exhausted by otherwise normal physical exercise.

For the Aymara Indians whose ancestors have inhabited the altiplano for many thousands of years, the situation is different. Through generations of natural selection, their bodies have become biologically adapted to the low oxygen levels. Short-legged and barrel-chested, their small bodies have an unusually large thoracic volume compared to their tropical lowland neighbors and most other humans. Remarkably, their expanded heart and lungs possess about 30 percent greater pulmonary diffusing capacity to oxygenate blood. In short, the distinctly broad chests of the Aymara Indians are biological evidence of their physiological adaptation to the low-oxygen atmosphere of a natural habitat in which they survive as high-altitude agropastoralists. *(See P. Baker (Ed.). (1978).* The biology of high altitude peoples. *London: Cambridge University Press; Rupert, J. L., & Hochachka, P. W. (2001). The evidence for hereditary factors contributing to high altitude adaptation in Andean natives: A review.* High Altitude Medicine & Biology 2 *(2), 235–256.)*

© Victor Englebert

to another and in adopting a new technology, the Comanche were able to take advantage of existing cultural capabilities to thrive in their new situation.

Sometimes societies that developed independently of one another find similar solutions to similar problems. For example, the Cheyenne Indians moved from the woodlands of the Great Lakes region to the Great Plains and took up a form of plains Indian culture resembling that of the Comanche, even though the cultural historical backgrounds of the two groups differed significantly. (Before they transformed into horse-riding bison hunters, the Cheyenne had cultivated crops and gathered

A Comanche bison hunt as painted by artist George Catlin. Plains Indians such as the Comanche and Lakota developed similar cultures, as they had to adapt to similar environmental conditions. (For a map of Native American culture areas, see Figure 7.1.)

wild rice, which fostered a distinct set of social, political, and religious practices.) This is an example of **convergent evolution**—the development of similar cultural adaptations to similar environmental conditions by different peoples with different ancestral cultures.

Especially interesting is that the Cheyenne gave up crop cultivation completely and focused exclusively on hunting and gathering after their move into the vast grasslands of the northern High Plains. Contrary to the popular notion of evolution as a progressive movement toward increased manipulation of the environment, this ethnographic example shows that cultural historical changes in subsistence practices do not always go from dependence on wild food to farming; they may go the other way as well.

Analogous to the phenomenon of convergent evolution is **parallel evolution,** in which similar cultural adaptations to similar environmental conditions are achieved by peoples whose ancestral cultures were already somewhat alike. For example, the development of farming in Southwest Asia and Mesoamerica took place independently, as people in both regions, whose lifeways were already comparable, became dependent on a narrow range of plant foods that required human intervention for their protection and reproductive success. Both developed intensive forms of agriculture, built large cities, and created complex social and political organizations.

It is important to recognize that stability as well as change is involved in cultural adaptation and evolution; episodes of major adaptive change may be followed by long periods of relative stability in a cultural system. For example, about 5,500 years ago a seasonal migratory way of life had evolved among indigenous peoples in New England and Quebec that was well attuned to the natural environmental conditions of the times.[3] Since those conditions remained fairly stable over the next 5,000 years or so, it is understandable that people's lifeways remained relatively unchanged.

This is not to say that culture change was entirely absent, for it was not. Periodically, people refined and enhanced their way of life: They replaced spears and spear-throwers with far-reaching bows and arrows; they enhanced cooking methods by using pottery vessels instead of containers made from bark, wood, or animal hide; they substituted heavy and cumbersome dugout boats with lightweight birch-bark canoes; and they supplemented foods gained in hunting, gathering, and fishing with cultivated corn, beans, and squash.

Despite these changes, however, the native peoples of the region retained the basic structure of their culture and maintained a balance with their resource base well into the 17th century, when the culture had to adjust to pressures associated with European invasions of North America. Such enduring stability suggests success. Had this culture not effectively satisfied people's physical and psychological needs, it would not have endured as it did for thousands of years.

That said, not every group has implemented the changes needed for long-term survival—and some have made changes that failed to bring expected benefits. Moreover, not everybody benefits from changes, especially if change is forced upon them. As history painfully demonstrates, all too often humans have made changes that have had disastrous results, leading to the deaths of thousands, even millions of people—not to mention other creatures—and to the destruction of the natural environment. In short, we must avoid falling into the ethnocentric trap of equating change with progress or seeing everything as adaptive.

Culture Areas

From early on, anthropologists recognized that ethnic groups living within the same broad habitat often share certain culture traits. This reflects the fact that neighboring peoples may easily borrow from each other and that there exists a basic relationship among their similar natural environment, available resources, and subsistence practices.

[3]Haviland, W. A., & Power, M. W. (1994). *The original Vermonters* (2nd ed.). Hanover, NH: University Press of New England.

convergent evolution In cultural evolution, the development of similar cultural adaptations to similar environmental conditions by different peoples with different ancestral cultures.
parallel evolution In cultural evolution, the development of similar cultural adaptations to similar environmental conditions by peoples whose ancestral cultures were already somewhat alike.

Classifying groups according to their culture traits, anthropologists have mapped culture clusters known as **culture areas**—geographic regions in which a number of societies have similar ways of life. Such areas often correspond to ecological areas. In sub-Arctic North America, for example, migratory caribou herds graze across the vast tundra. For dozens of different groups that have made this region their home, these animals provide a major source of food as well as material for shelter and clothing. Adapting to more or less the same ecological resources in this sub-Arctic landscape, these groups have developed similar subsistence technologies and practices in the course of generations. They may speak very different languages, but they may all be said to form part of the same culture area.

Because everything in nature is always in a state of flux—daily, seasonal, and annual cycles of abundance and scarcity, as well as permanent changes in the environment due to destruction of habitat and extinction of plant and animal species—culture areas are not always stable. Moreover, new species may be introduced and technologies invented or introduced from more distant cultures. Such was the case with the indigenous culture area of the Great Plains in North America (Figure 7.1). For thousands of years, many indigenous groups with similar ways of life existed in this vast ecological area between the Mississippi River and the Rocky Mountains. Until the mid-1800s, when European immigrants invaded the region and almost completely annihilated the millions of free-ranging bison, these large grazing herds provided an obvious and practical source of food and materials for clothing and shelter.

The efficiency of indigenous groups in the southern plains increased greatly in the 1600s when they gained access to Spanish horses on the northern Mexican frontier and became mounted bison hunters. During the next century, the new horse complex spread northward to almost every indigenous group ranging in the Great Plains culture area. A total of thirty-one politically independent peoples, including the Cheyenne and Comanche, reached a similar adaptation to this particular grassland region.

So it was that by the time of the Euramerican invasion of their vast hunting territories in the 19th century, the Indians of the Great Plains were all bison hunters, dependent upon this animal for food, clothing, shelter, and bone tools. Each native nation was organized into a number of warrior societies, and prestige came from hunting and fighting skills. Their villages were typically arranged in a distinctive circular pattern, and many re-

culture area   A geographic region in which a number of societies follow similar patterns of life.

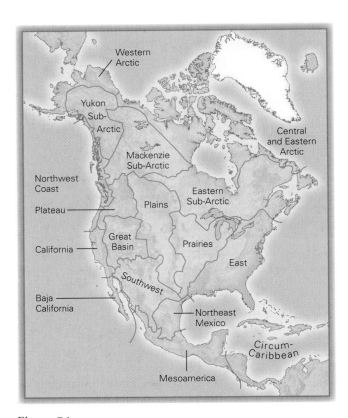

Figure 7.1

The culture area concept was developed by anthropologists in the early part of the 20th century. This map shows the culture areas that have been defined for North and Central America. Within each, there is an overall similarity of native cultures, as opposed to the differences that distinguish the cultures of one area from those of all others.

ligious rituals, such as the Sun Dance, were practiced throughout the region.

During the 1870s and 1880s, railroads were built across the Great Plains, and mass slaughter of bison followed. More than 1 million of these animals were killed every year, mostly by non-Indians interested only in their hides and tongues (tongues were a luxury meat commodity, easily removed and compact to ship). With their herds almost exterminated, Indians of the plains faced starvation, which made it impossible to effectively defend their homelands. This resulted in the near collapse of their traditional cultures from the 1890s onward.

Sometimes geographic regions are not uniform in climate and landscape, so new discoveries do not always spread from one group to another. Moreover, within a culture area, there are variations between local environments, and these favor variations in adaptation. One example of local variations in adaptation is the Great Basin of the western United States—a dry highland area embracing the states of Nevada and Utah, with adjacent portions of California, Oregon, Wyoming, and Idaho.[4]

---

[4]Steward, J. H. (1972). *Theory of culture change: The methodology of multilinear evolution.* Urbana: University of Illinois Press.

The Shoshone Indians who live there are divided into a northern and a western group. Traditionally, both subsisted as nomadic hunters and gatherers, but there were certain distinctions between them. In the north, a relative abundance of game animals made hunting primary and provided for the maintenance of large human populations, requiring a great deal of cooperation among local groups. In the west, by contrast, game was less plentiful so the western Shoshone depended especially upon rabbit hunting and the gathering of wild plants such as pine nuts for their subsistence. Since plants varied considerably in their seasonal and local availability, the western Shoshone were forced to cover vast distances in search of food. Under such conditions, it was most efficient to travel in groups of but a few families, only occasionally coming together with other groups and not always with the same ones.

The Shoshone were not the only inhabitants of the Great Basin. To the south lived the closely related Paiutes. They, too, were foragers (hunter–gatherers) living under similar environmental conditions as the Shoshone, but some Paiute bands inhabiting areas with swampy lowlands managed their food resources more actively by diverting small streams to irrigate wild crops such as wild hyacinth, nut grass, and spike rush. These bulbs and seeds were the mainstay of their food supply. Because this ecological adaptation provided them with higher yields than their northern neighbors, their populations were larger than those of the Shoshone, and they led a less nomadic existence.

Culture Core

Environment and technology are not the only factors that determine a society's pattern of subsistence; social and political organization also influence how technology is applied to the problem of staying alive. This given, if we wish to understand the rise of irrigation agriculture in the great centers of ancient civilization (such as in what are now Egypt, China, Peru, and Iraq), we need to know not only the technological and environmental factors that made the building of large-scale irrigation works possible but also the social and political organization that made it feasible to mobilize the many workers necessary to build and maintain the systems. For this understanding, we must examine the monarchies and priesthoods that coordinated the work, decided where the water would be used, and determined how the agricultural products of this collective venture would be distributed.

The cultural features that are fundamental in the society's way of making its living are called its **culture core.** This includes the society's food-producing techniques, knowledge of available resources in its environment, and the work arrangements involved in applying those techniques to the local environment. For example,

In Bali, gatherings for rituals at water temples allowed farmers to arrange schedules for flooding their rice paddies.

do people work every day for a fixed number of hours, or is most work concentrated during certain times of the year?

The culture core comprises other aspects of culture that bear on the production and distribution of food. Among these is worldview or ideology, evidenced in the ways religious beliefs sometimes prohibit the use of certain readily available and highly nutritious foods. For example, most Muslims and Jews abstain from eating pork because doing so is prohibited by their religion, and most Hindus do not eat beef because they revere cows as sacred animals. There are countless other food taboos, all varying across cultures: horse meat (regularly part of French fare but generally abhorred in England), dogs (not eaten by Europeans but a typical ingredient in Korean meals), monkeys (appreciated by Amazonian Indians but excluded from North American menus), insects (an important source of nutrition in many tropical cultures but considered creepy in most other parts of the world), and humans (not eaten by most humans).[5]

A number of anthropologists, known as *ethnoscientists,* focus on identifying the principles behind native idea systems, how they inform a people about their environment, and what role they play in survival. For example, on the Indonesian island of Bali, ritual meetings were held regularly at water temples, located at the forks of rivers. Part of the ritual included negotiating seasonal schedules for flooding the farmers' rice fields. When the

---

[5]Pelto, G. H., Goodman, A. H., & Dufour, D. L. (Eds.). (2000). *Nutritional anthropology: Biocultural perspectives on food and nutrition.* Mountain View, CA: Mayfield.

---

culture core Cultural features that are fundamental in the society's way of making its living—including food-producing techniques, knowledge of available resources, and the work arrangements involved in applying those techniques to the local environment.

Indonesian government forced abandonment of this traditional system in an effort to promote more productive growing techniques, disaster ensued. Without the water temple rituals, irrigation coordination fell apart, and water shortages and pest infestation became the norm. This led to lower and uneven field yields, plus resentment toward those with better harvests.[6] Eventually, the old system was restored because it worked better. The point of this example is that cultural beliefs, no matter how irrelevant they may seem to outsiders, are often anything but irrelevant if one is to understand another society's subsistence or any other long-established collective practice.

MODES OF SUBSISTENCE

Human societies all across the world have developed a cultural infrastructure that is compatible with the natural resources they have available to them and within the limitations of their various habitats. Each mode of subsistence involves not only resources but also the technology required to effectively capture and utilize them, as well as the kinds of work arrangements that are developed to best suit a society's needs. In the next few pages, we will discuss the major types of cultural infrastructure, beginning with the oldest and most universal mode of subsistence: food foraging.

FOOD-FORAGING SOCIETIES

Before the domestication of food plants and animals, all people supported themselves through **food foraging,** a mode of subsistence involving some combination of hunting, fishing, and gathering wild plant foods. When food foragers had the earth to themselves, they had their pick of the best environments. But gradually areas with rich soils and ample supplies of water were appropriated by farming societies and, more recently, by industrial and postindustrial societies. As a result, small foraging communities were edged out of their traditional habitats by these expanding groups.

Today at most a quarter of a million people (less then 0.005 percent of the world population of about 6 billion) still support themselves mainly as foragers. They are found only in the world's most marginal areas—frozen Arctic tundra, deserts, and inaccessible forests—and typically lead a migratory existence that makes it impractical

to accumulate many material possessions. Because foraging cultures have nearly disappeared in areas having a natural abundance of food and fuel resources, anthropologists are necessarily cautious when it comes to making generalizations about the ancient human past based on in-depth studies of still-existing foraging groups that have adapted to more marginal habitats.

Anthropological research shows that forager diets are typically ample and balanced and that foragers are less likely to experience severe famine than farmers. The material possessions of foragers may be limited, but so is their desire to amass things. Notably, they have plenty of leisure time for concentrating on family ties, social life, and spiritual development—apparently far more than people living in farming and industrial societies. Such findings clearly challenge the once widely held view that food foragers live a miserable existence.

All modern food foragers have had some degree of interaction with neighbors whose ways of life often differ radically from their own. For example, the food-foraging Mbuti pygmies of the Republic of Congo's Ituri rainforest have a complex interdependent relationship with their neighbors, Bantu- and Sudanic-speaking peoples who are farmers. They exchange meat and other products of the forest for farm produce and manufactured goods. During part of the year, these pygmies live in their trading partner's village and are incorporated into his kin group, even to the point of allowing him to initiate their sons.

It is important to note that present-day people who subsist by hunting, fishing, and wild plant collection are not following an ancient way of life because they do not know any better. Rather, they have been forced by circumstances into situations where foraging is the best means of survival or they simply prefer to live this way. In fact, foraging constitutes a rational response to particular ecological, economic, and sociopolitical realities. Moreover, for at least 2,000 years, hunters, fishers, and gatherers have met the demands for commodities such as furs, hides, feathers, ivory, pearls, fish, nuts, and honey within larger trading networks. Like everyone else, most food foragers are now part of a larger system with social, economic and political relations extending far beyond regional, national, or even continental boundaries.

Characteristics of Foraging Communities

The hallmarks of food-foraging societies, particularly those still (or until recently) surviving in marginal areas that are not as naturally rich in food and fuel, include mobility, small group size, flexible division of labor by gender, food sharing, egalitarianism, communal property, and rarity of warfare.

---

[6]Fountain, H. (2000, January 30). Now the ancient ways are less mysterious. *New York Times*, News of the Week, 5.

food foraging Hunting, fishing, and gathering wild plant foods.

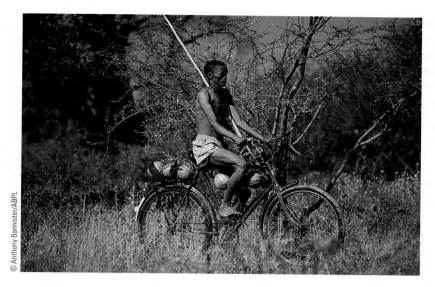

Human groups (including food foragers) do not exist in isolation except occasionally, and even then not for long. The bicycle this Bushman of southern Africa is riding is indicative of his links with the wider world. For 2,000 years, Bushmen have been interacting regularly with neighboring farmers and pastoralists. Much of the elephant ivory used for the keyboards on pianos so widely sought in 19th-century North America came from the Bushmen.

Although much has been written on the theoretical importance of hunting for shaping the supposedly competitive and aggressive nature of the human species, most anthropologists are unconvinced by these arguments. To be sure, warlike behavior on the part of food-foraging people is known, but such behavior is a relatively recent phenomenon in response to pressure from expansionist states. In the absence of such pressures, food-foraging peoples are remarkably nonaggressive and place more emphasis on peacefulness and cooperation than they do on violent competition. We touch on each of the other characteristics below.

Mobility

Food foragers move as needed within a circumscribed region that is their home range to tap into naturally available food sources. In pursuit of wild game, they are often aided by hunting dogs. Although there are countless varieties of dogs, they all descend from Asian wolves first domesticated more than 15,000 years ago.[7] Some groups, such as the Ju/'hoansi in the Kalahari Desert of southern Africa who depend on the reliable and highly drought-resistant mongongo nut, may keep to fairly fixed annual routes and cover only a restricted territory. Others, such as the traditional Shoshone in the western highlands of North America, had to cover a wider territory, their course determined by the local availability of the erratically productive pine nut.

A crucial factor in this mobility is availability of water. The distance between the food supply and water must not be so great that more energy is required to fetch water than can be obtained from the food.

Small Group Size

Another characteristic of the food-foraging adaptation is the small size of local groups, typically fewer than a hundred people. No completely satisfactory explanation for this has been offered, but both ecological and social factors are involved. Among the ecological factors is the **carrying capacity** of the land—the number of people that the available resources can support at a given level of food-getting techniques. This requires adjusting to seasonal and long-term changes in resource availability. A social factor is the **density of social relations** (the number and intensity of interactions among camp members). Higher social density means more opportunities for conflict.

Both carrying capacity and social density are complex variables. Carrying capacity involves not only the immediate presence of food and water but also the tools and work necessary to secure them, as well as short- and long-term fluctuations in their availability. Social density involves not only the number of people and their interactions but also the circumstances and quality of those interactions, as well as the mechanisms for regulating them. A mob of a hundred angry strangers has a different social density than the same number of neighbors enjoying themselves at a block party.

Among food-foraging populations, social density always seems in a state of flux as people spend more or less time away from camp and as they move to other camps, either on visits or more permanently. Among the Ju/'hoansi of southern Africa, for example, exhaustion

---

[7]Schwartz, M. (1997). *A history of dogs in the early Americas* (pp. 1–28). New Haven: Yale University Press.

carrying capacity The number of people that the available resources can support at a given level of food-getting techniques.
density of social relations The number and intensity of interactions among the members of a camp.

of local food resources, conflict within the group, or the desire to visit friends or relatives living elsewhere cause people to leave one group for another. As Canadian anthropologist Richard Lee notes, "Ju love to go visiting, and the practice acts as a safety valve when tempers get frayed. In fact, the Ju usually move, not when their food is exhausted, but rather when only their patience is exhausted."[8]

If a camp has so many children as to create a burden for the working adults, some young families may be encouraged to join others where fewer children live. Conversely, groups with few children may actively recruit families with young offspring in order to ensure the group's survival. Redistribution of people, then, is an important mechanism for regulating social density, as well as for assuring that the size and composition of local groups is suited to local variations in resources. Thus, cultural adaptations help transcend the limitations of the physical environment.

In addition to seasonal or local adjustments, food foragers must make long-term adjustments to resources. Most food-foraging populations stabilize at numbers well below the carrying capacity of their land. In fact, the home ranges of most food foragers can support from three to five times as many people as they typically do. In the long run, it may be more adaptive for a group to keep its numbers low rather than to expand indefinitely and risk destruction by a sudden and unexpected natural reduction in food resources. The population density of foraging groups surviving in marginal environments today rarely exceeds one person per square mile—a very low density.

How food-foraging peoples regulate population size relates to two things: how much body fat they accumulate and how they care for their children. Ovulation requires a certain minimum of body fat, and in traditional foraging societies, this is not achieved until early adulthood. Hence, female fertility peaks between the early and mid-20s, and teenage pregnancies—at least, successful ones—are virtually unknown.[9] Once a child is born, its mother nurses it several times each hour, even at night, and this continues over a period of four or five years. The constant stimulation of the mother's nipple suppresses the level of hormones that promote ovulation, making conception less likely, especially if work keeps the mother physically active, and she does not have a large store of body fat to draw on for energy.[10]

Frequent nursing of children over four or five years acts to suppress ovulation among food foragers such as Bushmen. As a consequence, women give birth to relatively few offspring at widely spaced intervals.

Continuing to nurse for several years, women give birth only at widely spaced intervals. Thus, the total number of offspring remains low but sufficient to maintain stable population size.

Flexible Division of Labor by Gender

Some form of division of labor has been observed in all human societies and is probably as old as human culture. Among food foragers, the hunting and butchering of large game as well as the processing of hard or tough raw materials are almost universally masculine occupations. By contrast, women's work in foraging societies usually focuses on collecting and processing a variety of plant foods, as well as other domestic chores that can be fit to the demands of breastfeeding and do not endanger pregnancy and childbirth.

Among food foragers today, the work of women is no less arduous than that of men. Ju/'hoansi women,

[8]Lee, R. (1993). *The Dobe Ju/'hoansi* (p. 65). Fort Worth: Harcourt Brace.

[9]Hrdy, S. B. (1999). Body fat and birth control. *Natural History 108* (8), 88. See also Frisch, R. (2002). *Female fertility and the body fat connection.* Chicago: University of Chicago Press.

[10]Small, M. F. (1997). Making connections. *American Scientist 85,* 503. See also Konner, M., & Worthman, C. (1980). Nursing frequency, gonadal function, and birth spacing among !Kung hunter-gatherers. *Science 207,* 788–791.

VISUAL COUNTERPOINT

Food foragers such as the Ju/'hoansi have a division of labor in which women gather and prepare "bush" food (here an ostrich egg omelette) and men usually do the hunting.

for example, may walk as many as 12 miles a day two or three times a week to gather food, carrying not only their children but also, on the return home, anywhere from 15 to 33 pounds of food. Still, they do not have to travel quite as far afield as do men on the hunt, and their work is usually less dangerous than hunting. Also, their tasks require less rapid mobility, do not need complete and undivided attention, and are readily resumed after interruption.

All of this is compatible with those biological differences that remain between the sexes. Certainly women who are pregnant or have infants to nurse cannot travel long distances in pursuit of game as easily as men can. By the same token, of course, women may have preferred and been better at the less risky task of gathering.

To say that differing gender roles among food foragers are compatible with the biological differences between men and women is *not* to say that they are biologically determined. Among the Great Plains Indians of North America, for example, are quite a few reported cases of women who gained fame as hunters and warriors—both historically regarded as men's activities. In fact, the division of labor by gender is often far less rigid among food foragers than it is in most other types of society. Thus, Ju/'hoansi males, willingly and without embarrassment, as the occasion demands, will gather wild plant foods, build huts, and collect water, even though all are regarded as women's work.

The nature of women's work in food-foraging societies is such that it can be done while taking care of chil-

dren. Typically, it is also work that can be in company with other women, which provides adult companionship and opportunities for sharing childrearing tasks and useful ideas, venting frustrations, idle chatter, gossip, and laughter. The food-gathering activities of women play a major role in the survival of their group: Research shows that contemporary food foragers may obtain up to 60 or 70 percent of their diets from plant foods, with perhaps some fish and shellfish provided by women (the exceptions tend to be food foragers living in Arctic regions, where plant foods are not available for much of the year).

Although women in food-foraging societies may spend some time each day gathering plant food, men do not spend all or even the greatest part of their time hunting. The amount of energy expended in hunting, especially in hot climates, is often greater than the energy return from the kill. Too much time spent searching out game might actually be counterproductive. Energy itself is derived primarily from plant carbohydrates, and it is usually the female gatherers who bring in the bulk of the calories. A certain amount of meat in the diet, though, guarantees high-quality protein that is less easily obtained from plant sources, for meat contains exactly the right balance of all of the amino acids (the building blocks of protein) the human body requires. No one plant food does this, and in order to get by without meat, people must hit on exactly the right combination of plants to provide the essential amino acids in the correct proportions.

Food Sharing

Another key feature of human social organization associated with food foraging is the sharing of food among adults. It is easy enough to see why sharing takes place, with women supplying one kind of food and men another. Among the Ju/'hoansi, women have control over the food they collect and can share it with whomever they choose. Men, by contrast, are constrained by rules that specify how much meat is to be distributed and to whom. Thus, a hunter has little effective control over the meat he brings into camp. For the individual hunter, meat sharing is really a way of storing it for the future: His generosity, obligatory though it might be, gives him a claim on the future kills of other hunters. As a cultural trait, food sharing has the obvious survival value of distributing resources needed for subsistence.

Relative to this is the importance of the camp as the center of daily activity and the place where food sharing actually occurs. Among nonhuman primates (and probably among human ancestors until they controlled the use of fire), activities tend to be divided between feeding areas and sleeping areas, and the latter tend to be shifted each evening. Historically known food-foraging people, however, live in camps of some permanence, ranging from the dry season camps of the Ju/'hoansi, which serve for the entire winter, to the wet season camps of the Hadza in Tanzania, which are centered on berry picking and honey collection and serve for a few days or weeks at most. Moreover, human camps are more than sleeping areas; people are in and out all day—eating, working, and socializing in camps to a greater extent than any other primates.

Egalitarian Social Relations

An important characteristic of the food-foraging society is its egalitarianism. Because food foragers are usually highly mobile and lack animal or mechanical transportation, they must be able to travel without many encumbrances, especially on food-getting expeditions. By necessity, the material goods they carry with them are limited to the barest essentials, which include implements for hunting, gathering, fishing, building, and cooking. (For example, the average weight of an individual's personal belongings among the Ju/'hoansi is just under 25 pounds.) In this context, it makes little sense for them to accumulate luxuries or surplus goods, and the fact that no one owns significantly more than another helps to limit status differences. Age and sex are usually the only sources of important status differences.

It is important to realize that status differences by themselves do not constitute inequality, a point that is all too easily misunderstood, especially where relations between men and women are concerned. In most tra-

ditional food-foraging societies, women did not and do not defer to men. To be sure, women may be excluded from some rituals that males participate in, but the reverse is also true. Moreover, the fruits of women's labor are not controlled by men but by the women themselves. Nor do women sacrifice their autonomy even in societies in which male hunting, rather than female gathering, brings in the bulk of the food.

Such was the case, for example, among the Innu (Montagnais) Indians of Labrador. Theirs was a society in which the hunt was of overwhelming importance. For their part, women manufactured clothing and other necessities but provided much less of the food than is common among food foragers. Until recently, women as well as men could be shamans. Nevertheless, women were excluded from ritual feasts having to do with hunting—but then, so were men excluded from ritual feasts held by women. Basically, each gender carried out its own activities, with neither meddling in those of the other. Early missionaries to the Innu hunting bands lamented that men had no inclination to make their wives obey them and worked long and hard to convince the Indians that civilization required men to impose their authority on women. But after 300 years of pressing this point, missionaries achieved only limited success.

Food foragers make no attempt to accumulate surplus foodstuffs, often an important source of status in agrarian societies. This does not mean that they live constantly on the verge of starvation, for their environment is their natural storehouse. Except in the coldest climates (where a surplus must be set aside to see people through the long, lean winter season) or in times of acute ecological disaster, some food can almost always be found in a group's territory. Because food resources are typically distributed equally throughout the group (share and share alike is the order of the day), no one achieves the wealth or status that hoarding might bring. In such a society, wealth is a sign of deviance rather than a desirable characteristic.

The food forager's concept of territory contributes as much to social equality as it does to the equal distribution of resources. Most groups have home ranges within which access to resources is open to all members. What is available to one is available to all. If an Mbuti hunter discovers a honey tree, he has first rights; but when he has taken his share, others have a turn. In the unlikely possibility that he does not take advantage of his discovery, others will. No individual within the community privately owns the tree; the system is first come, first served. Therefore, knowledge of the existence of food resources circulates quickly throughout the entire group.

Families move easily from one group to another, settling in any group where they have a previous kinship tie. As noted earlier, the composition of groups among food foragers is always shifting. This loose attitude toward group membership promotes the widest access to resources while maintaining a balance between populations and resources.

Cultural Adaptations and Technology among Foragers

Habitat as well as technology plays an important role in shaping the characteristics of foraging life discussed above. The mobility of food-foraging groups may depend on the availability of water, as among the Ju/'hoansi, or of game animals and other seasonal resources, as among the Mbuti in the Republic of Congo in Central Africa. Different hunting technologies and techniques may also play a part in determining movement, as well as population size, and division of labor by gender.

Consider, for example, the Mbuti pygmies in the Ituri tropical forest. All Mbuti bands hunt elephants with spears. However, for other game, some of the bands use bows and others use large nets. Those equipped with nets have a cooperative division of labor in which men, women, and children collaborate in driving antelope and other game into the net for the kill. Usually, this involves very long hours and movement over great distances as participants surround the animal(s) and beat the woods noisily to chase the game in one direction toward the great nets. Since this sort of "beat-hunt" requires the cooperation of seven to thirty families, those using this method have relatively large camps. Among Mbuti bow hunters, on the other hand, only men go after the game. These archers tend to stay closer to the village for shorter periods of time and live in smaller groups, typically of no more than six families. While there exists no significant difference in overall population densities of net and bow

hunting areas, archers generally harvest a greater diversity of animal species, including monkeys.[11]

FOOD-PRODUCING SOCIETIES

After tool making, which enabled humans to consume significant amounts of meat as well as plant foods, the next truly momentous event in human history was the domestication of plants and animals. Over time, this achievement transformed cultural systems, with humans developing new economic arrangements, social structures, and ideological patterns based either on plant cultivation, breeding and raising animals, or a mixture of both.

The gradual transition from food foraging to food production first took place about 10,000 years ago in Southwest Asia (the Fertile Crescent, including the Jordan River Valley and neighboring regions in the Middle East). This was the beginning of the **Neolithic** or New Stone Age, in which peoples possessed stone-based technologies and depended on domesticated plants and/or animals. Within the next few thousand years, similar early transitions to agricultural economies took place independently in other parts of the world where human groups began to grow and (later) alter wild cereal plants such as wheat, maize (corn), and rice; legumes such as beans; gourds such as squash; and tubers such as potatoes. They did the same with a number of wild animal species ranging in their hunting territories and began to domesticate goats, sheep, pigs, cattle, and llamas (Figure 7.2).

Because these activities brought about a radical transformation in almost every aspect of their cultural systems, Australian-born archaeologist Gordon Childe introduced the term *Neolithic revolution* to refer to the profound culture change associated with the early domestication of plants and animals. Today it is more commonly referred to as the **Neolithic transition.** Marking the beginning of what is traditionally known as the New

---

[11]Bailey, R. C., & Aunger, R. (1989). Net hunters vs. archers: Variation in women's subsistence strategies in the Ituri forest. *Human Ecology 17,* 273–297; Terashima, H. (1983). Mota and other hunting activities of the Mbuti archers: A socio-ecological study of subsistence technology. *African Studies Monograph* (Kyoto), 71–85.

Neolithic The New Stone Age; prehistoric period beginning about 10,000 years ago in which peoples possessed stone-based technologies and depended on domesticated plants and/or animals.

Neolithic transition Sometimes referred to as Neolithic revolution. The profound culture change beginning about 10,000 years ago and associated with the early domestication of plants and animals, and settlement in permanent villages.

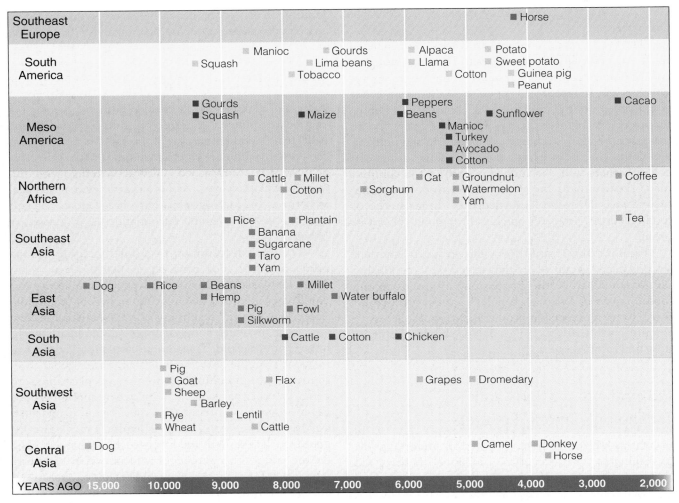

Figure 7.2

Appearance of domesticates in the archaeological record.

Stone Age, this shift changed the very nature of human society. As humans became increasingly dependent on domesticated crops, they mostly gave up their mobile way of life and settled down to till the soil, sow, weed, protect, harvest, and safely store their crops. No longer on the move, they could build more permanent dwellings and began to make pottery for storage of water, food, and so on.

Just why this change came about is one of the important questions in anthropology. Since food production by and large requires more work than food foraging, is more monotonous, is often a less secure means of subsistence, and requires people to eat more of the foods that foragers eat only when they have no other choice, it is unlikely that people voluntarily became food producers.

Initially, it appears that food production arose as a largely unintended by-product of existing food-management practices. Among many examples, we may

consider the Paiute Indians, whose desert habitat in the western highlands of North America includes some oasis-like marshlands. These foragers discovered how to irrigate wild crops in their otherwise very dry homeland, thus increasing the quantity of wild seeds and bulbs to be harvested. Although their ecological intervention was very limited, it allowed them to settle down for longer periods in greater numbers than otherwise would have been possible.

Unlike the Paiute, who just stopped short of a Neolithic transition, other groups elsewhere in the world continued to transform their landscapes in ways that favored the appearance of new varieties of particular plants and animals, which came to take on increasing importance for people's subsistence. Although probably at first accidental, it became a matter of necessity as growth outstripped people's ability to sustain themselves through food foraging. For them, food production became a subsistence option of last resort.

Crop Cultivation in Gardens: Horticulture

With the advent of plant domestication, some societies took up **horticulture** (*hortus,* "garden" in Latin) in which small communities of gardeners cultivate crops with simple hand tools, using neither irrigation nor the plow. Typically, horticulturists cultivate several varieties of food plants together in small, hand-cleared gardens. Because they do not usually fertilize the soil, they use a given garden plot for only a few years before abandoning it in favor of a new one. Horticulturists often can (and sometimes do) grow enough food for their subsistence, and many occasionally produce more than they need for purposes such as inter-village feasts and exchange.

Many horticulturists, however, do not depend exclusively on their gardens for their year-round subsistence. As already indicated by the example of Paiute Indian subsistence practices, societies categorized as food foragers by anthropologists may also engage in some wild food plant management. Likewise, horticulturists do not completely give up food foraging. Although their major food supplies may come from their gardens, they will also hunt game, fish, and collect wild plants foods in the forest whenever they need or get a chance.

One of the most widespread forms of horticulture, especially in the tropics, is **slash-and-burn cultivation,** also known as *swidden farming,* in which the natural vegetation is cut, the slash is subsequently burned, and crops then planted among the ashes. Unfortunately, widespread use of fire in connection with the clearing of vast tracts of Amazonian or Indonesian forest for cattle raising and other development schemes has led many people to see this kind of farming in a negative light. In fact, it is an ecologically sophisticated and sustainable way of raising food, especially in the tropics, when carried out under the right conditions: low population densities and adequate amounts of land. It mimics the diversity of the natural ecosystem, growing several different crops in the same field. Mixed together, the crops are less vulnerable to pests and plant diseases than a single crop.

Not only is the system ecologically sound, but it is far more energy efficient than modern farming methods used in developed countries such as the United States where natural resources such as land and fuel are still relatively cheap and abundant, and many farms operate with financial support in the form of government subsidies or tax breaks. While high-tech farming requires more energy input than it yields, swidden farming produces between 10 and 20 units of energy for every unit expended. A good example of how such a system works is provided by the Mekranoti Kayapo Indians of Brazil's Amazon forest, profiled in the following Original Study.

horticulture Cultivation of crops carried out with simple hand tools such as digging sticks or hoes.
slash-and-burn cultivation Also known as swidden farming. An extensive form of horticulture in which the natural vegetation is cut, the slash is subsequently burned, and crops are then planted among the ashes.

Reburning an old, overgrown slash-and-burn plot in the Amazon forest in Venezuela in preparation for new planting. Although it looks destructive, if properly carried out, slash-and-burn cultivation is an ecologically sound way of growing crops in the tropics.

© Jacques Jangoux/Alamy

Original Study • By Dennis Werner

Gardens of the Mekranoti Kayapo

The planting of a Mekranoti garden always follows the same sequence. First, men clear the forest and then burn the debris. In the ashes, both men and women plant sweet potatoes, manioc, bananas, corn, pumpkins, papaya, sugar cane, pineapple, cotton, tobacco, and annatto, whose seeds yield achiote, the red dye used for painting ornaments and people's bodies. Since the Mekranoti don't bother with weeding, the forest gradually invades the garden. After the second year, only manioc, sweet potatoes, and bananas remain. And after three years or so there is usually nothing left but bananas. Except for a few tree species that require hundreds of years to grow, the area will look like the original forest twenty-five to thirty years later.

This gardening technique, known as slash-and-burn, is one of the most common in the world. At one time critics condemned the technique as wasteful and ecologically destructive, but today we know that, especially in the humid tropics, slash-and-burn may be one of the best gardening techniques possible.

Continuous high temperatures encourage the growth of the microorganisms that cause rot, so organic matter quickly breaks down into simple minerals. The heavy rains dissolve these valuable nutrients and carry them deep into the soils, out of the reach of plants. The tropical forest maintains its richness because the heavy foliage shades the earth, cooling it and inhibiting the growth of the decomposers. A good deal of the rain is captured by leaves before ever reaching the ground.

When a tree falls in the forest and begins to rot, other plants quickly absorb the nutrients that are released. In contrast, with open-field agriculture, the sun heats the earth, the decomposers multiply, and the rains quickly leach the soils of their nutrients. In a few years a lush forest, if cleared for open one-crop agriculture, can be transformed into a barren wasteland.

A few months after the Mekranoti plant banana and papaya, these trees shade the soil, just as the larger forest trees do. The mixing of different kinds of plants in the same area means that

minerals can be absorbed as soon as they are released; corn picks up nutrients very fast, while manioc is slow. Also, the small and temporary clearings mean that the forest can quickly reinvade its lost territory.

Because decomposers need moisture as well as warmth, the long Mekranoti dry season could alter this whole picture of soil ecology. But soil samples from recently burned Mekranoti fields and the adjacent forest floor showed that, as in most of the humid tropics, the high fertility of the Indians' garden plots comes from the trees that are burned there, not from the soil, as in temperate climates.

Getting a good burn is a tricky operation. Perhaps for this reason its timing was left to the more experienced and knowledgeable members of the community. If the burn is too early, the rains will leach out the minerals in the ash before planting time. If too late, the debris will be too wet to burn properly. Then, insects and weeds that could plague the plants will not die and few minerals will be released into the soil. If the winds are too weak, the burn will not cover the entire plot. If they are too strong, the fire can get out of hand.

Shortly after burning the plots and clearing away of some of the charred debris, people began the long job of planting, which took up all of September and lasted into October. In the center of the circular garden plot the women dug holes and threw in a few pieces of sweet potatoes. After covering the tubers with dirt they usually asked a male—one of their husbands or anyone else who happened to be nearby—to stomp on the mound and make a ritual noise resembling a Bronx cheer. This magic would ensure a large crop, I was told. Forming a large ring around the sweet potatoes, the Indians rapidly thrust pieces of manioc stems into the ground, one after the other.

When grown, the manioc stems form a dense barrier to the sweet potato patch, and some of the plants must be cut down to gain entrance. Outside of the ring of manioc, the women plant yams, cotton, sugar cane, and annatto. Banana stalks

and papaya trees, planted by simply throwing the seeds on the ground, form the outermost circle. The Indians also plant corn, pumpkins, watermelons, and pineapple throughout the garden. These grow rapidly and are harvested long before the manioc matures. The garden appears to change magically from corn and pumpkins to sweet potatoes and manioc without replanting.

Mekranoti gardens grew well. A few Indians complained now and then about a peccary that had eaten a watermelon they were looking forward to eating, or that had reduced their corn harvest. Capybara, large rodents usually found near the river banks, were known for their love of sugar cane, but in general the animals seemed to leave the crops alone. Even the leaf-cutting ants that are problems in other areas did not bother the Mekranoti. Occasionally a neighbor who had not planted a new garden would make off with a prized first-year crop, such as pumpkin, watermelon, or pineapple. But even these thefts were rare. In general, the Mekranoti could depend on harvesting whatever they planted.

Eventually, I wanted to calculate the productivity of Mekranoti gardens. Western agronomists knew very little about slash-and-burn crop cultivation. They were accustomed to experiments in which a field was given over to one crop only, and in which the harvest happened all at once. Here, the plants were all mixed together, and people harvested piecemeal whenever they needed something. The manioc could stay in the ground, growing for several years before it was dug up.

I began measuring off areas of gardens to count how many manioc plants, ears of corn, or pumpkins were found there. The women thought it strange to see me struggling through the tangle of plants to measure off areas, 10 meters by 10 meters, placing string along the borders, and then counting what was inside. Sometimes I asked a woman to dig up all of the sweet potatoes within the marked-off area. The requests were bizarre, but the women cooperated just the same, holding on to the ends of the measuring tapes, or sending their children to help. For some plants, like bananas, I simply counted the number of clumps of stalks in the garden, and the number of banana bunches I could see growing in various

clumps. By watching how long it took the bananas to grow, from the time I could see them until they were harvested, I could calculate a garden's total banana yield per year.

After returning from the field, I was able to combine the time allocation data with the garden productivities to get an idea of how hard the Mekranoti need to work to survive. The data showed that for every hour of gardening one Mekranoti adult produces almost 18,000 kilocalories of food. (As a basis for comparison, people in the United States consume approximately 3,000 kilocalories of food per day.) As insurance against bad years, and in case they receive visitors from other villages, they grow far more produce than they need. But even so, they don't need to work very hard to survive. A look at

the average amount of time adults spend on different tasks every week shows just how easygoing life in horticultural societies can be:

8.5 hours	Gardening
6.0 hours	Hunting
1.5 hours	Fishing
1.0 hour	Gathering wild foods
33.5 hours	All other jobs

Altogether, the Mekranoti need to work less than 51 hours a week, and this includes getting to and from work, cooking, repairing broken tools, and all of the other things we normally don't count as part of our work week.

(Excerpted from D. Werner (1990). Amazon journey *(pp. 105–112). Englewood Cliffs, NJ: Prentice-Hall.)* ■

Crop Cultivation: Agriculture

In contrast to horticulture, **agriculture** (*agri,* "field" in Latin) is growing food plants like grains, tubers, fruits, and vegetables in soil prepared and maintained for crop production. This form of more intensive food production involves using technologies other than hand tools, such as irrigation, fertilizers, and the wooden or metal plow pulled by harnessed draft animals. The cultural ecological sophistication of some early agriculturalists is illustrated in this chapter's Anthropology Applied feature. In the so-called developed countries of the world, agriculture relies on fuel-powered tractors to produce food on larger plots of land.

Unlike horticulturists, agriculturists generally grow surplus crops—providing not only for their own needs but food for those of various full-time specialists and nonproducing consumers as well. This surplus may be traded or sold for cash, or it may be coerced out of the farmers through taxes, rent, or tribute (forced gifts acknowledging submission or protection) paid to landowners or other dominant groups. These landowners and specialists—such as traders, carpenters, blacksmiths, sculptors, basket makers, and stonecutters—typically reside in substantial towns or cities, where political power is centralized in the hands of a socially elite class. Dominated by more powerful groups and markets, much of what the farmers do is governed by political and economic forces over which they have little control.

The distinction between horticulture and agriculture is not always an easy one to make. For example, the Hopi Indians of the North American Southwest, in addition to flood plain farming, also irrigate plots near

springs, while using simple hand tools. Moreover, they produce for their own immediate needs and live in small towns without centralized political government.

Early food producers have developed several major crop complexes: two adapted to dry uplands and two to tropical wetlands. In the dry uplands of Southwest Asia, for example, farmers time their agricultural activities with the rhythm of the changing seasons, cultivating wheat, barley, oat, flax, rye, and millet. In the tropical wetlands of Southeast Asia, rice and tubers such as yams and taro are cultivated. In the Americas, people have adapted to natural environments similar to those of Africa and Eurasia, but have cultivated their own indigenous plants. Typically, maize, beans, squash, and the potato are grown in drier areas, whereas manioc is extensively grown in the tropical wetlands.

Characteristics of Agricultural Societies

One of the most significant correlates of plant cultivation was the development of fixed settlements, in which farming families reside together near their cultivated fields. While food foragers stay close to their food by moving around to follow nature's seasonal fluctuations, food producers stay close to theirs by not straying too far from their gardens or farmlands. The task of food production lent itself to a different kind of social organization. Because the hard work of some members of the

agriculture The cultivation of food plants in soil prepared and maintained for crop production. Involves using technologies other than hand tools, such as irrigation, fertilizers, and the wooden or metal plow pulled by harnessed draft animals.

Anthropology Applied

Agricultural Development and the Anthropologist ■ Ann Kendall

Gaining insight into the traditional practices of indigenous peoples, anthropologists have often been impressed by the ingenuity of their knowledge. This awareness has spread beyond the profession to the Western public at large, giving birth to the popular notion that indigenous groups invariably live in some sort of blissful oneness with the environment. But this was never the message of anthropologists, who know that traditional people are only human, and like all human beings, are capable of making mistakes. Yet, just as we have much to learn from their successes, so can we learn from their failures.

Archaeologist Ann Kendall is doing just this in the Patacancha Valley in the Andes Mountains of southern Peru. Kendall is director and founder of the Cusichaca Trust, near Oxford, England, a rural development organization that revives ancient farming practices. In the late 1980s, after working for ten years on archaeological excavations and rural development projects, she invited botanist Alex Chepstow-Lusty of Cambridge University to investigate climatic change and paleoecological data. His findings, along with Kendall's, provided evidence of in-

tensive farming in the Patacancha Valley, beginning about 4,000 years ago. The research showed that over time widespread clearing to establish and maintain farm plots, coupled with minimal terracing of the hillsides, had resulted in tremendous soil loss through erosion. By 1,900 years ago, soil degradation and a cooling climate had led to a dramatic reduction in farming. Then, about 1,000 years ago, farming was revived, this time with soil-sparing techniques.

Kendall's investigations have documented intensive irrigated terrace construction over two periods of occupation, including Inca development of the area. It was a sophisticated system, devised to counteract erosion and achieve maximum agricultural production. The effort required workers to haul load after load of soil up from the valley floor. In addition, they planted alder trees to stabilize the soil and to provide both firewood and building materials. So successful was this farming system by Inca times that the number of people living in the valley quadrupled to some 4,000, about the same as it is now. However, yet another reversal of fortune occurred when the Spanish took over Peru and the terraces

and trees here and elsewhere were allowed to deteriorate.

Armed with these research findings and information and insights gathered through interviews and meetings with locals, the Cusichaca Trust supported the restoration of the terraces and 5.8 km of canal. The effort relied on local labor working with traditional methods and materials—clay (with a cactus mix to keep it moist), stone, and soil. Local families

---

group could provide food for all, others became free to devote their time to inventing and manufacturing the equipment needed for a new sedentary way of life. Tools for digging and harvesting, pottery for storage and cooking, clothing made of woven textiles, and housing made of stone, wood, or sun-dried bricks all grew out of the new sedentary living conditions and the altered division of labor.

The Neolithic transition also brought important changes in social structure. At first, social relations were egalitarian and hardly different from those that prevailed among food foragers. As settlements grew, however, and large numbers of people had to share important resources such as land and water, society became more elaborately organized. Most likely, people formed multifamily kinship groups, each culturally elaborated to provide a socially convenient way to handle the distinctive and often thorny problems of individual and group land use and ownership that may arise in food-producing societies.

Mixed Farming: Crop Growing and Animal Breeding

As noted above, indigenous food-producing cultures in the western hemisphere depended primarily on growing domesticated indigenous crops such as manioc, corn, and beans. With some exceptions, including the Aymara and Quechua, who traditionally also keep llamas and alpacas in their high-altitude homeland in the Andes Mountains of South America (see the Biocultural Connection feature), American Indians obtained sufficient meat, fat, leather, and wool from wild game.

On the other side of both oceans, however, Eurasian and African food-producing peoples often do not have an opportunity to obtain enough vitally important animal proteins from wild game, fish, or fowl (although they would not pass up a rare chance to catch some). Instead, many of these farming cultures have developed a mixed subsistence strategy and combine have replanted 160 hectares of the renovated pre-conquest terraces with maize, potatoes, and wheat, finding the plots up to ten times more productive than they were. Among other related accomplishments, twenty-one water systems have been installed, which reach more than 800 large families, and a traditional concept of home-based gardens has been adapted to introduce European-style vegetable gardens to improve diet and health and to facilitate market gardening. Since 1997, these projects have been under a new and independent local rural development organization known as ADESA.

The Cusichaca Trust is now continuing its pioneering work in areas of extreme poverty in Peru further to the north, such as Apurimac and Ayacucho, using tried and tested traditional technology in the restoration of ancient canal and terrace systems.

(Adapted from K. Krajick (1998). Green-farming by the Incas? Science 281, *323. The 2003 update and elaboration by textbook authors is based on personal communication with Kendall and Cusichaca Trust reports. For more information see www .cusichaca.org.)*

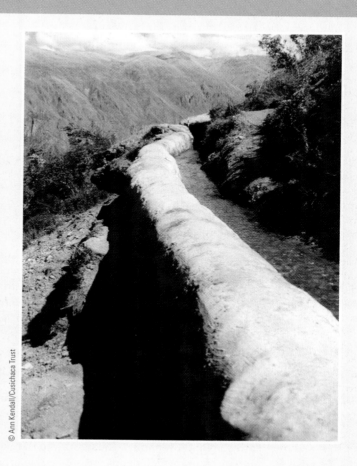
© Ann Kendall/Cusichaca Trust

crop cultivation with animal husbandry. Thus, in addition to growing crops like cereals, tubers, or vegetables, they may also breed and raise animals for food and other purposes, including selling or trading. The variety of wild animals domesticated by humans in Africa and Eurasia includes chickens, ducks, geese, rabbits, pigs, goats, sheep, cattle, camels, dromedaries, donkeys, and horses.

Depending on cultural traditions, ecological circumstances, and animal habits, some species are kept in barns or fenced-off fields, while others may range quite freely in and around the settlement or designated pastures, albeit under supervision, branded or otherwise marked by their owners as private property. For instance, in some English farming communities (not unlike Papua villages in New Guinea) it was historically not unusual to find ear-marked pigs freely roaming in the surrounding woodlands in search of acorns and any other food appealing to their omnivorous appetite.

Likewise, many ancient agricultural communities adapted to high altitude environments from the Alps to the Himalayas have traditionally herded livestock (cows, sheep, horses, and so on) in high summer pastures, leaving their narrow lowland valleys for alternative use—farming grains, keeping orchards, growing vegetables and hay for animal winter food. After the crop harvest, before the weather turns cold and snow covers the higher pastures, those who left the village to tend the herds bring the animals back to the valley for the winter season. This "vertical" seasonal movement of livestock between high altitude summer pastures and lowland valleys is known as *transhumance.*[12]

---

[12]Cole, J. W., & Wolf, E. R. (1999). *The hidden frontier: Ecology and ethnicity in an alpine valley* (with a new introduction). Berkeley: University of California Press; see also Jones, S. (2005). Transhumance re-examined. *Journal of the Royal Anthropological Institute* 11 (4), 841–842.

Pastoralism

One of the more striking examples of human adaptation to the environment is **pastoralism**—breeding and managing large herds of domesticated grazing (and browsing) animals, such as goats, sheep, cattle, horses, llamas, or camels. Unlike the forms of animal husbandry discussed above, pastoralism is a specialized way of life centered on breeding and herding animals.

Completely dependent on livestock for daily survival, families in pastoral cultures may own herds of hundreds of grazing animals whose needs for food and drink determine the pastoralists' everyday routines. When a dozen or more herding families join each other, their collective herds may number in the thousands and sometimes even a few hundred thousand. Unlike crop-cultivators who need to remain close to their fields, pastoral peoples do not usually establish permanent settlements since they must follow or drive their large herds to new pastures on a regular basis. Like their migratory herds, most pastoralists must be mobile and have adjusted their way of life accordingly.

Nomadic Pastoralism:
Bakhtiari Herders in the Zagros Mountains

Nomadic pastoralism is an effective way of living—far more so than sheep or cattle ranching—in environments that are too dry, cold, steep, or rocky for farming, such as the vast, arid grasslands that stretch eastward from northern Africa through the Arabian Desert, across the plateau of Iran and into Turkistan and Mongolia. Today, in Africa and Asia alone, more than 21 million people are pastoralists, still migrating with their herds. These nomadic groups regard movement as a natural part of life. Although some herding groups depend on nearby farmers for certain supplies, and may even earn more from other sources than from their own herds, the nomadic herding lifestyle remains central to their identities.

Counted among the world's pastoral groups are the Bakhtiari, a fiercely independent people who live in the unforgiving Zagros Mountains of western Iran.[13] The Bakhtiari way of life, uniquely adapted to the seasonal fluctuations in their rugged mountainous environment,

involves moving with their grazing animals from winter pastures in low steppe lands to summer pastures on high plateaus. For many thousands of years the Bakhtiari have tended herds of goats and fat-tailed sheep this way. Their lives revolve around these major seasonal migrations needed to provide good grazing lands for their flocks—long hazardous journeys that take them over mountains as high as 12,000 feet and through deep chasms and churning watercourses.

Each fall, before the harsh winter comes to the mountains, these nomads load their tents and other belongings on donkeys and drive their flocks down to the warm plains that border Iraq in the west. Here the grazing land is excellent and well watered during the winter months. In the spring, when the low-lying pastures dry up, the Bakhtiari return to the mountain valleys, where a new crop of grass is sprouting. For this trek, they split into five groups, each containing about 5,000 individuals and 50,000 animals.

The return trip north is especially dangerous because the mountain snows are melting and the gorges are full of turbulent, ice-cold water rushing down from the mountain peaks. This long trek is further burdened by the newborn spring lambs and goat kids. Where the watercourses are not very deep, the nomads ford them. Deeper channels, including one river that is a half-mile wide, are crossed with the help of inflatable goatskin rafts, on which they place infants and elderly or infirm family members, as well as lambs and kids. Men swim alongside the rafts, pushing them through the icy water. If they work from dawn to dusk, the nomads can get all of the people and animals across the river in five days. Not surprisingly, dozens of animals drown each day.

In the mountain passes, where a biting wind numbs the skin and brings tears to the eyes, the Bakhtiari trek a rugged slippery trail. Climbing the steep escarpments is dangerous, and often the stronger men must carry their children and the baby goats on their shoulders as they make their way over the ice and snow to the lush mountain valley that is their destination. During each

---

[13]Material on the Bakhtiari is drawn mainly from Barth, F. (1960). Nomadism in the mountain and plateau areas of Southwest Asia. *The problems of the arid zone* (pp. 341–355). UNESCO; Coon, C. S. (1958). *Caravan: The story of the Middle East* (2nd ed., ch. 13). New York: Holt, Rinehart & Winston; Salzman, P. C. (1967). Political organization among nomadic peoples. *Proceedings of the American Philosophical Society 111*, 115–131.

pastoralism Breeding and managing large herds of domesticated grazing animals, such as goats, sheep, cattle, horses, llamas, or camels.

In the Zagros Mountains region of Iran, pastoral nomads follow seasonal pastures, migrating with their flocks over rugged terrain that includes perilously steep snowy passes and fast ice-cold rivers.

© S. Eras/Images & Stories, Turkey

migration the nomads may cover as many as 200 miles. The journey is familiar but not predictable. It can take weeks, for the flocks travel slowly and require constant attention. Men and older boys walk the route, driving the sheep and goats as they go. Women and children usually ride atop donkeys, along with tents and other equipment.

Reaching their destination, the Bakhtiari set up tents—traditionally black goat-hair shelters woven by the women. The tents are a fine example of adaptation to a changing environment. The goat-hair cloth retains heat and repels water during the winter and keeps out heat during the summer. These portable homes are easy to erect, take down, and transport. Inside, the furnishings are sparse and functional, but also artful. Heavy felt pads or elaborate wool rugs, also woven by the women, cover the ground, and pressed against the inside walls of the tent are stacks of blankets, goatskin containers, copper utensils, clay jugs, and bags of grain.

Central to Bakhtiari subsistence, sheep and goats provide milk, cheese, butter, meat, hides, and wool. Women and girls spend considerable time spinning wool into yarn—sometimes doing so while riding atop donkeys on the less rugged parts of their migration. They use the yarn not only to make rugs and tents, but also clothing, storage bags, and other essentials.

Labor division among the Bakhtiari is according to gender. The chief task of the men is tending the flocks. The women cook, sew, weave, care for the children, and carry fuel and water. With men owning and controlling the animals, which are of primary importance in Bakhtiari life, women have generally lacked both economic and political power. The Bakhtiari live in the political state of Iran but have their own traditional system

of justice, including laws and a penal code. They are governed by tribal leaders, or *khans,* men who are elected or inherit their office. Most Bakhtiari *khans* grew wealthy when oil was discovered in their homeland around the start of the 20th century, and many of them are well educated, having attended Iranian or foreign universities.

Despite this, and although some of them own houses in cities, the *khans* spend much of their lives among their people in the mountains. Such prominence of men in both economic and political affairs is common among pastoral nomads; theirs is very much a man's world. That said, elderly Bakhtiari women eventually may gain a good deal of power. And some women of all ages today are gaining a measure of economic control by selling their beautiful handmade rugs to traders, which brings in cash to their households.

Although pastoral nomads like the Bakhtiari depend greatly on their large herds of grazing animals to meet their daily needs, they do trade surplus animals, wool, and woven rugs with farmers or merchants in exchange for crops and valued commodities such as flour, dried fruit, spices, tea, metal knives, pots and kettles, cotton or linen textiles, guns and (more recently) lightweight plastic containers, sheets, and so on. In other words, there are many ties that connect them to surrounding agricultural and industrial societies.

Intensive Agriculture and Nonindustrial Cities

With the intensification of agriculture, some farming villages grew into towns and even cities (Figure 7.3). In these larger population centers, individuals who had

Figure 7.3
Locations of major early civilizations. Those of Central and South America developed wholly independently of those in Africa and Eurasia. Chinese civilization may have developed independently of those that developed earlier in Mesopotamia, the Egyptian Valley, and the Indus Valley.

previously been engaged in farming were freed to specialize in other activities. Thus, craft specialists such as carpenters, blacksmiths, sculptors, basket makers, and stonecutters contribute to the vibrant, diversified life of the city.

Unlike horticulturists and pastoralists, city dwellers are only indirectly concerned with adapting to their natural environment. Far more important is the need to adapt to living and getting along with their fellow urbanites. Urbanization brings with it a new social order: Marked inequality develops as society becomes more complex, and people are ranked according to how much control they hold over resources, the kind of work they do, their gender, or the family they are born into. As social institutions cease to operate in simple, face-to-face groups of relatives, friends, and acquaintances, they become more formal and bureaucratic, with specialized political institutions.

With urbanization came a sharp increase in the tempo of human cultural change. Writing was invented, trade intensified and expanded, the wheel and the sail were invented, and metallurgy and other crafts were developed. In many early cities, monumental buildings, such as royal palaces and temples, were built by thousands of men, often slaves taken in war. These feats of engineering still amaze modern architects and engineers. The inhabitants of these buildings—the ruling class composed of nobles and priests—formed a central government that dictated the social and religious rules

peasant A rural cultivator whose surpluses are transferred to a dominant group of rulers that uses the surpluses both to underwrite its own standard of living and to distribute the remainder to groups in society that do not farm but must be fed for their specific goods and services in turn.

to be followed and carried out by the merchants, craft specialists, warriors, servants, and other city dwellers.

Notably, these urbanized populations mostly depend for much of their daily food (such as bread, tortillas, vegetables, meat, fish, fruit, milk, butter, and cheese) and fuel (especially firewood for cooking and heating their dwellings) on what is produced or foraged in surrounding areas. For this reason, the urban ruling class has sought to widen its territorial power and political control over rural populations. This is how farmers who raised their own crops and livestock as they saw fit, and who determined themselves if and how much surplus they would produce, lost that traditional self-determination.

Once a dominant group managed to impose its rules on the farmers, it also took control over their capacity to produce more food than the farmers actually needed to survive. In other words, these farmers turned into **peasants.** One of the first anthropologists to study peasant communities was Eric Wolf, who defined them as "rural cultivators whose surpluses are transferred to a dominant group of rulers that uses the surpluses both to underwrite its own standard of living and to distribute the remainder to groups in society that do not farm but must be fed for their specific goods and services in turn."[14]

The Aztec State

The Aztec state, which developed in the Mexican highlands in the 15th century, is a good example of a highly developed urban society among America's indigenous peoples and where an urban political elite also gained control over food production in the surrounding countryside.[15] Its capital city Tenochtitlán (modern-day Mexico City) was located in a fertile valley 7,000 feet above sea level. Its population, along with that of its sister city Tlatelolco, reached about 200,000 in the early 16th century.

[14]Wolf, E. R. (1966). *Peasants* (pp. 4–5). Englewood Cliffs: Prentice-Hall.

[15]Most of the following information is taken from Berdan, F. F. (1982). *The Aztecs of Central Mexico.* New York: Holt, Rinehart & Winston.

GLOBALSCAPE

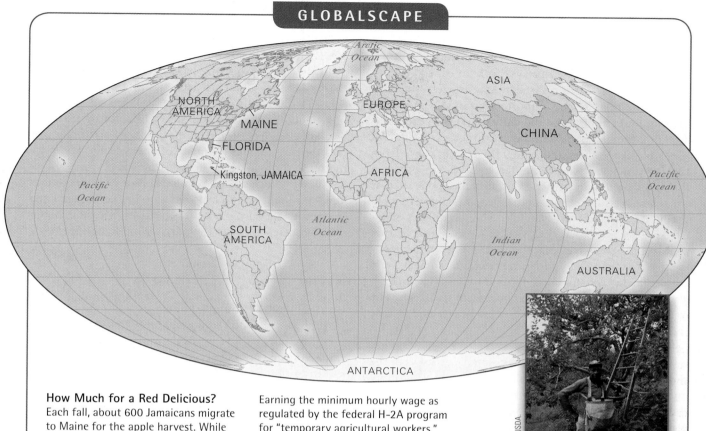

Ken Hammond/USDA.

How Much for a Red Delicious?

Each fall, about 600 Jamaicans migrate to Maine for the apple harvest. While plucking the trees with speed and skill, they listen to reggae music that reminds them of home. Calling each other "brother," they go by nicknames like "Rasta." Most are poor peasants from mountain villages in the Caribbean where they grow yams. But their villages don't produce enough to feed their families, so they go elsewhere to earn cash.

Before leaving Jamaica, they must cut their dreadlocks and shave their beards. Screened and contracted by a labor recruiter in Kingston, they receive a temporary foreign farm workers visa from the U.S. embassy and then fly to Miami. Traveling northward by bus, many work on tobacco farms en route to Maine's orchards (and in Florida's sugar cane fields on the way home).

Earning the minimum hourly wage as regulated by the federal H-2A program for "temporary agricultural workers," they work seven days a week, up to 10 hours daily. Orchard owners value these foreigners, for they are twice as productive as local pickers. Moreover, hand-picked apples graded "extra fancy" earn farmers eight times the price of apples destined for processing.

While in the United States, the Jamaicans remain quite isolated, trying to save as much as they can to send more money home. Just before leaving the country, Rasta and his "brothers" buy things like a television, refrigerator, clothes, and shoes to take home as gifts or as goods to be resold for profit. Lately, their cash-earning opportunities in Maine are disappearing due to a tide of cheaper illegal workers and a diminished demand for U.S.-grown apples due to increasing Chinese competition.

Although rural labor conditions for seasonal migrant workers in the United States have been likened to indentured service (causing some critics to call the federal H-2A program "rent-a-slave"), for Jamaicans like Rasta, it is an opportunity to escape from the dismal poverty on their Caribbean island.

Global Twister When you take a big bite from your next apple, think of a brother like Rasta and ask—what the heck is "fair value" anyway?
See Rathke, L. (1989). To Maine for apples. Salt Magazine 9 *(4),* 24–47.

This makes it five times more populous than the city of London at the same time.

The Aztec social order was stratified into three main classes: nobles, commoners, and serfs. The serfs were bound to the land and the lowest of this class were the slaves. Some had sold themselves into bondage; others were captives taken in war. The state was governed by an absolute monarch, assisted by a large number of government officials who oversaw various functions, such as maintenance of the tax system and the courts of justice, management of government storehouses, and control of military training.

As in early states elsewhere in the world, the foundation of Aztec society was intensive agriculture. Corn was the principal crop. Each family, allotted a plot of land by its kin group, cultivated any of a number of crops, including beans, squash, gourds, peppers, tomatoes, cotton, and tobacco. Only a few animals were domesticated; these included dogs and turkeys (both for eating).

As specialization increased in Aztec society, the market became an extremely important economic and social institution. In addition to the daily markets in each city, larger markets were held in the various cities at different times of year. Buyers and sellers traveled to these from the far reaches of the state. Trade networks between the Aztec capital and other cities brought goods such as chocolate, vanilla beans, and pineapples into Tenochtitlán. The market at Tlatelolco, Tenochtitlán's sister city, was so huge that the Spanish compared it to that of Rome. At the Aztec markets, barter was the primary means of exchange. At times, however, cacao beans and cotton cloaks were used as a form of money. The market also served social functions. People went there not only to buy or to sell but also to meet other people and to hear the latest news.

At Tenochtitlán, with a total area of about 20 square miles, a huge temple and two lavish palaces stood in the central plaza, also called the Sacred Precinct. Surrounding this area were other ceremonial buildings belonging to each kin group. In the city proper stood the houses of the more affluent—graceful, multiroomed, one- and two-story stone and mortar buildings, each surrounding a flower-filled patio and built on a stone platform for protection against floods. It is estimated that there were about 60,000 houses in Tenochtitlán. The focal points of the city were the large pyramidal temples, where religious ceremonies, including human sacrifice, were held.

The Aztec capital sat on an island in the middle of a lake, which has since been drained and filled, and two aqueducts brought in fresh water from springs on the mainland. A 10-mile dike rimmed the eastern end of the city to prevent nearby salty waters from entering the lake around Tenochtitlán. Since the city was surrounded by water, it was unfortified and connected to the mainland by three causeways. Communication among different parts of the city was easy, and people could travel either by land or by water. A series of canals, with footpaths beside them, ran throughout the city. Thousands of canoes plied the canals, carrying passengers and cargo around the city. As in a modern city, housing in Tenochtitlán ranged from squalid to magnificent. Farmers' huts made of wooden posts, thatched straw, and wattle plastered with mud were clustered on the outskirts of the city atop raised fields (*chinampas*) made of piles of mud and plant matter in the shallow lake and marshlands.

While the Spanish invaders were very impressed by Tenochtitlán's magnificence as one of the largest cities in the world, that did not prevent them from completely destroying it soon after their arrival in Mexico in 1519.

INDUSTRIAL SOCIETIES

Until about 200 years ago, human societies all across the world had developed a cultural infrastructure based on foraging, horticulture, agriculture, pastoralism, crafts, trade, or some combination of these. This changed with the invention of the steam engine in England, which brought about an industrial revolution that quickly spread to other parts of the globe. Machines and tools powered by water, wind, and steam (followed by oil, gas, and diesel fuel) replaced human labor and hand tools, increasing factory production and facilitating mass transportation.

Throughout the 1800s and 1900s, this resulted in large-scale industrialization of many societies. Technological inventions utilizing oil, electricity, and (since the 1940s) nuclear energy brought about more dramatic changes in social and economic organization on a worldwide scale. In the late 20th century, the electronic-digital revolution made the production and distribution of information the center of economic activity in some wealthy societies.

Questions for Reflection

1. Since the beginning of human history, our species has met the challenge of survival by adapting to different environments. In capturing essential natural resources, we have also modified these environments. Do you know any examples of landscapes radically transformed for economic reasons? Who benefits from such environmental changes in the long run?

2. What was so radical about the Neolithic transition that prompted some to refer to it as a revolution? Can you think of any equally radical changes in subsistence practices going on in the world today?

3. Consider the ideas of change and progress in light of the agricultural development project described in the Anthropology Applied box. Come up with your own definition of progress that goes beyond the standard idea of technological and material advancement.

4. Technological development in industrial societies often results in highly productive machines effectively replacing animal and human workers. Think of a useful mechanical device and consider its benefits and costs, not only to you but also to others.

5. When shopping for groceries in a supermarket, try to imagine the great chain of human hands that was involved in getting something as simple as a nice red apple from a distant orchard to your own mouth. How many people do you think handled the fruit to get it to you?

Suggested Readings

Bates, D. G. (2001). *Human adaptive strategies: Ecology, culture, and politics* (2nd ed.). Boston: Allyn & Bacon.

Explores different adaptive practices and their correlative political structures. Theoretical issues are made accessible through use of readable ethnographic case studies.

Bogucki, P. (1999). *The origins of human society.* Oxford, England: Blackwell.

Comprehensive global history of the human species, tracing the process of cultural evolution from our prehistoric beginnings as foragers to the creation of agricultural economies leading to complex societies and empires. As a record of human achievements, this book successfully incorporates the explosion in archaeological data accumulated since 1950.

Chatty, D. (1996). *Mobile pastoralists: Development planning and social change in Oman.* New York: Columbia University Press.

This study looks at the forces of modernization in a nomadic community and the resulting shift from herding to wage labor, as well as the changing role of women.

Lee, R. B., & Daly, R. H. (1999). *The Cambridge encyclopedia of hunters and gatherers.* New York: Cambridge University Press.

This is an essential reference text on foragers.

Lustig-Arecco, V. (1975). *Technology: Strategies for survival.* New York: Holt, Rinehart & Winston.

This text focuses especially on the technoeconomic adaptation of hunters, pastoralists, and farmers.

Schrire, C. (Ed.). (1984). *Past and present in hunter-gatherer studies.* Orlando: Academic Press.

This collection of papers demolishes many a myth (including several held by anthropologists) about food-foraging societies. Especially recommended is the editor's introduction, "Wild Surmises on Savage Thoughts."

Thomson Audio Study Products

Enjoy the MP3-ready Audio Lecture Overviews for each chapter and a comprehensive audio glossary of key terms for quick study and review. Whether walking to class, doing laundry, or studying at your desk, you now have the freedom to choose when, where, and how you interact with your audio-based educational media. See the preface for information on how to access this on-the-go study and review tool.

The Anthropology Resource Center

www.thomsonedu.com/anthropology
The Anthropology Resource Center provides extended learning materials to reinforce your understanding of key concepts in the four fields of anthropology. For each of the four fields, the Resource Center includes dynamic exercises including video exercises, map exercises, simulations, and "Meet the Scientists" interviews, as well as critical thinking questions that can be assigned and e-mailed to instructors. The Resource Center also provides breaking news in anthropology and interesting material on applied anthropology to help you link what you are learning to the world around you.

8 Economic Systems

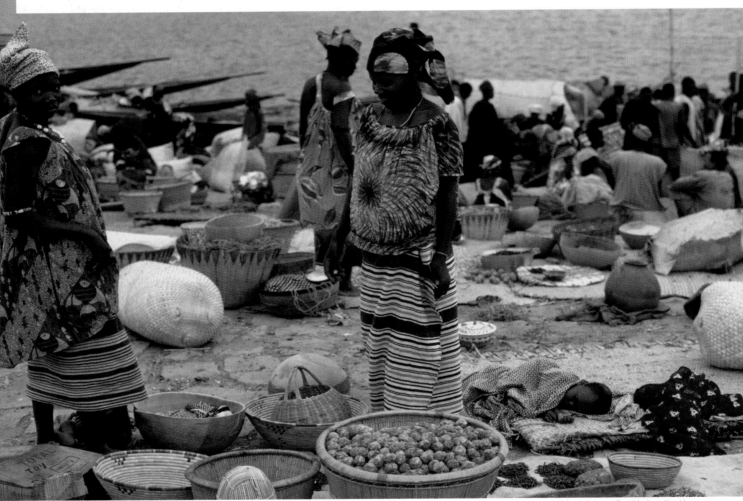

© Sarah Errington/Eye Ubiquitous/Hutchinson

CHALLENGE ISSUE

All humans face the challenge of gaining and maintaining access to resources needed for immediate and long-term survival. Whatever we lack, we may seek to get by peaceful means through exchange or trade. In today's capitalist societies people can exchange almost anything of value without ever actually meeting in person. But a fundamental characteristic of the market in traditional agricultural and pastoral cultures is that it is a specific location where people meet in person to exchange goods at designated times. In such economic transactions, humans forge and affirm social networks that play a key role in the search for safety and well-being. At this outdoor market by the Niger River in Mali, West Africa, people barter, buy, and sell goods in face-to-face encounters.

How Do Anthropologists Study Economic Systems?

Anthropologists study the means by which goods are produced, distributed, and consumed in the context of the total culture of particular societies. Although they have adopted theories and concepts from economists, most anthropologists recognize that theoretical principles derived from the study of capitalist market economies have limited applicability to economic systems in societies that are not industrialized and where people do not produce and exchange goods for private profit. This is because, in these nonstate societies, the economic sphere of behavior is not separate from the social, religious, or political spheres.

How Do Different Societies Organize Their Economic Resources and Labor?

In small-scale nonindustrial societies, land and other valuable resources are usually controlled by groups of relatives, and individual ownership is rare. Division of labor is by age and gender with some craft specialization. Production takes place in the quantity and at the time required, and most goods are consumed by the group that produces them. This is notably different from the economic arrangements in large-scale industrial and postindustrial societies where there is a much more complex division of labor, individuals or business corporations own property, producers and consumers rarely know each other, and transactions take place by means of money.

How and Why Are Goods Exchanged or Redistributed?

People exchange goods through reciprocity, redistribution, and/or market exchange. Reciprocity involves the exchange of goods and services of roughly equivalent value and is often undertaken for ritual or prestige purposes. Redistribution requires a government and/or religious elite to collect and reallocate resources, in the form of either goods or services. Leveling mechanisms ensure that no one accumulates significantly more goods than anyone else. Market exchange in nonindustrial societies takes place in designated locations where people trade goods, meet friends and strangers, and find entertainment. In industrial or capitalist societies, market exchange may be indirect, impersonal, and mediated by money or capital in the form of shares or stock. With the advent of digital technology, trading is also increasingly conducted on the Internet in an entirely impersonal manner.

An **economic system** is an organized arrangement for producing, distributing, and consuming goods. Since a people, in pursuing a particular means of subsistence, necessarily produces, distributes, and consumes things, it is obvious that our discussion of subsistence patterns in the previous chapter involved economic matters. Yet economic systems encompass much more than we have covered so far. Now comes the rest of the story.

ECONOMIC ANTHROPOLOGY

Studying the economies of traditional small-scale societies, researchers from industrial and postindustrial capitalist societies run the risk of interpreting anthropological data in terms of their own technologies, their own values of work and property, and their own determination of what is rational. Take, for example, the following statement from just one respected textbook in economics: "In all societies, the prevailing reality of life has been the inadequacy of output to fill the wants and needs of the people."[1] This ethnocentric assertion fails to take into consideration the fact that in many societies people's wants are maintained at levels that can be fully and continuously satisfied, and without jeopardizing the environment. In such societies, people gather or produce goods in the quantity and at the time required, and to do more than this makes no sense at all.

THOMSON AUDIO STUDY PRODUCTS Take advantage of the MP3-ready Audio Lecture Overviews and comprehensive audio glossary of key terms for each chapter. See the preface for information on how to access this on-the-go study and review tool.

Thus, no matter how hard they may work when hard work is called for, at other times they will have available hours, days, or even weeks on end to devote to "unproductive" (in the economic sense) activities. To observers from industrial or capitalist societies, such people may seem lazy—and if they happen to be hunters and gatherers, even the skillful or strenuous work they do is likely to be misinterpreted. To those whose livelihoods depend on farming, trading, factory or office work, hunting is typically defined as a sport. Hence, the male hunters in foraging societies are often perceived as spending virtually all of their time in recreational pursuits, while the female food gatherers are seen as working themselves to the bone.

To understand how the schedule of wants or demands of a given society is balanced against the supply of goods and services available, it is necessary to introduce a noneconomic variable—the anthropological variable of culture. In any given economic system, economic processes cannot be interpreted without culturally defining the demands and understanding the conventions that dictate how and when they are satisfied. The fact is, the economic sphere of behavior is *not* separate from the social, religious, and political spheres and thus is not completely free to follow its own purely economic logic. To be sure, economic behavior and institutions can be analyzed in strictly economic terms, but to do so is to ignore crucial noneconomic cultural considerations, which do, after all, have an impact on the way things are in real life. As a case in point, we may look briefly at yam production among the Trobriand Islanders, who inhabit a group of coral islands that lie in the southern Pacific Ocean off the eastern tip of New Guinea.[2]

The Yam Complex in Trobriand Culture

Trobriand men spend a great deal of their time and energy raising yams—not for themselves or their own households, but to give to others, normally their sisters and married daughters. The purpose of cultivating these starchy edible roots is not to provision the households that receive them, because most of what people eat they grow for themselves in gardens where they plant taro, sweet potatoes, tapioca, greens, beans, and squash, as well as breadfruit and banana trees. The reason a man gives yams to a woman is to show his support for her husband and to enhance his own influence.

Once received by the woman, the gift yams are loaded into her husband's yam house, symbolizing his worth as a man of power and influence in his community. He may use some of these yams to purchase a variety of things, including arm shells, shell necklaces and earrings, betel nuts, pigs, chickens, and locally produced goods such as wooden bowls, combs, floor mats, lime pots, and even magic spells. Some he must use to fulfill social obligations. For instance, a man is expected to present yams to the relatives of his daughter's husband when she marries and again when death befalls a member of the husband's family. Finally, any man who aspires to high status and power is expected to show his worth by organizing a yam competition, during which he gives away huge quantities of yams to invited guests. As anthropologist Annette Weiner explains: "A yam house,

[1]Heilbroner, R. L., & Thurow, L. C. (1981). *The economic problem* (6th ed., p. 327). Englewood Cliffs, NJ: Prentice-Hall.

economic system An organized arrangement for producing, distributing, and consuming goods.

[2]Weiner, A. B. (1988). *The Trobrianders of Papua New Guinea.* New York: Holt, Rinehart & Winston.

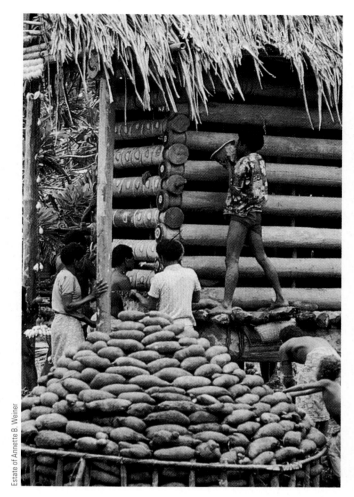

Estate of Annette B. Weiner

then, is like a bank account; when full, a man is wealthy and powerful. Until yams are cooked or they rot, they may circulate as limited currency. That is why, once harvested, the usage of yams for daily food is avoided as much as possible."[3]

By giving yams to his sister or daughter, a man not only expresses his confidence in the woman's husband, but he also makes the latter indebted to him. Although the recipient rewards the gardener and his helpers by throwing a feast, at which they are fed cooked yams, taro, and—what everyone especially looks forward to— ample pieces of pork, this in no way pays off the debt. The debt can only be repaid in women's wealth, which consists of bundles of banana leaves and skirts made of the same material dyed red.

Although the banana leaf bundles are of no utilitarian value, extensive labor is invested in their production, and large quantities of them, along with skirts, are regarded as essential for paying off all the members of other family groups who were close to a recently deceased relative in life and who assisted with the funeral. Also, the wealth and vitality of the dead person's family group is measured by the quality and quantity of the bundles and skirts so distributed. Because a man has received yams from his wife's brother, he is obligated to provide his wife with yams for purchasing the necessary bundles and skirts, beyond those she has produced, to help with payments following the death of a member of her family. Because deaths are unpredictable, and can occur at any time, a man must have yams available for his

Trobriand Island men devote a great deal of time and energy to raising yams, not for themselves but to give to others. These yams, which have been raised by men related through marriage to a chief, are about to be loaded into the chief's yam house.

wife when she needs them. This, and the fact she may require all of his yams, acts as an effective check on a man's wealth.

Like people the world over, the Trobriand Islanders assign meanings to objects that make those objects worth far more than their cost in labor or materials. Yams, for example, establish long-term relationships that lead to other advantages, such as access to land, protection, assistance, and other kinds of wealth. Thus, yam exchanges are as much social and political transactions as they are economic ones. Banana leaf bundles and skirts, for their part, are symbolic of the political status of families and of their immortality. In their distribution, which is related to rituals associated with death, we see how men in Trobriand society are ultimately dependent on women and their valuables.

So important are these matters to Trobrianders that even with the infiltration of Western culture—money, education, religion, and law—they remain as committed to yam cultivation and to the production of women's

[3]Weiner, A. B. (1988). *The Trobrianders of Papua New Guinea* (p. 86). New York: Holt, Rinehart & Winston.

wealth. Looked at in terms of modern capitalist economics, these activities appear meaningless, but viewed in terms of Trobriand values and concerns, they make a great deal of sense.

PRODUCTION AND ITS RESOURCES

In every society, particular customs and rules govern the kinds of work done, who does the work, attitudes toward the work, how it is accomplished, and who controls the resources necessary to produce desired goods, knowledge, and services. The primary resources in any culture are raw materials, technology, and labor. The rules directing the use of these are embedded in a people's culture and determine the way the economy operates within any given natural environment.

Control of Land and Water Resources

All societies regulate allocation of valuable natural resources—especially land and water. Food foragers must determine who will hunt game and gather plants in their home range and where these activities take place. Groups that rely on fishing or growing crops need to make similar decisions concerning who carries out which task on which stretch of water or land. Farmers must have some means of determining title to land and access to water supplies for irrigation. Pastoralists require a system that determines rights to watering places and grazing land, as well as the right of access to land where they move their herds.

In Western capitalist societies, a system of private ownership of land and rights to natural resources generally prevails. Although elaborate laws have been enacted to regulate the buying, owning, and selling of land and water resources, if individuals wish to reallocate valuable farmland to some other purpose, for instance, they generally can.

In traditional nonindustrial societies, land is often controlled by kinship groups such as the family or band rather than by individuals. For example, among the Ju/'hoansi of the Kalahari Desert, each band (a local group of anywhere from ten to thirty people) lives on roughly 250 square miles of land, which they consider to be their territory—their own country. These territories are defined not in terms of boundaries but in terms of water holes that are located within them. The land is said to be "owned" by those who have lived the longest in the band, usually a group of brothers and sisters or cousins. Their concept of ownership, however, is not something easily translated in modern Western terms. Suffice it to say that within their traditional worldview, no part of

their homeland can be sold for money or traded away for goods. Outsiders must ask permission to enter the territory—but denying the request would be unthinkable.

The practice of defining territories on the basis of core features—be they water holes (as among the Ju/'hoansi), watercourses (as among Indians of the northeastern United States), unique sites in the landscape where ancestral spirits are thought to dwell (as among the Aborigines in Australia), or whatever—is typical of food foragers. Typically, territorial boundaries are left rather vaguely defined. To avoid friction, foragers may designate part of their territory as a buffer zone between them and their neighbors. The adaptive value of this is obvious: The size of band territories, as well as the size of the bands, can adjust to keep in balance with availability of resources in any given place. Such adjustment would be more difficult under a system of individual ownership of clearly bounded land.

Among some West African farming groups, a tributary system of land ownership prevails. All land is said to belong to the head chief, who allocates it to various subchiefs, who in turn distribute it to family groups. Then the family group leaders assign individual plots to each farmer. Just as in traditional Europe, these African people owe allegiance to the subchiefs (or nobles) and the head chief (or king). The people who work the land must pay tribute in the form of products or special services such as fighting for the king when necessary.

These people do not really own the land; rather, it is a kind of lease. Yet as long as the land is kept in use, rights to such use will pass to their heirs. No user, however, can give away, sell, or otherwise dispose of a plot of land without approval from the elder of the family group. When an individual no longer uses the allocated land, it reverts to the head of the large family group, who reallocates it to some other group member. The important operative principle here is that the system extends the individual's right to use land for an indefinite pe-

© Irven DeVore/Anthro-Photo

A Ju/'hoansi water hole. The practice of defining territories on the basis of core features such as water holes is typical of food foragers, such as these people of the Kalahari Desert in southern Africa.

riod, but the land is not "owned" outright. This serves to maintain the integrity of valuable farmland as such, preventing its loss through subdivision and conversion to other uses.

Technology Resources

All societies have some means of creating and allocating tools that are used to produce goods, as well as traditions concerning passing them on to succeeding generations. The number and kinds of tools a society uses—which, together with knowledge about how to make and use them constitute its **technology**—are related to the lifestyles of its members. Food foragers and pastoral nomads who are frequently on the move are apt to have fewer and simpler tools than more settled peoples such as sedentary farmers. A great number of complex tools would hinder mobility. Thus, the average weight of an individual's personal belongings among the Ju'hoansi is just under 25 pounds, limited to the barest essentials such as implements for hunting, gathering, fishing, building, and cooking.

Food foragers make and use a variety of tools, many of which are ingenious in their effectiveness. Some of these they make for their individual use, but codes of generosity are such that a person may not refuse to give or loan what is requested. Tools may be given or loaned to others in exchange for the products resulting from their use. For example, a Ju/'hoansi who gives his arrow to another hunter has a right to a share in any animals the hunter kills. Game is considered to "belong" to the man whose arrow killed it, even when he is not present

on the hunt. In this context, it makes little sense for them to accumulate luxuries or surplus goods, and the fact that no one owns significantly more than another helps to limit status differences.

Among horticulturists, the axe, digging stick, and hoe are the primary tools. Since these are relatively easy to produce, almost everyone can make them. Whoever makes a tool has first rights to it, but when he or she is not using it, any family member may ask to use it, and the request is rarely denied. Refusal would cause people to treat the tool owner with scorn for this singular lack of concern for others. If a relative helps raise the crop traded for a particular tool, that relative becomes part owner of the implement, and it may not be traded or given away without his or her permission.

In permanently settled agricultural communities, tools and other productive goods are more complex, heavier, and costlier to make. In such settings, individual ownership tends to be more absolute, as are the conditions under which people may borrow and use such equipment. It is easy to replace a knife lost by a relative during palm cultivation but much more difficult to replace an iron plow or a diesel-fueled harvesting machine. Rights to the ownership of complex tools are more rigidly applied; generally the person who has funded the purchase of a complex piece of machinery is considered the sole owner and may decide how and by whom it will be used.

technology Tools and other material equipment, together with the knowledge of how to make and use them.

Labor Resources and Patterns

In addition to raw materials and technology, labor is a key resource in any economic system. A look around the world reveals many different labor patterns, but two features are almost always present in human cultures: a basic division of labor by gender and by age.

Division of Labor by Gender

Anthropologists have studied extensively the social division of labor by gender in cultures of all sorts. Whether men or women do a particular job varies from group to group, but typically work is divided into the tasks of either one or the other. For example, the practices most commonly regarded as "women's work" tend to be those that can be carried out near home and that are easily resumed after interruption. The tasks historically often regarded as "men's work" tend to be those requiring physical strength, rapid mobilization of high bursts of energy, frequent travel at some distance from home, and assumption of high levels of risk and danger.

Many exceptions occur, however, as in those societies where women regularly carry burdensome loads or put in long hours of hard work cultivating crops in the fields. In some societies, women perform almost three-quarters of all work, and in several societies they have served as warriors. For example, in the 19th-century West African kingdom of Dahomey, in what is now called Benin, thousands of women served in the armed forces of the Dahomean king, and some considered the women to be better fighters than their male counterparts. Also, there are references to female warriors in ancient Ireland, and archaeological evidence indicates their presence among Vikings. During World War II in

the early 1940s, some 58,000 Soviet women engaged in frontline combat defending their homeland against German invaders, and North Vietnamese women fought in mixed-gender army units during the Vietnam War in the 1960s and early 1970s.

Whether or not women should participate in direct combat operations is an ongoing issue in the United States. Clearly, the division of labor by gender cannot be explained simply as a consequence of sex differences, whether they be of male strength and expendability or female reproductive biology.

Instead of looking for key biological factors to explain the social division of labor, a more useful strategy is to examine the kinds of work that men and women do in the context of specific societies to see how it relates to other cultural and historical factors. Researchers find a continuum of patterns, ranging from flexible integration of men and women to rigid segregation by gender.[4]

The *flexible/integrated pattern* is exemplified by the Ju/'hoansi discussed above and is seen most often among food foragers (as well as communities where crops are traditionally cultivated primarily for family consumption). In such societies, men and women perform up to 35 percent of activities with approximately equal participation, and tasks deemed especially appropriate for one gender may be performed by the other, without loss of face, as the situation warrants. Where these practices prevail, boys and girls grow up in much the same way, learn to value cooperation over competition, and become equally habituated to adult men and women, who interact with one another on a relatively equal basis.

Societies following a *segregated pattern* define almost all work as either masculine or feminine, so men and women rarely engage in joint efforts of any kind. In such societies, it is inconceivable that someone would even think of doing something considered the work of the opposite sex. This pattern is frequently seen in pastoral nomadic, intensive agricultural, and industrial societies, where men's work keeps them outside the home for much of the time.

Typically, men in such societies are expected to be tough, aggressive, and competitive—and this often involves assertions of male superiority, and hence authority, over women. Historically, societies segregated by gender often have imposed their control on those featuring integration, upsetting the egalitarian nature of the latter.

In the third pattern of labor division by gender, sometimes called the *dual sex configuration,* men and women carry out their work separately, as in societies segregated

Often, work that is considered inappropriate for women (or men) in one society is performed by them in another. Here we see female stone construction laborers in Bangalore, India, who carry concrete atop their heads.

© David Wells/The Image Works

---

[4]Sanday, P. R. (1981). *Female power and male dominance: On the origins of sexual inequality* (pp. 79–80). Cambridge, England: Cambridge University Press.

by gender, but the relationship between them is one of balanced complementarity rather than inequality. Although competition is a prevailing ethic, each gender manages its own affairs, and the interests of both men and women are represented at all levels. Thus, as in integrated societies, neither gender exerts dominance over the other. The dual sex orientation may be seen among certain American Indian peoples whose economies were based upon subsistence farming, as well as among several West African kingdoms, including that of the aforementioned Dahomeans.

Division of Labor by Age

Division of labor according to age is also typical of human societies. Among the Ju/'hoansi, for example, children are not expected to contribute significantly to subsistence until they reach their late teens. Indeed, until they possess adult levels of strength and endurance, many "bush" foods are tough for them to gather.

The Ju/'hoansi equivalent of retirement comes somewhere around the age of 60. Elderly people, while they will usually do some foraging for themselves, are not expected to contribute much food. However, older men and women alike play an essential role in spiritual matters. Freed from food taboos and other restrictions that apply to younger adults, they may handle ritual substances considered dangerous to those still involved with hunting or having children. By virtue of their old age, they have memories of customary practices and events that happened far in the past. Thus, they are repositories of accumulated wisdom—the libraries of a nonliterate people—and are able to suggest solutions to problems younger adults have never before had to face. Considered useful for their knowledge, they are far from being unproductive members of society.

In some food-foraging societies, women do continue to make a significant contribution to provisioning in their later years. Among the Hadza of East Africa, the input of older women is critical to their daughters, whose foraging abilities are significantly impaired when they have new infants to nurse. This is because lactation is energetically expensive, along with the fact that holding, carrying, and nursing an infant all interfere with the mother's foraging efficiency. Those most immediately affected by this are a woman's weaned children not yet old enough to forage effectively for themselves. The problem is solved by the foraging efforts of grandmothers.[5]

In many traditional farming societies, children as well as older people may make a greater contribution to the economy in terms of work and responsibility than is

This Thai girl exemplifies the use of child labor in many parts of the world, often by large corporations. Even in Western countries, child labor plays a major economic role.

common in industrial or postindustrial societies. For instance, in Maya peasant communities in southern Mexico and Guatemala, children not only look after their younger brothers and sisters but also help with housework. Girls begin to make a substantial contribution to the work of the household by age 7 or 8. By age 11 they are constantly busy with an array of chores—grinding corn, making tortillas, fetching wood and water, sweeping, and so forth. Young boys have less to do but are given small tasks, such as bringing in the chickens or playing with a baby. However, by age 12 they are carrying toasted tortillas to the men out working in the fields and returning with loads of corn.[6]

Similar situations are not unknown in industrial societies. In Naples, Italy, children play a significant role in the economy. At a very young age, girls begin to take on responsibilities for housework, leaving their mothers and older sisters free to earn money for the household. Nor is it long before little girls are apprenticed out to neighbors and kin, from whom they learn the skills that enable them, by age 14, to enter a small factory or workshop. Typically, girls turn over earned wages to their mothers. Boys, too, are apprenticed out at an early age, but

[5]Hawkes, K., O'Connell, J. F., & Blurton Jones, N. G. (1997). Hadza women's time allocation, offspring, provisioning, and the evolution of long postmenopausal life spans. *Current Anthropology 38*, 551–577.

[6]Vogt, E. Z. (1990). *The Zinacantecos of Mexico, a modern Maya way of life* (2nd ed., pp. 83–87). Fort Worth: Holt, Rinehart & Winston.

they may achieve more freedom from adult control by becoming involved in various street activities not available to girls.[7]

The use of child labor has become a matter of increasing concern as large capitalist corporations rely more and more on the low-cost manufacture of goods in the world's poorer countries. Although reliable figures are hard to come by, it is estimated that there are some 15 million bonded child laborers in South Asia alone, including some as young as 4 years old. Although the United States long ago passed laws prohibiting institutionalized child labor, the country imports at least $100 million worth of products manufactured by poorly paid children, ranging from rugs and carpets to clothing and soccer balls.[8]

Cooperative Labor

Cooperative work groups can be found everywhere—in foraging as well as food-producing and in nonindustrial as well as industrial societies. Often, if the effort involves the whole community, a festive spirit permeates the work. Jomo Kenyatta (see Anthropologist of Note), who became president of the East African country of Kenya after it won independence from British colonial rule in 1963, describes a happy moment in a communal work day of a Kikuyu farming village such as his own:

> If a stranger happens to pass by, he will have no idea that these people who are singing and dancing have completed their day's work. This is why most Europeans have erred by not realizing that the African in his own environment does not count hours or work by the movement of the clock, but works with good spirit and enthusiasm to complete the tasks before him.[9]

In some parts of East Africa, work parties begin with the display of a pot of millet beer to be consumed after the tasks have been finished. Home-brewed from millet, their major cereal crop, the beer is not really payment for the work; indeed, the labor involved is worth far more than the beer consumed. Rather, drinking the low-alcohol but highly nutritious beverage together is more of a symbolic activity to celebrate the spirit of friendship and mutual support, whereas recompense comes as individuals sooner or later participate in work parties for others.

In most human societies, the basic unit within which cooperation takes place is the household. It is both a unit of production and consumption; only in industrial societies have these two things been separated. The Maya farmer in Guatemala, for example, unlike his North American counterpart (but like peasant and subsistence farmers everywhere), is not so much running a commercial enterprise as he is a household. He is motivated by a desire to provide for the welfare of his own family; each family, as an economic unit, works as a group for its own good. Cooperative work may be undertaken outside the household, however, for other reasons, though not always voluntarily. It may be part of fulfilling duties to in-laws, or it may be performed for political officials or priests by command. Thus, institutions of family, kinship, religion, and the state all may act as organizing elements that define the nature and condition of each worker's cooperative obligations.

Craft Specialization

In contemporary industrial and postindustrial societies, there is a great diversity of specialized tasks to be performed, and no individual can even begin to know all of those customarily seen as fitting for his or her age and gender. However, although specialization has increased in these societies, modern technologies are making labor divisions based on gender less relevant. By contrast, in small-scale foraging and traditional crop-cultivating societies, where division of labor typically occurs along lines of age and gender, each person has knowledge and competence in all aspects of work appropriate to his or her age and gender. Yet, even in these nonindustrial societies there is a measure of specialization.

One example of specialization in a traditional society is afforded by the Afar people of the desolate Danakil Depression of northeastern Ethiopia, one of the lowest and hottest places on earth. Afar men are miners of salt, which since ancient times has been traded widely in East Africa. It is mined from the crust of an extensive salt plain, and to get to it is a risky and difficult business. L. M. Nesbitt, the first European to successfully cross this desert, called it "the hell-hole of creation."[10] The heat is extreme during the day, with shade temperatures of 140 to 156 degrees Fahrenheit not unusual. Shade is not found on the salt plain unless a shelter of salt blocks is built. Nor is there food or water for man or beast. To add to the difficulty, until recently the Muslim Afars and the Christian Tigrians, who also mine salt, were sworn enemies.

Successful mining, then, requires specialized skill at planning and organization, as well as physical strength

---

[7]Goddard, V. (1993). Child labor in Naples. In W. A. Haviland & R. J. Gordon (Eds.), *Talking about people* (pp. 105–109). Mountain View, CA: Mayfield.

[8]It's the law: Child labor protection. (1997, November/December). *Peace and Justice News*, 11.

[9]Herskovits, M. (1952). *Economic anthropology: A study in comparative economics* (2nd ed., p. 103). New York: Knopf.

[10]Nesbitt, L. M. (1935). *Hell-hole of creation*. New York: Knopf.

Anthropologists of Note

Jomo Kenyatta (1889–1978)

Jomo Kenyatta, Kenya's first president, was academically trained in anthropology and took the concept of cooperation from the local level and applied it to the state. His national slogan was *Harambee* ("Pull Together"), and with that sentiment he led his country to freedom from British colonial rule.

Born a Kikuyu, Kenya's largest ethnic group, he was originally named Kamau Ngengi. Later in life he adopted the name Jomo Kenyatta—Jomo meaning "burning spear" in his own language and Kenyatta referring to the beaded belt (*kinyata*) that he always wore. After his father died in 1896, he went to live with his grandfather, a medicine man. As a teenager, he attended primary school at a Scottish mission, followed by work as an apprentice carpenter. In 1915, he found work on a sisal farm, and in 1917 he moved to Narok where he lived with Maasai relatives while employed by an Asian contractor. A year later he found a job as a storekeeper in the capital city of Nairobi and took evening classes at another mission school. In 1919 he and his new wife turned part of their home into a little shop, which became a gathering place for friends from different ethnic groups who, like Kenyatta, were hungry for independence. Living outside of Nairobi, he also kept a small farm.

In the late 1920s, while working for the Nairobi City Council water department, Kenyatta became actively involved in the politics of land control and edited a newspaper on Kikuyu culture and new farming methods. As president of the Kikuyu Central Association, he traveled to London in 1929 and again in 1931 to argue for his people's right to the land on which British colonials had settled. Staying on in England, he completed studies at a Quaker college. In the mid-1930s he studied anthropology at the London School of Economics under the famous Bronislaw Malinowski. During this time he also penned various anticolonialism articles, taught at

University College in London, and wrote anthropological studies about his people. Most significantly he published an autobiography titled *Facing Mount Kenya*, sometimes referred to as the bible of Kenya's independence movement.

After serving as a key organizer of the 1945 Pan African Congress held in Manchester, England, Kenyatta went home to Kenya. In 1946 he became president of the Kenya African Union, which pressed for voting rights, an end to racial discrimination, and the return of indigenous lands. Dissatisfied with what appeared to be dead-end diplomacy, radical natives launched the "Mau Mau" uprising against British colonial rule. Responding with

© Bruce Dale/National Geographic Image Collection

brutal force to guerrilla attacks that claimed about 100 British lives, British forces killed many thousands of native people and arrested those they suspected as instigators—including Kenyatta. During his seven years of imprisonment, Kenyatta gained all the more influence, and in 1960—just before his release—fellow natives in the colony elected him president of the newly founded Kenya African National Union. After his country finally won independence in 1963, he was elected as the republic's first president, holding that office until his death in 1978.

---

and the will to work under the most trying conditions.[11] Pack animals to carry the salt have to be fed in advance, for carrying sufficient fodder for them interferes with their ability to carry out salt. Food and water must be carried for the miners, who usually number thirty to forty per group. Travel is planned to take place at night to avoid the intense heat of day. In the past, measures to protect against attack had to be taken. Finally, timing is critical; a party has to return to sources of food and wa-

ter before their own supplies are too long exhausted and before their animals are unable to continue.

DISTRIBUTION AND EXCHANGE

In societies without a money economy, the rewards for labor are usually direct. The workers in a family group consume what they harvest, eat what the hunter or gatherer brings home, and use the tools they themselves make. But even where no formal medium of exchange such as money exists, some distribution of goods takes place. Anthropologists often classify the cultural sys-

---

[11]Mesghinua, H. M. (1966). Salt mining in Enderta. *Journal of Ethiopian Studies 4* (2); O'Mahoney, K. (1970). The salt trade. *Journal of Ethiopian Studies 8* (2).

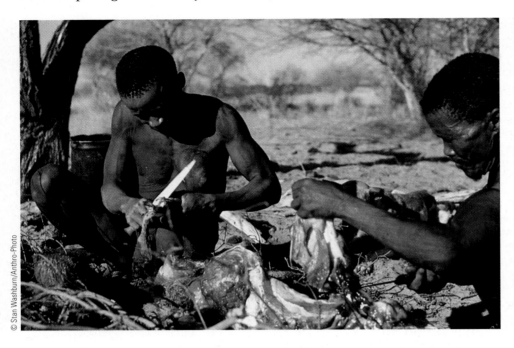

These Ju/'hoansi are cutting up meat that will be shared by others in the camp. Food distribution practices of such food foragers are an example of generalized reciprocity.

tems of distributing material goods into three modes: reciprocity, redistribution, and market exchange.[12]

Reciprocity

Reciprocity refers to a transaction between two parties whereby goods and services of roughly equivalent value are exchanged. This may involve gift giving. Notably, individuals or groups in most cultures like to think that the main point of the transaction is the gift itself, yet what actually matters are the social ties that are created or reinforced between givers and receivers. Because reciprocity is about a relationship between the self and others, gift giving is seldom really selfless. The overriding (if unconscious) motive is to fulfill social obligations and perhaps to gain a bit of prestige in the process. Cultural traditions dictate the manner and occasion of exchange.

For example, when an animal is killed by a group of indigenous hunters in Australia, the meat is divided among the hunters' families and other relatives. Each person in the camp gets a share, the size depending on the nature of the person's kinship tie to the hunters. Typically, if the animal is a kangaroo, the left hind leg goes to the brother of the hunter, the tail to his father's brother's son, the loins and the fat to his father-in-law, the ribs to his mother-in-law, the forelegs to his father's younger sister, the head to his wife, and the entrails and the blood to the hunter. If arguments were to arise over the apportionment, it would be because the principles of distribution were not followed properly. The hunter and his family seem to fare badly in this arrangement, but they have their turn when another man makes a kill. The giving and receiving is obligatory, as is the particularity of the distribution. Such sharing of food reinforces community bonds and ensures that everyone eats. By giving away part of a kill, the hunters get social credit for a similar amount of food in the future.

Reciprocity falls into several categories. The Australian food distribution example just noted constitutes an example of **generalized reciprocity**—exchange in which the value of what is given is not calculated, nor is the time of repayment specified. Gift giving, in the unselfish sense, also falls in this category. So, too, does the act of a kindhearted soul who stops to help a stranded motorist or someone else in distress and refuses payment with the admonition: "Pass it on to the next person in need."

Most generalized reciprocity, however, occurs among close kin or people who otherwise have very close ties with one another. Within such circles of intimacy, people give to others when they have the means and can count on receiving from others in time of need. Typically, participants will not consider such exchanges in economic terms but will couch them explicitly in terms of family and friendship social relations.

[12]Polanyi, K. (1968). The economy as instituted process. In E. E. LeClair, Jr., & H. K. Schneider (Eds.), *Economic anthropology: Readings in theory and analysis* (pp. 127–138). New York: Holt, Rinehart & Winston.

reciprocity The exchange of goods and services, of approximately equal value, between two parties.
generalized reciprocity A mode of exchange in which the value of what is given is not calculated, nor is the time of repayment specified.

Balanced reciprocity differs in that it is not part of a long-term process. The giving and receiving, as well as the time involved, are more specific. One has a direct obligation to reciprocate promptly in equal value in order for the social relationship to continue. Examples of balanced reciprocity in contemporary North American society include such customary practices as hosting a baby shower for young friends expecting their first baby; giving presents at birthdays, Christmas, and various other culturally prescribed "special" occasions; or buying drinks when one's turn comes at a gathering of friends or associates.

Examples from a traditional foraging society include those related by German American anthropologist Robert Lowie in his ethnography of the Crow (or Absaroke) Indians in Montana.[13] A woman skilled in the tanning of buffalo hides might offer her services to a neighbor who needed a new cover for her tepee. It took an expert to design and oversee the making of a tepee cover, which required from fourteen to twenty skins. The designer might need as many as twenty collaborators, whom she instructed in the sewing together of the skins and whom the tepee owner might thank by inviting them to be his guests at a feast. The designer herself would be given some special present of value by the tepee owner.

Giving, receiving, and sharing as so far described constitute a form of social security or insurance. A family contributes to others when they have the means and can count on receiving from others in time of need—promoting an egalitarian distribution of wealth over the long run.

Negative reciprocity is a third form of exchange, in which the aim is to get something for as little as possible. The parties involved have opposing interests and are not usually closely related; they may be strangers or even enemies. They are people with whom exchanges are often neither fair nor balanced and are usually not expected to be such. It may involve hard bargaining, manipulation, or outright cheating. An extreme form of negative reciprocity is to take something by force, while realizing that one's victim may seek compensation or retribution for losses.

Barter and Trade

Exchanges that occur within a group of relatives or between friends generally take the form of generalized or balanced reciprocity. However, when two or more partners from different groups negotiate a direct exchange of one trade good for another, we speak of *barter*. However, their arguing about the price and terms of the deal may well be in the form of negative reciprocity. This means

Scott Olson/Getty Images

Political fundraising in the United States involves elements of both balanced and negative reciprocity. Big contributors expect their generosity will buy influence with a candidate, resulting in benefits of equal value. The politician may seek to do as little as possible in return, but not so little as to jeopardize future donations. Those who accept too much and/or give too much in return risk legal repercussions. In 2006, a jury found former Illinois Governor George Ryan guilty of taking gifts and payoffs in return for government contracts, resulting in a prison sentence for this man who had been one of the most successful politicians in his state's history. Here we see Ryan speaking with the press outside the courtroom just after the guilty verdict was announced.

that there is the potential for suspicion and even the risk of hostility between both parties.

Although in barter each party seeks to get the best possible deal, both may negotiate until a relative balance has been found, and each feels satisfied at having achieved the better of the deal. Relative value is calculated, and despite an outward show of indifference, sharp trading is generally the rule, when compared to the more balanced nature of exchanges within a group.

An arrangement that combined elements of balanced reciprocity as well as barter existed in India between the Kota and three neighboring peoples. The Kota, the musicians and blacksmiths for the region, were able to provide their neighbors with tools and with music considered essential for ceremonial occasions. In exchange, the Toda, with whom they had an amicable relationship, offered *ghee* (a kind of butter used for certain ceremonies) and buffalo used for funerals. For grain, the Kota traded with the Badaga farmers, with whom they had a competitive relationship that sometimes led to one-sided trading practices (in which the Kota usually came out ahead). The forest-dwelling Kurumba, who were renowned as

---

balanced reciprocity A mode of exchange in which the giving and the receiving are specific as to the value of the goods and the time of their delivery.

negative reciprocity A form of exchange in which the aim is to get something for as little as possible. Neither fair nor balanced, it may involve hard bargaining, manipulation, and outright cheating.

---

[13]Lowie, R. (1956). *Crow Indians* (p. 75). New York: Holt, Rinehart & Winston. (orig. 1935)

sorcerers, had honey, canes, and occasionally fruits to of-fer, but their main contribution was protection against the supernatural. The Kota feared the Kurumba, and the Kurumba took advantage of this in their trade dealings, so that they always got more than they gave. Thus, great latent hostility existed between these two peoples.

Silent trade is a specialized form of barter in which no verbal communication takes place. In fact, it may in-volve no actual face-to-face contact at all. Such cases have often characterized the dealings between food-foraging peoples and their food-producing neighbors, as over the past 2,000 or so years, foragers have supplied various commodities in demand in a wider economy. A classic description of such trade follows:

> The forest people creep through the lianas to the trading place, and leave a neat pile of jungle products, such as wax, camphor, monkeys' gall bladders, birds' nests for Chinese soup. They creep back a certain distance, and wait in a safe place. The partners to the exchange, who are usually agriculturalists with a more elaborate and extensive set of material possessions but who cannot be bothered stumbling through the jungle after wax when they have someone else to do it for them, discover the little pile, and lay down beside it what they consider its equivalent in metal cutting tools, cheap cloth, bananas, and the like. They too discreetly retire. The shy folk then reappear, inspect the two piles, and if they are satisfied, take the second one away. Then the opposite group comes back and takes pile num-ber one, and the exchange is completed. If the forest people are dissatisfied, they can retire once more, and if the other people want to increase their offering they may, time and again, until everyone is happy.[14]

To speculate about the reasons for silent trade, in some situations it may be silent for lack of a common language. More often silent trade may serve to control situations of distrust so as to keep relations peaceful. Good relations are maintained by preventing direct con-tact. Another possibility that does not exclude the others is that it makes exchange possible where problems of sta-

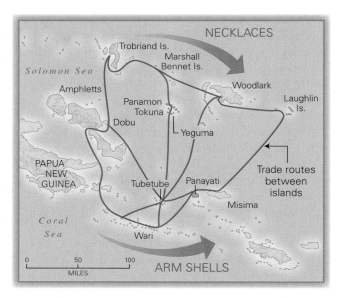

Figure 8.1

The ceremonial trading of shell necklaces and armbands in the Kula ring encourages trade throughout Melanesia.

tus might make verbal communication unthinkable. In any event, it provides for the exchange of goods between groups despite potential barriers.

The Kula Ring: Gift Giving and Trading in the South Pacific

Balanced reciprocity can take more complicated forms, whereby mutual gift giving serves to facilitate social interaction, "smoothing" social relations between trad-ers wanting to do business and make profits or between politicians seeking favorable deals for themselves, their parties, or their countries. One classic ethnographic ex-ample of balanced reciprocity between trading partners seeking to be friends and do business at the same time is the **Kula ring** in the southwestern Pacific Ocean, as first described by Bronislaw Malinowski. Involving thou-sands of seafarers going to great lengths to establish and maintain good trade relations, this centuries-old ceremo-nial exchange system continues to this day.[15]

Kula participants are men of influence who travel to islands within the Trobriand ring to exchange prestige items—red shell necklaces (*soulava*), which are circulated around the ring of islands in a clockwise direction, and white shell armbands (*mwali*), which are carried in the opposite direction (Figure 8.1). Each man in the Kula is linked to partners on the islands that neighbor his own. To a partner residing on an island in the clockwise direc-

---

[14]Coon, C. S. (Ed.) (1948). *A reader in general anthropology* (p. 594). New York: Holt, Rinehart & Winston.

silent trade A form of barter in which no verbal communication takes place.

Kula ring A form of balanced reciprocity that reinforces trade re-lations among the seafaring Trobriand people, who inhabit a large ring of islands in the southwestern Pacific Ocean off the eastern coast of Papua New Guinea, and other Melanesians.

---

[15]Malinowski, B. (1922). *Argonauts of the western Pacific* (p. 94). Lon-don: Routledge & Kegan Paul; Weiner, A. B. (1988). *The Trobriand-ers of Papua New Guinea* (pp. 139–157). New York: Holt, Rinehart & Winston.

In Melanesia, men of influence paddle and sail within a large ring of islands in the southwestern Pacific off the eastern coast of Papua New Guinea to participate in the ceremonial trading of Kula shells, which smoothes trade relations and builds personal prestige.

tion, he offers a *soulava* and receives in return a *mwali*. He makes the reverse exchange of a *mwali* for a *soulava* to a partner living in the counterclockwise direction. Each of these trade partners eventually passes the object on to a Kula partner further along the chain of islands. *Soulava* and *mwali* are ranked according to their size, their color, how finely they are polished, and their particular histories. Such is the fame of some that, when they appear in a village, they create a sensation.

Traditionally, men make their Kula journeys in elaborately carved dugout canoes, sailing and paddling these 20- to 25-feet long boats across open waters to shores some 60 miles or more away. The adventure is often dangerous and may take men away from their homes for several weeks, sometimes even months. Although men on Kula voyages may use the opportunity to trade for practical goods, acquiring such goods is not always the reason for these voyages—nor is Kula exchange a necessary part of regular trade expeditions.

Perhaps the best way to view the Kula is as an indigenous insurance policy in an economic order fraught with danger and uncertainty. It establishes and reinforces social partnerships between traders doing business on distant shores, ensuring a welcome reception from people who have similar vested interests. That said, this ceremonial exchange network does more than simply smooth or enhance the trade of foods and other goods essential for survival. Melanesians participating in the

Kula ring have no doubt that their social position has to do with the company they keep, the circles in which they move. They derive their social prestige from the reputations of their partners and the valuables that they circulate. By giving and receiving armbands and necklaces that accumulate the histories of their travels and names of those who have possessed them, men proclaim their individual fame and talent, gaining considerable influence for themselves in the process.

Like other forms of currency, *soulava* and *mwali* must flow from hand to hand; once they stop flowing, they may lose their value. A man who takes these valuables out of their inter-island circuit invites criticism. He may lose not only prestige or social capital as a man of influence, but may become a target of sorcery for unraveling the cultural fabric that holds the islands together as a functioning social and economic order.

As this example from the South Pacific illustrates, the potential tension between trading partners may be resolved or lessened when they engage in a ritual of balanced reciprocity. As an elaborate complex of ceremony, political relationships, economic exchange, travel, magic, and social integration, the Kula ring illustrates how inseparable economic matters are from the rest of culture. Although perhaps difficult to recognize, this is just as true in modern industrial societies as it is in traditional Trobriand society—as evident when heads of state engage in ceremonial gift exchanges at official visits.

Redistribution

Redistribution is a form of exchange in which goods flow into a central place where they are sorted, counted, and reallocated. Commonly, it involves an element of power. In societies with a sufficient surplus to support some sort of government, goods in the form of gifts, tribute, taxes, and the spoils of war are gathered into storehouses controlled by a chief or some other type of leader. From there they are handed out again. The leadership has three motives in redistributing this income: The first is to gain or maintain a position of power through a display of wealth and generosity; the second is to assure those who support the leadership an adequate standard of living by providing them with desired goods; and the third is to establish alliances with leaders of other groups by hosting them at lavish parties and giving them valuable goods.

The redistribution system of the ancient Inca empire in the Andean highlands of South America was one of the most efficient the world has ever known, both in the collection of tribute (obligatory contributions or gifts in the form of crops, goods, and services) and in its methods of administrative control.[16] Administrators kept inventories of resources and a census of the population, which at its peak reached 6 million. Each craft specialist had to produce a specific quota of goods from materials supplied by overseers. Required labor was used for some agricultural and mining work. Unpaid labor was also used in a program of public works that included a remarkable system of roads and bridges throughout the mountainous terrain, aqueducts that guaranteed a supply of water, temples for worship, and storehouses that held surplus food for times of famine.

Careful accounts were kept of income and expenditures. A central administration, regulated by the Inca emperor and his relatives, had the responsibility for ensuring that production was maintained and that commodities were distributed. Holding power over this command economy, the ruling elite lived in great luxury, but sufficient goods were redistributed to the common people to ensure that no one would be left in dire need or face the indignity of pauperism.

---

[16]Mason, J. A. (1957). *The ancient civilizations of Peru*. Baltimore: Penguin.

redistribution A form of exchange in which goods flow into a central place, where they are sorted, counted, and reallocated.
conspicuous consumption A showy display of wealth for social prestige.
potlatch On the northwest coast of North America, a ceremonial event in which a village chief publicly gives away stockpiled food and other goods that signify wealth.

Taxes imposed by central governments of countries all around the world today are one form of redistribution—required payments typically based on a percentage of one's income and property value. Typically, a portion of the taxes goes toward supporting the government itself while the rest are redistributed either in cash (such as welfare payments and government loans or subsidies to businesses) or in the form of services (such as military defense, law enforcement, food and drug inspection, schools, highway construction, and the like). Tax codes vary greatly among countries. In many European countries, wealthy citizens pay considerably higher percentages of their incomes than those in the United States.

Spending Wealth to Gain Prestige

In societies where people devote most of their time to subsistence activities, gradations of wealth are small, kept that way through various cultural mechanisms and systems of reciprocity that serve to spread quite fairly what little wealth exists. It is a different situation in ranked societies where substantial surpluses are produced, and the gap between the have-nots and the have-lots can be considerable. In these societies, showy display for social prestige—known as **conspicuous consumption**—is a strong motivator for the distribution of wealth.

Obviously, excessive efforts to impress others with one's wealth or status also play a prominent role in industrial and postindustrial societies, as individuals compete for prestige. Indeed, many North Americans and Europeans spend much of their lives trying to impress others. This requires the display of symbolic prestige items—designer clothes, substantial jewelry, mansions, big cars, private planes—and fits neatly into an economy based on consumer wants.

A form of conspicuous consumption also occurs in some crop-cultivating and foraging societies—as illustrated by potlatches hosted by the chiefs of various American Indian groups living along the Pacific northwest coast, including the Tlingit, Haida, and Kwakwaka'wakw (Kwakiutl) peoples. A **potlatch** is a ceremonial event in which a village chief publicly gives away stockpiled food and other goods that signify wealth. (The term comes from the Chinook Indian word *patshatl*, which means "gift.")

Traditionally, a chief whose village had built up enough surplus to host such a feast for other villages in the region would give away large piles of sea otter furs, dried salmon, blankets, and other valuables while making boastful speeches about his generosity, greatness, and glorious ancestors. While other chiefs became indebted to him, he reaped the glory of successful and generous leadership and saw his prestige rise. In the future, his own village might face shortages, and he would find

Among Native Americans living along the northwest coast of North America, one gains prestige by giving away valuables at the potlatch feast. Here we see Tlingit clan members dressed in traditional Chilkat and Raven's Tail robes during a recent potlatch in Sitka, Alaska.

himself on the receiving end of a potlatch. Should that happen, he would have to listen to the self-serving and pompous speeches of rival chiefs. Obliged to receive, he would temporarily lose prestige and status.

In extreme displays of wealth, chiefs even destroyed some of their precious possessions. This occurred with some frequency in the second half of the 19th century, after European contact triggered a process of culture change that included new trade wealth. Outsiders might view such grandiose displays as wasteful in the extreme. However, these extravagant giveaway ceremonies have played an ecologically adaptive role in a coastal region where villages alternately faced periods of scarcity and abundance and relied upon alliances and trade relations with one another for long-term survival. The potlatch provided a ceremonial opportunity to strategically redistribute surplus food and goods among allied villages in response to periodic fluctuations in fortune.

A strategy that features this sort of accumulation of surplus goods for the express purpose of displaying wealth and giving it away to raise one's status is known as a **prestige economy.** In contrast to conspicuous consumption in industrial and postindustrial societies, the emphasis is not on amassing goods that then become unavailable to others. Instead, it is on gaining wealth in order to give it away for the sake of prestige and status.

Leveling Mechanisms

The potlatch is an example of a **leveling mechanism**—a cultural obligation compelling prosperous members of a community to give away goods, host public feasts, provide free service, or otherwise demonstrate generosity so that no one permanently accumulates significantly more wealth than anyone else. With leveling mechanisms at work, greater wealth brings greater social pres-

prestige economy Creation of a surplus for the express purpose of gaining prestige through a public display of wealth that is given away as gifts.

leveling mechanism A cultural obligation compelling prosperous members of a community to give away goods, host public feasts, provide free service, or otherwise demonstrate generosity so that no one permanently accumulates significantly more wealth than anyone else.

sure to spend and give generously. In exchange for such demonstrated altruism, a person not only increases his or her social standing in the community, but may also keep disruptive envy at bay.

Underscoring the value of collective well-being over individual self-interest, leveling mechanisms are important in the long-term survival of traditional communities. The potlatch is just one of many cultural varieties of leveling mechanisms. Another example can be found in Maya Indian towns in the highlands of Guatemala and southern Mexico. In these traditional communities, the higher public offices are those of councilmen, judges, and mayors, in addition to various ceremonial leadership positions. Because the people who are called upon to fill these roles are not paid, the positions are known as *cargos* (Spanish for "burdens"). In fact, Maya Indian officeholders are expected to personally pay for the food, liquor, music, fireworks, or whatever is required for community festivals or for feast meals associated with their particular post. For some cargos, the cost can be as much as a man can earn in four years!

After holding a cargo position, a man usually returns to his normal life for a period, during which he may accumulate sufficient resources to campaign for a higher office. Each successful male citizen of the community is socially obliged to serve in the community's cargo system at least once, and the social pressure to do so drives individuals who have once again accumulated surplus wealth to apply for higher offices in order to raise their social status. Ideally, while some individuals gain appreciably more prestige than others in their community, no one has significantly more wealth in the long run than anyone else.

By pressuring members into sharing their wealth in their own community rather than keeping it to themselves or privately investing it elsewhere, such leveling mechanisms do more than keep resources in circulation. They also reduce social tensions among relatives, neighbors, and fellow town folk, promoting a collective sense of togetherness. An added practical benefit is that they ensure that necessary services within the community are performed.

Market Exchange

To an economist, **market exchange** has to do with the buying and selling of goods and services, with prices set by rules of supply and demand. Personal loyalties and moral values are not supposed to play a role, but they often do. Since the actual location of the transaction is not always relevant in today's world, we must distinguish between the "marketplace" and "market exchange."

Typically, until well into the 20th century, market exchange was carried out in specific localities or *marketplaces*. This is still the case in much of the nonindustrial world and even in numerous centuries-old European and Asian towns and cities. In food-producing societies, marketplaces overseen by a centralized political authority provide the opportunity for farmers or peasants in the surrounding rural territories to exchange some of their livestock and produce for needed items manufactured in factories or in the workshops of craft specialists living (usually) in towns and cities. Thus, some sort of complex division of labor as well as centralized political organization is necessary for the appearance of markets.

The traditional market is local, specific, and contained. Prices are typically set on the basis of face-to-face bargaining rather than by unseen market forces wholly removed from the transaction itself. Notably, sales do not necessarily involve money; instead, goods may be directly exchanged through some form of barter among the specific individuals involved.

In industrializing and industrial societies, many market transactions still take place in a specific identifiable location—including international trade fairs such as the semi-annual Canton Trade Fair in Guangzhou, China, which in spring 2005 featured some 10,000 Chinese enterprises and drew buyers from over 200 countries. However, it is possible and increasingly common for people living in technologically wired parts of the world to buy and sell everything from cattle to cars without ever being in the same city, let alone the same space. For example, think of Internet companies such as eBay where all buying and selling occurs electronically and irrespective of geographic distance. Thus, when people talk about a market in today's industrial or postindustrial world, the particular geographic location where something is bought or sold is often not important at all.

The faceless market exchanges that take place in industrial and postindustrial societies stand in stark contrast to experiences in the marketplaces of nonindustrial societies, which have much of the excitement of a fair. Traditional exchange centers are colorful places where a host of sights, sounds, and smells awaken the senses. Typically, vendors and/or their family members produced the goods they are selling, thereby personalizing the transactions. Dancers and musicians may perform, and feasting and fighting may mark the end of the day. In these markets social relationships and personal interactions are key elements, and noneconomic activities may even overshadow the economic. In short, such markets are gathering places where people renew friendships, see relatives, gossip, and keep up with the world,

market exchange The buying and selling of goods and services, with prices set by rules of supply and demand.

VISUAL COUNTERPOINT

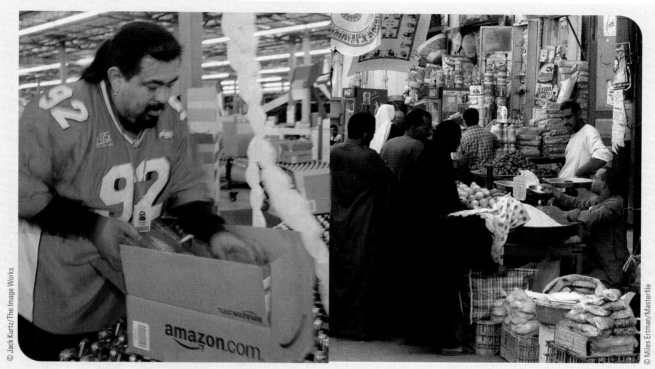

In many societies, particularly in developing countries, the market is an important focus of social as well as economic activity, as shown in the photo of a crowded outdoor marketplace in Aswan, Egypt. In contrast, the packer pictured on the left works at an Amazon.com distribution center in Fernley, Nevada, preparing orders purchased on the Internet. With the advent of online shopping, people can buy and sell with no social interaction whatsoever.

while procuring needed goods they cannot produce for themselves.[17]

Money: Invention and Spread of Coins as Means of Exchange

Although there have been marketplaces without money of any sort, money does facilitate trade. **Money** may be defined as something used to make payments for other goods and services as well as to measure their value. Its critical attributes are durability, transportability, divisibility, recognizability, and interchangeability. Items that have been used as money in various societies include salt, shells, precious stones, cacao beans, special beads, livestock, and of course valuable metals such as iron, copper, silver, and gold. Until recently, Indian Ocean cowry shells, for example, were widely used as a means of exchange in parts of Asia, Africa, and the Pacific Ocean. Indicative of its ancient use is the character for "money" in the Chinese writing system, which symbolically represents a cowry shell.

About 5,000 years ago, merchants and others in Mesopotamia (now part of Iraq) went beyond bartering in their trading activities and began using pieces of precious metal such as silver in their transactions. Once they agreed on the value of these pieces as a means of exchange, or money, at least within the boundaries of the political state, more complex commercial developments soon followed. As the means of exchange were standardized in terms of their value, it became easier to accumulate, lend, or borrow money for specified amounts and periods against payment of interest. In due time, some merchants began to do business with money itself and became bankers.

When the use of money began to spread far into neighboring territories and beyond, the metal units were adapted to long-term use, easy storage, and long-distance transportation. In many cultures, such pieces of iron, copper, or silver were cast as miniature models of especially valuable implements like sword blades, axes, or spades. In the ancient Mediterranean kingdom of

[17]Plattner, S. (1989). Markets and marketplaces. In S. Plattner (Ed.), *Economic anthropology* (p. 171). Stanford, CA: Stanford University Press.

money Something used to make payments for other goods and services as well as to measure their value.

Lydia (southwestern Turkey), however, these metal units took the shape of small metal disks, distinctively coined according to different size and weight, over 2,600 years ago.[18] Over the next few centuries, metal coins were also standardized in terms of the metal's purity and value, such as 100 units of copper equals 10 units of silver or 1 of gold.

By about 2,000 years ago, the commercial use of such coins was spreading throughout much of Europe and becoming increasingly common in parts of Asia and Africa, especially along trade routes and in urban centers. Meanwhile, new mines were opened to meet the growing demand for precious metals to produce more money. These mining operations, in turn, created growing demands for cheap human labor—demands that were often met by capturing people and forcing them to work as slaves.

About 500 years ago, Spanish explorers in search of wealth and glory discovered the great American civilizations of the Maya, the Aztecs, and the Incas, famous for their great cities, temples, and palaces. Impressed by the vast array of beautiful silver and gold objects, they not only looted Indian temples and palaces, but also lost no time locating the native gold and silver mines. During the first 150 years of Spanish colonial rule in the Americas, more than 7 million pounds of pure silver, much of it cast into heavy bars, was shipped to Spain's seaport city of Seville and later minted into Spanish or other coins. Having moved from hand to hand, pocket to pocket, and generation to generation, many of these coins have circulated around the globe more than once. In using them, merchants and bankers helped set into motion radical economic changes in many traditional societies and introduced what has been called merchant capitalism in many parts of the world.[19]

As revealed in this chapter's Biocultural Connection, there is much more to the story of some traditional non-Western forms of money than their economic exchange value.

LOCAL CULTURES AND ECONOMIC GLOBALIZATION

Failing to overcome cultural biases can have serious economic consequences, especially in this era of globalization. For example, it has led prosperous countries to impose inappropriate development schemes in parts of the world that they regard as economically underdeveloped. Typically, these schemes focus on increasing the target country's gross national product through large-scale pro-

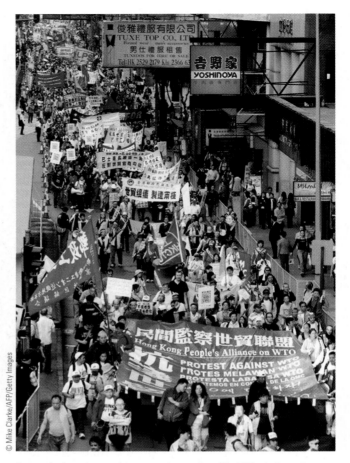

A crowd of protesters demonstrating against World Trade Organization (WTO) policies that favor rich countries over poor ones during the organization's December 2005 meeting in Hong Kong. Established in 1995 and headquartered in Geneva, Switzerland, the WTO has nearly 150 member-countries and is the only worldwide organization with rules of trade among countries.

duction that all too often boosts the well-being of a few but results in poverty, poor health, discontent, and a host of other ills for many.

In order to grow sisal for export to the United States, large-scale plantations were established in Brazil, taking over numerous small farms where peasants grew food to feed themselves. With this change, peasants were forced into the ranks of the unemployed or poorly paid wage laborers. Because they no longer had land for growing their own crops and did not earn enough to buy basic foodstuffs, they faced a dramatic increase in the incidence of malnutrition. Similarly, development projects in Africa, designed to bring about changes in local hydrology, vegetation, and settlement patterns—and even programs aimed at reducing certain diseases—have frequently led directly to *increased* disease rates.[20]

Such failures are tied to the fact that every culture is an integrated system (as illustrated by the barrel model)

[18]Davies, G. (2005). *A history of money from the earliest times to present day* (3rd ed.). Cardiff: University of Wales Press.

[19]See also Wolf, E. R. (1982). *Europe and the people without history* (pp. 135–141). Berkeley: University of California Press.

[20]Bodley, J. H. (1990). *Victims of progress* (3rd ed., p. 141). Mountain View, CA: Mayfield.

Biocultural Connection

Cacao: The Love Bean in the Money Tree

Several thousand years ago Indians in the tropical lowlands of southern Mexico discovered how to produce a hot brew from ground, roasted beans. They collected these beans from melon-shaped fruit pods growing in trees identified by today's scientists as *Theobroma cacao*. By adding honey, vanilla, and some flowers for flavoring, they produced a beverage that made them feel good and believed that these beans were gifts from their gods.

Soon, cacao beans became part of long-distance trade networks and appeared in the Mexican highlands, where the Aztec elite adopted this drink brewed from *cacahuatl*, calling it *chocolatl*. In fact, these beans were so highly valued that Aztecs also used them as money. When Spanish invaders conquered Guatemala and Mexico in the 1520s, they adopted the region's practice of using cacao beans as currency inside their new colony. They also embraced the custom of drinking chocolate, which they introduced to Europe, where it became a luxury drink as well as a medicine.[a]

In the next 500 years, chocolate developed into a $14 billion dollar global business, with the United States as top importer of cacao beans or cacao products. Women buy 75 percent of the chocolate products, and on Valentine's Day more than $1 billion worth of chocolate is sold.

What is it about chocolate that makes it a natural love drug? Other than carbohydrates, minerals, and vitamins, it contains about 300 chemicals, including some with mood-altering effects. For instance, cacao beans contain several chemical components that trigger feelings of pleasure in the human brain. In addition to tryptophan, which increases serotonin levels, chocolate also contains phenylethylamine, an amphetaminelike substance that stimulates the body's own dopamine and has slight antidepressant effects. Chocolate contains anandamide (*anan* means "bliss" in Sanskrit), a messenger molecule that triggers the brain's pleasure center. Also naturally pro-

duced in the brain, anandamide's mood-enhancing effect is the same as that obtained from marijuana leaves.[b] Finally, it also contains a mild stimulant called theobromine ("food of god"), which stimulates the human brain's production of natural opiates, reducing pain and increasing feelings of satisfaction and even euphoria.

These chemicals help explain why the last Aztec ruler Montezuma drank so much chocolate. A Spanish eyewitness, who visited his royal palace in the Aztec capital in 1519, later reported that Montezuma's servants sometimes brought their powerful lord "in cups of pure gold a drink made from the cocoaplant, which they said he took before visiting his wives. . . . I saw them bring in a good fifty large jugs of this chocolate, all frothed up, of which he would drink a little. They always served it with great reverence."[c]

[a] For an excellent cultural history of chocolate, see Coe, S. D., & Coe, M. D. (1996). *The true history of chocolate*. New York: Thames and Hudson; Grivetti, L. E. (2005). From aphrodisiac to health food: A cultural history of chocolate. *Karger Gazette* (68).

[b] Personal communication, Lawrence C. Davis, Kansas State U.
[c] del Castillo, B. D. (1963). *The conquest of New Spain* (pp. 226–227) (translation and introduction by J. M. Cohen). New York: Penguin.

and that a shift in the infrastructure, or economic base, impacts interlinked elements of the society's social structure and superstructure. As the ethnographic examples of the potlatch and the Kula ring show, economic activities in traditional cultures are intricately intertwined with social and political relations and even involve spiritual elements. Development programs that do not take such complexities into consideration may have unintended negative consequences on a society. Fortunately, there is now a growing awareness on the part of development officials that future projects are unlikely to succeed without the expertise that anthropologically trained people can bring to bear.

Achieving a cross-cultural understanding of the economic organizations of other peoples that is not distorted or limited by the logic, hopes, and expectations of one's own society has also become important for corporate executives in today's world.

Recognizing how the economic structures are intertwined with other aspects of a culture could help business corporations avoid problems of the sort experienced

by Gerber, when it began selling baby food in Africa. As in the United States, Gerber's labels featured a picture of a smiling baby. Only later did company officials learn that, in Africa, businesses routinely put pictures of the products themselves on the outside label, since many people cannot read. In a similar vein, Frank Perdue's line in ads for Perdue chickens, "It takes a strong man to make a tender chicken," was literally [mis]translated into Spanish as, "It takes an aroused man to make a chicken affectionate."[21]

As globalization increases so does corporate awareness of the cost of such cross-cultural miscues. So it is not surprising that business recruiters on college campuses in North America and elsewhere are now on the lookout for job candidates with the kind of cross-cultural understanding of the world anthropology provides. It is also of note that the business world has discovered that anthropological research methods are

[21] Madison Avenue relevance. (1999). *Anthropology Newsletter* 40 (4), 32.

Anthropology Applied

Anthropology in the Corporate Jungle ▪ By Karen Stephenson

For the first fifteen years of my career as an anthropologist, I did what most people in the discipline had done for more than a century: I focused my research on the cultures of "exotic" peoples living in remote, nonindustrial corners of the world. For me it was the rainforests of Central America and the deserts of the Sahara. Then I decided to turn the lens on my own culture and use anthropology's methods to study businesses, non-profit organizations, and governmental and educational institutions. I became part of a growing wave of corporate anthropologists, so-called because we study corporate groups.

What makes corporate anthropology an interesting addition to our discipline's repertoire is that fieldwork takes place in a contemporary organization rather than in the jungles of Guatemala, New Guinea, or Samoa. And when you think about it, you don't have to go far away to find the exotic. Many of us live in jungles, whether concrete or green and leafy. The challenge for all of us, not just anthropologists, is to critically see the most familiar and mundane cultural practice as a view from afar, and in that shift of perspective to gain new insight about how we live. Looking through an anthropological lens, some of those practices can at times seem quite bizarre!

Imagine, for example, observing a typical office meeting from an anthropological perspective. There are the tribal elders milling around a huge polished wooden slab, shaking hands and pounding each other on the back. The men are all dressed in the same costumes, their "loin cloths" held up by suspenders or a belt, their feet encased in black polished footwear. On occasion a female voice is heard, only to be drowned out by the bleating of the males. And then there's the question of what to do when you are the anthropologist and all of your informants are too busy to talk with you? I resorted to stocking my office

with exotic chocolates from all around the world and sprinkling Hershey's Kisses, like breadcrumbs, down the hallways so that people could find me easily. I was never lonely after that.

There are moments when this work is entertaining. That said, my research is serious business. It has a practical side, a purpose. It provides corporations with insights about their operations that can lead to problem-solving solutions that increase productivity and profitability. Let me offer a specific example.

I served as visiting anthropologist with IBM for ten years from 1990–2000. During that time IBM was struggling to respond to new market demands as the computer industry morphed from mainframes to personal computers in the late 1980s. Their slow reaction prompted their executives to seek help, and I was called in. I was placed in charge of developing a methodology for changing their culture, and, if successful, IBM would apply the same methodology on its many customers and vendors around the world (the inception of the IBM Consulting Group, now a part of Global Services). I explained how I had developed rapid analysis software that could "x-ray" the company's culture—the human

Courtesy of Karen Stephenson

networks of its current work processes. This was possible thanks to a database I'd created of more than 200 examples of corporate networks from all around the world. Using my database, I could quickly diagnose and benchmark IBM's culture to determine the nature of any pathology.

For the next several years, several divisions were analyzed, including their executive leadership. After a statistical analysis was performed, I developed a measure for cultural inertia (a resistance to change) and determined the sunk costs of operational inefficiencies. Fixing the problem was twofold:

1. Reorganizing the company by outsourcing divisions as independent companies partnering with IBM, reducing the overall employee population from 400,000 to 250,000.
2. Restructuring the pay and performance systems for the top executives so that they were rewarded for cooperating as a team rather than competing against neighboring divisions, perversely thwarting the overall organizational goals.

Both solutions were cultural in nature and difficult for those within the culture to detect. But with the help of my x-rays, IBMers saw for themselves how sometimes their best efforts were often misguided, hindering rather than helping. Accepting the findings and recommendations as objective and sound, they were willing to change their behaviors to improve productivity.

I also introduced another change at IBM: I was the first female executive to wear pants. When confronted with the news that I'd breached the fashion code, I just told them that females wearing pants was a more modest and conservative approach, totally in keeping with their cultural values. One vice president threw back his head and laughed: "I never thought of it that way!"

highly effective when it comes to identifying and analyzing what is and is not functioning within a particular corporate way of life. This has given rise to a career specialization known as business or corporate anthropology, as discussed in this chapter's Anthropology Applied.

That said, it is important to note that powerful corporations headquartered in the so-called developed world, often with subsidiaries overseas, are in business to make a profit, not to protect the weak, benefit the poor, support the sick, favor small producers, or save the environment. Their agenda is universally promoted through slogans such as "free trade," "free markets," and "free enterprise." The commercial success of such multinationals does not come without a price, and all too often that price is paid by still surviving indigenous foragers, small farmers, herders, fishermen, local artisans such as weavers and carpenters, and so on. From the viewpoint of these structurally disadvantaged groups of people, such slogans of freedom have the ring of "savage capitalism," a term now often used in Latin America for a new world order in which the powerless feel condemned to dependency and poverty.

Although political authorities in state-organized societies seek to govern and control economic activities for regulation and taxation purposes, they don't always succeed. Either because of insufficient government resources, bureaucratic mismanagement, and official corruption, or because of people seeking to escape from government regulations and tax-collectors, state-organized societies also possess a largely undocumented **informal economy**—a network of producing and circulating marketable commodities, labor, and services that for various reasons escape government control (enumeration, regulation, or other types of public monitoring or auditing). Such enterprises may encompass a range of activities: house cleaning, child care, gardening, repair or construction work, making and selling alcoholic beverages, street peddling, money lending, begging, prostitution, gambling, drug dealing, pick-pocketing, and labor by illegal foreign workers, to mention just a few.

These off-the-books or black market activities have been known for a long time but generally have long been dismissed by economists as of marginal importance. Yet, in many countries of the world, the informal economy is, in fact, more important than the formal economy. In many places, large numbers of under- and unemployed people who have only limited access to the formal economic sector in effect improvise, "getting by" on scant resources. Meanwhile, more affluent members of society may dodge various regulations in order to maximize returns and/or to vent their frustrations at their perceived loss of self-determination in the face of increasing government regulation.

And now that globalization is connecting national, regional, and local markets in which natural resources, commodities, and human labor are bought and sold, people everywhere in the world face new economic opportunities and confront new challenges. Not only are natural environments more quickly and radically transformed by means of new powerful technologies, but long-established subsistence practices, economic arrangements, social organizations, and associated ideas, beliefs, and values are also under enormous pressure.

What is the future for the world's last remaining food-foraging societies? What about the hundreds of millions of independent herders, farmers, and peasants trying to make a living off the land like their ancestors? How will communities traditionally dependent on manufacturing handmade crafts—like basketry, pottery, weaving, blacksmithing, saddle or furniture making, and so on—fare now that mass-produced machine-made commodities are sold cheaper in nearby stores and markets?

informal economy A network of producing and circulating marketable commodities, labor, and services that for various reasons escape government control.

Questions for Reflection

1. Imagine that you have gone to live with a group of nomadic foragers who meet the challenges of survival by hunting, fishing, and gathering, rather than by shopping. How would that way of life challenge your current attitude on social relations, possessions, and the natural environment?

2. Consider the differences between reciprocity and market exchange. What role does each play in your own society?

3. As the potlatch ceremony shows, prestige may be gained by giving away wealth. Does such a prestige-building mechanism exist in your own society? If so, how does it work?

4. In the Kula ring, men of influence participate in a wide social network based on balanced reciprocity. Why would such a system not survive if individuals in this ring begin to operate on the basis of negative reciprocity?

5. As discussed in this chapter, economic relations in traditional cultures are usually wrapped up in social, political, and even spiritual issues. Can you think of any examples in your own society in which the economic sphere is inextricably intertwined with other structures in the cultural system? Would tinkering with the economic sphere affect these other aspects of your culture?

Suggested Readings

Blumberg, R. L. (1991). *Gender, family, and the economy: The triple overlap*. Newbury Park, CA: Sage.

A look at the interrelationship of gender, domestic life, and the economy.

Dalton, G. (1971). *Traditional tribal and peasant economies: An introductory survey of economic anthropology*. Reading, MA: Addison-Wesley.

This is just what the title says it is, by a major specialist in economic anthropology.

Halperin, R. H. (1994). *Cultural economies: Past and present*. Austin: University of Texas Press.

A cross-cultural approach to analyzing economic processes in cultural systems.

Plattner, S. (Ed.). (1989). *Economic anthropology*. Stanford, CA: Stanford University Press.

A collection of essays from twelve scholars in the field concerning a variety of issues ranging from economic behavior in foraging, horticultural, and "preindustrial" state, peasant, and industrial societies; to gender roles, common property resources, informal economics in industrial societies; and mass marketing in urban areas.

Wilk, R. R. (1996). *Economics and cultures: An introduction to economic anthropology*. Boulder, CO: Westview Press.

This lively primer traces the history of the dialogue between anthropology and economics and identifies the subdiscipline's basic practical and theoretical problems.

Thomson Audio Study Products

Enjoy the MP3-ready Audio Lecture Overviews for each chapter and a comprehensive audio glossary of key terms for quick study and review. Whether walking to class, doing laundry, or studying at your desk, you now have the freedom to choose when, where, and how you interact with your audio-based educational media. See the preface for information on how to access this on-the-go study and review tool.

The Anthropology Resource Center

www.thomsonedu.com/anthropology

The Anthropology Resource Center provides extended learning materials to reinforce your understanding of key concepts in the four fields of anthropology. For each of the four fields, the Resource Center includes dynamic exercises including video exercises, map exercises, simulations, and "Meet the Scientists" interviews, as well as critical thinking questions that can be assigned and e-mailed to instructors. The Resource Center also provides breaking news in anthropology and interesting material on applied anthropology to help you link what you are learning to the world around you.

9 Sex, Marriage, and Family

© Chao-Yang Chan/Alamy

CHALLENGE ISSUE

All around the world humans face the challenge of managing sexual relations and establishing social alliances essential to the survival of individuals and their offspring. Marriage and family, in various forms, provide cultural structures for meeting this challenge. Because each new generation becomes responsible for maintaining a group's overall well-being and advancing its collective interests, essential cultural know-how must be passed on to children to ensure the group's long-term survival. Adjusting to distinct environments and facing specific challenges, each group establishes its own arrangements in terms of child-rearing tasks, gender relations, household and family structures, and residence patterns. Because marriage, in all its varied forms, has played a fundamental role in determining these arrangements, wedding rituals are usually public—and often elaborate—events. In China they often include a procession, as pictured here.

What Is Marriage?

A nonethnocentric definition of marriage is a culturally sanctioned union between two or more people that establishes certain rights and obligations between the people, between them and their children, and between them and their in-laws. Although most marriages around the world involve unions between one woman and one man, numerous other arrangements exist. For example, many cultures not only permit but encourage marriage of one man to multiple wives. The specific form marriage takes is related to who has rights and obligations to offspring that may result from the marital union, as well as how property is distributed. In contrast to mating—the sexual bonding that all animal species do—marriage is a cultural institution, backed by economic, social, legal, and ideological forces.

What Is the Family?

Although the idea of family means different things to different people, in anthropological terms it is a group of two or more people related by blood, marriage, or adoption. The family may take many forms, ranging from a single parent with one or more children, to a married couple or polygamous spouses with offspring, to several generations of parents and their children. The particular form family takes within a society is related to distinct social, historical, and ecological circumstances.

What Is the Difference Between Family and Household?

Households are task-oriented residential units within which economic production, consumption, inheritance, child rearing, and shelter are organized and accomplished. In the vast majority of human societies, a household consists of a family or part of a family or their core members, even though some household members may not be relatives of the family around which it is built. In some societies, families may be less important in people's thinking than the households in which they live.

Among Trobriand Islanders in the southwestern Pacific, whose Kula voyages we examined in the previous chapter, children who have reached the age of 7 or 8 years begin playing erotic games and imitating adult seductive attitudes. Within another four or five years they begin to pursue sexual partners in earnest—experimenting sexually with a variety of individuals. By the time they are in their mid-teens, meetings between lovers may take up most of the night, and affairs are apt to last for several months. Ultimately, lovers begin to meet the same partner again and again, rejecting the advances of others. When the couple is ready, they appear together one morning outside the young man's house as a way of announcing their intention to be married.

For young Trobrianders, attracting sexual partners is an important matter, and they spend a great deal of time making themselves look attractive and seductive. Youthful conversations during the day are loaded with sexual innuendo, and magical spells as well as small gifts are employed to entice a prospective sex partner to the beach at night or to the house in which boys sleep apart from their parents. Because girls, too, sleep apart from their parents, youths and adolescents have considerable freedom in arranging their love affairs. Boys and girls play this game as equals, with neither having an advantage over the other.

Until the latter part of the 20th century, the Trobriand attitude toward adolescent sexuality was in marked contrast to that of most Western cultures in Europe and North America where individuals were not supposed to have sexual relations before or outside of marriage. Since

© Hideo Haga/HAGA/The Image Works

To attract lovers, young Trobriand men and woman must look as attractive and seductive as possible. This woman's beauty has been enhanced by face painting and adornments given by her father.

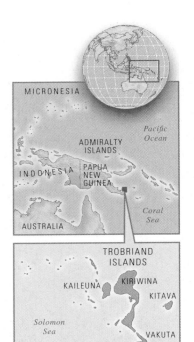

then, practices in much of Europe and North America have converged toward those of the Trobrianders, even though the traditional ideal of premarital abstinence has not been abandoned entirely.

As noted by anthropologist Annette Weiner who did ethnographic research among Trobrianders, all of this sexual activity is not a frivolous, adolescent pastime. Instead, she proposes that attracting lovers is:

> the first step toward entering the adult world of strategies, where the line between influencing others while not allowing others to gain control of oneself must be carefully learned. . . . Sexual liaisons give adolescents the time and occasion to experiment with all the possibilities and problems that adults face in creating relationships with those who are not relatives. Individual wills may clash, and the achievement of one's desire takes patience, hard work, and determination. The adolescent world of lovemaking has its own dangers and disillusionments. Young people, to

the degree they are capable, must learn to be both careful and fearless.[1]

CONTROL OF SEXUAL RELATIONS

One important human characteristic is the ability for the human female, like the human male, to engage in sexual relations at any time she wants or whenever her culture deems it appropriate. Although this ability to perform at any time when provided with the appropriate cue is not unusual for male mammals in general, it is unusual for females. Among most primate species, females whose offspring are weaned but who have not yet become pregnant again are likely to engage in sexual activity around the time of ovulation (approximately once a month), at which time they advertise their availability through highly visible physical signs. Otherwise, they are little interested in such activity. Bonobos, one of the species most closely related to us, are an exception. Whereas among chimpanzees, female genital swelling indicates ovulation and signals readiness for sexual activity, female bonobos are in a constant state of genital swelling, so that sexual activity may occur before, during, and after ovulation. Moreover, it may take place between individuals in virtually all combinations of ages and sex.

Among humans, female fertility is not signaled by any visible display, and couples are likely to engage in sex at any time, even when the female is pregnant. In some human societies, intercourse during pregnancy is thought to promote the growth of the fetus. Among Trobriand Islanders, for example, a child's identity is thought to come from its mother, but it is the father's job to build up and nurture the child, which he begins to do before birth through frequent intercourse with its mother.

As for the homosexual behavior seen among bonobos, that, too, is not uncommon among humans. While such behavior is absolutely condemned in some societies, many others are indifferent about such personal practices and openly tolerate individuals who engage in homosexual activities. Most languages do not even have a special term to distinguish such behavior as significant in its own right. In fact, in some cultures certain prescribed male-to-male sexual acts are part of male initiation rituals required of all boys to become respected adult men.[2] Certain New Guinea societies, for example, see the transmission of semen from older to younger boys, through oral sex, as vital for building up the strength needed to

protect against the supposedly debilitating effects of adult heterosexual intercourse.[3]

Even in the United States, with its long-standing obsession about and hostility toward homosexuality, the phenomenon is far from uncommon. Homosexuality is found in diverse contexts: from lifelong loving relationships to casual sexual encounters to supposedly celibate clergy to inmate populations in both men's and women's prisons. During the past few decades, public denigration or condemnation of homosexuality has diminished in general, and same-sex relationships have become an openly accepted part of the cosmopolitan lifestyle in urban cultural centers such as Amsterdam, London, and San Francisco. That said, the social rules and cultural meanings of *all* sexual behavior are subject to great variability from one society to another.

The ability of females as well as males to engage in sex at any time would have been advantageous to early humans and their ancestors to the extent that it acted, not alone but with other factors, to tie members of both sexes more firmly to the social groups so crucial to their survival. However, although sexual activity can reinforce group ties, it can also disrupt harmonious social relationships. The solution to this problem is to bring sexual activity under cultural control. Thus, just as a culture tells people what, when, and how they should eat, so does it tell them when, where, how, and with whom they should have sex.

Marriage and the Regulation of Sexual Relations

Given the potential for violent conflict resulting from unregulated sexual competition and the challenges of rearing and socializing the children that result from sexual contact, it is not surprising that all societies have cultural rules that seek to regulate those relations.

In much of North America and Europe, the traditional ideal was that all sexual activity outside of marriage was taboo. Individuals were expected to establish a family through marriage, by which one gained an exclusive right of sexual access to another person. According to strict Judeo-Christian law, as prescribed in the Book of Leviticus (20:10), adultery was punishable by death: "And the man that committeth adultery with another man's wife . . . , the adulterer and the adulteress shall surely be put to death." Deuteronomy (22:24) adds: "Then ye shall bring them both out unto the gate of that city, and ye shall stone them with stones that they die."

---

[1]Weiner, A. B. (1988). *The Trobrianders of Papua New Guinea* (p. 17). New York: Holt, Rinehart & Winston.

[2]Kirkpatrick, R. C. (2000). The evolution of human homosexual behavior. *Current Anthropology 41*, 385.

[3]Herdt, G. H. (1993). Semen transactions in Sambia culture. In D. N. Suggs & A. W. Mirade (Eds.), *Culture and human sexuality* (pp. 298–327). Pacific Grove, CA: Brooks/Cole.

VISUAL COUNTERPOINT

Although homosexuality is a widespread human phenomenon, in some societies it faces repression or ridicule. In parts of the United States, for example, public displays of same-sex affection between men in particular are often looked upon as distasteful or even disgusting. One nationwide exception is the football field, where an extreme measure of rough-and-tumble masculine behavior makes it possible for players to pat each other on the behind, exchange celebratory hugs, and even leap into each other's arms without bringing their sexual orientation into question.

Many centuries later, among Christian colonists in 17th- and 18th-century New England, adultery by women remained a serious crime. While it did not lead to stoning, women so accused were shunned by the community and could even be imprisoned. As recounted in *The Scarlet Letter* by Nathaniel Hawthorne, the adulteress was forced to have the letter "A" stitched on her dress, publicly signifying her transgression.

THOMSON AUDIO STUDY PRODUCTS Take advantage of the MP3-ready Audio Lecture Overviews and comprehensive audio glossary of key terms for each chapter. See the preface for information on how to access this on-the-go study and review tool.

Such restrictions exist today in many traditional Muslim societies in northern Africa and western Asia, where age-old Shariah law continues or has been reinstated to regulate social behavior in strict accordance with religious standards of morality. Under this law,

marriage A culturally sanctioned union between two or more people that establishes certain rights and obligations between the people, between them and their children, and between them and their in-laws. Such marriage rights and obligations most often include, but are not limited to, sex, labor, property, child rearing, exchange, and status.

women found guilty of having sexual relations outside marriage can be sentenced to death by stoning. In northern Nigeria, for example, a Muslim woman who committed adultery and had a child outside marriage was sentenced to death in 2002. Her sentence was ultimately overturned by an Islamic appeals court, but it nonetheless drove home the rule of Shariah law. Turning legal transgressions into a public spectacle, authorities reinforce public awareness of the rules of social conduct.

One positive side effect of such restrictive rules of sexual behavior is that they may limit the spread of sexually transmitted diseases. For instance, the global epidemic of HIV/AIDS has had relatively little impact in sexually restrictive societies. Such societies, however, are a minority. In fact, most cultures in the world are much more relaxed about sexuality and do not sharply regulate personal practices. Indeed, a majority of all cultures are considered sexually permissive or semi-permissive (the former having few or no restrictions on sexual experimentation before marriage, the latter allowing some experimentation but less openly). A minority of known societies—about 15 percent—have rules requiring that sexual involvement take place only within marriage.

This brings us to an anthropological definition of **marriage**—a culturally sanctioned union between two or more people that establishes certain rights and obligations between the people, between them and their children, and between them and their in-laws. Such marriage rights and obligations most often include, but are not limited to, sex, labor, property, child rearing, exchange, and status. Thus defined, marriage is universal. Notably, our definition of marriage refers to "people" rather than "a man and a woman" because in some countries same-sex marriages are considered socially acceptable and allowed by law, even though opposite-sex marriages are far more common. We will return to this point later in the chapter.

Sexual and Marriage Practices among the Nayar

In many cultures, marriage is considered the central and most important social institution. In such cultures, people will spend considerable time and energy on maintaining this institution. They may do so in various ways, including highlighting the ritual moment when the wedding takes place, festively memorializing the event at designated times such as anniversaries, and making it difficult to divorce.

In some societies, however, marriage is a relatively marginal institution and is not considered central to the establishing and maintenance of family life and society. For instance, marriage has lost much of its traditional significance in the Scandinavian societies of Iceland, Norway, Sweden, and Denmark, in part due to changes in the political economy, more balanced gender relations, and, last but not least, the shared public benefits of these capitalist welfare states.

But the relative insignificance of marriage is not unique to these wealthy European nations. For instance, this institution is also of marginal significance in the family life of the Nayar of Southwest India. Like the Scandinavians and Trobriand Islanders noted above, the Nayar are one of many examples of sexually permissive cultures.[4] A landowning warrior caste, their estates are held by corporations of sorts made up of kinsmen related in the female line. These blood relatives live together in a large household, with the eldest male serving as manager. Traditionally, Nayar boys began military training around the age of 7, and from this time through much of their young adulthood, they were away from home for significant stretches of time for military purposes.

Three traditional Nayar transactions are of interest in our discussion of sexual and marriage practices. The first occurred shortly before a girl experienced her first menstruation. It involved a ceremony that joined her with a "ritual husband" in a temporary union. This union, which did not necessarily involve sexual relations, lasted for a few days and then broke up. (Neither indi-

vidual had any further obligation, although later, when the girl became a woman, she and her children typically participated in ritual mourning for the man when he died.) This temporary union established the girl as an adult ready for motherhood and eligible for sexual activity with men approved by her household.

The second transaction took place when a young Nayar woman entered into a continuing sexual liaison with a man approved by her family. This was a formal relationship that required the man to present her with gifts three times each year until the relationship was terminated. In return, the man could spend the nights with her. In spite of continuing sexual privileges, however, this "visiting husband" had no obligation to support his sex partner economically, nor was her home regarded as his home. In fact, she may have had such an arrangement with more than one man at the same time. Regardless of the number of men with whom she was involved, this second Nayar transaction, their version of marriage, clearly specified who had sexual rights to whom and included rules that deterred conflicts between the men.

In the absence of effective birth control devices, the usual outcome of sexual activity between individuals of opposite sex is that, sooner or later, the woman becomes pregnant. When this happens among the Nayar, one of the men with whom she has a relationship (who may or may not be the biological father) must formally acknowledge paternity. He does this by making gifts to the woman and the midwife. This third transaction establishes the child's birth rights. In this sense, it is the counterpart of the registration of birth in Western societies, which clearly establishes motherhood and fatherhood. However, once a man has formally acknowledged fatherhood by gift giving, he may continue to take interest in the child, but he has no further obligations. Support and education for the child are the responsibility

---

[4]Our interpretation of the Nayar follows Goodenough, W. H. (1970). *Description and comparison in cultural anthropology* (pp. 6–11). Chicago: Aldine.

of the mother and her brothers with whom she and her offspring live.

Indeed, unlike most other cultural groups in the world, the Nayar household includes only the mother, her children, and her other blood relatives, technically known as **consanguineal kin.** It does not include any of the "husbands." Nor does it include any other people related through marriage, technically known as **affinal kin.** In other words, sisters and their offspring all live together with their brothers and their mother and her brothers. This arrangement answers the need for security in a cultural group where, traditionally, warfare repeatedly pulled young men away from their homes. Among the Nayar, sexual relations are forbidden between consanguineal relatives and thus are permitted only with individuals who live in other households. This brings us to another human universal: the incest taboo.

The Incest Taboo

Just as marriage in its various forms is found in all cultures, so is the **incest taboo**—the prohibition of sexual contact between certain close relatives. But, what is defined as "close" is not the same in all cultures. Moreover, such definitions may be subject to change over time. The scope and details of the taboo vary across cultures and time, but almost all societies past and present strongly forbid sexual relations at least between parents and children and nearly always between siblings. In some societies the taboo extends to other close relatives, such as cousins, and even some relatives linked through marriage.

Anthropologists have long been fascinated by the incest taboo and have proposed many explanations for its cross-cultural existence and variation. The simplest explanation, based on the idea of "human nature," is that our species has an "instinctive" repulsion for incest. It has been documented that human beings raised together have less sexual attraction for one another. However, by itself this "familiarity breeds contempt" argument may simply substitute the result for the cause. The incest taboo ensures that children and their parents, who are constantly in close contact, avoid regarding one another as sexual objects. Besides this, if an instinctive horror of incest exists, how do we account for the far from rare violations of the incest taboo? (In the United States, for instance, an estimated 10 to 14 percent of children under 18 years of age have been involved in incestuous relations.[5])

Moreover, so-called instinctive repulsion doesn't explain institutionalized incest, such as that requiring the divine ruler of the Inca empire in ancient Peru be married to his own (half) sister. Sharing the same father, both siblings belonged to the political dynasty that derived its sacred right to rule the empire from Inti, its ancestral Sun God. And by virtue of this royal lineage's godly origin, their children could claim the same sacred political status as their human god father and mother. Ancient emperors in Egypt also practiced such religiously prescribed incest based on a similar claim to godly status.

Early students of genetics argued that the incest taboo prevents the harmful effects of inbreeding. While this is so, it is also true that, as with domestic animals, inbreeding can increase desired characteristics as well as detrimental ones. Furthermore, undesirable effects will show up sooner than without inbreeding, so whatever genes are responsible for them are quickly eliminated from the population. That said, a preference for a genetically different mate does tend to maintain a higher level of genetic diversity within a population, and in evolution this variation works to a species' advantage. Without genetic diversity a species cannot adapt biologically to environmental change.

The inbreeding- or biological-avoidance theory can be challenged on several fronts. Detailed census records made in Roman Egypt about 2,000 years ago show that brother–sister marriages were not uncommon among ordinary members of the farming class.[6] Moreover, in a sample of 129 societies, anthropologist Nancy Thornhill found that only fifty-seven had specific rules against parent–child or sibling incest. Twice that number (114) had explicit rules to control activity with cousins, in-laws, or both.[7]

Some anthropologists have argued that the incest taboo exists as a cultural means to preserve the stability and integrity of the family, which is essential to maintaining social order. Sexual relations between members other than the husband and wife would introduce competition, destroying the harmony of a social unit fundamental to social order. A truly convincing explanation of the incest taboo has yet to be advanced.

---

consanguineal kin Biologically related relatives, commonly referred to as blood relatives.
affinal kin People related through marriage.
incest taboo The prohibition of sexual contact between certain close relatives, usually parent and child and sibling relations at a minimum.

[5]Whelehan, P. (1985). Review of incest, a biosocial view. *American Anthropologist 87*, 678. See also Langan, P., & Harlow, C. (1994). *Child rape victims, 1992*. Washington, D.C.: Bureau of Justice Statistics, U.S. Department of Justice.

[6]Leavitt, G. C. (1990). Sociobiological explanations of incest avoidance: A critical review of evidential claims. *American Anthropologist 92*, 982.

[7]Thornhill, N. (1993). Quoted in W. A. Haviland & R. J. Gordon (Eds.), *Talking about people* (p. 127). Mountain View, CA: Mayfield.

Biocultural Connection

Marriage Prohibitions in the United States
By Martin Ottenheimer

In the United States, every state has laws prohibiting some type of relatives from marrying each other. There is complete agreement when it comes to prohibiting parent–child marriage and preventing full siblings from marrying, but the laws vary when it comes to more distant relatives. Thirty-one states prohibit first cousins from marrying while nineteen do not. Furthermore, the prohibitions are not limited to people related by birth. A dozen states also forbid certain step-relatives and in-laws from intermarrying.

Although the marriage prohibitions apply to people not related by birth, North Americans commonly believe that these prohibitions are based on biological factors. It is assumed that the prohibitions protect families from potential genetic defects in children of parents who are biologically "too close." The first-cousin prohibitions, in particular, are often defended for this reason.

There are two major problems with this idea. First, the cousin prohibitions began to be enacted in the United States around the middle of the 19th century, long before the emergence of modern genetics. Second, modern genetic research has shown that first-cousin marriage does not present any significantly greater risk to offspring than that from parents who are not related. Why, then, do some North Americans maintain this myth?

In the 19th-century United States, an evolutionary model of humans that included a notion about human progress dependent upon outbreeding became widely accepted. Cousin marriage was thought to be characteristic of savagery, considered a form of degeneration based on inbreeding, believed to inhibit the intellectual development of humans, and feared as a threat to civilized life. With the development of modern genetics, it was wrongly assumed that genetic data supported this now-discredited evolutionary dogma.

Human reproduction is a biological process situated in a cultural context. Each culture develops a particular understanding about the nature of reproduction. This can change over time. At present, the Western model of reproduction is undergoing a transformation stimulated by the recent discovery of mitochondrial DNA and the introduction of new reproductive technologies.

The process well illustrates that biological processes and culture are intimately intertwined, each affecting and being affected by the other.

Endogamy and Exogamy

Whatever its cause, the utility of the incest taboo can be seen by examining its effects on social structure. Closely related to prohibitions against incest are cultural rules against **endogamy** (from Greek *endon,* "within," and *-gamos,* "marriage"), or marriage within a particular group of individuals (cousins and in-laws, for example). If the group is defined as one's immediate family alone, then societies generally prohibit or at least discourage endogamy, thereby promoting **exogamy** (from Greek *exo,* "outside," and *-gamos,* "marriage"), or marriage outside the group. Yet, a society that practices exogamy at one level may practice endogamy at another. Among the Trobriand Islanders, for example, each individual has to marry outside of his or her own clan and lineage (exogamy). However, since eligible sex partners are to be found within one's own community, village endogamy is commonly practiced.

Interestingly, societies vary widely concerning which relatives are or are not covered by rules of exogamy. For example, first cousins are prohibited from marrying each other in many countries where the Roman Catholic Church has long been a dominant institution. Such marriages are also illegal in thirty-one of the United States. Yet, in numerous other societies, first cousins are preferred spouses.[8] (See a discussion of U. S. marriage prohibitions in the Biocultural Connection.)

Early anthropologists suggested that our ancestors discovered the advantage of intermarriage as a means of creating bonds of friendship. French anthropologist Claude Lévi-Strauss elaborated on this idea. He saw exogamy as a form of inter-group social exchange in which "wife-giving" and "wife-taking" created social networks and alliances between distinct communities. By widening the human network, a larger number of people could pool natural resources and cultural information, including technology and other useful knowledge. (For more on this, see Anthropologist of Note.)

Building on Lévi-Strauss' theory, other anthropologists have proposed that exogamy is an important means of building and maintaining political alliances and promoting trade between groups, thereby ensuring mutual

---

[8]Ottenheimer, M. (1996). *Forbidden relatives: The American myth of cousin marriage* (pp. 116–133). Champaign: University of Illinois Press.

endogamy Marriage within a particular group or category of individuals.
exogamy Marriage outside the group.

Anthropologists of Note
Claude Lévi-Strauss (b. 1908)

Claude Lévi-Strauss is the leading exponent of French structuralism, which posits that the human mind imposes order by separating the perceived world into elementary bits of basic information. From this theoretical perspective, culture is viewed as the product of an underlying universal pattern of thought. Each culture is shaped and influenced by its unique physical and social environment as well as its history. Thus, cultures may vary considerably, even though the basic structure of the human thought processes responsible for them is the same for all people everywhere. The task of the anthropologist is to explain the fundamental principles by which humans accomplish this process and to uncover these underlying patterns.

According to Lévi-Strauss, human thought processes are structured into contrastive pairs of polar opposites, such as light versus dark, good versus evil, nature versus culture, dry versus wet, raw versus cooked, and male versus female. The ultimate contrastive pair is that of "self" versus "others," which is necessary for true symbolic communication to occur and upon which culture depends. Communication is a reciprocal exchange, which is extended to include goods and marital partners. Hence, the incest taboo stems from this fundamental contrastive pair of "self" versus "others." From this universal taboo are built the many and varied marriage rules ethnographers have described.

© Brissard Figaro/Getty Images

protection and access to needed goods and resources not otherwise available. Forging wider kinship networks, exogamy also functions to integrate distinctive groups and thus potentially reduces violent conflict.

Distinction Between Marriage and Mating

Having defined marriage, in part, in terms of sexual access, we must make clear the distinction between marriage and mating. All animals, including humans, mate—some for life and some not, some with a single individual and some with several. Mates are secured and held solely through personal effort and mutual consent. (Rape occurs when someone is pressured by one or more other individuals to submit to sexual acts, in particular sexual intercourse, by force. There exist a variety of cross-cultural differences in whether and how rapes are condoned or condemned.)

In contrast to mating, which is a personal affair, marriage is a culturally recognized right. Only marriage is backed by social, political, and ideological factors that regulate sexual relations as well as reproductive rights and obligations. Even among the Nayar, discussed above,

monogamy Marriage in which both partners have just one spouse.

where marriage seems to involve little other than a sexual relationship, a woman's husband is legally obligated to provide her with gifts at specified intervals. Nor may a Nayar woman legally have sex with a man to whom she is not married. Thus, while mating is biological, marriage is cultural. This is evident when we consider the various forms that marriage takes cross-culturally.

FORMS OF MARRIAGE

Within societies, and all the more so across cultures, we see contrasts in the constructs and contracts of marriage. Indeed, as evident in the definition of marriage given above, this institution comes in various forms—and these forms are distinct in terms of the number and gender of spouses involved.

Monogamy

Monogamy—marriage in which both partners have just one spouse—is the most common form of marriage worldwide. In North America and most of Europe, it is the only legally recognized form of marriage. Not only are other forms prohibited there, but also systems of inheritance, whereby property and wealth are transferred from one generation to the next, are based on the institution of monogamous marriage. In some parts of the world, such as North America and Europe where divorce rates are high and divorcees typically remarry, an increasingly common form of marriage is **serial monogamy,** whereby an individual marries a series of partners in succession.

Polygamy

While monogamy is the most common marriage form worldwide, it is not the most preferred. That distinction goes to **polygamy** (one individual having multiple spouses)—specifically to **polygyny,** in which a man is married to more than one woman. Favored in about 80 to 85 percent of the world's cultures, polygyny is commonly practiced in parts of Asia and much of sub-Saharan Africa.[9]

Although polygyny is the favored marriage form in these places, monogamy exceeds it, and the reason for this is economic rather than moral. In many polygynous societies, where a groom is usually expected to compensate a bride's family in cash or kind, a man must be fairly wealthy to be able to afford more than one wife. Recent multiple surveys of twenty-five sub-Saharan African countries where polygyny is common show that it declined by about half between the 1970s and 2001 but nonetheless remains highly significant with an overall average of 25 percent of married women in polygynous unions.[10]

Polygyny is particularly common in traditional food-producing societies that support themselves by herding grazing animals or growing crops and where women do the bulk of cultivation. Under these conditions, women are valued both as workers and as child bearers. Because the labor of wives in polygynous households generates wealth, and little support is required from husbands, the wives have a strong bargaining position within the household. Often, they have considerable freedom of movement and some economic independence from the sale of crafts or crops. Wealth-generating polygyny is found in its fullest elaboration in parts of sub-Saharan Africa and southwestern Asia, though it is known elsewhere as well.[11]

In societies practicing wealth-generating polygyny, most men and women do enter into polygynous marriages, although some are able to do so earlier in life than others. This is made possible by a female-biased sex ratio and/or a mean age at marriage for females that is significantly below that for males. In fact, this marriage pattern is frequently found in societies where violence, including war, is common and where many young males lose their lives in fighting. Their high combat mortality results in a population where women outnumber men.

By contrast, in societies where men are more heavily involved in productive work, generally only a small minority of marriages are polygynous. Under these circumstances, women are more dependent on men for support, so they are valued as child bearers more than for the work they do. This is commonly the case in pastoral nomadic societies where men are the primary owners and tenders of livestock. This makes women especially vulnerable if they prove incapable of bearing children, which is one reason a man may seek another wife.

Another reason for a man to take on secondary wives is to demonstrate his high position in society. But where men do most of the productive work, they must work extremely hard to support more than one wife, and few actually do so. Usually, it is the exceptional hunter or male shaman ("medicine man") in a food-foraging society or a particularly wealthy man in a horticultural, agricultural, or pastoral society who is most apt to practice polygyny. When he does, it is usually of the *sororal* type, with the co-wives being sisters. Having lived their lives together before marriage, the sisters continue to do so with their husband, instead of occupying separate dwellings of their own.

Polygyny also occurs in a few places in Europe. In 1972, for example, English laws concerning marriage changed to accommodate immigrants who traditionally practiced polygyny. Since that time polygamous marriages have been legal in England for some specific religious minorities, including Muslims and Sephardic Jews. According to one family law specialist, the real impetus behind this law change was a growing concern that "destitute immigrant wives, abandoned by their husbands, [were] overburdening the welfare state."[12]

[9]Lloyd, C. B. (Ed.). (2005). *Growing up global: The changing transitions to adulthood in developing countries* (pp. 450–453). Washington, D.C.: National Academies Press, Committee on Population, National Research Council, and Institute of Medicine of the National Academies.

[10]Lloyd, C. B. (Ed.). (2005). *Growing up global: The changing transitions to adulthood in developing countries* (pp. 450–453). Washington, D.C.: National Academies Press, Committee on Population, National Research Council, and Institute of Medicine of the National Academies.

[11]White, D. R. (1988). Rethinking polygyny: Co-wives, codes, and cultural systems. *Current Anthropology 29,* 529–572.

[12]Cretney, S. (2003). *Family law in the twentieth century: A history* (pp. 72–73). New York: Oxford University Press.

serial monogamy A marriage form in which an individual marries or lives with a series of partners in succession.
polygamy One individual having multiple spouses at the same time; from the Greek words *poly* ("many") and *gamous* ("marriage").
polygyny Marriage of a man to two or more women at the same time; a form of polygamy.

VISUAL COUNTERPOINT

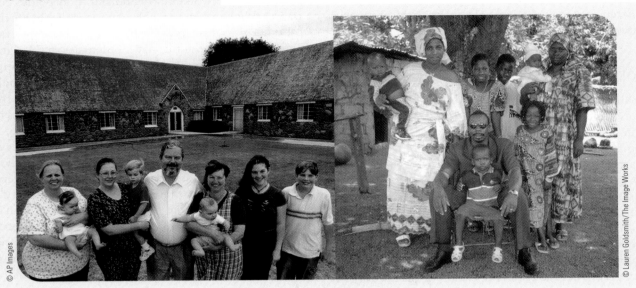

A U.S. Christian polygamist with his three wives and children in front of their dormitory-style home in Utah, and a Baranarna man of Upper Guinea with his two wives and children.

Even in the United States where it is illegal, somewhere between 20,000 and 60,000 people in the Rocky Mountain states live in households made up of a man with two or more wives.[13] Most consider themselves Mormons, even though the official Mormon Church does not approve of the practice. A growing minority, however, call themselves "Christian polygamists," citing the Bible as justification.[14] Despite its illegality, regional law enforcement officials have adopted a "live and let live" attitude toward polygyny in their region. One woman—a lawyer and one of nine co-wives—expresses her attitude toward polygyny as follows:

> I see it as the ideal way for a woman to have a career and children. In our family, the women can help each other care for the children. Women in monogamous relationships don't have that luxury. As I see it, if this lifestyle didn't already exist, it would have to be invented to accommodate career women.[15]

In some societies, if a husband dies leaving a wife and children, it is customary that the wife marry the dead man's brother—but this does not preclude the brother having another wife then or in the future. This custom, called the *levirate,* not only provides social security for the widow and her children but also is a way for the husband's family to maintain the established relationship with her family and their rights over her sexuality and her future children. In short, it acts to preserve relationships previously established. When a man marries the sister of his dead wife, it is called the *sororate;* in essence, a family of "wife givers" supplies one of "wife takers" with another spouse to take the dead one's place. In societies that have the levirate and sororate, the established in-law relationship between the two families is maintained even after the spouse's death.

Although monogamy and polygyny are the most common forms of marriage in the world today, other forms do occur. **Polyandry,** the marriage of one woman to two or more men simultaneously, is known in only a few societies, perhaps in part because a woman's life expectancy is usually longer than a man's, and female infant mortality is somewhat lower, so a surplus of women in a society is likely.

Fewer than a dozen societies are known to have favored this form of marriage, but they involve people as widely separated from one another as the eastern Inuit (Eskimos), Marquesan Islanders of Polynesia, and Tibet-

[13]Egan, T. (1999, February 28). The persistence of polygamy. *New York Times Magazine,* 52.

[14]Wolfson, H. (2000, January 22). Polygamists make the Christian connection. *Burlington Free Press,* 2c.

[15]Johnson, D. (1996). Polygamists emerge from secrecy, seeking not just peace but respect. In W. A. Haviland & R. J. Gordon (Eds.),

polyandry Marriage of a woman to two or more men at one time; a form of polygamy.

Talking about people (2nd ed., pp. 129–131). Mountain View, CA: Mayfield.

ans. In Tibet, where inheritance is in the male line and arable land is limited, the marriage of brothers to a single woman (*fraternal polyandry*) keeps the land together by preventing it from being repeatedly subdivided among sons from one generation to the next. Unlike monogamy, it also holds down population growth, thereby avoiding increased pressures on resources. Finally, among Tibetans who practice a mixed economy of farming, herding, and trading, fraternal polyandry provides the household with an adequate pool of male labor for all three subsistence activities.[16]

Other Forms of Marriage

There are several other marriage forms, each with its own particular cultural expressions and reasons for being. For instance, in a few societies the social practice of **group marriage** exists. Also known as *co-marriage,* this is a rare arrangement in which several men and women have sexual access to one another. Among Eskimos in northern Alaska, for instance, sexual relations between unrelated individuals implied ties of mutual aid and support. In order to create or strengthen such ties, a man could share his wife with another man for temporary sexual relationships:

> Thus, in attracting and holding members of a hunting crew, an *umialik* [whaleboat headman] could lend his wife to a crew member and borrow that man's wife in turn. These men thereafter entered into a partnership relationship, one virtually as strong as kinship. The children of such men, in fact, retained a recognized relationship to each other by virtue of the wife exchange of their parents.[17]

In contrast to group marriage, there are also arrangements anthropologists categorize as **fictive marriage**—marriage by proxy to the symbols of someone not physically present in order to establish a social status for a spouse and heirs. One major reason for such a marriage is to control rights to property in the next generation. One type of fictive marriage occurs in several traditional African societies, most famously among Nuer cattle herders of southern Sudan, where a woman can marry a man who has died without heirs. In such situations the deceased man's brother may become his stand-in, or proxy, and marry a woman on his behalf. The biological offspring will be considered as having been fathered by the dead man's spirit. Recognized as his

legitimate children, they are his rightful heirs. Because such spouses are absent in the flesh yet believed to exist in spirit form, anthropologists refer to these fictive unions as *ghost marriages*.[18]

Fictive marriage variations also exist outside Africa. For instance, a form of ghost marriage can be found in traditional Christianity, in particular Roman Catholic monasteries, where women who remain virgins devote their lives to religious service. When a young woman decides to become a nun, she may enter a religious order as a novice. Being promised in spiritual marriage to Jesus Christ, deemed to be the divine bridegroom, she makes vows of celibacy and chastity, abstaining from regular marriage and renouncing all sexual pleasures. In a special marriage by proxy ceremony, such women are "wedded" as spouses of Christ, who they believe died as a human but lives on as divine spirit in heaven. Veiled and clothed as divine spouses, these nuns also receive a new name, thus completely shedding their old social identities.[19]

Other cultural forms of wedding by proxy can be found throughout the world. In the Netherlands, for example, a legal custom exists known as "marriage with the glove" (*huwelijk met de handschoen*). In this official ceremony, just one of the marriage partners appears before the civil authorities—the other is represented symbolically by an imaginary glove and physically by someone formally authorized as a legal proxy. Traditionally, such proxy marriage ceremonies accommodated physically separated partners such as Dutch seafarers or nationals residing in remote territories.

In several states in the United States, including Colorado and Texas, we find yet another example of marriage by proxy. It involves citizens who are incarcerated, deployed in the military, residing in a foreign country, or otherwise prevented from being physically present at the formal ceremony. In California, this legal wedding option is restricted to members of the U.S. armed forces in war or deployed in combat operations abroad.

Since the 1860s, a *double-proxy marriage* has been possible in Montana, where partners may become legally married in a civil wedding ceremony with neither party appearing before the official authorities. Because

---

[16]Levine, N. E., & Silk, J. B. (1997). Why polyandry fails. *Current Anthropology 38,* 375–398.

[17]Spencer, R. F. (1984). North Alaska Coast Eskimo. In D. Damas (Ed.), *Arctic: Handbook of North American Indians* (Vol. 5, pp. 320–337). Washington, D.C.: Smithsonian Institution.

[18]Evans-Pritchard, E. E. (1951). *Kinship and marriage among the Nuer.* New York: Oxford University Press.

[19]See also Pope Pius XII. (1954). *Sacra Virginitas. Encyclical on consecrated virginity.* The Catholic Encyclopedia Online: www.newadvent.org.

group marriage Marriage in which several men and women have sexual access to one another. Also called co-marriage.

fictive marriage Marriage by proxy to the symbols of someone not physically present to establish the social status of a spouse and heirs.

proxy marriages that take place in states where they are legal are officially recognized by the U.S. federal government and in all member states, these options are gaining acceptance in the military, especially among troops deployed in dangerous overseas combat operations. In cases of injury or death, a military person married in a proxy wedding ceremony may leave a partner (with or without children) with full military benefits. Those who survive and return home may opt to celebrate their already legal marriage in a religious or otherwise meaningful ceremony with family and friends.[20]

CHOICE OF SPOUSE

The Western egalitarian ideal that an individual should be free to marry whomever he or she chooses is a distinct arrangement, certainly not universally embraced.

---

[20]Shane III, L. (2005). Happy couple both no-show wedding: Deployed troops make use of double-proxy ceremony. *Stars & Stripes 3* (17), 6; see also www.MarriageByProxy.com.

In many societies, marriage and the establishment of a family are considered far too important to be left to the whims of young people. The individual relationship of two people who are expected to spend their lives together and raise their children together is viewed as incidental to the more serious matter of making allies of two families through the marriage bond. Marriage involves a transfer of rights between families, including rights to property and rights over children, as well as sexual rights. Thus, marriages tend to be arranged for the economic and political advantage of the family unit.

Although arranged marriages are rare in North American society, they do occur. Among ethnic minorities, they may serve to preserve traditional values that people fear might otherwise be lost. Among families of wealth and power, marriages may be arranged by segregating their children in private schools and carefully steering them toward "proper" marriages. The following Original Study illustrates how marriages may be arranged in societies where such practices are commonplace.

Original Study ▪ By Serena Nanda

Arranging Marriage in India

Six years [after my first field trip to India] I returned to do fieldwork among the middle class in Bombay [Mumbai], a modern, sophisticated city. From the experience of my earlier visit, I decided to include a study of arranged marriages in my project. By this time I had met many Indian couples whose marriages had been arranged and who seemed very happy. Particularly in contrast to the fate of many of my married friends in the United States who were already in the process of divorce, the positive aspects of arranged marriages appeared to me to outweigh the negatives. In fact, I thought I might even participate in arranging a marriage myself. I had been fairly successful in the United States in "fixing up" many of my friends, and I was confident that my matchmaking skills could be easily applied to this new situation, once I learned the basic rules. "After all," I thought, "how complicated can it be?"

An opportunity presented itself almost immediately. A friend from my previous Indian trip was in the process of arranging for the marriage of her eldest son. Since my friend's family was eminently respectable and the boy him-

self personable, well educated, and nice looking, I was sure that by the end of my year's fieldwork, we would have found a match.

The basic rule seems to be that a family's reputation is most important. It is understood that matches would be arranged only within the same caste and general social class, although some crossing of subcastes is permissible if the class positions of the bride's and groom's families are similar. Although dowry is now prohibited by law in India, extensive gift exchanges took place with every marriage. Even when the boy's family does not "make demands," every girl's family nevertheless feels the obligation to give the traditional gifts, to the girl, to the boy, and to the boy's family. Particularly when the couple would be living in the joint family—that is, with the boy's parents and his married brothers and their families, as well as with unmarried siblings, which is still very common even among the urban, upper-middle class in India—the girl's parents are anxious to establish smooth relations between their family and that of the boy. Offering the proper gifts, even when not called "dowry," is often an important factor in

influencing the relationship between the bride's and groom's families and perhaps, also, the treatment of the bride in her new home.

In a society where divorce is still a scandal and where, in fact, the divorce rate is exceedingly low, an arranged marriage is the beginning of a lifetime relationship not just between the bride and groom but between their families as well. Thus, while a girl's looks are important, her character is even more so, for she is being judged as a prospective daughter-in-law as much as a prospective bride. . . .

My friend is a highly esteemed wife, mother, and daughter-in-law. She is religious, soft-spoken, modest, and deferential. She rarely gossips and never quarrels, two qualities highly desirable in a woman. A family that has the reputation for gossip and conflict among its womenfolk will not find it easy to get good wives for their sons. Parents will not want to send their daughter to a house in which there is conflict.

Originally from North India, my friend's family had lived for forty years in Bombay, where her husband owned a business. The family had delayed in seeking a match for their eldest son because he had been an air force pilot for several years, stationed in such remote places that it had seemed fruitless to try to find a girl who would be willing to accompany him. In their social class, a military career, despite its economic security, has little prestige and is considered a drawback in finding a suitable bride. Many families would not allow their daughters to marry a man in an occupation so potentially dangerous and that requires so much moving around.

The son had recently left the military and joined his father's business. Since he was a college graduate, modern, and well traveled, from such a good family, and, I thought, quite handsome, it seemed to me that he, or rather his family, was in a position to pick and choose. I said as much to my friend. While she agreed that there were many advantages on their side, she also said, "We must keep in mind that my son is both short and dark; these are drawbacks in finding the right match." While the boy's height had not escaped my notice, "dark" seemed to me inaccurate; I would have called him "wheat" colored perhaps, and in any case, I did not realize that color would be a consideration. I discovered, however, that while a boy's skin color is a less important consideration than a girl's, it is still a factor.

An important source of contacts in trying to arrange her son's marriage was my friend's social club in Bombay. Many of the women had daughters of the right age, and some had already expressed an interest in my friend's son. I was most enthusiastic about the possibilities of one particular family who had five daughters, all of whom were pretty, demure, and well educated. Their mother had told my friend, "You can have your pick for your son, whichever one of my daughters appeals to you most." I saw a match in sight. "Surely," I said to my friend, "we will find one there. Let's go visit and make our choice." But my friend held back; she did not seem to share my enthusiasm, for reasons I could not then fathom.

When I kept pressing for an explanation of her reluctance, she admitted, "See, Serena, here is the problem. The

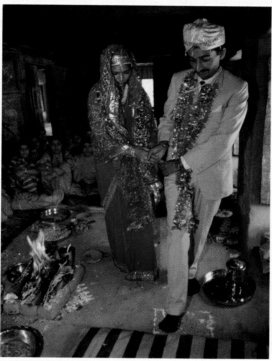

© Earl & Nazima Kowall/Corbis

family has so many daughters, how will they be able to provide nicely for any of them? We are not making any demands, but still, with so many daughters to marry off, one wonders whether she will even be able to make a proper wedding. Since this is our eldest son, it's best if we marry him to a girl who is the only daughter, then the wedding will truly be a gala affair." I argued that surely the quality of the girls themselves made up for any deficiency in the elaborateness of the wedding. My friend admitted this point but still seemed reluctant to proceed.

Is there something else," I asked her, "some factor I have missed?" "Well," she finally said, "there is one other thing. They have one daughter already married and living in Bombay. The mother is always complaining to me that the girl's in-laws don't let her visit her own family often enough. So it makes me wonder, will she be that kind of mother who always wants her daughter at her own home? This will prevent the girl from adjusting to our house. It is not a good thing." And so, this family of five daughters was dropped as a possibility.

Somewhat disappointed, I nevertheless respected my friend's reasoning and geared up for the next prospect. This was also the daughter of a woman in my friend's social club. There was clear interest in this family and I could see why. The family's reputation was excellent; in fact, they came from a subcaste slightly higher than my friend's own. The girl, who was an only daughter, was pretty and well educated and had a brother studying in the United States. Yet, after expressing an interest to me in this family, all talk of them suddenly died down and the search began elsewhere.

What happened to that girl as a prospect?" I asked one day. "You never mention her anymore. She is so pretty and so educated, what did you find wrong?"

"She is too educated. We've decided against it. My husband's father saw the girl on the bus the other day and thought her forward. A girl who 'roams about' the city by herself is not the girl for our family." My disappointment this time was even greater, as I thought the son would have liked the girl very much. . . . I learned that if the family of the girl has even a slightly higher social status than the family of the boy, the bride may think herself too good for them, and this too will cause problems. Later my friend admitted to me that this had been an important factor in her decision not to pursue the match. . . .

After one more candidate, who my friend decided was not attractive enough for her son, almost six months had passed and I had become anxious. My friend laughed at my impatience: "Don't be so much in a hurry," she said.

CONTINUED

"You Americans want everything done so quickly. You get married quickly and then just as quickly get divorced. Here we take marriage more seriously. We must take all the factors into account. It is not enough for us to learn by our mistakes. This is too serious a business. If a mistake is made we have not only ruined the life of our son or daughter, but we have spoiled the reputation of our family as well. And that will make it much harder for their brothers and sisters to get married. So we must be very careful."

What she said was true and I promised myself to be more patient. I had really hoped and expected that the match would be made before my year in India was up. But it was not to be. When I left India my friend seemed no further along in finding a suitable match for her son than when I had arrived.

Two years later, I returned to India and still my friend had not found a girl for her son. By this time, he was close to 30, and I think she was a little worried. Since she knew I had friends all over India, and I was going to be there for a year, she asked me to "help her in this work" and keep an eye out for someone suitable. I was flattered that my judgment was respected, but I had lost my earlier confidence as a matchmaker. Nevertheless, I promised that I would try.

It was almost at the end of my year's stay in India that I met a family with a marriageable daughter whom I felt might be a good possibility for my friend's son. . . . This new family had a successful business in a medium-sized city in central India and were from the same subcaste as my friend. The daughter was pretty and chic; in fact, she had studied fashion design in college. Her parents would not allow her to go off by herself to any of the major cities in India where she could make a career, but they had compromised with her wish to work by allowing her to run a small dress-making boutique from their home. In spite of her desire to have a career, the daughter was both modest and home-loving and had had a traditional, sheltered upbringing.

I mentioned the possibility of a match with my friend's son. The girl's parents were most interested. Although their daughter was not eager to marry just yet, the idea of living in Bombay—a sophisticated, extremely fashion-conscious city where she could continue her education in clothing design—was a great inducement. I gave the girl's father my friend's address and suggested that when they went to Bombay on some business or whatever, they look up the boy's family.

Returning to Bombay on my way to New York, I told my friend of this newly discovered possibility. She seemed to feel there was potential but, in spite of my urging, would not make any moves herself. She rather preferred to wait for the girl's family to call upon them.

A year later I received a letter from my friend. The family had indeed come to visit Bombay, and their daughter and my friend's daughter, who were near in age, had become very good friends. During that year, the two girls had frequently visited each other. I thought things looked promising.

Last week I received an invitation to a wedding: My friend's son and the girl were getting married. Since I had found the match, my presence was particularly requested at the wedding. I was thrilled. Success at last! As I prepared to leave for India, I began thinking, "Now, my friend's younger son, who do I know who has a nice girl for him . . . ?"

(Excerpted from S. Nanda (1992). Arranging a marriage in India. In P. R. De Vita (Ed.). The naked anthropologist (pp. 139–143). Belmont, CA: Wadsworth.) ■

Cousin Marriage

While cousin marriage is prohibited in some societies, certain cousins are the preferred marriage partners in others. A **parallel cousin** is the child of a father's brother or a mother's sister (Figure 20.1). In some societies, the preferred spouse for a man is his father's brother's daughter (or, from the woman's point of view, her father's brother's son). This is known as *patrilateral parallel-cousin marriage*. Although not obligatory, such marriages have been favored historically among Arabs, the ancient Israelites, and the ancient Greeks. All of these societies are (or were) hierarchical in nature—that is, some people are ranked higher than others because they have more power and property—and although male dominance and descent are emphasized, property of value to men is inherited by daughters as well as sons. Thus, when a man marries his father's brother's daughter (or a woman marries her father's brother's son), property is retained within the single male line of descent. In these societies, generally speaking, the greater the property, the more this form of parallel-cousin marriage is apt to occur.

A **cross cousin** is the child of a mother's brother or a father's sister (Figure 9.1). Some societies favor *matrilateral cross-cousin marriage*—marriage of a man to his mother's brother's daughter, or a woman to her father's sister's son. This preference exists among food foragers (such as the Aborigines of Australia) and some farming cultures (including various peoples of South India). Among food foragers, who inherit relatively little in the way of property, such marriages help establish and maintain ties of solidarity between social groups. In agricultural societies, however, the transmission of property is an important determinant. In societies that trace descent exclusively in the female line, for instance, property and other important rights usually pass from a man to his sister's son; under cross-cousin marriage, the sister's son is also the man's daughter's husband.

parallel cousin Child of a father's brother or a mother's sister.
cross cousin Child of a mother's brother or a father's sister.

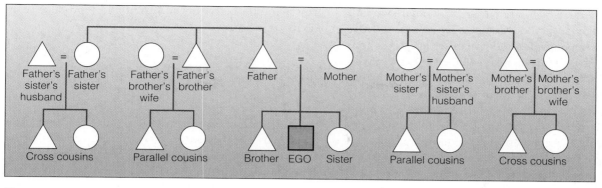

Figure 9.1

Anthropologists use diagrams of this sort to illustrate kinship relationships. Shown in this one is the distinction between cross cousins and parallel cousins. In such diagrams, males are always shown as triangles, females as circles, marital ties by an equal sign (=), sibling relationships as a horizontal line, and parent–child relationships as a vertical line. Terms are given from the perspective of the individual labeled EGO, who can be female or male.

Same-Sex Marriage

As noted earlier in this chapter, our definition of marriage refers to a union between "people" rather than "a man and a woman" because in some societies same-sex marriages are socially acceptable and officially allowed by law. Marriages between individuals of the same sex may provide a way of dealing with problems for which opposite-sex marriage offers no satisfactory solution. This is the case with woman–woman marriage, a practice permitted in many societies of sub-Saharan Africa, although in none does it involve more than a small minority of all women.

Details differ from one society to another, but woman–woman marriages among the Nandi of western Kenya may be taken as representative of such practices in Africa.[21] The Nandi are a pastoral people who also do considerable farming. Control of most significant property and the primary means of production—livestock and land—is exclusively in the hands of men and may only be transmitted to their male heirs, usually their sons. Since polygyny is the preferred form of marriage, a man's property is normally divided equally among his wives for their sons to inherit. Within the household, each wife has her own home in which she lives with her children, but all are under the authority of the woman's husband, who is a remote and aloof figure within the household. In such situations, the position of a woman who bears no sons is difficult; not only does she not help perpetuate her husband's male line—a major concern among the Nandi—but also she has no one to inherit the proper share of her husband's property.

To get around these problems, a woman of advanced age who bore no sons may become a female husband by marrying a young woman. The purpose of this arrangement is for the young wife to provide the male heirs her female husband could not. To accomplish this, the woman's wife enters into a sexual relationship with a man other than her female husband's male husband; usually it is one of his male relatives. No other obligations exist between this woman and her male sex partner, and her female husband is recognized as the social and legal father of any children born under these conditions.

In keeping with her role as female husband, this woman is expected to abandon her female gender identity and, ideally, dress and behave as a man. In practice, the ideal is not completely achieved, for the habits of a lifetime are difficult to reverse. Generally, it is in the context of domestic activities, which are most highly symbolic of female identity, that female husbands most completely assume a male identity.

---

[21]The following is based on Obler, R. S. (1982). Is the female husband a man? Woman/woman marriage among the Nandi of Kenya. *Ethnology 19*, 69–88.

The individuals who are parties to woman–woman marriages enjoy several advantages. By assuming male identity, a barren or sonless woman raises her status considerably and even achieves near equality with men, who otherwise occupy a far more favored position in Nandi society than women. A woman who marries a female husband is usually one who is unable to make a good marriage, often because she (the female husband's wife) has lost face as a consequence of premarital pregnancy. By marrying a female husband, she too raises her status and also secures legitimacy for her children. Moreover, a female husband is usually less harsh and demanding, spends more time with her, and allows her a greater say in decision making than a male husband does. The one thing she may not do is engage in sexual activity with her marriage partner. In fact, female husbands are expected to abandon sexual activity altogether, including with their male husbands to whom they remain married even though the women now have their own wives.

In contrast to woman–woman marriages among the Nandi are same-sex marriages that include sexual activity between partners. Over the past decade, the legal recognition of such unions has become a matter of vigorous debate in some parts of the world. Several countries, including Spain, Belgium, Canada, and the Netherlands, have passed laws legalizing gay marriages. Meanwhile numerous U.S. states have adopted constitutional amendments barring same-sex marriage.

The arguments most commonly marshaled by opponents of same-sex unions are, first, that marriage has always been between males and females—but as we have just seen, this is not true. Same-sex marriages have been documented not only for a number of societies in Africa but in other parts of the world as well. As among the Nandi, they provide acceptable positions in society for individuals who might otherwise be marginalized.

A second argument against same-sex unions is that they legitimize gays and lesbians, whose sexual orientations have been widely regarded as unnatural. But again, as discussed in earlier chapters, neither cross-cultural studies nor studies of other animal species suggest that homosexual behavior is unnatural.

A third argument, that the function of marriage is to produce children, is at best a partial truth, as marriage involves economic, political, and legal considerations as well. Moreover, it is increasingly common for same-sex partners to have children through adoption or by turning to modern reproductive technologies. There is also the fact that in many societies, such as the Nandi, there is a separation between the sexual and reproductive attributes of women.

MARRIAGE AND ECONOMIC EXCHANGE

In the Trobriand Islands, when a young couple decides to get married, they sit in public on the veranda of the young man's adolescent retreat, where all may see them. Here they remain until the bride's mother brings the couple cooked yams, which they then eat together, making their marriage official. A day later the bride is presented with three long skirts by the husband's sister, a symbol of the fact that the sexual freedom of adolescence is now over for the newlywed woman. This is followed by a large presentation of uncooked yams by the bride's father and her mother's brother, who represent both her father's and her own lineages.

Meanwhile, the groom's father and mother's brother collect such valuables as stone axe blades, clay pots, money, and the occasional Kula shell (see Chapter 19) to present to the young wife's maternal kin and father. After the first year of the marriage, during which the bride's mother continues to provide the couple's meals of cooked yams, each of the young husband's relatives who provided valuables for his father and mother's brother to present to the bride's relatives will receive yams from her maternal relatives and father. All of this gift giving back and forth between the husband's and wife's lineages, as well as those of their fathers, serves to bind the four parties together in a way that makes people respect and honor the marriage and that creates obligations on the part of the woman's kin to take care of her husband in the future.

As among the Trobriand Islanders, marriages in many human societies are formalized by some sort of economic exchange. Among the Trobrianders, this takes the form of a gift exchange, as just described. Far more common is **bride-price,** sometimes called *bride wealth,* which involves payments of money or valuable goods to a bride's parents or other close kin. This usually happens in patrilineal societies where the bride will become a member of the household where her husband grew up; this household will benefit from her labor as well as from the offspring she produces. Thus, her family must be compensated for their loss.

Not only is bride-price *not* a simple "buying and selling" of women, but the bride's parents may use the money to purchase jewelry or household furnishings for her or to finance an elaborate and costly wedding celebration. It also contributes to the stability of the marriage, because it usually must be refunded if the couple separates. Other forms of compensation are an exchange of women between families—"My son will marry your

bride-price Money or valuable goods paid by the groom or his family to the bride's family upon marriage. Also called bride wealth.

In some societies when a woman marries, she receives her share of the family inheritance (her dowry), which she brings to her new family (unlike bride-price, which passes from the groom's family to the bride's family). Shown here are Slovakian women carrying the objects of a woman's dowry.

daughter if your son will marry my daughter." Yet another is **bride service,** a period of time during which the groom works for the bride's family.

In a number of societies more or less restricted to the western, southern, and eastern margins of Eurasia, where the economy is based on agriculture, women often bring a dowry with them at marriage. A form of dowry in the United States is the custom of the bride's family paying the wedding expenses. Another example is that a Roman Catholic woman joining a religious order as a consecrated nun, and thus entering into a spiritual marriage, as discussed earlier, also traditionally brings a dowry (*dos religiosa*) to that institution. In effect, a **dowry** is a woman's share of parental property that, instead of passing to her upon her parents' death, is distributed to her at the time of her marriage. This does not mean that she retains control of this property after marriage. In some European countries, for example, a woman's property traditionally falls exclusively under her husband's control. Having benefited by what she has brought to the marriage, however, he is obligated to look out for her future well-being, including her security after his death.

Thus, one of the functions of dowry is to ensure a woman's support in widowhood (or after divorce), an important consideration in a society where men carry out the bulk of productive work, and women are valued for their reproductive potential rather than for the work they do. In such societies, women incapable of bearing children are especially vulnerable, but the dowry they bring with them at marriage helps protect them against desertion. Another function of dowry is to reflect the economic status of the woman in societies where differ-

ences in wealth are important. It also permits women, with the aid of their parents and kin, to compete through dowry for desirable (that is, wealthy) husbands.

DIVORCE

Like marriage, divorce in most societies is a matter of great concern to the couple's families. Since marriage is less often a religious matter than it is an economic one, divorce arrangements can be made for a variety of reasons and with varying degrees of difficulty. Among the Gusii farmers of western Kenya, for instance, sterility and impotence are grounds for a divorce. Among certain aboriginal peoples in northern Canada and Chenchu foragers inhabiting the thickly forested hills in central India, divorce was discouraged after children were born; couples usually were urged by their families to adjust their differences. By contrast, in the southwestern United States, a Hopi Indian woman in Arizona could divorce her husband at any time merely by placing his belongings outside the door to indicate he was no longer welcome.

An adult unmarried woman is very rare in most non-Western societies where a divorced woman usually soon remarries. In many societies, economic considerations are often the strongest motivation to wed. On the island

bride service A designated period of time after marriage when the groom works for the bride's family.

dowry Payment of a woman's inheritance at the time of her marriage, either to her or to her husband.

of New Guinea, a man does not marry because of sexual needs, which he can readily satisfy out of wedlock, but because he needs a woman to make pots and cook his meals, to fabricate nets and weed his plantings. Likewise, women in communities that depend for security upon males capable of fighting need husbands who are raised to be able warriors as well as good hunters.

Although divorce rates may be high in various corners of the world, they have become so high in Western industrial and postindustrial societies that many worry about the future of what they view as traditional and familiar forms of marriage and the family. It is interesting to note that although divorce was next to impossible in Western societies between 1000 and 1800, few marriages lasted more than about ten or twenty years, due to high mortality rates caused in part by inadequate health care and medical expertise.[22] With increased longevity, separation by death has diminished, and separation by legal action has grown. In the United States today, some 50 percent of first marriages end in divorce—twice the 1960 divorce rate but slightly less than the high point in the early 1980s.[23]

---

[22]Stone, L. (1998). *Kinship and gender: An introduction* (p. 235). Boulder, CO: Westview Press.

[23]Whitehead, B. D. & Popenoe, D. (2004). *The state of our unions: The social health of marriage in America 2004.* Rutgers, NJ: Rutgers University National Marriage Project.

family   Two or more people related by blood, marriage, or adoption. The family may take many forms, ranging from a single parent with one or more children, to a married couple or polygamous spouses with offspring, to several generations of parents and their children.

FAMILY AND HOUSEHOLD

Dependence on group living for survival is a basic human characteristic. We have inherited this from primate ancestors, although we have developed it in our own distinctly human way—through culture. However each culture may define what constitutes a family, this social unit forms the basic cooperative structure that ensures an individual's primary needs and provides the necessary care for children to develop as healthy and productive members of the group and thereby help ensure its future.

Comparative historical and cross-cultural studies reveal a wide variety of family patterns, and these patterns may change over time. Thus, the definition of **family** is necessarily broad: two or more people related by blood, marriage, or adoption. The family may take many forms, ranging from a single parent with one or more children, to a married couple or polygamous spouses with offspring, to several generations of parents and their children.

In all known cultures, past and present, gender plays at least some role in determining the division of labor. An effective way to facilitate economic cooperation between men and women and simultaneously provide for a close bond between mother and child is through the establishment of residential groups that include adults of both sexes. The differing nature of male and female roles, as defined by different cultures, makes it advantageous for a child to have an adult of the same sex available to serve as a proper model for the appropriate adult role. The presence of adult men and women in the same residential group provides for this. The men, however, need not be the women's husbands. In some societies

A celebration at the palace in the Yoruba city of Oyo, Nigeria. As is usual in societies where royal households are found, that of the Yoruba includes many individuals not related to the ruler, as well as the royal family.

they are the women's brothers—as in the case of the Nayar, discussed earlier in this chapter, where sisters and their children live together with their brothers and their mother and her brothers.

For purposes of cross-cultural comparison, anthropologists define the **household** as the basic residential unit where economic production, consumption, inheritance, child rearing, and shelter are organized and carried out. In the vast majority of human societies, most households are made up of families, but there are many other arrangements. For instance, among the Mundurucu Indians, a horticultural people living in the center of Brazil's Amazon rainforest, married men and women are members of separate households, meeting periodically for sexual activity. At age 13 boys join their fathers in the men's house. Meanwhile, their sisters continue to live with their mothers and the younger boys in two or three houses grouped around the men's house. Thus, the men's house constitutes one household inhabited by adult males and their sexually mature sons, and the women's houses, inhabited by adult women and prepubescent boys and girls, constitute others.

An array of other domestic arrangements can be found in other parts of the world, including situations in which co-residents of a household are not related biologically or by marriage—such as the service personnel in an elaborate royal household, apprentices in the household of craft specialists, low-status clients in the household of rich and powerful patrons, or groups of children being raised by paired teams of adult male and female community members in an Israeli kibbutz (a collectively owned and operated agricultural settlement). So it is that *family* and *household* are not always synonymous.

Forms of the Family

To discuss the various forms families take in response to particular social, historical, and ecological circumstances, we must, at the outset, make a distinction between a **conjugal family** (in Latin *conjugere* means "to join together"), which is formed on the basis of marital ties, and a **consanguineal family** (based on the Latin word *consanguineus*, literally meaning "of the same blood"), which consists of related women, their brothers, and the women's offspring.

Consanguineal families are not common, but there are more examples than the classic case of the Nayar described at the beginning of the chapter. Among these are the Musuo of southwestern China and the Tory Islanders, a Roman Catholic, Gaelic-speaking fisherfolk living off the coast of Ireland. The Tory Islanders, who do not marry until they are in their late 20s or early 30s, look at it this way: "Oh well, you get married at that age, it's too late to break up arrangements that you have already known for a long time. . . . You know, I have my sisters

Figure 9.2

This diagram shows the relationships in a traditional nuclear family, a form that is common but declining in North America and much of Europe.

and brothers to look after, why should I leave home to go live with a husband? After all, he's got his sisters and his brothers looking after him."[24] Because the community numbers but a few hundred people, husbands and wives are within easy commuting distance of each other.

According to a cross-cultural survey of family types in 192 cultures around the world, the extended family is most common, present in about 48 percent of those cultures, compared to the nuclear family at 25 percent, and polygamous at 22 percent.[25] Each of these is discussed below.

The Nuclear Family

The smallest family unit is known as the **nuclear family,** a group consisting of one or two parents and dependent offspring, which may include a stepparent, stepsiblings, and adopted children (Figure 9.2). Until recently, the term *nuclear family* referred solely to the mother, father, and child(ren) unit—the family form that most Americans, Europeans, and many others now regard as the normal or natural nucleus of larger family units. In the United States father–mother–child(ren) nuclear fam-

[24]Fox, R. (1981, December 3). [Interview]. Coast Telecourses, Inc., Los Angeles.

[25]Winick, C. (Ed.). (1970). *Dictionary of anthropology* (p. 202). Totowa, NJ: Littlefield, Adams.

household The basic residential unit where economic production, consumption, inheritance, child rearing, and shelter are organized and carried out.
conjugal family A family established through marriage.
consanguineal family A family of "blood relatives" consisting of related women, their brothers, and the women's offspring.
nuclear family A group consisting of one or two parents and dependent offspring, which may include a stepparent, stepsiblings, and adopted children. (Until recently this term referred only to the father–mother–child(ren) unit.)

ily households reached their highest frequency around 1950, when 60 percent of all households conformed to this model.[26] Today such families comprise only 24 percent of U.S. households,[27] and the term *nuclear family* is used to cover the social reality of several types of small parent–child units, including single parents with children and same-sex couples with children.

Industrialization and market capitalism have played a historical role in shaping the nuclear family most of us are familiar with today. One reason for this is that factories, mining and transportation companies, warehouses, shops, and other businesses generally only pay individual wage earners for the jobs they are hired to do. Whether these workers are single, married, divorced, have siblings or children is really not a concern to the profit-seeking companies. Because jobs may come and go, individual wage earners must remain mobile to adapt to the labor markets. And since few wage earners have the financial resources to support large numbers of relatives without incomes of their own, industrial or postindustrial societies do not favor the continuance of larger extended families (discussed below), which are standard in most societies traditionally dependent on pastoral nomadism, agriculture, or horticulture.

Interestingly, the nuclear family is also likely to be prominent in traditional foraging societies such as that of the Eskimo people who live in the barren Arctic environments of eastern Siberia, Alaska, Greenland, and Canada (where Eskimos are now known as Inuit). In the winter the traditional Inuit husband and wife, with their children, roam the vast Arctic Canadian snowscape in their quest for food. The husband hunts and makes shelters. The wife cooks, is responsible for the children, and

[26]Stacey, J. (1990). *Brave new families* (pp. 5, 10). New York: Basic Books

[27]Irvine, M. (1999, November 24). Mom-and-pop houses grow rare. *Burlington Free Press; Current population survey.* (2002). U.S. Census Bureau.

makes the clothing and keeps it in good repair. One of her chores is to chew her husband's boots to soften the leather for the next day so that he can resume his quest for game. The wife and her children could not survive without the husband, and life for a man is unimaginable without a wife.

Similar to nuclear families in industrial societies, those living under especially harsh environmental conditions must be prepared to fend for themselves. Such isolation comes with its own set of challenges, including the difficulties of rearing children without multigenerational support and a lack of familial care for the elderly. Nonetheless, this form of family is well adapted to a mode of subsistence that requires a high degree of geographic mobility. For the Inuit in Canada, this mobility permits the hunt for food; for other North Americans, the hunt for jobs and improved social status requires a mobile form of family unit.

Not even among the Inuit, however, is the nuclear family as independent from other kin as it has become among most non-native North Americans. When Inuit families are off by themselves, it is regarded as a mat-

Among Inuit people in Canada who still hunt for much of their food, nuclear families such as the one shown here are typical. Their isolation from other relatives is usually temporary. Much of the time they are found in groups of at least a few related families.

© Joe Cavanaugh/DDB Stock

Extended family households exist in many parts of the world, including among the Maya people of Central America and Mexico.[30] In many of their communities, sons bring their wives to live in houses built on the edges of a small open plaza, on one edge of which their father's house already stands. Numerous household activities are carried out on this plaza—children play, while adults weave, do some other productive work, or socialize with guests. The head of the family is the sons' father, who makes most of the important decisions. All members of the family work together for the common good and deal with outsiders as a single unit.

ter of temporary expediency; most of the time, they are found in groups of at least a few families together, with members of one family having relatives in all of the others.[28] Thus families cooperate with one another on a daily basis, sharing food and other resources, looking out for one another's children, and sometimes even eating together.

The sense of shared responsibility for one another's children and for the general welfare in Inuit multifamily groups contrasts with families in the United States, which are basically "on their own." Here the states assign sole responsibility to individual families for child care and the welfare of family members, with relatively little assistance from outside.[29] To be sure, families can and often do help one another out, but they are under no obligation to do so, and even if they wish to may find it impossible due to geographic separation born of high mobility. In fact, once children reach the age of majority (18), parents have no further legal obligation to them, nor do the children to their parents. When families do have difficulty fulfilling their assigned functions—as is increasingly the case even though it be through no fault of their own—less support is available to them from the community at large than in most of the world's "stateless" societies, including that of the Inuit.

The Extended Family

When two or more closely related nuclear families cluster together into a large domestic group, they form a unit known as the **extended family.** This larger family unit,

common in traditional horticultural, agricultural, and pastoral societies around the world, typically consists of siblings with their spouses and offspring, and often their parents. All of these kin, some related by blood and some by marriage, live and work together for the common good and deal with outsiders as a single unit.

Because members of the younger generation bring their husbands or wives to live in the family, extended families have continuity through time. As older members die off, new members are born into the family. Extended families have built into them particular challenges. Among these are difficulties that the in-marrying spouse is likely to have in adjusting to his or her spouse's family.

In North America, extended families can still be found on many American Indian reservations. They also exist in some non-Indian communities, for example along the Maine coast,[31] where they developed in response to a unique economy featuring a mix of farming and seafaring, coupled with an ideal of self-sufficiency. Because family farms were incapable of providing self-sufficiency, seafaring was taken up as an economic alternative. Sea-going commerce, however, was periodically afflicted by depression, so family farming remained important as a cushion against economic hard times. The need for a sufficient labor pool to tend the farm, while at the same time furnish officers, crew, or (frequently) both for locally owned vessels, was satisfied by the practice of

[28]Graburn, N. H. H. (1969). *Eskimos without igloos: Social and economic development in Sugluk* (pp. 56–58). Boston: Little Brown.

[29]Collier, J., Rosaldo, M. Z., & Yanagisako, S. (1982). Is there a family? New anthropological views. In B. Thorne & M. Yalom (Eds.), *Rethinking the family: Some feminist questions* (pp. 34–35). New York: Longman.

[30]Vogt, E. Z. (1990). *The Zinacantecos of Mexico, A modern Maya way of life* (2nd ed., pp. 30–34). Fort Worth: Holt, Rinehart & Winston.

[31]Haviland, W. A. (1973). Farming, seafaring and bilocal residence on the coast of Maine. *Man in the Northeast 6*, 31–44.

extended family Two or more closely related nuclear families clustered together into a large domestic group.

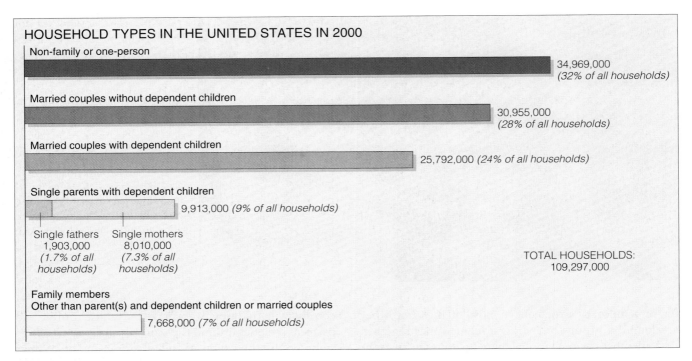

Figure 9.3
Household types in the United States, based on U.S. Census Bureau figures for 2000.

a newly married couple settling on the farm of either the bride's or the groom's parents. Thus, most people spent their lives cooperating on a day-to-day basis in economic activities with close relatives, all of whom lived together (even if in separate houses) on the same farm.

Nontraditional Families and Nonfamily Households

In North America and parts of Europe, increasing numbers of people live in nonfamily households, either alone or with nonrelatives. In fact, some 32 percent of households in the United States fall into this category (Figure 9.3). Many others live as members of what are often called *nontraditional families*. These include single-parent households. Such households are often the result of divorce or a marriage partner's death. They also stem from increased sexual activity outside of wedlock, combined with declining marriage rates among women of childbearing age, as well as a rise in the number of women actively choosing single motherhood. About a third of all births in the United States occur outside of marriage, and in several northwestern European countries, the nonmarital birthrate is close to 50 percent.[32]

The percentage of single-parent households in the United States has grown to 9 percent, while the number

comprised of married couples with children has dropped to 24 percent. Although single-parent households account for just 9 percent of all households in the United States, they are home to 28 percent of all children (under 18 years of age) in the country.[33] In the vast majority of cases, a child living in a single-parent household is with his or her mother. Fathers are usually required to pay child support but are not always able or willing to do so. And when they do pay, the amount is often insufficient for essential food, clothing, and medical care, let alone the cost of child care so that the woman can seek or continue income-producing work to support herself. Notably, single fathers in the United States are three times more likely to have a cohabiting partner in the home than are single mothers.

Not surprisingly, as the number of female-headed households has increased, so has the number of women (and, of course, their children) living below the poverty line. More than one-third of all female-headed households in the United States now fall into this category, and one-quarter of all children are poor.

Single-parent households headed by women are neither new nor restricted to industrial or postindustrial societies. They have been known and studied for a long time in the countries of the Caribbean Sea, where men historically have been exploited as a cheap source of la-

---

[32]*Recent demographic developments in Europe—2000.* Council of Europe.

[33]*Current population survey.* (2002). U.S. Census Bureau.

bor on sugar, coffee, or banana plantations. In more recent decades, many of these men are now also working as temporary migrant laborers in foreign countries, primarily in the United States. Under such seasonal or temporary work conditions, men are absent from their families for many months each year, have no social or political power and few economic rewards. Hence they are tenuously attached at best to any particular household. These are held together by women, who as producers of subsistence foods provide the means of economic survival for households. Similar female-headed households are becoming increasingly common in other "underdeveloped" countries, too, as development projects restrict the ability of women to earn a living wage (reasons for this are discussed in later chapters).

Residence Patterns

Where some form of conjugal or extended family is the norm, family exogamy requires that either the husband or wife, if not both, must move to a new household upon marriage. There are five common patterns of residence that a newly married couple may adopt—the prime determinant being ecological circumstances, although other factors enter in as well. Thus, postmarital residence arrangements, far from being arbitrary, are adaptive in character. Here we will mention only the four most common arrangements.

Patrilocal residence is when a married couple lives in the husband's father's place of residence. This arrangement is favorable in situations where men play a predominant role in subsistence, particularly if they own property that can be accumulated, if polygyny is customary, if warfare is prominent enough to make cooperation among men especially important, and if an elaborate political organization exists in which men wield authority. These conditions are most often found together in societies that rely on animal husbandry and/or intensive agriculture for their subsistence. Where patrilocal residence is customary, the bride often must move to a different band or community. In such cases, her parents' family is not only losing the services of a useful family member, but they are losing her potential offspring as well. Hence, some kind of compensation to her family, most commonly bride-price, is usual.

Matrilocal residence, in which a married couple lives in the wife's mother's place of residence, is a likely result if ecological circumstances make the role of the woman predominate for subsistence. It is found most often in horticultural societies, where political organization is relatively uncentralized and where cooperation among women is important. The Hopi Indians provide one example. Although it is the Hopi men who do the farming, the women control access to land and "own" the harvest. Indeed, men are not even allowed in the gra-

naries. Under matrilocal residence, men usually do not move very far from the family in which they were raised so they are available to help out there from time to time. Therefore, marriage usually does not involve compensation to the groom's family.

Ambilocal residence (*ambi* in Latin means "both"), a pattern in which a married couple may choose either matrilocal or patrilocal residence, is adaptive in situations where economic cooperation of more people than are available in the nuclear family is needed but where resources are limited in some way. Because the couple can join either the bride's or the groom's family, family membership is flexible, and the two can live where the resources look best or where their labor is most needed. This was once the situation on the peninsulas and islands along the coast of Maine, where, as already noted, extended family households were based upon ambilocal residence.

The same residential pattern is particularly common among food-foraging peoples, as among the Mbuti pygmies of Africa's Ituri forest. Typically, a Mbuti marries someone from another band, so that one spouse always has in-laws who live elsewhere. Thus, if foraging is bad in their part of the tropical rainforest, the couple has somewhere else to go where food may be more readily available. Ambilocality greatly enhances the Mbutis' opportunity to find food. It also provides a place to go if a dispute breaks out with someone in the band where the couple is currently living. Consequently, Mbuti camps are constantly changing their composition as people split off to go live with their in-laws, while others are joining from other groups. For a people like food foragers, who find their food in nature and who maintain an egalitarian social order, ambilocal residence can be a crucial factor in both survival and conflict resolution.

Under **neolocal residence,** a married couple forms a household in a separate location. This occurs where the independence of the nuclear family is emphasized. In industrial societies such as the United States, where most economic activity occurs outside rather than inside the family and where it is important for individuals to be able to move where jobs can be found, neolocal residence is better suited than any of the other patterns.

patrilocal residence A residence pattern in which a married couple lives in the husband's father's place of residence.
matrilocal residence A residence pattern in which a married couple lives in the wife's mother's place of residence.
ambilocal residence A residence pattern in which a married couple may choose either matrilocal or patrilocal residence.
neolocal residence A pattern in which a married couple establish their household in a location apart from either the husband's or the wife's relatives.

© Edward Burtynsky

Many of China's 114 million migrant laborers work in factories and live in factory dormitories such as this.

MARRIAGE, FAMILY, AND HOUSEHOLD IN OUR GLOBALIZED AND TECHNOLOGIZED WORLD

In many countries the mosaic of marriage, family, and household forms has become more varied in recent decades. Many factors contribute to this, including global capitalism and large-scale emigration of peoples moving across cultural boundaries. Also significant are high rates of divorce and remarriage, resulting in *blended families* comprised of a married couple together raising children from previous unions. And although it has not been uncommon for childless couples in many cultures throughout human history to adopt children, including orphans and even captives, today it is a transnational practice for adults from industrial and postindustrial countries to travel across the world in search of infants to adopt, regardless of their ethnic heritage. Other contributing factors include *new reproductive technologies* (NRTs), such as in vitro fertilization, as well as open adoption, which make it possible for a child to have a relationship with both the biological and adoptive parents.

Also of note, worldwide, is the ever-growing number of households comprised of temporary and migrant workers. Today, China alone has 114 million of them, mostly young people who have quit the peasant villages

of their childhood and traveled to fast-growing cities to work in factories, shops, restaurants, and other such places. Some pile into apartments with friends or co-workers, others live in factory dormitories—new, single-generation households that stand in stark contrast to the multigeneration extended family households in which they were raised. Similar scenes are repeated all around the world as individuals in this transient workforce set up house together far away from home in order to make a living. Although many countries have passed legislation intended to provide migrants with protections concerning housing, as well as work conditions and pay (such as the 1983 Migrant and Seasonal Agricultural Worker Protection Act in the United States), living conditions for these workers are often miserable.[34]

As the various ethnographic examples in this chapter illustrate, our species has invented a wide variety of marriage, family, and household forms, each in correspondence with related features in the social structure and conforming to the larger cultural system. In the face of new challenges, we explore and tinker in search of solutions, sometimes resulting in finding completely new forms, and other times returning to time-tested formulas of more traditional varieties.

---

[34]Chang, L. (2005, June 9). A Migrant worker sees rural home in new light. *Wall Street Journal.*

Questions for Reflection

1. Members of traditional communities in countries where the state is either weak or absent depend on relatives to help meet the basic challenges of survival. In such traditional societies, why would it be risky to choose marriage partners exclusively on the basis of romantic love? Can you imagine other factors playing a role if the long-term survival of your community is at stake?

2. Although most women in Europe and North America probably view polygyny as a marriage practice exclusively benefiting men, women in cultures where such marriages are traditional may stress more positive sides of sharing a husband with several co-wives. Under which conditions do you think polygyny could be considered as relatively beneficial for women?

3. Many people in North America and Europe choose to have children outside marriage. Considering some of the major functions of marriage, do you think there is a relationship

between the type of society an individual belongs to and the choice to forgo the traditional benefits of marriage? Under what cultural conditions might the choice to remain unmarried present serious challenges?

4. Raising children is a challenge not only for parents but also for the larger community. Why do you think your own culture has developed the kind of family and household organization most familiar to you? Why do you think those particular organizational forms came into being? Can you imagine under which circumstances these arrangements may become inadequate?

5. Single motherhood in North America has typically been seen as something tied to low income, yet it is becoming increasingly common among women across the economic spectrum. What do you consider to be the reasons for this, based on the barrel model of culture with its three tiers of infrastructure, social structure, and superstructure?

Suggested Readings

Coontz, S. (2005). *Marriage, a history: From obedience to intimacy, or how love conquered marriage*. New York: Viking Adult.

Challenging the idea that marriage is in crisis due to rising divorce rates, out-of-wedlock births, and same-sex unions, Coontz argues that marriage has always been in a state of flux and that "almost every marital and sexual arrangement we have seen in recent years . . . has been tried somewhere before." Placing current concepts of marriage in broad historical context, Coontz explains marriage as a political tool, a means of ensuring a domestic labor force, and a flexible reflection of changing social standards.

Holy, L. (1996). *Anthropological perspectives on kinship*. London: Pluto Press.

Holy investigates changes in the conceptualization of kinship brought about by new reproductive technologies and the growing interest in culturally specific notions of personhood and gender. Considering the extent to which Western assumptions have guided anthropological studies of kinship, the author offers critical reflection on cultural bias in approaches to the subject.

Hutter, M. (Ed.) (2003). *The family experience: A reader in cultural diversity* (4th ed.). Boston: Allyn & Bacon.

This readable anthology examines the cultural diversity of the American family by providing relevant articles integrating race, class, gender, and ethnicity. Taken as a whole, these readings reveal both historical trends and unique variations that widen our understanding of the diversity, patterns, and dynamics of the American family.

Modell, J. (1994). *Kinship with strangers: Adoption and interpretations of kinship in American culture*. Berkeley: University of California Press.

The author, an adopter and an anthropologist, analyzes the "core symbols" of kinship in American culture—birth, biology, and blood—and examines their impact on people who experience the "fictive" kinship of adoption.

Stockard, J. E. (2002). *Marriage in culture: Practice and meaning across diverse societies*. Ft. Worth: Harcourt College Publishers.

This innovative, accessible text explores the meaning of marriage in different cultures, using compelling ethnographic accounts of the !Kung San (Bushman), Chinese, Iroquois, and Tibetan societies to familiarize students with anthropologists' unique perspective on marriage in culture. Each chapter explores the ways in which different economic, political, family, and gender systems shape the practice and meaning of marriage.

Stone, L. (2005). *Kinship and gender: An introduction* (3rd ed.). Boulder, CO: Westview Press.

Focusing on gender, Stone considers the cross-cultural variations in marriage practices in the broader context of kinship studies. A particular strength is the inclusion of specific case studies to illustrate general principles. The book ends with a thought-provoking discussion of new reproductive technologies and their repercussions for both kinship and gender. This revised and updated edition features new case studies on primate kinship, American kinship, and new reproductive technologies.

Thomson Audio Study Products

 Enjoy the MP3-ready Audio Lecture Overviews for each chapter and a comprehensive audio glossary of key terms for quick study and review. Whether walking to class, doing laundry, or studying at your desk, you now have the freedom to choose when, where, and how you interact with your audio-based educational media. See the preface for information on how to access this on-the-go study and review tool.

The Anthropology Resource Center

www.thomsonedu.com/anthropology
The Anthropology Resource Center provides extended learning materials to reinforce your understanding of key concepts in the four fields of anthropology. For each of the four fields, the Resource Center includes dynamic exercises including video exercises, map exercises, simulations, and "Meet the Scientists" interviews, as well as critical thinking questions that can be assigned and e-mailed to instructors. The Resource Center also provides breaking news in anthropology and interesting material on applied anthropology to help you link what you are learning to the world around you.

10 Kinship and Descent

© Graeme Matthews/Photo New Zealand

All humans face the challenge of creating and maintaining a social network that reaches beyond the capabilities of immediate family or household to provide support and security. On a very basic level that network is arranged by kinship. We see such a kin-ordered arrangement with the Maori of New Zealand today. About seven centuries ago, their Polynesian ancestors arrived on the shores of this island country in a small fleet of large sailing canoes called *waka.* The chiefs and crewmembers of these canoes had children. Their offspring, in the course of generations, formed large descent groups known as *iwi* ("tribe"). Each Maori today belongs to such an *iwi* and can trace his or her family's genealogy back about twenty-five generations to a founding ancestor in one of these legendary canoes. For this reason, Maori refer to groups of related *iwi* sharing a territorial district as *waka,* and membership in one of these "canoes" gives them certain rights to cultural and natural resources as the indigenous heirs of New Zealand's first human settlers.

What Is Kinship?

Kinship is a social network of relatives within which individuals possess certain mutual rights and obligations. One's place in this network, or kinship status, determines what these rights and obligations are. Providing groups of relatives with a social structure, kinship helps shield them from the dangers of disorganization and fracture. Kinship is especially important in societies where other institutions such as a centralized government, a professional military, or financial banks are absent or do not function effectively. In such societies, individuals must depend on a wide network of relatives for support and protection.

What Are Descent Groups?

A descent group is a kind of kinship group in which being in the direct line of descent from a particular real or mythical ancestor is a criterion of membership. Descent may be traced exclusively through men or women, or through either at the discretion of the individual. Two different means of tracing descent may be used at the same time to assign individuals to different groups for different purposes. In societies without descent groups, such as many food-foraging as well as industrial and postindustrial societies, people rely instead on the kindred: an individual's close blood relatives on the maternal and paternal sides of his or her family. Because each kindred is an ego-centered family group, it is a less stable social unit than the descent group.

What Functions Do Kin-Ordered Groups Serve?

Kin-ordered groups of various kinds are social organizational devices for solving a number of specific challenges that commonly confront human societies: maintaining the integrity of resources that cannot be divided without being destroyed; providing work forces for tasks that require a labor pool larger than households can provide; and rallying support for purposes of self-defense or offensive attack. Kin-ordered organizations such as descent groups arise from extended family organization. Kinship terminology is affected by and adjusts to the kinds of descent or other kinship groups that are important in a society.

Åll societies rely on some form of family and/or household organization to effectively deal with basic human challenges: regulating sexual activities, co-ordinating work, and organizing child rearing. As efficient and flexible as family and household organization may be for meeting such challenges, many societies confront problems that are beyond the coping ability of family and household organization.

For example, members of one independent local group often need some means of interacting with neighboring groups, of claiming support and protection from individuals in another group. This can be important for defense against natural or human-made disasters. Also, a group frequently needs to share rights to a natural resource that is difficult to divide or exclusively control, such as a large tract of land, stretch of water, or a wild herd of migratory animals. Further, people often need some means of providing cooperative work forces for tasks that require more participants than households alone can provide. Finally, larger social units may be essential for pulling together support for self-defense against outside aggressors or offensive attacks against neighboring groups in order to gain control over scarce or choice resources.

THOMSON AUDIO STUDY PRODUCTS Take advantage of the MP3-ready Audio Lecture Overviews and comprehensive audio glossary of key terms for each chapter. See the preface for information on how to access this on-the-go study and review tool.

Humans have come up with many ways to widen their circles of support to meet such challenges. One is through a formal political system, with personnel to make and enforce laws, keep the peace, allocate resources, and perform other regulatory and societal functions. But the predominant way in societies not (or not effectively) organized as political states—especially foraging, crop-cultivating, and pastoral societies—is by means of **kinship,** a network of relatives within which individuals possess certain mutual rights and obligations.

kinship A network of relatives within which individuals possess certain mutual rights and obligations.
descent group Any kin-ordered social group with a membership in the direct line of descent from a real (historical) or fictional common ancestor.
unilineal descent Descent that establishes group membership exclusively through either the male or female line.
matrilineal descent Descent traced exclusively through the female line to establish group membership.
patrilineal descent Descent traced exclusively through the male line to establish group membership.

DESCENT GROUPS

A common way of organizing a society along kinship lines is by creating what anthropologists call descent groups. Found in many societies, a **descent group** is any kin-ordered social group with a membership in the direct line of descent from a real (historical) or fictional common ancestor. Members of a descent group trace their shared connections back to such an ancestor through a chain of parent–child links. The addition of a few culturally meaningful obligations and taboos acts as a kind of glue to help hold the structured social group together.

Membership in a descent group provides individuals with a wider social network of relatives without whom it is difficult or even impossible to effectively deal with the multiple challenges of survival hurled at them, including securing vitally important natural resources for food, fuel, shelter, and other necessities. Although many important functions of the descent group are taken over by other institutions when a society becomes politically organized as a state, elements of such kin-ordered groups may continue.

We see this with many traditional indigenous societies that have become part of larger state societies yet endure as distinctive kin-ordered communities. So it is with the Maori of New Zealand, featured in this chapter's Challenge Issue and the Biocultural Connection. Retaining key elements of their traditional social structure, they are still organized in about thirty large descent groups known as *iwi* ("tribes"), which form part of larger social and territorial units known as *waka* ("canoes").

Descent group membership must be sharply defined in order to operate effectively in a kin-ordered society. If membership is allowed to overlap, it is unclear where someone's primary loyalty belongs, especially when different descent groups have conflicting interests. Membership can be restricted in a number of ways. The most common way is what anthropologists refer to as *unilineal descent,* in which membership is determined by a direct line of descent from a common ancestor exclusively through one's male or female ancestors, but not both. In this way, each individual is automatically assigned from the moment of birth to his or her mother's or father's group and to that group only.

Unilineal Descent

Unilineal descent (sometimes called *unilateral descent*) establishes descent group membership exclusively through the male or the female line. In non-Western societies, unilineal descent groups are quite common. The individual is assigned at birth to membership in a specific descent group, which may be traced either by **matrilineal descent,** through the female line, or by **patrilineal descent,** through the male line, depending on the culture.

Biocultural Connection

Maori Origins: Ancestral Genes and Mythical Canoes

Anthropologists have been fascinated to find that the oral traditions of Maori people in New Zealand fit quite well with scientific findings. New Zealand, an island country whose dramatic geography served as the setting for the *Lord of the Rings* film trilogy, lies in a remote corner of the Pacific Ocean some 1,200 miles southeast of Australia. Named by Dutch seafarers who landed on its shores in 1642, it was claimed by the British as a colony about 150 years later. Maoris, the country's indigenous people, fought back but were outgunned, outnumbered, and forced to lay down their arms in the early 1870s. Today, nearly 600,000 of New Zealand's 4.1 million citizens claim some Maori ancestry.

Maori have an age-old legend about how they came to Aotearoa ("Land of the Long White Cloud"), their name for New Zealand: More than twenty-five generations ago, their Polynesian ancestors arrived in a great fleet of sailing canoes from Hawaiki, their mythical homeland sometimes identified with Tahiti where the native language closely resembles their own. According to chants and genealogies passed down through the ages, this fleet consisted of at least seven (perhaps up to thirteen) seafaring canoes. Estimated to weigh about 5 tons, each of these large dugouts had a single claw-shaped sail and may have carried fifty to 120 people, plus food supplies, plants, and animals.

As described by Maori anthropologist Te Rangi Hiroa (Peter Buck), the seafaring skills of these voyagers enabled them to navigate by currents, winds, and stars across vast ocean expanses.[a] Perhaps escaping warfare and tribute payments in Hawaiki, they probably made the five-week long voyage around 1350 AD, although there were earlier and later canoes as well.

Traditional Maori society is organized into about thirty different *iwi* ("tribe"),

grouped in thirteen *waka* ("canoe"), each with its own traditional territory. Today, prior to giving a formal talk, Maoris still introduce themselves by identifying their *iwi*, their *waka*, and the major sacred places of their ancestral territory. Their genealogy connects them to their tribe's founding ancestor who was a crew member or perhaps even a chief in one of the giant canoes mentioned in the legend of the Great Fleet.[b]

Maori oral traditions about their origins fit quite well with scientific data based on anthropological and more recent genetic research. Study by outsiders can be controversial because Maori equate an individual's genes to his or her genealogy, which belongs to one's *iwi* or ancestral community. Considered sacred and entrusted to the tribal elders, genealogy is traditionally surrounded by *tapu* ("sacred prohibitions").[c] The Maori term for genealogy is *whakapapa* ("to set layer upon layer"), which is also a word for "gene." This Maori term captures something of the original *genous*, the Greek word for "offspring." Another Maori word for gene is *ira tangata* ("life spirit of mortals"), and for them, a gene has *mauri* (a "life force"). Given these spiritual associations, genetic investigations of Maori human DNA could not proceed until the Maori themselves became actively involved in the research.

Together with other researchers, Maori geneticist Adele Whyte has examined sex-linked genetic markers, namely mitochondrial DNA in women and Y chromosomes in men.[d] She recently calculated that the number of Polynesian females required to found New Zealand's

Maori population probably ranged between 170 to 230 women. If the original fleet sailing to Aotearoa consisted of seven large canoes, it may have carried a total of about 600 people (men, women, and children).

A comparison of the DNA of Maori with that of Polynesians across the Pacific Ocean and peoples from Southeast Asia reveals a genetic map of very ancient Maori migration routes. Mitochondrial DNA, which is passed along virtually unchanged from mothers to their children, provides a genetic clock linking today's Polynesians to southern Taiwan's indigenous coastal peoples, showing that female ancestors originally set out from that island off the southeast coast of China about 6,000 years ago.[e] In the next few thousand years, they migrated by way of the Philippines and then hopped south and east from island to island.

Adding to their gene pool in the course of later generations, Melanesian males from New Guinea and elsewhere joined the migrating bands before arriving in Aotearoa. In short, Maori cultural traditions in New Zealand are generally substantiated by anthropological as well as molecular biological data.

[a]Buck, P. H. (1938). *Vikings of the Pacific.* Chicago: University Press of Chicago.

[b]Hanson, A. (1989). The making of the Maori: Culture invention and its logic. *American Anthropologist 91* (4), 890–902.

[c]Mead, A. T. P. (1996). Genealogy, sacredness, and the commodities market. *Cultural Survival Quarterly 20* (2).

[d]Whyte, A. L. H. (2005). Human evolution in Polynesia. *Human Biology 77*(2), 157–177.

[e]Gene study suggests Polynesians came from Taiwan. (2005 , July 4). Reuters.

Unlike the Han, the dominant ethnic majority in China who are patrilineal, several ethnic minorities in southwestern China are matrilineal, including the Mosuo. The women in the Mosuo family shown here are blood relatives of one another, and the men are their brothers. As among the Nayar, discussed in the previous chapter, Mosuo husbands live apart from their wives, in the households of their sisters.

In matrilineal societies females are culturally recognized as socially significant, for they are considered responsible for the group's continued existence. In patrilineal societies, this responsibility falls on the male members of the group, thereby enhancing their social importance.

The two major forms of a unilineal descent group, be it patrilineal or matrilineal, are the lineage and the clan. A **lineage** is a unilineal kinship group descended from a common ancestor or founder who lived four to six generations ago and in which relationships among members can be exactly stated in genealogical terms. A **clan** is an extended unilineal kinship group, often consisting of several lineages, whose members claim common descent from a remote ancestor, usually legendary or mythological.[1]

There is a close relationship between the descent system and a cultural system's infrastructure. Generally, patrilineal descent predominates where male labor is considered of prime importance, as among pastoralists and agriculturalists. Matrilineal descent predominates mainly among horticulturists in societies where female

work in subsistence is especially important. Numerous matrilineal societies are found in southern Asia, one of the earliest cradles of food production in the world. They are also prominent in parts of indigenous North America, South America's tropical lowlands, and parts of Africa.

Patrilineal Descent and Organization: A Chinese Example

Patrilineal descent (sometimes called *agnatic* or *male descent*) is the more widespread of the two unilineal descent systems. The male members of a patrilineal descent group trace through forefathers their descent from a common ancestor (Figure 10.1). Brothers and sisters belong to the descent group of their father's father, their father, their father's siblings, and their father's brother's children. A man's son and daughter also trace their descent back through the male line to their common ancestor. In the typical patrilineal group, authority over the children rests with the father or his elder brother. A woman belongs to the same descent group as her father and his brothers, but her children cannot trace their descent through them.

Patrilineal kinship organization is traditionally embedded in many cultures throughout the world and often endures despite radical political and economic changes. Such is also the case among the Han, the dominant ethnic majority in modern China. Until the communist takeover in 1949, most of rural Chinese society was strongly patrilineal, with a few exceptions such as the Mosuo in the southwestern part of the country. Since then, considerable changes have occurred, although vestiges of the old system persist in different regions. Traditionally, the basic unit for economic cooperation among the Han Chinese was the large extended family, typically including aged parents and their sons, their sons' wives, and their sons' children.[2]

Residence, therefore, was patrilocal, as defined in the previous chapter, so Han Chinese children grew up in a household dominated by their father and his male relatives. The father was a source of discipline from whom a child would maintain a respectful social distance. Often, the father's brother and his sons were members of the same household. Thus, one's paternal uncle was like a second father and deserving of obedience and respect, while his sons were like one's brothers. Accordingly, the Han Chinese kinship term applied to one's own father was extended to the father's brother, and the term for a brother was extended to the father's brother's sons. When families became too large and unwieldy, as frequently happened, one or more sons would move elsewhere to establish separate households. When a son did

---

[1]See Hoebel, E. A. (1949). *Man in the primitive world: An introduction to anthropology* (pp. 646, 652). New York: McGraw-Hill.

lineage A unilineal kinship group descended from a common ancestor or founder who lived four to six generations ago, and in which relationships among members can be exactly stated in genealogical terms.

clan An extended unilineal kinship group, often consisting of several lineages, whose members claim common descent from a remote ancestor, usually legendary or mythological.

---

[2]Most of the following is from Hsiaotung, F. (1939). *Peasant life in China*. London: Kegan, Paul, Trench & Truber.

so, however, the tie to the household in which he was born remained strong.

While family membership was important for each individual, the primary social unit was the lineage, or the *tsu,* as it is known among the Han in China. Each *tsu* consisted of men who traced their ancestry back through the male line to a common ancestor, usually within about five generations. Although a woman belonged to her father's *tsu,* for all practical purposes she was absorbed by the *tsu* of her husband, with whom she lived after marriage. Nonetheless, members of her natal (birth) *tsu* retained some interest in her after her departure. Her mother, for example, would assist her in the birth of her children, and her brother or some other male relative would look after her interests, perhaps even intervening if her husband or other members of his family treated her badly.

The function of the *tsu* was to help its members economically and to gather on ceremonial occasions such as weddings and funerals or to make offerings to the ancestors. Recently deceased ancestors, up to about three

generations back, were given offerings of food and paper money on the anniversaries of their births and deaths, while more distant ancestors were collectively worshiped five times a year. Each *tsu* maintained its own shrine for storage of ancestral tablets on which the names of all members were recorded. In addition to its economic and ritual functions, the *tsu* also functioned as a legal body, passing judgment on misbehaving members.

Just as families periodically split up into new ones, so would the larger descent groups periodically splinter along the lines of their main family branches. Causes included disputes among brothers over management of landholdings and suspicion of unfair division of profits. When such fissions occurred, a representative of the new *tsu* would return periodically to the ancestral temple in order to pay respect to the ancestors and record recent births and deaths in the official genealogy.

Ultimately, though the lineage tie to the old *tsu* still would be recognized, a copy of the old genealogy would be made and brought home to the younger *tsu,* and then only its births and deaths would be recorded. In this way, over many centuries, a whole hierarchy of descent groups developed, with all persons having the same surname considering themselves to be members of a great patrilineal clan. With this went surname exogamy, meaning that none of the many bearing the same clan name could marry anyone else within that large group. This marriage rule is still widely practiced today even though clan members no longer carry on ceremonial activities together.

The patrilineal system permeated all of rural Han Chinese social relations. Children owed obedience and respect to their fathers and older patrilineal relatives in life and had to marry whomever their parents chose for them. It was the duty of sons to care for their parents when they became old and helpless, and even after death

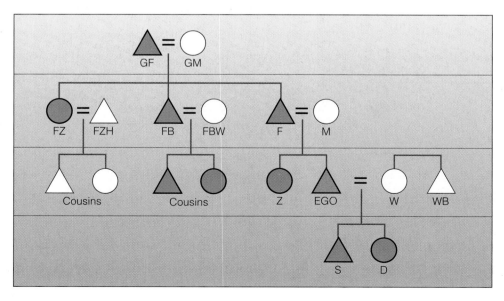

Figure 10.1

How patrilineal descent is traced. Only the individuals symbolized by a filled-in circle or triangle are in the same descent group as EGO (the central person from whom the degree of each kinship relationship is traced). The abbreviation F stands for father, B for brother, H for husband, S for son, M for mother, Z for sister, W for wife, D for daughter, and G for grand.

In traditional Han Chinese society, offerings were made to the ancestors in special ancestral halls or temples such as the one pictured here, located in a family home in Taishun, Zhejiang Province. Among the Han, the dominant ethnic majority in China, almost all ancestral temples, or clan houses, are dedicated to male forebears, reflecting the country's long-established patrilineal rules of descent and cultural values.

sons had ceremonial obligations to them. Inheritance passed from fathers to sons, with an extra share going to the eldest, since he ordinarily made the greatest contribution to the household and had the greatest responsibility toward his parents after their death. Han Chinese women, by contrast, had no claims on their families' heritable property. Once married, a woman was in effect cast off by her own patrilineal kin (even though they might continue to take an interest in her) in order to produce children for her husband's family and *tsu*.

As the preceding suggests, a patrilineal society is very much a man's world. No matter how valued women may be, they inevitably find themselves in a difficult position. Far from resigning themselves to a subordinate position, however, they actively manipulate the system to their own advantage as best they can.

Matrilineal Descent and Organization: An American Indian Example

As the term implies, matrilineal descent is traced exclusively through the female line (Figure 10.2), just as patrilineal descent is through the male line. However, the matrilineal pattern differs from the patrilineal in that it does not automatically confer gender authority.

Although descent passes through the female line and women may have considerable power, they do not hold exclusive authority in the descent group. They share it with men. Usually, these are the brothers, rather than the husbands, of the women through whom descent is traced. Apparently, the adaptive purpose of matrilineal systems is to provide continuous female solidarity within the female work group. Matrilineal systems are usually found in horticultural societies in which women perform much of the work in the house and nearby gardens. In part because women's labor as crop cultivators is regarded as so important to the society, matrilineal descent prevails.

In a matrilineal system, brothers and sisters belong to the descent group of the mother, the mother's mother, the mother's siblings, and the mother's sisters' children. Thus, every male belongs to the same descent group as his mother, and a man's own children belong to his wife's descent group, not his.

Although not true of all matrilineal systems, a common feature is the relative weakness of the social tie between wife and husband. A woman's husband lacks au-

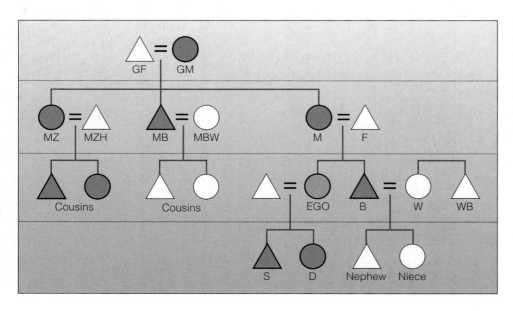

Figure 10.2

This diagram, which traces descent matrilineally, can be compared with that in Figure 10.1, showing patrilineal descent. The two patterns are virtually mirror images. Note that a man cannot transmit descent to his own children.

thority in the household they share. Her brother, and not the husband-father, distributes goods, organizes work, settles disputes, supervises rituals, and administers inheritance and succession rules. Meanwhile, her husband fulfills the same role in his own sister's household. Furthermore, his property and status are inherited by his sister's son rather than his son. Thus, brothers and sisters maintain lifelong ties with one another, whereas marital ties are easily severed. In matrilineal societies, unsatisfactory marriages are more easily ended than in patrilineal societies.

Among Hopi Indians, a farming people whose ancestors have lived in *pueblos* (villages) in northeastern Arizona for many centuries, society is divided into a number of clans based strictly on matrilineal descent.[3] (This is also true of many other Native American groups, such as the White Mountain Apache of Arizona.) At birth, every Hopi is assigned to his or her mother's clan. This affiliation is so important that, in a very real sense, a person has no social identity in the community apart from it. Two or more clans together constitute larger supraclan units, which anthropologists refer to as *phratries* (discussed later in this chapter). There are nine phratries in Hopi society, and within each phratry member clans are expected to support one another and observe strict exogamy. Because people from all nine phratries can be found living in any given Hopi village, marriage partners usually can be found in one's home community. This same dispersal of membership provides individuals with rights of entry into villages other than their own.

Although phratries and clans are the major kinship units in Hopi culture, the actual functional social units consist of lineages, and there are several in each village. Each Hopi lineage is headed by a senior woman (usually the eldest), although it is her brother or mother's brother who keeps the sacred "medicine bundle" (objects of spiritual power considered essential for peoples' well-being) and plays an active role in running lineage affairs. However, the senior woman is no mere figurehead. She may act as mediator to help resolve disputes among group members. Also, although her brother or mother's brother have the right to offer her advice and criticism, they are equally obligated to listen to what she has to say, and she does not yield her authority to them.

Most female authority, however, is exerted within the household, which is the smallest distinct unit of Hopi society, and here men clearly take second place. These households consist of the women of the lineage with their husbands and unmarried sons, all of whom used to live in sets of adjacent rooms in single large buildings.

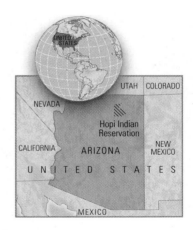

Nowadays, nuclear families often live (frequently with a maternal relative or two) in separate houses, but motorized vehicles enable related households to maintain close contact and cooperation as before.

Hopi lineages function as landholding corporations, allocating land for the support of member households. These lands are farmed by "outsiders," the husbands of the women whose lineage owns the land, and the harvest belongs to these women. Thus, Hopi men spend their lives laboring for their wives' lineages, and in return they are given food and shelter. Although sons learn from their fathers how to farm, a man has no real authority over his son. This is because a man's own children belong to his wife's lineage while his sister's children form part of his. Thus, when parents have difficulty with an unruly child, the mother's brother is called upon to mete out discipline. A man's loyalties are therefore divided between his wife's household on the one hand and his sisters' on the other. According to tradition, if a man is perceived as being an unsatisfactory husband, his wife merely has to place his personal belongings outside the door, and the marriage is over.

In addition to their economic and legal functions, lineages play a role in Hopi ceremonial activities. Although membership in the associations that actually perform ceremonies is open to all who have the proper qualifications, clans own and manage all the associations, and in each village, a leading lineage acts as its clan's representative. This lineage owns a special house where the clan's religious paraphernalia are stored and cared for by the "clan mother." Together with her brother, the clan's "big uncle," she helps manage ceremonial activity. Although men control most of the associations that do the actual performing, women still have vital roles to play. For example, they provide the cornmeal, symbolic of natural and spiritual life that is a necessary ingredient in virtually all ceremonies.

Traditionally, each Hopi village was politically autonomous, with its own chief and village council. Here again, however, descent group organization made itself

---

[3]Most of the following is from Connelly, J. C. (1979). Hopi social organization. In A. Ortiz (Ed.), *Handbook of North American Indians, Vol. 9, Southwest* (pp. 539–553). Washington, D.C.: Smithsonian Institution.

White Mountain Apaches in Arizona are organized in dozens of matrilineal clans. Closely related through the maternal line, small groups of these American Indian women lived and worked together, farming on the banks of streams in the mountains and gathering wild foods in ancestral territories. They trace their ancestry to *Is dzán naadleeshe'* (Changing Woman), a mythological founding mother. This photo shows three generations in prayer during a traditional puberty ceremony known as *na'ii'ees* ("getting her ready"), also called a Sunrise Dance. During this event, marking a girl's transition into womanhood, the sacred power of her clan's founding mother ritually passes to her.

felt, for the council was made up of men who inherited their positions through their clans. Moreover, the powers of the chief and his council were limited; the chief's major job was to maintain harmony between his village and the spiritual world, and whatever authority he and his council wielded was directed at coordination of community effort, not enforcement of official decrees. Decisions were made on a consensual basis, and women's views had to be considered, as well as those of men.

Once again, although men held positions of authority, women had considerable control over their decisions in a behind-the-scenes way. These men, after all, lived in households women controlled, and their position within them depended largely on how well they got along with the senior women. Outside the household, women's refusal to play their part in the performance of ceremonies gave them veto power. Small wonder, then, that Hopi men readily admit that "women usually get their way."[4]

Other Forms of Descent

Among Samoan Islanders (and many other cultures in the Pacific as well as in Southeast Asia) a person has the option of affiliating with either the mother's or the father's descent group. Known as *ambilineal descent,* such a kin-ordered system provides a measure of flexibility. However, this flexibility also introduces a possibility of dispute and conflict as unilineal groups compete for members.

This problem does not arise under *double descent,* or double unilineal descent, a very rare system whereby de-

scent is reckoned both patrilineally and matrilineally at the same time. Here descent is matrilineal for some purposes and patrilineal for others.

Generally, where double descent is traced, the matrilineal and patrilineal groups take action in different spheres of society. For example, among the Yakö of eastern Nigeria, property is divided into both patrilineal possessions and matrilineal possessions.[5] The patrilineage owns perpetual productive resources, such as land, whereas the matrilineage owns consumable property, such as livestock. The legally weaker matriline is somewhat more important in religious matters than the patriline. Through double descent, a Yakö might inherit grazing lands from the father's patrilineal group and certain ritual privileges from the mother's matrilineal group.

Finally, when descent derives from both the mother's and father's families equally, anthropologists use the term *bilateral descent.* In such a system people trace their descent from all ancestors, regardless of their gender or side of the family. We may recognize bilateral descent when individuals apply the same genealogical terms to identify similarly related individuals on both sides of the family—when they speak of a "grandmother" or "grandfather," for instance, no indication is given whether these relatives are on the paternal or maternal side of the family.

Bilateral descent exists in various foraging cultures and is also quite common in many contemporary state societies with agricultural, industrial, or postindustrial economies. For example, although most people in Eu-

[4]Schlegel, A. (1977). Male and female in Hopi thought and action. In A. Schlegel (Ed.), *Sexual stratification* (p. 254). New York: Columbia University Press.

[5]Forde, C. D. (1968). Double descent among the Yakö. In P. Bohannan & J. Middleton (Eds.), *Kinship and social organization* (pp. 179–191). Garden City, NY: Natural History Press.

rope, Australia, and North America typically inherit their father's family name (indicative of a culture's history in which patrilineal descent was the norm), they usually consider themselves as much a member of their mother's as their father's family.

DESCENT INTEGRATED IN THE CULTURAL SYSTEM

Regardless of how descent is traced, descent groups are usually more than mere sets of relatives providing emotional support and a sense of belonging. In nonindustrial societies they are tightly organized working units providing security and services in what can be a difficult, uncertain life. The tasks descent groups perform are manifold. Besides acting as economic units providing mutual aid to their members, they may act to support the aged and infirm and help with marriages and deaths. Often, they play a role in determining who an individual may or may not marry. The descent group also may act as a repository of religious traditions. Ancestor worship, for example, is often a powerful force acting to reinforce group solidarity.

In many societies an individual has no legal or political status except as a lineage member. Since "citizenship" is derived from lineage membership and legal status depends on it, political powers are derived from it as well. Because a lineage endures after the deaths of members with new members continually born into it, it has a con-

tinuing existence that enables it to act like a corporation, as in owning property, organizing productive activities, distributing goods and labor power, assigning status, and regulating relations with other groups. Thus it is a strong, effective base of social organization.

Beyond providing an important structure for social organization in kin-ordered societies, the descent group is also culturally represented in a society's worldview (superstructure), which provides relevant explanation and direction to its members. That is to say, there are certain important cultural ideas and values that members collectively subscribe to and reinforce by means of culturally appropriate rituals, ceremonies, and a range of social practices. As a traditional institution in a kin-ordered society, the descent group often endures in state-organized societies where political institutions are ineffective or weakly developed. Such is the case in many countries of the world today, especially in remote mountain or desert villages difficult to reach by state authorities.

Because the cultural ideas, values, and practices associated with traditional descent groups may be deeply embedded, such patterns of culture often endure in *diasporic communities* (among immigrants who have relocated from their ancestral homelands and retain their distinct cultural identities as ethnic minority groups in their new host countries). In such situations, it is not uncommon to find people seeking familiar kin-ordered cultural solutions to challenges faced in unfamiliar state-organized settings. We see an example of this in the following Original Study.

Original Study ▪ By Clementine van Eck

Honor Killings in The Netherlands

When I first told my anthropology professors I wanted to write my dissertation on honor killing among Turkish immigrants in the Netherlands, they told me no way. It was the mid-1990s, and everyone seemed to feel that writing negative things about struggling immigrants was discriminatory. Better to choose a subject that would help them deal with the challenges of settling in Dutch society, such as the problems they experienced as foreigners in school or at work. But I was quite determined to investigate this issue and finally found a professor who shared my interest—Dr. Anton Blok. He himself was specialized in Italian mafia,[a]

_____
[a]Blok, A. (1974). *The mafia of a Sicilian village 1860–1960.* New York: Harper & Row.

so quite used to violence of the cultural sort.

Before getting into some of the details of my research, I need to set the stage. Until the 1960s, the Netherlands was a relatively homogenous society (despite its colonial past). The major differences among its people were not ethnic but religious, namely their distinct ties to Catholicism or Protestantism (of various kinds). The country's population makeup began to change dramatically after the economic boom of the 1960s created a need for cheap labor and led to an influx of migrants from poor areas in Mediterranean countries seeking wage-earning opportunities.

These newcomers came not as immigrants but as "guest laborers"

(*gastarbeiders*) expected to return to their countries of origin, including Italy, Yugoslavia, Turkey, and Morocco. While many did go back home, numerous others did not. In contrast to most of the guest workers from southern European nations, those from Turkey and Morocco are mainly Muslim. And unlike southern European workers who stayed on as immigrants and successfully assimilated into Dutch society, many of the Muslim newcomers formed isolated, diasporic communities.

During the past three decades, these communities have expanded in size and are concentrated in certain areas of various cities. Today, the Turkish population in the Netherlands is about

CONTINUED

350,000. Most of them have become Dutch citizens, but they maintain some key cultural features of their historical "honor-and-shame" traditions. And this is what is at stake when we are dealing with the problem of honor killing.

Anthropologists have identified honor-and-shame traditions in many parts of the world, especially in remote traditional herding and farming societies where the power of the political state is either absent or ineffective. People in such areas, my professor, Dr. Blok, explained,

> cannot depend on stable centers of political control for the protection of life and patrimony. In the absence of effective state control, they have to rely on their own forces—on various forms of self-help. These conditions . . . put a premium on self-assertive qualities in men, involving the readiness and capacity to use physical force in order to guarantee the immunity of life and property, including women as the most precious and vulnerable part of the patrimony of men. The extremes of this sense of honour are reached when even merely glancing at a woman is felt as an affront, an incursion into a male domain, touching off a violent response.[b]

Beyond serving as a means of social control in isolated areas, honor-and-shame traditions may be used in situations where state mechanisms are alien to a certain group of people, as among some Turkish and Moroccan migrants in the Netherlands. Focusing on the latter, I tried to make sense of certain cultural practices that often baffle indigenous Dutch citizens accustomed to a highly organized bureaucratic state where our personal security and justice are effectively managed by social workers, police, courts, and so on. Most of all, I wanted to understand honor killings.

Honor killings are murders in the form of a ritual and they are carried out to purify tarnished honor—specifically honor having to do with something Turks refer to as *namus*. Both men and women pos-

sess *namus*. For women and girls *namus* means chastity, while for men it means having chaste family members. A man is therefore dependent for his *namus* on the conduct of the womenfolk in his family. This means in effect that women and girls must not have illicit contact with a member of the opposite sex and must avoid becoming the subject of gossip, since gossip alone can impugn *namus*. The victim of an honor killing can be the girl or woman who tarnished her honor, or the man who did this to her (usually her boyfriend). The girl or woman is killed by her family members, the man is killed by the family of the girl/woman whose honor he has violated.

As I was wrapping up my Ph.D. in 2000, Dutch society still didn't seem quite ready to acknowledge the phenomenon of honor killing. That year a Kurdish boy whose parents were born in Turkey tried to shoot the boyfriend of his sister. Because the attempt took place in a high school and resulted in injury to several students and a teacher, authorities focused on the issue of school safety rather than on the cultural reasons behind the murder attempt.

A shift in government and public awareness of honor killing took place in 2004. That year three Muslim Turkish women were killed by their former husbands on the street. Coming in quick succession, one after the other, these murders did not escape the attention of government officials or the media. Finally, honor killing was on the national agenda. In November of that year I was appointed as cultural anthropologist at the Dutch police force in The Hague district and began working with law enforcers on honor killing cases there (and soon in other areas of the country).

On 2 November 2004, the day I gave an opening speech about honor killings to colleagues at my new job, a radical Muslim migrant from Morocco shot the famous Dutch author and film director Theo van Gogh, well known for his critical, often mocking, views on Islam. Although his murder was not an honor killing, it had key elements of that cleansing ritual: It occurred in a public place (on the street) in front of many people, the victim had to die (injury would not suffice), the killer used many shots (or knife thrusts), the killing was planned (it was not the product of a sudden outburst), and the killer had no remorse.

Let me tell you about a recent and quite typical case. On a Friday evening the local police in an eastern Dutch community called in the help of our police team. A 17-year-old Turkish girl had run away to the family home of her Dutch boyfriend, also 17. Her father, who had discovered that this boy had a police record, telephoned his parents and asked them to send the daughter home. The parents tried to calm him down and told him his daughter was safe at their house. But as he saw it, she was in the most unsafe place in the world, for she was with the boy she loved. This could only mean that her virginity was in jeopardy and therefore the *namus* of the whole family.

My colleagues and I concluded that the girl had to be taken out of her boyfriend's home that same night: the father knew the place, he didn't want the boy as a son-in-law, and he believed his daughter not mature enough to make a decision about something as important as marriage. ("Just having a boyfriend" was not allowed. You either marry or you don't have a boyfriend, at least not an obvious one.) Because of my honor killing research, I was well aware of similar situations that ended in honor killings. To leave the girl where she was would invite disaster.

After we persuaded the prosecutor that intervention was necessary, the girl was taken from her boyfriend's house and brought to a guarded shelter to prevent her from fleeing back to him the next day. This is anthropology-in-action. You cannot always just wait and see what will happen (although I admit that as a scholar this is very tempting); you have to take responsibility and take action if you're convinced that a human life is at stake.

When I took up the study of cultural anthropology, I did so just because it intrigued me. I never imagined that what I learned might become really useful. So, what I would like to say to anthropology students is: Never give up on an interesting subject. One day it might just matter that you have become an expert in that area. At this moment I am analyzing all kinds of threatening cases and drawing up genealogies of the families involved—all in the effort to deepen our understanding of and help prevent honor killings. ∎

[b]Blok, A. (1981). Rams and billy-goats: A key to the Mediterranean code of honour. *Man, New Series 16* (3), 427–440. See also Van Eck, C. (2003). *Purified by blood: honour killings amongst Turks in the Netherlands.* Amsterdam University Press.

Clearly, descent carries codes of conduct. And, whatever form of descent predominates, the kin of both mother and father are important components of the social structure in all societies. Just because descent may be traced patrilineally, for example, does not mean that matrilineal relatives are necessarily unimportant. It simply means that, for purposes of group membership, the mother's relatives are excluded. Similarly, under matrilineal descent, the father's relatives are excluded for purposes of group membership.

By way of example, we have seen in preceding chapters how important paternal relatives are among the matrilineal Trobriand Islanders of the southern Pacific. Although children belong to their mother's descent groups, fathers play an important role in nurturing and educating them. Upon marriage, the bride's and groom's paternal relatives contribute to the exchange of gifts, and, throughout life, a man may expect his paternal kin to help him improve his economic and political position in society. Eventually, sons may expect to inherit personal property from their fathers.

In some cultures, lineages facing exceptional challenges to their survival may choose to ritually adopt individuals not related by birth. Such was the case among Iroquois Indians in Northeast America, for instance. In the 17th and 18th centuries, they often incorporated specially selected war captives and other valued strangers, including some Dutch, French, English, and other non-Indians, into their lineages in order to make up for population losses due to warfare and diseases. As soon as these newcomers were ceremonially naturalized, they acquired essentially the same birthright status as those actually born into the lineage.

Lineage Exogamy

A common characteristic of lineages is *exogamy*. As defined in the previous chapter, this means that lineage members must find their marriage partners in other lineages. One advantage of exogamy is that competition for desirable spouses within the group is curbed, promoting the group's solidarity. Lineage exogamy also means that each marriage is more than a union between two individuals; it is as well a new alliance between lineages. This helps to maintain them as components of larger social systems. Finally, lineage exogamy maintains open communication within a society, promoting the diffusion of knowledge from one lineage to another.

In contemporary North American Indian communities, kinship and descent play an essential role in tribal membership—as illustrated in this chapter's Anthropology Applied.

From Lineage to Clan

In the course of time, as generation succeeds generation and new members are born into the lineage, the kinship group's membership may become too large to be manageable or too much for the lineage's resources to support. When this happens, as we have seen with the Chinese *tsu,* **fission** occurs; that is, the original lineage splits into new, smaller lineages. Usually the members of the new lineages continue to recognize their original relationship to one another. The result of this process is the appearance of a larger kind of descent group: the clan.

As already noted, a clan—typically consisting of several lineages—is an extended unilineal descent group whose members claim common descent from a distant ancestor (usually legendary or mythological) but are unable to trace the precise genealogical links back to that ancestor. This stems from the great genealogical depth of the clan, whose founding ancestor lived so far in the past that the links must be assumed rather than known in detail. A clan differs from a lineage in another respect: It lacks the residential unity generally—although not invariably—characteristic of a lineage's core members. As with the lineage, descent may be patrilineal, matrilineal, or ambilineal.

Because clan membership is dispersed rather than localized, it usually does not involve a shared holding of tangible property. Instead, it involves shared participation in ceremonial and political matters. Only on special occasions will the membership gather together for specific purposes. Clans, however, may handle important integrative functions. Like lineages, they may regulate marriage through exogamy. Because of their dispersed membership, they give individuals the right of entry into local groups other than their own. Members usually are expected to give protection and hospitality to others in the clan. Hence, these can be expected in any local group that includes people who belong to a single clan.

Clans, lacking the residential unity of lineages, frequently depend on symbols—of animals, plants, natural forces, colors, and special objects—to provide members with solidarity and a ready means of identification. These symbols, called *totems,* often are associated with the clan's mythical origin and reinforce for clan members an awareness of their common descent.

The word *totem* comes from the Ojibwa American Indian word *ototeman,* meaning "he is a relative of mine." **Totemism** was defined by the British anthropologist A. R. Radcliffe-Brown as a set of customary beliefs

fission The splitting of a descent group into two or more new descent groups.

totemism The belief that people are related to particular animals, plants, or natural objects by virtue of descent from common ancestral spirits.

Anthropology Applied

Resolving a Native American Tribal Membership Dispute ■ By Harald E. L. Prins

In autumn 1998, I received a call from the tribal chief of the Aroostook band of Micmacs in Northern Maine asking for help in resolving a bitter tribal membership dispute. The conflict centered on the fact that several hundred individuals had become tribal members without proper certification of their Micmac kinship status. Traditionalists in the community argued that their tribe's organization was being taken over by "non-Indians." With the formal status of so many members in question, the tribal administration could not properly determine who was entitled to benefit from the available health, housing, and education programs. After some hostile confrontations between the factions, tribal elders requested a formal inquiry into the membership controversy, and I was called in as a neutral party with a long history of working with the band.

My involvement as an advocacy anthropologist began in 1981, when these Micmacs (also spelled Mi'kmaq) first employed me (with Bunny McBride) as Co-Director of Research and Development. At the time, they formed a poor and landless community not yet officially recognized as a tribe. During that decade, we helped the band define its political strategies, which focused on petitioning for federal recognition of their Indian status, claiming traditional rights to hunt, trap, and fish, and even demanding return of lost ancestral lands.

To generate popular support for the effort, I co-produced a film about the community (*Our Lives in Our Hands*, 1986). Most important, we gathered oral histories and detailed archival documentation to address kinship issues and other government criteria for tribal recognition. The latter included important

genealogical records showing that most Micmac adults in the region were at least "half-blood" (having two of their grandparents officially recorded as Indians).

Based on this evidence, we effectively argued that Aroostook Micmacs could claim aboriginal title to lands in the region and convinced politicians in Washington, D.C., to introduce a special bill to acknowledge their tribal status and settle their land claims. When formal hearings were held in 1990, I testified in the U.S. Senate as expert witness for the Micmacs. The following year, the Aroostook band of Micmacs Settlement Act became federal law. This made the band eligible for the financial assistance (health, housing, education and child welfare) and economic development loans available to all federally recognized tribes in the United States. Moreover, it provided the band with funding to buy a 5,000-acre territorial base in Maine.

Flush with federal funding and rapidly expanding its activities, the 500-member band became overwhelmed by complex

© Donald Sanipass

The Sanipass-Lafford family cluster in Chapman, Maine, represents a traditional Micmac residential kin group. Such extended families typically include grandchildren and bilaterally related family members such as in-laws, uncles, and aunts. Taken from the Sanipass family album, this picture shows a handful of members in the mid-1980s: Marline Sanipass Morey with two of her nephews and uncles.

bureaucratic regulations now governing their existence. Without formally established ground rules determining who could apply for tribal membership, and overlooking federally imposed regulations, hundreds of new names were rather casually added to its tribal rolls.

By 1997, the Aroostook band population had ballooned to almost 1,200 members, and Micmac traditionalists were questioning the legitimacy of many whose names had been added to the band roll. With mounting tension threatening to destroy the band, the tribal chief invited me to evaluate critically the membership claims of more than half the tribe. In early 1999, I reviewed kinship records submitted by hundreds of individuals whose membership on the tribal rolls was in question. Several months later, I offered my final report to the Micmac community.

After traditional prayers, sweetgrass burning, drumming, and a traditional meal of salmon and moose, I formally presented my findings: Based on the official criteria, about 100 lineal descendants of the original members and just over 150 newcomers met the minimum required qualifications for membership; several hundred would have to be stripped from the tribal rolls. After singing, drumming, and closing prayers, the Micmac gathering dispersed.

Today, the band numbers about 850 members and is doing well. It has purchased several tracts of land (collectively over 600 acres), including a small residential reservation near Presque Isle, now home to about 200 Micmacs. Also located here are new tribal administration offices, a health clinic, and a cultural center.

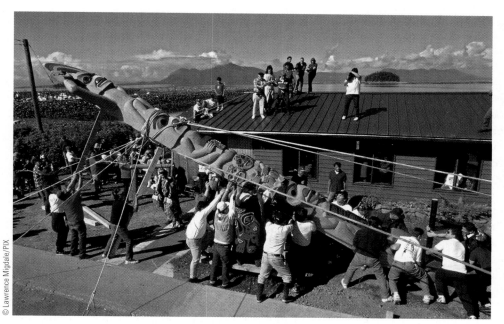

Tsimshian people of Metlakatla, Alaska, raise a memorial totem pole gifted to the community by noted carver David Boxley, a member of the Eagle clan. The tradition of erecting totem poles to commemorate special events endures in several Native American communities in the Pacific Northwest. Carved from tall cedar trees, these spectacular monuments display a clan or lineage's ceremonial property and are prominently positioned as frontal house posts, as markers at grave sites, or at some other place of significance. Often depicting legendary ancestors and mythological animals, the painted carvings symbolically represent a descent group's cultural status and associated privileges in the community.

© Lawrence Migdale/PIX

and practices "by which there is set up a special system of relations between the society and the plants, animals, and other natural objects that are important in the social life."[6] For example, Hopi Indian matrilineal clans in Arizona bear such totemic names as Bear, Bluebird, Butterfly, Lizard, Spider, and Snake.

Totemism varies among cultures. A reductive variation of totemism may be found in contemporary industrial and postindustrial societies, where sports teams are often given the names of such powerful wild animals as bears, lions, and wildcats. In the United States, this extends to the Democratic Party's donkey and the Republican Party's elephant, to the Elks, the Lions, and other fraternal and social organizations. These animal emblems, or mascots, however, do not involve the notion of biological descent and the strong sense of kinship that they have for clans, nor are they linked with the various ritual observances associated with clan totems.

In addition to the above-mentioned matrilineal clans (or matriclans), there are also patrilineal clans (or patriclans) tracing descent exclusively through men from a founding ancestor. Historically, a few dozen of such clans existed in the Scottish highlands, often identified with the prefix "Mac" or "Mc" (from an old Celtic word meaning "son of"). During the past few hundred years, large Scottish clans such as McGregor and Mackenzie broke apart as many members moved away in search of economic opportunity. Today, their descendants are dispersed all across the globe, especially in countries such as Australia, Canada, England, New Zealand, and the United States. During the past few decades, widely scattered descendants have sought to re-establish their kinship ties to ancestral clans, and many travel from afar to attend the annual gathering of their clan, preferably in their traditional ancient homeland in the highlands of Scotland. These clan members express their kinship with one another by wearing woolen shawls, kilts, or other pieces of clothing made of their clan tartan—a distinct plaid pattern and color identifying their particular clan membership.

© Wally Turnbull

In the highlands of Scotland, as among many traditional peoples around the world, large kinship groups known as clans have been important units of social organization. Now dispersed all over the world, clan members gather and express their sense of kinship with one another by wearing a tartan skirt, or kilt, with a distinct plaid pattern and color identifying clan membership. Shown here is a Turnbull clan gathering in Stone Mountain, Georgia.

[6]Radcliffe-Brown, A. R. (1931) Social organization of Australian tribes. *Oceana Monographs 1*, 29.

Phratries and Moieties

Larger kinds of descent groups are phratries and moieties (Figure 10.3). A **phratry** (after the Greek word for "brotherhood") is a unilineal descent group composed of at least two clans that supposedly share a common ancestry, whether or not they really do. Like individuals in the clan, phratry members cannot trace precisely their descent links to a common ancestor, although they firmly believe such an ancestor existed.

If the entire society is divided into only two major descent groups, whether they are equivalent to clans or phratries, each group is called a **moiety** (after the French word *moitié,* for "half"). Members of the moiety believe themselves to share a common ancestor but cannot prove it through definite genealogical links. As a rule, the feelings of kinship among members of lineages and clans are stronger than those of members of phratries and moieties. This may be due to the much larger size and more diffuse nature of the latter groups.

Since feelings of kinship are often weaker between people from different clans, the moiety system is a cultural invention that keeps clan-based communities together by binding the clans into a social network of obligatory giving and receiving. That is to say, by institutionalizing reciprocity between groups of clans, the moiety system binds together families who otherwise would not be sufficiently invested in maintaining the commonwealth.

Like lineages and clans, phratries and moieties are often exogamous and so are bound together by marriages between their members. And like clans, they provide members rights of access to other communities as among the Hopi. In a community that does not include one's clan members, one's phratry members are still there to turn to for hospitality. Finally, moieties may perform reciprocal services for one another. Among them, individuals turn to members of the opposite "half" in their community for the necessary mourning rituals when a member of their own moiety dies. Such interdependence between moieties, again, serves to maintain the cohesion of the entire society.

The kin-ordered social structure of the Winnebago Indian nation (since 1993, known as the Ho-Chunk Nation—"People of the Sacred Language") offers an interesting ethnographic example of the moiety system. Organized in twelve patrilineal clans, these North American

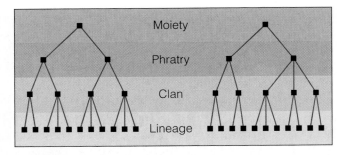

Figure 10.3
This diagram shows how lineages, clans, phratries, and moieties form an organizational hierarchy. Each moiety is subdivided into phratries, each phratry is subdivided into clans, and each clan is subdivided into lineages.

Indians, traditionally ranging the woodlands and prairies of southern Wisconsin, were divided between "those who are above" (Sky) and "those who are below" (Earth). The Sky moiety included the Eagle, Hawk, Pigeon, and Thunder clans, whereas those belonging to the Earth "half" consisted of the Bear, Buffalo, Deer, Elk, Fish, Snake, Water Spirit, and Wolf clans. These exogamous moieties not only regulated marriage and leadership positions among the Ho-Chunk, but even structured their traditional settlement patterns, with Sky clans inhabiting the southwest half of each village and those of the Earth moiety the northeast.[7] For archaeologists excavating ancient Ho-Chunk village sites, of course, the physical reflection in a traditional village layout of such clearly demarcated kinship patterns has considerable interpretive potential.

The principle of institutionalized reciprocity between groups of matrilineal clans organized into two equal halves, or moieties, is beautifully illustrated in the circular settlement pattern of many traditional Indian villages in the tropical forest of South America's Amazon region. Dwellings located in one-half of the village are those of clans belonging to one exogamous moiety, and those on the opposite side are the dwellings of clans belonging to the other. Since their clans are often matrilineal, the institutionalized rules of reciprocity in this kin-ordered community traditionally require that a woman marry a man from a clan house on the opposite side of the village, who then moves into her ancestral clan house. Their son, however, will one day have to find a wife from his father's original moiety and will have to move to his father's mother's side of the village. That is to say, the moiety system of institutionalized reciprocity functions like a social "zipper" between otherwise unconnected clans.

---

phratry A unilineal descent group composed of at least two clans that supposedly share a common ancestry, whether or not they really do.
moiety Each group that results from a division of a society into two halves on the basis of descent.

---

[7] Radin, P. (1923). The Winnebago tribe. In *37th annual report of the Bureau of American Ethnology, 1915–1916* (pp. 33–550). Washington, D.C.: Government Printing Office.

Many Amazonian Indians in South America's tropical woodlands traditionally live in circular villages socially divided into moieties. Here we see the Canela Indians' Escalvado village as it was in 1970. (Behind it is a smaller abandoned village where part of the tribe lived before uniting under one chief.) The village is 300 meters (nearly 1,000 feet) in diameter with a central plaza about 50 meters (165 feet) wide. The community's "upper" moiety meets in the eastern part (right) of the village, and the "lower" moiety meets in the western part. Nearly all 1,800 members of the Canela tribe reside in the village during festival seasons, but otherwise they are largely dispersed to their smaller, farm-centered circular villages. Missionaries built the landing strip. (P.c., William H. Crocker, Smithsonian Institution.)

© Ray Roberts Brown/Smithsonian Institution

BILATERAL KINSHIP AND THE KINDRED

Important though descent groups are in many societies, they are not found in all societies, nor are they the only kinds of extended kinship groups to be found. *Bilateral kinship,* a characteristic of most contemporary European and American societies as well as a number of food-foraging cultures, affiliates a person with genetically close relatives (but not in-laws) through both sexes. In other words, the individual traces descent through both parents, all four grandparents, and so forth, recognizing multiple ancestors. Theoretically, one is associated equally with all "blood" relatives on both the mother's and father's sides of the family. Thus, this principle relates an individual lineally to all eight great-grandparents and laterally to all third and fourth cousins.

Since such a huge group is too big to be socially practical, it is usually reduced to a smaller circle of paternal and maternal relatives, called the kindred. The **kindred** may be defined as an individual's close blood relatives on the maternal and paternal side of his or her family. Since the kindred is laterally rather than lineally organized—that is, **EGO,** or the central person from whom the degree of each relationship is traced, is the center of the group—it is not a true descent group (Figure 10.4).

Most North Americans are familiar with the kindred; those who belong are simply referred to as relatives. It includes those blood relatives on both sides of the family who are seen on important occasions, such as family weddings, reunions, and funerals. They can iden-

tify the members of their kindred up to grandparents and first, if not always second, cousins.

The limits of the kindred, however, are variable and indefinite. No one ever can be absolutely certain which relatives to invite to every important function and which to exclude. Inevitably, situations arise that require some debate about whether or not to invite particular, usually distant, relatives. Kindreds are thus not clearly bounded and lack the distinctiveness of the lineage. (They are also temporary, lasting only as long as the functions for which they are assembled.)

Unlike a descent group, the kindred is not self-perpetuating—it ceases with EGO's death. It has no constant leader, nor can it easily hold, administer, or pass on property. Because of its vagueness, temporary nature, and changing affiliation, the kindred cannot function as a group except in relation to EGO. In most cases, it cannot organize work, nor can it easily administer justice or assign status.

It can, however, be turned to for aid. In non-Western societies, for example, raiding or trading parties may be composed of kindreds. The group comes together to perform some particular function, shares the results, and then disbands. It also can act as a ceremonial group for rites of passage: initiation ceremonies and the like. In traditional European societies, kindreds acted

kindred An individual's close blood relatives on the maternal and paternal sides of his or her family.
EGO The central person from whom the degree of each relationship is traced.

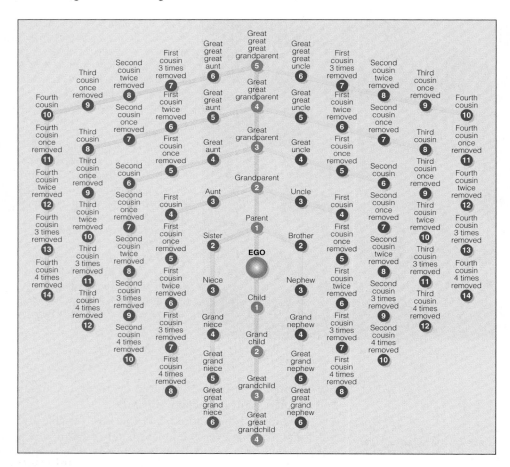

Figure 10.4
The kindred is traditionally of importance in many European cultures. It designates a person's exact degree of being related by blood to other relatives in the family. This degree of blood relatedness determines not only one's social obligations toward relatives but also one's rights. For instance, when a wealthy widowed great-aunt has died without children and without a will, specific surviving members of her kindred will be legally entitled to inherit from her.

to raise bail, compensate a victim's family, or take revenge for the murder or injury of someone in one's own kindred. Finally, kindreds also can regulate marriage through exogamy.

Kindreds are frequently found in industrial and postindustrial state societies where capitalist wage labor conditions bring on mobility and promote individualism, thereby weakening the importance of a strong kinship organization.

CULTURAL EVOLUTION OF THE DESCENT GROUP

Just as different types of families occur in different societies, so do different kinds of non-family kin groups. Descent groups, for example, are not a common feature of food-foraging societies, which are usually small. In many crop-cultivating or herding societies, however, the descent group usually provides the basic structural framework of the social system.

It is generally agreed that lineages arise from extended family organization, so long as organizational challenges exist that such structures help solve. All that is required, really, is that as members of existing ex-

tended families find it necessary to split off and establish new households elsewhere, they not move too far away; that the core members of such related families explicitly acknowledge their descent from a common ancestor; and that they continue to participate in common activities in an organized way. As this process proceeds, lineages will develop, and these may with time give rise to clans and ultimately moieties.

Another way that clans may arise is as fictive kin groups to politically integrate otherwise autonomous ethnic groups. The six Iroquois Indian nations of what now is New York State, for example, developed clans by simply behaving as if lineages of the same name in different villages were related. Thus, their members became fictitious "brothers" and "sisters." By this device, members of, say, a Bear clan in a Mohawk village could travel to a nearby Oneida village, or more distant Onondaga, Cayuga, Tuscarora, or even Seneca villages some 200 miles west of their homeland, and be welcomed in and hosted in any of these Iroquois settlements by members of local Bear clans. In this way, the six neighboring Iroquois nations achieved a wider cultural unity than had previously existed.

As larger, dispersed descent groups develop, the conditions that gave rise to extended families and lineages

Clans among the Six Nations of the Iroquois confederacy in New York State are a kinship construct that allowed people to freely travel among multiple member villages. This portrait, done in 1710, shows Sa Ga Yeath Qua Pieth Tow, a chief of the Mohawk Nation. Behind him stands a bear, which represents his clan.

KINSHIP TERMINOLOGY AND KINSHIP GROUPS

Any system of organizing people who are relatives into different kinds of groups—whether kindreds, lineages, or clans—influences how relatives are labeled in any given society. Kinship terminology systems vary considerably across cultures, reflecting the positions individuals occupy within their respective societies and helping to differentiate one relative from another. Distinguishing factors include gender, generational differences, or genealogical differences. In the various systems of kinship terminology, any one of these factors may be emphasized at the expense of others.

By looking at the terms people in a particular society use for their relatives, an anthropologist can tell how kinship groups are structured, what relationships are considered especially important, and sometimes what the prevailing attitudes are concerning various relationships. For instance, a number of languages use the same term to identify a brother and a cousin, and others have a single word for cousin, niece, and nephew. Some cultures find it useful to distinguish an oldest brother from his younger brothers and have different words for these brothers. And unlike English, many languages distinguish between an aunt who is mother's sister and one who is father's sister.

Regardless of the factors emphasized, all kinship terminologies accomplish two important tasks. First, they classify similar kinds of individuals into single specific categories; second, they separate different kinds of individuals into distinct categories. Generally, two or more kin are merged under the same term when the individuals have more or less the same rights and obligations with respect to the person referring to them as such. Such is the case among most English-speaking North Americans, for instance, when someone refers to a mother's sister and father's sister both as an "aunt." As far as the speaker is concerned, both relatives possess a similar status.

Several different systems of kinship terminology result from the application of the above principles just mentioned, including the Eskimo, Hawaiian, Iroquois, Crow, Omaha, Sudanese, Kariera, and Aranda systems, each named after the ethnographic example first or best described by anthropologists. The last five of these systems are fascinating in their complexity and are found among only a few of the world's societies. However, to illustrate some of the basic principles involved, we will focus our attention on the first three systems.

Eskimo System

The Eskimo system, comparatively rare among all the world's systems, is the one used by Euramericans, as well as by a number of food-foraging peoples (including

may change. For example, lineages may lose their economic bases if developing political institutions take control of resources. In such circumstances, lineages would be expected to disappear as important organizational units. Clans, however, might survive, if they continue to provide an important integrative function. Such is the case with the Scottish clans discussed earlier. This helps explain their continued strength and vitality even far outside Scotland today. They perform an integrative function among kin who are geographically dispersed as well as socially diverse—and they do this in a way that does not conflict with the mobility characteristic of industrial or postindustrial societies.

In societies where small domestic units—nuclear families or single-parent households—are of primary importance, bilateral kinship and kindred organization are likely to result. This can be seen in modern industrial and postindustrial societies, in newly emerging societies in the "underdeveloped" world, and in still-existing food-foraging societies throughout the world.

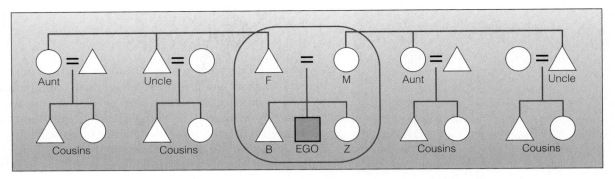

Figure 10.5
The Eskimo system of kinship terminology emphasizes the nuclear family (circled). EGO's father and mother are distinguished from EGO's aunts and uncles, and siblings from cousins.

the Inuit and other Eskimos; hence the name). Sometimes referred to as the *lineal system,* the **Eskimo system** emphasizes the nuclear family by specifically identifying mother, father, brother, and sister while lumping together all other relatives into a few large categories (Figure 10.5). For example, the father is distinguished from the father's brother (uncle); but the father's brother is not distinguished from the mother's brother (both are called "uncle"). The mother's sister and father's sister are treated similarly, both called "aunt." In addition, all the sons and daughters of aunts and uncles are called "cousin," thereby making a generational distinction but without indicating the side of the family to which they belong or even their gender.

Unlike other terminologies, the Eskimo system pro-

vides separate and distinct terms for the nuclear family members. This is probably because the Eskimo system is generally found in bilateral societies where the dominant kin group is the kindred, in which only immediate family members are important in day-to-day affairs. This is especially true of modern North American societies, where many families are independent, living apart from, and not directly involved with, other relatives except on special occasions. Thus, most North Americans (and others) generally distinguish between their closest kin (parents and siblings) but lump together (as aunts, uncles, cousins) other kin on both sides of the family.

Hawaiian System

The **Hawaiian system** of kinship terminology, common (as its name implies) in Hawaii and other islands in the southern central Pacific Ocean but found elsewhere as well, is the least complex system, in that it uses the fewest terms. The Hawaiian system is also called the *generational system,* since all relatives of the same generation and sex are referred to by the same term (Figure 10.6). For example, in one's parents' generation, the

Eskimo system Kinship reckoning in which the nuclear family is emphasized by specifically identifying the mother, father, brother, and sister, while lumping together all other relatives into broad categories such as uncle, aunt, and cousin. Also referred to as lineal system.
Hawaiian system Kinship reckoning in which all relatives of the same sex and generation are referred to by the same term.

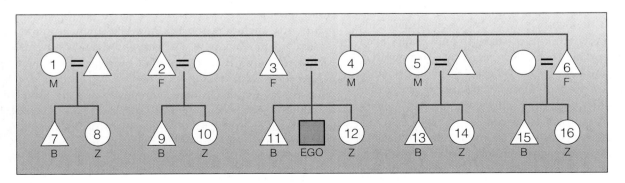

Figure 10.6
In the Hawaiian kinship system the men numbered 2 and 6 are called by the same term as father (3) by EGO; the women numbered 1 and 5 are called by the same term as mother (4). All cousins of EGO's own generation (7–16) are considered brothers (B) and sisters (Z).

Polynesian societies throughout the Pacific Ocean are traditionally structured conforming to the Hawaiian system of kinship terminology. With so many relatives identified as their fathers and mothers, children growing up in hamlets on islands such as Hawaii, as well as Tahiti, Samoa, Tonga, or Fiji are welcome in many homes where they share in meals and find a place to sleep like other brothers and sisters.

term used to refer to one's father is used as well for the father's brother and mother's brother. Similarly, one's mother, mother's sister, and father's sister are all lumped together under a single term. In EGO's generation, male and female cousins are distinguished by gender and are equated with brothers and sisters.

The Hawaiian system reflects the absence of strong unilineal descent, and members on both the father's and the mother's side are viewed as more or less equal. Thus, someone's father's and mother's siblings are all recognized as being similar relations and are merged under a single term appropriate for their gender. In like manner, the children of the mother's and father's siblings are related to EGO in the same way brother and sister are. Falling under the incest taboo, they are ruled out as potential marriage partners.

Iroquois System

In the **Iroquois system** of kinship terminology, the father and father's brother are referred to by a single term, as are the mother and mother's sister; however, the father's sister and mother's brother are given separate terms (Figure 10.7). In one's own generation, brothers, sisters, and parallel cousins (offspring of parental siblings of the same sex, that is, the children of the mother's sis-

Iroquois system Kinship reckoning in which a father and father's brother are referred to by a single term, as are a mother and mother's sister, but a father's sister and mother's brother are given separate terms. Parallel cousins are classified with brothers and sisters, while cross cousins are classified separately but not equated with relatives of some other generation.

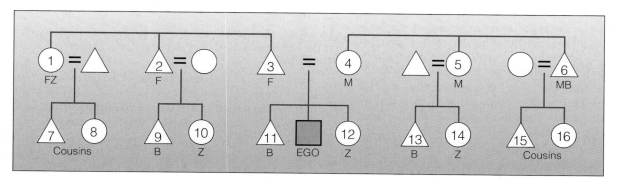

Figure 10.7

According to the Iroquois system of kinship terminology, EGO's father's brother (2) is called by the same term as the father (3); the mother's sister (5) is called by the same term as the mother (4); but the people numbered 1 and 6 are each referred to by a distinct term. Those people numbered 9 to 14 are all considered siblings, but 7, 8, 15, and 16 are considered cousins.

ter or father's brother) of the same sex are referred to by the same terms, which is logical enough considering that they are the offspring of people who are classified in the same category as EGO's actual mother and father. Cross cousins (offspring of parental siblings of opposite sex; that is, the children of the mother's brother or father's sister) are distinguished by terms that set them apart from all other kin. In fact, cross cousins are often preferred as spouses, for marriage to them reaffirms alliances between related lineages or clans.

Iroquois terminology, named for the Iroquoian Indians of northeastern North America's woodlands, is in fact very widespread and is usually found with unilineal descent groups. It was, for example, the terminology in use until recently in rural Chinese society.

Kinship Terms and New Reproductive Technologies

If systems of kinship reckoning other than one's own seem strange and complex, consider the implications of an event that took place in 1978: the production of the

new reproductive technologies (NRTs)   Alternative means of reproduction such as surrogate motherhood and in vitro fertilization.

world's first test-tube baby, outside the womb, without sexual intercourse. Since then, thousands of babies have been created in this way, and all sorts of new technologies have become part of the reproductive repertoire. **New reproductive technologies** (NRTs) are alternative means of reproduction such as surrogate motherhood and in vitro fertilization.

These technologies have opened up a large—and sometimes mind-boggling—array of reproductive possibilities. For example, if a child is conceived from a donor egg, implanted in another woman's womb to be raised by yet another woman, who is its mother? To complicate matters even further, the egg may have been fertilized by sperm from a donor not married to, or in a sexual relationship with, any of these women. Indeed, it has been suggested that we need nearly a dozen different terms to cover the concepts of mother and father in today's changing societies.[8]

Clearly, the new reproductive technologies are impacting traditional notions of kinship. Beyond transforming our sense of being human, they force us to redefine established ideas about the status of relatives—challenging us to rethink what being "related" to others is about and, specifically, what our rights and obligations are toward such unfamiliar categories of kin.

---

[8]Stone, L. (1998) *Kinship and gender* (p. 272). Boulder, CO: Westview Press.

Questions for Reflection

1. Suppose that for reasons of support and security, you were forced to create and maintain a social network of relatives beyond your immediate family or household. How would you meet that challenge?

2. People growing up in modern industrial and postindustrial societies generally treasure ideas of personal freedom, individuality, and privacy as essential in their pursuit of happiness. Considering the social functions of kinship relations in traditional non-state societies, why do you think that such ideas may be considered unsociable and even dangerously selfish?

3. Why do you think that one of the simplest kinship terminology systems imaginable, namely the Eskimo system, is functionally adequate for most Europeans, North Americans, and others living in complex modern societies?

4. One major reason anthropologists are so interested in getting a handle on a culture's kinship terminology system is that it offers them a quick but crucially important insight into a group's social structure. Why do you think this is especially true for traditional communities of foragers, herders, and farmers but is less so for urban neighborhoods in industrial and postindustrial societies?

5. In some North American Indian languages, the English word for "loneliness" is translated as "I have no relatives." What does that tell you about the importance of kinship in these Native cultures?

Suggested Readings

Carsten, J. (Ed.). (2000). *Cultures of relatedness: New approaches to the study of kinship*. Cambridge, England: Cambridge University Press.

A cross-cultural examination of what it means to be a "relative" at a time when established ideas about kinship are being transformed by radical changes in marriage arrangements and gender relations, as well as new reproductive technologies.

Finkler, K. (2000). *Experiencing the new genetics: Family and kinship on the medical frontier*. Philadelphia: University of Pennsylvania Press.

An exploration of medical and genetic aspects of kinship and debates concerning the social impact of modern medical/genetic knowledge and practices.

Fox, R. (1968). *Kinship and marriage in an anthropological perspective*. Baltimore: Penguin.

This excellent book outlines some of the methods of analysis used in the anthropological treatment of kinship and marriage. It updates Radcliffe-Brown's *African Systems of Kinship and Marriage* and features a perspective focused on kinship groups and social organization.

Parkin, R. (1997). *Kinship: An introduction to basic concepts.* Cambridge, MA: Blackwell.

A solid, useful, readable text on the basics of kinship study.

Schusky, E. L. (1983). *Manual for kinship analysis* (2nd ed.). Lanham, MD: University Press of America.

This useful book discusses the elements of kinship, diagramming, systems classification, and descent with specific examples.

Thomson Audio Study Products

 Enjoy the MP3-ready Audio Lecture Overviews for each chapter and a comprehensive audio glossary of key terms for quick study and review. Whether walking to class, doing laundry, or studying at your desk, you now have the freedom to choose when, where, and how you interact with your audio-based educational media. See the preface for information on how to access this on-the-go study and review tool.

The Anthropology Resource Center

www.thomsonedu.com/anthropology
The Anthropology Resource Center provides extended learning materials to reinforce your understanding of key concepts in the four fields of anthropology. For each of the four fields, the Resource Center includes dynamic exercises including video exercises, map exercises, simulations, and "Meet the Scientists" interviews, as well as critical thinking questions that can be assigned and e-mailed to instructors. The Resource Center also provides breaking news in anthropology and interesting material on applied anthropology to help you link what you are learning to the world around you.

11 Grouping by Gender, Age, Common Interest, and Class

© Jeffrey David Ehrenreich

CHALLENGE ISSUE

Because ties of kinship and household are not always sufficient to handle all the challenges of human survival, people also establish other kinds of social groups. Such groups can be based on gender, age, common interest, and class or social rank. The latter—tied to differences in wealth, prestige, and power—may take the social form of class, caste, or "race" groups. Some groups embody more than one of these, as illustrated by this photo of "Black Indians" marching in the famous New Orleans' Mardi Gras parade. Usually Americans of African descent and belonging to the poor working class, these "Indians" are members of neighborhood social clubs or "tribes" that are, in part, spiritual and secret. During carnival week, when the normal social order is suspended, they publicly express ethnic pride in spectacular fashion.

What Principles Do People Use to Organize Societies?

Besides kinship and marriage, people group themselves by gender, age, common interest, and class or social rank within a society to deal with problems not conveniently handled by marriage, the family and/or household, descent group, or kindred.

What Is Age Grading?

Age grading—the formation of groups on an age basis—is a widely used means of organizing people in societies, including those of Europe and North America. In addition to age grades, some societies feature age sets—formally established groups of people born during a certain time span who move through the series of age-grade categories together.

What Are Common-Interest Associations?

Common-interest associations are formed to deal with specific challenges or opportunities. Membership may be voluntary to compulsory. Common-interest associations have been a feature of human societies since the appearance of the first farming villages several thousand years ago. They have become especially prominent in contemporary postindustrial, industrial, or industrializing societies. Assisted by electronic media, associations are also increasingly transnational in our globalizing world.

What Is Social Stratification?

Stratification is the division of society into two or more social classes of people who do not share equally in basic resources, power, or prestige. Such a hierarchical social structure is characteristic of all of the world's societies having large and heterogeneous populations with centralized political control. Among others, these include ancient kingdoms and empires, but also modern republics. Social classes can be relatively open, as in North America where membership is based primarily on personal achievement or wealth. They can also be closed, as in India where membership in hierarchically ranked groups known as castes is determined by birth and remains fixed for life.

Social organization based on kinship and marriage has received considerable attention from anthropologists. There are several reasons for this: In one way or another, kinship and marriage operate as organizing principles in all societies, and in the small stateless societies so often studied by anthropologists they are usually the most important organizational principles. There is, too, a certain fascination in the almost mathematical way kinship systems at least appear to work.

To the unwary, all this attention to kinship and marriage may give the impression that these are the only principles of social organization that really matter. Yet it is obvious from analyzing modern industrial societies that other principles of social organization not only exist but also may be quite important. These include grouping by gender, age, common interest, and class or social rank—each of which we will examine in this chapter.

GROUPING BY GENDER

As shown in preceding chapters, division of labor along gender lines occurs in all human societies. In some cultures—the previously discussed Ju/'hoansi in southern Africa for example—many tasks that men and women undertake may be shared. People may perform work normally assigned to the opposite sex without loss of face. In others, however, men and women are rigidly segregated in what they do. Such is the case in many maritime cultures, where seafarers aboard fishing, whaling, and trading ships are usually men. For instance, we find temporary all-male communities aboard ships of coastal Basque fishermen in northwest Spain, Yupik Eskimo whalers in Alaska, and Swahili merchants sailing along the East African coast. These seafarers commonly leave their wives, mothers, and daughters behind in their home ports, sometimes for months at a time.

Clearly demarcated grouping by gender also occurs in many traditional horticultural societies. For instance, among the Mohawk, Oneida, Onondaga, Cayuga, Seneca, and Tuscarora Indians of New York—the famous Six Nations of the Iroquois—society was divided into two parts consisting of sedentary women on the one hand and highly mobile men on the other. Women who were blood relatives to one another lived in the same village and shared the job of growing the corn, beans, and squash that all Iroquois relied upon for subsistence. Although men built the houses and the wooden palisades that protected villages and also helped women clear fields for cultivation, they did their most important work some distance away from the villages. This consisted of hunting, fishing, trading, warring, and diplomacy. As a consequence, men were mostly transients in the villages, being present for only brief periods.

Traditionally, the Iroquois viewed women's activities as less prestigious than those of men, but they explicitly acknowledged women as the sustainers of life. Moreover, women headed the longhouses (dwellings occupied by matrilocal extended families), descent and inheritance passed through women, and ceremonial life centered on women's activities. Although men held all leadership positions outside households—sitting on the councils of the villages, tribes, and the league of Six Nations—the women of their clans were the ones who nominated them for these positions and held veto power over them. Thus, Iroquois male leadership was balanced by female authority.

Overall, the phrase "separate but equal" accurately describes relations between the sexes in Six Nations Iroquois society, with members of neither sex being dominant nor submissive to the other. Related to this seems to have been a low incidence of rape, for outside observers in the 19th century widely commented upon its apparent absence within Iroquois communities. Even in warfare, sexual violation of female captives was virtually unheard of—as noted in this back-handed compliment made by U.S. Brigadier General James Clinton in 1779: "Bad as the savages are, they never violate the chastity of any women of their prisoners."[1]

Although Iroquoian men were often absent from the village, when present they ate and slept with women. This contrasts the habits of Mundurucu Indians of Brazil's Amazon rainforest. Mundurucu men and women work, eat, and sleep separately. From age 13 onward males live together in one large house, while women, girls, and preteen boys occupy two or three houses grouped around the men's house. For all intents and purposes, men associate with men, and women with women.

Among the Mundurucu, relations between the sexes is not harmonious but rather one of opposition. According to their belief, sex roles were once reversed: Women ruled over men and controlled the sacred trumpets that are the symbols of power and represent the reproductive capacities of women. But because women could not hunt, they could not supply the meat demanded by the ancient spirits that abided in the trumpets. This enabled the men to take the trumpets from the women, establishing their dominance in the process. Ever since, the trumpets have been carefully guarded and hidden in the men's house, and traditionally women were prohibited from even seeing them.

Thus, Mundurucu men express fear and envy toward women and seek to control them by force. For their part, the women neither like nor accept a submissive status,

---

[1]Littlewood, R. (1997). Military rape. *Anthropology Today 13* (2), 14.

Gender-based groups are common among the Mundurucu as well as numerous other Amazonian Indian nations such as the Yawalapiti pictured here, who live on the Tuatuari River in Brazil's upper Xingu region. Gender issues are symbolically worked out in their mythologies and ceremonial dances. One common theme concerns ownership of the sacred trumpets, which represents spiritual power. These trumpets are zealously guarded by the tribesmen, and traditionally women were forbidden to see them.

© Reuters/Corbis

and even though men occupy all formal positions of political and religious leadership, women are autonomous in the economic realm.

Alongside notable differences, there are also interesting similarities between the Mundurucu beliefs and those of traditional European and Euramerican cultures. For example, many 19th-century European and Euramerican intellectuals held to the idea that patriarchy (rule by men) had replaced an earlier state of matriarchy (rule by women). Moreover, the idea that men may use force to control women is deeply embedded in both Judaic, Christian, and Muslim traditions (and even today, despite changing attitudes, one out of three women in the United States is sexually assaulted at some time in her life). A major difference between Mundurucu and traditional European societies is that, in the latter, women often have not had control over their own economic activities. This has changed significantly over the past few decades, but women in North America and other Western countries still have some distance to go before they achieve economic parity with men.

GROUPING BY AGE

Age grouping is so familiar and so important that it and sex have been called the only universal factors that determine a person's positions in society. In North America today, for instance, a child's first friends are usually children of his or her own age. They begin preschool or kindergarten with age mates and typically move through a dozen or more years in the educational system together. At specified ages they are allowed to see certain movies, drive a car, and do things reserved for adults, such as voting, drinking alcoholic beverages, and serving in the military. Ultimately, North Americans retire from their jobs at a specified age and, increasingly, spend the final years of their lives in retirement communities, segregated from the rest of society. As North Americans age, they are labeled "teenagers," "middle-aged," and "senior citizens," whether they like it or not and for no other reason than the number of years they have lived.

Age classification also plays a significant role in non-Western societies, which, at a minimum, make a distinction between immature, mature, and older people whose physical powers are waning. In these societies old age often has profound significance, bringing with it the period of greatest respect (for women it may mean the first social equality with men). Rarely are the elderly shunted aside or abandoned. Even the Inuit of the Canadian Arctic, who are often cited as a people who literally abandon their aged relatives, do so only in truly desperate circumstances, when the group's physical survival is at stake. In all oral tradition societies, elders are the repositories of accumulated wisdom for their people. Recognized as such and no longer expected to carry out many subsistence activities, they play a major role in passing on cultural knowledge to their grandchildren.

In North America, however, elder status is becoming problematic because senior citizens 65 years and older now constitute 12 percent of the overall population, and experts predict their numbers will swell to about 70 million (20 percent of the overall population) by 2030.[2] With more and more people living longer, achieving old age seems less of an accomplishment than it once did and so commands less respect. An increasingly common view of the elderly is that they are unproductive and, even worse, a serious economic burden. The ultimate irony is that in the United States all of the ingenuity of modern science is used to keep alive the bodies of individuals who, in virtually every other way, society pushes aside.

All human societies recognize a number of life stages. The demarcation and duration of these stages vary across cultures. Each successive life stage provides distinctive social roles and comes with certain cultural features such as specific patterns of activity, attitudes, prohibitions, and obligations. In many cultures, the social position of an individual in a specific life stage is also marked by a distinctive outward appearance in terms of dress, hairstyle, body paint, tattoos, insignia, or some other symbolic distinction. Typically, these stages are designed to help the transition from one age to another, to teach needed skills, or to lend economic assistance. Often they are taken as the basis for the formation of organized groups.

THOMSON AUDIO STUDY PRODUCTS Take advantage of the MP3-ready Audio Lecture Overviews and comprehensive audio glossary of key terms for each chapter. See the preface for information on how to access this on-the-go study and review tool.

Institutions of Age Grouping

An organized category of people with membership on the basis of age is known as an **age grade.** Theoretically speaking, membership in an age grade ought to be automatic: One reaches the appropriate age and so is included, without question, in the particular age grade. Just such situations exist, for example, among the East African Tiriki, whose system we will examine shortly. Sometimes, though, individuals must buy their way into the age grade for which they are eligible. This was the case among some of the Indians of North America's plains, who required boys to purchase the appropriate

---

[2]U.S. Census Bureau News. (2004, March 18).

age grade An organized category of people based on age; every individual passes through a series of such categories over his or her lifetime.
age set A formally established group of people born during a certain time span who move through the series of age-grade categories together.

costumes, dances, and songs for age-grade membership. In societies where entrance fees are expensive, not all people eligible for membership in a particular age grade may actually be able to join.

Entry into and transfer out of age grades may be accomplished individually, either by a biological distinction, such as puberty, or by a socially recognized status, such as marriage or childbirth. Whereas age-grade members may have much in common, may engage in similar activities, may cooperate with one another, and may share the same orientation and aspirations, their membership may not be entirely parallel with physiological age. A specific time is often ritually established for moving from a younger to an older grade. An example of this is the traditional Jewish ceremony of the bar mitzvah (a Hebrew term meaning "son of the commandment"), marking that a 13-year-old boy has reached the age of religious duty and responsibility. (*Bat mitzvah,* meaning "daughter of the commandment," is the term for the equivalent ritual for a girl.)

Although members of senior groups commonly expect deference from and acknowledge certain responsibilities to their juniors, this does not necessarily mean that one grade is seen as better, or worse, or even more important than another. There can be standardized competition (opposition) between age grades, such as that traditionally between first-year students and sophomores on U.S. college campuses.

In addition to age grades, some societies feature age sets (sometimes referred to as *age classes*). An **age set** is a formally established group of people born during a certain time span who move through the series of age-grade categories together. Age sets, unlike age grades, end after a specified number of years; age set members usually remain closely associated throughout their lives. This is akin to but distinct from the broad and informal North American practice of identifying generation clusters comprised of all individuals born within a particular time frame—such as baby boomers (1946–1964), Gen-Xers (1961–1981), and the Internet generation (1986–1999) (year spans approximate).

The age-set notion implies strong feelings of loyalty and mutual support. Because such groups may possess property, songs, shield designs, and rituals and are internally organized for collective decision making and leadership, age sets are distinct from simple age grades. One also may distinguish between transitory age grades—and the comprehensive systems that affect people through the whole of their lives.

Age Grouping in African Societies

Although age is a criterion for group membership in many parts of the world, its most varied and elaborate use is found in Africa, south of the Sahara. An example may be seen among the Tiriki, one of several pastoral

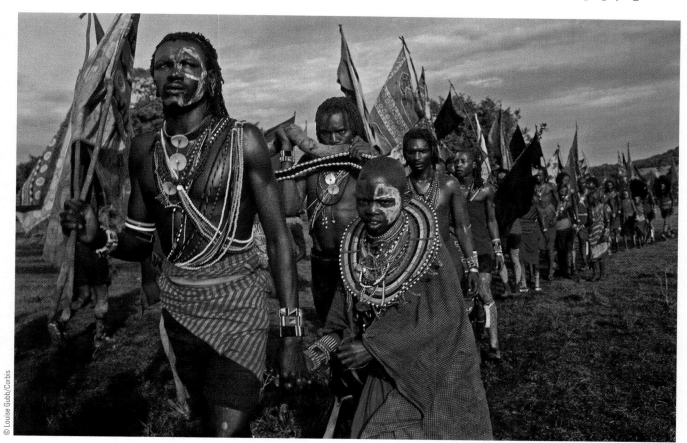

Maasai subclans of western Kenya at the opening parade of the elaborate *eunoto* ceremony, marking the coming of age of *morans* (warriors). At the end of the ceremony, these men will be in the next age grade—junior adults—ready to marry and start families. Members of the same age set, they were initiated together into the warrior age grade as teenagers. They spent their warrior years raiding cattle (an old tradition that is now illegal, but nonetheless still practiced) and protecting their community homes and animal enclosures (from wild animals and other cattle raiders). The *eunoto* ceremony includes the ritual shaving of a warrior's hair by his mother, symbolizing the end of many freedoms and the passage to manhood.

nomadic groups living in Kenya.[3] In this culture of herders, each boy born within a 15-year period becomes a member of a particular age set then open for membership. Seven such named age sets exist, only one of which is open for membership at a time; when membership in one is closed, the next one is open for a 15-year period, and so on until the passage of 105 years (7 times 15), when the first set's membership is gone due to death, and it opens once again to take in new "recruits."

Members of Tiriki age sets remain together for life as they move through four successive age grades: Advancement in age grades occurs at fifteen-year intervals, coinciding with the closing of the oldest age set and the opening of a new one. Each age group has its own particular duties and responsibilities. Traditionally, the first, or Warrior age grade, served as guardians of the country, and members gained renown through fighting. Under British colonial rule, however, this traditional function fell by the wayside with the cessation of warfare, and members of this age grade now find excitement and adventure by leaving their community for extended employment or study elsewhere.

The next age grade, the Elder Warriors, had few specialized tasks in earlier days beyond learning skills they would need later on by assuming an increasing share of administrative activities. For example, they would chair the postfuneral gatherings held to settle property claims after someone's death. Traditionally, Elder Warriors also served as envoys between elders of different communities. Nowadays, they hold nearly all of the administrative and executive roles opened up by the creation and growth of a centralized Tiriki administrative bureaucracy.

Judicial Elders, the third age grade, traditionally handled most tasks connected with the administration and settlement of local disputes. Today, they still serve as the local judiciary body. Members of the "Ritual Elders,

[3]Sangree, W. H. (1965). The Bantu Tiriki of western Kenya. In J. L. Gibbs, Jr. (Ed.), *Peoples of Africa* (pp. 69–72). New York: Holt, Rinehart & Winston.

VISUAL COUNTERPOINT

The range of common-interest associations is astounding, as suggested by these photos of Shriners and Crips. The Shriners are a secret fraternal order of middle-class males in the United States committed to "fun, fellowship, and service" and named after the "Ancient Arabic Order of Nobles of the Mystic Shrine." The Crips are a violent urban gang, originating in poor Los Angeles neighborhoods, whose trademark is a blue bandana—in contrast to the red bandana of their rival gang, the Bloods. The notoriety of the Crips spread as a result of sensational stories in the media, spawning a network of independent satellite Crip gangs in other U.S. cities as well as in Europe and Central America.

the senior age grade, used to preside over the priestly functions of ancestral shrine observances on the household level, at subclan meetings, at semiannual community appeals, and at rites of initiation into the various age grades. They also were credited with access to special magical powers. With the decline of ancestor worship

common-interest associations Associations that result from an act of joining based on sharing particular activities, objectives, values, or beliefs.

over the past several decades, many of these traditional functions have been lost, and no new ones have arisen to take their places. Nonetheless, Ritual Elders continue to hold the most important positions in the initiation ceremonies, and their power as sorcerers and expungers of witchcraft are still recognized.

GROUPING BY COMMON INTEREST

The rise of urban, industrialized societies in which individuals are often separated from their kin has led to a proliferation of **common-interest associations**—associations that result from an act of joining and are based on sharing particular activities, objectives, values, or beliefs. As U.S. anthropologist Meredith Small observes,

> We often imprint lines of kinship on friends and colleagues, transferring familial expectations onto those with whom we share time but not blood or genes or vows, so that we can have the experience of an extended family. Young people join gangs, older people join clubs, and even babies are put into play groups. Pushed by a culture that favors independence and self-reliance, the social animal in us nonetheless seeks connections, even if they are bloodless and fragile.[4]

[4]Small, M. F. (2000). Kinship envy. *Natural History 109* (2), 88.

Moreover, common-interest associations help people meet a range of needs from companionship to safe work conditions to learning a new language and customs upon moving from one country to another.

Because common-interest associations are by nature flexible, they have often been turned to, both in cities and in traditional villages, as a way of meeting these needs. Common-interest associations are not, however, restricted to modernizing societies alone. They also are found in many traditional societies, and there is reason to believe they arose with the emergence of the first horticultural villages. Furthermore, associations in traditional societies may be just as complex and highly organized as those of countries such as the United States and Canada.

Common-interest associations have often been referred to in the anthropological literature as *voluntary associations,* but this term is misleading. The act of joining may range from fully voluntary to one required by law. For example, in the United States, under previous draft laws, individuals often became members of the armed forces without choosing to join. It is not really compulsory to join a labor union, but unless one does, one cannot work in a union shop. What the term *voluntary association* really refers to are those associations not based on sex, age, kinship, marriage, or territory that result from an act of joining. The act often may be voluntary, but it does not have to be.

Kinds of Common-Interest Associations

The variety of common-interest associations is astonishing. In the United States, they include such diverse entities as street gangs, private militias, sport and service clubs, churches and other religious organizations, political parties, labor unions, environmental organizations, women's and men's clubs of all sorts—the list could go on and on. Their goals may include the pursuit of friendship, recreation, and the promotion of certain values, as well as governing, seeking peace on a local or global scale, and the pursuit or defense of economic interests.

Associations also have served to preserve traditional songs, history, language, moral beliefs, and other customs among members of various ethnic minorities. A unique example can be found in the following Original Study, which illustrates how one ethnic minority group establishes a sense of traditional community within modern cities by means of symbolic geographic boundary markers.

Original Study ▪ By Susan Lees

The Jewish *Eruv:* Symbolic Place in Public Space

Cultural anthropologists are interested in how a geographic *space* becomes a culturally meaningful *place*—an area that we may think of as "our territory" or that we designate for one particular purpose or another, such as pasturing animals, playing football, gardening, or worshiping. As in a tennis court or baseball diamond, there are certain boundaries to such places. We may mark them off with symbols not readily comprehensible to outsiders, who may not understand why a ball has been hit "out of bounds" or is a "foul ball" until we explain the rules and the symbols.

At times, two different cultural groups may occupy the same geographic space, but each will see and divide it differently in terms that are meaningful only within their group. We see this on maps where the borders of many modern nation-states often cut through the traditional tribal or ethnic group territories. And we see it in various urban communities that may divide up their spaces in ways perceptible only to themselves.

An intriguing example can be found among Orthodox Jews who practice an ancient tradition by ritually defining the boundaries of their communities for the purpose of Sabbath observance: On the Sabbath, the area enclosed by the boundaries becomes, by definition, a single shared symbolic domain. This symbolically enclosed space is called an *eruv*, which means "combination" or "amalgamation" of public and private space—that is, the private spaces of the household and the public areas of the sidewalks, streets, and perhaps parks are combined on the Sabbath as one big communal household.

The purpose of the *eruv* for Orthodox communities is to accommodate one of the many Sabbath prohibitions on religiously defined "work": the work of "carrying" objects from a private domain to a public one, or vice versa, or carrying objects for any distance in a public domain. On the Sabbath, if there is an *eruv*, observant Orthodox Jews are permitted to treat carrying within the entire *eruv* enclosure as if they were in their own homes. Having an *eruv* means that strictly Orthodox Jews may push a baby stroller or a wheelchair within the ritually enclosed neighborhood—activities otherwise restricted by the "carrying" prohibition. This makes it possible for whole families—including small children and disabled individuals—to attend religious services in the synagogue or to socialize with one another and still be faithful to traditional law.

In ancient times, the boundaries of the *eruv* were in fact the walls of houses and courtyards and city walls within which communities were enclosed. But today, where there are no walls, communities sometimes erect thin strings or wires, or sometimes just use wires already there on utility poles (such as

CONTINUED

CONTINUED

phone or electricity wires) to demarcate the boundaries. These are known to members of the community but usually invisible to outsiders because they are part of the urban landscape anyway.

I was first drawn to the subject of the *eruv* nearly three decades ago, when I leafed through my mother's copy of the Code of Jewish Law still found in many Jewish households. Much of this text concerns rules about observing the Sabbath (the seventh day, the Lord's day reserved for worship and obligatory rest). Many of these seemed exotic and mysterious to me and hard to reconcile with life in the modern world.

As an anthropologist, I was intrigued by explanations given for certain practices because they heightened awareness of the special character of the Sabbath itself and *also* of the uniqueness of Jewish identity in a world where temptations to assimilate with the larger, dominant culture were strong. Most of all, the *eruv* captured my interest because it seemed to create, not just prohibit something. It transformed a group of diverse urban households into one common household, not just a community but a real "private" home. The symbolic "walls" around this collective domain were erected not to keep others out but to enclose its members and thus erase the actual walls of each individual household.

The ritual that creates an *eruv* requires that one member take a loaf of bread and make other members co-owners of that loaf; the symbolism of a household is shared ownership (not consumption) of this most symbolically meaningful food. The boundaries of the *eruv* "household" they co-inhabit must be contiguous, broken only by symbolic doorways through which they can pass as if through doorways of their individual homes. As long as the contiguity is maintained, they can extend the *eruv* to incorporate hundreds or even thousands of other houses. It occurred to me then that in a highly urbanized mass society of mostly strangers, this symbolic unification of sometimes widely separated

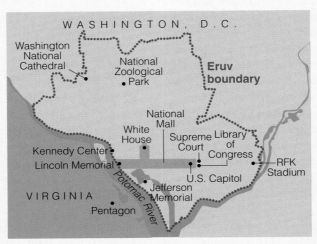

Boundaries of *eruv* in Washington, D.C.

Jewish households was an extraordinary thing.

The majority of North American Jews who are members of religious congregations belong to Reform synagogues (the other major groups are Conservative and Orthodox), and American Reform Judaism officially abandoned the *eruv* as a Sabbath practice in 1846. When I first became interested in the subject, there were rather few *eruvin* anywhere. Most Orthodox Jewish communities were still concentrated in a few large cities, particularly on the East Coast. After WWII, many Jews were able to move to the suburbs, where they integrated for the first time into the mainstream as "white folks."

But it was in the early 1970s that a shift in Jewish identity issues occurred, and some younger generation Jews began to turn purposefully to traditional practices that distinguished them from mainstream society and more assimilated Jews. Coming on the heels of the 1960s civil rights movement, this shift echoed the "Black Pride" movement of African Americans affirming their African roots. Other ethnic minorities developed their own distinct cultural expressions as the wider society seemed first to tolerate and then to respect such expressions. In this changing social climate young Orthodox Jews began to assert themselves as their forebears had not dared to. It was in this context that a proliferation of new *eruvin* occurred both in urban and suburban contexts. Meanwhile, some Jews resisted this expression of difference,

and within the wider Jewish community there was considerable strife over the question of the "authenticity" of the beliefs and practices of more assimilated Jews.

Most *eruvin* have been established without conflict, but a handful have been highly controversial, including one effort in North London, England, which faced a dozen years of legal struggles. The question of why a virtually invisible boundary that enables believers to exercise their religious obligations would be of such great significance to nonbelievers has generated considerable debate and touches on issues that are especially important in a globalized world of pluralistic societies that include many diasporic groups (people dispersed from their ancestral homeland). In these societies, diasporic cultures are created and developed through interaction with their surrounding communities, reacting in part to discrimination against them and in part to their own desire for continuity and connection with others sharing their origins and beliefs.

In my research, I was interested to find that Jews are among the principal parties on *both* sides of *eruv* conflicts. Opponents of the *eruv* appear to fear the creation, or re-creation, of ghettos of inassimilable Jews who neither conform to nor respect the ideals of the dominant or mainstream culture—who appear "foreign" in appearance and practices. Thus the *eruv* conflict appears on one level to be an argument among Jews adhering to different beliefs about how they should live in modern society with other groups and among themselves. (Interestingly, when Jewish religious leaders were first developing the laws of the *eruv* more than 2,000 years ago, this problem of how Jews could maintain a communal identity while living among others was among their primary concerns.)

Jews are not alone among diasporic groups in having this argument about assimilation and distinctiveness in the modern world, though the specifics of their conflict are their own. Like many others, they wish to live comfortably and without fear in a plural society with full rights of membership, yet also in communities of others like themselves, in which they can socialize and build institutions that tie them together.

The *eruv* is one symbolic device to reinforce community as neighborhood—to establish a meaningful *place* for a distinct group in a diverse society. Ethnic church parishes often have done the same for other urban groups. Neigh-

borhood identities like these can be the basis for disputes about exclusivity, but they can also ease the maintenance of cultural traditions and humanize life in the city.   ■

Sometimes operating secretly, common-interest associations have helped maintain traditions. So it is among North American Indians, who since the late 1960s have been experiencing a resurgence of ethnic pride after generations of forced assimilation and schooling designed to stamp out their cultural identity. A very satisfying way of publicly expressing pride in their ethnic identity and cultural heritage is by way of ceremonial gatherings known as *powwows,* which take place not only on reservations but also in cities where most American Indians now live. Usually "pan-tribal," these festive gatherings feature American Indians from dozens of different nations or "tribes" dancing together in traditional regalia as the sounds of traditional songs and drumming fill the air. Gift offerings are part of the event, along with traditional Native foods such as frybread and the selling of Native crafts.[5]

Men's and Women's Associations

In some societies women have not established formal common-interest associations to the extent men have because they live in male-dominated cultures that re-

strict them or because women are absorbed on the domestic front with the constant and often unpredictable demands of rearing children. Moreover, some functions of men's associations—such as military duties—often are culturally defined as purely for men or repugnant to women.

Still, as cross-cultural research makes clear, women often play important roles in associations of their own as well as in those in which men predominate. Among the Crow (Apsaroke) Indians, women participated in the secret Tobacco Society, in addition to their own exclusive groups. Throughout Africa women's social clubs complement the men's and are concerned with educating women and with crafts, charitable, and wealth-generating activities—and increasingly with politics. In Sierra Leone, once-simple dancing societies have developed under urban conditions into complex organizations with a set of new objectives. The resulting dancing *compin* is made up of young women as well as men who together perform plays based on traditional music and dancing and raise money for various mutual benefit causes.[6]

[5]Ellis, C. (2006). *A dancing people: Powwow culture on the southern plains.* Lawrence: University Press of Kansas

[6]See Steady, F. C. (2001). *Women and the Amistad connection, Sierra Leone Krio Society* (pp. 71–80). Rochester, VT: Schenkman Books.

Courtesy of Women's Promotion and Assistance Association of Cameroon. Photo by Mousa.

Since the United Nations Decade for Women (1976–1985), the number of women's associations all around the world has grown significantly, from the local to the global. These associations often function as support systems for women while focusing on a range of issues and activities, including economic opportunities. For example, here we see members of a women's craft association in Bakingili, Cameroon (Africa), tie-dying fabric together.

Women's rights organizations, consciousness-raising groups, and professional organizations for women are examples of some of the associations arising directly or indirectly out of an ever-expanding feminist movement. These groups cover the entire range of association formation, from simple friendship and support groups to associations centered on politics, sports, the arts, spirituality, charity, and economic endeavors—on a national and even international scale. If an unresolved point does exist in the matter of women's participation, it is in determining why women are excluded from certain associations in some societies, while in others their participation is essentially equal to that of men.

Associations in the Postindustrial World

In spite of the diversity and vitality of common-interest associations, some have noted a recent decline in participation in all sorts of these groups, at least in North America. Those who have observed this trend see it as part of a more general drop in civic participation. People are spending less time socializing with others in bars, at dinner parties, having friends over, and so on.

One can only speculate on the causes, but they likely include further isolation of individuals as they spend more and more of their free time with an ever-growing array of electronic home entertainment options. For example, in the United States, adults spend an average of 4 hours each day watching television. Then, too, the frequency with which people move interferes with their ability to establish more than superficial friendships with others. Add to this the fact that North Americans work longer hours on average than people in almost all industrialized countries, leaving less time for socialization. In this connection, some have noted a 10 percent drop in civic participation for every 10 minutes of commuting time.

Finally, there is the rise of the Internet; as people spend more and more time online, they can stay in touch without having to leave home. The cyberworld has seen an explosion of what are, in effect, virtual common-interest associations, many of which are transnational, with members in far-flung corners of the world. In short, common-interest associations may not be showing a decline so much as a transformation.

stratified societies Societies in which people are hierarchically divided and ranked into social strata, or layers, and do not share equally in basic resources that support survival, influence, and prestige.
egalitarian societies Societies in which everyone has about equal rank, access to, and power over basic resources.
social class A category of individuals in a stratified society who enjoy equal or nearly equal prestige according to the system of evaluation.

With computer technology has come the rise of online common-interest associations, involving everything from ethnicity to hobbies to special education needs. Here, Inuit students in Canada use a computer to learn the Inuktitut syllabary—a phonetic writing system consisting of symbols representing syllables.

GROUPING BY CLASS OR SOCIAL RANK IN STRATIFIED SOCIETIES

Social stratification is a common and powerful structuring force in many of the world's societies. Basically, **stratified societies** are those in which people are hierarchically divided and ranked into social strata, or layers, and do not share equally in basic resources that support survival, influence, and prestige. Members of low-ranked strata typically have fewer privileges and less power than those in higher ranked strata. In addition, the restrictions and obligations they face are usually more oppressive, and they must work harder for less reward.

In short, social stratification amounts to institutionalized inequality. Without ranking—high versus low—no stratification exists; social differences without this do not constitute stratification. In the United States, Hispanic, African American, and American Indian groups are among those who have struggled with their positions in the low-ranked strata. As profiled in this chapter's Anthropology Applied, their needs are often ignored in development efforts.

Stratified societies stand in sharp contrast to **egalitarian societies,** in which everyone has about equal rank, access to, and power over basic resources. As we saw in earlier chapters, foraging societies are characteristically egalitarian, although there are some exceptions.

Social Class and Caste

A **social class** may be defined as a category of individuals in a stratified society who enjoy equal or nearly equal prestige according to the system of evaluation. The quali-

Anthropology Applied

Anthropologists and Social Impact Assessment ■ Sue Ellen Jacobs

Anthropologists frequently do a type of policy research called a social impact assessment, which entails collecting data about a community or neighborhood for planners of development projects. Such an assessment seeks to determine a project's effect by determining how and upon whom its impact will fall and whether the impact is likely to be positive or negative.

In the United States, any project requiring a federal permit or license, or using federal funds, by law must be preceded by a social impact assessment as part of the environmental review process. Examples of such projects include highway construction, urban renewal, water diversion schemes, and land reclamation. Often, such projects are sited so that their impact falls most heavily on neighborhoods or communities inhabited by people in low socioeconomic strata—sometimes because the projects are seen as a way of improving the lives of poor people and sometimes because the poor people are seen as having less political power to block proposals that others conceive as in "the public interest."

As an illustration of this kind of work, anthropologist Sue Ellen Jacobs was hired to do a social impact assessment of a water diversion project in New Mexico planned by the Bureau of Land Recla-

mation in cooperation with the Bureau of Indian Affairs. This project proposed construction of a diversion dam and an extensive canal system for irrigation on the Rio Grande. Affected by this would be twenty-two communities inhabited primarily by Hispanic Americans, as well as two Indian pueblos. Unemployment was high in the region, and the project was seen as a way to promote a perceived trend to urbanism (which theoretically would be associated with industrial development), while bringing new land into production for intensive agriculture.

What the planners failed to take into account was that both the Hispanic and Indian populations were heavily committed to farming for household consumption (with some surpluses raised for the market), using a system of irrigation canals established as long as 300 years ago. These canals are maintained by elected supervisors familiar with the communities and knowledgeable about water laws, ditch management, and sustainable crop production. Such individuals can resolve conflicts concerning water allocation and land use—and often other issues as well. Under the proposed project, this system was to be given up in favor of one in which fewer people would control larger tracts of land, and water allocation would be in the hands of a government tech-

nocrat. One of the strongest measures of local government would be lost.

Not surprisingly, Jacobs discovered widespread community opposition to this project, and her report helped convince Congress that any positive impact was far outweighed by negative effects. One of the major objections to the construction of the project was that it would result in the obliteration of the centuries-old irrigation system structures. Project planners did not seem to recognize the antiquity and cultural significance of these traditional irrigation structures, referring to them as "temporary diversion structures." The fact that the old dams associated with the ditches were attached to local descent groups was simply not recognized by the official documents.

Beyond infringing on local control, the project threatened the community with a range of negative side effects: problems linked to population growth and relocation, a loss of fishing and other river-related resources, and new health hazards, including increased threat of drowning, insect breeding, and airborne dust.

(Adapted from J. van Willigen (1986). Applied anthropology (p. 169). South Hadley, MA: Bergin & Garvey.)

fication "nearly equal" is important, for a certain amount of inequality may occur even within a given class. Class distinctions are not always clear-cut and obvious in societies that have a wide and continuous range of differential privileges.

A **caste** is a closed social class in a stratified society in which membership is determined by birth and fixed for life. The opposite of the principle that all humans are born equal, the caste system is based on the principle that humans neither are nor can be equal. Castes are strongly endogamous, and offspring are automatically members of their parents' caste.

The classic ethnographic example is the traditional Hindu caste system of India. Perhaps the world's longest surviving social hierarchy, it encompasses a complex ranking of social groups on the basis of "ritual purity." Each of some 2,000 different castes considers itself as a distinct community higher or lower than other castes,

although their particular ranking varies among geographic regions and over time. The different castes are associated with specific occupations and customs, such as food habits and styles of dress, along with rituals involving notions of purity and pollution. Differences in status are traditionally justified by the religious doctrine of karma, a belief that one's place in life is determined by one's deeds in previous lifetimes.

All of these castes, or *jatis,* are organized into four basic orders or *varnas* (literally meaning "colors"), distinguished partly by occupation and ranked in order of descending religious status of purity. The religious foundation for this social hierarchy is found in a sacred text known as the Laws of Manu, an ancient work about

caste A closed social class in a stratified society in which membership is determined by birth and fixed for life.

cal affairs. In an effort to bestow some dignity on these poverty-stricken victims of the caste system, Hindu nationalist leader Mahatma Gandhi renamed them *harijan* or "children of God."

Although India's national constitution of 1950 sought to abolish caste discrimination and the practice of untouchability, the caste system remains deeply entrenched in Hindu culture and is still widespread throughout southern Asia, especially in rural India. In what has been called India's "hidden apartheid," entire villages in many Indian states remain completely segregated by caste. Representing about 15 percent of India's population—or some 160 million people—the widely scattered Dalits endure near complete social isolation, humiliation, and discrimination based exclusively on their birth status. Even a Dalit's shadow is believed to pollute the upper castes. They may not cross the line dividing their part of the village from that occupied by higher castes, drink water from public wells, or visit the same temples as the higher castes. Dalit children are still often made to sit at the back of classrooms.

Castelike situations are known elsewhere in the world. In Bolivia, Ecuador, and several other South and Central American countries, for example, the wealthy upper class is almost exclusively white and rarely intermarries with people of non-European descent. In contrast, the lower class of working poor in those countries is primarily made up of American Indian laborers and peasants. Segregation also existed in the United States, where the nation's upper class was made up exclusively of individuals of European descent.

After the American Revolution, several states in New England joined Virginia and other southern states and made it illegal for whites to marry blacks or Ameri-

2,000 years old and considered by traditional Hindus as the highest authority on their cultural institutions. It defines the Brahmans as the purest and therefore highest *varna*. As priests and lawgivers, Brahmans represent the world of religion and learning. Next comes the order of fighters and rulers, known as the Kshatriyas. Below them are the Vaisyas (merchants and traders), who are engaged in commercial, agricultural, and pastoral pursuits. At the bottom are the Shudras (artisans and laborers), an order required to serve the other three *varnas* and who also make a living by handicrafts.

Falling outside the *varna* system is a fifth category of degraded individuals known as "untouchables" or Dalits. Considered the most impure of all people, these outcasts can own neither land nor the tools of their trade. Untouchables constitute a large pool of cheap labor at the beck and call of those controlling economic and politi-

Dalits, known as "untouchables" in India's traditional caste system, light 100 "candles of freedom" at the 2004 World Social Forum held in Mumbai. Tens of thousands of activists from 130 countries attended the forum, debating and demonstrating against social, economic, and political inequality around the world.

© AFP/Getty Images

can Indians. After the U.S. federal government officially abolished slavery in 1863, these anti-miscegenation laws remained in force in many states from Maine to Florida for several decades.

In 1924, Virginia's General Assembly passed the Racial Integrity Act to prevent light-skinned individuals with some African ancestry from "passing" as whites. Known as the "one drop" rule, it codified the idea of white racial purity by classifying individuals as black if just one of their multiple ancestors was of African origin ("one drop of Negro blood"). However light-skinned, they were subject to a wide range of discriminatory practices not applicable to whites. Such institutionalized racial discrimination continued for a century after slavery was abolished, and today self-segregation exists in many parts of the United States.

Despite U.S. civil rights laws passed in the 1960s (prohibiting discrimination in accommodations, schools, employment, and voting for reasons of color, race, religion, or national origin), ethnic inequality persists in which the typical African American household has 54 cents of income and 12 cents of wealth for every corresponding dollar in the typical white American household[7] (Figure 11.1).[8]

Another castelike social system based on skin color and wealth officially existed in South Africa where until recently a minority of European origin imposed a political regime known as apartheid (an Afrikaans-Dutch term meaning "segregation" or "separation"). Based on a racist white superiority ideology, it relegated indigenous dark-skinned Africans to a low-ranking stratum in a racially divided society. Although the foundations for the policy of strict racial segregation were laid earlier, apartheid became national law in 1948.

During the next few decades, the European minority in control of the South African government enacted a series of racist laws and regulations creating a social order privileging themselves and discriminating against the indigenous African peoples. From then on, the government policy of segregation based on differences in skin color affected every level of social existence. In addition to prohibiting "racially mixed" marriages, apartheid laws also stipulated where "blacks" and "coloreds" were allowed to live, work, and play. Invading private lives, these laws even made "interracial" sexual relations a crime.

In the early 1960s, South Africa's apartheid regime declared that territories historically inhabited by South Africa's indigenous nations such as the Swazi, Xhosa, and Zulu were to become semi-independent countries

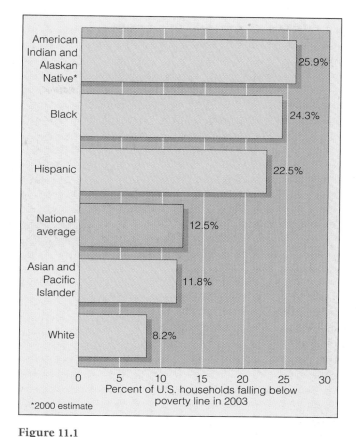

Figure 11.1

In the United States 70 percent of all wealth is in the hands of 10 percent of the population. The country's official poverty rate has increased for four consecutive years, from a 26-year low of 11.3 percent in 2000 to 12.7 percent in 2004. In real numbers 37 million people were below the official poverty thresholds in 2004—5.4 million more than in 2000. As this chart shows, poverty rates are much higher for minorities.

known as homelands. According to the apartheid regime, dark-skinned Africans were allowed to own property in these black homelands but could not own land in vast areas exclusively reserved for white settlement.

Internationally isolated and facing growing problems within the country, the South African government finally agreed to abolish the apartheid system in 1993. A year later, following the deeply divided country's first all-race multiparty elections, anti-apartheid activist Nelson Mandela, a lawyer born into the Xhosa-speaking Thembu nation, became the Republic of South Africa's first indigenous president. Today, more than a decade after the abolition of apartheid, the white minority no longer controls the government, and racial policies are no longer in effect. In daily practice, however, segregation still exists; few people of European descent can be found in South Africa's vast underclass of have-nots, who are almost all people of color.

All of this brings to mind the concepts of ritual purity and pollution so basic to the Indian caste system. In South Africa, whites feared pollution of their purity

[7]Boshara, R. (2003, January/February). Wealth inequality: The $6,000 solution. *Atlantic Monthly*.

[8]Kennickell, A. B. (2003, November). *A rolling tide: Changes in the distribution of wealth in the U.S. 1989–2001.* Levy Economics Institute.

VISUAL COUNTERPOINT

Homeless men sleeping on sidewalks—one in India, one in the United States. Outcast groups such as India's untouchables are a common feature of stratified societies. In the United States, nearly 13 percent of the population is trapped in poverty—according to the 2004 U.S. Census, which defined poverty as having an income under $19,300 for a four-person household, under $15,000 for three persons. Many sociologists and government officials argue that U.S. poverty is understated and that as much as 30 percent of Americans have trouble making ends meet. A disproportionate number in this underclass are African Americans, many still victimized by discrimination that is a remnant of slavery.

through improper contact with blacks. In India and South Africa, untouchables and blacks comprised categories of landless or near-landless people who served as a body of mobile laborers, always available for exploitation by those in political control. A similar mobile labor force of landless men at the state's disposal emerged in China as many as 2,200 years ago.

The basis of social class structure is role differentiation. Since great role diversity is most characteristic of civilizations—centrally organized state societies in which large numbers of people live in cities—it is not surprising they provide the greatest opportunities for stratification. Furthermore, the large size and heterogeneity of populations in civilizations create a need for classifying people into a manageable number of social categories. Small wonder, then, that social stratification is one of the defining characteristics of an urban civilization.

Social classes are manifest several ways. One is through *verbal evaluation*—what people say about others in their own society. For this, anything can be singled out for attention and spoken of favorably or unfavorably: political, military, religious, economic, or professional roles; wealth and property; kinship; physical qualities (skin color, for example); community activity; linguistic dialect; and a host of other traits. Cultures do this differently, and what may be spoken of favorably in one may be spoken of unfavorably in another and ignored in a third.

Furthermore, cultural values may change, so that something regarded favorably at one time may not be

at another. This is one reason why a researcher may be misled by verbal evaluation, for what people say may not correspond completely with social reality. As an example, the official language of Egypt is Classical Arabic, the language of the Koran (the holiest of Islamic texts). Though it is highly valued, no one in Egypt uses this language in daily interaction; rather, it is used for official documents or on formal occasions. Those most proficient in it are not of the upper class but, rather, of the lower middle classes. These are the people educated in the public schools (where Classical Arabic is the language of schooling) and who hold jobs in the government bureaucracy (which requires the most use of Classical Arabic). Upper-class Egyptians, by contrast, go to private schools, where they learn the foreign languages essential for success in diplomacy and in the global economy of business and industry.[9]

Social classes also are manifest through *patterns of association*—not just who interacts with whom but how and in what context. In Western society, informal, friendly relations take place mostly within one's own class. Relations with members of other classes tend to be more formal and occur in the context of specific situations. For example, a corporate executive and a janitor normally are members of different social classes. They may have frequent contact with each other, but it occurs in the setting of the corporate of-

---

[9]Haeri, N. (1997). The reproduction of symbolic capital: Language, state, and class in Egypt. *Current Anthropology 38*, 795–816.

Biocultural Connection

African Burial Ground Project ▪ By Michael Blakey

In 1991, construction workers in lower Manhattan unearthed what turned out to be an African burial ground, the final resting place of some 10,000 enslaved African captives brought to New York in the 17th and 18th centuries to build the city and provide the labor for its thriving economy. The discovery sparked controversy as the African American public held protests and prayer vigils to stop the part of a federal building project that nearly destroyed the site.

As a biological anthropologist and African American, I had a unique opportunity to work together with the descendant African American community to develop a plan that included both extensive biocultural research and the humane retention of the sacred nature of the site, ultimately through reburial and the creation of a fitting memorial. The research also involved archaeological and historical studies that used a broad African diasporic context for understanding the lifetime experiences of these people who were enslaved and buried in New York.

Studying a sample population of 419 individuals from the burial ground, our team used an exhaustive range of skeletal biological methods, producing a database

containing more than 200,000 observations of genetics, morphology, age, sex, growth and development, muscle development, trauma, nutrition, and disease. The bones revealed an unmistakable biocultural connection: physical wear and tear of an entire community brought on by the social institution of slavery.

We now know, based on this study, that life for Africans in colonial New York was characterized by poor nutrition, grueling physical labor that enlarged and often tore muscles, and death rates that were unusually high for 15- to 25-year-olds. Many of these young adults died soon after arriving on slaving ships. Few Africans lived past 40 years of age, and less than 2 percent lived beyond 55. Church records show strikingly different mortality trends

for the Europeans of New York: About eight times as many English as Africans lived past 55 years of age, and mortality in adolescence and the early 20s was relatively low.

Skeletal research also showed that those Africans who died as children and were most likely to have been born in New York exhibited stunted and disrupted growth and exposure to high levels of lead pollution—unlike those who had been born in Africa (and were distinguishable because they had filed teeth). Fertility was very low among enslaved women in New York, and infant mortality was high. In these respects, this northern colonial city was very similar to South Carolina and the Caribbean to which its economy was tied—regions where conditions for African captives were among the harshest.

© J. A. Giordano/Corbis SABA

Individuals in this deeply troubling burial ground came from warring African states including Calibar, Asante, Benin, Dahomey, Congo, Madagascar, and many others—states that wrestled with the European demand for human chattel. They resisted their enslavement through rebellion, and they resisted their dehumanization by carefully burying their dead and preserving what they could of their cultures.

---

fices and usually requires certain stereotyped behavior patterns.

A third way social classes are manifest is through *symbolic indicators*. For example, in the United States certain activities and possessions are indicative of class: occupation (a garbage collector has different class status than a medical specialist); wealth (rich people are generally in a higher social class than poor people); dress ("white collar" versus "blue collar"); form of recreation (upper-class people are expected to play golf rather than shoot pool down at the pool hall—but they can shoot pool at home or in a club); residential location (upper-class people do not ordinarily live in slums); kind of car; and so on. All sorts of status symbols are indicative of class position, including measures such as the number of

bathrooms in a person's house. That said, class rankings do not fully correlate with economic status or pay scales. The local garbage collector or unionized car-factory laborer typically makes more money than an average college professor with a doctorate.

Symbolic indicators involve factors of lifestyle, but differences in life chances may also signal differences in class standing. Life is apt to be less hard for members of an upper class as opposed to a lower class. This shows up in a tendency for lower infant mortality and longer life expectancy for the upper class. There is also a tendency for greater physical stature and robustness among upper-class people, the result of better diet and protection from serious illness in their juvenile years (see Biocultural Connection).

Social Mobility

Most stratified societies offer at least some **social mobility**—upward or downward change in one's social class position in a stratified society. For those who move upward in social ranking, this helps to ease the strains inherent in any system of inequality. Even the Indian caste system, with its guiding ideology that all hierarchical social arrangements within it are fixed, has a degree of flexibility and mobility, not all of it associated with the recent changes modernization has brought to India. Although individuals cannot move up or down the caste hierarchy, whole groups can do so depending on claims they can make for higher status and on how well they can manipulate others into acknowledging their claims.

Nonetheless, caste-structured societies exemplify *closed-class societies,* because of the limits on social mobility. Those that permit a great deal of mobility are referred to as *open-class societies.* Yet even in these, mobility is apt to be more limited than one might suppose. In the United States, despite its rags-to-riches ideology, most mobility involves a move up or down only a notch, although if this continues in a family over several generations, it may add up to a major change. Nonetheless, U.S. society makes much of relatively rare examples of great upward mobility consistent with its cultural values and does its best to overlook the numerous cases of little or no upward, not to mention downward, mobility.

The degree of mobility in a stratified society is related to the prevailing kind of family organization. Social mobility is most common in societies made up of independent nuclear families where the individual is closely tied to fewer people—especially when neolocal residence is the norm, and it is assumed that individuals will leave their family of birth when they become adults. In such social settings, through careful marriage, occupational success, and disassociation from the lower-class family in which they grew up, individuals can more easily move up in society.

In societies where the extended family is the usual form, mobility tends to be more difficult, because each individual is strongly tied to many relatives. Typically, if a person in such a society moves up to a higher social class, it is expected that he or she will help the rest of the family move up as well. In all likelihood, the extended families of the highly successful Ivory Coast soccer players described in this chapter's Globalscape have experienced upward social mobility through their ties to these athletes.

social mobility Upward or downward change in one's social class position in a stratified society.

Maintaining Stratification

Because social stratification of any kind generally makes life more difficult for large segments of a population, the lower classes are usually kept quiet through the cultural system's superstructure or worldview. This superstructure may be governed and directed by ruling elites, who impose their own ideas and values on a society by controlling information, staging public ceremonies, and other forms of ideological expression.

In India, for example, belief in reincarnation and the existence of an incorruptible supernatural power that assigns people to a particular caste position as a reward or punishment for the deeds and misdeeds of past lives justifies one's position in this life. If, however, individuals faithfully perform the duties appropriate to their caste in this lifetime, then they can expect to be reborn into a higher caste in a future existence. Truly exemplary performance of their duties may even release them from the cycle of rebirth, to be reunited with the divinity from which all existence springs.

In the minds of orthodox Hindus, then, one's caste position is something earned rather than the accident of birth as it appears to outside observers. Thus, although the caste system explicitly recognizes (and accepts as legitimate) inequality among people, an implicit assumption of ultimate equality underlies it. This contrasts with the situation in the United States, where the equality of all people is proclaimed even while various groups are repressed or otherwise discriminated against.

Although the cost is great—social classes do, after all, make life oppressive for large numbers of people—classes may nevertheless perform an integrative function in society. By cutting across some or all lines of kinship, residence, occupation, and age group, depending on the particular society, they counteract potential tendencies for society to fragment into separate entities. For instance, in India a succession of conquerors succeeded in moving into the caste hierarchy near its top as warriors. Coming from diverse ethnic and religious groups, they were incorporated into the larger state society by certification of their leaders as warriors and by marriage of their women to upper-caste Brahmans.

Nonetheless, stratification, by its very nature, provides a means by which one, usually small, group of people may dominate and make life miserable for large numbers of others. It provided 4.5 million people of European descent with justification to dominate 25 million indigenous people in South Africa and sanctioned the horrors of slavery in the United States and other parts of the world. Even without conquest or slavery, ethnic differences often are a factor in the definition of social classes, as not only African Americans but also members of other North American minorities have experienced

GLOBALSCAPE

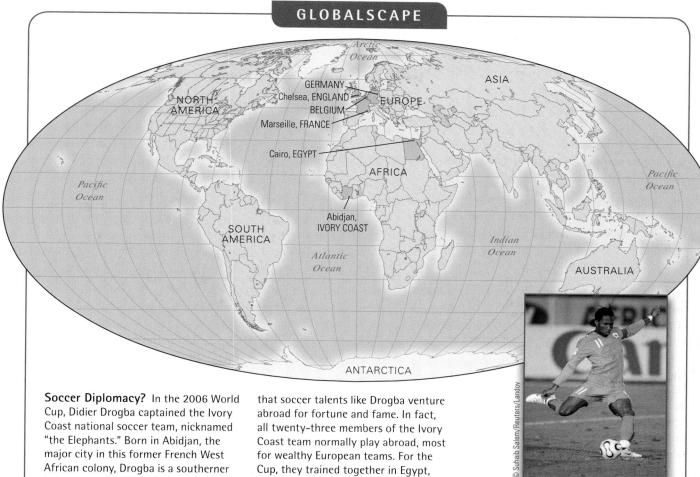

Soccer Diplomacy? In the 2006 World Cup, Didier Drogba captained the Ivory Coast national soccer team, nicknamed "the Elephants." Born in Abidjan, the major city in this former French West African colony, Drogba is a southerner belonging to the Bete, one of the country's sixty-five ethnic groups. He was recruited at an early age to play for a Belgian club. Emerging as a powerful striker, he was drafted by a French club for $8 million and moved to Marseille. Chosen French Player of the Year in 2004, after just one season he signed with England's champion team, Chelsea Football Club, for a record $42 million multi-year contract. In England, his annual salary (not counting endorsements) is more than $6 million.

Given that the average Ivorian earns just $1,600 per year, it is not surprising that soccer talents like Drogba venture abroad for fortune and fame. In fact, all twenty-three members of the Ivory Coast team normally play abroad, most for wealthy European teams. For the Cup, they trained together in Egypt, under a French coach. Meanwhile, their home country has been wracked by a brutal civil war in which southern ethnic groups are pitted against northern ones.

Ninety percent of the Ivory Coast's foreign exchange earnings come from cocoa beans. An international sports star, Drogba appears in ads promoting the sale of Ivorian chocolate in France and Germany. He also promotes peace: During the 2006 World Cup games in Germany, enthusiastically watched on television by millions of fellow Ivorians back home, he and his national soccer team (representing both southern and northern Ivory Coast) pleaded that the unity of the Elephants in the stadium would inspire fellow Ivorians to settle their conflict and reunite as a country.

Global Twister Why does the captain of Ivory Coast's national soccer team competing for the World Cup think that the Elephants can help bring together fellow Ivorians from rival factions?

© Suhaib Salem/Reuters/Landov

---

through the racist stereotyping that leads to social and economic disadvantages.

In any system of stratification, those who dominate proclaim their supposedly superior status, commonly asserting it through intimidation or propaganda (in the form of gossip, media, religious doctrine, and so forth) that presents their position as normal, natural, divinely guided, or at least well-deserved. As U.S. anthropologist Laura Nader of the University of California, Berkeley, points out, "Systems of thought develop over time and reflect the interests of certain classes or groups in the society who manage to universalize their beliefs and values."[10]

---

[10]Nader, L. (1997). Controlling processes: Tracing the dynamic components of power. *Current Anthropology 38,* 271.

So it is with certain religious ideologies that effectively assert that the social order is divinely fixed and therefore not to be questioned. With the aid of institutionalized thought structures, religious and otherwise, those in power hope that members of the lower classes will thereby "know their place" and not contest their domination by the "chosen elite." If, however, this domination is contested, the elite usually control the power of the state and use its institutions to protect their privileged position.

Questions for Reflection

1. When teenagers leave their parental home to go to college or find employment in a distant part of the country, they face the challenge of establishing social relationships that are not based on kinship but on common interest. To which common-interest associations do you belong and why?

2. At what point do you think kinship ceases to be the major organizational principle in a social structure?

3. Do you think that members of an upper class or caste in a socially stratified system have a greater vested interest in the idea of law and order than those forced to exist on the bottom of such societies? Why or why not?

4. Slavery in the United States was officially abolished in 1863, caste-based discrimination of untouchables became constitutionally outlawed in India in 1950, and race-based segregation in South Africa officially ended with the abolition of apartheid in 1993. Considering these important political changes, do you think that social repression against these groups has now ended for good?

5. In your own life, have you personally seen and experienced grouping by gender, age, and class? What do you see as the positive and negative aspects of these groupings?

Suggested Readings

Bernardi, B. (1985). *Age class systems: Social institutions and policies based on age.* New York: Cambridge University Press.

This is a cross-cultural analysis of age as a device for organizing society and seeing to the distribution and rotation of power.

Bradfield, R. M. (1998). *A natural history of associations.* New York: International Universities Press.

First published in 1973, this major anthropological study of common-interest associations attempts to provide a comprehensive theory of the origin of associations and their role in kin-based societies.

De Mott, B. (1990). *The imperial middle: Why Americans can't think straight about class.* New York: Morrow.

This critical commentary on the myth that the United States is a classless society demonstrates the great social and political costs of buying into that idea.

Lenski, G. E. (1984). *Power and privilege: A theory of social stratification.* New York: McGraw-Hill.

In this classic text, the author uses a historical and broadly comparative approach to analyze how stratification develops in societies.

Price, T. D., & Feinman, G. M. (Eds.). (1995). *Foundations of social inequality.* New York: Plenum.

A collection of essays by various contributors examining the emergence of social inequality.

Sanday, P. R. (1981). *Female power and male dominance: On the origins of sexual inequality.* Cambridge, England: Cambridge University Press.

A cross-cultural study of various ways that male–female relations are organized in human societies. Demonstrating that male dominance is not inherent in those relations, the author suggests that dominance emerges in situations of stress as a result of chronic food shortages, migration, and colonial domination.

Steady, F. C. (2005). *Women and collective action in Africa.* New York: Palgrave Macmillan.

This examination of women's movements and collective action in Africa begins in pre-colonial times and moves through to the present. It identifies and discusses the various arenas in which collective action has and can influence, including women's traditional, mutual-aid, and religious associations.

Thomson Audio Study Products

 Enjoy the MP3-ready Audio Lecture Overviews for each chapter and a comprehensive audio glossary of key terms for quick study and review. Whether walking to class, doing laundry, or studying at your desk, you now have the freedom to choose when, where, and how you interact with your audio-based educational media. See the preface for information on how to access this on-the-go study and review tool.

The Anthropology Resource Center

www.thomsonedu.com/anthropology
The Anthropology Resource Center provides extended learning materials to reinforce your understanding of key concepts in the four fields of anthropology. For each of the four fields, the Resource Center includes dynamic exercises including video exercises, map exercises, simulations, and "Meet the Scientists" interviews, as well as critical thinking questions that can be assigned and e-mailed to instructors. The Resource Center also provides breaking news in anthropology and interesting material on applied anthropology to help you link what you are learning to the world around you.

12 Politics, Power, and Violence

© Reuters/Corbis

CHALLENGE ISSUE

In all societies, from the largest to the smallest, people must decide who gets what, when, where, and how. This is the basic challenge of politics. Political organization takes many forms, of which the state is just one. Often, states are controlled by wealthy elites who use their positional power to defend their vested interests. They do so by means of government institutions, administrative bureaucracies, and armed forces equipped with the means of violence to impose or maintain law and order. Citizens seeking political change by staging public demonstrations, as in this photo of protestors in Japan, may be stopped by state security forces authorized to use violence, if necessary, to prohibit, control or even eliminate such opposition.

How Are Power and Political Organization Different?

All social relations involve power, which essentially refers to the ability of individuals or groups to impose their will upon others and make them do things even against their own wants or wishes. Power also operates on the level of entire societies. The ability to impose or maintain order and to resolve conflicts requires political organization, which refers to the means by which a society maintains order internally and manages its affairs with other societies externally. It may be relatively uncentralized and informal, as in bands and tribes, or more centralized and formal, as in chiefdoms and states.

How Are Social and Political Order Formed and Maintained?

Social controls may be internalized—in cultural values that are "built into" individuals—or externalized, in the form of sanctions. Positive sanctions encourage approved behavior, while negative sanctions discourage unacceptable behavior. Negative sanctions are called laws if they are formalized and enforced by an authorized political agency. Force may be employed to impose or maintain order within a society or between groups. Although states and chiefdoms frequently practice warfare as a means of achieving political objectives, some groups avoid such organized violence.

How Do Political Systems Obtain Popular Support?

In uncentralized systems people give loyalty and cooperation freely because everyone participates in making most decisions. Centralized systems, by contrast, rely more heavily on power, even coercion, although in the long run these may lessen the system's effectiveness. To a greater or lesser extent, political organizations all over the world seek to legitimize their power through recourse to supernatural ideas.

An irony of human life is that something as fundamental to our existence as cooperation should contain within it the seeds of its own destruction. It is nonetheless true that the groups people form to fulfill important organizational needs do not just facilitate cooperation among the members of those groups; they also create conditions that may lead to the disruption of society. We see this in a wide range of situations: in riots among fans rooting for different soccer teams, in the gang violence that takes place in many North American cities, and all the more seriously in bloody conflicts between neighboring ethnic groups such as Serbs and Albanians in southern Europe and Tutsi and Hutu in East Africa.

The attitude that "my group is better than your group" is not confined to any one of the world's cultures, and it commonly takes the form of rivalry between groups: descent group against descent group, men against women, age grade against age grade, social class against social class, and so forth. This does not mean that such rivalry has to be disruptive; indeed, it may function to ensure that the members of groups perform their jobs well so as not to lose face or be subject to ridicule. Rivalry, however, can become a serious problem if it erupts into violence.

The fact is, social living inevitably entails a certain amount of friction—not just between groups but between individual members of groups as well. Thus, any society can count on a degree of disruptive behavior by some of its members at one time or another. Yet, no one can know precisely when such outbursts will occur or what form they will take. Not only does this uncertainty go against the predictability social life demands, but it also goes against the deep-seated psychological need each individual has for structure and certainty. Therefore, every society must have means by which conflicts can be resolved and breakdown of the social order prevented. Today, throughout the world, state governments play a central role in maintaining social order.

THOMSON AUDIO STUDY PRODUCTS
Take advantage of the MP3-ready Audio Lecture Overviews and comprehensive audio glossary of key terms for each chapter. See the preface for information on how to access this on-the-go study and review tool.

power The ability of individuals or groups to impose their will upon others and make them do things even against their own wants or wishes.

political organization The way power is distributed and embedded in society; the means through which a society creates and maintains social order.

Complex political structures known as states first began to emerge over 5,000 years ago. Commonly unstable, many have disappeared in the course of history, some temporarily and others forever. Some were annexed by other states, and others collapsed or fragmented into smaller political units. Although some present-day states are very old—such as Japan, which has endured as a state for almost 1,500 years—few are older than the United States, an independent country since 1783.

Despite the predominance of state societies today, there are still groups where political organization consists of flexible and informal kinship systems whose leaders lack real **power**—the ability of individuals or groups to impose their will upon others and make them do things even against their own wants or wishes. Between these two polarities of kin-ordered and state-organized political systems lies a world of variety.

KINDS OF POLITICAL SYSTEMS

The term **political organization** refers to the way power is distributed and embedded in society, whether in organizing a giraffe hunt, managing irrigated farmlands, or raising an army. In short, it is the means through which a society creates and maintains social order. It assumes a variety of forms among the peoples of the world, but anthropologists have simplified this complex subject by identifying four basic kinds of political systems: bands, tribes, chiefdoms, and states (Figure 12.1). The first two are uncentralized systems; the latter two are centralized.

Uncentralized Political Systems

Until recently, many non-Western peoples have had neither chiefs with established rights and duties nor any fixed form of government, as those who live in modern states understand the term. Instead, marriage and kinship have formed their principal means of social organization. The economies of these societies are primarily of a subsistence type, and populations are typically small.

Leaders do not have real power to force compliance with the society's customs or rules, but if individuals do not conform, they may become targets of scorn and gossip or even be banished. Important decisions are usually made in a collective manner by agreement among adults. Dissenting members may decide to act with the majority, or they may choose to adopt some other course of action, including leaving the group. This egalitarian form of political organization provides great flexibility, which in many situations offers an adaptive advantage. Since power in these kin-ordered communities is shared, with nobody exercising exclusive control over collective

TYPES OF POLITICAL ORGANIZATION

The symbol → indicates that the attribute varies between less and more complex societies of that type.

	BAND	TRIBE	CHIEFDOM	STATE
MEMBERSHIP				
Number of people	Dozens and up	Hundreds and up	Thousands and up	Tens of thousands and up
Settlement pattern	Mobile	Mobile or fixed: 1 or more villages	Fixed: 2 or more villages	Fixed: Many villages and cities
Basis of relationships	Kin	Kin, descent groups	Kin, rank, and residence	Class and residence
Ethnicities and languages	1	1	1	1 or more
GOVERNMENT				
Decision making, leadership	"Egalitarian"	"Egalitarian" or Big Man	Centralized, hereditary	Centralized
Bureaucracy	None	None	None, or 1 or 2 levels	Many levels
Monopoly of force and information	No	No	No → Yes	Yes
Conflict resolution	Informal	Informal	Centralized	Laws, judges
Hierarchy of settlement	No	No	No → Paramount village or head town	Capital
ECONOMY				
Food production	No	No → Yes	Yes → Intensive	Intensive
Labor specialization	No	No	No → Yes	Yes
Exchanges	Reciprocal	Reciprocal	Redistributive ("tribute")	Redistributive ("taxes")
Control of land	Band	Descent group	Chief	Various
SOCIETY				
Stratified	No	No	Yes, ranked by kin	Yes, by class or caste
Slavery	No	No	Some, small-scale	Some, large-scale
Luxury goods for elite	No	No	Yes	Yes
Public architecture	No	No	No → Yes	Yes
Indigenous literacy	No	No	No → Some	Often

Figure 12.1

Four Kinds of Political Systems

resources or public affairs, individuals typically enjoy much more freedom than those who form part of larger and more complex political systems.

Band Organization

The **band** is a relatively small and loosely organized kin-ordered group that inhabits a specific territory and that may split periodically into smaller extended family groups that are politically independent. Typically, bands are found among food foragers and other nomadic societies where people organize into politically autonomous extended-family groups that usually camp together, although the members of such families may periodically break up into smaller groups to forage for food or visit other relatives. Thus, bands are kin groups, composed of men and/or women who are related (or are assumed to be) with their spouses and unmarried children.

Bands may be characterized as associations of related families who occupy a common (often loosely de-fined) territory and who live there together as long as environmental and subsistence circumstances are favorable. The band is probably the oldest form of political organization, since all humans were once food foragers and remained so until the development of farming and pastoralism over the past 10,000 years.

Since bands are egalitarian and small, numbering at most a few hundred people, no real need exists for formal, centralized political systems. Because everyone is related to—and knows on a personal basis—everyone else with whom dealings are required, there is high value placed on "getting along." Conflicts that do arise are usually settled informally through gossip, ridicule, direct negotiation, or mediation. When negotiation or

band A relatively small and loosely organized kin-ordered group that inhabits a specific territory and that may split periodically into smaller extended family groups that are politically independent.

mediation are used, the focus is on reaching a solution considered fair by all concerned parties, rather than on conforming to some abstract law or rule. Where all else fails, disgruntled individuals have the option of leaving to go live in another band where they may have relatives or trying to establish a new community of their own.

Decisions affecting a band are made with the participation of all its adult members, with an emphasis on achieving consensus—a collective agreement—rather than a simple majority. Individuals become leaders by virtue of their abilities and serve in that capacity only as long as they retain the confidence of the community. They have no real power to force people to abide by their decisions. A leader who exceeds what people are willing to accept quickly loses followers.

An example of the informal nature of band leadership is found among the Ju/'hoansi Bushmen of the Kalahari Desert mentioned in earlier chapters. Each Ju/'hoansi band is composed of a group of families that live together, linked through kinship to one another and to the headman (or, less often, headwoman). Although each band has rights to the territory it occupies and the resources within it, two or more bands may range over the same land. The head, called the *kxau,* or "owner," is the focal point for the band's claims on the territory. He or she does not personally own the land or resources but symbolically represents the rights of band members to them. If the head leaves the area to live elsewhere, people turn to someone else to lead them.

The head coordinates band migration when resources are no longer adequate for subsistence in a particular habitat. This leader's major duty is to plan when and where the group will move, and when the move

begins his or her position is at the head of the line. The leader selects the site for the new settlement and has the first choice of a spot for his or her own fire.

There are few other material rewards or duties. For example, a Ju/'hoansi head is not a judge and does not punish other band members. Wrongdoers are judged and held accountable by public opinion, usually expressed by gossip—which can play an important role in curbing socially unacceptable behavior. In small-scale communities where everyone is interdependent, public scolding or open expression of irritation may escalate into serious anger and lead to splits that jeopardize everyone's security.

Through gossip—talking behind someone's back and spreading rumors about behavior considered disruptive, shameful, or ridiculous—people accomplish several objectives while avoiding the potential disruption of open confrontation: They underscore and reinforce the cultural standards of "normal" people who abide by the unwritten rules of proper conduct; they punish those who violate standards of socially acceptable behavior; moreover, since gossip can damage a person's reputation and is often fueled by hidden jealousy or a secret desire to retaliate against someone considered too accomplished or successful, it may function like a leveling mechanism.

Another prime technique in small-scale societies for resolving disputes, or even avoiding them in the first place, is mobility. Those unable to get along with others of their group may choose or feel pressured to move to another group where existing kinship ties may give them rights of entry.

Tribal Organization

The second type of uncentralized authority system is the tribe. This term is problematic because it has many meanings. The English term is derived from the Latin word *tribus,* which referred to each of the three original divisions of the Roman people more than 2,500 years ago. Even after the number of Roman tribes increased to thirty-five, this term stuck, still referring to a major subdivision of a nation. When the biblical texts were translated from Hebrew into Latin, and much later into English, the term *tribe* was also applied to the twelve subdivisions of Israel. Over time, it came to be widely used as a label for any people not organized into states.

In the past few centuries, when the English and other Europeans expanded their powerful reach across the globe, the term gained popularity as a way to contrast people whom they regarded as inferior to their own supposedly superior civilization. The term was even applied to non-Western peoples who in fact had strongly centralized states (the Aztecs, for example).

The word is still often used in a negative or degrading way. For instance, political unrest in many parts of

Toma, a Ju/'hoansi headman, is known to many people worldwide through the ethnographic film *The Hunters.*

Shown here is a meeting of the Navajo Tribal Council, a nontraditional governing body created in response to requirements set by the U.S. government in order for the Navajo to exercise national sovereignty.

© AP Photo/Matt York

the world is often blamed on "tribalism," when in fact the strife is usually the direct consequence of the creation of states that make it possible for the governing elite of one ethnic group or nationality to exploit others for their own benefit.[1]

To complicate matters, the term *tribe* also has a distinct legal meaning in some countries, including the United States. For instance, lumping together for administrative purposes a variety of groups historically organized as bands, tribes, or chiefdoms, U.S. law defines *tribe* as "any Indian tribe, band, nation, or other organized group or community . . . recognized as eligible for the special programs and services provided by the United States to Indians because of their status as Indians."[2]

In anthropology, this problematic term **tribe** refers to a wide range of kin-ordered groups that are politically integrated by some unifying factor and whose members share a common ancestry, identity, culture, language, and territory. In these larger political entities, people sacrifice a degree of household autonomy in return for greater security against such perils as enemy attacks or starvation.

Typically, though not invariably, a tribe has an economy based on some form of crop cultivation or herding.

Since these subsistence methods usually yield more food than those of the food-foraging band, tribal membership is usually larger than band membership. While band population densities are usually less than one person per square mile, tribal population densities generally exceed that and may be as high as 250 per square mile. Greater population density brings a new set of problems to be solved as opportunities for bickering, begging, adultery, and theft increase markedly, especially among people living in permanent villages.

Each tribe consists of one or more self-supporting and self-governing local communities that may then form alliances with others for various purposes. As in the band, political organization in the tribe is informal and temporary. Whenever a situation requiring political integration of all or several groups within the tribe arises—perhaps for defense, to carry out a raid, to pool resources in times of scarcity, or to capitalize on a windfall that must be distributed quickly lest it spoil—groups join to deal with the situation in a cooperative manner. When the problem is satisfactorily solved, each group then resumes autonomy.

In many tribal societies the organizing unit and seat of political authority is the clan, comprised of people who consider themselves descended from a common an-

---

[1]Whitehead, N. L., & Ferguson, R. B. (1993, November 10). Deceptive stereotypes about tribal warfare (p. A48). *Chronicle of Higher Education;* Van Den Berghe, P. L. (1992). The modern state: Nation builder or nation killer? *International Journal of Group Tensions 92*(3), 199–200.

[2]25 U.S. Code, par.450–450n.

tribe In anthropology, refers to a range of kin-ordered groups that are politically integrated by some unifying factor and whose members share a common ancestry, identity, culture, language, and territory.

cestor. Within the clan, elders or headmen and/or head-women regulate members' affairs and represent their clan in interactions with other clans. As a group, the elders of all the clans may form a council that acts within the community or for the community in dealings with outsiders. Because clan members usually do not all live together in a single community, clan organization facilitates joint action with members of related communities when necessary.

Leadership among tribes is also relatively informal, as evident in a wide array of past and present examples. The Navajo Indians in the southwestern United States, for example, traditionally did not think of government as something fixed and all-powerful, and leadership was not vested in a central authority. A local leader was a man respected for his age, integrity, and wisdom. Therefore, people sought his advice frequently, but he had no formal means of control and could not force any decision on those who asked for his help. Group decisions were made by public consensus, although the most influential man usually played a key role in reaching a decision. Social mechanisms that induced members to abide by group decisions included gossip, criticism, withdrawal of cooperation, and the belief that antisocial actions caused sickness and other misfortune.

Another example of tribal leadership is the Big Man. Common in the southern Pacific, such men are leaders of localized descent groups or of a territorial group. The Big Man combines a small amount of interest in his tribe's welfare with a great deal of cunning and calculation for his own personal gain. His authority is personal; he does not come to office in any formal sense, nor is he elected. His status is the result of acts that raise him above most other tribe members and attract to him a number of loyal followers.

The Kapauku of Western New Guinea typify this form of political organization. Among them, the Big Man is called the *tonowi*, or "rich one." To achieve this status, one must be male, wealthy, generous, and eloquent. Physical bravery and an ability to deal with the supernatural are also common *tonowi* characteristics,

but they are not essential. The *tonowi* functions as the headman of the village unit in a wide variety of situations within and beyond the community. He represents his group in dealing with outsiders and other villages and acts as negotiator and/or judge when disputes break out among his followers.

Because Kapauku culture places a high value on wealth, a well-to-do man is considered successful and admirable—provided he is also generous when it comes to making loans. Those who refuse to lend money to other villagers may be ostracized, ridiculed, and, in extreme cases, actually executed by a group of warriors. Such responses to tightfistedness ensure that economic wealth is distributed throughout the group.

The *tonowi* acquires political power through his loans. Other villagers comply with his requests because they are in his debt (often interest-free), and they do not want to have to repay their loans. Those who have not yet borrowed from him may wish to do so in the future, so they, too, want to keep his goodwill.

The *tonowi* gains further support by taking into his household young male apprentices who receive business

This Big Man from New Guinea is wearing his official regalia.

training along with food and shelter. He also gives them a loan that enables them to marry when the apprenticeship ends. In return, they act as messengers and bodyguards. After leaving, they remain tied to the *tonowi* by bonds of affection and gratitude. Political support also comes from the *tonowi*'s kinsmen, whose relationship brings with it varying obligations.

The *tonowi* functions as a leader in a wide variety of situations. He represents his group in dealing with outsiders and other villages and acts as negotiator and/or judge when disputes break out among his followers. As discussed in an earlier chapter, the *tonowi*'s wealth comes from his success at breeding pigs—the focus of the entire Kapauku economy. It is not uncommon for a *tonowi* to lose his fortune rapidly due to bad management or bad luck with his pigs. Thus the Kapauku political structure shifts frequently; as one man loses wealth and consequently power, another gains it and becomes a *tonowi*. These changes confer a degree of flexibility on the political organization and prevent any one *tonowi* from holding political power for too long.

Although it is far more common for tribal chiefs to be men, in some cultures women serve in such leadership positions, as discussed later in this chapter.

Political Integration Beyond the Kin Group

Age sets, age grades, and common-interest groups discussed in the previous chapter are among the mechanisms used by tribal societies as means of political integration. Cutting across territorial and kin groupings, these organizations link members from different lineages and clans. For example, among the Tiriki of East Africa (mentioned in the previous chapter) the Warrior age grade guards the village and grazing lands, while Judicial Elders resolve disputes. The oldest age grade, the Ritual Elders, advise on matters involving the well-being of all the Tiriki people. With the tribe's political affairs in the hands of the various age grades and their officers, this type of organization enables the largely independent kin groups to solve conflicts and sometimes even avoid feuding between the lineages.

Another system of political integration found among tribes in many parts of the world is the common-interest association, also discussed in the previous chapter. For example, among many Indian nations inhabiting North America's Great Plains in the 19th century, the band comprised the basic territorial and political unit. In addition, however, there existed a number of military societies or warrior clubs.

Among the Cheyenne, for instance, there were seven of these groups. A boy might be invited to join one of these societies when he achieved warrior status, whereupon he became familiar with the society's particular insignia, songs, and rituals. Beyond military functions, the warrior societies also had ceremonial and social functions.

The Cheyenne warriors' daily tasks consisted of overseeing activities in the village, protecting families on the move to the next camping site, and enforcing rules against individual hunting when the whole tribe was on a buffalo hunt. In addition, each warrior society had its own repertoire of dances, performed on special ceremonial occasions. Since each Cheyenne band had identical military societies bearing identical names, the societies served to integrate the entire tribe for military and political purposes.[3]

Centralized Political Systems

In bands and tribes, political authority is not centralized, and each group is economically and politically autonomous. Political organization is vested in kinship, age, and common-interest groups. Populations are small and relatively homogeneous, with people engaged for the most part in the same sorts of activities throughout their lives. However, as a society's social life becomes more complex—as population rises, technology becomes more intricate, and specialization of labor and trade networks produce surplus goods—the opportunity increases for some individuals or groups to exercise control at the expense of others. In such societies, political authority and power are concentrated in a single individual (the chief) or in a body of individuals (the state).

Chiefdoms

A **chiefdom** is a regional polity (a politically organized society) in which two or more local groups are organized under a single ruling individual—the chief—who is at the head of a ranked hierarchy of people. An individual's status in such a polity is determined by the closeness of his or her relationship to the chief. Those closest are officially superior and receive deferential treatment from those in lower ranks.

The office of the chief is usually for life and often hereditary. Typically, it passes from a man to his son or his sister's son, depending on whether descent is traced patrilineally or matrilineally. Unlike the headmen or headwomen in bands and tribes, the leader of a chiefdom is generally a true authority figure, whose authority serves to unite members in all affairs and at all times. For

---

[3]Hoebel, E. A. (1960). *The Cheyennes: Indians of the Great Plains*. New York: Holt, Rinehart & Winston.

chiefdom A regional polity in which two or more local groups are organized under a single chief, who is at the head of a ranked hierarchy of people.

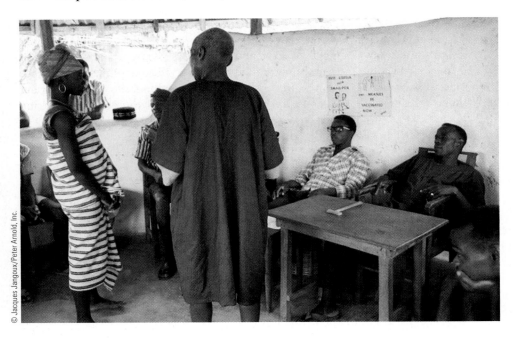

A Kpelle town chief in Liberia, West Africa, listens to a dispute in his district. Settling disputes is one of several ongoing traditional tasks that fall to paramount chiefs among Kpelle people.

example, a chief can distribute land among community members and recruit people into military service. Chiefdoms have a recognized hierarchy consisting of major and minor authorities who control major and minor subdivisions. Such an arrangement is, in effect, a chain of command, linking leaders at every level. It serves to bind groups in the heartland to the chief's headquarters, be it a mud and dung hut or a marble palace.

Although leaders of chiefdoms are almost always men, in some cultures a politically astute wife, sister, or single daughter of a deceased male chief could inherit such a powerful position as well. One historical example is Aimata, who succeeded her deceased half-brother Pomare III as leader of the Polynesian chiefdom of Tahiti in 1827, ruling as Queen Pomare IV until her death fifty years later.

Chiefs usually control the economic activities of those who fall under their political rule. Typically, chiefdoms involve redistributive systems, and the chief has control over surplus goods and perhaps even over the community's labor force. Thus, he (and sometimes she) may demand a quota of rice from farmers, which will then be redistributed to the entire community. Similarly, laborers may be recruited to build irrigation works, a palace, or a temple.

The chief may also amass a great amount of personal wealth and pass it on to offspring. Land, cattle, and luxury goods produced by specialists can be collected by the chief and become part of the power base. Moreover, high-ranking families of the chiefdom may engage in the same practice and use their possessions as evidence of noble status. An example of this form of political organi-

zation may be seen among the Kpelle of Liberia in West Africa.[4] Among them is a class of paramount chiefs, each of whom presides over one of the Kpelle chiefdoms (each of which is now a district of the Liberian state). The paramount chiefs' traditional tasks are hearing disputes, preserving order, seeing to the upkeep of trails, and various other supervising functions. In addition, they are now salaried officials of the Liberian government, mediating between it and their own people. Also, a paramount chief receives government commissions on taxes and court fees collected within his chiefdom, plus a commission for furnishing the rubber plantations with laborers. Moreover, he gets a stipulated amount of rice from each household and gifts from people who come to request favors and intercessions. In keeping with his exalted station in life, a paramount chief has at his disposal uniformed messengers, a literate clerk, and the symbols of wealth: many wives, embroidered gowns, and freedom from manual labor.

In a ranked hierarchy beneath each Kpelle paramount chief are several lesser chiefs: one for each district within the chiefdom, one for each town within a district, and one for each quarter of all but the smallest towns. Each acts as a kind of lieutenant for his chief of the next higher rank and also serves as a liaison between him and those of lower rank. Unlike paramount or district chiefs, who are comparatively remote, town and quarter chiefs are readily accessible to people at the local level.

[4]Gibbs, J. L., Jr. (1965). The Kpelle of Liberia. In J. L. Gibbs, Jr. (Ed.), *Peoples of Africa* (pp. 216–218). New York: Holt, Rinehart & Winston.

Traditionally, chiefdoms in all parts of the world have been highly unstable, with lesser chiefs trying to take power from higher ranking chiefs or paramount chiefs vying with one another for supreme power. In precolonial Hawaii, for example, war was the way to gain territory and maintain power; great chiefs set out to conquer one another in an effort to become paramount chief of all the islands. When one chief conquered another, the loser and all his nobles were dispossessed of all property and were lucky if they escaped alive. The new chief then appointed his own supporters to positions of political power. As a consequence, there was very little continuity of governmental or religious administration.

State Systems

The **state** is a centralized polity involving large numbers of people within a defined territory who are divided in social classes and organized and directed by a formal government that has the capacity and authority to make laws and to use force to defend the social order. This is the most formal of political organizations and represents one of the hallmarks of what is commonly referred to as *civilization*. From the perspective of the political elite in control of the state, its formation and endurance are typically represented as something positive—as progress. This view is not necessarily shared by those who exist on the political underside and do not possess much personal freedom to say and do as they please.

A large population in a state-organized society requires increased food production and wider distribution networks. Together, these lead to a transformation of the landscape by way of irrigation and terracing, carefully managed crop rotation cycles, intensive competition for clearly demarcated lands, roads, and enough farmers and other rural workers to support market systems and a specialized urban sector. Under such conditions, cor-

porate groups that stress exclusive membership proliferate, ethnic differentiation and ethnocentrism become more pronounced, and the potential for social conflict increases dramatically. Given these circumstances, state institutions, which minimally involve a bureaucracy, a military, and (usually) an official religion, provide the means for numerous and diverse groups to function together as an integrated whole.

Although their guiding ideology is that they are permanent and stable, since their first appearance some 5,000 years ago, states have been anything but permanent. Whatever stability they have achieved has been short term at best; over the long term, they show a clear tendency toward instability and transience. Nowhere have states even begun to show the staying power exhibited by less centralized political systems, the longest lasting social forms invented by humans.

An important distinction to make at this point is between state and nation. As noted in Chapter 1, a **nation** is a people who share a collective identity based on a common culture, language, territorial base, and history.[5] Today, there are roughly 200 internationally recognized states in the world, most of which did not exist before the end of World War II (1945). By contrast, there are about 5,000 nations (including tribes), many of which have existed since "time immemorial." Rarely do state and nation coincide, as they do, for example, in Iceland, Japan, and Swaziland.

About 73 percent of the world's states are pluralistic societies, having within their boundaries peoples of more than one nation.[6] Often, smaller nations (including tribes) and other groups find themselves at the mercy of one or more dominant nations or ethnic groups controlling the state. Frequently facing discrimination, even repression, some minority nations seek to improve their political position by founding an independent state. In the process, they usually encounter stiff opposition, even violent confrontations.

So it is with the Kurdish people inhabiting the borderlands of Iran, Iraq, and Turkey (Figure 12.2), the Pal-

---

[5]Clay, J. W. (1996). What's a nation? In W. A. Haviland & R. J. Gordon (Eds.), *Talking about people* (2nd ed., p. 188). Mountain View, CA: Mayfield.

[6]Van Den Berghe, P. L. (1992). The modern state: Nation builder or nation killer? *International Journal of Group Tensions* 92 (3), 193.

---

state In anthropology, a centralized polity involving large numbers of people within a defined territory who are divided into social classes and organized and directed by a formal government that has the capacity and authority to make laws, and use force to defend the social order.
nation A people who share a collective identity based on a common culture, language, territorial base, and history.

Figure 12.2
The Kurds, most of whom live in Iran, Iraq, and Turkey, are an example of a nation without a state.

estinians whose lands have been occupied by Israel for several decades, and the Chechens in the Russian federation, to cite but a few examples. While the outcome of armed struggle may be the formation of a new state (such as Bosnia's recent split from Serb-dominated Yugoslavia), some nations have forged their own states without open violence. Papua New Guinea in the southern Pacific, which became an independent state in 1975, is one example of this.

An important aspect of the state is its delegation of authority to maintain order within and outside its borders. Police, foreign ministries, war ministries, and other bureaucracies function to control and punish disruptive acts of crime, dissension, and rebellion. By such agencies the state asserts authority impersonally and in a consistent, predictable manner. Western forms of government, like that of the United States (in reality, a superstate), of course, are state governments, and their organization and workings are undoubtedly familiar to most everyone.

An example of a not-so-familiar state is Swaziland in southern Africa. One of the world's few true nation-states, it is home to the Swazi—a Bantu-speaking people.[7] Although the Swazi are primarily farmers, cattle raising is also practiced—and highly esteemed. In fact, the ritual, wealth, and power of their authority system are all intricately linked with cattle. In addition to farming and cattle raising, there is some specialization of

labor; certain people are specialists in ritual activities, metal smithing, wood carving, and pottery making. Their goods and services are traded, although the Swazi do not have elaborate markets.

The traditional Swazi authority system was characterized by a highly developed dual monarchy (now a thing of the past), a hereditary aristocracy, and elaborate kinship rituals, as well as by statewide age sets. The king and his mother were the central figures of all national activity, linking all the people of the Swazi state: They presided over higher courts, summoned national gatherings, controlled age classes, allocated land, disbursed national wealth, took precedence in ritual, and helped organize important social events.

Advising the king were the senior princes, who were usually his uncles and half-brothers. Between the king and the princes were two specially created *tinsila,* or "blood brothers," who were chosen from certain common clans. These men were his shields, protecting him from evildoers and serving him in intimate personal situations. In addition, the king was guided by two *tindvuna,* or counselors, one civil and one military. The people of the state made their opinions known through two councils: the *liqoqo,* or privy council (dissolved in 1986), composed of senior princes, and the *libanda,* or council of state, composed of chiefs and headmen and open to all adult males of the state. The *liqoqo* could advise the king, make decisions, and carry them out. For example, they could rule on questions about land, education, traditional ritual, court procedure, and transport.

Swazi government extended from the smallest local unit—the homestead—upward to the central administration. The head of a homestead had legal and administrative powers; he was responsible for the crimes of those under him, controlled their property, and spoke for them before his superiors. On the district level, political organization was similar to that of the central government. The relationship between a district chief, however, and his subjects was personal and familiar; he knew all the

[7]Kuper, H. (1965). The Swazi of Swaziland. In J. L. Gibbs, Jr. (Ed.), *Peoples of Africa* (pp. 475–512). New York: Holt, Rinehart & Winston.

Anthropologists of Note

Laura Nader (b. 1930)

Laura Nader has stood out among her peers from the start of her career in 1960, when she became the first woman faculty member in the anthropology department at the University of California, Berkeley.

Nader and her three siblings grew up in Winsted, Connecticut, children of immigrants from Lebanon. As she recalls, "My dad left Lebanon for political reasons, and when he came to the land of the free, he took it seriously. So we were raised to believe that you should be involved in public issues." They were also taught to question assumptions. Both Nader and her younger brother Ralph have made careers of doing this. She is an anthropologist noted for her cross-cultural research on law, justice, and social control and their connection to power structures. He is a consumer advocate and former U.S. presidential candidate who is a watchdog on issues of public health and the safety and quality of life.

Laura Nader's undergraduate studies included a study-abroad year in Mexico. Later, while earning her doctorate in anthropology at Radcliffe College, she returned to Mexico to do fieldwork in a Zapotec Indian peasant village in the Sierra Madre Mountains of Oaxaca. Re-

Courtesy of Laura Nader

flecting on this and subsequent research, she says, "In the 1950s, when I went to southern Mexico, I was studying how the Zapotec organize their lives, what they do with their problems, what they do when they go to court. And when I came back to this country, I started looking at American equivalents, at how Americans solve their consumer and service complaints."

Nader's first decade of teaching at Berkeley coincided with the Vietnam War, an era when the campus was in a perpetual state of turmoil with students demonstrating for peace and civil rights. Turning into a scholar-activist, she called upon colleagues to "study up" and do research on the world's power elite. "The

study of man," she wrote in 1972, "is confronted with an unprecedented situation: Never before have a few, by their actions and inactions, had the power of life and death over so many members of the species."

To date, the results of Nader's own research have appeared in over a hundred publications. Among these are her numerous books, including *Naked Science—Anthropological Inquiry into Boundaries, Power, and Knowledge* (1996), and *The Life of the Law: Anthropological Projects* (2002).

Playing a leading role in the development of the anthropology of law, Nader has taken on specialists in the fields of law, children's issues, nuclear energy, and science (including her own profession), critically questioning the basic assumptions ("central dogmas") under which these experts operate. She presses her students to do the same—to think critically, question authority, and break free from the "controlling processes" of the power elite. In 2000, Nader accepted one of the highest honors of the American Anthropological Association—an invitation to give the distinguished lecture at its annual gathering.

(Adapted from Interview with Laura Nader. California Monthly. November 2000.)

families in his district. The main check on any autocratic tendencies he might have exhibited rested in his subjects' ability to transfer their allegiance to a more responsive chief. Swazi officials held their positions for life and were dismissed only for treason or witchcraft. Incompetence, drunkenness, and stupidity were frowned upon, but they were not considered to be sufficient grounds for dismissal.

POLITICAL SYSTEMS AND THE QUESTION OF LEGITIMACY

Whatever form a society's political system may take, it must find some way to obtain and retain the people's allegiance. In uncentralized systems, where every adult participates in all decision making, loyalty and coopera-

tion are freely given, since each person is considered a part of the political system. As the group grows larger, however, and the organization becomes more formal, the problem of obtaining and keeping public support becomes greater.

Centralized political systems may rely upon coercion as a means of social control. This, however, carries a measure of risk since the personnel needed to apply force often must be numerous and may grow to be a political power. Also, the emphasis on force may create resentment and lessen cooperation. Thus, police states are generally short-lived; most societies choose less extreme forms of social coercion. In the United States, this is reflected in the increasing emphasis placed on cultural, as opposed to social, control. Laura Nader (see Anthropologist of Note) is well known for her anthropological research concerning issues of power, including social and cultural control.

VISUAL COUNTERPOINT

In contrast to countries such as the United States, where religion and state are constitutionally separated, countries such as Iran and Great Britain permit a much closer relationship between political and religious affairs. For instance, Shiite Muslim religious leader Ayatollah Khamenei is not only Iran's supreme spiritual leader but also his country's highest political authority. In England, Queen Elizabeth is not only her country's nominal head of state but also head of the Anglican Church.

Also basic to the political process is the concept of **legitimacy,** or the right of political leaders to govern— to hold, use, and allocate power. Like force, legitimacy is a form of support for a political system; unlike force, legitimacy is based on the values a particular society holds. For example, among the Kapauku of western New Guinea discussed above, the legitimacy of the *tonowi's* power comes from his wealth; the kings of Hawaii, and of England and France before their revolutions, were thought to have a divine right to rule; and the head of the traditional Dahomey state in what is now Benin, West Africa, acquired legitimacy through his age, as he was always the oldest living male.

While the basis for legitimacy varies across cultures, power based on legitimacy always results in authority. It is distinct from power based solely on force: Obedience to authority results from the belief that obedience is "right"; compliance to power based on force results from

legitimacy The right of political leaders to govern—to hold, use, and allocate power—based on the values of a particular society.

fear of being deprived of liberty, physical well-being, life, or material property. Thus, power based on legitimacy is symbolic and depends upon the positive expectations of those who recognize and accept it. If the expectations are not met regularly (if the head of state fails to deliver economic prosperity or the leader is continuously unsuccessful in preventing or dealing with calamities), the legitimacy of the recognized power figure erodes or may collapse altogether.

POLITICS AND RELIGION

Religion is often intricately connected with politics. Frequently it is religion that legitimizes the political order and leadership. Religious beliefs may influence or provide authoritative approval to customary rules and laws. For example, acts that people believe to be sinful, such as murder, are often illegal as well.

In both industrial and nonindustrial societies, belief in the supernatural is important and is reflected in people's political institutions. One place where the effect of religion on politics was well exemplified was in medieval Europe: Holy wars were fought over the smallest matter; labor was mobilized to build immense cathedrals in honor of the Virgin Mary and other saints; kings and queens ruled by "divine right" and (in the West) pledged allegiance to the pope and asked his blessing in all important ventures, were they marital or martial.

In Peru, the divine ruler of the Inca empire proclaimed absolute authority based on the proposition that he was descended from the Sun God. Mexico's ancient Aztec state was also a politico-religious one, having a divine ruler and engaging in nearly constant warfare to procure captives for human sacrifices thought necessary to assuage or please the gods. Modern Iran was proclaimed an "Islamic republic," and its first head of state was the most holy of all Shiite Muslim holy men.

The fact that the president of the United States takes the oath of office by swearing on the Bible is another instance of the use of religion to legitimize political power, as is the phrase "one nation, under God" in the Pledge of Allegiance. On U.S. coins is the phrase "In God We Trust," many meetings of government bodies begin with a prayer or invocation, and the phrase "so help me God" is routinely used in legal proceedings. In spite of an official separation of church and state, religious legitimization of government lingers.

POLITICAL LEADERSHIP AND GENDER

Irrespective of cultural configuration or type of political organization, women hold important positions of political leadership far less often than men. Furthermore, when they do occupy publicly recognized offices, their power and authority rarely exceed those of men. But significant exceptions occur. Historically, one might cite the female chiefs, or *sachems,* of Algonquian Indian communities in southern New England, as well as powerful queens in several Asian, African, and European monarchies.

Perhaps most notable is Queen Victoria, the long-reigning queen of England, Scotland, Wales, and Ireland. Also recognized as monarch in a host of colonies all over the world, Victoria even acquired the title Empress of India. Ruling the British empire from 1837 until 1901, she was perhaps the world's most powerful leader.

In addition to inheriting high positions of political leadership, growing numbers of women have also been elected as presidents or prime ministers. Countries with female heads of state now or in recent years include Indonesia, Pakistan, Ireland, Sri Lanka, Norway, India, Turkey, Liberia, Chile, Germany, and the Philippines, to mention just a few. While such high-profile female leadership is still relatively rare, women regularly enjoy as much political power as men in a number of societies. In band societies, for example, it is common for females to have as much of a say in public affairs as males, even though more often than not the latter are the nominal leaders of their groups.

Among the Iroquois nations of New York State, all leadership positions above the household and clan level were, without exception, filled by men. Thus men held all positions on the village and tribal councils, as well as on the great council of the Iroquois Confederacy. However, they were completely beholden to women, for only women could nominate men to high office. Moreover, women actively lobbied the men on the councils and could have someone removed from office whenever it suited them.

Lower visibility in politics does not necessarily indicate that women lack power in political affairs. And just as there are various ways in which women play a role behind the scenes, so it is when they have more visible roles, as in the dual-sex system of the Igbo in Nigeria, West Africa. Among the Igbo, each political unit has separate political institutions for men and women, so that both have an autonomous sphere of authority, as well as an area of shared responsibility.[8] At the head of each political unit was a male *obi,* considered the head of government although in fact he presided over the male community, and a female *omu,* the acknowledged mother of the whole community but in practice concerned with the female section of the community. Unlike a queen (though both she and the *obi* were crowned), the *omu* was neither the *obi*'s wife nor the previous *obi*'s daughter.

[8]Okonjo, K. (1976). The dual-sex political system in operation: Igbo women and community politics in midwestern Nigeria. In N. Hafkin & E. Bay (Eds.), *Women in Africa.* Stanford, CA: Stanford University Press.

© AFP/Getty Images

Liberian President Ellen Johnson Sirleaf inspects members of the Liberian police after taking the presidential oath in January 2006. Founded through the efforts of the American Colonization Society in 1821, this small West African country was settled mainly by freed slaves from the United States whose descendants became a powerful elite controlling Liberia's multi-ethnic population. After a military coup in 1980, the misgoverned state plunged into civil war. The first female president on the African continent, Sirleaf is a Harvard-educated economist who took the world by surprise when she won the elected head office in her war-torn and poverty-stricken country.

Just as the *obi* had a council of dignitaries to advise him and act as a check against any arbitrary exercise of power, the *omu* was served by a council of women in equal number to the *obi's* male councilors. The duties of the *omu* and her councilors involved such tasks as establishing rules and regulations for the community market (marketing was a woman's activity) and hearing cases involving women brought to her from throughout the town or village. If such cases also involved men, then she and her council would cooperate with the *obi* and his council. Widows also went to the *omu* for the final rites required to end their period of mourning for dead husbands. Since the *omu* represented all women, she had to be responsive to her constituency and would seek their approval and cooperation in all major decisions.

In addition to the *omu* and her council, the Igbo women's government included a representative body of women chosen from each quarter or section of the village or town. Moreover, political pressure groups of women acted at the village or lineage level to stop quarrels and prevent wars. These pressure groups included women born into a community (most of whom lived elsewhere since villages were exogamous and residence was patrilocal) and women who had married into the community. Their duties included helping companion wives in times of illness and stress and meting out discipline to lazy or recalcitrant husbands.

In the Igbo system, then, women managed their own affairs, and their interests were represented at all levels of government. Moreover, they had the right to enforce their decisions and rules with sanctions similar to those employed by men, including strikes, boycotts,

and "sitting on" someone. Political scientist Judith Van Allen, senior fellow at Cornell University's Institute for African Development, describes the latter:

> To "sit on" or "make war on" a man involved gathering at his compound, sometimes late at night, dancing, singing scurrilous songs which detailed the women's grievances against him and often called his manhood into question, banging on his hut with the pestles women used for pounding yams, and perhaps demolishing his hut or plastering it with mud and roughing him up a bit. A man might be sanctioned in this way for mistreating his wife, for violating the women's market rules, or for letting his cows eat the women's crops. The women would stay at his hut throughout the day, and late into the night if necessary, until he repented and promised to mend his ways.[9]

Given the high visibility of women in the Igbo political system, it may come as a surprise to learn that when the British imposed colonial rule on the Igbo in the late 1800s, they failed to recognize the autonomy and power of the women. One reason is that the British were blinded by their own cultural values, reflecting a male-dominated society in which the domestic sphere was seen as the ideal place for women. This is ironic because the long-reigning and powerful head of the British empire

---

[9]Van Allen, J. (1997). Sitting on a man: Colonialism and the lost political institutions of Igbo women. In R. Grinker & C. Steiner (Eds.), *Perspectives on Africa* (p. 450). Boston: Blackwell Press.

at the time was, as mentioned earlier, Queen Victoria. Nevertheless, unable to imagine that Igbo women might play important roles in politics, the British introduced "reforms" that destroyed traditional forms of female autonomy and power without providing alternative forms in exchange. As a result, Igbo women lost much of their traditional equality and became subordinate to men.

POLITICAL ORGANIZATION AND THE MAINTENANCE OF ORDER

Political organization always includes means of maintaining order that ensure people behave in acceptable ways and define what action will be taken when they do not. In chiefdoms and states, some sort of authority has the power to regulate the affairs of society. In bands and tribes, however, people behave generally as they are expected to, without the direct intervention of any centralized political authority. To a large degree, gossip, criticism, fear of supernatural forces, and the like serve as effective deterrents to antisocial behavior.

As an example of how such seemingly informal considerations serve to keep people in line, we may look at the Wape people of Papua New Guinea, who believe the spirits of deceased ancestors roam lineage lands, protecting them from trespassers and helping their hunting descendants by driving game their way.[10] These ancestral spirits also punish those who have wronged them or their descendants by preventing hunters from finding game or causing them to miss their shots, thereby depriving people of much needed meat.

Nowadays, the Wape hunt with shotguns, which the community purchases for the use of one man, whose job it is to hunt for all the others. The cartridges used in the hunt, however, are invariably supplied by individual community members. Thus, if the gunman shoots and misses, it is not viewed as his failing. Rather, it is because the owner of the fired shell, or some close relative, has quarreled or wronged another person whose deceased relative is securing revenge by causing the hunter to miss. Or, if the gunman cannot even find game, it is because vengeful ancestors have chased the animals away. As a proxy hunter for the villagers, the gunman is potentially subject to sanctions by ancestral spirits in response to collective wrongs by those for whom he hunts.

For the Wape, then, successful hunting depends upon avoiding quarrels and maintaining tranquility within the community so as not to antagonize anybody's deceased ancestor. Unfortunately, complete harmony is impossible to achieve in any human community, and the Wape are no exception. Thus, when hunting is poor, the gunman must discover what quarrels and wrongs have occurred within his village to identify the proper ancestral spirits to appeal to for renewed success. Usually, this is done in a special meeting where confessions of wrongdoing may be forthcoming. If not, questioning accusations are bandied about until resolution occurs, but even with no resolution, the meeting must end amicably to prevent new antagonisms. Thus, everyone's behavior comes under public scrutiny, reminding all of what is expected of them and encouraging all to avoid acts that will cast them in an unfavorable light.

Internalized Controls

The Wape concern about ancestral spirits is a good example of internalized, or cultural, controls—beliefs that are so thoroughly ingrained that each person becomes personally responsible for his or her own conduct. **Cultural control** may be thought of as control through beliefs and values deeply internalized in the minds of individuals, as opposed to **social control,** which involves external enforcement through open coercion.

Cultural controls are embedded in our consciousness and may rely on deterrents such as fear of supernatural punishment—ancestral spirits sabotaging the hunting, for example—and magical retaliation. Like the devout Christian who avoids sinning for fear of hell, the individual expects some sort of punishment, even though no one in the community may be aware of the wrongdoing.

Cultural controls can also be framed in positive terms, with customary ways and means that encourage individual sacrifice for the common good. For example, many cultures honor traditions of giving to, or volunteering for, charitable or humanitarian institutions. Performed out of a desire to help those in need, such personal sacrifices (Latin: *sacer,* "holy"; *facere,* "making") may be motivated by a spiritual or religious worldview. Often deeply rooted in basic ideas of a wider community and reciprocity, they are also cultural controls against self-seeking, self-serving, greedy opportunism that threaten the well-being of a larger community.

Externalized Controls

Because internalized controls are not wholly sufficient even in bands and tribes, every society develops externalized social controls known as **sanctions** designed to

---

[10]Mitchell, W. E. (1973, December). A new weapon stirs up old ghosts. *Natural History Magazine,* 77–84.

cultural control Control through beliefs and values deeply internalized in the minds of individuals.
social control External control through open coercion.
sanction An externalized social control designed to encourage conformity to social norms.

Formal sanctions may involve some form of regulated combat, seen here as armed dancers near Mount Hagen in New Guinea demand redress for murder.

encourage conformity to social norms. Operating within social groups of all sizes and involving a mix of cultural and social controls, sanctions may vary significantly within a given society, but they fall into one of two categories: positive or negative. Positive sanctions consist of incentives to conformity such as awards, titles, and recognition by one's neighbors. Negative sanctions consist of threats such as imprisonment, fines, corporal punishment, or ostracism from the community for violation of social norms.

For sanctions to be effective, they cannot be arbitrary. They must be applied consistently, and they must be generally known among members of the society. If some individuals are not convinced of the advantages of social conformity, they are still more likely to obey society's rules than to accept the consequences of not doing so.

Sanctions may also be categorized as either formal or informal, depending on whether or not a legal statute is involved. In the United States, the man who goes shirtless in shorts to a church service may be subject to a variety of informal sanctions, ranging from disapproving glances from the clergy to the chuckling of other parishioners. If, however, he were to show up without any clothing at all, he would be subject to the formal negative sanction of arrest for indecent exposure. Only in the second instance would he have been guilty of breaking the law.

Formal sanctions, such as laws, are always organized, because they attempt to precisely and explicitly regulate people's behavior, whether they are peacefully trading with each other or confronting each other on a battlefield. Other examples of organized sanctions include, on the positive side, military decorations and monetary rewards. On the negative side are loss of face, exclusion from social life and its privileges, seizure of property, imprisonment, and even bodily mutilation or death. Informal sanctions emphasize cultural control and are diffuse in nature, involving spontaneous expressions of approval or disapproval by members of the group or community. They are, nonetheless, very effective in enforcing a large number of seemingly unimportant customs. Because most people want to be accepted, they are willing to acquiesce to the rules that govern dress, eating, and conversation, even in the absence of actual laws.

Social Control through Witchcraft

In societies with or without centralized political systems, witchcraft sometimes functions as an agent of social control and involves both internal and external controls. An individual will think twice before offending a neighbor if convinced that the neighbor could retaliate by resorting to black magic. Similarly, individuals may not wish to be accused of practicing witchcraft, and so they behave with greater circumspection.

Among the Azande of the Sudan, people who think they have been bewitched may consult an oracle, who, after performing the appropriate mystical rites, then may establish or confirm the identity of the offending witch.[11] Confronted with this evidence, the "witch" will usually agree to cooperate in order to avoid any additional trouble. Should the victim die, the relatives of the deceased may choose to make magic against the witch, ultimately accepting the death of some villager both as evidence of guilt and of the efficacy of their magic.

For the Azande, witchcraft provides not only a sanction against antisocial behavior but also a means of dealing with natural hostilities and death. No one wishes to be thought of as a witch, and surely no one wishes to be victimized by one. By institutionalizing their emotional responses, the Azande successfully maintain social order.

SOCIAL CONTROL THROUGH LAW

Among the Inuit of northern Canada, all offenses are considered to involve disputes between individuals; thus, they must be settled between the disputants themselves. A traditional way of doing this is through a song duel, in which the individuals involved heap insults upon one another in songs specially composed for the occasion. Although society does not intervene, its interests are represented by spectators, whose applause determines the outcome. If, however, social harmony cannot be restored—and that is the goal, rather than assigning and punishing guilt—one or the other disputant may move to another band. Ultimately, there is no binding legal authority.

In Western society, by contrast, someone who commits an offense against another person may become subject to a series of complex legal proceedings. In criminal cases the primary concern is to assign and punish guilt rather than to help out the victim. The offender will be arrested by the police; tried before a judge and, perhaps, a jury; and, depending on the severity of the crime, may be fined, imprisoned, or even executed. Rarely does the victim receive restitution or compensation. Throughout this chain of events, the accused party is dealt with by police, judges, jurors, and jailers, who may have no personal acquaintance whatsoever with the plaintiff or the defendant. How strange this all seems from the standpoint of traditional Inuit culture! Clearly, the two systems operate under distinctly different assumptions.

Definition of Law

Once two Inuit settle a dispute by engaging in a song contest, the affair is considered closed; no further action is expected. Would we choose to describe the outcome of such a contest as a legal decision? If every law is a sanction but not every sanction is a law, how are we to distinguish between social sanctions in general and those to which we apply the label "law"?

The definition of law has been a lively point of contention among anthropologists. In 1926, Bronislaw Malinowski argued that the rules of law are distinguished from the rules of custom in that "they are regarded as the obligation of one person and the rightful claim of another, sanctioned not by mere psychological motive, but by a definite social machinery of binding force based . . . upon mutual dependence."[12] In other words, laws exemplify social control because they employ overt coercion.

An example of one rule of custom in contemporary North American society might be the dictate that guests at a dinner party should repay the person who gave the party with entertainment in the future. A host or hostess who does not receive a return invitation may feel cheated out of something thought to be owed but has no legal claim against the ungrateful guest for the $30 spent on food and drinks. If, however, an individual was cheated out of the same sum by the grocer when shopping, the law could be invoked. Although Malinowski's definition introduced several important elements of law, his failure to distinguish adequately between legal and nonlegal sanctions left the problem of formulating a workable definition of law in the hands of later anthropologists.

According to E. Adamson Hoebel, an important pioneer in the anthropological study of law, "A social norm is legal if its neglect or infraction is regularly met, in threat or in fact, by the application of physical force by an individual or group possessing the socially recognized privilege of so acting."[13] In stressing the legitimate use of physical coercion, Hoebel de-emphasized the traditional association of law with a centralized court system. Although rules enacted by an authorized legislative body and enforced by the judicial mechanisms of the state are fundamental features of Western jurisprudence, they are not the universal backbone of human law. Can any concept of law be applied to societies for whom the notion of a centralized judiciary is virtually meaningless? How shall we categorize Inuit song duels and other socially condoned forms of self-help that seem to meet some but not all of the criteria of law?

Ultimately, it is always of greatest value to consider each case within its cultural context. After all, law reflects a society's basic postulates, so to understand any society's laws, one must understand the underlying values and assumptions. Nonetheless, a working definition of law is useful for purposes of discussion and cross-

[11]Evans-Pritchard, E. E. (1937). *Witchcraft, oracles and magic among the Azande.* London: Oxford University Press.

[12]Malinowski, B. (1951). *Crime and custom in savage society* (p. 55). London: Routledge.

[13]Hoebel, E. A. (1954). *The law of primitive man: A study in comparative legal dynamics* (p. 28). Cambridge, MA: Harvard University Press.

Having a song duel is the traditional approach to dispute resolution among the Inuit of northern Canada.

cultural comparison, and for this, **law** is adequately characterized as formal rules of conduct that, when violated, lead to negative sanctions.

Functions of Law

In Hoebel's 1954 book, *The Law of Primitive Man,* he described the generous sharing of private property as a fundamental principle in traditional Cheyenne Indian culture. However, he wrote, this principle shifted after some men assumed the privilege of borrowing other men's horses without bothering to obtain permission. When Wolf Lies Down complained of such unauthorized borrowing to the members of the Elk Soldier Society, the Elk Soldiers not only had his horse returned to him but also secured an award for damages from the offender. The Elk Soldiers then announced that, to avoid such difficulties in the future, horses no longer could be borrowed without permission. Furthermore, they declared their intention to retrieve any such property and whip anyone who resisted the return of improperly borrowed goods.

This case illustrates three basic functions of law. First, it defines relationships among society's members

and marks out proper behavior under specified circumstances. Knowledge of the law permits each person to know his or her rights and duties with respect to every other member of society. Second, law allocates the authority to employ coercion in the enforcement of sanctions. In societies with centralized political systems, such authority is generally vested in the government and its judiciary system. In societies that lack centralized political control, the authority to employ force may be allocated directly to the injured party. Third, law functions to redefine social relations and to ensure social flexibility. As new situations arise, law must determine whether old rules and assumptions retain their validity and to what extent they must be altered. Law, if it is to operate efficiently, must allow room for change.

In practice, law is never as neat as a written description about it. In any given society, people are usually members of various subgroups—and fall under the varied dictates of these diverse groups. For example, among the Kapauku of Papua New Guinea, discussed earlier in this chapter, each individual is simultaneously a member of a family, a household, a sublineage, and a confederacy—and is subject to all the (sometimes conflicting) rules and regulations of each. Furthermore, the power to employ sanctions may vary from level to level within a given society. Thus, the head of a Kapauku household in Papua New Guinea may punish a household member by slapping or beating, but the authority to confiscate prop-

law Formal rules of conduct that, when violated, effectuate negative sanctions.

erty is vested exclusively in the headman of the lineage. Analogous distinctions exist in the United States among municipal, state, and federal jurisdictions. The complexity of legal jurisdiction within each society makes it difficult to generalize about law.

Crime

As we have observed, an important function of negative sanctions, legal or otherwise, is to discourage the breach of social norms. A person contemplating theft is aware of the possibility of being caught and punished. Yet, even in the face of severe sanctions, individuals in every society sometimes violate the norms and subject themselves to the consequences of their behavior.

In Western societies a clear distinction is made between offenses against the state and offenses against an individual. However, in non-state societies such as bands and tribes, all offenses are viewed as transgressions against individuals or kin-groups (families, lineages, clans, and so on).

Disputes between individuals or kin-groups may seriously disrupt the social order, especially in small groups where the number of disputants, though small in absolute numbers, may be a large percentage of the total population. For example, although the Inuit traditionally have no effective domestic or economic unit beyond the family, a dispute between two people will interfere with the ability of members of separate families to come to one another's aid when necessary and is consequently a matter of wider social concern. The goal of judicial proceedings in such instances is restoring social harmony rather than punishing an offender. When distinguishing between offenses of concern to the community as a whole and those of concern only to a few individuals, we may refer to them as *collective* or *personal*.

Basically, disputes are settled in one of two ways. First, disputing parties may, through argument and compromise, voluntarily arrive at a mutually satisfactory agreement. This form of settlement is referred to as **negotiation** or, if it involves the assistance of an unbiased third party, **mediation.** In bands and tribes a third party mediator has no coercive power and thus cannot force disputants to abide by such a decision, but as a person who commands great personal respect, the mediator frequently may help bring about a settlement.

Second, in chiefdoms and states, an authorized third party may issue a binding decision that the disputing parties will be compelled to respect. This process is referred to as **adjudication.** The difference between mediation and adjudication is basically a difference in authorization. In a dispute settled by adjudication, the disputing parties present their positions as compellingly as they can, but they do not participate in the ultimate decision making.

Although the adjudication process is not universally characteristic, every society employs some form of negotiation to settle disputes. Often negotiation acts as a prerequisite or an alternative to adjudication. For example, in the resolution of U.S. labor disputes, striking workers may first negotiate with management, often with the mediation of a third party. If the state decides the strike constitutes a threat to the public welfare, the disputing parties may be forced to submit to adjudication. In this case, the responsibility for resolving the dispute is transferred to a presumably impartial judge.

The judge's work is difficult and complex. In addition to sifting through evidence presented, he or she must consider a wide range of norms, values, and earlier rulings to arrive at a decision intended to be considered just not only by the disputing parties but by the public and other judges as well.

In many politically centralized societies, incorruptible supernatural, or at least nonhuman, powers are thought to make judgments through a "trial by ordeal." Among the Kpelle of Liberia, for example, when guilt is in doubt an "ordeal operator" licensed by the government may apply a hot knife to a suspect's leg. If the leg is burned, the suspect is guilty; if not, innocence is assumed. But the operator does not merely heat the knife and apply it. After massaging the suspect's legs and determining the knife is hot enough, the operator then strokes his own leg with it without being burned, demonstrating that the innocent will escape injury. The knife is then applied to the suspect.

Up to this point—consciously or unconsciously—the operator has read the suspect's nonverbal cues: gestures, the degree of muscular tension, amount of perspiration, and so forth. From this the operator can judge whether or not the accused is showing so much anxiety as to indicate probable guilt; in effect, a psychological stress evaluation has been made. As the knife is applied, it is manipulated to either burn or not burn the suspect, once this judgment has been made. The operator does this manipulation easily by controlling how long the knife is in the fire, as well as the pressure and angle at which it is pressed against the leg.[14]

Similar to this is the use of the lie detector (polygraph) in the United States, although the guiding ideol-

---

[14]Gibbs, J. L., Jr. (1983). [Interview]. *Faces of culture: Program 18.* Fountain Valley, CA: Coast Telecourses.

negotiation The use of direct argument and compromise by the parties to a dispute to arrive voluntarily at a mutually satisfactory agreement.
mediation Settlement of a dispute through negotiation assisted by an unbiased third party.
adjudication Mediation with an unbiased third party making the ultimate decision.

ogy is scientific rather than supernaturalistic. Nevertheless, an incorruptible nonhuman agency is thought to establish who is lying and who is not, whereas in reality the polygraph operator cannot just "read" the needles of the machine. He or she must judge whether or not they are registering a high level of anxiety brought on by the testing situation, as opposed to the stress of guilt. Thus, the polygraph operator has much in common with the Kpelle ordeal operator.

Restorative Justice and Conflict Resolution

Punitive justice, such as imprisonment, may be the most common approach to justice in North America, but it has not proven to be an effective way of changing criminal behavior. There are cultural alternatives.

For a number of years, Native American communities in Canada urged their federal government to reform justice services to make them more consistent with indigenous values and traditions. In 1999 Canada's Supreme Court amended sentencing law in the country's Criminal Code to include the following principle: "All available sanctions other than imprisonment that are reasonable in the circumstances should be considered for all offenders, with particular attention to the circumstances of aboriginal offenders."[15]

Native communities have pressed especially for restorative justice techniques such as the Talking Circle, traditionally used by Native American groups. For this, parties involved in a conflict come together in a circle with equal opportunity to express their views—one at a time, free of interruption. Usually, a "talking stick" (or eagle feather or some other symbolic tool) is held by whoever is speaking to signal that she or he has the right to talk at that moment and others have the responsibility to listen.

In the United States, over the past three decades there has been significant movement away from the courts in favor of outside negotiation and mediation to resolve a wide variety of disputes. Many jurists see this as a means to clear overloaded court dockets so as to concentrate on more important cases. A correlate of this move is a change in ideology, elevating order and harmony to positive values and replacing open coercion (seen as undemocratic) with control through persuasion.

In the abstract, this seems like a good idea and suggests a return to a system of cultural control characteristic of band and tribal societies. However, a crucial difference exists. In tribal and band societies, agreement is less likely to be coercive because all concerned individuals can negotiate and mediate on relatively equal terms. The

United States, by contrast, has great disparities in power, and evidence indicates that it is the stronger parties that prefer mediation and negotiation.

As anthropologist Laura Nader points out, there is now less emphasis on justice and concern with causes of disputes than on smoothing things over in ways that tend to be pacifying and restrictive—an emphasis that produces order of a repressive sort.[16] That said, leaders in the field of dispute resolution in the United States and other parts of the industrial and postindustrial world are finding effective ways to bring about balanced solutions to conflict. An example of this appears in the Anthropology Applied feature.

VIOLENT CONFLICT AND WARFARE

Although the regulation of internal affairs is an important function of any political system, it is by no means the sole function. Another is the management of external affairs—relations not just among different states but among different bands, lineages, clans, or whatever the largest autonomous political unit may be. And just as the threatened or actual use of force may be used to maintain order within a society, it also may be used in the conduct of external affairs.

Humans have a horrific track record when it comes to violence. Far more lethal than spontaneous and individual outbursts of aggression, organized violence in the form of war is responsible for enormous suffering and deliberate destruction of life and property. In the past 5,000 years or so, some 14,000 wars have been fought, resulting in many hundreds of millions of casualties.

Generally, we may distinguish among different motives, objectives, methods, and scales of warfare as organized violence. For instance, some societies engage in defensive wars only and avoid armed confrontations with others unless seriously threatened or actually attacked. Others initiate aggressive wars to pursue particular strategic objectives, including material benefits in the form of precious resources such as slaves, gold, or oil, as well as territorial expansion or control over trade routes. In some cultures, aggressive wars are waged for ideological reasons, such as spreading one's own worldview or religion and defeating "evil" ideas or heresies elsewhere.

The scope of violent conflict is wide, ranging from individual fights, local feuds, and raids to formally declared international wars fought by professional armed forces. In addition, we may distinguish among various civil wars (in which armies from different geographic

---

[15]Criminal Code of Canada, s.718.2(e).

[16]Nader, L. (1997). Controlling processes: Tracing the dynamic components of power. *Current Anthropology 38*, 714–715.

Anthropology Applied

Dispute Resolution and the Anthropologist ▪ William Ury

In an era when the consequences of violent approaches to dispute resolution are more far-reaching than ever, conflict management is of growing importance. A world leader in this profession is anthropologist William L. Ury, an independent negotiations specialist.

In his first year at graduate school, Ury began looking for a way to apply anthropology to practical problems, including conflicts of all dimensions. He wrote a paper about the role of anthropology in peacemaking and on a whim sent it to Roger Fisher, a law professor noted for his work in negotiation and world affairs. Fisher, in turn, invited the young graduate student to co-author a kind of how-to book for international mediators. The book they researched and wrote together turned out to have a far wider audience, for it presented basic principles of negotiation that could be applied to household spats, management–employee conflicts, or international crises. Titled *Getting to Yes: Negotiating Agreement Without Giving In* (1981), it sold millions of copies, was translated into twenty-one languages, and earned the nickname "negotiator's bible."

While working on *Getting to Yes,* Ury and Fisher co-founded the Program on Negotiation (PON) at Harvard Law School, pulling together an interdisciplinary group of academics interested in new approaches to and applications of the negotiation process. Today this applied research center is a multiuniversity consortium that trains mediators, businesspeople, and government officials in negotiation skills. It has four key goals: (1) design, implement, and evaluate better dispute resolution practices; (2) promote collaboration among practitioners and

© Jay Dickman

scholars; (3) develop education programs and materials for instruction in negotiation and dispute resolution; (4) increase public awareness and understanding of successful conflict resolution efforts.

In 1982, Ury earned his doctorate in anthropology from Harvard with a dissertation titled *Talk Out or Walk Out: The Role and Control of Conflict in a Kentucky Coal Mine.* Afterward, he taught for several years while maintaining a leadership role at PON. In particular, he devoted himself to PON's Global Negotiation Project (initially known as the Project on Avoiding War). Today, having left his teaching post at Harvard, Ury continues to serve as director of the Global Negotiation Project, writing, consulting, and running regular workshops on dealing with difficult people and situations.

Utilizing a cross-cultural perspective sharpened through years of anthropo-

logical research, he specializes in ethnic and secessionist disputes, including those between white and black South Africans, Serbs and Croats, Turks and Kurds, Catholics and Protestants in Northern Ireland, and Russians and Chechens in the former Soviet Union.

Among the most effective tools in Ury's applied anthropology work are his books on dispute resolution. In 1993 he wrote *Getting Past No: Negotiating Your Way from Confrontation,* which explores ways to reach out to hostile parties who are not interested in negotiation. His 1999 book, *Getting to Peace: Transforming Conflict at Home, at Work, and in the World,* examines what he calls the "third side," which is the role that the surrounding community can play in preventing, resolving, and containing destructive conflict between two parties.[a]

His 2002 edited volume *Must We Fight?* challenges entrenched ideas that violence and war are inevitable and presents convincing evidence that human beings have as much inherent potential for cooperation and co-existence as they do for violent conflict. The key point in this book is that violence is a choice. In Ury's words, "Conflict is not going to end, but violence can."[b]

What Ury and others in this field are doing is helping create a culture of negotiation in a world where adversarial, win–lose attitudes are out of step with the increasingly interdependent relations between people.

---

[a]Pease, T. (2000, Spring). Taking the third side. *Andover Bulletin.*
[b]Ury, W. (2002, Winter). A global immune system. *Andover Bulletin;* see also www.PON.harvard.edu and www.thirdside.org.

---

sections, ethnic or religious groups, or political parties within the same state are pitted against each other) and low-intensity guerrilla warfare involving small-scale hit-and-run tactical operations instead of pitched battles.

Why do wars occur? Some argue that males of the human species are naturally aggressive (see this chapter's Biocultural Connection). As evidence, they point to aggressive group behavior exhibited by chimpanzees in Tanzania where researchers observed one group sys-

tematically destroy another and take over their territory. Also, they cite the behavior of people such as the Yanomami Indians who range on either side of the border between Brazil and Venezuela. These tropical horticulturalists and foragers have been described as living in a chronic state of war, and some scientists suggest this exemplifies the way all humans once behaved. However, as discussed in earlier chapters, warfare among humans, as well as aggressive group behavior among apes, may be

VISUAL COUNTERPOINT

Public displays of human skulls may serve to commemorate victory over enemies slain in battle or sacrificed as war captives—as depicted on this stone wall in the ancient Maya city of Chichen Itza in southeastern Mexico. Such displays may also serve as a gruesome monument of organized violence as in this Cambodian map made of skulls belonging to victims of the ruthless Khmer Rouge regime that claimed the lives of some 1.7 million innocent Cambodians in the 1970s.

situation specific rather than an unavoidable expression of biological predisposition.

This is not to say that violence was unknown among ancient humans. The occasional discovery of stone spear points embedded in human skeletons, such as that of a more than 9,000-year-old man found in Kennewick in the northwestern United States or even older ones from the Grimaldi caves in Italy prove otherwise. Nevertheless, it is clear that war is not a universal phenomenon, for in various parts of the world there are societies that do not practice warfare as we know it. Examples include people as diverse as the Ju/'hoansi Bushmen and pygmy peoples of southern Africa, the Arapesh of New Guinea, and the Jain of India, as well as the Amish of North America. Among societies that do practice warfare, levels of violence may differ dramatically.

We have ample reason to suppose that war has become a problem only in the last 10,000 years, since the invention of food-production techniques and especially since the formation of centralized states 5,000 years ago. It has reached crisis proportions in the past 200 years, with the invention of modern weaponry and increased direction of violence against civilian populations. In contemporary warfare, casualties not just of civilians but also of *children* far outnumber those of soldiers. Thus, war is not so much an age-old problem as it is a relatively recent one.

Among food foragers, with their uncentralized political systems, violence may erupt sporadically, but warfare was all but unknown until recent times. There are several reasons for this. First of all, since territorial boundaries and membership among food-foraging bands are usually fluid and loosely defined, a man who hunts with one band today may hunt with a neighboring band next month. This renders warfare impractical.

So, too, does the systematic exchange of marriage partners among food-foraging groups, which makes it likely that someone in each band will have a sister, a brother, or a cousin in a neighboring band. Moreover, the absence of a food surplus among foragers makes prolonged combat difficult. Finally, a worldview in which people perceive themselves as part of the natural world rather than superior to it tends to work against exploitation of other people. In sum, where populations are small and see themselves as part of the natural world, where food surpluses are absent, property ownership minimal, and no state organization exists, the likelihood of organized violence by one group against another is small.[17]

Despite the traditional view of the gardener or farmer as a gentle tiller of the soil, it is among such people, along with pastoralists, that warfare becomes prominent. One reason may be that food-producing peoples have a more exploitative worldview than do food foragers. Another is that they are far more prone to population growth than are food foragers, whose numbers are generally maintained well below carrying capacity. This population growth, if unchecked, can lead to resource depletion, one solution to which may be seizure of some other people's resources.

In addition, the commitment to a fixed piece of land inherent in farming makes such societies somewhat less

---

[17]Knauft, B. M. (1991). Violence and sociality in human evolution. *Current Anthropology 32*, 391–409.

Biocultural Connection

Sex, Gender, and Human Violence

At the start of the 21st century, war and violence are no longer the strictly male domains that they were in many societies in the past. War has become embedded in civilian life in many parts of the world and impacts the daily lives of women and children. Moreover, women now serve in the military forces of several states, although their participation in combat is often limited. Some female soldiers in the United States argue that gender should not limit their participation in combat as they consider themselves as strong, capable, and well trained as their male counterparts. Others believe that biologically based sex differences make war a particularly male domain.

Scientists have long argued that males are more suited to combat because natural selection has made them on average larger and stronger than females. This idea, known as sexual selection, was first put forth by Darwin in the 19th century. At that time he proposed that the physical specializations of males in animal species—such as horns, vibrant plumage, and, in the case of humans, intelligence and tool use—demonstrate selection acting upon males to aid in the competition for mates. In these scenarios, male reproductive success is thought to be optimized through a strategy of "spreading seed"—in other words, by being sexually active with as many females as possible.

Females, on the other hand, are considered gatekeepers who optimize their reproductive success through car-

ing for individual offspring. According to this theory of sexual selection, in species where male–male competition is high, males will be considerably larger than females, and aggression will serve males well. In monogamous species, males and females will be of similar sizes.

Primatologist Richard Wrangham has taken the idea of sexual selection even further. In his book *Demonic Males,* he explores the idea that both male aggression and patriarchy have an evolutionary basis. He states that humans, like our close cousins the chimpanzees, are "party gang" species characterized by strong bonds among groups of males who have dominion over an expandable territory. These features "suffice to account for natural selection's ugly legacy, the tendency to look for killing opportunities when hostile neighbors meet."[a] Violence in turn generates a male-dominated social order: "Patriarchy comes from biology in the sense that it emerges from men's temperaments out of their evolutionarily derived efforts to control women and at the same time have solidarity with fellow males in competition against outsiders."[b] While Wrangham allows that evolutionary forces have shaped women as well, he suggests that females' evolutionary interests

cannot be met without cooperation with males.

Feminist scholars have pointed out that these scientific models are "gendered" in that they incorporate the gender norms derived from the scientists' culture. Darwin's original model of sexual selection incorporated the Victorian gender norms of the passive female and active male. U.S. primatologist Laura Fedigan suggests that in Darwinian models women evolved in positive directions only by a "coat tails" process whereby females were "pulled along" toward improved biological states by virtue of the progress of the genes they shared with males.[c] Wrangham's more recent *Demonic Males* theory is similarly shaped by culture. It incorporates the dominant world order (military states) and the gender norms (aggressive males) it values. In both cases, the putatively scientific theory has created a natural basis for a series of social conventions.

This does not mean that biological differences between the sexes cannot be studied in the natural world. Instead, scientists studying sex differences must be especially aware of how they may project cultural beliefs onto nature. Meanwhile, the attitudes of some women soldiers continue to challenge generalizations regarding "military specialization" by gender.

[a]Wrangham, R., & Peterson, D. (1996). *Demonic males* (p. 168). Boston: Houghton Mifflin.
[b]Wrangham, R., & Peterson, D. (1996). *Demonic males* (p. 125). Boston: Houghton Mifflin.

[c]Fedigan, L. M. (1986). The changing role of women in models of human evolution. *Annual Review of Anthropology 15,* 25–66.

---

fluid in their membership than those of food foragers. Instead of marrying distantly, farmers marry locally, depriving them of long-distance kin networks. In rigidly matrilocal or patrilocal societies, each new generation is bound to the same territory, no matter how small it may be or how large the group trying to live within it.

The availability of unoccupied lands may not serve as a sufficient detriment to the outbreak of war. Among swidden farmers, for example, competition for land cleared of old growth forest frequently leads to hostility and armed conflict. The centralization of political control and the possession of valuable property among farming people provide many more stimuli for warfare.

It is among such peoples, especially those organized into states, where the violence of warfare is most apt to result in indiscriminate killing. This development has reached its peak in modern states. Indeed, much (but not all) of the warfare that has been observed in recent stateless societies (so-called tribal warfare) has been induced by states as a reaction to colonial expansion.[18]

For example, although warfare was certainly present in northeastern America before the arrival of Europeans, intergroup conflicts began to increase and intensify in

---

[18]Whitehead, N. L., & Ferguson, R. B. (1993, November). Deceptive stereotypes about tribal warfare. *Chronicle of Higher Education,* A48.

© Dan Connell/The Image Works

Many armies around the world recruit children. Today, there are more than 250,000 child soldiers, many as young as 12 years old. Among them are these boys training to be guerrillas in Sahel, Eritrea.

the 16th century as a direct consequence of dispossession of Indian lands and the huge demand in Europe for precious furs, especially beaver ("soft gold"). Competition over game-rich territories, intensified by the availability of muskets and other deadly European weapons, led to violence. Alcohol introduced by Europeans as a trade commodity no doubt fueled the aggression, and each killing called for revenge. All of this triggered a cycle of bloody warfare commonly referred to as the Beaver Wars, involving virtually all native groups—food foragers and horticulturalists alike—from Cape Breton Island down to Chesapeake Bay and as far inland as the Great Lakes. These wars—periodic vicious outbursts—continued throughout much of the 17th century.[19]

Among the many American Indian groups involved in the Beaver Wars were the Iroquoian nations—Mohawk, Oneida, Onondaga, Cayuga, and Seneca. Before Europeans landed on their shores, these neighboring groups had resolved to end warfare among themselves by creating an alliance and directing their aggressive activities against outsiders. In this way the famous Iroquois Confederacy came into being.

Warring frequently against their immediate and more distant neighbors, members of the confederacy gained dominance and forced their victims to acknowledge Iroquoian superiority. The relation between victim and victor, however, was not outright subordination. Imposed payment of tribute purchased "protection" from the Iroquois. The price of protection went further than this, though; it included constant and public ceremonial

deference to the Iroquois, free passage for their war parties through the subordinate group's country, and the contribution of young men to Iroquoian war parties.

An instructive comparison can be made between the Iroquois nations and European Christians. In the year 1095 the Roman Catholic Pope Urban II launched the first crusade ("War of the Cross"), with a speech urging the Christian nobles of Europe to end their ceaseless wars against each other by directing their hostilities toward Muslim Turks and Arabs in the Middle East, who Europeans saw as infidels. In the same speech the pope also alluded to the economic benefits to be realized by seizing the resources of the "infidels." Although it is clear that the Crusades were motivated by more than religious ideology, they were justified as a holy war to liberate Jerusalem and the Holy Land from Muslims. Their success was limited, and twenty years after the ninth and final crusade of 1271 to 1272, the last Christian stronghold in Palestine surrendered to a Muslim army.

Within the next few centuries, however, Europe's Christian powers turned their attention to state building and colonial expansion in other parts of the world. Proceeding in concert with this growth and outward expansion was the development of the technology and organization of warfare. With the emergence of states (not just in Europe but in other parts of the world as well) has come a dramatic increase in the scale of warfare. Perhaps this is not surprising, given the state's acceptance of force as a legitimate tool for regulating human affairs and its ability to organize large numbers of people.

Consider, for example, the Aztec state in the central Mexican highlands, which engaged in continuous warfare from the mid-1400s until its demise in the early

[19]Prins, H. E. L. (1996). *The Mi'kmaq: Resistance, accommodation, and cultural survival* (p. 106). Orlando: Harcourt Brace.

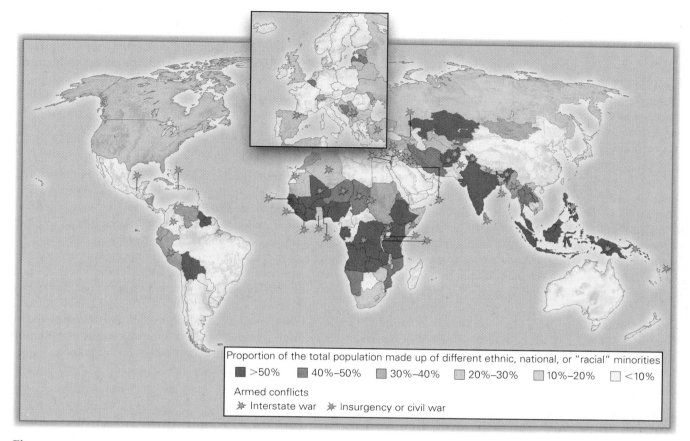

Figure 12.3

In multinational states, warfare is common as one nationality suppresses others within the country.

1520s. By way of battle, the state collected tribute and achieved regional dominance. Moreover, by waging war against their neighbors, Aztecs obtained prisoners to use as offerings for gods that they believed required human sacrifice to maintain the cosmic order: "The warrior slated for sacrifice was a *teomiqui,* 'he who dies in godlike fashion,' and would feed the sun so that it might shine upon the world and keep it in motion."[20]

Among Aztecs, this worldview justified, even sanctified, perpetual aggression. In fact, according to the noted anthropologist Eric Wolf, priests bearing the images of the Aztec war god Huitilopochtli and other deities walked ahead of the army and gave the signal to commence combat by lighting a fire and blowing on shell trumpets. The victory that followed, Wolf wrote, "always had the same results: long lines of captives, wooden collars about their necks, made the long journey to Tenochtitlán to be offered upon the altars of the gods."[21] Several thousand captives could be sacrificed after a

military campaign, and within a single year as many as 20,000 may have been offered to the gods in that capital city of the Aztec state.

This Aztec example, as well as that of the Christian Crusades, shows that ideological motivations and justifications for war are embedded in a society's worldview—the collective body of ideas that members of a culture generally share concerning the ultimate shape and substance of their reality. We will discuss other aspects of worldview in the following chapter, which focuses on religion and the supernatural.

Currently, there are several dozen wars going on in the world, often resulting in massive killing fields (Figure 12.3). And many contemporary wars are not between states but often occur within countries where the government is either corrupt, ineffective, or without popular support. Notably, many armies around the world recruit not only men, but also women and children. Today, more than 250,000 child soldiers, many as young as 12 years old, are participating in armed conflicts around the world.[22]

---

[20]Keen, B. (1971). *The Aztec image in Western thought* (p. 13). New Brunswick, NJ: Rutgers University Press.

[21]Wolf, E. R. (1999). *Envisioning power: Ideologies of dominance and crisis* (p. 263). Berkeley: University of California Press.

[22]Study estimates 250,000 active child soldiers. (2006, July 26). Associated Press.

The following examples offer some specific data. Between 1975 and 1979, Khmer Rouge soldiers in Cambodia murdered 1.7 million fellow citizens, or 20 percent of that country's population. In the 1990s, between 2 and 3 million died due to warfare in the southern Sudan. Another 5 million died in the recent war in Congo (1998–2003), which involved armies from a handful of neighboring states as well.

Moreover, the Middle East is in political turmoil, especially since the U.S. invasion of Iraq's oil-rich dictatorship in 2003, which has plunged that multi-ethnic country into violent chaos. In addition to many tens of thousands of fatalities, the vast majority of whom are Iraqi civilians, there is also massive destruction of the country's infrastructure. In the summer of 2006, Israel used its air force, army, and navy to fight an enemy Hezbollah (Shia Islamist) force on its northern border. Retaliating against a raid in which guerrillas kidnapped two Israeli soldiers, Israel staged a full-force invasion of the multi-ethnic country of Lebanon. Within a month of punishing warfare, much of which consisted of bombs, missiles, and small rockets, over a million people on both sides of the border were made refugees. The vast majority of fatalities in this war, which the state of Israel considers part of the global war against terror, were civilians; much of Lebanon's infrastructure—bridges, harbors, airports, roads, and other structures that make civilized life possible—was destroyed, along with countless homes.

Beyond these wars there are numerous so-called low-intensity wars involving guerrilla organizations, rebel armies, resistance movements, terrorist cells, and a host of other armed groups engaged in violent conflict with official state-controlled armed forces. Every year, confrontations result in hundreds of hot spots and violent flashpoints, most of which are never reported in Western news media.[23]

As the above examples show, the causes of warfare are complex, involving economic, political, and ideological factors. The challenge of eliminating human warfare has never been greater than it is in today's world—nor has the cost of *not* finding a way to do so. In the age of globalization, a new category—crimes against humanity—has been adopted by most countries in order to punish those responsible for mass murder; these crimes may be prosecuted in an international court of justice.

---

[23]icasualties.org.

Questions for Reflection

1. In many states, political power is concentrated in the hands of a wealthy elite—the have-lots. Imagine you belong to a group that is losing its traditional freedom or quality of life due to government policies but feel that your political representatives are unwilling or unable to defend your interests. Would you challenge the state authorities, as the Japanese demonstrators did in the chapter opening photo, or accept your degenerating condition without public protest?

2. Given the basic definition of politics presented in the beginning of this chapter, why do you think that power in egalitarian societies plays a relatively insignificant role?

3. If political organization functions to impose or maintain order and to resolve conflicts, why do you think that a government in a country such as yours is so interested in legitimizing its power? What happens when a government loses such legitimacy?

4. Which nationalities or ethnic groups do you know that are dominant, and which can you identify that are in a minority position or are repressed? What is the basis for this inequality?

5. When your own government declares war against another country, on which basis does it seek to justify its decision to send soldiers into battle? Do you know the death ratio of noncombatants to soldiers in your country's most recent war?

Suggested Readings

Cheater, A. (2005). *The anthropology of power*. London: Routledge.

Presents case studies from a wide range of societies to examine the issues surrounding power and empowerment and to question whether power is actually being transferred to the powerless. Explores how traditionally disempowered groups gain influence in postcolonial and multicultural settings. Surveys the relationships between empowerment and economic development, gender, and environmentalism.

Gledhill, J. (2000). *Power and its disguises: Anthropological perspectives on politics* (2nd ed.). Boulder, CO: Pluto Press.

Exploring the power relations that shape the global order, the author discusses the politics of agrarian civilizations and societies without indigenous states and then turns to the politics of domination and resistance within the colonial context, followed by an examination of contemporary politics of Africa, Asia, and Latin America.

Kertzer, D. I. (1989). *Ritual, politics, and power*. New Haven, CT: Yale University Press.

Using numerous examples from traditional and modern societies and writing in clear accessible prose, the author argues that political symbols manifested through rituals explain much of the political life of modern nations, contrary to the usual rational, utilitarian, and interest-group explanations. He discusses how elites use rituals to support the existing order, while revolutionaries use them to replace it.

Nader, L. (Ed.) (1997). *Law in culture and society*. Berkeley: University of California Press.

Classic anthology of studies on the process, structure, comparison, and perception of the law—reflecting the shift from what law is to what law does.

Ury, W. (Ed.). (2002). *Must we fight? From the battlefield to the schoolyard—A new perspective on violent conflict and its prevention*. Hoboken, NJ: Jossey-Bass.

This fresh exploration of the question of whether violence and war are inevitable presents evidence from leading anthropologists and others that human beings have as much inherent potential for cooperation and coexistence as they do for violent conflict.

Vincent, J. (2002). *The anthropology of politics: A reader in ethnography, theory, and critique*. Boston: Blackwell.

This sweeping historical and theoretical introduction to the field features readings from noted anthropologists past and present, enriched by Vincent's insightful headnotes.

Whitehead, N., & Ferguson, R. B. (Eds.) (1992). *War in the tribal zone*. Santa Fe: School of American Research Press.

The central point of this book is that the transformation and intensification of war, as well as the formation of tribes, result from complex interaction in the "tribal zone" that begins where centralized authority makes contact with stateless peo-ple it does not rule. In such zones, newly introduced plants, animals, diseases, and technologies often spread widely, even before colonizers appear. These and other changes disrupt existing social and political relationships, fostering new alliances and creating conflicts.

Thomson Audio Study Products

 Enjoy the MP3-ready Audio Lecture Overviews for each chapter and a comprehensive audio glossary of key terms for quick study and review. Whether walking to class, doing laundry, or studying at your desk, you now have the freedom to choose when, where, and how you interact with your audio-based educational media. See the preface for information on how to access this on-the-go study and review tool.

The Anthropology Resource Center

www.thomsonedu.com/anthropology
The Anthropology Resource Center provides extended learning materials to reinforce your understanding of key concepts in the four fields of anthropology. For each of the four fields, the Resource Center includes dynamic exercises including video exercises, map exercises, simulations, and "Meet the Scientists" interviews, as well as critical thinking questions that can be assigned and e-mailed to instructors. The Resource Center also provides breaking news in anthropology and interesting material on applied anthropology to help you link what you are learning to the world around you.

13 Spirituality, Religion, and the Supernatural

c-print, copyright Kuo-ming Sung

CHALLENGE ISSUE

As self-aware and self-reflecting beings, humans face challenges beyond biological survival. We face emotional and intellectual ones born of the need to make sense of our place in the universe. Among other fundamental concerns, each of us wrestles with basic existential questions about our own fate, life, and death. More broadly, we puzzle over human origin and destiny and truly big questions about time and space, the earth, and the universe. Throughout time and across the globe, humans have creatively addressed these ponderings and worked out answers articulated in sacred narratives and associated ceremonies, rituals, and other cultural forms of religious or spiritual expression. Here we see a Buddhist monk in crimson red robes walking alongside a row of prayer wheels in a temple gallery—spinning the wheels on the wall (and perhaps in his soul) as he goes.

What Are Religion and Spirituality?

Religion and spirituality form part of a cultural system's superstructure, which comprises a society's worldview. Religion is an organized system of ideas about spiritual reality, or the supernatural, along with associated beliefs and ceremonial practices. Spirituality, which also concerns the supernatural, involves less formalized spiritual beliefs and practices and is often individual rather than collective. Both guide humans in their attempts to give meaning to the world and their place in it and to deal with problems that defy ordinary explanation or solution through direct means. To overcome these challenges, people appeal to, or seek to influence and even manipulate, spiritual or supernatural beings and powers.

What Are the Identifying Features of Religion and Spirituality?

Religion (and spiritual practices in general) consists of various beliefs and rituals—prayers, songs, dances, offerings, and sacrifices—that people use to interpret, appeal to, and manipulate supernatural beings and powers to their advantage. These beings and powers may consist of gods and goddesses, ancestral and other spirits, or impersonal powers, either by themselves or in various combinations. In all societies certain individuals are especially skilled at dealing with these beings and powers and assist other members of society in their ritual activities. A body of myths rationalizes or explains the system in a manner consistent with people's experience in the world in which they live.

What Functions Do Religion and Spirituality Serve?

Whether or not a particular religion accomplishes what people believe it does, all religions serve a number of important emotional, psychological, and social functions. They reduce anxiety by explaining the unknown and offer comfort with the belief that supernatural aid is available in times of crisis. They provide notions of right and wrong, setting precedents for acceptable behavior and transferring the burden of decision making from individuals to supernatural powers. Through ritual, religion may be used to enhance the learning of oral traditions. Finally, religion plays an important role in maintaining social solidarity. Spirituality also serves emotional, psychological, and social functions, but it tends to be fitted to more personal preferences, and its form and expression are often uniquely creative.

From an anthropological point of view, spirituality and religion are part of a cultural system's superstructure, earlier defined as the collective body of ideas, beliefs, and values by which a group of people makes sense of the world and their place in it. In their studies of different religious and spiritual beliefs and practices, anthropologists seek to remain unbiased regarding any particular cultural tradition. Instead, they examine spirituality and religion in terms of a society's **worldview**— the collective body of ideas that members of a culture generally share concerning the ultimate shape and substance of their reality.

Among people in all cultures, particular spiritual or religious beliefs and practices fulfill numerous social and psychological needs, such as the need to confront and explain suffering and death. Religion gives meaning to individual and group life, drawing power from spiritual forces or beings and offering continuity of existence beyond death. It can provide the path by which people transcend their burdensome and mortal existence and attain, if only momentarily, spiritual hope and relief.

THOMSON AUDIO STUDY PRODUCTS
Take advantage of the MP3-ready Audio Lecture Overviews and comprehensive audio glossary of key terms for each chapter. See the preface for information on how to access this on-the-go study and review tool.

Religion and spirituality also serve an array of social needs. A traditional religion reinforces group norms, provides moral sanctions for individual conduct, and furnishes the ideology of common purpose and values that support the well-being of the community. Also of note, people often turn to religion or spirituality in the hope of reaching a specific goal, such as the healing of physical, emotional, or social ills.

Perhaps it is because they fulfill these and numerous other social and psychological needs shared by humans across cultures that supernatural beliefs are universal. While recognizing that not all individuals believe in a supernatural force or entity, anthropologists know of no group of people anywhere on the face of the earth who, at any time over the past 100,000 years, has been without some manifestation of spirituality or religion. Not even in Russia and Albania, where atheism was the communist state dogma during much of the 20th century, did religion entirely disappear.

In the 19th century, the European intellectual tradition gave rise to the idea that modern science would ultimately replace religion by showing people the irrationality of their spiritual beliefs and practices. The expectation was that as valid scientific explanations became available, people would abandon their religious beliefs and rituals as superstitious myths and false worship. But to date, despite tremendous scientific advancements, that has not occurred. In fact, in many places, the opposite trend seems to prevail.

Far from causing religion's death, the growth of scientific knowledge in rapidly changing societies may have contributed to the continuing practice of religion in modern life by producing new anxieties and raising new questions about human existence. Although traditional, mainline Christian religions have shown some decline, nondenominational spirituality is on the rise. Also on the rise are fundamentalist religions, which often take a strong antiscience position. Examples include Islamic fundamentalism in countries such as Afghanistan, Algeria, and Iran; Jewish fundamentalism in Israel and the United States; and Hindu fundamentalism in India. Christian fundamentalism is represented in the dramatic growth of evangelical denominations in the United States, Central America, and sub-Saharan Africa.

Among the fastest-growing religious communities in the world are the indigenous churches of Africa. Over the last half century, the number of registered indigenous denominations in southern Africa alone has doubled from about 5,000 to about 10,000. There, it is estimated that more than half of Christian church members belong to indigenous churches, like the Amanazaretha Church founded by a Zulu prophet and popular among fellow Zulus in Natal.[1]

Within the United States, non-Christian religions are also growing. Islam (3 to 5 million followers—up from 527,000 in 1990), Buddhism (2 to 3 million—up from 401,000 in 1990), Hinduism (1.28 million—up from 227,000 in 1990), not to mention various new age options such as Wicca (a modern, nature-oriented religion that draws upon ancient western European and pre-Christian beliefs and now counting about 310,000 adherents).[2] Notably, just 16 percent of the adult population throughout the world claims to be nonreligious (Figure 13.1). This is not to say that those classified as nonreligious are all atheists, because this miscellaneous "negative" category actually includes many millions of individuals in dozens of countries who may reject or not fit under the label of any organized religion, but are metaphysically involved in creative arrangements of spiritual beliefs and practices of their own choosing.

worldview The collective body of ideas that members of a culture generally share concerning the ultimate shape and substance of their reality.

[1]Kunnie, J. (2003). Africa's fast growing indigenous churches. http://coh.arizona.edu/newandnotable/kunnie/kunnie.html

[2]U.S. Census 2000; www.adherents.com. See also *World Almanac*. (2004). New York: Press Publishing Co.; and pluralism.org (The Pluralism Project, Harvard University).

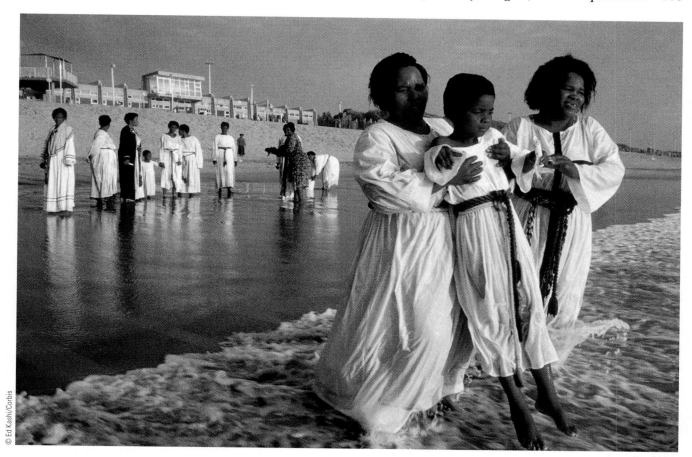

Members of the Church of Zion, an indigenous Christian church with a primarily Zulu congregation, perform a baptism in the Indian Ocean near Durban, South Africa. Over half of all Christian church members in South Africa belong to indigenous churches that combine some elements of their traditional African beliefs and rituals with those of Christianity.

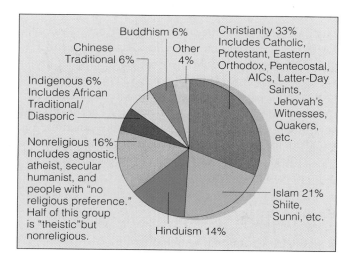

Figure 13.1

Major religions of the world and their percentage of all believers, 2005. (Note: Total adds up to more than 100 percent due to rounding and due to the upper-bound estimates used for each group.)

SOURCE: Adherents.com.

An inventory of the technological applications of modern science reveals the range of new anxieties facing our species. These include nuclear catastrophe, threats of chemical or biological terrorism, health hazards from pollution, and uneasiness about the consequences of developments in biotechnology such as cloning, production of new strains of genetically engineered organisms, ability to store human sperm and eggs for future fertilization, and manipulation of human DNA. On top of these, many people face emotional turmoil and psychological upheaval brought on by the breakup of traditional communities due to globalization, plus invasions of foreign ideas and values through mass media controlled by unfamiliar powers. In the face of these and other modern anxieties confronting the human species, religion offers social and psychological support.

The continuing strength of religion in the face of Western scientific rationalism clearly reveals that it remains a dominant and dynamic force in most contemporary societies. It is not the role of anthropologists to rank or pass judgment on the metaphysical truth of any particular religion or spiritual belief, but it is their task to show how each embodies a number of revealing facts about humans and the particular cultural system within which it is embedded.

THE ANTHROPOLOGICAL APPROACH TO RELIGION

Anthropologist Anthony F. C. Wallace defined religion as "a set of rituals, rationalized by myth, which mobilizes supernatural powers for the purpose of achieving or preventing transformations of state in man and nature."[3] Behind his definition lies a recognition that when people are unable to "fix" serious, anxiety-causing problems through technological or organizational means, they try to do so through manipulation of supernatural or spiritual beings and powers. This requires ritual, or "religion in action," which can be seen as a basic expression of religion. Its major functions are to reduce anxiety and boost confidence, thereby helping people cope with reality. It is this that gives religion survival value.

With these aspects in mind, we offer a somewhat simpler definition of **religion:** an organized system of ideas about the spiritual sphere or the supernatural, along with associated ceremonial practices by which people try to interpret and/or influence aspects of the universe otherwise beyond their control. Similar to religion, **spirituality** is also concerned with the sacred, as distinguished from material matters, but it is often individual rather than collective and does not require a distinctive format or traditional organization. Both are indicators that many aspects of the human experience are thought to be beyond scientific explanation.

Since no known culture, including those of modern industrial societies, has achieved complete certainty in controlling existing or future conditions and circumstances, spirituality and/or religion play a role in all known cultures. However, considerable variability exists here.

At one end of the spectrum are food-foraging peoples, whose technological ability to manipulate their en-

vironment is limited and who tend to see themselves as part of, rather than masters of, nature. This may be referred to as a *naturalistic worldview.* Among food foragers religion is likely to be inseparable from the rest of daily life. It also mirrors and confirms the egalitarian nature of social relations in their societies, in that individuals do not plead with high-ranking deities for aid the way members of stratified societies do.

At the other end of the spectrum is Western civilization, with its ideological commitment to overcoming problems through technological and organizational skills. Here religion is less a part of daily activities and is restricted to more specific occasions. Moreover, with its hierarchy of supernatural beings—for instance, God, and (in some religions) the angels, saints, or holy people—it reflects and confirms the stratified nature of the society in which it is embedded.

Religious activity may be less prominent in the lives of social elites, who may see themselves as more in control of their own destinies, than it is in the lives of peasants or members of lower classes. Among the latter, religion may afford some compensation for a dependent position in society. Yet religion is still important to elite members of society, in that it rationalizes the system in such a way that less advantaged people are not as likely to question the existing social order as they might otherwise be. With hope for a better existence after death, one may be more willing to put up with a disadvantaged position in life. Thus, religious beliefs serve to influence and perpetuate certain ideas about the relationships, if not actual relations, between different classes of people.

THE PRACTICE OF RELIGION

Much of religion's value comes from the activities called for by its prescriptions and rules. Participation in religious ceremonies may bring a sense of personal lift—a wave of reassurance, a feeling of overwhelming joy, and even a sense of moving into a trancelike state—or a feeling of closeness to fellow participants. The beliefs and ceremonial practices of religions vary considerably. Yet, rituals that seem bizarre to an outsider can be shown to serve the same basic social and psychological functions as do his or her own distinct rituals.

Supernatural Beings and Powerss

A hallmark of religion is belief in supernatural beings and forces. In attempting to control by religious means what cannot be controlled in other ways, humans turn to prayer, sacrifice, and other religious or spiritual rituals. These presuppose the existence of spiritual forces that can be tapped into, or spiritual beings interested in human affairs and available for aid.

---

[3]Wallace, A. F. C. (1966). *Religion: An anthropological view.* New York: Random House.

religion An organized system of ideas about the spiritual sphere or the supernatural, along with associated ceremonial practices by which people try to interpret and/or influence aspects of the universe otherwise beyond their control.

spirituality Concern with the sacred, as distinguished from material matters. In contrast to religion, spirituality is often individual rather than collective and does not require a distinctive format or traditional organization.

Beginning with spiritual beings, we may divide them into three categories: major deities (gods and goddesses), ancestral spirits, and other sorts of spirit beings. Although the variety of deities and spirits recognized by the world's cultures is tremendous, it is possible to make certain generalizations about them.

Gods and Goddesses

Gods and goddesses are the great and more remote beings. They are usually seen as controlling the universe. If more than one is recognized (known as **polytheism**), each has charge of a particular part of the universe. Such was the case with the gods and goddesses of ancient Greece: Zeus was lord of the sky, Poseidon was ruler of the sea, and Hades was lord of the underworld and ruler of the dead.

In addition to these three brothers, Greek mythology features a host of other deities, female as well as male, each similarly concerned with specific aspects of life and the universe. A **pantheon,** or the collection of gods and goddesses such as those of the Greeks, is common in non-Western states as well. Since states typically have grown through conquest, often their pantheons have expanded as local deities of conquered peoples were incorporated into the official state pantheon. Another frequent though not invariable feature of pantheons is the presence of a supreme deity, who may be all but totally ignored by humans. The Aztecs of the Mexican highlands, for instance, recognized a supreme pair to whom they paid little attention. After all, being so remote, this divine duo was unlikely to be interested in human affairs. The sensible practice, then, was to focus attention on less remote deities who were more directly concerned with human affairs.

Whether or not a people recognize gods, goddesses, or both has to do with how men and women relate to each other in everyday life. Generally speaking, societies that subordinate women to men define the supreme deity in masculine terms. For instance, in traditional Chris-

tian religions believers speak of God as a "father" who had a divine "son" but do not entertain thoughts of God as a "mother" nor of a divine "daughter." Such male-privileging religions developed in traditional societies with economies based upon the herding of animals or intensive agriculture carried out or controlled by men, who are dominating figures to their children.

Goddesses, by contrast, are likely to be most prominent in societies where women play a significant role in the economy, where women enjoy relative equality with men, and where men are less controlling figures to their wives and children. Such societies are most often those that depend upon crop cultivation carried out solely or mostly by women.

As an illustration, the early Israelites, like other pastoral nomadic groups of the Middle East, described their god in masculine, authoritarian terms. By contrast, goddesses played central roles in religious ritual and in the popular imagination of the region's farming peoples. Associated with these goddesses were concepts of light, fertility, and procreation. About 3,200 years ago, the Israelite tribes crossed the Jordan River and entered the land of Canaan (Palestine) where they began to till the soil and grow crops, requiring them to establish a new kind of relationship with the land. As they settled down and became sedentary, dependent upon rainfall and concerned about seasonal cycles and soil fertility (as the region's Canaanites already were), they adopted many of the region's already established Canaanite goddess cults. Although diametrically opposed to the original Israelite supreme male deity cult, worship of these Canaanite female deities appealed to the farming people's desire for security by seeking to control the forces of fertility.

polytheism Belief in several gods and/or goddesses (as contrasted with monotheism—belief in one god or goddess).
pantheon The several gods and goddesses of a people.

The patriarchal nature of many traditional Euramerican societies is expressed in its Judeo-Christian theology, in which a supreme male deity gives life to the first man, as depicted here on the ceiling of the Sistine Chapel in Rome. Only later is the first woman created from the first man.

© Visual Arts Library (London)/Alamy

Later on, when the Israelite tribes sought national unity in the face of a military threat by neighboring nations and when they ethnocentrically strengthened their own identity as a supernaturally "chosen people," the goddess cults lost out to followers of the old masculine tribal god. This ancient masculine-authoritarian concept of god has been perpetuated down to the present, not just in the Judaic tradition but also by most Christians and Muslims, whose religions stem from the old Israelite religion. As a consequence, this masculine-authoritarian model has played an important role in perpetuating a relationship between men and women in which the latter traditionally have been expected to submit to the rule of men at every level of Jewish, Christian, and Islamic society.

Ancestral Spirits

A belief in ancestral spirits is consistent with the widespread notion that human beings are made up of two closely intertwined parts: a physical body and some mental component or spiritual self. For example, traditional belief of the Penobscot Indians in Maine holds that each person has a vital spirit capable of traveling apart from the body. Given such a concept, the idea of the spirit being freed from the body in trance and dreams or by death, and having an existence thereafter, seems quite reasonable. Frequently, where a belief in ancestral spirits exists, these beings are seen as retaining an active interest and even membership in society.

In the previous chapter, for instance, we discussed how the Wape Papuans in New Guinea believe that ancestral spirits act to provide or withhold meat from their living descendants. Like living persons, such spirit beings are viewed as benevolent or malevolent, but no one is ever quite sure what their behavior will be. The same feeling of uncertainty—How will they react to what I have done?—may be displayed toward ancestral spirits as it often is toward people of an older generation who hold authority over individuals. Beyond this, ancestral spirits closely resemble living humans in their appetites, feelings, emotions, and behavior. Thus, they reflect and reinforce social reality.

Belief in ancestral spirits of one sort or another is found in many parts of the world, especially among people having unilineal descent systems with their associated ancestor orientation. In several such African societies, the concept is highly elaborate. Here one frequently finds ancestral spirits behaving just like humans. They are able to feel hot, cold, and pain, and they may be capable of dying a second death by drowning or burning. They even may participate in family and lineage affairs, and seats will be provided for them, even though the spirits are invisible. If they are annoyed, they may send sickness or death. Eventually, they are reborn as new members of their lineage, and, in societies that hold such beliefs, adults need to observe infants closely to determine just who has been reborn. Such beliefs provide a strong sense of continuity that links the past, present, and future.

Ancestor spirits played an important role in the patrilineal society of traditional China. For the gift of life, a boy was forever indebted to his parents, owing them obedience, deference, and a comfortable old age. Even after their death, he had to provide for them in the spirit world, offering them food, money, and incense on the anniversaries of their births and deaths. In addition, people collectively worshiped all lineage ancestors periodically throughout the year. Giving birth to sons was regarded as an obligation to the ancestors, because boys inherited their father's ancestral duties.

To fulfill his ancestors' needs for descendants (and his own need to be respectable in a culture that demanded satisfying the needs of one's ancestors), a man would go so far as to marry a girl who had been adopted into his family as an infant so she could be raised as a dutiful wife for him, even when this arrangement went against the wishes of both parties. Furthermore, a father readily would force his daughter to marry a man against her will. In fact, a female child raised to be cast out by her natal family might not find acceptance in her husband's family for years. Not until after death, when her vital spirit was carried in a tablet and placed in the shrine of her husband's family, was she an official member of it. As a consequence, once a son was born to her, a woman worked long and hard to establish the strongest possible tie between herself and her son to ensure she would be looked after in life.

Strong beliefs in ancestral spirits are particularly appropriate in a society of descent-based groups with their associated ancestor orientation. But, more than this, as noted above, these beliefs provide a strong sense of continuity that links the past, present, and future.

Sacred Places

In addition to revering special supernatural figures such as deities, ancestral spirits, and other special beings, some religious traditions consider certain geographic places to be spiritually significant or even sacred. Typically, such sites are rivers, lakes, waterfalls, islands, forests, caves, and—especially—mountains. Often, their status is due to some unique shape or outstanding feature, such as a conical volcano capped with snow. Numerous mountains around the world fall into this category. Often they are associated with origin myths as splendid abodes of the gods. Or they are revered as dwelling places for the spirits of the dead, heights where prophets received their divine directions, or retreats for prayer, meditation, and vision quests.

Three sacred mountains are shared by the Jewish, Christian, and Muslim traditions: Mount Ararat in the Caucasus Mountain Range between Russia and Turkey where the ark of the ancient patriarch Noah is said to have landed after the Great Flood; Mount Horeb, the "mountain of God" in the Sinai Desert where the prophet Moses received the stone tablets with the ten sacred rules of behavior from his god; and Mount Zion at the old city of Jerusalem where Solomon, the Israelite king, is believed to have been divinely ordered to build the Great Temple and where an important Muslim mosque is also located. Another sacred mountain in that region is Mount Tabor in northern Israel where Christians believe the change in the appearance of Jesus as God's son took place.

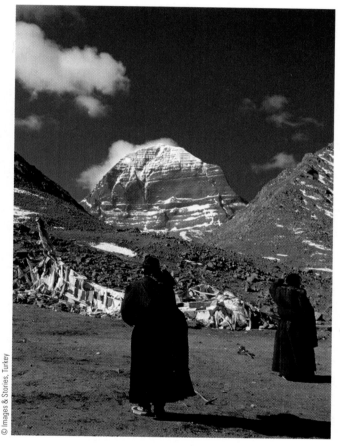

Pilgrims at Mount Kailash in Tibet. Rising 6,700 meters (about 22,000 feet), this mountain has been held sacred for thousands of years by Hindus, Buddhists, Jains, and followers of Bön (Tibet's indigenous religion). Year after year pilgrims follow the ancient tradition of circling the mountain on foot. The rugged, 52-kilometer (32-mile) trek, known as *parikarma*, is seen as a holy ritual that removes sins and brings good fortune. The most devout pilgrims make the journey lying down: Prostrating their bodies full-length, they extend their hands forward and make a mark on the ground with their fingers; then they rise, pray, crawl ahead on hands and knees to the mark, and then repeat the process again and again.

Similar traditions exist in many other cultures. For instance, the Japanese view the snow-capped perfect volcanic cone of Mount Fuji ("ever-lasting life") as a sacred place. Likewise, the Aztecs held several snow-capped volcanoes sacred, including Popocatepetl ("Smoking Mountain") just outside Mexico City. And the same can be said for Kirinyaga (Mount Kenya) in East Africa. Straddling the equator, it is seen as a holy place by the Kikuyu people who believe this "Mountain of Brightness" to be the earthly dwelling place of their creator god Ngai. Similarly, the ancient Greeks considered Mount Olympus to be the mythological abode of Zeus, the king of all their gods. In some religious traditions, such as among the Aymara of the Bolivian highlands, a volcanic mountain like Kaata is not only considered sacred, but is actually deified and worshiped as a living god.

Symbolic of the supreme being, or associated with various important deities or ancestral spirits, sacred mountains may feature in religious ceremonies or spiritual rituals. In some religious traditions, these towering geographic features are places of worship, like shrines, or are sacred destinies for spiritual journeys or pilgrimages. For example, every year thousands of Buddhist and Hindu worshipers make a long pilgrimage to the foot of Mount Kailash in Tibet. They do not deify this peak, but they believe it to be the sacred abode of Lord Shiva, a member of the supreme divine trinity—so sacred that they would not even dream of trying to climb it.

Among the many other mountains considered sacred is Bear Butte in the Paha Sapa, or Black Hills, of South Dakota. This mythological place is of great religious significance to dozens of American Indian nations in the Great Plains, especially the Lakota and Cheyenne who come to this domed mountain for meditation, prayers, and sacred vision quests. For outsiders unfamiliar with (or unsympathetic to) the indigenous religious traditions, these sacred mountains may be valued for commercial or recreational purposes, thus leading sometimes to bitter controversies and unfortunate consequences.

Animism

One of the most widespread concepts concerning supernatural beings is **animism,** a belief that nature is animated (enlivened or energized) by distinct personalized spirit beings separable from bodies. Spirits such as souls and ghosts are thought to dwell in humans and animals but also in human-made artifacts, plants, stones, mountains, wells, and other natural features. So too the woods may be full of a variety of unattached or free-ranging spirits.

animism A belief that nature is animated (enlivened or energized) by distinct personalized spirit beings separable from bodies.

The various spirits involved are a highly diverse lot. Generally speaking, though, they are less remote than gods and goddesses and are more involved in people's daily affairs. They may be benevolent, malevolent, or just plain neutral. They also may be awesome, terrifying, lovable, or mischievous. Since they may be pleased or irritated by human actions, people are obliged to be concerned about them.

Animism is typical of those who see themselves as being a part of nature rather than superior to it. This includes most food foragers, as well as those food-producing peoples who acknowledge little qualitative difference between a human life and any living entity from turtles to trees, or even rivers and mountains. In such societies, gods and goddesses are relatively unimportant, but the woods are full of spirits. Gods and goddesses, if they exist at all, may be seen as having created the world and perhaps making it fit to live in; but in animism, spirits are the ones to beseech when ill, the ones to help or hinder the shaman, and the ones who the ordinary hunter may meet when off in the woods.

Animatism

Although supernatural power is often thought of as being vested in supernatural beings, it does not have to be. Such is the case with **animatism**—the belief that nature is enlivened or energized by an impersonal spiritual power or supernatural potency.

The Melanesians, for example, think of *mana* as a force inherent in all objects—not unlike the idea of a cosmic energy passing into and through everything, affecting living and nonliving matter alike (similar to "the Force" in the *Star War* films). It is not in itself physical, but it can reveal itself physically. A warrior's success in fighting is not attributed to his own strength but to the *mana* contained in an amulet that hangs around his neck. Similarly, a farmer may know a great deal about horticulture, soil conditioning, and the correct time for sowing and harvesting, but nevertheless may depend upon *mana* for a successful crop, often building a simple altar to this power at one end of the field. If the crop is good, it is a sign that the farmer has in some way appropriated the necessary *mana*. Far from being a personalized force, *mana* is abstract in the extreme, a power or potency lying always just beyond reach of the senses.

This concept of impersonal potency or energy was widespread among North American Indians. The Algonquins called it *manitou*; to the Mohawk it was *orenda*; to the Lakota, *wakonda*. For instance, Bear Butte in the Black Hills, mentioned earlier, is a mountain where Lakota believers feel a strong presence of spirit power, or *wakonda*, which makes it a sacred site.

Nevertheless, though found on every continent, the concept of impersonal spirit power is not necessarily universal. In some cultures this energy is turned to for healing purposes. Notably, *animism* (as a belief in distinct spirit beings) and *animatism* (which lacks particular substance or individual form) are not mutually exclusive. They are often found in the same culture, as in Melanesian societies and also in the North American Indian societies just mentioned.

People trying to comprehend beliefs in the supernatural beings and powers that others recognize frequently ask how such beliefs are maintained. In part, the answer is through manifestations of power. Given a belief in animatism and/or the powers of supernatural beings, one is predisposed to see what appear to be results of the application of such powers. For example, if a Melanesian warrior is convinced of his power because he possesses the necessary *mana* and he is successful, he is likely to interpret this success as proof of the power of *mana*: "After all, I would have lost had I not possessed it, wouldn't I?" Beyond this, because of his confidence in his *mana*, he may be willing to take more chances in his fighting, and this indeed could mean the difference between success or failure.

Failures, of course, do occur, but they can be explained. Perhaps one's prayer was not answered because a deity or spirit was still angry about some past insult. Or perhaps the Melanesian warrior lost his battle because he was not as successful in bringing *mana* to bear or his opponent had more of it. In any case, humans generally emphasize successes over failures, and long after many of the latter have been forgotten, tales will still be told of striking cases of the workings of supernatural powers.

Beliefs are also maintained through myths—explanatory narratives that rationalize and reinforce religious beliefs and practices. We will discuss myths in more detail later in this chapter.

Religious Specialists

All human societies include individuals who guide and supplement the religious practices of others. Such individuals are seen to be highly skilled at contacting and influencing supernatural beings and manipulating supernatural forces. Often their qualification for this is that they have undergone special training. In addition, they may display certain distinctive personality traits that make them particularly well suited to perform these tasks.

animatism A belief that nature is enlivened or energized by an impersonal spiritual power or supernatural potency.

Priests and Priestesses

Within societies with the resources to support a full-time occupational specialist, a **priest** or **priestess** will have the role of guiding religious practices and influencing the supernatural. He or she is the socially initiated, ceremonially inducted member of a recognized religious organization, with a rank and function that belong to him or her as the holder of a position others have held before. The sources of power are the society and the institution within which the priest or priestess functions.

The priest, if not the priestess, is a familiar figure in Western societies; he is the priest, minister, imam, lama, rabbi, or whatever the official title may be in an organized religion. With their god defined historically in masculine, authoritarian terms, it is not surprising that, in the Judaic, Christian, and Islamic religions, the most important positions traditionally have been filled by men. Female religious specialists are likely to be found only in societies where women are acknowledged to contribute in a major way to the economy and where gods and goddesses are both recognized. In western Europe and North America, for instance, where women are now wage earners in almost every profession and occupy leadership positions in the workforce, they now have an increasing presence in the leadership of many Judeo-Christian religious groups.[4]

Although women still do not occupy the highest ranking religious leadership positions in the Roman Catholic Church (headed by a male pope and his all-male council, the College of Cardinals), this Christian religion does recognize important female saints. Most significant among these is the Virgin Mary, held to be the human mother of God's son. In many places where Roman Catholicism has spread, worshipers have created cults around this female saint. Moreover, all around the world women devoted to a religious life have formed their own places for religious exclusion as nuns jointly belonging to a cloister or convent, headed by an abbess. Such all-female religious institutions are not unique to Roman Catholicism. Convents of nuns are also part of Buddhist religious traditions and can be found in several Asian countries, including Thailand, as described by U.S. anthropologist Hillary Crane in this chapter's Biocultural Connection.

Shamans

Societies that lack full-time occupational specialization have existed far longer than those with such specialization, and they have always included individuals with special powers and skills that enable them to connect with and manipulate supernatural beings and forces. These powers have come to them through some personal experience, usually in solitude. In an altered state of consciousness, they receive a vision that empowers them to heal the sick, change the weather, control the movements of animals, and foretell the future. As they perfect these and related skills, they assume the role of shaman.

The word *shaman* originally referred to medical-religious specialists, or spiritual guides, among the Tungus and other Siberian pastoral nomads with animist beliefs. By means of various techniques such as fasting, drumming, chanting, or dancing, as well as hallucinogenic mushrooms, these Siberian shamans enter into a trance, or altered state of consciousness. While in this waking dream state, they experience visions of an alternate reality inhabited by spirit beings such as guardian animal spirits who may assist in the healing.

Cross-cultural research of shamanism shows that similar medical-religious healing practices also exist in traditional cultures outside Siberia. For that reason, the term *shaman* has also been applied to a variety of part-time spiritual leaders and traditional healers ("medicine men") active in North and South American indigenous communities and beyond.

As defined by U.S. anthropologist Michael Harner, famous for his participant observation among Shuar (or Jivaro) Indian shamans in the Amazon rainforest, a **shaman** is "a man or woman who enters an altered state of consciousness—at will—to contact and utilize an ordinarily hidden reality in order to acquire knowledge, power, and to help other persons. The shaman has at least one, and usually more, 'spirits' in his or her personal service."[5]

The term *shaman* has become so popular in recent decades that any non-Western local priest, healer, or diviner is often loosely referred to as one.[6] In the United States millions of people learned something about shamans through the popular autobiography of Black Elk, a traditional Lakota Indian Holy Man, and Carlos Castañeda's largely fictional accounts of his experiences with Don Juan, the Yaqui Indian shaman. Numerous books

---

[4]Lehman, E. C., Jr. (2002, Fall). Women's path into the ministry. *Pulpit & Pew Research Reports 1,* 4.

[5]Harner, M. (1980). *The way of the shaman: A guide to power and healing* (p. 20). San Francisco: Harper & Row.

[6]Kehoe, A. (2000). *Shamans and religion: An anthropological exploration in critical thinking.* Prospect Heights, IL: Waveland Press.

---

priest or **priestess** A full-time religious specialist formally recognized for his or her role in guiding the religious practices of others and for contacting and influencing supernatural powers.
shaman A person who enters an altered state of consciousness—at will—to contact and utilize an ordinarily hidden reality in order to acquire knowledge, power, and to help others.

Change Your Karma and Change Your Sex?

By Hillary Crane

As Mahayana Buddhists, Taiwanese Chan (Zen) monastics believe that all humans are able to reach enlightenment and be released from reincarnation. But they believe it is easier for some because of the situation into which they are born—for example, if one is born in a country where Buddhism is practiced, in a family that teaches proper behavior, or with exceptional mental or physical gifts.

Chan monastics view contrasting human circumstances as the result of the karma accrued in previous lives. They believe certain behavior—such as diligently practicing Buddhism—improves karma and the chances of attaining spiritual goals in this lifetime or coming back in a better birth. Other behavior—such as killing a living being, eating meat, desiring or becoming attached to things or people—accrues bad karma.

One way karma manifests itself is in one's sex. Taiwanese Buddhists believe that being born female makes it harder to attain spiritual goals. This idea comes, in part, from the inferior status of women in Taiwan and the belief that their "complicated bodies" and monthly menstruation cycles can distract them. Moreover, they believe, women are more enmeshed in their families than men, and their emotional ties keep them focused on worldly rather than spiritual tasks.

Taiwanese Buddhists who decide to become monks and nuns must break from their families to enter a monastery. Since women are thought to be more attached to their families than are men, leaving home is seen as a particularly big step for nuns and a sign that they are more like men than most women. In fact, a nun's character is considered masculine, unlike the frightened, indecisive, and emotional traits usually associated with women in Taiwan. When they leave home nuns even stop referring to themselves as women and call one another *shixiong* ("dharma brother"). They use this linguistic change to signal that they identify themselves as men and to remind one another to behave like men, particularly like the monks at the temple.

Monastics also reduce their attachments to worldly things like music and food. Nuns usually emphasize forsaking food and eat as little as possible. Their appearance, already quite masculine because they shave their heads and wear loose, gray clothing, becomes even more so when they lose weight—particularly in their hips, breasts, and thighs. Also, after becoming monastics, they often experience a slowing or stopping of their menses. Although these physical changes can be attributed to change in diet and lifestyle, the nuns point to them as signs they are becoming men, making progress toward their spiritual goals, and improving their karma.

(For a more detailed treatment of this topic, see H. Crane (2001). Men in spirit: The masculinization of Taiwanese Buddhist nuns. *Doctoral dissertation, Brown University.)*

VISUAL COUNTERPOINT

Shamanism is by no means absent in modern industrial societies. Here we see a new age shaman in North America (left) and a traditional shaman in Mongolia. The Mongolian shaman's drum is crafted from the wood of a tree struck by lightning and covered with leather made from a female red deer. It is believed that when the shaman goes into trance, her drum transforms into a magic steed that carries her into the dark sky of her ancestors.

and other publications on shamanism have appeared over the past four decades, and some Euramericans have gone into practice as shamans, a development that has triggered considerable resentment among some Native Americans. ("They stole our land, now they are stealing our religion.") In addition to so-called new age enthusiasts, among whom shamanism is particularly popular, faith healers and other evangelists among fundamentalist Christians share many of the characteristics of shamanism.

Typically, one becomes a shaman by passing through stages of learning and practical experience, often involving psychological and emotional ordeals brought about by isolation, fasting, physical torture, sensory deprivation, and/or hallucinations. These hallucinations (derived from the Latin word for "mental wandering") occur when the shaman is in a trance, which may occur spontaneously but can also be induced by drumming or consuming mind-altering drugs such as psychoactive vines or mushrooms.

Among the Penobscot Indians in northern New England, for example, any person could become a shaman, since no formal institution provided rules and regulations to guide religious consciousness. The search for shamanic visions was pursued by most adult Penobscot males, who would go off alone and—through meditation, sensory deprivation, and hyperventilation—induce an altered state of consciousness in which they hoped to receive a vision. Not all were successful, but failure did not result in social disgrace. Those who did achieve success experienced a sense of being freed from their bodily existence in which they established a special relationship with a particular animal spirit that appeared in their trance state. This became the shaman's animal helper—a common element in shamanism—who thereafter would assist the individual in performing shamanic tasks.

Because shamanism is rooted in altered states of consciousness and the human nervous system that produces these trance states is universal, individuals involved in shamanism experience similarly structured visual, auditory, somatic (touch), olfactory (smell), and gustatory (taste) hallucinations. The widespread occurrence of shamanism and the remarkable similarities among shamanic traditions everywhere are consequences of this universal neurological inheritance. At the same time, the meanings ascribed to sensations experienced in altered states and made of their content are culturally determined; hence, despite their overall similarities, local traditions always vary in their details.

The shaman is essentially a religious go-between who acts on behalf of some human client, often to bring about healing or to foretell some future event. To do so, the shaman intervenes to influence or impose his or her will on supernatural powers. The shaman can be contrasted with the priest or priestess, whose "clients" are the deities. Priests and priestesses frequently tell people what to do; the shaman tells supernaturals what to do. In return for services rendered, the shaman may collect a fee—fresh meat, yams, or a favorite possession. In some cases, the added prestige, authority, and social power attached to the shaman's status are reward enough.

When a shaman acts on behalf of a client, he or she may put on something of a show—one that heightens the basic drama with a sense of danger. Typically, the shaman enters a trance state, in which he or she experiences the sensation of traveling to the alternate world and seeing and interacting with spirit beings. The shaman tries to impose his or her will upon these spirits, an inherently dangerous contest, considering the superhuman powers spirits usually are thought to possess.

An example of this can be seen in the trance dances of the Ju/'hoansi Bushmen of Africa's Kalahari Desert. Among the Ju/'hoansi, shamans constitute, on average, about half the men and a third of the older women in any group. Their most common reasons for going into trance are to bring rain, control animals, and to heal the sick. Healing is an important activity of shamans across cultures, and the following Original Study offers insight into shamanic healing as practiced among the Ju/'hoansi.

Original Study ▪ By Marjorie Shostak

Healing among the Ju/'hoansi of the Kalahari

One way the spirits affect humans is by shooting them with invisible arrows carrying disease, death, or misfortune. If the arrows can be warded off, illness will not take hold. If illness has already penetrated, the arrows must be removed to enable the sick person to recover. An ancestral spirit may exercise this power against the living if a person is not being treated well by others. If people argue with her frequently, if her husband shows how little he values her by carrying on blatant affairs, or if people refuse to cooperate or share with her, the spirit may conclude that no one cares whether or not she remains alive and may "take her into the sky."

CONTINUED

CONTINUED

Ju/'hoansi healers, when entering trance, are assisted by others among the trance dancers.

Interceding with the spirits and drawing out their invisible arrows is the task of [Ju/'hoansi] healers, men and women who possess the powerful healing force called *n/um* [the Ju/'hoansi equivalent of *mana*]. *N/um* generally remains dormant in a healer until an effort is made to activate it. Although an occasional healer can accomplish this through solo singing or instrumental playing, the usual way of activating *n/um* is through the medicinal curing ceremony or trance dance. To the sound of undulating melodies sung by women, healers dance around and around the fire, sometimes for hours. The music, the strenuous dancing, the smoke, the heat of the fire, and the healers' intense concentration cause their *n/um* to heat up. When it comes to a boil, trance is achieved.

At this moment the *n/um* becomes available as a powerful healing force, to serve the entire community. In trance, a healer lays hands on and ritually cures everyone sitting around the fire. His hands flutter lightly beside each person's head or chest or wherever illness is evident; his body trembles; his breathing becomes deep and coarse; and he becomes coated with a thick sweat—also considered to be imbued with power. Whatever "badness" is discovered in the person is drawn into the healer's own body and met by the *n/um* coursing up his spinal column. The healer gives a mounting cry that culminates in a soul-wrenching shriek as the illness is catapulted out of his body and into the air.

While in trance, many healers see various gods and spirits sitting just outside the circle of firelight, enjoying the spectacle of the dance. Sometimes the spirits are recognizable—departed relatives and friends—at other times they are "just people." Whoever these beings are, healers in trance usually blame them for whatever misfortune is being experienced by the community. They are barraged by hurled objects, shouted at, and aggressively warned not to take any of the living back with them to the village of the spirits.

To cure a very serious illness, the most experienced healers may be called upon, for only they have enough knowledge to undertake the dangerous spiritual exploration that may be necessary to effect a cure. When they are in a trance, their souls or vital spirits are said to leave their bodies and to travel to the spirit world to discover the cause of the illness or the problem. An ancestral spirit or a god is usually found responsible and asked to reconsider. If the healer is persuasive and

the spirit agrees, the sick person recovers. If the spirit is elusive or unsympathetic, a cure is not achieved. The healer may go to the principal god, but even this does not always work. As one healer put it, "Sometimes, when you speak with God, he says, 'I want this person to die and won't help you make him better.' At other times, God helps; the next morning, someone who has been lying on the ground, seriously ill, gets up and walks again."

These journeys are considered dangerous because while the healer's soul is absent his body is in half-death. Akin to loss of consciousness, this state has been observed and verified by medical and scientific investigators. The power of other healers' *n/um* is all that is thought to protect the healer in this state from actual death. He receives lavish attention and care—his body is vigorously massaged, his skin is rubbed with sweat, and hands are laid on him. Only when consciousness returns—the signal that his soul has been reunited with his body—do the other healers cease their efforts. *(Excerpted from M. Shostak. (1983). Nisa: The life and words of a !Kung woman (pp. 291–293). New York: Vintage.)* ∎

In many human societies, sleight-of-hand tricks and ventriloquism occur at the same time as trancing. Among Arctic peoples, for example, a shaman may summon spirits in the dark and produce flapping noises and strange voices to impress the audience. Some Western observers regard this kind of trickery as evidence of the fraudulent nature of shamanism. However, those who have studied shamanic practices agree that even though shamans know perfectly well that they are manipulating people with their tricks, they really believe in their power to deal with supernatural forces and spirit beings. Their power, verified by the trance experience, gives them the right as well as the ability to manipulate people in minor technical matters. In short, the shaman regards his or her ability to perform extraordinary tricks as further proof of superior powers.

The importance of shamanism in a society should not be underestimated. It promotes, through the drama of performance, a trancelike feeling and a release of tension. And it provides psychological assurance that prevailing upon supernatural powers and spirits otherwise beyond human control can bring about invulnerability from attack, success at love, or the return of health. In fact, a frequent reason for a shamanic performance is poor health—a concept that is difficult to define effectively in cross-cultural terms. Not only do people in diverse cultures recognize and experience different types of illnesses, they may also view and explain them in different terms. The culturally defined diagnosis of an illness, in turn, determines how the patient will be treated according to the beliefs of the culture, in order to achieve healing.

Although the psychological effects of the shamanic treatment are not known, the connection between mind and body may contribute to the patient's recovery. From an anthropological perspective, shamanic healings can be understood by means of a three-cornered model we call the *shamanic complex* (Figure 13.2). This triangle is created by the relationships among the shaman and the patient and the community to which both belong.

For healing to take place, the shaman needs to be convinced of the effectiveness of his or her spiritual powers and techniques. Likewise, the patient must see the

shaman as a genuine healing master using appropriate techniques. Finally, to close the triangle's "magic field," the community within which the shaman operates on the patient must view the healing ceremony and its practitioner as potentially effective and beneficial.

Such dynamics are not unique to shamanic healing ceremonies, for similar social psychological processes are involved in Western medical treatments as well. Some people involved in modern medicine work collaboratively with practitioners of traditional belief systems toward the healing of various illnesses—as illustrated in this chapter's Anthropology Applied feature.

RITUALS AND CEREMONIES

Rituals, or ceremonial acts, are not all religious in nature (consider, for example, college graduation ceremonies in North America), but those that are play a crucial role in religious activity. Religious ritual is the means through which people relate to the supernatural; it is religion in action. Ritual serves to relieve social tensions and reinforce a group's collective bonds. More than this, it provides a means of marking many important events and lessening the social disruption and individual suffering of crises, such as death. Anthropologists have classified several different types of ritual. These include rites of passage and rites of intensification.

Rites of Passage

Rites of passage are rituals that mark important stages in an individual's life cycle. In one of anthropology's classic works, French social scientist Arnold van Gennep analyzed the rites of passage that help individuals through the crucial crises or major social transitions in their lives, such as birth, puberty, marriage, parenthood, advancement to a higher class, occupational specialization, and death.[7] He found it useful to divide ceremonies for all of these life crises into three stages: **separation, transition,** and **incorporation;** the first being ritual removal of the individual from everyday society, followed by a period

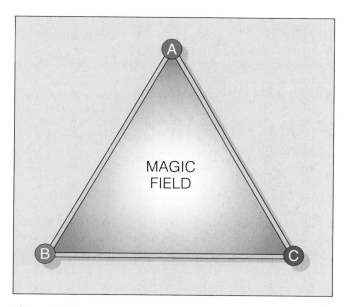

Figure 13.2

The shamanic complex. Shamanic healing takes place within a "magic field" created when the shaman (A) and patient (B), as well as their community (C), are all convinced that the shaman is a genuine healing master using appropriate techniques that are effective and beneficial. Similar psychological processes are involved in Western medical treatments.

[7]Van Gennep, A. (1960). *The rites of passage.* Chicago: University of Chicago Press.

rite of passage A ritual that marks an important stage in an individual's life cycle, such as birth, marriage, and death.
separation In a rite of passage, the ritual removal of the individual from society.
transition In a rite of passage, isolation of the individual following separation and prior to incorporation into society.
incorporation In a rite of passage, reincorporation of the individual into society in his or her new status.

Anthropology Applied

Reconciling Modern Medicine with Traditional Beliefs in Swaziland ▪ By Edward C. Green

Although the biomedical germ theory is generally known and accepted in Western societies today, this is not the case in many other societies around the world. In southern Africa's Swaziland, for example, many illnesses are generally thought to be caused by sorcery or by loss of ancestral protection. (Sexually transmitted diseases—STDs—and other contagious diseases are exceptions to these beliefs.)

Even where the effectiveness of Western medicine is recognized, the ultimate question remains: Why did a disease come to a particular person in the first place? Thus, for the treatment of disease, the Swazi have traditionally relied upon herbalists, diviner mediums through whom ancestor spirits are thought to work, and (more recently) Christian faith healers. Unfortunately, such individuals have usually been regarded as quacks and charlatans by the medical establishment. Yet, the herbal medicines used by traditional healers are effective in several ways, and the reassurance provided patient and family alike through rituals that reduce stress and anxiety plays an important role in the patient's recovery. In a country where there is one traditional healer for every 110 people, but only one physician for every 10,000, the potential benefit of cooperation between physicians and healers seems self-evident. Nevertheless, it was largely unrecognized until proposed by anthropologists D. M. Warren (in Ghana) and later, myself.

It was in 1981, when I was a Washington-based independent consultant, that I first went to Swaziland as a researcher for the Rural Water-Borne

Disease Control Project, funded by the United States Agency for International Development. Assigned the task of finding out about knowledge, attitudes, and practices related to water and sanitation, and aware of the serious deficiencies of conventional surveys that rely on pre-coded questionnaires, I used instead the traditional anthropological techniques of open-ended interviews with key informants, along with participant observation. The key informants were traditional healers, their patients, and rural health motivators (women chosen by communities to receive eight weeks of training in preventive health care in regional clinics). Without such anthropological research, it would have been impossible to design and interpret a reliable survey instrument, but the added payoff was that I learned a great deal about Swazi theories of illness and its treatment.

Disposed at the outset to recognize the positive value of many traditional practices, I could also see how cooperation with physicians might be achieved. For example, traditional healers already recognized the utility of Western medicines for treatment of diseases considered not indigenous to Africa, and traditional preventive medicines were routinely given to children through inhalation, something like childhood vaccinations. Thus, nontraditional medicines and vaccinations might be accepted, if presented in ways that resembled traditional medicine.

Realizing the suspicion existing on both sides, I and my Swazi associate Lydia Makhubu (a chemist who had

studied the properties of indigenous medicines) recommended to the minister of health a cooperative project focusing on a problem of concern to both health professionals and native healers: infant diarrheal diseases. These had recently become a health problem of high concern to the general public; healers wanted a means to prevent such diseases, and a means of treatment existed—oral rehydration therapy—that was compatible with traditional treatments for diarrhea (herbal preparations taken orally over a period of time). Packets of oral rehydration salts, along with instructions, were provided to healers in a pilot project, with positive results. This helped convince health professionals of the benefits of cooperation, while the healers saw the distribution of packets to them as a gesture of trust and cooperation on the part of their government.

Since then, further steps toward cooperation have been taken, such as work in prevention of AIDS, STDs, and TB. All of this demonstrates the importance of finding how to work in ways compatible with existing belief systems. Directly challenging traditional beliefs, as all too often happens, does little more than create stress, confusion, and resentment among people.

(See E. C. Green (1987). The planning of health education strategies in Swaziland, and the integration of modern and traditional health sectors in Swaziland. In R. M. Wulff & S. J. Fiske (Eds.), Anthropological praxis: Translating knowledge into action *(pp. 15–25, 87–97). Boulder, CO: Westview Press.)*

of isolation, and, finally, formal return and readmission back into society in his or her new status.

This sequence of stages is something that takes place in many forms in all cultures around the world, from military boot camps to college fraternity and sorority initiation ceremonies in the United States to a global array of puberty ceremonies that mark the transition from childhood to adulthood. For example, take the male initiation rites of the Aborigines of Australia. When the elders decide the time for initiation, the boys are taken from the village (separation), while the women cry and

make a ritual show of resistance. At a place distant from the camp, groups of men from many villages gather. The elders sing and dance, while the initiates act as though they are dead. The climax of this part of the ritual is a bodily operation, such as circumcision or the knocking out of a tooth. Australian anthropologist A. P. Elkin comments:

This is partly a continuation of the drama of death. The tooth-knocking, circumcision or other symbolical act "killed" the novice; after this he does not return to the general camp and normally may not be seen by any woman. He is dead to the ordinary life of the tribe.[8]

In this transitional stage, the novice may be shown secret ceremonies and receive some instruction, but the most significant element is his complete removal from society. In the course of these Australian puberty rites, the initiate must learn the lore that all adult men are expected to know; he is given, in effect, a "cram course." The trauma of the occasion is a pedagogical technique that ensures he will learn and remember everything; in a nonliterate society the perpetuation of cultural traditions requires no less, and so effective teaching methods are necessary.

On his return to society (incorporation), the novice is welcomed with ceremonies, as though he had returned from the dead. This alerts the society at large to the individual's new status—that people can expect him to act in certain ways, and in return they must act in the appropriate ways toward him. The individual's new rights and duties are thus clearly defined. He is spared, for example, the problems of a teenager in North America, a time when an individual is neither adult nor child, a person whose status is ill defined.

In the Australian case just cited, boys are prepared not just for adulthood but also for *manhood*. In their society, for example, courage and endurance are considered important masculine virtues, and the pain of tooth-knocking and circumcision help instill these in initiates. In a similar way, female initiation rites help prepare Mende girls in West Africa for womanhood. After they have begun to menstruate, the girls are removed from society to spend weeks, or even months, in seclusion. There they discard the clothes of childhood, smear their bodies with white clay, and dress in short skirts and many strands of beads.

Shortly after entering this transitional stage, the girls undergo clitoridectomy, a form of female circumcision that they and Mende in general believe enhances their reproductive potential. Until their incorporation back into society, they are trained in the moral and practical responsibilities of potential child bearers by experienced women in the Sande association, an organization to which the initiates will belong once their training has ended. This training is not all harsh, however, for it is accompanied by a good deal of singing, dancing, and storytelling, and the initiates are very well fed. Thus, they acquire both a positive image of womanhood and a strong sense of sisterhood. Once their training is complete, a medicine made by brewing leaves in water is used for a

ritual washing, removing the magical protection that has shielded them during the period of their confinement.

Mende women emerge from their initiation, then, as women in knowledgeable control of their sexuality, eligible for marriage and childbearing. The pain and danger of the surgery, endured in the context of intense social support from other women, serves as a metaphor for childbirth, which may well take place in the same place of seclusion, again with the support of women in the Sande association. It also has been suggested that, symbolically, the clitoridectomy (excision of the clitoris, the feminine version of the penis) removes sexual ambiguity.[9] Having gone through this ritual, a traditional Mende woman knows she is "all woman." Thus we have symbolic expression of gender as something important in people's cultural lives.

Anthropological commitment to cultural relativism permits an understanding of the practice of clitoridectomy in the Mende female initiation rites. However, as discussed early on in this book, cultural relativism does not preclude the anthropologist from criticizing a given practice. Apart from the pain and the effect of the operation on a woman's future sexual satisfaction, significant numbers of young women die from excessive bleeding, shock, various infections, or damage to the urethra or anus brought on by the procedure. Others face later risks when giving birth as scar tissue tears.

Not surprisingly, female circumcision—commonly referred to as female genital mutilation (FGM) and practiced in various forms in Asia and Africa especially—has been much condemned as a human rights violation in recent years. Committees to end the practice have been set up in twenty-two African countries.[10] (Notably, women's breast implant surgery has been compared to FGM as Western industrialized society's version of what it takes to be "all woman." The Original Study in the final chapter of this book addresses this issue in detail.)

Rites of Intensification

Rites of intensification are rituals that take place during a crisis in the life of the group and serve to bind individuals together. Whatever the precise nature of the crisis—a

---

[8]Elkin, A. P. (1964). *The Australian Aborigines.* Garden City, NY: Doubleday/Anchor Books.

---

[9]MacCormack, C. P. (1977). Biological events and cultural control. *Signs 3*, 98.

[10]Female genital mutilation. (2000). Fact sheet no. 241. World Health Organization; Dirie, W., & Miller, C. (1998). *Desert flower: The extraordinary journey of a desert nomad* (pp. 218, 219). New York: William Morrow.

rite of intensification A ritual that takes place during a crisis in the life of the group and serves to bind individuals together.

drought that threatens crops, the sudden appearance of an enemy war party, the onset of an epidemic—mass ceremonies are performed to ease the sense of danger. This unites people in a common effort so that fear and confusion yield to collective action and a degree of optimism. The balance in the relations of all concerned is restored to normal, and the community's values are celebrated and affirmed.

While an individual's death might be regarded as the ultimate crisis in that person's life, it is, as well, a crisis for the entire group, particularly if the group is small. A member of the community has been removed, so its composition has been seriously altered. The survivors, therefore, must readjust and restore balance. They also need to reconcile themselves to the loss of someone to whom they were emotionally tied.

Funerary ceremonies, then, can be regarded as rites of intensification that permit the living to express in nondisruptive ways their upset over the death while providing for social readjustment. Frequently such ceremonies feature ambivalence toward the dead person. For example, one part of the funerary rites of certain Melanesians was the eating of the dead person's flesh. This ritual cannibalism, witnessed by anthropologist Malinowski, was performed with "extreme repugnance and dread and usually followed by a violent vomiting fit. At the same time it is felt to be a supreme act of reverence, love, and devotion."[11] This custom and the emotions accompanying it clearly reveal an ambiguous attitude toward death: On the one hand, there is the survivors' desire to maintain the tie to the dead person, and, on the other hand, they feel disgust and fear at the transformation wrought by death. According to Malinowski, funeral ceremonies provide an approved collective means for individuals to express these feelings while maintaining social cohesiveness and preventing disruption of society.

The performance of rites of intensification does not have to be limited to times of overt crisis. In regions where the seasons differ enough that human activities must change accordingly, they will take the form of annual ceremonies. These are particularly common among horticultural and agricultural people, with their planting and harvest ceremonies. These are critical times in the lives of people in such societies, and the ceremonies express a reverent attitude toward nature's forces of generation and fertility upon which people's very existence depends.

Participation in rituals of reverence and celebration during planting and harvest seasons reinforces group involvement. It also serves as a kind of dress rehearsal for crisis situations by promoting the habit of relying on supernatural forces—a habit that may make a crucial difference under stressful circumstances when it is important not to give way to fear and despair.

MAGIC

Among the most fascinating of ritual practices is application of the belief that supernatural powers can be compelled to act in certain ways for good or evil purposes by recourse to certain specified formulas. This is a classical anthropological notion of magic. Many societies have magical rituals to ensure good crops, the replenishment of game, the fertility of domestic animals, and the avoidance or healing of illness in humans.

Although many Western peoples today—seeking to objectify and demythologize their world—have tried to suppress magic mysteries in their own consciousness, they continue to be fascinated by them. Not only are books and films about demonic possession and witchcraft avidly devoured and discussed, but horoscope columns are a regular feature of daily newspapers in the United States. And magical rituals are still commonly practiced by many Westerners seeking some "luck"

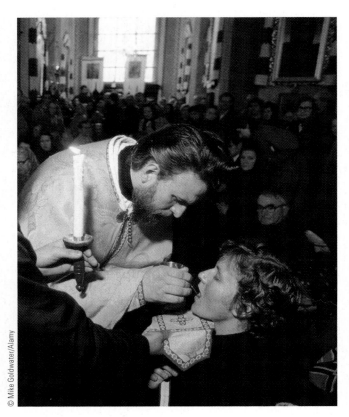

Ritual cannibalism appears in various societies in diverse forms. In Christianity, it is symbolic rather than actual, although millions of orthodox believers subscribe to the doctrine of transubstantiation, which holds that in Holy Communion the consecrated red wine and wafer or bread actually change into the divine blood and flesh of Christ, the Son of God.

© Mike Goldwater/Alamy

[11]Malinowski, B. (1954). *Magic, science, and religion* (p. 50). Garden City, NY: Doubleday.

where the outcome is in doubt or beyond factual influence—from lighting a votive candle for someone going through a hard time, to wearing lucky boxers on a hot date, to the curious gesturing baseball pitchers do before each throw.

While it may raise few eyebrows that Abraham Lincoln's wife invited psychics to the White House, it caused a considerable stir when it was learned that President Reagan's wife regularly conferred with an astrologer. As for psychics or spirit mediums, they are consulted by growing numbers of people in the United States today. A 1996 Gallup poll found that 20 percent of the respondents believed the dead could contact the living, and another 22 percent thought it might be possible. Anthropologist Lauren Kendall notes,

> Many witches, wizards, druids, Cabalists, and shamans . . . practice modern magic in contemporary England and the United States, where their ranks are comfortably reckoned in the tens of thousands. . . . The usual magician is ordinary, generally middle class, and often highly intelligent—a noticeable number of them have something to do with computers.[12]

In the 19th century Scottish anthropologist Sir James George Frazer made a useful distinction between two fundamental principles of magic. The first principle, that "like produces like," he named **imitative magic** (sometimes called *sympathetic magic*). In Burma (Myanmar) in Southeast Asia, for example, a rejected lover might engage a sorcerer to make an image of his would-be love. If this image were tossed into water, to the accompaniment of certain charms, it was expected that the hapless girl would go mad. Thus, the girl would suffer a fate similar to that of her image.

Frazer called the second principle of thought on which magic is based **contagious magic**—the idea that things or persons once in contact can influence each other after the contact is broken. The most common example of contagious magic is the permanent relationship between an individual and any part of his or her body, such as hair, fingernails, or teeth. Frazer cited the Basutos of Lesotho in southern Africa, who were careful to conceal their extracted teeth, because these might fall into the hands of certain mythical beings who could harm the owners of the teeth by working magic on them. Related to this is the custom, in Western societies, of treasuring things that have been touched by special people. Such things range from a saint's relics to possessions of other admired or idolized individuals, such as the U.S. basketball star Michael Jordan or England's rock musician Mick Jagger of the Rolling Stones.

© SSPL/The Image Works

A hundred-year old carved wooden figure from the Congo believed to have magical powers. During a special ritual, based on the principle of imitative magic, iron nails were driven into this traditional African fetish with the motive of causing pain, disease, or even death to someone feared or detested.

WITCHCRAFT

In Salem, Massachusetts, 200 innocent citizens suspected of being witches were arrested in 1692; of these, thirteen women and six men were hanged, and one 80-year-old farmer was tortured to death. Despite awarding damages to descendants of some of the victims nineteen

---

[12]Kendall, L. (1990, October). In the company of witches. *Natural History*, 92.

imitative magic Magic based on the principle that like produces like; sometimes called sympathetic magic.
contagious magic Magic based on the principle that things or persons once in contact can influence each other after the contact is broken.

years later, it was not until 1957 that the last of the Salem witches were exonerated by the Massachusetts legislature. **Witchcraft** is an explanation of events based on the belief that certain individuals possess an innate psychic power capable of causing harm, including sickness and death.

Although many North Americans suppose it to be something that belongs to a less enlightened past, witchcraft is alive and well in the United States today. Indeed, starting in the 1960s, a "witch cult" known as Wicca began to undergo something of a boom in this country, including among highly educated segments of society. And, contrary to popular belief, the self-styled witches belonging to this neo-pagan religion are *not* concerned with "working evil."

Ibibio Witchcraft

North Americans are by no means alone in this. For example, as the Ibibio of Nigeria have become increasingly exposed to modern education and scientific training, their reliance on witchcraft as an explanation for misfortune has increased.[13] Furthermore, it is often the younger, more educated members of Ibibio society who accuse others of bewitching them. Frequently, the accused are older, more traditional members of society; thus, we have an expression of the intergenerational hostility that often exists in fast-changing traditional societies.

Ibibio witchcraft beliefs are highly developed and long-standing—as they are among most traditional peoples of sub-Saharan Africa. A rat that eats a person's crops is not really a rat but a witch that changed into one; if a young and enterprising man cannot get a job or fails an exam, he has been bewitched; if someone's money is wasted or if the person becomes sick, is bitten by a snake, or is struck by lightning, the reason is always the same—witchcraft.

Indeed, traditional Ibibio attribute virtually all misfortune, illness, or death to the malevolent activity of witches. The modern Ibibio's knowledge about the role microorganisms play in disease has little impact on this; after all, it says nothing about why these were sent to the afflicted individual. Although Ibibio religious beliefs provide alternative explanations for misfortune, those carry negative connotations and do not elicit nearly as

much sympathy from others. Thus, if evil befalls a person, witchcraft is a far more satisfying explanation than something such as offspring disobedience or violation of a taboo.

Ibibio witches are thought to be men or women who have within them a special substance acquired from another established witch. From swallowing this substance—made up of needles, colored threads, and other ingredients—one is believed to become endowed with a special power that causes injury, even death, to others regardless of whether its possessor intends harm or not. The power is purely psychic, and witches do not perform rites or make use of "bad medicine." It is believed to give them the ability to transform into animals and travel any distance at incredible speed to get at their unsuspecting victims, whom they may torture or kill by transferring the victim's soul or vital spirit into an animal, which is then eaten.

To identify a witch, an Ibibio looks for any person living in the region whose behavior is considered odd, out of the ordinary, immoral, or unsocial. Any combination of the following may cause someone to be labeled a witch: not being fond of greeting people; living alone in a place apart from others; charging too high a price for something; enjoying adultery or committing incest; walking about at night; not showing sufficient grief upon the death of a relative or other member of the community; taking improper care of one's parents, children, or wives; and hard-heartedness. Witches are apt to look and act mean and to be socially disruptive people in the sense that their behavior exceeds the range of variance considered acceptable.

The Ibibio make a distinction between *sorcerers,* whose acts are especially diabolical and destructive, and benign *witches,* whose witchcraft is relatively harmless, even though their powers are thought to be greater than those of their malevolent counterparts. Sorcerers are the very embodiment of a society's conception of evil—beings that flout the rules of sexual behavior and disregard

---

[13]Offiong, D. (1985). Witchcraft among the Ibibio of Nigeria. In A. C. Lehmann & J. E. Myers (Eds.), *Magic, witchcraft, and religion* (pp. 152–165). Palo Alto, CA: Mayfield.

witchcraft An explanation of events based on the belief that certain individuals possess an innate psychic power capable of causing harm, including sickness and death.

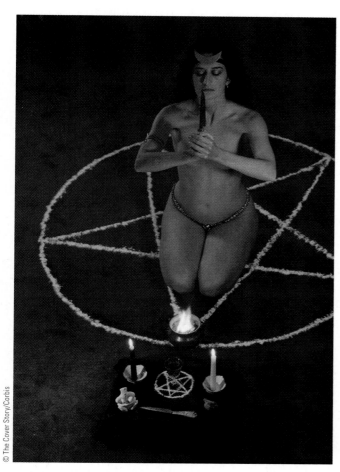

In North America, interest in and practice of witchcraft have grown significantly over the past thirty years, often among highly educated segments of society. Contrary to popular belief, witchcraft is *not* concerned exclusively, or even primarily, with working evil.

by a witch's curse, then magical countermeasures should cure it.

Not only does the idea of personalized evil answer the problem of unmerited suffering, but it also provides an explanation for many happenings for which no cause can be discovered. Witchcraft, then, cannot be refuted. Even if we could convince a person that his or her illness was due to natural causes, the victim would still ask, as the Ibibio do, Why me? Why now? Such a view leaves no room for pure chance; everything must be assigned a cause or meaning. Witchcraft offers an explanation and, in so doing, also provides both the basis and the means for taking counteraction.

Nor is witchcraft always entirely harmful. Its positive functions are noted in many African societies where people traditionally believe sickness, death, or other harm may be caused by witches. If people in the community agree that evildoing magic is in play, the ensuing search for the perpetrator of the misfortune becomes, in effect, a communal probe into dysfunctional social behavior. A witch-hunt is, in fact, a systematic investigation, through a public hearing, into all social relationships involving the victim of the sickness or death. Was a husband or wife unfaithful or a son lacking in the performance of his duties? Were an individual's friends uncooperative, or was the victim guilty of any of these wrongs? Accusations are reciprocal, and before long just about every unsocial or hostile act that has occurred in that society since the last outbreak of witchcraft (as manifested in sickness, death, or some other misfortune) is brought into the open.[16]

Through such periodic public scrutiny of everyone's behavior, people are reminded of what their society regards as both strengths and weaknesses of character. This encourages individuals to suppress as best they can those personality traits that are looked upon with disapproval, for if they do not, they at some time may be accused of being a witch. A belief in witchcraft thus serves a function of social control.

Witchcraft among the Navajo

Widely known among American Indians are the Navajo of the southwestern United States, who possess a highly developed concept of witchcraft. Several types of witchcraft are distinguished. *Witchery* encompasses the practices of witches, who are said to meet at night to practice cannibalism and kill people at a distance. *Sorcery* is distinguished from witchery only by the methods used by the sorcerer, who casts spells on individuals using the victim's fingernails, hair, or discarded clothing. *Wizardry* is not distinguished so much by its effects as by its manner of working: Wizards kill by injecting a cursed

every other standard of decency. Benign witches are often the community's nonconformists. Typically, they are morose, arrogant, and unfriendly people who keep to themselves but otherwise cause little disturbance. Such witches are thought to be dangerous when offended—likely to retaliate by causing sickness, death, crop failure, cattle disease, or any number of lesser ills. Not surprisingly, people viewed as witches are usually treated with considerable caution, respect, and even fear.[14]

The Functions of Witchcraft

Why witchcraft? We might better ask, why not? In a world where there are few proven techniques for dealing with everyday crises, especially sickness, a belief in witches is not foolish; it is indispensable.[15] No one wants to resign oneself to illness, and if the malady is caused

[14]See Mair, L. (1969). *Witchcraft* (p. 37). New York: McGraw-Hill.

[15]Mair, L. (1969). *Witchcraft*. New York: McGraw-Hill.

[16]Turnbull, C. M. (1983). *The human cycle* (p. 181). New York: Simon & Schuster.

substance, such as a tooth from a corpse, into the victim's body.

Whether or not a particular illness results from Navajo witchcraft is determined by **divination**—a magical procedure or spiritual ritual designed to find out about what is not knowable by ordinary means. Once a person is charged with witchcraft, he or she is publicly interrogated—in the past, possibly even tortured until there is a confession. It is believed the witch's own curse will turn against the witch once this happens, so it is expected that the witch will die within a year. Some confessed witches have been allowed to live in exile.

According to Clyde Kluckhohn, Navajo witchcraft serves to channel anxieties, tensions, and frustrations caused by the pressures from Euramericans.[17] The rigid rules of proper behavior among the Navajo allow little means for expression of hostility, except through accusations of witchcraft. Such accusations funnel pent-up negative emotions against individuals without upsetting the wider society. Another function of witchcraft accusations is that they permit direct expression of hostile feelings against people toward whom one ordinarily would be unable to express anger or enmity.

On a more positive note, individuals strive to behave in ways that will prevent them from being accused of witchcraft. Since excessive wealth is believed to result from witchcraft, individuals are encouraged to redistribute their assets among friends and relatives, thereby leveling economic differences. Similarly, because the Navajo believe elders, if neglected, will turn into witches, people are strongly motivated to take care of aged relatives. And because leaders are thought to be witches, people are understandably reluctant to go against their wishes, lest they suffer supernatural retribution.

The Consequences of Witchcraft

Anthropological research suggests that witchcraft, in spite of its often negative image, frequently functions in a very positive way to manage tensions within a society. Nonetheless, events may get out of hand, particularly in crisis situations, when widespread accusations may cause great suffering. This certainly was the case in the Salem witch trials, but even those pale in comparison to the half a million individuals executed as witches in Europe from the 15th through the 17th centuries. This was a time of profound change in European societies, marked by a good deal of political and religious conflict. At such times, it is all too easy to search out scapegoats to blame for what people believe are undesirable changes.

THE FUNCTIONS OF RELIGION

Just as belief in witchcraft may serve a variety of psychological and social functions, so too do religious beliefs and practices in general. Here we may summarize these functions in a somewhat more systematic way.

One psychological function is to provide an orderly model of the universe, which plays a key role in establishing orderly human behavior. Through special stories, or myths, people find answers to important questions such as: What does the universe look like, how does it work, and what is my place in it? To many Euramericans, the word *myth* conjures up the idea of an invented story about imaginary events, something that did not factually happen. This is not true for those people for whom a particular myth comprises part of their worldview. To them myths are sacred and true stories, not unlike historical documents in contemporary European or North American culture. And even in these literate societies, myths exist, such as the accounts of creation in the Book of Genesis. Invariably, myths are full of accounts about the doings of various supernatural beings and thus serve to reinforce beliefs in them.

Beyond this, by explaining the unknown and making it understandable, religion reduces the fears and anxieties of individuals. As we have seen, these explanations typically assume the existence of supernatural beings and powers, which people may potentially appeal to or manipulate as a means for dealing with crises. Thus, at least theoretically, divine aid is available when all else fails.

A social function of religion is to prompt reflection concerning conduct. In this context, religion plays a role in social control, which, as we saw in the last chapter, does not rely on law alone. This is done through notions of right and wrong, good and evil. Right actions earn the approval of whatever supernatural powers are recognized by a particular culture. Wrong actions may cause revenge or punishment through supernatural agencies. In short, by deliberately *raising* people's feelings of guilt and anxiety about their actions, religion helps keep them in line.

Religion does more than this, though; it sets guidelines for acceptable behavior. We have noted already the connection between myths and religion. Usually, myths feature tales of extraordinary or supernatural beings that in various ways illustrate the society's ethical code in action. So it is that Gluskabe, the Penobscot Indian culture hero, is portrayed in that society's traditions as tricking and punishing those who lie, mock others, behave

---

[17]Kluckhohn, C. (1944). Navajo witchcraft. *Papers of the Peabody Museum of American Archaeology and Ethnology 22* (2).

divination A magical procedure or spiritual ritual designed to find out about what is not knowable by ordinary means, such as foretelling the future by interpreting omens.

c-print, copyright Kuo-ming Sung

Buddhist monk prostrating in front of Jokhang temple in Lhasa, Tibet. Some religious devotees prostrate themselves for hours or days in an effort to demonstrate humility, transcend pain, and seek enlightenment. Some who make pilgrimages to sacred sites crawl the distance in a ritually prescribed ordeal for similar reasons.

the way things are rests with the gods or spirit forces rather than with themselves.

Another social function of religion is its role in the maintenance of social solidarity. In our discussion of shamans, we saw how such individuals provide focal points of interest, thus supplying one ingredient of assistance for maintaining group unity. In addition, common participation in rituals, coupled with a basic uniformity of beliefs, helps to bind people together and reinforce their identification with their group. Particularly effective may be their joint participation in rituals, when the atmosphere is charged with emotion. The ecstatic feelings people may experience in such circumstances serve as a positive reinforcement in that they feel good as a result. Here, once again, we find religion providing psychological assurance while fulfilling the needs of society.

One other area in which religion serves a social function is education. In our discussion of rites of passage, we noted that puberty rituals of Aborigines in Australia served as a kind of cram course in traditional lore. By providing a memorable occasion, initiation rites can enhance learning and so help ensure the perpetuation of a nonliterate culture. And as we saw in the female initiation rites among the Mende, they ensure that individuals have the knowledge they will need to fulfill their adult roles in society.

Education also may be served by rites of intensification. Frequently, such rites involve dramas that portray matters of cultural importance. For example, among a food-foraging people, dances may imitate the movement of game and techniques of hunting. Among farmers a fixed round of ceremonies may emphasize the steps necessary for good crops. All of this helps preserve knowledge important to a people's material well-being, gives expression to their worldview, and thereby reinforces their collective self-understanding.

In addition to all of the above, people often turn to religion in the hope of reaching a specific goal, such as the healing of physical, emotional, or social ills—as illustrated in this chapter's Original Study and the Anthropology Applied features.

greedily, overreact, or engage in other behaviors deemed inappropriate in Penobscot culture. Moreover, the specific situations relayed in myths serve as guidelines for human behavior in similar circumstances. The Old and New Testaments of the Bible are rich in the same sort of material, as is the Koran. Related to this, by the models religion presents and the morals it espouses, religion serves to justify and perpetuate a particular social order. Thus, in the Jewish, Christian, and Islamic traditions, a masculine-authoritarian godhead along with a creation story that portrays a woman as responsible for a fall from grace serve to justify a social order in which men exercise control over women.

A psychological function also is tied up in this. A society's moral code, since it is considered to be divinely ordained, lifts the burden of responsibility for conduct from the shoulders of the society's individual members, at least in important situations. It can be a tremendous relief to individuals to know that the responsibility for

RELIGION AND CULTURE CHANGE: REVITALIZATION MOVEMENTS

No anthropological consideration of religion is complete without some mention of **revitalization movements**— movements for radical culture reform in response to

revitalization movement A movement for radical cultural reform in response to widespread social disruption and collective feelings of great stress and despair.

A Sufi *sema* (prayer dance) in Istanbul, Turkey. Sufism, a mystical Muslim movement that emerged in the late 10th century, borrowing ideas from Buddhism, Christianity, and Neoplatonism, emphasizes the surrender of individual ego and attachment to worldly things in order to be receptive to God's grace. Known as "Whirling Dervishes," these Sufi dancers are part of the Mevlevi brotherhood founded by Mevlana Rumi in the 13th century. According to Mevlevi tradition, during the *sema* the soul is freed from earthly ties and able to jubilantly commune with the divine. (*Dervish* literally means "doorway" and is thought to be an entrance from the material world to the spiritual.) The felt hat represents personal ego's tombstone, and the wide skirt symbolizes its shroud.

widespread social disruption and collective feelings of great stress and despair. Many such movements developed in indigenous societies where European colonial exploitation caused enormous upheaval.

Among the various types of revitalization movements is the **cargo cult**—a spiritual movement (especially noted in Melanesia in the Southwest Pacific) in reaction to disruptive contact with Western capitalism, promising resurrection of deceased relatives, destruction or enslavement of white foreigners, and the magical arrival of utopian riches. Indigenous Melanesians referred to the white man's wealth as "cargo" (pidgin English for European trade goods). In times of great social stress, native prophets emerged, predicting that the time of suffering would come to an end, and a new paradise on earth would soon arrive. Their deceased ancestors would return to life, and the rich white man would magically disappear—swallowed by an earthquake or swept away by a huge wave. However, their cargo would be left for the

prophets and their cult followers who performed rituals to hasten this supernatural redistribution of wealth.[18]

One of many cargo cults took place in 1931 at Buka, in the Solomon Islands (in the Pacific Ocean). A native religious movement suddenly emerged there when prophets predicted that a deluge would soon engulf all whites, and a ship would then arrive filled with Western industrial commodities. The prophets told their followers to construct a storehouse for the goods and to prepare themselves to repulse the colonial police. They also spread word that the ship would come only after the natives had used up all their own supplies, and for this reason believers ceased working in the fields. Although the leaders of the movement were arrested, the cult continued for some years.

As deliberate efforts to construct a more satisfying culture, revitalization movements aim to reform not just the religious sphere of activity but an entire cultural system. Such drastic measures are taken when a group's anxiety and frustration have become so intense that the

cargo cult A spiritual movement (especially noted in Melanesia) in reaction to disruptive contact with Western capitalism, promising resurrection of deceased relatives, destruction or enslavement of white foreigners, and the magical arrival of utopian riches.

[18]For more on cargo cults, see Lindstrom, L. (1993). *Cargo cult: Strange stories of desire from Melanesia and beyond.* Honolulu: University of Hawaii Press; and Worsley, P. (1957). *The trumpet shall sound: A study of "cargo" cults in Melanesia.* London: Macgibbon & Kee.

only way to reduce the stress is to overturn the entire social system and replace it with a new one. From the cargo cults of Melanesia to the 1890 Ghost Dance of many North American Indians to the Mau Mau of the Kikuyu in Kenya in the 1950s, extreme and sometimes violent religious reactions to European domination are so common that anthropologists have sought to formulate their underlying causes and general characteristics.

Revitalization movements are by no means restricted to the colonial world, and in the United States alone hundreds of them have sprung up. These range from Mormonism, which began in the 19th century, to the more recent Unification Church led by Reverend Sun Myung Moon, the Branch Davidians led by Seventh-Day Adventist prophet David Koresh, and the Black Muslims led by Prophet Elijah Muhammad. Recent U.S. revitalization movements also include the American Indian revival of the spectacular Sun Dance ceremony, now held each summer at various reservations in the Great Plains.

Anthropologist Anthony Wallace outlined a sequence common to all expressions of the revitalization process.[19] First is the normal state of society, in which stress is not too great, and sufficient cultural means exist to satisfy needs. Under certain conditions, such as domination by a more powerful group or severe economic depression, stress and frustration are steadily amplified; this ushers in the second phase, or period of increased individual stress. If there are no significant adaptive changes, a period of cultural distortion follows in which stress becomes so chronic that socially approved methods of releasing tension begin to break down. This steady deterioration of the culture may be checked by a period of revitalization, during which a dynamic cult or religious movement grips a sizable portion of the population.

Sometimes the movement will be so out of touch with existing circumstances that it is doomed to failure from the beginning. This was the case with the Heaven's Gate cult, which mixed bits and pieces of apocalyptic Christian beliefs predicting destruction of the world at the end of the millennium with folk myths of contemporary North American culture, in particular those having to do with UFOs (alien spaceships). Its followers committed mass suicide out of a conviction that their spiritual essences would reunite with higher extraterrestrial beings in a spaceship that awaited them behind the tail of the Hale-Bopp comet, ready to take them "home." A similar case of self-destruction took place among the Branch Davidians, whose hostility toward government authorities prompted an official assault on the cult's compound in Waco, Texas. In reaction, cult members set fire to their own headquarters, sending their movement and their lives up in flames.

More rarely, a movement may tap long-dormant adaptive forces underlying a culture, and an enduring religion may result. Such was the case with Mormonism. Though heavily persecuted at first and hounded from place to place, Mormons adapted to the point that their religion thrives in the United States today. Indeed, revitalization movements lie at the root of all known religions—Judaism, Christianity, and Islam included.

In Africa, during and following the period of foreign colonization and missionization, indigenous groups resisted or creatively revised Christian teachings and formed culturally appropriate religious movements. Since the 1970s, thousands of indigenous Christian churches have been founded, often born of alternative theological interpretations, new divinely inspired revelations, or cultural disagreements between African Christians and European or North American missionaries over the extent to which traditional African practices (such as animism, ancestor worship, and polygamy) were permissible. Today the African continent is as religiously diverse as ever. Although at least 40 percent of the population is Christian and more than another 40 percent is Muslim, African indigenous religious traditions persist and are often merged with Christianity and Islam.

Persistence of Religion

From the ongoing need to make sense of their existence, humans continue to explore metaphysically or spiritually as well as scientifically. All around the globe we see indications of the effort, not only in buildings and other structures created for religious purposes but in natural places that people have designated as sacred sites. The search for meaning is also evident in many works of art, as discussed in the next chapter.

[19]Wallace, A. F. C. (1970). *Culture and personality* (2nd ed., pp. 191–196). New York: Random House.

Questions for Reflection

1. Beyond biological survival, humans face mental challenges born of the need to make meaningful sense of their existence. Do you ever ponder questions such as the meaning of your life and big issues such as the origin or destiny of the human species? How does your culture, including your religious or spiritual beliefs, offer you guidance in finding meaningful answers to such big questions?

2. You have read about female genital mutilation as a rite of passage in some cultures. Do you know of any genital mutilation practices in your society? Why are so many boys in the United States circumcised immediately after their birth?

3. Do the basic dynamics of the shamanic complex also apply to preachers or priests in modern churches and medical doctors working in modern hospitals? Can you think of some similarities among the shaman, preacher, and medical doctor in terms of their respective fields of operation?

4. Revitalization movements occur in reaction to the upheavals caused by rapid colonization and modernization. Do you think that the rise of Christian fundamentalism in the North American Bible Belt today is a response to such upheavals as well?

5. In postindustrial societies such as western Europe, the United States, and Canada, there is growing interest in shamanism and alternative healing techniques. Is there any relationship between globalization and this phenomenon?

Suggested Readings

Behrend, H., & Luig, U. (Eds.). (2000). *Spirit possession, modernity, and power in Africa*. Madison: University of Wisconsin Press.

This fascinating collection investigates how African spirit possession cults respond to local circumstances in a globalizing world. Contributors focus on power, histories, gender roles, and images of the Other in shaping these beliefs and practices, introducing pantheons of new holy spirits—such as spirits of airplanes and guitars in Central Africa or Christian spirits with names like "Hitler" fighting against the government of Uganda.

Bowen, J. R. (2004). *Religions in practice: An approach to the anthropology of religion* (3rd ed.). Boston: Allyn & Bacon.

Investigates how people from an array of spiritual traditions engage in special and everyday religious practices (prayer, sacrifice, pilgrimage, dress, rituals related to death) and discusses major issues of gender, states, and laws with respect to religion. Includes a review of religious studies theories from Hegel and Tylor to Geertz.

Bowie, F. (2006). *The anthropology of religion: An introduction* (2nd ed.). Malden, MA: Blackwell.

This readable introductory text presents the central theoretical ideas in the anthropology of religion, illustrating them with specific case studies. This edition features new chapters on mythology and pilgrimage, plus coverage of topics such as spirit possession and cargo cults.

Lambek, Michael (2002). *A reader in the anthropology of religion*. London: Blackwell.

This ambitious reader encompasses the breadth, depth, and complexity of anthropology's investigations into religion—

and aims to create a conversation between Western and non-Western cultures, as well as between anthropology and other disciplines in the social sciences and humanities. It features a general introduction, a comprehensive range of classical and recent readings, and an extensive bibliography that is indexed according to both ethnographic region and religious topics and practices.

Stein, R. L., & Stein, P. L. (2004). *Anthropology of religion, magic, and witchcraft*. Boston: Allyn & Bacon.

This concise introductory text emphasizes the major concepts of anthropology in general and the anthropology of religion in particular. Concepts are illustrated primarily with examples drawn from tribal or traditional societies, but the "world's great religions" are also included.

Tedlock, B. (2005). *The woman in the shaman's body: Reclaiming the feminine in religion and medicine*. New York: Random House.

Tracing the history of shamanism around the globe and illuminating the roles of women, the author integrates scholarship and her personal experience as a practicing shaman.

Thomson Audio Study Products

 Enjoy the MP3-ready Audio Lecture Overviews for each chapter and a comprehensive audio glossary of key terms for quick study and review. Whether walking to class, doing laundry, or studying at your desk, you now have the freedom to choose when, where, and how you interact with your audio-based educational media. See the preface for information on how to access this on-the-go study and review tool.

The Anthropology Resource Center

www.thomsonedu.com/anthropology
The Anthropology Resource Center provides extended learning materials to reinforce your understanding of key concepts in the four fields of anthropology. For each of the four fields, the Resource Center includes dynamic exercises including video exercises, map exercises, simulations, and "Meet the Scientists" interviews, as well as critical thinking questions that can be assigned and e-mailed to instructors. The Resource Center also provides breaking news in anthropology and interesting material on applied anthropology to help you link what you are learning to the world around you.

14 The Arts

© Vince Hemingson

CHALLENGE ISSUE

Humans in all cultures throughout time face the challenge of creatively articulating their feelings and ideas about themselves and the world around them. Although not all societies distinguish "art" as a special cultural domain, people everywhere have developed aesthetic forms—visual, verbal, musical, movement, and so on—to symbolically express, appreciate, and share experiences of beauty in all its variety. Several art forms are represented in this photo—dance, music, weaving, beadwork, and tattoos. Tattooing—puncturing and ingraining with indelible pigment the skin with special designs—is a widespread form of body art practiced by humans for thousands of years.

What Is Art?

Although difficult to define, art may be understood as the creative use of the human imagination to aesthetically interpret, express, and engage life, modifying experienced reality in the process. Many contemporary Western peoples consider art as exclusively aesthetic, serving no practical purpose, but most societies past and present have used art to give meaningful expression to almost every part of their culture, including ideas about religion, kinship, and ethnic identity. In fact, almost anything humans can lay their hands on can become an object of artistic creativity— skin, hair, dress, dwellings, vehicles, weapons, utensils, and so on.

Why Do Anthropologists Study Art?

Anthropologists have found that art often reflects a society's collective ideas, values, and concerns. From myths, songs, dances, paintings, carvings, and so on, anthropologists may learn how a people imagine their reality and understand themselves as well as other beings around them. Through the cross-cultural study of art and creativity, we discover much about different worldviews, religious beliefs, political ideas, social values, kinship structures, economic relations, and historical memory as well.

What Are the Functions of Art?

Aside from adding beauty and pleasure to everyday life, art serves a number of functions. Myths, for example, may offer basic explanations about the world and set cultural standards for right behavior. The verbal arts generally transmit and preserve a culture's customs and values. Songs, too, may do this within the structures imposed by musical form. And any art form, to the degree that it is characteristic of a particular society, may contribute to the cohesiveness or solidarity of that society. Yet, art may also express political themes and be used to influence events and create social change. Often it is created for religious purposes, to honor or beseech the aid of a divine power, a sacred being, an ancestral spirit, or an animal spirit.

Humans in all cultures throughout time have expressed feelings and ideas about themselves and the world around them through **art**—the creative use of the human imagination to aesthetically interpret, express, and engage life, modifying experienced reality in the process. It comes in many forms: visual, verbal, musical, dance, and so on. Most societies, past and present, have used art to symbolically express almost every part of their culture, including ideas about religion, kinship, and ethnic identity.

In North America, the arts often are seen as a luxury, an aesthetic pleasure that people engage in for personal or collective enjoyment quite apart from more useful or productive pursuits. This attitude becomes apparent whenever public funds are in short supply. On the local level, for example, in battles over school budgets, art programs are often the first to be cut. On the national level, fiscal conservatives repeatedly seek to curb funds for theater performances, museum exhibits, concerts, and other fine arts to be enjoyed by the general public on the premise that these lack the practical importance of roads, sewers, police, warplanes, office bureaucracies, and other governmental priorities.

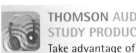

THOMSON AUDIO STUDY PRODUCTS Take advantage of the MP3-ready Audio Lecture Overviews and comprehensive audio glossary of key terms for each chapter. See the preface for information on how to access this on-the-go study and review tool.

Indeed, a significant portion of the society views artists and their supporters as an elite group subsidized at the expense of "practical" tax-paying citizens. This is due in large part to the rather recent Western concept of *fine art* as a distinct cultural category of art for art's sake, unrelated to society at large but relished by specialists and wealthy collectors who chatter about, purchase, or even commission works of art for enjoyment in the privacy of their homes or showings in selective galleries and museums.

The idea of art serving purely aesthetic but non-practical purposes seems firmly entrenched in the thinking of many contemporary Western peoples. Today, for example, the objects from the ancient tomb of the young Egyptian king Tutankhamen are on display in a museum, where they may be seen and admired as the exquisite works of art that they are. They were made, however, not for human eyes but to guarantee the eternal life of the king and protect him from evil forces that might enter his body and gain control over it.

art The creative use of the human imagination to aesthetically interpret, express, and engage life, modifying experienced reality in the process.

Similarly, we may listen to the singing of a sea chantey purely for aesthetic pleasure, as a form of entertainment. But, in fact, in the days of sailing by wind power alone, sea chanteys served very useful and practical purposes. They set the appropriate rhythm for the performance of specific shipboard tasks such as hoisting or reefing sails, and the same qualities that make them pleasurable to listen to today served to coordinate joint tasks or relieve the boredom of those jobs.

Such links between art and other aspects of everyday life are common in human societies around the world. This can also be seen in the way that art has commonly been incorporated into everyday, functional objects—from pottery and baskets used to carry or store food to carpets and mats woven by herders to cover the ground inside their dwellings. Designs painted on or woven or carved into such objects typically express ideas, values, and things that have meaning to an entire community.

All of this goes to show that artistic expression is as basic to human beings as talking and is by no means limited to a special category of people called "artists." For example, all human beings adorn their bodies in certain ways and by doing so make a statement about who they are, both as individuals and as members of society. Similarly, people in all cultures tell stories in which they express their values, hopes, and concerns and in the process reveal much about themselves and the nature of the world as they see it. In short, all peoples engage in artistic expression. What's more, they have been doing this for at least 40,000 years. Far from being a luxury to be afforded or appreciated by a minority of sophisticated experts or frivolous lovers of art, creativity is a necessary activity in which everyone participates in one way or another.

Whether a particular work of art is intended to be appreciated purely for beauty or to serve some practical purpose, it will in every case require the same special combination of the symbolic representation of form and the expression of feeling that constitute the creative imagination. Since the creative use of the human ability to symbolize is universal, and both expresses and is shaped by cultural values and concerns, it is an important subject for anthropological study.

THE ANTHROPOLOGICAL STUDY OF ART

Anthropologists have found that art often reflects a society's collective ideas, values, and concerns. Indeed, through the cross-cultural study of art—myths, songs, dances, paintings, carvings, designs, and so on—we may discover much about different worldviews and religious beliefs, as well as political ideas, social values, kinship structures, economic relations, and historical memory.

VISUAL COUNTERPOINT

© Indiana University Art Museum, Bloomington

© Giraudon/Art Resource

On the left is a wooden spoon used by the Dan people of Ivory Coast, West Africa, carver unknown. On the right is a bronze sculpture, "Spoon Woman," created by Italian artist Alberto Giacometti in 1926. Both may be beautiful, but one is functional, the other purely aesthetic. Usually, traditional utilitarian objects, no matter how exquisite, are identified only in terms of the "primitive" or "tribal" cultures in which they were made. In contrast, "works of art" created for the sake of art itself are typically tied to the name of the person who made them. How curious it is that this great modern piece credited to the famous Giacometti was inspired by a now nameless West African person.

In approaching art as a cultural phenomenon, anthropologists have the pleasant task of cataloguing, photographing, recording, describing, and analyzing all possible forms of imaginative activity in any particular culture. An enormous variety of forms and modes of artistic expression exists in the world. Because people everywhere continue to create and develop in ever-new ways, there is no end in sight to the interesting process of collecting and describing the world's ornaments, ceremonial masks, body decorations, clothing variations, blanket and rug designs, pottery and basket styles, monuments, architectural embellishments, legends, work songs, dances, and other art forms—many of them rich with religious symbolism.

To study and analyze art, anthropologists employ a combination of aesthetic, narrative, and interpretive approaches. The distinction between these methods can be illustrated through a brief look at a famous work of West-

ern art, Leonardo da Vinci's painting *The Last Supper*.[1] A non-Christian viewing this late 15th-century mural in Italy will see thirteen people at a table, apparently enjoying a meal. Although one of the men clutches a bag of money and appears to have knocked over a dish of salt, nothing else in the scene seems out of the ordinary.

Aesthetically, our non-Christian observer may admire the way the composition fits the space available, the way the attitudes of the men are depicted, and the way the artist conveys a sense of movement. As *narrative*, the painting may be seen as a record of customs, table manners, dress, and architecture. But to *interpret* this picture—to perceive its real meaning—the viewer must be aware that in Western culture money symbol-

[1]This example is drawn from Lewis-Williams, J. D. (1990). *Discovering southern African rock art* (p. 9). Cape Town and Johannesburg: David Philip.

Leonardo da Vinci's *The Last Supper*. To really understand this painting, one must know something about Christianity and about the general cultural symbols and beliefs of the famous Italian artist (1452–1519) in his own place and time.

© Scala/Art Resource, NY

izes the root of all evil and spilling the salt symbolizes impending disaster. But even this is not enough; to fully understand this work of art, one must know something of the beliefs of Christianity. In other words, moving to the interpretive level of studying art requires knowledge of the symbols and beliefs of the people responsible for the art.

A good way to deepen our insight into the relationship between art and the rest of culture is to examine critically some of the generalizations that have already been made about specific art forms. Since it is impossible to cover all art forms in the space of a single chapter, we shall concentrate on just a few: visual, verbal, and musical—in that order.

VISUAL ART

For many people, the first thing that springs to mind in connection with the word *art* is some sort of visual image, be it a painting, drawing, sketch, or whatever. And indeed, in many parts of the world, people have been making pictures in one way or another for a very long time—etching in bone, engraving in rock, painting on cave walls and rock surfaces, carving and painting on wood, gourds, and clay pots, or painting on textiles, bark cloth, animal hide, or even their own bodies. Some form of visual art is a part of every historically known human culture.

As a type of symbolic expression, visual art may be representational (imitating closely the forms of nature)

or abstract (drawing from natural forms but representing only their basic patterns or arrangements). In some of the Indian art of North America's northwest coast, for example, animal figures may be so highly stylized as to be difficult for an outsider to identify. Although the art appears abstract, the artist has created it based on nature, even though he or she has exaggerated and deliberately transformed various shapes to express a particular feeling toward the animals. Because artists do these exaggerations and transformations according to the aesthetic principles of their Indian culture, their meanings are understood not just by the artist but by other members of the community as well.

This collective understanding of symbols is a hallmark in traditional art. Unlike modern Western art, which is judged in large part on its creative originality and the unique vision of an individual artist, traditional art is all about community and shared symbolism. As discussed in several earlier chapters, hunter–gatherers, nomadic herders, slash-and-burn horticulturists, and others living in small-scale traditional societies are profoundly interested in kinship relations—who is related to whom and how. In such societies, concerns about kinship may be symbolically expressed in stylized motifs and colorful designs. As described by North American art historian Carl Schuster and anthropologist Edmund Carpenter, cross-cultural and historical comparisons of certain widespread and recurrent geometric motifs—etched or painted on human skin, animal hides or bones, clay pottery, wood, rocks, or almost any other surface imaginable—indicate that many designs that we perceive as

In the figure at left, the two rows of diagrams at the top show the stylized human figures that are the basic "bricks" used in the construction of genealogical patterns. Each figure is designed to be joined limb-and-limb with adjacent figures to illustrate descent or other kin relationships. The diagrams in the two bottom rows show how these basic figures are linked arm-and-leg with diagonally adjacent figures to depict descent. For thousands of years people all over the world have linked such figures together, creating the familiar geometric patterns that we see in countless art forms, from pottery to sculpture to weaving—patterns that informed eyes recognize as genealogical.

purely decorative, ornamental, or abstract are actually symbolic. This symbolism, they show, can often be decoded in terms of a genealogical iconography primarily illustrating social relations of marriage and descent.[2]

[2]Schuster, C., & Carpenter, E. (1996). *Patterns that connect: Social symbolism in ancient and tribal art.* New York: Abrams; see also

Shared symbolism has also been fundamental to the traditional art of tattooing—although that is changing in some parts of the world, as discussed in the following Original Study.

Prins, H. E. L. (1998). Book review of Schuster, C., & Carpenter, E. *American Anthropologist 100* (3), 841.

Original Study ▪ By Margo DeMello

The Modern Tattoo Community

As an anthropology graduate student in the early 1990s, I had no idea what (or, more accurately, whom) to study for my field research. Working as an animal advocate, I had a house full of creatures to care for, which left me in no position for long-term travel to a far-off field site.

Then one of my professors suggested a topic that was literally under

my nose—tattooing. I myself had several tattoos and spent quite a bit of time with other tattooed people, including my husband who had just become a professional tattooist. Yet, I had never thought about this as a research topic. Part of my everyday life, it didn't seem "exotic" enough. My professor assured me I was wrong, and I began my research assuming that it would not be difficult since I was already accustomed to attending tattoo conventions, getting tattooed, and hanging around tattoo studios.

As it turned out I had unanticipated obstacles to overcome. Early on in my research, I, along with my husband, strove to find a way to "join" what is known as

CONTINUED

CONTINUED

the "tattoo community," finding that it was not as friendly and open as we had imagined it to be. As a tattooed person, married to a fledgling tattooist, I often felt excluded. But as an anthropologist I came to see that what I was experiencing was the lower rungs of a highly stratified social group, in which an artist's status is based on such features as class, geography, and professional and artistic credentials, and a "fan" might be judged on the type and extent of his or her tattoos, the artist(s) who created them, the level of media coverage achieved, and more. It was my personal experiences as both insider (tattooed person) and outsider (anthropologist) with this community that in fact led to one of the major focuses of my work: how class and status increasingly came to define this once working-class art form.

Ultimately, I spent almost five years studying and writing about tattooing, finding my "community" wherever tattooed people talked about themselves and each other—within the pages of tattoo magazines and mainstream newspapers, on Internet newsgroups, and at tattoo-oriented events across the country. I spent countless hours in tattoo shops watching the artists work; I collected what I call "tattoo narratives," which are often elaborate, sometimes spiritual, stories that people tell about their tattoos; and I followed the careers of seminal artists. I even learned to tattoo a bit myself, placing a few particularly ugly images on my patient husband's body.

Tattoos are created by inserting ink or some other pigment through the epidermis (outer skin) into the dermis (the second layer of skin) through the use of needles. They may be beautiful as designs in and of themselves, but they can also express a multitude of meanings about the wearer and his or her place within the social group. Whether used in an overt punitive fashion (as in the tattooing of

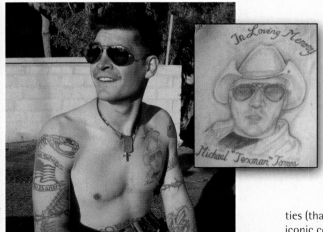

Michael M. Phillips

For many U.S. Marines in Iraq, memorial tattoos are becoming a way to give ink-and-skin permanence to fallen friends. In memory of fellow Marine Lance Cpl. Michael Torres, Curt Stiver of Oshkosh, Wisconsin, had a tattoo artist copy onto his left chest a photograph taken of Torres in infantry school.

slaves or prisoners) or to mark clan or cult membership, religious or tribal affiliation, social status, or marital position, tattoos have historically been a social sign. They have long been one of the simplest ways of establishing humans as social beings. In fact, tattooing is one of the most persistent and universal forms of body art and may date back as far as the Upper Paleolithic era (10,000–40,000 years ago).

Tattoos as signs derive their communicative power from more than a simple sign-to-meaning correspondence: They also communicate through color, style, manner of execution, and location on the body. Traditionally inscribed on easily viewable parts of the body, tattoos were designed to be "read" by others and were part of a collectively understood system of inscription. However, for many middle-class North Americans today tattoos are more about private statement than public sign, and these individuals, especially women, tend to favor smaller tattoos in private spots.

The process by which tattooing has expanded in the United States from a working-class folk art into a more widespread and often refined aesthetic practice is related to a number of shifts in North American culture that occurred during the 1970s and 1980s. This time

period saw the introduction of finely trained artists into tattooing, bringing with them radically different backgrounds and artistic sensibilities to draw from. More and more middle-class men and women began getting tattooed, attracted by the expanded artistic choices and the new, more spiritual context of body decoration.

Tattoos have been partially transformed into fine art by a process of redefinition and framing based on formal qualities (that is, the skill of the artist, the iconic content of the tattoo, the style in which the tattoo is executed, and so on) and ideological qualities (the discourses that surround "artistic" tattoos, discourses that point to some higher reality on which the tattoo is based). When it is judged that a tattoo has certain formal artistic qualities as well as expresses a higher, often spiritual, reality, then it is seen as art.

While it may seem as though tattoos are not good candidates to be defined as art, due to their lack of permanence (the body, after all, ages and dies) and their seeming inability to be displayed within a gallery setting, modern tattoo art shows get around these problems by photographing tattoos and displaying them in a way that showcases the "art" and often minimizes the body. By both literally and figuratively "framing" tattoos in a museum or gallery setting, or within an art book, the tattoo is removed from its social function and remade into art.

The basic working-class American tattoo designs (such as "Mother" or "Donna" inscribed alongside a heart) have been relegated to the bottom rung of today's tattoo hierarchy in the United States. Such tattoos are now seen by middle-class artists and fans as too literal, too transparently obvious, and too grounded in everyday experience and social life to qualify as art. The modern, artistic tattoos that have increasingly gained favor are less "readable" and no longer have an easily recognizable function. Often derived from foreign (or "exotic") cultures (such as Polynesia) and custom-drawn for the wearer, they tend to eliminate the social aspect in favor of the highly individualistic. Some are purely decorative, and those that are intended to signify meaning often do so only for the individual or those in his or her intimate circle.

Tattoos in the United States have traveled a long way from the tattoo of old: brought to North America by way of Captain James Cook's 18th-century explorations of the Pacific, moving, over time, from a mark of affiliation to a highly individual statement of personal identity, losing and regaining function, meaning, and content along the way. In our increasingly global world, tattoo designs and motifs move swiftly and easily across cultural boundaries. As this happens, their original, communal meanings are often lost—but they are not meaningless. An animal crest tattoo traditionally worn by Indians on the Northwest Coast of North America to signify clan membership may now be worn by a non-Native in Boston as an artful, often private, sign of rebellion against Western "coat and tie" consumer culture.

(For a more detailed discussion of this topic, see DeMello, M. (2000). Bodies of inscription: A cultural history of the modern tattoo community. (2000). Durham: Duke University Press.) ■

Southern Africa Rock Art

Rock art—paintings and engravings made on the faces of rock outcrops and on the interior walls of rock shelters—is one of the world's oldest art traditions. Bushmen in southern Africa practiced this art continually from at least 27,000 years ago until the beginning of the 20th century when European colonization led to the demise of their societies. Their art depicted humans and animals in highly sophisticated ways, sometimes in static poses but often in highly animated scenes. It also featured what appear to be abstract signs—dots, zigzags, nested curves, and the like. Until fairly recently, the significance of these abstract features puzzled non-Bushmen, as did the fact that new pictures were quite often created directly over existing images.

Because Bushman rock art, especially the paintings, are generally seen as beautiful and pleasurable to look at, it is not surprising that the specialists who first studied them took the aesthetic approach—analyzing *how* things were depicted. Investigating the various colored pigments, they found that the Bushmen had used charcoal and specularite for black; silica, china clay, and gypsum for white; and ferric oxide for red and reddish-brown hues—and that they had mixed the colors with fat, blood, and perhaps water. The paint had been applied to the rough rock with great skill. Indeed, the effectiveness of line and the way shading was used to suggest the contours of the animals' bodies elicits admiration, as does the realistic rendering of details such as the twist of an eland's horns or the black line running along its back.

In addition to the aesthetic approach of analyzing *how* Bushman rock paintings and engravings are created, specialists also study the art as "narrative," investigating *what* it depicts. Certainly, aspects of Bushman life are shown, as in several hunting scenes of men with bows, arrows, quivers, and hunting bags. Some depictions show hunting nets and also fish traps. Women are also portrayed—identifiable by their visible sexual characteristics and the stone-weighted digging sticks they carry.

Taking an interpretive approach to studying Bushman rock art—looking at it in light of contemporary ethnographic research among modern-day Bushman communities—we see that certain designs relate to the trance dance discussed in the previous chapter. This is symbolically indicated by several features: the numbers of people shown and the arrangement of hand-clapping women surrounding dancing men whose bodies are bent forward (in the distinctive posture caused by the cramping of abdominal muscles as they go into trance), whose noses are bleeding (common today when Bushmen trance), whose arms are stretched behind their backs (present-day Bushmen do this to gather more of the supernatural potency—*n/um*), and who are wearing dance rattles and carrying fly whisks (used to extract invisible arrows of sickness).

A fuller interpretation of this scene requires more than ethnographic knowledge about the Bushman trance dance. It calls for knowledge about the nature of trance gained through laboratory experiments in altered states of consciousness.

Laboratory research shows that humans typically move through three stages when entering a trance. In the first stage, the nervous system generates images of luminous, pulsating, revolving, and constantly shifting geometric patterns known as *entoptic phenomena*—similar to images seen during a migraine headache. Typically these include dots, zigzags, grids, filigrees, nested curves, and parallel lines, often in a spiral pattern.

In the second stage, the brain tries to make sense of these abstract forms (a process known as *construal*). Here, cultural influences come into play, so a trancing Bushman in southern Africa's Kalahari is likely to construe a grid pattern as markings on the skin of a giraffe, nested curves as a honeycomb (honey is a Bush delicacy), and so forth. A New York police officer or a Chinese priest would construe the patterns in very different ways.

During the third and deepest trance stage, people tend to feel as if they are at one with their visions, passing into a rotating tunnel or vortex. Typically, the tunnel

Bushmen in southern Africa created rock paintings and engravings depicting animals they believed possessed great supernatural powers. Shamans appear as well: In the painted example at the right, we see rain shamans with swallowtails acting in the spirit realm to protect people from the dangers of storms. Like contemporary Bushman shamans, several of these hold paired dance sticks. The idea of shamans transforming into birds, as well as being elongated and weightless as in flight or water, is based on altered states of consciousness experienced in trance.

has latticelike sides where **iconic images** of animals, humans, and monsters appear, merging with the entoptic forms of the early trance stages. Because these images are culture specific, individuals usually see things that have high significance within their culture. Thus, Bushmen often see the eland, a massive antelope they believe carries supernatural powers for rain-making. This given, one of the things shamans try to do in trance is to "capture" these envisioned elands ("rain animals") for purposes of making rain.

All of this helps us understand why elands are so prominent in the Bushman rock art. Moreover, it reveals the significance of the zigzags, dots, grids, and so forth that are so often a part of the compositions. It also leads to an understanding of other puzzling features of the art. For example, the third trance stage includes such sensations as being stretched out or elongated, weightlessness as in flight or in the water, and difficulty breathing as when under water. Hence we find depictions in the art of humans who appear to be abnormally long, as well as individuals who appear to be swimming or flying.

Another well-documented trance phenomenon is the sense of being transformed into some sort of animal. Such sensations are triggered in the deepest stage of trance if the individual sees or thinks of an animal, and the sensation accounts for the part human–part animal (therianthropes) in the art. Finally, the superpositioning of one work of art over another becomes comprehensible; not only are the visions seen in trance commonly superimposed on one another as they rotate and move,

but if the trancer stares at a painting or engraving of an earlier vision, the new one will appear as if projected on the old.

The interpretive approach makes clear, then, that the rock art of southern Africa—even in the case of compositions that otherwise might appear to be scenes of everyday life—is intimately connected with the practices and beliefs of shamanism. After shamans came out of trance and reflected on their visions, they proceeded to paint or engrave their recollections on the rock faces. But these were more than records of important visions; they had their own innate power, owing to their supposed supernatural origin. This being so, when the need arose for a new trance experience, it might be held where the old vision was recorded to draw power from it.

A similar interpretive analysis is needed to fully understand the art of Huichol Indians living in Mexico and profiled in this chapter's Biocultural Connection feature.

VERBAL ART

The verbal arts include narratives, dramas, poetry, incantations, proverbs, riddles, word games—as well as naming procedures, compliments, and insults, when these take structured and special forms. Narrative seems to be one of the easiest kinds of the verbal arts to record or collect. Perhaps because they also are the most reproducible of the arts and have considerable popular appeal, they have received considerable attention from linguists and anthropologists.

In the 19th century, when scholars began studying the unwritten stories (and other artistic traditions) of ru-

iconic images Culturally specific people, animals, and monsters seen in the deepest stage of trance.

Biocultural Connection

Peyote Art: Divine Visions among the Huichol

For generations, Huichol Indians living in Mexico's mountainous western Sierra Madre region have created art remarkable for its vibrant colors. They are especially noted for their spectacular beadwork and embroidery. Although many people far and wide appreciate the intricate beauty of Huichol art, most are probably unaware that the colorful designs express a religious worldview tied to the chemical substance of a sacred plant: a small cactus "button" known as peyote (*Lophophora williamsii*).[a]

Among the many Huichol gods and goddesses, all addressed in kinship terms, is Our Grandfather Fire. His principal spirit helper is Our Elder Brother Deer, a messenger between the gods and humans. Serving the Huichol as their spiritual guide, this divine deer is also the peyote cactus itself. Huichol Indians refer to peyote as *yawéi hikuri*, the "divine flesh of Elder Brother Deer." Guided by their shamans on a pilgrimage to harvest peyote, they "hunt" this "deer" in Wirikúta, the sacred desert highlands

where their ancestor deities dwell. Having found and "shot" the first cactus button with an arrow, they gather many more, later to be consumed in fresh, dried, or liquid form.

Participating in a holy communion with the creator god, Huichol shamans consume peyote (the divine flesh) as a

© Benjamin Chodroff

sacrament. Doing so, they enter into an ecstatic trance. With the help of peyote, their spiritual guide, they become hawks or eagles soaring high in the sky. Having visions extending far across the world, they interact directly with their gods and seek advice on behalf of those who need help in dealing with illness and other misfortunes.

From a purely chemical point of view, peyote contains a psychotropic substance identified by modern chemists as an alkaloid. By consuming some of this toxic organic substance, the Huichol move into an altered state of consciousness. In this dreamlike psychological state, which is also profoundly emotional, they experience religiously inspired, brilliantly colored visions from their spirit world.

These are reflected in Huichol art, such as the piece pictured here in which a stylized peyote button and deer have been rendered in rainbow-hued beading. The sacred cactus with its starlike shape is the most prominent symbolic design in Huichol art. Beaded onto fabric and objects of all kinds or embroidered on clothing, shoulder bags, and so forth, it can be found in almost all of their artwork—much of it now produced for sale abroad.

[a]Schaeffer, S. B., & Furst, P. T. (Eds.). (1996). *People of the peyote: Huichol Indian history, religion, and survival.* Albuquerque: University of New Mexico Press.

---

ral peoples, they coined the word **folklore** to distinguish between "folk art" and the "fine art" of the literate elite. Today, many linguists and anthropologists prefer to speak of a culture's oral traditions and verbal arts rather than its folklore and folktales, recognizing that the distinction between folk and fine art is a projection imposed by European and Euramerican elites. Generally, the narratives comprising the verbal arts have been divided into several basic and recurring categories, including myth, legend, and tale.

Myth

Derived from the Greek word *mythos,* meaning "speech" or "story," a **myth** is a sacred narrative that explains the fundamentals of human existence—where we and everything in our world came from, why we are here, and where we are going. Beyond this explanatory function, a myth provides a rationale for religious beliefs and

practices and sets cultural standards for "right" behavior. A typical creation or origin myth, traditional with the western Abenaki of northwestern New England and southern Quebec, goes as follows:

> In the beginning, *Tabaldak,* "The Owner," created all living things but one—the spirit being who was to accomplish the final transformation of the earth. Man and woman *Tabaldak* made out of a piece of stone, but he didn't like the result, their hearts being cold and hard. This being so,

folklore A term coined by 19th-century scholars studying the unwritten stories and other artistic traditions of rural peoples to distinguish between "folk art" and the "fine art" of the literate elite.

myth A sacred narrative that explains the fundamentals of human existence—where we and everything in our world came from, why we are here, and where we are going.

he broke them up, and their remains today can be seen in the many stones that litter the landscape of the Abenaki homeland. But *Tabaldak* tried again, this time using living wood, and from this came all later Abenakis. Like the trees from which the wood came, these people were rooted in the earth and (like trees when blown by the wind) could dance gracefully. The one living thing not created by *Tabaldak* was *Odzihózo*, "He Makes Himself from Something." This being seems to have created himself out of dust, but since he was a transformer, rather than creator, he wasn't able to accomplish it all at once. At first, he managed only his head, body, and arms; the legs came later, growing slowly as legs do on a tadpole. Not waiting until his legs were grown, he set out to transform the shape of the earth. He dragged his body about with his hands, gouging channels that became the rivers. To make the mountains, he piled dirt up with his hands. Once his legs grew, *Odzihózo's* task was made easier; by merely extending his legs, he made the tributaries of the main streams.

Odzihózo, then, was the Abenaki transformer who laid out the river channels and lake basins and shaped the hills and mountains. Just how long he took is a subject which Abenakis have discussed for as long as any can remember. Once he was finished, he surveyed his handiwork and found it was good. The last work he made was Lake Champlain and this he found especially good. He liked it so well that he climbed onto a rock in Burlington Bay and changed himself into stone so that he could sit there and enjoy his masterpiece through the ages. He still likes it, because he is still there and he is still given offerings of tobacco as Abenakis pass this way. The Abenaki call the rock *Odzihózo*, since it is the Transformer himself.[3]

Such a myth, insofar as it is believed, accepted, and perpetuated in a culture, may be said to express part of a people's traditional *worldview* (the collective body of ideas that members of a culture generally share concerning the ultimate shape and substance of their reality). Extrapolating from the details of this particular Abenaki myth, we might arrive at the conclusion that these people recognize a kinship among all living things; after all,

---

[3]Haviland, W. A., & Power, M. W. (1994). *The original Vermonters: Native inhabitants, past and present* (2nd ed., p. 193). Hanover, NH: University Press of New England.

legend A story about a memorable event or figure handed down by tradition and told as true but without historical evidence.

they were all part of the same creation, and humans even were made from living wood. Moreover, an attempt to make them of nonliving stone was not satisfactory.

This idea of closeness among all living things led the Abenaki to show special respect to the animals they hunted in order to sustain their own lives. For example, after killing a beaver, muskrat, or waterfowl, one could not unceremoniously toss its bones into the nearest garbage pit. Proper respect required that the bones be returned to the water, with a request to continue its kind. Similarly, before eating meat, the Abenaki placed an offering of grease on the fire to thank *Tabaldak*. More generally, waste was to be avoided so as not to offend the animals. Failure to respect their rights would result in an unwillingness to sacrifice their lives that people might live.

By transforming himself into stone in order to enjoy his work for all eternity, *Odzihózo* may be seen as setting an example for people; they should see the beauty in things as they are and not seek to alter what is already good. To question the goodness of existing reality would be to call into question the judgment of a powerful deity. A characteristic of explanatory myths, such as this one, is that the unknown is simplified and explained in terms of the known. This myth, in terms of human experience, accounts for the existence of rivers, mountains, lakes, and other features of the landscape, as well as of humans and all other living things. It also sanctions particular attitudes and behaviors. It is a product of creative imagination, and is a work of art, as well as a potentially religious statement.

The analysis of myths has been carried to great lengths, becoming a field of study almost unto itself. Myth making is an extremely significant kind of human creativity, and studying the myth-making process and its results can give valuable clues to the way people perceive and think about their world. The problems of interpretation, however, are great, as evidenced in these questions: Are myths literally believed or perhaps accepted symbolically or emotionally as a different kind of truth? To what extent do myths actually determine or reflect human behavior? Can an outsider discover the meaning that a myth has in its own culture? How do we account for contradictory myths in the same culture (such as the two distinct accounts of creation in the first and second chapters of the Bible's Book of Genesis)? New myths arise and old ones die. Is it then the myth's content or the structure that is important? All of these questions deserve, and are currently receiving, serious consideration.

Legend

A **legend** is a story about a memorable event or figure handed down by tradition and told as true but without historical evidence. An example of a modern urban legend in the United States is one that was often told by Ronald Reagan when he was president, about an African American woman on welfare in Chicago. Supposedly, her ability to collect something like 103 welfare checks under different names enabled her to live lavishly. Although proved to be false, the story was told as if true (by the president even after he was informed that it was not true) as legends are.

This particular legend illustrates a number of features all such narratives share: They cannot be attributed to any known author; they always exist in multiple versions, but, in spite of variation, they are told with sufficient detail to be plausible; and they tell us something about the cultures in which they are found. In this case, we learn something about popular anger against wasteful government spending of taxpayer dollars ("big government" policies to help the poor), mainstream society's views on self-reliant individualism and hard work (distrust, if not dislike of the poor), and last but not least, enduring racism in U.S. society (the story is told by whites, who identify the woman as African American).

As this illustration shows, legends (no more than myths) are not confined to nonliterate, nonindustrialized societies. Commonly, legends consist of pseudo-historical narratives that account for the deeds of heroes, the movements of peoples, and the establishment of local customs, typically with a mixture of realism and the supernatural or extraordinary. As stories, they are not necessarily believed or disbelieved, but they usually serve to entertain as well as to instruct and to inspire or bolster pride in family, community, or nation. Legends all around the world tell us something about the cultures in which they are found.

To a degree, in literate societies, the function of legends has been taken over by history. The trouble is that history does not always tell people what they want to hear about themselves, or, conversely, it tells them things that they would prefer not to hear. By projecting their culture's hopes and expectations onto the record of the past, they seize upon and even exaggerate some past events while ignoring or giving scant attention to others. Although this often takes place unconsciously, so strong is the motivation to transform history into legend that states often have gone as far as to deliberately rewrite it.

There are countless examples of the fact that different groups often recall and recount the same historical event in highly contrasting ways. For instance, white colonists and their descendants who settled in New England portrayed the region's 17th-century Indian rebellion led by Chief Metacomet (better known in American history books as "King Philip") as a treacherous uprising and described his defeat as a divinely guided military victory over heathen savages. In this violent conflict, thousands on both sides lost their lives. Although many Indian survivors found refuge among neighboring indigenous na-

tions, hundreds of Indian captives were sold as slaves and died in foreign lands. Unable to resist English colonial land grabs and repression, Indians who were allowed to remain in their homeland were confined to small reservations where they came under the administrative control of white agents.

In public commemorations and written historical accounts, the Indian side of this conflict remains largely unvoiced and unknown to the general public.[4] For this reason, American Indians sometimes joke bitterly about such one-sided versions of the past as *"his* story," and scholars attempting to separate historical fact from fiction frequently incur the wrath of people who refuse to abandon what they wish to believe is true, whether or not it really is.

A long dramatic narrative recounting the celebrated deeds of a historic or legendary hero—often sung or recited in poetic language—is known as an **epic**. In parts of western and central Africa, people hold remarkably elaborate and formalized recitations of extremely long legends, lasting several hours and even days. These long narratives have been described as veritable encyclopedias of a culture's most diverse aspects, with direct and indirect statements about history, institutions, relationships, values, and ideas. Epics are typically found in nonliterate societies with some form of state political organization; they serve to transmit and preserve a culture's legal and political precedents and practices.

Legends may incorporate mythological details, especially when they make an appeal to the supernatural, and are therefore not always clearly distinct from myth. Legends may also incorporate proverbs and incidental tales and thus be related to other forms of verbal art as well.

For the anthropologist, a major significance of the secular and apparently realistic portions of legends, whether long or short, is the clues they provide as to what constitutes a culture's approved or ideal ethical behavior. The subject matter of legends is essentially problem solving and mentoring, and the content is likely to include physical and psychological trials of many kinds. Certain questions may be answered explicitly or implicitly. In what circumstances, if any, does the culture permit homicide? What kinds of behavior are considered heroic or cowardly? Does the culture stress forgiveness over retaliation as an admirable trait?

---

[4]Calloway, C. (1997). Introduction: Surviving the dark ages. In C. G. Calloway (Ed.), *After King Philip's war: Presence and persistence in Indian New England* (pp. 1–28). Hanover, NH: University Press of New England.

---

epic A long dramatic narrative recounting the celebrated deeds of a historic or legendary hero—often sung or recited in poetic language

Here again, however, there are pitfalls in the process of interpreting art in relation to life. It is always possible that certain behaviors are acceptable or even admirable, with the distance or objectivity afforded by art, but are not at all so approved in daily life. In Euramerican culture, murderers, charlatans, and rascals sometimes have become popular heroes and the subjects of legends; North Americans would object, however, to an outsider's inference that they necessarily approved or wanted to emulate the morality of the notorious 19th-century Wild West outlaws Billy the Kid or Jesse James.

Tale

A third type of creative narrative, the **tale,** is recognized as fiction that is for entertainment but may also draw a moral or teach a practical lesson. Consider this brief summary of a tale from Ghana in West Africa, known as "Father, Son, and Donkey":

> A father and his son farmed their corn, sold it, and spent part of the profit on a donkey. When the hot season came, they harvested their yams and prepared to take them to storage, using their donkey. The father mounted the donkey and they all three proceeded on their way until they met some people. "What? You lazy man!" the people said to the father. "You let your young son walk barefoot on this hot ground while you ride on a donkey? For shame!" The father yielded his place to the son, and they proceeded until they came to an old woman. "What? You useless boy!" said the old woman. "You ride on the donkey and let your poor father walk barefoot on this hot ground? For shame!" The son dismounted, and both father and son walked on the road, leading the donkey behind them until they came to an old man. "What? You foolish people!" said the old man. "You have a donkey and you walk barefoot on the hot ground instead of riding?" And so it goes. Listen: when you are doing something and other people come along, just keep on doing what you like.

This is precisely the kind of tale that is of special interest in traditional folklore studies. It is an internationally popular "numbskull" tale. Versions of it have been recorded in India, Southwest Asia, southern and western Europe, and North America, as well as in West Africa. It is classified or catalogued as exhibiting a basic **motif**

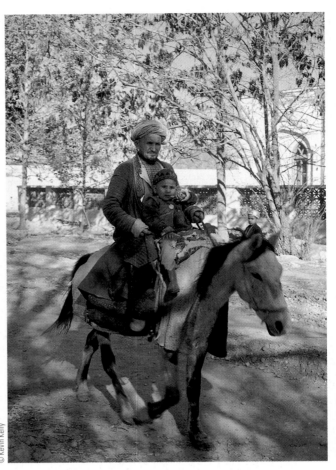

© Kevin Kelly

A scene such as this may bring to mind the internationally popular "Father, Son, and Donkey" tale. Told in different versions featuring localized draft animals, this tale conveys a basic motif or story situation—father and son trying in vain to please everyone.

or story situation—father and son trying to please everyone—one of the many thousands that have been found to recur in tales around the world. Despite variations in detail, every version follows the same basic structure in the sequence of events, sometimes called the *syntax* of the tale: A peasant father and son work together, a beast of burden is purchased, the three set out on a short excursion, the father rides and is criticized, the son rides and is criticized, both walk and are criticized, and a conclusion is drawn.

Tales of this sort (not to mention myths and legends) that are found to have wide geographic distribution raise the question: Where did they originate? Did the story arise only once and then pass from one culture to another (*diffusion*)? Or did the stories arise independently (*independent invention*) in response to like causes in similar settings, or perhaps as a consequence of inherited mental preferences and images deeply embedded in the evolutionary construction of the human brain? Or is it merely that there are logical limits to the structure

tale A creative narrative that is recognized as fiction for entertainment but may also draw a moral or teach a practical lesson.
motif A story situation in a tale.

of stories, so that, by coincidence, different cultures are bound to come up with similar motifs and syntax?[5]

A surprisingly large number of motifs in European and African tales are traceable to ancient sources in India, evidence of diffusion of tales. Of course, purely local tales also exist. Within any particular culture, anthropologists usually can categorize local types of tales: animal, human experience, trickster, dilemma, ghost, moral, scatological, nonsense tales, and so on. In West Africa, for example, there is a remarkable prevalence of stories with animal protagonists. Many were carried to the slaveholding areas of the Americas; the Uncle Remus stories about Brer Rabbit and Brer Fox may be part of this tradition.

The significance of tales for the anthropologist rests partly in this matter of their distribution. They provide evidence of either cultural contacts or cultural isolation and of limits of influence and cultural cohesion.

Anthropologists are interested, however, in more than these questions of distribution. Like legends, tales very often illustrate local solutions to universal human ethical problems, and in some sense they state a moral

philosophy. Anthropologists see that whether the tale of the father, the son, and the donkey originated in West Africa or arrived there from Europe or the Middle East, the very fact it is told in West Africa suggests that it states something valid for that culture. The tale's lesson of a necessary degree of self-confidence in the face of arbitrary social criticism is therefore something that can be read into the culture's values and beliefs.

Other Verbal Art

Myths, legends, and tales, prominent as they are in anthropological studies, in many cultures turn out to be no more important than many other verbal arts. In the culture of the Awlad 'Ali Bedouins of Egypt's western desert, for example, poetry is a lively and active verbal art, especially as a vehicle for personal expression and private communication. These people use two forms of poetry. One is the elaborately structured and heroic poems men chant or recite only on ceremonial occasions and in specific public contexts. The other is the *ghinnáwas* or "little songs" that punctuate everyday conversations. Simple in structure, these deal with personal matters and feelings more appropriate to informal social situations, and

---

[5]Gould, S. J. (2000). The narthex of San Marco and the pangenetic paradigm. *Natural History 109* (6), 29.

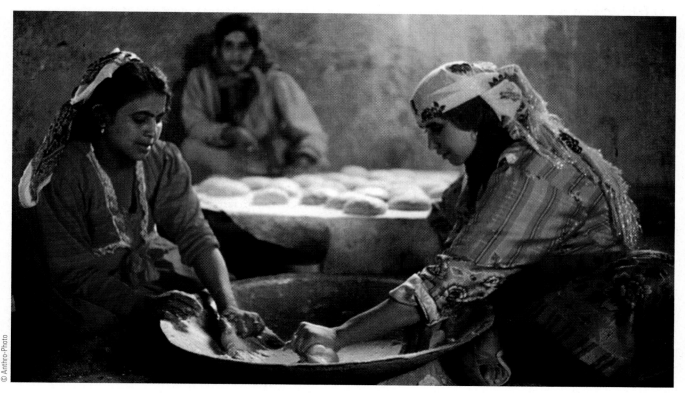

© Anthro-Photo

The *ghinnáwas* or "little songs" of the Awlad 'Ali Bedouins in Egypt punctuate conversations carried out while the people perform everyday chores, such as making bread, as these young women are doing. Through these "little songs," they can express what otherwise are taboo topics.

older men regard them as the unimportant productions of women and youths.

Despite this official devaluation in the male-dominated Bedouin society, however, "little songs" play a vital part in people's daily lives. In these poems individuals are shielded from the consequences of making statements and expressing sentiments that contravene the moral system. Paradoxically, by sharing these "immoral" sentiments only with intimates and veiling them in impersonal traditional formulas, those who recite them demonstrate that they have a certain control, which actually enhances their moral standing. As is often true of folklore in general, the "little songs" of the Awlad 'Ali provide a culturally appropriate outlet for otherwise taboo thoughts or opinions.[6] Disaster jokes are an example of this in contemporary North American society.

In all cultures the words of songs constitute a kind of poetry. Poetry and stories recited with gesture, movement, and props become drama. Drama combined with dance, music, and spectacle becomes a public celebration. The more we look at the individual arts, the clearer it becomes that they often are interrelated and interdependent. The verbal arts are, in fact, simply differing manifestations of the same creative imagination that produces music and the other arts.

MUSICAL ART

The study of music in specific cultural settings, beginning in the 19th century with the collection of folksongs, has developed into a specialized field of anthropological study called **ethnomusicology.** Like the study of folktales for their own sake, ethnomusicology is both related to and somewhat independent of anthropology. Nevertheless, it is possible to sort out several concerns that are of interest to the general discipline of anthropology.

To begin, we may ask, How does a culture conceive of music? What is considered of primary importance when distinguishing music from other modes of expression? Music to one person may be merely noise to another. Music is a form of communication that includes a nonverbal auditory component. The information it transmits is often abstract emotion rather than concrete ideas and is experienced in a variety of ways by different listeners. Such factors make music tough to define. In fact, no single definition of music can be agreed upon,

because different peoples may include or exclude different ideas within that category. Ethnomusicologists often distinguish between "music" and that which is "musical." The way to approach an unfamiliar kind of musical expression is to define it either in indigenous terms or in orthodox musicological terms such as melody, rhythm, and form.

Much of the historical development of ethnomusicology has been based upon musicology, which is primarily the study of European music. One problem has been the tendency to discuss music in terms of elements considered important in European music (tonality, rhythm, melody, and so on), when these may be of little importance to the practitioner. European music is defined, primarily, in terms of the presence of melody and rhythm. Melody is a function of tonality, and rhythm is an organizing concept involving tempo, stress, and measured repetition. Although these can be addressed in non-European music, they may not be the defining characteristics of a performance.

Early investigators of non-European song were struck by the apparent simplicity of *pentatonic* (five-tone) scales and a seemingly endless repetition of phrases. They often did not give sufficient credit to the formal function of repetition in such music, confusing repetition with lack of invention. A great deal of complex, sophisticated, non-European music was dismissed as primitive and formless and typically treated as trivial. Repetition, nevertheless, is a fact of music, including European music, and a basic formal principle.

In general, human music is said to differ from natural music—the songs of birds, wolves, and whales, for example—by being almost everywhere perceived in terms of a repertoire of tones at fixed or regular intervals: in other words, a scale. Scale systems and their modifications comprise what is known as **tonality** in music. These vary cross-culturally, so it is not surprising that something that sounds musical to one group of people may come across as noise to another.

Humans make closed systems out of a formless range of possible sounds by dividing the distance between a tone and its first *overtone* or sympathetic vibration (which always has exactly twice as many vibrations as the basic tone) into a series of measured steps. In the Western or European system, the distance between the basic tone and the first overtone is called the *octave;* it consists of seven steps—five *whole* tones and two *semitones.* The whole tones are further divided into semitones for a total working scale of twelve tones. Interestingly, some birds pitch their songs to the same scale as Western music,[7] perhaps influencing the way these people developed their scale.

---

[6]Abu-Lughod, L. (1986). *Veiled sentiments: Honor and poetry in a Bedouin society* (p. 252). Berkeley: University of California Press.

ethnomusicology The study of a society's music in terms of its cultural setting.
tonality In music, scale systems and their modifications.

---

[7]Gray, P. M., et al.. (2001). The music of nature and the nature of music. *Science 291,* 52.

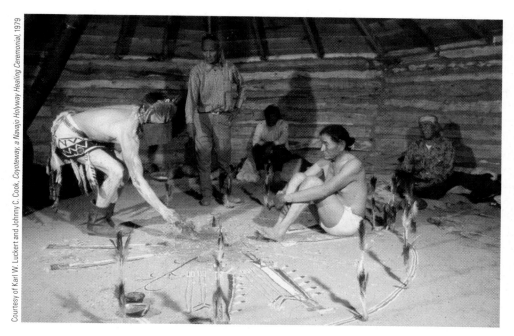

Navajo Indian sand paintings, created for sacred healing rituals, are among countless examples of the interconnection of art, religion, and healing. A Navajo ceremonial "singer" directs the communal creation of these intricate works. Each painting features supernatural images "dry painted" with powders made from ground sandstone, ochre, lime, and charcoal on a surface of smooth clean sand. As shown in this photo, the patient sits at the painting's center, where a masked *yé'ii* (supernatural being) impersonator replaces illness with supernatural essences. Ritual acts include singing, anointing, and drinking medicine. When the ceremony is over, the supernatural presences depicted in the sand painting are brushed from the surface and sent home.

One of the most common alternatives to the semitonal system is the pentatonic system, which, as noted, divides the scale into five nearly equidistant tones. Such scales may be found all over the world, including in much European folk music. Arabic and Persian music have smaller units of a third of a tone with scales of seventeen and twenty-four steps in the octave. Even quarter-tone scales are used in India with subtleties of shading that are nearly indistinguishable to a Western ear. Small wonder, then, that even when Westerners can hear what sounds like melody and rhythm in these systems, the total result may sound peculiar to them, or "out of tune." Anthropologists need a practiced ear to learn to appreciate some of the music they hear, and only some of the most skilled folksong collectors have attempted to notate and analyze music that is not semitonal.

Another organizing factor in music, rhythm—whether regular or irregular—may be more important than tonality. One reason for this may be our constant exposure to natural pulses, such as our own heartbeat and rhythms of breathing and walking. Even before we are born, we are exposed to our mother's heartbeat and rhythms of her movements, and as infants we experience rhythmic touching, petting, stroking, and rocking.[8]

The rhythms of traditional European music are most often measured into recurrent patterns of two, three, and four beats, with combinations of weak and strong beats to mark the division and form patterns. Non-European music is likely to move in patterns of five, seven, or eleven beats, with complex arrangements of internal beats and sometimes *polyrhythms:* one instrument or singer using a pattern of three beats, for example, while another uses a pattern of five or seven. Polyrhythms are frequent in the drum music of West Africa, which shows remarkable precision in the overlapping of rhythmic lines. Non-European music also may contain shifting rhythms: a pattern of three beats, for example, followed by a pattern of two or five beats with little or no regular recurrence or repetition of any one pattern, although the patterns are fixed and identifiable as units.

Like other art forms, music is often created for religious purposes. Shamans drum to help create a trance state, Buddhist monks chant to focus their meditation, Christians sing hymns to praise God, and so on. Indeed, the division between art and religion is by no means sharply defined. However uniquely imagined or creatively expressed, art and religion are about feelings, values, and ideas people have about themselves and the world around them and as such form part of a culture's superstructure.

FUNCTIONS OF ART

Art in all its many forms has countless functions beyond providing aesthetic pleasure, some of which have been touched upon or hinted at in the preceding paragraphs. For anthropologists and others seeking to understand cultures beyond their own, art offers insights into a culture's worldview, giving clues about everything from gender and kinship relations to religious beliefs, political ideas, historical memory, and so on.

For those within a society, art may serve to display social status, spiritual identity, and political power. An

---

[8]Dissanayake, E. (2000). Birth of the arts. *Natural History 109* (10), 89.

example of this can be seen in the totem poles of Indians living along America's northwest coast. Erected in front of the homes of chiefs, these poles are inscribed with symbols that are visual reminders of the social hierarchy. Similarly, art is used to mark kinship ties, as seen in Scottish tartans designed to identify clan affiliation. It can also affirm group solidarity and identity beyond kinship lines, as evidenced in national emblems such as the dragon (Bhutan), bald eagle (United States), maple leaf (Canada), crescent moon (Turkey), or cedar tree (Lebanon) that typically appear on coins, government buildings, and so on. Sometimes art is employed to express political themes and influence events, as in the counterculture rock and folk music of the 1960s in the United States. Other times it is used to transmit traditional culture and ancestral ties, as in epic poems passed down from generation to generation.

As an activity or behavior that contributes to human well-being and that helps give shape and significance to life, art is related to, yet distinct from, religion. In an elaborate ceremony involving ornamentation, masks, costumes, songs, dances, and effigies, it is not easy to say precisely where art stops and religion begins. Furthermore music, dance, and other arts may be used, like magic, to "enchant"—to take advantage of the emotional or psychological predispositions of another person or group so as to cause them to perceive reality in a way favorable to the interests of the "enchanter." Often it is created to honor or beseech the aid of a deity, an ancestral spirit, or an animal spirit. Indeed, the arts may be used to manipulate a seemingly inexhaustible list of human passions, including desire, terror, wonder, love, fantasy, and vanity.[9] (Marketing specialists, of course, are well aware of this, which is why they routinely employ certain music and images in their advertising.)

Clearly, art in all its varied forms is used in a vast number of ways for a great array of purposes. To simplify our discussion of its numerous functions, we will consider a particular art form as embedded in a cultural system: music.

Functions of Music

Evidence of humans making music reaches far back in time. Bone flutes and whistles that date back some 40,000 years and resemble today's recorders have been found by archaeologists. And historically known food-foraging peoples were not without music. In the Kalahari Desert, for example, a Ju/'hoansi hunter off by himself would play a tune on his bow simply to help while

[9]Gell, A. (1988). Technology and magic. *Anthropology Today 4* (2), 7; Lewis-Williams, J. D. (1997). Agency, art and altered consciousness: A motif in French (Quercy) upper Paleolithic parietal art. *Antiquity, 71*, 810–830.

away the time (long before anyone thought of beating swords into plowshares, some genius discovered that bows could be used not just to kill but to make music as well). In northern New England, Abenaki shamans used cedar flutes to call game, lure enemies, and attract women. In addition, shamans would use a drum—over which two rawhide strings were stretched to produce a buzzing sound, representing singing—to allow communication with the spirit world.

Music is also a powerful identifier. Many marginalized groups have used it for purposes of self-identification—as a means of building group solidarity and distinguishing themselves from dominant culture and sometimes as a channel for direct social and political commentary. Examples of this range from ethnic groups sponsoring music festivals to rock bands such as Britain's Rolling Stones, Coldplay, and Radiohead to North American rap artists OutKast, Eminem, and Jay-Z. Music plays an important role in Native American potlatches and powwows where Native American groups gather to reaffirm and celebrate their ethnic identities. And Scottish gatherings would not be Scottish without the sound of the highland bagpipes and the fiddle.

This power of music to shape identity has had varying consequences. The English understood that the bagpipes created a strong sense of identity among the highland regiments of the British army and encouraged it within certain bounds, even as they suppressed piping in Scotland itself under the Disarming Act. Over time, the British military piping tradition was assimilated into the Scottish piping tradition and so was accepted and spread by Scottish pipers. As a result, much of the supposedly Scottish piping one hears today consists of marches written within the conventions of the musical tradition of England, though shaped to fit the physical constraints of the instrument. Less often heard is the "classical" music known in Scottish Gaelic as *Pibroch* ("pipering") or, as some prefer to call traditional pipe music, *Ceòl Mòr* ("great music"). This more traditional Scottish pipe music has been revived over the past century and is now often romantically associated with rising cultural pride and even nationalist sentiment.

The English adoption of the highland bagpipe into Scottish regiments is an instance of those in authority employing music to further a political agenda. So, too, in Spain, former dictator Francisco Franco (who came to power in the 1930s) established community choruses in even the smallest towns to promote the singing of patriotic songs. Similarly, in Ireland Comhaltas Ceoltoiri Eireann has promoted the collection and performance of traditional Irish music, and in Brittany and Galicia music is playing an important role in attempts to revive the spirits of the indigenous Celtic cultures in these regions of France and Spain.

R. Todd Hoffman

Laborers in Mali, West Africa, working to the beat of a drum, which serves to set the pace of work, unify the workforce, and relieve boredom.

The social function of music is perhaps most obvious in song, since these contain verbal text. Like other verbal forms, songs often express a group's values, beliefs, and concerns, but they do so with an increased formalism resulting from adherence to the restrictions of systematic rules or conventions of pitch, rhythm, timbre, and musical genre. For this reason, music plays an important part in the cultural preservation and revitalization efforts of indigenous peoples around the world whose traditions were repressed or nearly exterminated through colonialism.

Work songs have played an important part in manual labor, serving to coordinate efforts in heavy or dangerous labor (such as weighing anchor and furling sail on board ships), to synchronize axe or hammer strokes, and to pass time and relieve tedium as with oyster-shucking songs. Songs also have been used to soothe babies to sleep, to charm animals into giving more milk, to keep witchcraft at bay, and to advertise goods. Songs may also serve social and political purposes, spreading particular ideas swiftly and effectively by giving them a special form involving poetic language and rhythm and by attaching a pleasing and appropriate tune, be it solemn or light.

In the United States numerous examples exist of marginalized social and ethnic groups attempting to gain a larger audience and more compassion for their plight through song. Perhaps no better example exists than African Americans, whose ancestors were cap-

tured and carried across the Atlantic Ocean to be sold as slaves. Out of their experience emerged spirituals and, ultimately gospel, jazz, blues, rock and roll, and rap. These forms all found their way into the North American mainstream, and white performers such as Elvis Presley and Benny Goodman (the latter with integrated bands—unusual in the 1930s) presented their own versions of this music to white audiences. Even composers of so-called serious music ranging from Leonard Bernstein to George Gershwin to Antonin Dvořák to Francis Poulenc were influenced by the music of African Americans. In short, music of a marginalized group of former slaves eventually captivated the entire world, even while the descendants of those slaves have had to struggle continually to escape their subordinate status.

In the 1950s and 1960s performers such as Pete Seeger and Joan Baez gained great visibility when supporting civil and human rights causes in the United States. Indeed, both performers' celebrity status led to the broader dissemination of their social and political beliefs. Such celebrity status comes from skill in performing and communicating with the intended audience. So powerful a force was music in the civil rights and peace movements of the time that Seeger was targeted by right-wing Senator Joseph McCarthy's anti-Communist crusade, which aimed to discredit the political left as anti-American and unpatriotic. Seeger became one of many performers blacklisted by the entertainment industry due to this political witch-hunt.

GLOBALSCAPE

Do Coffins Fly? In his workshop in Nungua, Ghana, master carpenter Paa Joe makes unique painted wooden coffins for his clients in his Ga society and beyond. Some are spectacular, representing a richly colored tropical fish or even luxury cars, such as Mercedes-Benz. Celebrating the life accomplishments of the deceased, these designer coffins show off the family's prominent status and wealth.

As a collective expression of culturally shared ideas about the afterlife, a Ga funeral ceremony reminds the mourners of important values embodied in the departed individual. Seeing the deceased off on a journey to the afterlife, Ga mourners call out praises to this person, and some may even pour schnapps on the coffin. Hence-

forth, the deceased will continue to be ritually honored as an ancestor by descendants.

The 747 jumbo jet coffin pictured here confers upon the deceased the prestige and mystique of air travel. Its colors, blue and white, are those of the KLM Royal Dutch Airline, a long-time provider of air service between this West African country and the rest of the world. Its creator, Paa Joe, began working at age 15 for his cousin Kane Quaye, a carpenter known for designer coffins. Later, Joe started his own workshop, and before too long he began receiving orders from other parts of the world—not only from individuals but also from museums. Using wood, enamel paint, satin, and Christmas wrapping paper, Joe created this KLM airplane coffin in

1997 for the Smithsonian National Museum of Natural History in Washington, DC, where millions of visitors from all over the globe now admire this Ghanian funereal ritual object.

Global Twister When the Smithsonian museum purchased one of Paa Joe's remarkable coffins for public display, did this West African funereal ritual object transform into a work of art?
SOURCE: Based on script for African Voices *exhibition at NMNH, Smithsonian courtesy of Dr. Mari Jo Arnoldi.*

In Australia, certain ceremonial songs of the Aborigines have taken on a new legal function, as they are being introduced into court as evidence of early settlement patterns. These songs carry ancient stories recounting adventures of mythic ancestors who lived in "Dreamtime" and created waterholes, mountains, valleys, and other significant features in the landscape. The ancestors' tracks are known as *songlines,* and through ceremonial songs about them countless generations of Aborigines

have passed on sacred ecological knowledge. This oral tradition helps Aborigines to claim extensive indigenous land ownership, thus allowing them greater authority to use the land, as well as to negotiate and profit from the sale of natural resources. This had been impossible before. The British, upon their annexation of Australia, declared the land ownerless (*Terra Nullius*). Although the Aborigines had preserved their records of ownership in song and story, these were not admissible in the British

Anthropologists of Note

Frederica de Laguna (1906–2004)

A concern with the arts of non-Western people has always been an important part of anthropology, as illustrated by the work of anthropologist Frederica de Laguna. Educated at Bryn Mawr College and Columbia University, where she earned her doctorate, she made her first trip into the field with a Danish expedition to Greenland in 1929. A year later, she began work in southeastern Alaska, a region to which she returned repeatedly until the end of the 20th century. Her first research there was archaeological, and she was a pioneer in southeastern Alaskan prehistory. But as her interest in native peoples grew, she became increasingly involved with ethnographic work as well. She found out that to understand the past, one had to know what it led to, just as to understand the present native people, one had to know their past.

In 1949, after many seasons of work in different localities, de Laguna began a project to trace the roots of the lifeways of the Tlingit Indians of Yakutat through combining archaeological and ethnographic research. This resulted in a monumental three-volume work published in

Laura Bliss Spaan

1972, *Under Mount St. Elias.* Considerable space in this trilogy is devoted to transcriptions of Tlingit songs and stories just as they were related and performed by elders now long dead. Beyond its

scientific anthropological value, this work has come to be of enormous importance to the Tlingit themselves.

When "Freddy" de Laguna began to work at Yakutat, Tlingit children were being sent to government boarding schools, where they were told nothing of their own culture and were harshly punished for even speaking their own language. The aim was to stamp out native culture to facilitate assimilation into mainstream American culture. Thus, as the elders died out, many traditions were being lost. But with the publication of de Laguna's trilogy, the community has been able to revitalize much that they were in danger of losing. As de Laguna said, songs and stories are for giving back, and so it was that in 1997 the Tlingit of Yakutat honored her with a potlatch ceremony in recognition of what she gave back to them.

Since her death at age 98 in 2004, generations of Tlingit with whom she worked readily acknowledge that much of their present-day cultural vigor and pride in who they are is due to "Grandmother Freddy's" work.

---

courts. In the early 1970s, however, the Aborigines exposed the injustice of the situation, and the Australian government began responding in a more favorable, if still limited, fashion, granting the claims of traditional ownership to groups in the Northern Territory. In 1992 the legitimacy of the concept of *Terra Nullius* was overturned, and native claims are now being presented in the other territories as well. These newer claimants are granted equal partnership with developers and others. Sacred sites are being recognized, and profits are being shared with the traditional owners. Proof of native ownership includes recordings of Aborigine songs indicative of traditional patterns of settlement, travel, and land use.[10]

Music gives basic human ideas a concrete form, made memorable and attractive with melody and rhythm, to basic human ideas. Whether a song's content is didactic,

satirical, inspirational, religious, political, or purely emotional, the formless has been given form, and feelings hard to express in words alone are communicated in a symbolic and memorable way that can be repeated and shared. The group is consequently united and has the sense that their shared experience, whatever it may be, has shape and meaning. This, in turn, shapes and gives meaning to the community.

ART, GLOBALIZATION, AND CULTURAL SURVIVAL

Clearly, there is more to art than meets the eye or ear (not to mention the nose and tongue—consider how burning incense or tobacco are part of the artfulness of sacred ceremonies, and imagine the cross-cultural array of smells and tastes in the cooking arts). In fact, art is such a significant part of any culture that many indigenous groups around the world whose lifeways have been threatened—first by colonialism and now by globaliza-

---

[10]Koch, G. (1997). Songs, land rights, and archives in Australia. *Cultural Survival Quarterly 20* (4). See also Berndt, R. M., & Berndt, C. H. (1989). *The Speaking Land: Myth and story in Aboriginal Australia.* New York: Penguin.

tion—are using aesthetic expressions as part of a cultural survival strategy. They are finding that a traditional art form—a dance, a song, a dress, a basket, a carving, or anything that is distinctly beautiful and well-made or performed—can serve as a powerful symbol that conveys the vital message, "We're still here, and we're still a culturally distinct people with our own particular beliefs and values." (See Anthropologist of Note box.)

There are many examples of art playing a role in indigenous rights efforts. Consider the native rights case of the Aroostook Band of Micmac Indians in northern Maine, described in the Anthropology Applied box in the Kinship and Descent chapter. Building support for this particular case involved making a documentary film to inform politicians and the general public about the band's cultural identity and tribulations.[11] At the time,

only a dozen or so families in this band still practiced traditional wood-splint basketry. However, it had been a common livelihood for many generations, and almost every band member had parents or grandparents who had made baskets.

Emblematic of Micmac identity, including their stubborn desire for self-determination, basketry became a focal point of the film, which ultimately played a key role in the success of the band's native rights case. More than this, the film helped create a wider market for Micmac baskets, and by conveying the diligence and real skill involved in making them, it justified raising the prices of the baskets to levels that make the craft a viable livelihood. This, in turn, has prompted young people to take up basketry and strengthened their relationships with Micmac elders who are now passing the age-old art on to a new generation.

A great array of similar examples of the link between art and cultural survival can be found all around the world.

[11]Prins, H. E. L., & Carter, K. (1986). *Our lives in our hands*. Video and 16mm. Color. 50 min. Distributed by Watertown, MA: Documentary Educational Resources and Bucksport, ME: Northeast Historic Film; see also Prins, H. E. L. (2002). Visual media and the primitivist perplex: Colonial fantasies, indigenous imagination, and advocacy in North America. In F. D. Ginsburg et al., *Media*

worlds: Anthropology on new terrain (pp. 58–74). Berkeley: University of California Press.

Questions for Reflection

1. Throughout history humans worldwide have creatively articulated their feelings and ideas about themselves and the world around them. Considering the range of possible art forms, how have people in your home community met this particular challenge? Can you identify specific examples in music, dance, imagery, or sculpture that are not only beautiful but also meaningful?

2. Among the Maori in New Zealand, tattooing is a traditional form of skin art, and their tattoo designs are typically based on cultural symbols understood by all members in the community. Are the tattoo designs in your culture based on traditional motifs that have a shared symbolic meaning?

3. Because kinship relations are important in small-scale traditional societies, these relationships are often symbolically represented in artistic designs and motifs. What are some of the major concerns in your society, and are these concerns reflected in any of your culture's art forms?

4. In some cultures art is produced not to be preserved and enjoyed by the living but to be buried along with the dead. In fact, in some cultures highly valued art objects may also be burned or otherwise destroyed. Can you think of any reason for such seemingly irrational cultural practices?

5. Many museums and private collectors in Europe and North America are interested in so-called tribal art, such as African statues or American Indian masks originally used in sacred rituals. Are there sacred objects such as paintings or carvings in your religion that might also be collected, bought, or sold as art?

Suggested Readings

Dundes, A. (1980). *Interpreting folklore*. Bloomington: Indiana University Press.

A collection of articles that assesses the materials folklorists have amassed and classified, this book seeks to broaden and refine traditional assumptions about the proper subject matter and methods of folklore.

Hannah, J. L. (1988). *Dance, sex, and gender*. Chicago: University of Chicago Press.

Like other art forms, dance is a social act that contributes to the continuation and emergence of culture. One of the oldest art forms, dance shares the same instrument, the human body, with sexuality. This book, written for a broad nonspecialist audience, explicitly examines sexuality and the construction of gender identities as they are played out in the production and visual imagery of dance.

Layton, R. (1991). *The anthropology of art* (2nd ed.). Cambridge, England: Cambridge University Press.

This readable introduction to the diversity of non-Western art deals with questions of aesthetic appreciation, the use of art, and the big question: What *is* art?

Morphy, H., & Perkins, M. (Eds.). (2006). *Anthropology of art: A reader*. Boston: Blackwell.

This illustrated anthology explores the art of different cultures at different times, covering the essential theoretical debates in the anthropology of art—including definitions of art and aesthetics, the nature of authenticity and representational processes, the Primitivism controversy, and the history of trade and commodification.

Seeger, A. (2004). *Why Suya sing: A musical anthropology.* Champaign: University of Illinois Press.

Examining the myth telling, speech making, and singing of Suyá Indians in Mato Grosso, Brazil, Seeger considers why music is important for them—and by extension for other groups. He reveals how Suyá singing creates euphoria out of silence, a village community out of a collection of houses, a socialized adult out of a boy, and contributes to the formation of ideas about time, space, and social identity.

Venbrux, E., Rosi, P. S., & Welsch, R. L. (Eds.) (2006). *Exploring world art.* Longrove, IL: Waveland Press.

Ethnographic case studies examine the contemporary art world from local and comparative global perspectives, spanning topics such as artistic agency, new art forms and media, arenas of cultural production, and the role of gender in these innovative traditions.

Thomson Audio Study Products

Enjoy the MP3-ready Audio Lecture Overviews for each chapter and a comprehensive audio glossary of key terms for quick study and review. Whether walking to class, doing laundry, or studying at your desk, you now have the freedom to choose when, where, and how you interact with your audio-based educational media. See the preface for information on how to access this on-the-go study and review tool.

The Anthropology Resource Center

www.thomsonedu.com/anthropology
The Anthropology Resource Center provides extended learning materials to reinforce your understanding of key concepts in the four fields of anthropology. For each of the four fields, the Resource Center includes dynamic exercises including video exercises, map exercises, simulations, and "Meet the Scientists" interviews, as well as critical thinking questions that can be assigned and e-mailed to instructors. The Resource Center also provides breaking news in anthropology and interesting material on applied anthropology to help you link what you are learning to the world around you.

15 Processes of Change

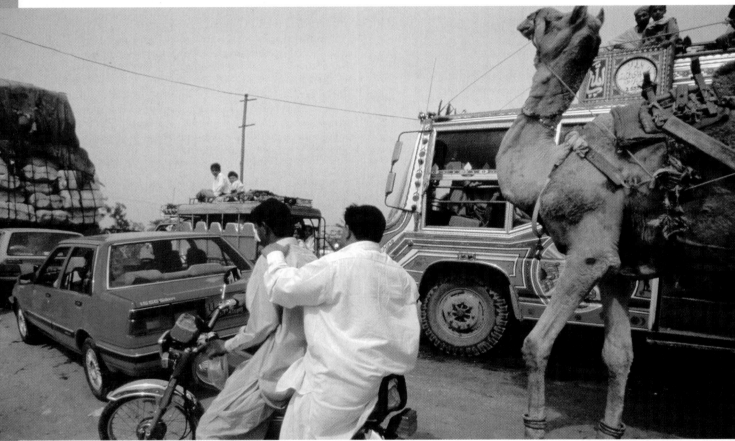

© Randy Olson/National Geographic Image Collection

CHALLENGE ISSUE

For long-term survival, human cultures have had to adapt to different environments and shifting circumstances. Today's technological and other major changes challenge us to adjust at an ever-faster pace. The challenge is all the more unsettling for traditional peoples around the world, for whom changes are often imposed by powerful outside forces undermining their customary ways of life. However, there are also many examples of traditional peoples confronting change on their own terms, welcoming certain new ideas, products, or practices into their lives as improvements. So it is with the means of transportation in developing countries such as Pakistan where the heavily-packed mules and camels that travel desert and mountain trails may also be found on city streets among cars, trucks, and buses. Since city traffic is often congested and slow-paced, it does not really matter whether one's transportation is a shrub-eating camel or a gas-fed vehicle.

Why Do Cultures Change?

All cultures change at one time or another for a variety of reasons. Although people may deliberately alter their ways in response to problems or challenges, much change is unforeseen, unplanned, and undirected. Changes in existing values and behavior may also come about due to contact with other peoples who introduce new ideas or tools. This may even involve the massive imposition of foreign ideas and practices through conquest of one group by another. Through cultural change, societies can adapt to altered conditions; however, not all change is positive or adaptive.

How Do Cultures Change?

The mechanisms of culture change include innovation, diffusion, cultural loss, and acculturation. Innovation is the discovery or creation of something that is then accepted by fellow members in a society. Diffusion is the borrowing of something from another group, and cultural loss is the abandonment of an existing practice or trait, with or without replacement. Acculturation is a massive change that comes about in a group due to intensive firsthand contact with another, usually more powerful, group. Typically, it occurs when dominant societies forcefully expand their activities beyond their borders, pressuring other societies to abandon their traditional cultures in favor of the foreign.

What Is Modernization?

Modernization is a problematic term referring to a process of change by which traditional, nonindustrial societies acquire characteristics of technologically complex societies. Accelerated modernization interconnecting all parts of the world is known as globalization. Although commonly assumed to be a good thing, modernization has also led to the destruction of treasured customs and values, leaving many people unsettled, disoriented, and demoralized.

Culture has become the primary medium through which the human species adapts to changes and solves the problems of existence. Various cultural institutions—such as religion, kinship and marriage, and political and economic organization—mesh to form an integrated cultural system. Because systems generally work to maintain stability, cultures are often fairly stable and remain so unless there is a critical change in one or more significant factors such as natural environment, technology, population density—or in human perceptions of the various conditions to which they are adapted.

Archaeological studies reveal how elements of a culture may persist for long periods. In northeastern North America, for example, the cultures of indigenous inhabitants remained relatively consistent over thousands of years because they successfully adapted to relatively minor fluctuations in their social conditions and natural environments, making changes from time to time in tools, utensils, and other material support.

Although stability may be a striking feature of many traditional cultures, all cultures are capable of adapting to changing conditions—climatic, economic, political, or ideological. Adaptation is a consequence of change that happens to work favorably for a population.

However, not all change is positive or adaptive, and not all cultures are equally well equipped for making the necessary adjustments in a timely fashion. In a stable society, change may occur gently and gradually, without altering in any fundamental way the culture's underlying structures, as was the case in much of North America before the European invasion several centuries ago. Sometimes, though, the pace of change may increase dramatically, to the point of destabilizing or even wrecking a cultural system. The modern world is full of examples of such radical changes, from the disintegration of the Soviet Union to the utter devastation of many indigenous communities in the Amazon caused by state efforts to develop Indian homelands and capitalize on the vast rainforest's natural resources.

The causes of change are many, including accidental discoveries, deliberate attempts to solve a perceived problem, and interaction with other people who introduce—or force—new ideas or tools or ways of life. Sometimes change is caused by the unexpected outcome of particular actions or events. Among countless examples is the establishment of European colonies in the homelands of Algonquian-speaking natives in northeastern America nearly 500 years ago. Many people today assume this came about because the culture of the newcomers was better or more advanced than that of the region's original inhabitants. However, one could just as well argue that it was the reverse, for at the time, these Indians had higher quality diets, enjoyed better health, and experienced less violence in their lives than did most Europeans.[1]

A deeper look at American history shows that the colonial settlements in New England were actually the outcome of a series of unrelated historical events that happened to coincide at a critical time. In the 1500s, economic and political developments in England drove large numbers of small farmers off the land during a period of population growth, thereby forcing an outward migration. By pure chance, this took place shortly after the European discovery of the Americas. Seeing the New World as an answer to its overpopulation, the English attempted to establish overseas colonies in lands they claimed and renamed New England. Early efforts failed, until an epidemic of unprecedented scope resulted in the sudden death of 75 to 90 percent of the indigenous inhabitants.

This devastating epidemic occurred because the region's native communities were exposed to a host of foreign diseases through contact with European fishermen and traders. It left the weakened remnants of indigenous survivors with few defenses against aggressive colonizers, many of whom possessed natural immunity to the diseases. (For centuries, Europeans had been living under conditions that were ideal for the incubation and spread of infectious diseases, which periodically killed off up to 80 percent of local populations. Since those who survived had a higher resistance to the diseases than those who succumbed, such resistance became more common in European populations over time. Indians at the time of the European invasion, by contrast, lacked all resistance to these diseases.)

Although the crucial issue of immunity played a huge role in England's North American colonization efforts, it is unlikely the English could have dispossessed the surviving indigenous peoples from their land were it not for one other important factor: They crossed the Atlantic Ocean equipped with the political and military techniques for dominating other peoples—tactics previously used to impose rule over the Scots, Irish, and Welsh. In addition, they came with the ideology of a "just war," which they believed justified dispossessing America's indigenous peoples who fought back in defense.

Change imposed upon one group by another continues in much of the world today as culture contact intensifies between societies unequal in power. Among those who have the power to drive and direct change in their favor, it is typically referred to as "progress." But progress is a relative term that implies improvement as de-

---

[1]Stannard, D. E. (1992). *American holocaust* (pp. 57–67). Oxford: Oxford University Press.

Anthropologists of Note
Eric R. Wolf (1923–1999)

Like the millions of peasants about whom he wrote, Eric Wolf personally experienced radical upheaval in his life due to powerful outside political forces. A war refugee in his teens, he went on to survive the battlefields and mass murders of Nazi-occupied Europe. Driven by the inequities and atrocities he witnessed during World War II, he turned to anthropology to sort through issues of power. Viewing anthropology as the most scientific of the humanities and the most humane of the sciences, he became famous for his comparative historical studies on peasants, power, and the transforming impact of capitalism on traditional nations.

Eric Wolf's life began in Austria shortly after the First World War. During that terrible conflict, his Austrian father had been a prisoner of war in Siberia, where he met Wolf's mother, a Russian exile. When peace returned, the couple married and settled in Vienna, where Eric was born in 1923. Growing up in Austria's capital and then (because of his father's job) in Sudetenland in what is now the Czech Republic, young Eric enjoyed a life of relative ease. He relished summers spent in the Alps among local peasants in exotic costumes, and he drank in his mother's tales about her father's adventures with Siberian nomads.

Life changed for Eric in 1938 when Adolf Hitler grabbed power in Germany, annexed Austria and Sudetenland, and threatened Jews like the Wolfs. Seek-

ing security for their 15-year-old son, Eric's parents sent him to high school in England. In 1940, a year after World War II broke out, British authorities believed invasion was imminent and ordered aliens, including Eric, into an internment camp. There he met other refugees from Nazi-occupied Europe and had his first exposure to Marxist theories. Soon, he left England for New York City and enrolled at Queens College, where Professor Hortense Powdermaker, a former student of Malinowski, introduced him to anthropology.

In 1943, the 20-year-old refugee enlisted in the U.S. Army's 10th Mountain Division. Fighting in the mountains of Tuscany, Italy, he won a Silver Star for combat bravery. At the war's end, Wolf returned to the United States, completed his bachelor's degree, and went on to

graduate school at Columbia University, studying anthropology under Julian Steward and Ruth Benedict. After earning his doctorate in 1951, based on fieldwork in Puerto Rico, he did extensive research on Mexican peasants.

Following short stints at various U.S. universities, he became a professor at the University of Michigan in 1961. A prolific writer, Wolf gained tremendous recognition for his fourth book, *Peasant Wars of the Twentieth Century,* published in 1969 during the height of the Vietnam War. Against that war, he headed a newly founded ethics committee in the American Anthropological Association and helped expose counter-insurgency uses of anthropological research in Southeast Asia.

Wolf left Michigan in 1971, accepting a distinguished professorship at Lehman College in the Bronx, New York. There his classes were filled with working-class students of all ethnic backgrounds, including many who took the courses he taught in Spanish. In addition, he taught anthropology at the Graduate School of the City University of New York. After many more publications, Wolf wrote his award-winning book, *Europe and the People Without History* (1982). In 1990, he received a MacArthur "genius" prize. Shortly before his death of cancer in 1999, he published *Envisioning Power: Ideologies of Dominance and Crisis,* which explores how ideas and power are connected though the medium of culture.

fined by the people who profit or otherwise benefit from the changes set into motion. In other words, progress is in the eye of the beholder.

In recent decades, some anthropologists have focused on the historical impact European capitalist expansionism has had on indigenous cultures all around the world, radically changing or even destroying them. One of the first and most prominent among these anthropologists was Eric Wolf, who personally experienced the global havoc and upheaval of the 20th century (see Anthropologist of Note).

MECHANISMS OF CHANGE

Anthropologists are not only interested in the structures of cultures as systems of adaptation, which help us understand how a population maintains itself in a certain habitat, but also in explaining processes of culture change. Some of the major mechanisms involved in culture change are innovation, diffusion, and cultural loss. These types of change are typically voluntary and are not imposed on a population by outside forces.

A Hopi Indian woman firing pottery vessels. The earliest discovery that firing clay vessels makes them more durable took place in Asia, probably when clay-lined basins next to cooking fires were accidentally fired. Later, a similar innovation took place in the Americas.

© Stephen Trimble

Innovation

The ultimate source of all culture change is innovation: any new idea, method, or device that gains widespread acceptance in society. **Primary innovation** is the creation, invention, or chance discovery of a completely new idea, method, or device. A **secondary innovation** is a deliberate application or modification of an existing idea, method, or device.

An example of a primary innovation is the discovery that firing clay makes it permanently hard. Presumably, accidental firing of clay occurred frequently in ancient cooking fires—but a chance occurrence is of no account unless someone perceives an application of it. This perception took place about 25,000 years ago, when people began making figurines of fired clay. However, it was not until some time between 8,500 and 9,000 years ago that people recognized a highly practical application of fired clay and began using it to make pottery containers and cooking vessels—a secondary innovation.

THOMSON AUDIO STUDY PRODUCTS Take advantage of the MP3-ready Audio Lecture Overviews and comprehensive audio glossary of key terms for each chapter. See the preface for information on how to access this on-the-go study and review tool.

primary innovation The creation, invention, or chance discovery of a completely new idea, method, or device.
secondary innovation A new and deliberate application or modification of an existing idea, method, or device

As nearly as we can reconstruct it, the development of the earliest known pottery vessels came about in the following way:[2] About 9,000 years ago, people in Southwest Asia still relied upon stone bowls, baskets, and animal-hide bags for containers. However, they were familiar with the working of clay, using it to build houses, line storage pits, and model figurines. In addition, their cooking areas included clay-lined basins built into the floor and clay ovens and hearths, making the accidental firing of clay inevitable. Once the significance of fired clay—the primary innovation—was understood, then the application of known techniques to it—secondary innovation—became possible. Clay could be modeled in the familiar way but now into the known shapes of existing containers. It could then be fired, either in an open fire or in the same facilities used for cooking food. The earliest known Southwest Asian pottery imitates leather and stone containers, but over time potters developed shapes and decorative techniques specifically suited to the new technology.

Archaeological research shows that the earliest known clay vessels produced were initially handmade, and the earliest furnaces or kilns were the same ovens used for cooking. As people became more adept at making pottery, they refined the technology. To aid in production, the clay could be modeled on a mat or other surface that could be turned as work progressed. Hence, the potter could sit in one place while working, without having to get up to move around the clay. A further re-

[2]Amiran, R. (1965). The beginnings of pottery-making in the Near East. In F. R. Matson (Ed.), *Ceramics and man* (pp. 240–247). Viking Fund Publications in Anthropology, 41.

Once one's reflexes become adjusted to doing something one way, it becomes difficult to do it differently. Thus, when a North American visits one of the world's many left-side drive countries (about sixty) such as Great Britain (or vice versa), learning to drive on the "wrong" side of the road is difficult.

finement was to mount the movable surface on a vertical rotating shaft—an application of a known principle used for drills—creating the potter's wheel and permitting mass production. Kilns, too, were modified for better heat circulation by separating the firing chamber from the fire itself. By chance, these improved kilns produced enough heat to smelt metal ores such as copper, tin, gold, silver, and lead. Presumably, this discovery was made by accident—another primary innovation—and set the stage for the eventual development of the forced-draft furnace out of the earlier pottery kiln.

The accidental discoveries responsible for primary innovations are not generated by environmental change or some other need, nor are they necessarily adaptive. They are, however, given structure by the cultural context. Thus, the outcome of the discovery of fired clay by migratory food foragers 25,000 years ago was very different from what it was when discovered later by more sedentary farmers in Southwest Asia, where it set off a cultural chain reaction as one invention led to another. Indeed, given particular sets of cultural goals, values, and knowledge, certain innovations are nearly inevitable.

Although a culture's internal dynamics may encourage certain innovative tendencies, they may discourage or remain neutral about others. Indeed, Polish astronomer Nicolaus Copernicus's discovery in the early 1500s of the rotation of the planets around the sun and the discovery of the basic laws of heredity in the early 1860s by botanist Gregor Mendel, a Roman Catholic monk in what is now the Czech Republic, are instances of genuine creative insights out of step with the established needs, values, and goals of their times and places. In fact, Mendel's work remained obscure until sixteen years

after his death, when three scientists working independently rediscovered, all in the same year (1900), the same laws of heredity. Thus, in the context of turn-of-the-century Western culture, Mendel's laws were bound to be discovered, even if Mendel's botanical experiments had not revealed them earlier.

Although an innovation must be reasonably consistent with a society's needs, values, and goals in order to gain acceptance, it takes more than this. Force of custom or habit tends to obstruct ready acceptance of the new or unfamiliar, for people typically stick with what they are used to rather than adopt something strange that requires adjustment on their part.

An example of this can be seen in the continued use of the QWERTY keyboard, named for the lineup of the top row of letters and familiar to all who use English language keyboards today. Devised in 1874, the QWERTY system was the first commercially successful typewriter. In 1932, after extensive study, U.S. education professor August Dvorak developed a more efficient system known as the Dvorak keyboard (Figure 15.1). Tests have shown that it can be learned in one-third the time it takes to master QWERTY. Moreover, once learned, the Dvorak system is less fatiguing and increases the average keyboard operator's accuracy by 68 percent and speed by 74 percent. So why has not Dvorak replaced QWERTY? The answer is commitment.

Because QWERTY had a head start, by the time Dvorak came along manufacturers, typists, teachers, salespeople, and office managers were committed to the old keyboard. It was what they were used to, and to this day it remains the standard on English language keyboards incorporated in a growing array of techno-

Figure 15.1

Dvorak and QWERTY keyboards, compared. Although superior to the latter in virtually every way, the Dvorak keyboard has not been adopted owing to the head start enjoyed by QWERTY.

Change, whether generated within a society or introduced from the outside, may encounter unexpected cultural obstacles. Such obstacles are often ideologically embedded in religious faith-based traditions, such as some conservative Mennonite sects in North America rejecting motorized vehicles in their rural communities. In several Asian and African countries primarily inhabited by Muslims, orthodox religious groups oppose modern development and the spread of what they consider immoral foreign influences. Instead, they seek to return to or maintain a society based on Muslim traditions. Here we see a class of traditional Muslim students in Lahore, Pakistan, studying the holy scriptures of the Koran at a *madrassah* (religious school).

logical innovations—from PCs and laptops to handheld computers.[3]

Obviously, an innovation is not assured of acceptance simply because it is notably better than the thing, method, or idea it might replace. Much depends on the prestige of the innovator and potential adopters. If the innovator's prestige is high, this will help gain more general acceptance for the innovation. If it is low, acceptance is less likely, unless the innovator can attract a sponsor who has high prestige.

Diffusion

The spread of certain ideas, customs, or practices from one culture to another is known as **diffusion.** So common is cross-cultural borrowing that North American anthropologist Ralph Linton suggested that it accounts

[3]Diamond, J. (1997). The curse of QWERTY. *Discover 18* (4), 34–42.

diffusion The spread of certain ideas, customs, or practices from one culture to another.

for as much as 90 percent of any culture's content. People are creative about their borrowing, however, picking and choosing from multiple possibilities and sources. Usually their selections are limited to those compatible with the existing culture. In Guatemala in the 1960s, for example, Maya Indians, who then (as now) made up more than half of that country's population, would adopt Western ways if the practical advantage of what they adopted was self-evident and did not conflict with deeply rooted traditional values and customs. The use of metal hoes, shovels, and machetes became standard early on, for they are superior to stone tools and yet compatible with the cultivation of corn in the traditional way by men using hand tools.

Yet, certain other modern practices that might seem advantageous to the Maya were resisted if they were perceived to be in conflict with Indian tradition. Pursuing these practices could make one a social outcast. This happened to a young farmer who tried using chemical fertilizers and pesticides to grow cash crops of vegetables not eaten by the Maya to sell in the city. He found he could not secure a "good" woman for a wife—a "good" woman (in his cultural context) being one who has never had sex with another man and is hard-working, skilled at

Figure 15.2
The diffusion of tobacco. Having spread from the tropics of the western hemisphere to much of the rest of North and South America, it spread rapidly to the rest of the world after Italian explorer Christopher Columbus first crossed the Atlantic in 1492.

domestic chores, and willing to attend to her husband's needs. However, after abandoning his unorthodox ways, he gained acceptance in his community as a "real" man— one who provides for his household by working steadily at farming and making charcoal in the traditional ways. No longer conspicuous as someone different from other local men, he married well within a short time.[4]

An awareness of the extent of cultural borrowing can be eye opening. Take, for example, the numerous things that people all around the globe have borrowed from American Indians. Domestic plants developed ("invented") by the Indians—potatoes, avocados, beans, squash, tomatoes, peanuts, manioc, chili peppers, chocolate, sweet potatoes, and corn or maize, to name a few— furnish a major portion of the world's food supply. In fact, American Indians are recognized as primary contributors to the world's varied cuisine and credited with developing the largest array of nutritious foods.[5]

As for drugs and stimulants introduced by Indians, tobacco is the best known (Figure 15.2), but others include the coca in cocaine, ephedra in ephedrine, datura

in pain relievers, and cascara in laxatives. Early on, Europeans discovered that Indians had a most sophisticated pharmacy. For instance, Spanish Jesuit missionaries in Peru and Ecuador in the 17th century learned from indigenous healers about the medicinal properties of the bitter tree bark of which quinine is extracted to treat malaria. All told, 200 plants and herbs used by Native Americans for medicinal purposes have at one time or another been included in official government-approved prescription and over the counter drugs.

On top of this, varieties of cotton developed by Indians supply much of the world's clothing needs, while the woolen poncho, the parka, and moccasins are universally familiar items. These borrowings are so thoroughly integrated into contemporary societies across the globe that few people are aware of their source.

Despite the obvious importance of diffusion, an innovation from another culture probably faces more obstacles when it comes to being accepted than does one that is "homegrown" simply because it is foreign. In the United States, for example, this is one reason why people have been so reluctant to abandon the cumbersome English system of weights and measures for the far more logical metric system. While all other countries in the world have essentially converted to metric, in the United States the switchover is still less than about 50 percent.

---

[4]Reina, R. E. (1966). *The law of the saints* (pp. 65–68). Indianapolis: Bobbs-Merrill.

[5]Weatherford, J. (1988). *Indian givers: How the Indians of the Americas transformed the New World* (p. 115). New York: Ballantine.

Hence, ethnocentrism may act as a barrier to cultural diffusion.

Cultural Loss

Most often people look at culture change as an accumulation of innovations. Frequently, however, the acceptance of a new innovation results in **cultural loss**—the abandonment of an existing practice or trait. For example, in ancient times chariots and carts were used widely in northern Africa and southwestern Asia, but wheeled vehicles virtually disappeared from Morocco to Afghanistan about 1,500 years ago. They were replaced by camels, not because of some reversion to the past but because camels used as pack animals worked better. The old Roman empire roads had deteriorated, and these sturdy animals traveled well with or without roads. Their endurance, longevity, and ability to ford rivers and traverse rough ground made pack camels admirably suited for the region. Plus, they were economical in terms of labor: A wagon required a man for every two draft animals, but a single person could manage up to six pack camels.

Reflecting on this, U.S. paleontologist Stephen Jay Gould commented that this surprises most Westerners because:

> Wheels have come to symbolize in our culture . . . intelligent exploitation and technological progress. . . . The success of camels reemphasizes a fundamental theme. . . . Adaptation, be it biological or cultural, represents a better fit to specific, local environments, not an inevitable stage in a ladder of progress. Wheels were a formidable invention, and their uses are manifold. . . . But camels may work better in some circumstances. Wheels, like wings, fins, and brains, are exquisite devices for certain purposes, not signs of intrinsic superiority.[6]

Often overlooked is another facet of losing apparently useful traits: loss without replacement. An example of this is the historical absence of boats among the indigenous inhabitants of the Canary Islands, a group of small islands isolated off North Africa's Atlantic coast. The ancestors of these people must have had boats, for without them they could never have transported themselves and their domestic livestock to the islands in the first place.

Later, without boats, they had no way to communicate between islands or with the mainland. This loss of something useful came about due to the islands' lack of stone suitable for making polished stone axes, which in turn limited the islanders' carpentry.[7]

REPRESSIVE CHANGE

Innovation, diffusion, and cultural loss all may take place among peoples who are free to decide for themselves what changes they will or will not accept. Not always, however, do people have the liberty to make their own choices. Frequently, changes they would not willingly make have been forced upon them by some other group, usually in the course of conquest and colonialism. A direct outcome in many cases is repressive culture change, which anthropologists call acculturation. The most radical form of repressive culture change is ethnocide.

Acculturation and Ethnocide

Acculturation is the massive culture change that occurs in a society when it experiences intensive firsthand contact with a more powerful society. It always involves an element of force, either directly, as in conquests, or indirectly, as in the implicit or explicit threat that force will be used if people refuse to make the demanded changes. Other variables include degree of cultural difference; circumstances, intensity, frequency, and hostility of contact; relative status of the agents of contact; who is dominant and who is submissive; and whether the nature of the flow is reciprocal or nonreciprocal. *Acculturation* and *diffusion* are not equivalent terms; one culture can borrow from another without being in the least acculturated.

In the course of cultural contact, any number of things may happen. Merger or fusion occurs when two cultures lose their separate identities and form a single culture, as historically expressed by the melting pot ideology of English-speaking, Protestant Euramerican culture in the United States. Sometimes, though, one of the cultures loses its autonomy but retains its identity as a subculture in the form of a caste, class, or ethnic group. This is typical of conquest or slavery situations, and the United States has examples of this in spite of its melting pot ideology—we need look no further than the nearest American Indian reservation.

In virtually all parts of the world today, people are faced with the tragedy of forced removal from their traditional homelands, as entire communities are uprooted to make way for hydroelectric projects, grazing lands for cattle, mining operations, or highway construction. In Brazil's rush to develop the vast Amazon rainforest,

---

[6]Gould, S. J. (1983). *Hens' teeth and horses' toes* (p. 159). New York: Norton.

cultural loss The abandonment of an existing practice or trait.
acculturation Massive culture change that occurs in a society when it experiences intensive firsthand contact with a more powerful society.

[7]Coon, C. S. (1954). *The story of man* (p. 174). New York: Knopf.

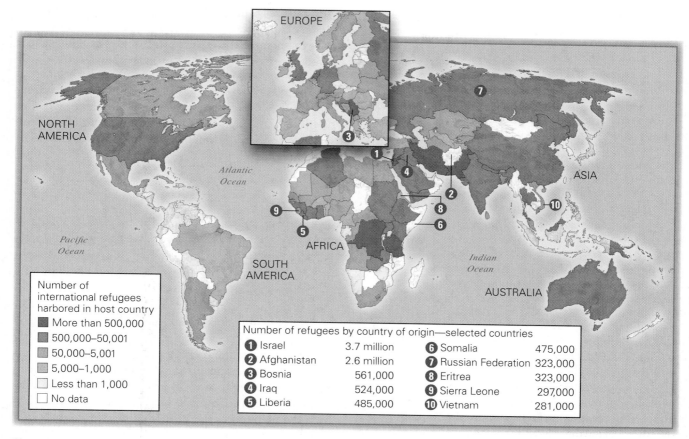

Figure 15.3

Increasing refugee populations, a consequence of conflict between nationalities living in multinational states, have become a burden and source of instability in the states to which they have fled.

for instance, entire indigenous communities have been relocated to "national parks," where resources are inadequate for the number of people and where former enemies are often forced to live in close proximity.

Ethnocide, the violent eradication of an ethnic group's collective cultural identity as a distinctive people, occurs when a dominant society deliberately sets out to destroy another society's cultural heritage. This may take place when a powerful nation aggressively expands its territorial control by annexing neighboring peoples and their territories, incorporating the conquered groups as subjects. A policy of ethnocide typically includes forbidding a subjugated nation's ancestral language, criminalizing their traditional customs, destroying their religion and demolishing sacred places and practices, breaking up their social organizations, and dispossessing or removing the survivors from their homelands—in essence, stopping short of physical extermination while removing all traces of their unique culture.

One tragic current example is Tibet, which could not defend itself against an invasion by the Chinese communist army in 1950. The Chinese government then initiated its ethnocidal policies by means of systematic attacks

against traditional Tibetan culture. Seeking to stamp out deeply rooted religious beliefs and practices, it ordered the demolition of most Buddhist temples and monasteries. Following a mass uprising, hundreds of thousands of Tibetans were killed or forced into exile abroad. Seeking to annihilate Tibetan identity, China sought to turn the surviving Tibetans into political subjects who would culturally identify themselves as Chinese nationals.[8]

Ethnocide may also take place when so many carriers of a culture die that those who manage to survive become refugees, living among peoples of different cultures. Examples of this may be seen in many parts of the world today (Figure 15.3). A particularly well-

---

[8]http://www.savetibet.org/tibet/us/proceedings/senatefrmaur amoynihan.php. See also Avedon, John F. (1997). *In exile from the land of snows: The definitive account of the Dalai Lama and Tibet since the Chinese conquest.* New York: Harper.

ethnocide The violent eradication of an ethnic group's collective cultural identity as a distinctive people; occurs when a dominant society deliberately sets out to destroy another society's cultural heritage.

documented case occurred in Brazil's Amazon basin in 1968, when developers hired killers to wipe out several Indian groups, using arsenic, dynamite, and machine guns from light planes.

Violence continues to be used in Brazil as a means of dealing with indigenous peoples. For example, according to conservative estimates, at least 1,500 Yanomami Indians died in the 1980s, many the victims of deliberate massacres, as cattle ranchers and gold miners poured into northern Brazil. By 1990, 70 percent of Yanomami land in Brazil had been illegally expropriated; fish supplies were poisoned by mercury contamination of rivers; and malaria, venereal disease, and tuberculosis were running rampant. The Yanomami were dying at the rate of 10 percent a year, and their fertility had dropped to near zero. Many villages were left with no children or old people, and the survivors awaited their fate with a profound terror of extinction.[9]

The typical attitude of many Brazilians toward such situations is illustrated by their government's reaction to a diplomatic journey that two Kayapó Indian leaders and an anthropologist made to the United States. They ventured north to speak with World Bank authorities and various government officials in the U.S. Congress and State Department concerning the destruction of their land and way of life caused by internationally financed development projects. All three were charged with vio-

---

[9]Turner, T. (1991). Major shift in Brazilian Yanomami policy. *Anthropology Newsletter 32* (5), 1, 46.

---

genocide The physical extermination of one people by another, either as a deliberate act or as the accidental outcome of activities carried out by one people with little regard for their impact on others.

lating Brazil's Foreign Sedition Act, which prohibits foreigners from secretly stirring up discontent, resistance, or revolt against the government in power. This charge and other relevant atrocities provoked international outrage, which in turn prompted Brazilian authorities to recommend policy changes that could favorably impact the country's indigenous peoples. However, whether their recommendations will be sufficient to effect positive change, or will even be acted upon fully, remains to be seen.

Genocide

The Brazilian Indian case just cited raises the issue of **genocide**—the physical extermination of one people by another, either as a deliberate act or as the accidental outcome of activities carried out by one people with little regard for their impact on others. Genocide, like ethnocide, is not new in the world. In North America in 1637, for example, a deliberate attempt was made to destroy the Pequot Indians by setting fire to their village at Mystic, Connecticut, and then shooting down all those—primarily unarmed elders, women, and children—who sought to escape the fire. To ensure that even their very memory would be stamped out, colonial authorities forbade the mention of the Pequot name. Numerous other massacres of Indian peoples occurred thereafter, up until the last one at Wounded Knee, South Dakota, in 1890.

Of course, such acts were by no means restricted to North America. One of the most famous 19th-century acts of genocide was the extermination of the indigenous inhabitants of Tasmania, a large island just south of Australia. In this case, the use of military force failed to achieve the complete elimination of the Tasmanians, but what the military could not achieve was done by George Augustus Robinson, a British Protestant missionary. He rounded up the surviving natives and brought them to his mission station, where they died from the combination of psychological depression and lack of resistance to European disease. Robinson retired to Britain to contemplate the horrible if unintended consequences of his actions, having brought about the demise of the last full-blooded Tasmanians.

The most widely known act of genocide in recent history was the attempt of the Nazis during World War II to wipe out European Jews and Roma (Gypsies) in the name of racial superiority and improvement of the human species. Unfortunately, the common practice of referring to this as "*the* Holocaust"—as if it were something unique, or at least exceptional—tends to blind us to the fact that this thoroughly monstrous act is but one example of an all-too-common phenomenon. Among many examples of mass murder in more recent years, Khmer Rouge soldiers in Cambodia killed 1.7 million fellow citi-

VISUAL COUNTERPOINT

Two of many examples of attempted genocide in the 20th century: Hitler's Germany against Jews and Gypsies in the 1930s and the 1940s; and Hutus against Tutsis in Rwanda, as in this 1994 massacre.

zens in the 1970s. In the following decade, government-sponsored terrorism against indigenous communities in Guatemala reached its height, and Saddam Hussein's government used poison gas against the Kurdish ethnic minority in northern Iraq. In the 1990s, more than half a million Tutsi people were slaughtered by their Hutu neighbors in the African country of Rwanda, and today a genocidal campaign is waged against the non-Arab black peoples in the Darfur desert region of western Sudan. Estimates vary, but during the 20th century, as many as 83 million people died of genocide and tyranny.[10]

If such ugly practices are ever to end, we must gain a better understanding of what is behind them. Anthropologists are actively engaged in this, carrying out cross-cultural as well as specific case studies. One finding to

emerge is the regularity with which religious, economic, and political interests are allied in cases of genocide. In Tasmania, for example, British wool growers wanted the indigenous peoples off the island so that they could have it for their sheep. The government advanced their interests through its military campaigns against the natives, but it was the British missionary work that finally secured Tasmania for the commercial wool interests.

Directed Change

As we have seen, genocide is not about change but annihilation. The most extreme cases of forced cultural change, or acculturation, occur as a result of military conquest or massive invasion and breaking up of traditional political structures by dominant newcomers who know or care nothing about the culture they control. The indigenous people—unable to effectively resist imposed changes and obstructed in carrying out many of their own social, religious, and economic activities—may be

---

[10]White, M. (2001). *Historical atlas of the twentieth century.* http://users.erols.com/mwhite28/20centry.htm; see also Van Den Berghe, P. (1992). The modern state: Nation builder or nation killer? *International Journal of Group Tensions* 22 (3), 198.

forced into new practices that tend to isolate individuals and destroy the integrity of their societies.

So it was with the Ju/'hoansi of Namibia in southern Africa. Rounded up in the early 1960s, these Bushmen were confined to a reservation in Tsumkwe where they could not possibly provide for their own needs. The government supplied them with rations, but these were insufficient to meet basic nutritional needs. In poor health and prevented from developing meaningful alternatives to traditional activities, the Ju/'hoansi became embittered and depressed, and their death rate came to exceed the birthrate. Within the next few years, however, surviving Ju/'hoansi began to take matters into their own hands. They returned to water holes in their traditional homeland, where, assisted by anthropologists and others concerned with their welfare, they are trying to sustain themselves by raising livestock. Whether this will succeed or not remains to be seen, as there are still many obstacles to success.

One by-product of colonial dealings with indigenous peoples has been the growth of *applied anthropology,* defined in Chapter 1 as the use of anthropological techniques and knowledge for the purpose of solving practical problems. For example, in the United States, the Bureau of American Ethnology was founded in 1876 to gather reliable data the government might use to formulate Indian policies. At the time, anthropologists were convinced of the practicality of their discipline, and many who did ethnographic work among Indians devoted a great deal of time, energy, and even money to assisting their informants, whose interests were frequently threatened from outside.

In the 20th century, the scope and intent of applied anthropology expanded. In the first part of that century, the applied work of Franz Boas—who almost single-handedly trained an entire generation of anthropologists in the United States—proved instrumental in reforming the country's immigration policies. With impressive statistical data based on comparative skull measurements and related physical anthropological studies, this German Jewish immigrant challenged popular race theories of the day. He demonstrated that theories privileging non-Jewish immigrants from western Europe and discriminating against Jews and others deemed undesirable as newcomers in the United States were based not on fact but on deeply rooted racial prejudice.

In the 1930s, anthropologists with clearly pragmatic objectives did a number of studies in industrial and other institutional settings in the United States. With World War II came increased involvement at colonial administration beyond U.S. borders, especially in the Pacific, by American officers trained in anthropology. The rapid postwar recovery of Japan was due in no small measure to the influence of anthropologists in structuring the U.S. occupation. Anthropologists continue to play an active role today in administering U.S. trust territories in the Pacific.

All too often, however, states and other powerful institutions directly intervening in the affairs of different ethnic groups or foreign societies fail to seek professional advice from anthropologists who possess relevant cross-cultural expertise and deeper insights. Such failures have contributed to a host of avoidable errors in planning and executing nation-building programs in ethnically divided countries such as Iraq and Afghanistan, both of which are now devastated by war and violence.

Today, applied anthropologists are in growing demand in the field of international development because of their specialized knowledge of social structure, value systems, and the functional interrelatedness of cultures targeted for development. Those working in this arena face a particular challenge: As anthropologists, they are bound to respect other peoples' dignity and cultural integrity, yet they are asked for advice on how to change certain aspects of those cultures. If the request comes from the people themselves, that is one thing, but more often than not, it comes from outsiders. Supposedly, the proposed change is for the good of the targeted population, yet members of that community do not always see it that way. Just how far applied anthropologists should go in advising outsiders how to manipulate people—especially those without the power to resist—to embrace changes proposed for them is a serious ethical question.

In direct response to such critical questions concerning the application and benefits of anthropological research, an alternative type of practical anthropology has emerged during the last half century. Known by a variety of names—including action anthropology and committed, engaged, involved, and advocacy anthropology—this involves community-based research and action in collaboration and solidarity with indigenous societies, ethnic minorities, and other besieged or repressed groups. In sum, the practical applications of anthropology are not only necessary, but there is a growing demand for anthropologically informed pragmatic solutions.

REACTIONS TO REPRESSIVE CHANGE

The reactions of indigenous peoples to the changes outsiders have thrust upon them have varied considerably. Some have responded by moving to the nearest available forest, desert, or other remote places in hopes of being left alone. In Brazil, a number of communities once located near the coast took this option a few hundred years ago and were successful until the great push to develop

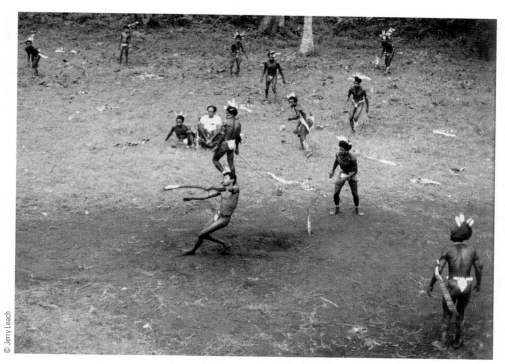

© Jerry Leach

Indigenous peoples have reacted to colonialism in many different ways. When British missionaries pressed Trobriand Islanders of Melanesia to celebrate their regular yam harvests with a game of "civilized" cricket rather than traditional "wild" erotic dances, Trobrianders responded by transforming the staid British sport into an exuberant event that featured sexual chants and dances between innings. This is an example of syncretism—the creative blending of indigenous and foreign beliefs and practices into new cultural forms.

the Amazon forest began in the 1960s. Others, like many Indians of North America, took up arms to fight back but were ultimately forced to sign treaties and surrender much of their ancestral lands, after which they were reduced to an impoverished underclass in their own land. Today, they continue to fight through nonviolent means to retain their identities as distinct peoples and to regain control over natural resources on their lands.

In addition, ethnic groups may try to retain their distinctive identities by maintaining cultural boundaries such as holding on to traditional language, festive ceremonies, customary dress, ritual songs and dances, unique food, and so on. Indeed, in opposing modernization, people often seek cultural protection and emotional comfort from **tradition**—customary ideas and practices passed on from generation to generation, which in a modernizing society may form an obstacle to new ways of doing things.

When people are able to hold on to some of their traditions in the face of powerful outside domination, the result may be **syncretism**—the creative blending of indigenous and foreign beliefs and practices into new cultural forms. A fine illustration of this is the game of cricket as played by the Trobriand Islanders of Melanesia, some of whose practices we looked at in earlier chapters. When Trobrianders were under British rule, missionaries introduced them to this rather reserved British game to replace the erotic dancing and open sexuality that normally followed the yam harvests. Traditionally,

this was the season when chiefs sought to spread their fame by hosting nights of dancing, providing food for the hundreds of young married people who participated. For several months, there would be night after night of provocative dancing, accompanied by chanting and shouting full of sexual innuendo, each night ending as couples disappeared into the bush together.

Since no chief wished to be outdone by any other (being outdone brought into question the strength of one's magic), the dancing had a strong competitive element, and fighting sometimes erupted. To the British Protestant missionaries, cricket seemed a good way to end all of this in a way that would encourage conformity to "civilized" comportment in dress, religion, and sportsmanship. The Trobrianders, however, were determined to "rubbish" (throw out) the British rules of the game. They did this by turning it into the same kind of distinctly Trobriand event that their thrilling dance competitions had once been.

Making cricket their own, Trobrianders added battle dress and battle magic and incorporated erotic dancing into the game. Instead of inviting dancers each night,

tradition Customary ideas and practices passed on from generation to generation, which in a modernizing society may form an obstacle to new ways of doing things.
syncretism In acculturation, the creative blending of indigenous and foreign beliefs and practices into new cultural forms.

chiefs now arrange cricket matches. Pitching has been modified from the British style to one closer to their old way of throwing a spear. Following the game, they hold massive feasts, where wealth is displayed to enhance their prestige.

Cricket, in its altered form, has been made to serve traditional systems of prestige and exchange. Neither primitive nor passively accepted in its original form, Trobriand cricket was thoughtfully and creatively adapted into a sophisticated activity reflecting the importance of basic indigenous cultural premises. Exuberance and pride are displayed by everyone associated with the sport, and the players are as much concerned with conveying the full meaning of who they are as with scoring well. From the sensual dressing in preparation for the game to the team chanting songs full of sexual metaphors to the erotic chorus-line dancing between the innings, it is clear that each participant is playing for his own importance, for the fame of his team, and for the hundreds of attractive young women who watch the game.

Revitalization Movements

Another common reaction to repressive change is revitalization. As noted in an earlier chapter, revitalization movements are efforts for radical culture reform in response to widespread social disruption and collective feelings of anxiety and despair. When primary ties of culture, social relationships, and activities are broken and meaningless activity is imposed by outside forces, individuals and groups characteristically react by rejecting newly introduced cultural elements and reclaiming historical roots and traditional identity, as well as with spiritual imagination.

In the United States, revitalization movements have occurred often—whenever significant segments of the population have found their conditions in life to be at odds with the values of the American Dream. For example, the 1960s saw the emergence of revitalization movements among young people of middle-class and even upper-class families. In their case, the professed cultural values of peace, equality, and individual freedom were seen to be at odds with the realities of persistent war, poverty, and constraints on individual action imposed by a variety of impersonal institutions. Youths countered these realities by advocating free love, joining hippie communes, celebrating new forms of rock and folk music, using mind-altering drugs, challenging authority, growing their hair long, and wearing unconventional clothes.

By the 1980s revitalization movements were becoming prominent even among older, more affluent segments of U.S. society, as in the rise of the so-called religious right. In these cases, the reaction is not so much

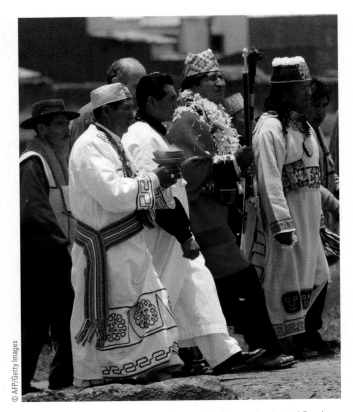

© AFP/Getty Images

Flanked by indigenous spiritual leaders, Bolivia's newly elected President Evo Morales was ceremonially inaugurated at the archaeological site of Tiwanaku, the ancient capital of a large indigenous empire in the Bolivian highlands surrounding Lake Titicaca. The first indigenous head of state elected since the Spanish conquest of Bolivia, Morales was dressed in traditional royal clothing. In their native tongue, he addressed a crowd that included thousands of Bolivian Indians, telling them, "Today begins a new era for the native peoples of the world." Morales chose this symbolic event to officially launch an indigenous cultural revitalization movement in a country where most citizens are members of Indian nations. Mostly poverty-stricken, these Bolivian Indians have seen their ancestral traditions repressed, marginalized, or ridiculed by Spanish-speaking European invaders and their descendants during the past five centuries.

against a perceived failure of the American Dream as it is against perceived threats to that dream by dissenters and activists within their society, by foreign governments, by new ideas that challenge other ideas they prefer to believe, and by the sheer complexity of modern life.

Clearly, when value systems are out of step with existing realities, a condition of cultural crisis is likely to build up that may breed reactive movements. Not all suppressed, conquered, or colonized people eventually rebel against established authority, although why they do not is debatable. When they do, however, cultural resistance may take one of several forms, all of which are varieties of revitalization movements. Some of these revitalization movements take on a revolutionary character, as did the Taliban in Afghanistan.

REBELLION AND REVOLUTION

When the scale of discontent within a society reaches a certain level, the possibilities are high for **rebellion**—organized armed resistance to an established government or authority in power. For instance, there have been many peasant rebellions around the world in the course of history. Often, such rebellions are triggered by repressive regimes imposing new taxes on the already struggling small farmers unable to feed their families under such unacceptable levels of exploitation.

One current example is the Zapatista Maya Indian uprising in southern Mexico, which began in the mid-1990s and has not yet been resolved. This rebellion involves thousands of poor Indian farmers whose livelihoods have been threatened by the disruptive outside changes imposed on them and whose human rights under the Mexican constitution have never been fully implemented.

In contrast to rebellions, which have rather limited objectives, a **revolution**—a radical change in a society or culture—involves a more radical transformation. Revolutions occur when the level of discontent in a society is very high. In the political arena, revolution involves the forced overthrow of an old government and the establishment of a completely new one.

Such was the case when Muslim fundamentalists in Iran toppled the imperial regime of the shah in 1979 and replaced him with Ayatollah Khomeini, a high-ranking Shiite Muslim religious leader. Returning to his homeland from exile and becoming Iran's new leader, he instituted a new social and political order.

The question of why revolutions erupt, as well as why they frequently fail to live up to the expectations of the people initiating them, is unsolved. It is clear, however, that the colonial policies of countries such as Britain, France, Spain, Portugal, and the United States during the 19th and early 20th centuries have created a worldwide situation in which revolution is nearly inevitable. Despite the political independence most colonies have gained since World War II, powerful countries continue to exploit many of these "underdeveloped" countries for their natural resources and cheap labor, causing a deep resentment of rulers beholden to foreign powers. Further discontent has been caused as governing elites in newly independent states try to assert their control over peoples living within their boundaries. By virtue of a common ancestry, possession of distinct cultures, persistent occupation of their own territories, and traditions of self-determination, the peoples they aim to control identify themselves as distinct nations and refuse to recognize the legitimacy of what they regard as a foreign government.

Thus, in many a former colony, large numbers of people have taken up arms to resist annexation and absorption by imposed state governments run by people of other nationalities. As they attempt to make their multiethnic states into unified countries, ruling elites of one nationality set about stripping the peoples of other nations within their states of their lands, resources, and particular cultural identities. The phenomenon is so common that it led Belgian sociologist Pierre van den Berghe to label what modern states refer to as "nation building" as, in fact, "nation killing."[11]

One of the most important facts of our time is that the vast majority of the distinct peoples of the world have never consented to rule by the governments of states within which they find themselves living.[12] In many newly emerging countries, such peoples feel they have no other option than to fight.

From an examination of various revolutions of the past, the following conditions have been offered as causes of rebellion and revolution:

1. Loss of prestige of established authority, often from the failure of foreign policy, financial difficulties, dismissals of popular ministers, or alteration of popular policies.

2. Threat to recent economic improvement. In France and Russia, sections of the population (professional classes and urban workers) whose economic fortunes previously had taken an upward swing were radicalized by unexpected setbacks, such as steeply rising food prices and unemployment.

3. Government indecisiveness, as exemplified by a lack of consistent policy. Such governments appear to be controlled by, rather than in control of, events.

4. Loss of support from the intellectual class. Such a loss deprived the prerevolutionary governments of France and Russia of philosophical support and popularity among the literate public.

5. A leader or group of leaders with enough charisma, or popular appeal, to mobilize a substantial part of the population against the establishment.

Apart from resistance to internal authority, such as in the Chinese, French, and Russian revolutions, many

---

[11]Van Den Berghe, P. (1992). The modern state: Nation builder or nation killer? *International Journal of Group Tensions 22* (3), 191–207.

[12]Nietschmann, B. (1987). The third world war. *Cultural Survival Quarterly 11* (3), 3.

---

rebellion Organized armed resistance to an established government or authority in power.
revolution Radical change in a society or culture. In the political arena, it involves the forced overthrow of an old government and establishment of a completely new one.

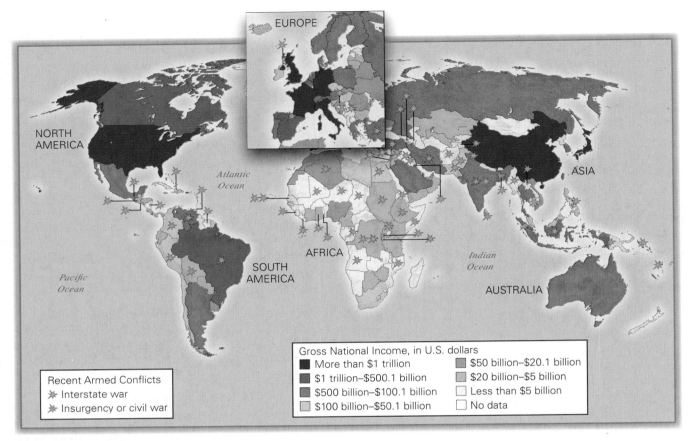

Figure 15.4
Today, the majority of armed conflicts are in the economically poor countries of Africa, Asia, Central and South America, many of which were at one time under European colonial domination. Most are between the state and one or more nations or ethnic groups within the state's borders who are seeking to maintain or regain control over their lives, lands, and resources.

revolutions in modern times have been struggles against an authority imposed by outsiders. Such resistance usually takes the form of independence movements that wage campaigns of armed defiance against colonial powers. The Algerian struggle for independence from France is a relevant example. Of the hundreds of armed conflicts in the world today, almost all are in the economically poor countries of Africa, Asia, Central and South America, many of which were at one time under European colonial domination (Figure 15.4). Of these wars, the majority are between the state and one or more nations or ethnic groups within the state's borders who are seeking to maintain or regain control of their personal lives, communities, lands, and resources in the face of what they regard as repression or subjugation by a foreign power.[13]

Revolutions do not always accomplish what they set out to do. One of the stated goals of the 1949 Chi-nese communist revolution, for example, was to liberate women from the oppression of a strongly patriarchal society in which a woman owed lifelong obedience to some male relative—first her father, later her husband and, after his death, her oldest son. Although changes were (and continue to be) made, the transformation overall has been frustrated by the cultural lens through which the revolutionaries viewed their work. A tradition of deeply rooted patriarchy extending back at least 2,200 years is not easily overcome and has influenced many of the decisions made by communist China's leaders since the revolution.

In many parts of rural China today, as in the past, a woman's life is still largely determined by her relationship to a man, be it her father, husband, or son, rather than by her own efforts or failures. What's more, many rural women face official local policies that identify their primary roles as wives and mothers. When they do work outside the house, it is generally at jobs with low pay, low status, and no benefits. Indeed, the 1990s saw a major outbreak of the abduction and sale of women from ru-

---

[13] Nietschmann, B. (1987). The third world war. *Cultural Survival Quarterly* 11 (3), 7.

In China, women's labor has become critical to economic expansion. Much of this labor is controlled by male heads of families, who act as agents of the state in allocating labor.

© A. Ramey/PhotoEdit

ral areas as brides and workers. Women's no-wage home labor (and low-wage outside labor) for their husbands' households have been essential to China's economic expansion, which relies on the allocation of labor by the heads of patrilineal households.[14]

This situation shows that the undermining of revolutionary goals, if it occurs, is not necessarily by political opponents. Rather, it may be a consequence of the revolutionaries' own traditional cultural background. In rural China, as long as women marry out and their labor is controlled by male heads of families, women will be seen as a commodity.

It should be understood that revolution is a relatively recent phenomenon, occurring only during the past 5,000 years or so. The reason is that political rebellion requires a centralized political authority to rebel against, and states did not exist before 5,000 years ago. Obviously, then, in kin-ordered societies organized as tribes and bands, without a centralized government, there could be no rebellion or political revolution.

MODERNIZATION

One of the most frequently used terms to describe social and cultural changes as they are occurring today is **modernization.** This is most clearly defined as an all-encompassing and global process of political and socioeconomic change, whereby developing societies acquire some of the cultural characteristics common to Western industrial societies.

Derived from the Latin word *modo* ("just now"), modernization literally refers to something "in the pres-

ent time." The dominant idea behind this concept is that "becoming modern" is becoming like North American and other industrial societies, with the very clear implication that not to do so is to be stuck in the past—backward, inferior, and needing to be improved. It is unfortunate that the term *modernization* continues to be so widely used. Since we seem to be stuck with it, the best we can do at the moment is to recognize its problematic one-sidedness, even as we continue to use it.

The process of modernization may be best understood as consisting of four subprocesses, of which one is *technological development.* In the course of modernization, traditional knowledge and techniques give way to the application of scientific knowledge and techniques borrowed mainly from the industrialized West.

Another subprocess is *agricultural development,* represented by a shift in emphasis from subsistence farming to commercial farming. Instead of raising crops and livestock for their own use, people turn with growing frequency to the production of cash crops, with increased reliance on a cash economy and on global markets for selling farm products and purchasing goods.

A third subprocess is *industrialization,* with a greater emphasis placed on material forms of energy—especially fossil fuels—to drive machines. Human and animal power becomes less important, as do handicrafts in general. The fourth subprocess is *urbanization,* marked particularly by population movements from rural settlements into cities. Although all four subprocesses are interrelated, there is no fixed order of appearance.

[14]Gates, H. (1996). Buying brides in China—again. *Anthropology Today* 12 (4), 10.

modernization The process of political and socioeconomic change, whereby developing societies acquire some of the cultural characteristics of Western industrial societies.

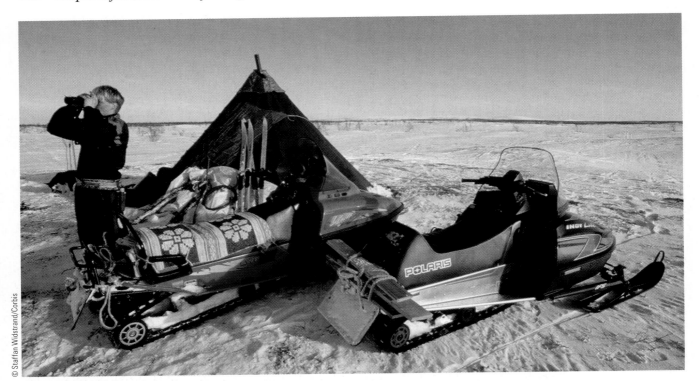

In the 1960s, Saami reindeer herders in Scandinavia's Arctic tundra adopted newly invented snowmobiles, convinced that these modern machines would make traditional herding physically easier and economically more advantageous. Here, a young Saami man stands beside his tent and snowmobile, searching for his reindeer with binoculars.

As modernization proceeds, other changes are likely to follow. In the political realm, political parties and some sort of electoral apparatus frequently appear, along with the development of an administrative bureaucracy. In formal education, institutional learning opportunities expand, literacy increases, and an indigenous educated elite develops. Religion becomes less important in many areas of thought and behavior, as traditional beliefs and practices are undermined. Many traditional rights and duties connected with kinship are altered, if not eliminated, especially where distant relatives are concerned. Finally, where social stratification is a factor, social mobility increases as ascribed status becomes less important and personal achievement counts for more.

Self-Determination

A closer examination of traditional cultures that have felt the impact of modernization or other culture changes will help to pinpoint some of the problems such cultures have met. We will focus here on the Shuar Indians of Ecuador and the Skolt Lapps, one of several groups of Saami people living in the Arctic and sub-Arctic tundra of northwest Russia and Scandinavia.

Saami Herders: The Snowmobile Revolution and Its Unintended Consequences

In the 1960s Saami reindeer herders in Scandinavia eagerly adopted snowmobiles, expecting that the new technology would make herding physically easier and economically more advantageous. The choice to modernize was essentially theirs, but in Finland it backfired.

As snowmobile technology replaced traditional skills, the ability of the Saami (historically also known as Lapps) to creatively survive on their own diminished, and their dependency on the outside world grew. Given the high cost of buying, maintaining, and fueling the machines, they faced a sharp rise in their need for money. To obtain cash, men began going outside their communities for wage labor more than just occasionally, as had previously been the case.

One might argue that dependency on the larger economy and the need for cash are prices worth paying for an improved system of reindeer herding. However, snowmobiles contributed in a significant way to a disastrous decline in reindeer herding in some Saami communities, such as among the Skolt Lapps of northern Finland. Traditionally Skolt men tended the animals, moving about on wooden skis and associating closely with the herds—intensively from November to January and periodically from January to April. But once snowmobiles were introduced, the familiar, prolonged, and largely peaceful relationship between herder and beast changed into a noisy, traumatic one. The humans reindeer encountered came speeding out of the woods on noisy, smelly machines that invariably chased the animals, often for long distances. Instead of helping the reindeer in their winter food quest, aiding does with their calves, and protecting the herd from predators, men appeared periodically, either to slaughter or castrate the animals.

The reindeer became wary of people, resulting in de-domestication, with reindeer scattering and running off to less accessible areas. In addition, snowmobile harassment seemed to adversely affect birthing and the survival of calves. Within a decade the average size of the family herd among the Skolts had dropped from fifty to twelve—a number that is not economically viable.

This is a classic illustration that change, even when initiated by a community on its own volition, is not always advantageous. The financial cost of mechanized herding and the decline in domesticated herd size have led many to abandon herding altogether. Now, the majority of men are no longer herders at all. This constitutes a serious economic problem, since few local subsistence alternatives are available.[15]

Shuar Indians and Cattle in the Amazon: A Successful Experiment in Controlled Adaptation

In contrast to the Saami, the Shuar Indians of Ecuador's tropical forest deliberately avoided modernization until they felt that they had no other option if they were to

fend off the same outside forces that had destroyed whole societies elsewhere in the Amazon Basin. Traditionally organized in small autonomous groups that engaged in constant feuding, the Shuar (historically better known as Jivaro) survived on a mixed subsistence strategy of foraging and gardening. In 1964, threatened with the loss of their land base as more and more Ecuadoran colonists intruded into their territory, leaders from the many, widely scattered Shuar communities came together and founded a fully independent ethnic organization—the Shuar Federation—to take control over their own future.

Recognized by Ecuador's government, albeit reluctantly, the federation is officially dedicated to promotion of the social, economic, and moral advancement of the growing Shuar population and to coordinating development with official governmental agencies. Since its founding, the federation has secured title to more than 96,000 hectares of communal land; established a cattle herd of more than 15,000 head as the people's primary source of income; taken control of their own education, using their own language and mostly Shuar teachers; and established their own bilingual radio station and a bilingual newspaper.

Obviously, all of this has transformed daily life among the Shuar, but they have been able to maintain a variety of distinctive cultural markers, including their language, communal land tenure, cooperative production and distribution, a basically egalitarian economy, and kin-based communities that retain maximum autonomy. Thus, for all the changes, they feel they are still Shuar and distinct from other Ecuadorans.[16]

The Shuar case shows that indigenous peoples are capable of taking control of their own destinies even in the face of intense outside pressures, *if* allowed to do so. Unfortunately, until recently, few have had that op-

---

[15]Pelto, P. J. (1973). *The snowmobile revolution: Technology and social change in the Arctic.* Menlo Park, CA: Cummings.

[16]Bodley, J. H. (1990). *Victims of progress* (3rd ed., pp. 160–162). Mountain View, CA: Mayfield.

Anthropology Applied

Development Anthropology and Dams ■ Michael M. Horowitz

Over a 35-year career in scholarly and applied work, Michael M. Horowitz, president and executive director of the Institute for Development Anthropology (IDA) and Distinguished Professor of Anthropology at the State University of New York at Binghamton, has made pioneering contributions to applied anthropology. His work has focused on achieving equitable economic growth, environmental sustainability, conflict resolution, and participatory government in the former colonial world.

Since co-founding IDA in 1976, Horowitz has been its principal leader. He has played a key role in bringing anthropology forward as an applied science in international development organizations such as the World Bank, the United Nations Fund for Women, and the US Agency for International Development (USAID), as well as nongovernmental organizations (NGOs) such as Oxfam and the International Union for the Conservation of Nature. He has mentored several generations of young scholars and professionals—paying particular attention to those from developing countries— encouraging the application of anthropology's comparative and holistic methodologies and theories to empower low-income majorities in the so-called underdeveloped world.

Horowitz's work with pastoralists and floodplain dwellers has had substantial positive impact on the well-being of small producers and small landholders in developing countries. A clear example of this is the impact of his work on the lives and livelihoods of people living downstream of a hydropower dam in West Africa. Beginning in the 1980s, he and his IDA team carried out rigorous anthropological research along the Senegal River, which flows through Mali, Senegal, and Mauritania. Their study showed that traditional, pre-dam, flood-recession

© AP Images

A local woman eats her breakfast overlooking the ship locks of China's Three Gorges hydroelectric dam on the Yangtze River. Under construction since 1992 and due for completion in 2009, the dam has been controversial since its inception, raising concerns among environmentalists around the world, not to mention among peasant farmers living downstream. If completed, the dam will result in the largest forced displacement of people in the world's history. Close to 2 million people are being relocated to make way for its 365-mile-long reservoir, and bitter complaints abound among those who have already been moved. *Unlike* the dam described in this Anthropology Applied box, not one social scientist was consulted in the planning and assessment phase of Three Gorges Dam.

farming yielded better results than irrigated agriculture and was better for the environment.

This finding influenced decisions made by these countries and affiliated NGOs to manage the system with a controlled release from the Manatali Dam in Mali in order to reproduce as nearly as possible the pre-dam flow system. Horowitz's long-term field research demonstrated that seasonal flooding would provide economic, environmental, and sociocultural benefits for nearly a million small producers.

Recognized by national governments, NGOs, and development funding agencies, the work of Horowitz and his IDA colleagues on the Senegal River Basin Monitoring Activity (SRBMA) was a breakthrough in the concepts of resettlement and river management, and it continues to influence development policy. Prior to IDA's work in West Africa, no hydropower dam had ever been managed with a controlled flood. Since then, IDA has been asked to help apply the SRMBA model to other parts of the world, including the lower Zambezi River in Mozambique and the Mekong River in Laos, Cambodia, and Vietnam.
(Adapted from W. Young (Ed.). (2000). Kimball Award winner. Anthropology News 41(8), 29, with update based on personal communication with IDA, November 2003.)

tion. Prior to European invasions of the Amazon rainforest, more than 700 distinct ethnic groups inhabited this vast region. By 1900 in Brazil, the number was down to 270, and today something like 180 remain.[17] Many of these survivors find themselves in situations not unlike that of the Yanomami, described earlier in this chapter. Nevertheless, some are showing resourcefulness in resisting the outside forces of destruction arrayed against

them. Some receive help from anthropologists, as discussed in this chapter's Anthropology Applied feature.

Globalization in the "Underdeveloped" World

Throughout the so-called underdeveloped world, in Africa, Asia, South and Central America, and elsewhere, whole countries are in the throes of radical political and

[17]*Cultural Survival Quarterly.* (1991). *15* (4), 38.

economic change and overall cultural transformation. In fact, inventions and major advances in industrial production, mass transportation, and communication and information technologies are transforming societies in Europe and North America as well. This worldwide process of accelerated modernization in which all parts of the earth are becoming interconnected in one vast interrelated and all-encompassing system is known as globalization—as defined in Chapter 1.

All around the globe we are witnessing the removal of economic activities—or at least their control—from the family and community setting. And we are seeing the altered structure of the family in the face of the changing labor market: young children relying increasingly on parents alone for affection, instead of on the extended family; parental authority generally declining; schools replacing the family as the primary educational unit; old people spending their last days in nursing homes rather than with family members; and many other changes.

In traditional societies, these changes are now happening very fast, without the time to adjust gradually. Changes that took generations to accomplish in Europe and North America are attempted within the span of a single generation in developing countries. In the process they frequently face the erosion of a number of dearly held values they had no intention of giving up. Anthropologists doing fieldwork in distant communities throughout the world have witnessed how these traditional cultures have been affected, and often destroyed, by powerful global forces.

Commonly, the burden of modernization falls most heavily on women. For example, the commercialization of agriculture often involves land reforms that overlook or ignore women's traditional land rights. This reduces their control of and access to resources at the same time that mechanization of food production and processing drastically reduces their opportunities for employment. As a consequence, women are confined more and more to traditional domestic tasks, which, as commercial production becomes peoples' dominant concern, are increasingly downgraded in value.

Moreover, the domestic workload tends to increase, because men are less available to help out, while tasks such as fuel gathering and water collection are made more difficult as common land and resources come to be privately owned and as woodlands are reserved for commercial exploitation. To top it all off, the growing of nonfood crops such as cotton and sisal or luxury crops such as tea, coffee, and cacao (source of chocolate) for the world market makes households vulnerable to wide price fluctuations. As a result, people cannot afford the high-quality diet subsistence farming provided and become malnourished. In short, with modernization, women frequently find themselves in an increasingly inferior position. As their workload increases, the value assigned to the work they do declines, as does their relative educational status, not to mention their health and nutrition.

Globalization: Must It Be Painful?

Most anthropologists see the radical changes that affect traditional non-Western peoples caught up in the modern technological world as an ordeal. Yet, the more common attitude in the industrial West has been that modernization is both inevitable and good—that however disagreeable the "medicine" may be, it is worth it for the "backward" people to become just like people in the West. (For a serious look at the consequences of these changes, see the Biocultural Connection.)

This Western view has little to do with the cold political and economic realities of the contemporary world. It overlooks the stark fact that the standard of middle- and upper-class living in the Western world is based on a rate of consumption of nonrenewable resources whereby a small fraction of the world's population uses the vast majority of these precious resources. The imbalance continues, suggesting that it is impossible for most peoples of the world to achieve a material standard of living at all comparable to that of many people in Western countries in the near future. At the very least, the peoples of the industrial and postindustrial West would have to cut drastically their unrelenting and often wasteful consumption of resources. So far, few have shown a willingness to seriously adjust their standard of living in order to do this.

Countless people around the world today have been led to aspire to a material standard of living like that enjoyed by the middle class and well-to-do in many industrialized and postindustrialized countries, even as the gap between the rich and the poor continues to widen. Every year, many millions of people slide below the poverty level.[18] This has led to the development of what U.S. anthropologist Paul Magnarella called a new "culture of discontent" in which aspirations far exceed the bounds of local opportunities.

No longer satisfied with traditional values and often unable to sustain themselves in the rural backlands, people all over the world are moving to the large cities to find a better life. All too often they live out their days in poor, congested, and diseased slums while attempting to achieve what is usually beyond their reach. Unfortunately, despite rosy predictions about a better future, hundreds of millions of people in our world remain trapped in a wretched reality, struggling against poverty, hunger, poor health, and other dangers. In the next and final chapter of this book, we further explore the underlying structures and deeper causes of these problems, and look at the role anthropology can and does play in helping to meet these challenges.

---

[18]Kurth, P. (1998, October 14). Capitol crimes. *Seven Days*, 7.

Since the Neolithic, humans have had to cope with a host of new diseases that began as a consequence of changes in human behavior. Recently, this has become a renewed source of concern following the resurgence of infectious diseases and the spread of a host of new and lethal diseases.[a]

All told, more than thirty diseases new to medicine have emerged in the past twenty-five years. Perhaps the best known of these is AIDS, which has become a top killer among infectious diseases. Since 1981, more than 25 million people have died of AIDS, and today some 40 million people around the world are living with AIDS/HIV.[b] But there are others—like Ebola hemorrhagic fever, which causes victims to bleed to death; hemorrhagic fevers like dengue fever, Lassa fever, and hantavirus; invasive Streptococcus A, which consumes the victims' flesh; Legionnaire's disease; and Lyme disease.

What has sparked the appearance and spread of these new diseases remains a mystery, but one theory is that some are the result of human activities. In particular, the intrusion of people into new ecological settings, such as rainforests, along with construction of roads allows viruses and other infectious microbes to spread

rapidly to large numbers of people. It is now generally accepted that the HIV virus responsible for AIDS transferred to humans from chimpanzees in the forests of the Democratic Republic of Congo as a consequence of hunting and butchering these animals for food. For the first thirty years, few people were affected; it was not until people began congregating in cities like Kinshasa that conditions were ripe for an epidemic.

To gain a better understanding of the interplay between ecological disturbance and the emergence of new diseases, U.S. medical anthropologist Carol Jenkins obtained a grant from the MacArthur Foundation in 1993. From her base at the Papua New Guinea Institute of Medical Research, she is tracking the health of local people in the wake of a massive logging operation. Her work should provide a better understanding of how disease organisms spread from animal hosts to humans.

Since most of the "new" viruses that have suddenly afflicted humans are in fact old ones that have been present in animals like monkeys (monkey pox), rodents (hantavirus), deer (Lyme disease), and insects (West Nile virus); it appears that something new has enabled them to jump from their animal hosts to humans.

A recent example comes from the Democratic Republic of Congo. Here civil war created a situation where villagers in the central part of the country were

faced with starvation. Their response was to increase the hunting of animals, including monkeys, squirrels, and rats that carry a disease called monkey pox. Related to smallpox, the disease transfers easily to humans, resulting in the largest outbreak of this disease ever seen among humans. What makes this outbreak even more serious is an apparently new strain of the infection, enabling it to spread from person to person, instead of only from an animal host.[c]

Large-scale habitat disturbance is an obvious candidate for such disease transfers, but this needs to be confirmed and the process understood. So far, it is hard to make more than a circumstantial case, by looking back after a disease outbreak. The work of Jenkins and her team is unique in that she was able to get baseline health data on local people before their environment was disturbed. Thus, she is in a position to follow events as they unfold.

It will be some time before conclusions can be drawn from Jenkins's study. Its importance is obvious; in an era of globalization, as air travel allows diseases to spread worldwide, we need a fuller understanding of how viruses interact with their hosts if we are to devise effective preventive and therapeutic strategies to deal with them.

[a]Gibbons, A. (1993). Where are new diseases born? *Science 261*, 680–681.
[b]See www.avert.org/worldstats.htm.

[c]Cohen, J. (1997). Is an old virus up to new tricks? *Science 277*, 312–313.

Questions for Reflection

1. A people's ability to change their culture has always been a key requirement for long-term human survival. However, globalization radically challenges us to adjust at an ever-faster pace within increasingly complex transnational settings. Considering your own situation, can you identify any powerful outside force such as a government agency or large corporation that has had caused changes for your own family, community, or neighborhood? Do you feel that these changes are good for everyone?

2. What are some of the driving forces of culture change in the world today? Which groups are benefiting the most from free markets all across the globe?

3. On a regular basis, the news media are reporting about violent uprisings or rebellion and armed conflicts that result in death and destruction. Why do you think many people feel the need to fight?

4. When societies become involved in the modernizing process, all levels of their cultural systems are affected by these changes. Do you think that people are fully aware of the long-term consequences of the changes they themselves may have welcomed? Can you come up with any examples of unforeseen changes in your own community or neighborhood?

5. In many Muslim countries, orthodox religious groups may oppose modern developments that they associate with moral corruption and seek to maintain or return to a culture based on Muslim traditions. Do you know any religious groups that

identify themselves as fundamentalist, having similar tradition-based values and ideals? Would you feel comfortable if these groups controlled your country's government?

Suggested Readings

Bodley, J. H. (1999). *Victims of progress* (4th ed.). New York: McGraw-Hill.

Few North Americans are aware of the devastation unleashed upon indigenous peoples in the name of progress, nor are they aware that this continues on an unprecedented scale today and the extent of their own society's contributions to it. For most, this book will be a real eye-opener.

Spindler, G., & Stockard, J. E. (Eds.). (2006). *Globalization and change in fifteen cultures*. Belmont, CA: Wadsworth.

This collection of original articles reflects a world changed by globalization and an anthropology committed to documenting the effects of the vast cultural flows of people, information, goods, and technology, now in motion the world over. Spindler and Stockard's introduction frames the topic of cultural change, and the fifteen anthropologists in the anthology take readers on a return visit to their original field sites, asking questions for a new era and writing of peoples familiar to them yet transformed by global forces.

Inda, J. X., & Renato, R. (Eds.). (2001). *The anthropology of globalization: A reader*. Malden, MA, and Oxford: Blackwell.

This wide-ranging reader focuses simultaneously on the large-scale processes through which various cultures are becoming increasingly interconnected and on the ways that people around the world—from Africa and Asia to the Caribbean and North America—mediate these processes in culturally specific ways.

Maybury-Lewis, D. (2001). *Indigenous peoples, ethnic groups, and the state* (2nd ed.). Boston: Allyn & Bacon.

The author, who founded the organization Cultural Survival, summarizes modernization's effect on "tribalism and ethnic parochialism." Revealing the peculiar situation of indigenous peoples as ethnic minorities alien to the states in which they live, he describes the worldwide proliferation of ethnic conflicts and the growing demands for indigenous rights. The book stands on its own, while serving as introduction to a series of individual ethnographies on indigenous peoples and their struggles.

Prins, H. E. L. (1996). *The Mi'kmaq: Resistance, accommodation, and cultural survival*. Belmont, CA: Wadsworth.

This content-rich case study spans 500 years of history, chronicling the endurance of a tribal nation—its ordeals in the face of colonialism and its current struggle for self-determination and cultural revitalization. Rare for its multi-vocality.

Stannard, D. E. (1992). *American holocaust*. Oxford: Oxford University Press.

Stannard deals with 500 years of culture change in the Americas arising from contact between European and native cultures. In doing so, he focuses on genocide, relates it to the Holocaust of World War II, and demonstrates how deeply rooted the phenomenon is in Western culture and Christianity.

Thomson Audio Study Products

 Enjoy the MP3-ready Audio Lecture Overviews for each chapter and a comprehensive audio glossary of key terms for quick study and review. Whether walking to class, doing laundry, or studying at your desk, you now have the freedom to choose when, where, and how you interact with your audio-based educational media. See the preface for information on how to access this on-the-go study and review tool.

The Anthropology Resource Center

www.thomsonedu.com/anthropology

The Anthropology Resource Center provides extended learning materials to reinforce your understanding of key concepts in the four fields of anthropology. For each of the four fields, the Resource Center includes dynamic exercises including video exercises, map exercises, simulations, and "Meet the Scientists" interviews, as well as critical thinking questions that can be assigned and e-mailed to instructors. The Resource Center also provides breaking news in anthropology and interesting material on applied anthropology to help you link what you are learning to the world around you.

16

Global Challenges, Local Responses, and the Role of Anthropology

© Yann Arthus-Bertrand/Corbis

CHALLENGE ISSUE

For at least 10,000 years humans have met the challenges of survival not only by adapting to their natural environment but by transforming it to fit their needs. They have turned deserts, forests, swamps, and mountainsides into pastures and farmland, creating new survival opportunities for an ever-growing human population. During the past 200 years, global cultural development has relied on burning increasing quantities of fossil fuels such as coal, oil, and gas, which has had dire results: massive deforestation and desertification, along with severe air, water, and soil pollution threatening the health of all life. Fossil fuel use has dramatically increased carbon dioxide levels, trapping more heat in the earth's atmosphere. Rising temperatures are causing more and greater storms, droughts, and heat waves, devastating populations in vulnerable areas. And if the massive meltdown of Arctic ice now underway continues, rising sea levels will inundate low coastal areas worldwide. Entire islands may soon disappear, including thousands of villages and even large cities. Among those threatened is Malé, pictured here. It is the capital island of the Maldives, an Indian Ocean archipelago comprised of 1,200 low-lying islands (199 inhabited), home to 70,000 people.

What Can Anthropologists Tell Us of the Future?

Although anthropologists cannot accurately predict future cultural forms, they can identify certain patterns and trends and foresee some of the consequences these might have if they continue. Moreover, they can shed light on already identified problems by showing how they relate to each other and to cultural features and structures that are often below the radar of experts in other disciplines. This ability to systematically consider cultural facts and their underlying structures in a wider context and from a comparative perspective is a recognized anthropological specialty.

What Are the Cultural Trends in Our Globalizing World?

One major cultural trend is globalization, including worldwide adoption of the products, technologies, ideas, and cultural practices of powerful Western countries. This move toward a homogenized, global culture is countered by an opposite trend of ethnic and religious groups all over the world reasserting their distinctive cultural identities and emphasizing their unique historical traditions. A third trend is the growing concern that rising populations, spiraling energy use, and expanding consumption are devastating our natural resources, overwhelming us with waste, and poisoning our environment.

What Problems Must Be Solved for Humans to Have a Viable Future?

Creative, effective, and responsible solutions need to be found to deal with a host of serious problems posed by demographic shifts, unequal distribution of wealth, vanishing natural resources, environmental destruction, ever-more powerful technologies, and explosive population growth. One difficulty is that most people fail to recognize that many problems facing us are interconnected. Anthropology provides us with a critical and realistic understanding of the emergence of a global cultural system and its radical impact on local communities. Its cross-cultural and historically informed perspective is essential for solving problems and ensuring a future in which all peoples enjoy basic human rights.

Anthropology is superficially described by those who know little about it as an exotic discipline interested mainly in what happened long ago and far away. The most common popular stereotype is that anthropologists devote all of their attention to digging up the past and describing the last surviving tribal peoples with traditional ways of life. Yet, as noted earlier in this book, neither archaeologists nor paleoanthropologists (the anthropologists most devoted to looking into the past) limit their interests to ancient times, nor do ethnographers (who focus on contemporary cultures) overlook the ways and workings of industrial and postindustrial societies. Indeed, anthropologists are interested in the entire range of human cultures past and present—in their similarities and differences and in the multiple ways they influence one another.

Moreover, many anthropologists have a special concern with the future and the changes it may bring. They wonder what today's globalizing processes will create and what will be transformed, disrupted, or damaged beyond repair. As we saw in the preceding chapter, when traditional peoples are exposed to intense contact with technologically empowered Western peoples, their cultures typically change with unprecedented speed, often for the worse, becoming both less supportive and less adaptive. Since globalization seems unstoppable, we are compelled to ask: How can the thousands of different cultures, developed in the course of centuries if not millennia, deal successfully with the multiple challenges hurled at them?

THE CULTURAL FUTURE OF HUMANITY

To comprehend anthropology's role in understanding and solving problems in times to come, we must look at flaws frequently seen in publications and planning efforts focused on the future. First of all, rarely do futurists look more than about fifty years ahead, and more often than not the trends they project are those of recent history. This predisposes people to think that a trend that seems acceptable today will always be so. The danger of this assumption is neatly captured in anthropologist George Cowgill's comment: "It is worth recalling the story of the person who leaped from a very tall building and on being asked how things were going as he passed the 20th floor replied 'Fine, so far.'"[1]

A second flaw typical in futurist projections is a tendency to treat subjects in isolation, without reference to pertinent trends outside an expert's field of competence. For example, agricultural planning is often based on the

assumption that a certain amount of water is available for irrigation, whether or not urban planners or others have designs upon that same water. Thus, people may be counting on natural resources in the future that will not, in fact, be available.

This brings us to a third flaw common among futurists: The tendency to project the hopes and expectations of one's own social group or culture into the future interferes with the scientific objectivity necessary to see and address emerging problems. A recent example is the war in Iraq, where the hopes and expectations of the official U.S. and British planners blinded them to the complex problems that would emerge.

Against this background, anthropology's contribution to our understanding of the future is clear. With their holistic and integrative perspective, anthropologists are specialists at seeing how parts fit together into a larger whole. With their comparative and long-term historical perspective, they can place short-term trends in deeper and wider perspective. With more than a hundred years of cross-cultural research behind them—based on ancient archaeological finds, linguistic information, biological data, as well as participant observation within living cultures—anthropologists can recognize culture-bound assertions when they encounter them. Last but not least, they are familiar with alternative ways of dealing with a wide variety of problems.

Global Culture

Human populations have always been on the move. But today, more people travel faster and farther than ever before due to modern means of transportation (Figure 16.1). Moreover, revolutions in communication technology—from print media to telegraph and telephone to radio, television, satellites, and the Internet—make it possible to exchange more information with more people faster and over greater distances. Obviously, this global flow of humans, their products, and their ideas plays a major role in culture change.

A popular belief since the mid-1900s has been that the future world will see the development of a single homogeneous world culture. This idea is based largely on the observation that technological developments in communication, transportation, and trade are causing peoples of the world to increasingly watch the same television programs, read the same newspapers, eat the same foods, wear the same types of clothes, and communicate via satellites and the Internet.

Also of note, at least 175 million people (2.5 percent of the world's population) now live outside their countries of birth—not as refugees but as migrants who earn their living in one country while being citizens of another. The continuation of such trends, so this thinking goes, would mean that North Americans who travel in

---
[1]Cowgill, G. L. (1980). Letter, *Science 210*, 1,305.

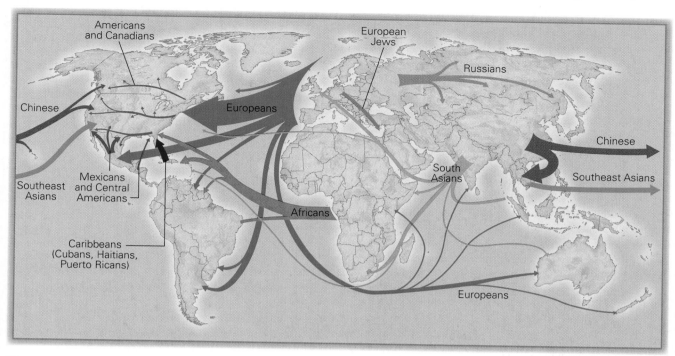

Figure 16.1

World Migrations Migration has had and continues to have a significant effect on world social geography, contributing to culture change and development, to the diffusion of ideas and innovations, and to the complex mixture of people and cultures found in the world today. Internal migration occurs within the boundaries of a country; external migration is movement from one country or region to another. Over the last fifty years, the most important migrations in the world have been internal, largely the rural-to-urban migration that has been responsible for the recent rise of global urbanization. Prior to the mid-20th century, three types of external migration were most important: voluntary, most often in search of better conditions and opportunities; involuntary or forced, involving people who have been driven from their homelands by war, political unrest, or environmental disasters, or transported as slaves or prisoners; and imposed, not entirely forced but made advisable by the circumstances.

SOURCE: From *Student Atlas of Anthropology* by John L. Allen and Audrey Shalinsky, p. 73. Copyright © 2003 McGraw-Hill/Dushkin Publishing.

the year 2100 to Afghanistan, Botswana, Colombia, or Denmark would find the local inhabitants living in a manner identical or similar to theirs. Yet, looking at ethnic conflicts around the world, we must ask if this prediction is likely to be accurate.

Is the World Coming Together or Coming Apart?

Certainly it is striking—the extent to which such items as Western-style clothing, bicycles, cars, cameras, computers, and soft drinks have spread to virtually all parts of the world. And many countries—Japan, for example—appear to have gone a long way toward becoming Westernized. Moreover, looking back over the past 5,000 years of human history, we see that political units have tended to become larger, more all-encompassing, and fewer in number. The logical outcome of this trend would be a further reduction of autonomous political units into a single one taking in the entire globe.

Informed by comparative historical and cross-cultural research, anthropologists call attention to something that all large states throughout time have had in common: a tendency to come apart. Not only have the great empires of the past, without exception, broken up into numbers of smaller independent states, but states in virtually all parts of the world today show this same tendency to fragment, usually along major geographic and ethnic divisions.

The threat of political collapse is ever-present in multi-ethnic states, especially when these countries are large, difficult to travel in, and lack major unifying cultural forces such as a common national language. Such has been the case, for instance, with Afghanistan. This vast, mountainous country is inhabited by several major ethnic groups, including Pashtun who live mainly in the south, and Tajik, Uzbek, Hazara, and Turkmen who live

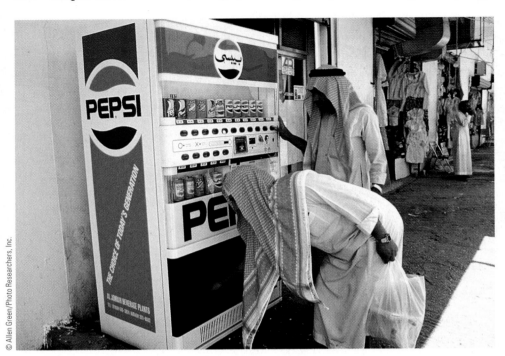

The worldwide spread of such products as Pepsi is taken by some as a sign that a homogeneous world is developing. Pepsi beverages include not only cola, but Mountain Dew, Lipton's Iced Tea, and Aquafina water—generating more than $26 billion in sales.

mainly in the north. Although the Pashtun are greatest in number and most dominant in the past 200 years, they were never able to successfully impose their political will on the other ethnic groups who maintain a great deal of independence; nor did they succeed in making their own native tongue, Pashto, the country's national language.

The tendency of multi-ethnic states to break apart has been especially noteworthy since the end of the Cold War between the United States and the former Soviet Union around 1990. For example, 1991 saw the dramatic breakup of the Soviet Union into about a dozen independent republics—Russia, Armenia, Kazakhstan, and Ukraine, among others. In 1992 Czechoslovakia split into the Czech and the Slovak republics. That same year the Republic of Yugoslavia began splintering into what are now six independent states in the Balkan Mountains.

The splintering tendency of multi-ethnic states can also be seen in separatist movements such as that of French-speaking peoples in Canada; Basques in Spain; Tibetans in China; the Karen in Burma (Myanmar); Tamils in Sri Lanka; Kurds in Turkey, Iran, and Iraq, and so on— this list is far from exhaustive. Nor is the United States immune, as can be seen in Native American nations seeking to secure greater political self-determination on their reservations.

All of these examples involve peoples who see themselves as members of distinct nations by virtue of their birth and their cultural and territorial heritage—nations over whom peoples of some other ethnic background have tried to assert political control. An estimated 5,000 such national groups exist in the world today, as opposed to a mere 192 states formally admitted as members of the

United Nations (up from fewer than fifty in the 1940s).[2] Although some of these ethnic groups are small in population and area—100 or so people living on a few acres— many others are quite large. The Karen people inhabiting southern Burma (Myanmar), for example, number some 4.5 to 5 million, exceeding the population of nearly half of the countries in the world.

The reactions of such groups to forced annexation and domination by state regimes controlled by people of other nations range all the way from the nonviolence of Scottish and Welsh nationalism to bloody fights for national independence by the Irish, Algerians, Vietnamese, or Palestinians. Many struggles for independence have been going on for years. Today, about 35 million people in almost half of the world's countries are either internally displaced or have crossed international borders as refugees. Some 9 million of these unfortunates have been forced outside their countries, most of them suffering in makeshift camps where they cannot make a living.

In some cases, a large proportion of an ethnic group's entire population finds itself forced to abandon their homes and flee for their lives. For instance, some 18 million Africans are currently uprooted. In war-torn Sudan alone, more than 2.5 million people have been driven from their homes.

It is possible that we are reaching a point where the tendency for political units to increase in size while decreasing in number is being canceled out by the tendency for such units to fragment into a greater number of smaller ones. Despite these examples, there are also a

[2]*Cultural Survival Quarterly* (1991). *15* (4), 38.

Reuters/Corbis

Almost fifty years ago, when the Chinese communist government in Beijing annexed Tibet and imposed its rule over the Buddhist people in this Himalayan region, tens of thousands of Tibetans were forced to flee to neighboring Nepal and India, where they found safety in refugee camps. Among the many refugees is the Dalai Lama (left), Tibet's spiritual leader, who escaped his homeland across the freezing cold and snow-covered mountains in 1959 and still lives in exile.

few instances of reunification. Best known among these is the 1990 reunification of Germany, divided since the end of World War II as East and West Germany, into one large federal republic. Another notable exception is the recent integration of twenty-seven European countries into the European Union—however hindered by linguistic differences, distinctive cultural traditions, and bureaucratic red tape.

Global Culture: A Good Idea or Not?

The idea of a shared global culture may have a degree of popular appeal, in that it might diminish chances for the kinds of misunderstandings and conflicting viewpoints that so often in the past few hundred years have led to violent clashes and even full-scale wars. Anthropologists greet this prognosis with skepticism, though, suspecting that distinctive worldviews will persist as they have for hundreds of years, even in the face of massive changes. Indeed, one might argue that the chance for conflicting viewpoints actually increases, given the intensified interactions among people in the world today.

Some have argued that perhaps a generalized world culture would be desirable in the future, because some traditional cultures may be too specialized to adjust to a changed environment. For instance, when Amazonian Indians pursuing traditional ways of life that are well adapted to South America's tropical rainforest are confronted with sudden, radical changes brought on by

foreign invaders, their long-established cultures often collapse. The reason for this, it is argued, is that the forest dwellers' traditions and political and social organizations are not adapted to modern ways and that they are naturally destined to give way to the new.

A problem with this argument is that, far from being unable to adapt, such traditional peoples have been robbed repeatedly of the opportunity to work out their own adaptations based on their own agendas. Their demise is caused not by laws of nature but rather by the political and economic choices of the powerful, fueled by arrogance, intolerance, and greed, along with a willingness to invade and exploit lands already owned and long inhabited by indigenous people.

The possibility of Amazonian Indians adapting to the changing realities, if allowed to do so, without losing their distinctive ethnic and cultural identity, is demonstrated by the Shuar case in Ecuador, noted in the preceding chapter. However, the pressures to "develop" the Amazon rainforest in Brazil are so great that whole indigenous communities are dispossessed, swept aside, or even destroyed so that global timber, energy, and mining corporations and agribusinesses are free to pursue their unrestrained profit-making activities. People do not have much chance to work out their own adaptations to the globalizing world if they are driven from their homelands and abruptly deprived of their means of survival so that more acreage can be devoted to the raising of beef cattle. Much of this meat is refrigerated and shipped directly to Europe. And much of the profits also leave the country since the major ranches are owned and operated by foreign corporations. Although large tracts of land have been set aside as Indian reservations since the mid-1990s, the devastation process continues. In the globalization process, economically and technologically empowered people have defined others—indeed, whole societies—as inferior, subservient, irrelevant, and not entitled to human rights, including self-determination.

Ethnic Resurgence

Despite the worldwide adoption of such products as blue jeans, sunglasses, Coca-Cola, and the Big Mac, and despite ever-growing pressures on traditional cultures to disappear, it is clear that cultural differences are still with us in the world today. In fact, resistance to many aspects of globalization is growing in many parts of the world. We see evidence of this in examples already noted, as well as in repeated public protests around the globe against policies of the Geneva-based World Trade Organization. In addition, Greenpeace and a host of less radical environmental groups can be found demonstrating worldwide against such practices as French nuclear testing in the Pacific or Japanese commercial whaling. Other examples include symbolic attacks by small farmers in France against corporate control, genetically modified crops, industrial agriculture, and McDonald's fast-food outlets. Resistance to globalization is also evident in political movements in Bolivia and Venezuela, as well as Muslim fundamentalist movements from Algeria in northwest Africa to Indonesia in Southeast Asia. The remarkable recent revival of shamanism in former communist Mongolia is yet another example, as is the increasing political activism of many other indigenous peoples from every corner of the world.

During the 1970s the world's indigenous peoples (almost all of whom are minorities suffering repression or discrimination by more dominant nations or ethnic groups politically controlling the countries within which the indigenous groups have always lived) began to organize self-determination movements. Joining together across international borders, they established the World Council of Indigenous Peoples in 1975. This global organization now has official status as a nongovernmental organization of the United Nations, which allows it to present the plight of indigenous peoples before the world community. Movement leaders see their own traditional societies as community based, egalitarian, and close to the natural environment, and they are intent upon keeping them that way.

Representing 5 percent of the world's population, indigenous peoples gained important symbolic ground in 1992 when Rigoberta Menchú, a Maya Indian woman from Guatemala who won the Nobel Peace Prize in 1992 for her activism on behalf of indigenous rights. Receiving this honor in 1992 had particular political significance, because it was the year of the Columbian quincentennial in which people in Europe and the Americas commemorated the pioneering journey of Christopher Columbus across the Atlantic ocean—a journey that had devastating consequences for American Indians. The prize focused international attention on the ongoing repression of indigenous peoples in Guatemala and helped pave the way to peace accords in late December 1996.

In 1993, representatives of some 124 indigenous groups and organizations agreed to a draft Declaration of the Rights of Indigenous Peoples that had taken a decade to produce. Presented to the UN General Assembly, it contains some 150 articles urging respect for indigenous cultural heritages, calling for recognition of indigenous land titles and rights of self-determination, and demanding an end to all forms of oppression and discrimination as a principle of international law. So far, this drafted document is largely symbolic. It remains under consideration by the UN, which to date has agreed to only a handful of its articles. Whether it will be adopted remains to be seen.

The struggle by indigenous groups against domination and discrimination by more powerful peoples with different cultures is not only in defense of their human rights, but also resistance against imposed cultural values and foreign ethnocentrism—the belief that the ways of one's own culture are the only proper ones. North Americans, Europeans, and people in many other industrial or postindustrial societies often have difficulty adjusting to the fact that not everyone wants to be just like they are. In the United States, for example, children are taught to believe that the "American way of life" is one to which all other peoples aspire. Although it is true that many peoples from poor countries across the world seek to improve their living conditions and enjoy the fruits of freedom, such aspirations should not be confused with wanting to become "American." Moreover, in the globalizing world dominated by the United States, Japan, and a handful of European capitalist states today, whole countries that once valued Western ways are now drawing the line or even turning against many of these ideas, trends, and practices.

One striking case of such a cultural reaction was that of a group of Muslim religious fundamentalists in Afghanistan known as the Taliban (the Pashto word for "students," specifically of Islam). After helping to force the Russian army out of their country and ending the subsequent civil war, they rose to power in the 1990s and imposed a radical version of traditional Islamic law (Shariah) in an effort to create an Islamic republic based on strict religious values. A similar, though less radical, reaction against modernity is taking place in the United States, where "born again" and other fundamentalist politicians have been elected in recent years on a plat-

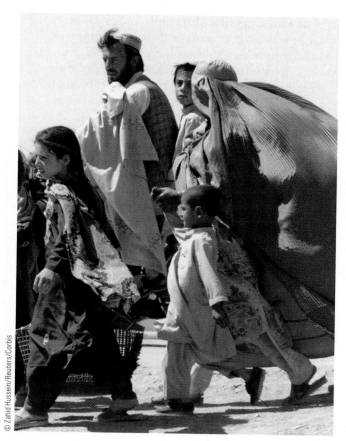

Often resistance to modernization takes the form of cultural traditionalism and religious fundamentalism, as in Afghanistan during recent decades. This reactionary practice is evident in this family's clothing, the mother's veil, and the father's beard.

form of creating a national culture based on what they see as traditional Christian values.[3]

Cultural Pluralism and Multiculturalism

If a single homogenous global culture is not necessarily the wave of the future, what is? Some predict a world in which ethnic groups will become more nationalistic in response to globalization, each group stressing its unique cultural heritage and emphasizing differences with neighboring groups. But not all ethnic groups organize themselves politically as distinctive nations with their own state. In fact, it has been common for two or more neighboring ethnic groups or nations to draw together in a loose political union while maintaining their particular cultural identities. However, because such pluralistic societies lack a common cultural identity and

heritage, and often do not share the same language or religion, political relationships between them can be fraught with tension. When feelings of ethnonationalism are not far from the surface, political pressure may build up and result in separation and independence.

One way of curbing divisive pressures in pluralistic or multi-ethnic societies is the adoption of a public policy based on mutual respect and tolerance for cultural differences. Known as **multiculturalism,** such an official policy or doctrine asserts the value of different cultures co-existing within a country and stresses the reciprocal responsibility of all citizens to accept the rights of others to freely express their views and values. In contrast to state policies in which a dominant ethnic group uses its power to impose its own culture as the national standard, forcing other groups within the same state to assimilate, multiculturalism involves a public policy for managing a society's cultural diversity. Examples of long-established multiculturalism may be seen in states such as Switzerland (where German-, French-, Italian-, and Romansh-speaking peoples co-exist under the same government) and Canada (where French- and English-speaking Canadians, as well as dozens of indigenous nations live side by side).

THOMSON AUDIO STUDY PRODUCTS Take advantage of the MP3-ready Audio Lecture Overviews and comprehensive audio glossary of key terms for each chapter. See the preface for information on how to access this on-the-go study and review tool.

Although cultural pluralism is still more common than multiculturalism, several multi-ethnic countries have recently changed their official melting pot ideology and associated policies of assimilation. One example of a country that is moving toward multiculturalism is the United States, which now has over 120 different ethnic groups within its borders (in addition to hundreds of federally recognized American Indian groups). Another is Australia, now counting over a hundred ethnic groups and with eighty languages spoken within its territorial boundaries. Similar changes are also underway in many European countries where millions of foreign immigrants have settled during the past few decades. Such changes are not easy, and often engender protests along the way. In many pluralistic societies, however, governments lack the ideological commitment or political capacity to successfully structure a national cultural system.

We cannot ignore the fact that, historically, what has been called "nation building" in all parts of the world

[3]Marsella, J. (1982). Pulling it together: Discussion and comments. In S. Pastner & W. A. Haviland (Eds.), *Confronting the creationists* (pp. 79–80). *Northeastern Anthropological Association, Occasional Proceedings,* 1.

multiculturalism Public policy for managing cultural diversity in a multi-ethnic society, officially stressing mutual respect and tolerance for cultural differences within a country's borders.

In 1982 United Nations Sub-Commission on the Promotion and Protection of Human Rights established a Working Group on Indigenous Populations (WGIP). Eleven years later WGIP completed a draft Declaration of the Rights of Indigenous Peoples. The document has yet to be ratified, but indigenous peoples all around the world are increasingly organizing to defend their own interests against both developers and governments. Here we see delegates from Japan's ethnic Ainu community in the UN assembly hall at a recent WGIP gathering.

almost always involves attempts to destroy the cultures of peoples whose nationalities differ from those controlling the governments in those countries.[4] During the last two decades of the 20th century, states were borrowing more money to fight peoples within their own boundaries than for all other programs combined. Nearly all state debt in Africa and nearly half of all other debt in "underdeveloped" countries comes from the cost of weapons purchased by states to fight their own citizens.[5] The more divergent cultural traditions are, the more difficult it is to make pluralism work.

That said, states as political constructs are products of human imagination, and nothing prevents us from imagining in ways that are more tolerant of cultural pluralism or multiculturalism. For example, consider once again Switzerland, where multiculturalism has worked out to the satisfaction of all four ethnic groups. In this confederation of small states (cantons), a political tradition of direct democracy is combined with a political organization that does not interfere with the country's regional, linguistic, and religious differences.

Obviously, replicating such a success in other political arenas will take a good deal of work, but at least the international community recognizes the concept of *group* rights. Even though it often fails to act on it, the UN General Assembly's 1966 Covenant of Human Rights states unequivocally:

In those states in which ethnic, religious or linguistic minorities exist, persons belonging to such minorities shall not be denied the rights, in community with the other members of their group, to enjoy their own culture, to profess and practice their own religion or to use their own language.[6]

Ethnocentrism and Cultural Pluralism

The major problem associated with cultural pluralism has to do with ethnocentrism. To function effectively, we may expect a society to embrace at least a degree of ethnic pride and a loyalty to its unique cultural traditions, from which its people derive psychological support and a firm social bond to their group. In societies where one's self-identification derives from the group, belief that one's own distinct customs and cultural practices are ideal is essential to a sense of personal worth.

As illustrated again and again in this book, the problem with ethnocentrism is that it is all too easy to take it as a charter for condemning other cultures as inferior and to denigrate and exploit them for the benefit of one's own. Although this does have to be the result, when it is, unrest, hostility, and violence commonly result.

In the world today, powerful governments frequently operate on the basis of the political idea that no group has the right to stand in the way of "the greater good for the greater number." This concept is commonly used to justify the expropriation of natural resources in regions traditionally occupied by subsistence farmers, pastoral nomads, or food foragers—without any respect for the rights, concerns, or wishes of these peoples. But is it truly the greater good for the greater number? A look at the rise of global corporations helps to answer this question.

The Rise of Global Corporations

The resistance of the world to political integration might seem to be offset to some extent by the rise and ongoing growth of global corporations. Because these cut across the international boundaries between states, they are a force for worldwide integration despite the political, linguistic, religious, and other cultural differences that separate people.

Global corporations, rare before the latter half of the 20th century, now are a far-reaching economic and political force in the world. Modern-day business giants such as General Electric, Shell, and Toyota are actually clusters of several corporations joined by ties of com-

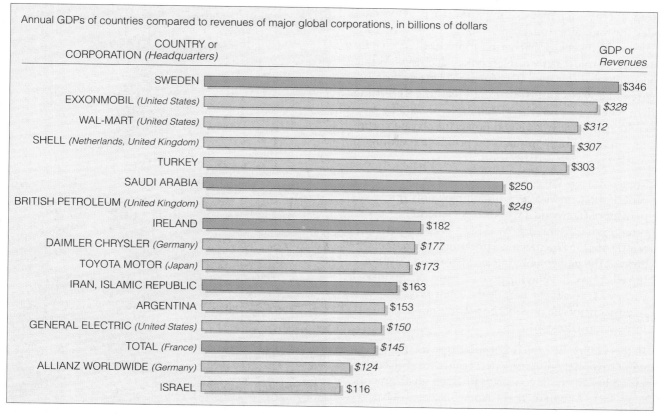

Annual GDPs of countries compared to revenues of major global corporations, in billions of dollars

COUNTRY or CORPORATION (Headquarters)	GDP or Revenues
SWEDEN	$346
EXXONMOBIL (United States)	$328
WAL-MART (United States)	$312
SHELL (Netherlands, United Kingdom)	$307
TURKEY	$303
SAUDI ARABIA	$250
BRITISH PETROLEUM (United Kingdom)	$249
IRELAND	$182
DAIMLER CHRYSLER (Germany)	$177
TOYOTA MOTOR (Japan)	$173
IRAN, ISLAMIC REPUBLIC	$163
ARGENTINA	$153
GENERAL ELECTRIC (United States)	$150
TOTAL (France)	$145
ALLIANZ WORLDWIDE (Germany)	$124
ISRAEL	$116

Figure 16.2

In today's consumer-driven world, it is not uncommon for the yearly revenues of large multinational corporations to equal and even exceed the total value of all goods and services produced within a country per year, known as a country's gross domestic product (GDP). This graph shows the annual GDPs of selected countries alongside the annual revenues of leading global corporations (Note: GDP says nothing about the unequal distribution of wealth within a country.)

SOURCE: Based on 2005 sales figures (www.forbes.com, May 2006) and GDP figures (www.worldbank.org, May 2006).

mon ownership and responsive to a common management strategy. Usually tightly controlled by a head office in one country, these enterprises organize and integrate production across the international boundaries of different countries for interests formulated in corporate boardrooms, irrespective of whether these are consistent with the interests of people in the countries where they operate. These megacorporations are the products of the technological revolution, for without sophisticated data-processing equipment and electronic communication, they could not keep adequate track of their worldwide operations.

Though typically thought of as responding impersonally to outside market forces, large corporations are in fact controlled by an increasingly smaller number of wealthy capitalists who benefit directly from their operations. Yet, unlike political leaders, the world's largest individual stockholders and most powerful directors are known to few people. For that matter, most people cannot even name the world's major global corporations,

which include Wal-Mart, British Petroleum, Shell, Exxon-Mobil, DaimlerChrysler, Toyota, and General Electric (Figure 16.2). Each of these business giants currently generates annual revenues above $150 billion, and three of them have passed the $300 billion mark.[7]

So great is the power of large businesses operating all across the globe that they increasingly thwart the wishes of national governments or international organizations such as the United Nations, Red Cross, International Court of Justice, or the World Council of Churches. Because the information these corporations process is kept from flowing in a meaningful way to the population at large, or even to lower levels within the organization, it becomes difficult for governments to get the information they need for informed policy decisions. It took years for the U.S. Congress to extract the information it needed from tobacco companies to decide what to do about tobacco legislation—and it is nearly as slow-going today

---

[7]Forbes International 500 List.

getting energy and media companies to provide data needed for regulatory purposes.

Beyond this, the global corporations have repeatedly shown they can overrule foreign policy decisions. While some might see this as a hopeful signal for getting beyond national vices and rivalries, it raises the unsettling issue of whether or not the global arena should be controlled by immensely large and powerful private corporations interested only in financial profits. According to one market research organization,

> Today, the top 100 companies control 33 percent of the world's assets, but employ only one percent of the world's workforce. General Motors is larger than Denmark, Wal-Mart bigger than South Africa. The mega-corporations roam freely around the globe, lobbying legislators, bankrolling elections and playing governments off against each other to get the best deals. Their private hands control the bulk of the world's news and information flows.[8]

If the ability of global corporations to ignore the wishes of sovereign governments is cause for concern, so is their ability to act in concert with such governments. Here, in fact, is where their worst excesses have occurred. One example took place in Brazil, where the situation is hardly unique but is especially well documented. After a 1964 military coup in that country, a partnership emerged between the new government, which was anxious to proceed as rapidly as possible with development of the Amazon rainforest, and a number of global corporations and international lending institutions. (The corporations included ALCOA, Borden, Union Carbide, Swift-Armour, and Volkswagen, among others, and the lending institutions included the Export-Import Bank, the Inter-American Development Bank, and the World Bank.[9])

To help bring about what they liked to call the Brazilian miracle, these allies initiated new road construction projects and introduced inappropriate technology and ecologically unsound practices into the region, converting vast woodlands into semi-desert. Far more shocking, however, has been the practice of uprooting whole human societies because they were seen as obstacles to economic growth.

Eager to alleviate acute land shortages in the country's impoverished northeastern region, but unwilling to break up the huge rural estates owned by a powerful elite and embark on much-needed land reform, govern-

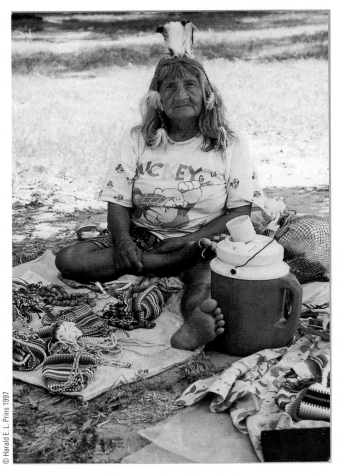

© Harald E. L. Prins 1997

Maká Indian woman in Paraguay, South America. The poorest people in the world often wear clothing discarded by those who are better off—and people from all walks of life can be found wearing clothes with corporate logos. The power that big business (such as the Disney media corporation) has over individuals is illustrated by the ability of corporations to get consumers to pay for goods that advertise corporate products.

ment officials launched massive resettlement schemes. They lured millions of Brazilian peasants to the Amazon to clear the forest and settle as farmers in territories traditionally owned and long inhabited by many different indigenous nations. Soon, however, it became obvious that few of these newcomers could adequately support their families, so tens of thousands turned to gold mining. This, in turn, resulted in poisoning the rivers with mercury, creating serious health problems.

Bad as this was for these poor peasants, the disease, death, and human suffering that such schemes and policies unleashed upon the native Indians can only be described as massive. Entire indigenous groups have been (and are still being) destroyed with a thoroughness not achieved even by the communist dictator Stalin during his "Great Terror" in the Soviet Union of the 1930s or the Nazis in World War II. Were it not so well documented, it would be beyond belief.

---

[8]www.adbusters.org, accessed January 10, 2003. See also Hertz, N. (2001). *The silent takeover: Global capitalism and the death of democracy* (p. 43). New York: Arrow Books.

[9]Davis, S. H. (1982). *Victims of the miracle.* Cambridge, England: Cambridge University Press.

Megacorporations are changing the shape of the world and the lives of individuals from every walk of life, including those they employ. Anthropologist Jules Henry, in a classic 1965 study of life in the United States, observed that working for any large corporation—global or not—tends to generate "hostility, instability, and fear of being obsolete and unprotected. For most people their job was what they had to do rather than what they wanted to do, . . . taking a job, therefore, meant giving up part of their selves."[10]

Since Henry's day such feelings have grown in the ever more "sprawling, anonymous, networks" of global corporations.[11] Not only are business decisions typically made in corporate headquarters very far removed from where the actual business operations take place, but also, because corporations depend on sophisticated data-processing systems, many decisions can be and are being made by computers programmed for particular contingencies and strategies. In the face of such coldly calculating systems for making decisions exclusively in the corporate interest, workers become fearful that, if they ask too much of the company, it simply may shift its operations to another part of the world where it can find cheaper, more submissive personnel.

In the never-ending search for cheap labor, multinational corporations have returned to a practice once seen in the textile mills of 19th-century Britain and New England, but now on a much larger scale. More than ever before, they have come to favor women for low-skilled assembly jobs. In so-called underdeveloped countries, as subsistence farming gives way to mechanized agriculture for production of crops for export, women are less able to contribute to their families' survival. Together with the devaluation of domestic work, this places pressure on women to seek jobs outside the household to contribute to its support. Since most women in these countries do not have the time or resources to get an education or to develop special job skills, only low-paying jobs are open to them.

Corporate officials, for their part, assume female workers are strictly temporary, and high turnover means that wages can be kept low. Unmarried women are especially favored for employment, for it is assumed that they are free from family responsibilities until they marry, whereupon they will leave the labor force. Thus, the increasing importance of the multinationals in developing countries is contributing to the emergence of a marked gender-segregated division of labor. On top of their housework, women hold low-paying jobs that require little skill; altogether, they may work as many as 15 hours a day. Higher-paying jobs, or at least those that require special skills, are generally held by men, whose workday may be shorter since they do not have additional domestic tasks to perform. Men who lack special skills—and many do—are often doomed to lives of unemployment.

Big business has created problems for consumers as well as workers. In a ten-year intensive study of relations between producers and consumers of products and services, anthropologist Laura Nader found repeated and documented offenses by North American businesses that could not be handled by existing complaint mechanisms, either in or out of court. Faceless relations between producers and consumers, among whom there is a grossly unequal distribution of power, have exacted a high cost: a terrible sense of apathy, even a loss of faith in the system itself.

In recent years, the power of corporations has become all the greater through media expansion. Over the past two decades, a global commercial media system has developed, dominated by a few megacorporations, most based in the United States. One such global media corporation is NBC, now owned by General Electric (GE), which is among the world's leading electronics and manufacturing firms with $150 billion in sales. In addition to NBC, GE owns various other broadcasting companies, including Paxson Communications and the Telemundo Communications Group. It also owns and operates a host of television stations in major urban markets such as New York, Los Angeles, Chicago, and Washington, D.C.—not to mention a digital media firm and three cable network companies, including CNBC and MSNBC. Moreover, GE owns companies such as GE Aircraft Engines, GE Commercial Finance, GE Consumer Products, GE Industrial Systems, GE Insurance, GE Medical Systems, GE Plastics, GE Power Systems, GE Specialty Materials, and GE Transportation Systems, and so on.

Having control of television and other media, as well as the advertising industry, gives global corporations such as GE and Disney enormous influence on the ideas and behavior of hundreds of millions of ordinary people across the world in ways most people little suspect and can hardly imagine.

Consider, for example, the powerful marketing messages that shape cultural standards concerning the ideal human body. The widespread nature of this concern is evident in highly popular reality TV programs like *Extreme Makeover,* which feature a few individuals chosen from many thousands of applicants to have their dream come true—to change their looks in an effort to lead better lives. They receive free plastic surgery and other radical cosmetic procedures in exchange for undergoing the knife on camera and allowing the details of their makeover to be broadcast on international television. The following Original Study offers details on what has become a lucrative cosmetic surgery industry.

[10]Henry, J. (1965). *Culture against man* (p. 127). New York: Vintage Books.

[11]Pitt, D. (1977). Comment. *Current Anthropology 18,* 628.

Original Study ▪ By Laura Nader

Standardizing the Body: The Question of Choice

The question of choice is central to the story of how medicine and business generate controlling processes in the shaping of women's bodies. Images of the body appear natural within their specific cultural milieus. For example, breast implants are not seen as odd within the cultural milieu of the United States, and female circumcision and infibulation (also known as female genital mutilation or FGM) are not considered odd among people from the Sudan and several other African countries. However, many feminist writers differentiate FGM from breast implantation by arguing that North American women *choose* to have breast implants whereas in Africa women are presumably subject to indoctrination since they experience circumcision as young girls.

One of the most heated debates arising from the public health concern over breast implants is whether the recipients are freely situated—that is, whether their decision is voluntary or whether control is disguised as free will.

An informed response to the free choice argument requires knowing how the beauty-industrial complex works. Toward this end, corporate accountability researcher Linda Coco carried out fieldwork in multiple sites, gaining insights into the inner workings of a multibillion-dollar industry that segments the female body and manufactures commodities of and for the body.

Coco's research shows how some women get caught in the official beauty ideology, and in the case of silicone-gel breast implants some hundreds of thousands of women have been ensnared. But who gets caught and when are important to an understanding of the ecology of power. The average age of a woman having breast implantation is 36 years, and she has an average of two children. She is

the beauty industry's insecure consumer recast as a patient with an illness the industry defines as hypertrophy (small breasts).

Coco quotes a past president of the American Society of Plastic and Reconstructive Surgery (ASPRS): "There is substantial and enlarging medical knowledge to the effect that these deformities [small breasts] are really a disease which result in the patient's feelings of inadequacies, lack of self-confidence, distortion of body image, and a total lack of well-being due to a lack of self-perceived femininity. . . . Enlargement . . .

is therefore . . . necessary to ensure the quality of life for the patient." In other words, cosmetic surgery is necessary to the patient's psychological health.

The plastic surgeon regards the construction of the official breast as art, the aim being to reform the female body according to the ideals of classic Western art. One surgeon pioneering procedures for correcting deformity took as his ideal female figure that of ancient Greek statues, which he carefully measured, noticing the exact size and shape of the breasts, their vertical location between the third and seventh ribs, the horizontal between the line of the sternal (breast bone) border and the anterior axillary line, and so forth. In Coco's analysis the exercise of the plastic surgeon's technoart recreates a particular static, official breast shape and applies this creation ostensibly to relieve women's mental suffering. The surgeon becomes a psychological healer as well as an artist.

Along with art and psychology, there is, of course, the business of organized plastic surgery, which responds to the demands and opportunities of market economics (see figure). By the late 1970s and early 1980s there was a glut of plastic surgeons. The ASPRS began to operate like a commercial enterprise instead of a medical society, saturating the media with ads and even providing low-cost financing. The discourse became a sales pitch. Women "seek" breast implants to keep their husbands or their jobs, to attract men, or to become socially acceptable. Coco calls this "patriarchal capitalism" and questions whether this is free choice or "mind colonization."

Understanding "choice" led Coco to an examination of the power both in the doctor–patient relationship and in the control of information. She

PROCEDURE	NUMBER DONE PER YEAR	PERCENT DONE FOR WOMEN
Chemical peel	1,033,581	89%
Eyelid surgery	230,697	86%
Nose reshaping	298,413	67%
Botox injection	3,839,387	92%
Face lift	150,401	90%
Breast enlargement	291,350	100%
Tummy tuck	134,746	96%
Liposuction	323,605	89%

Cosmetic surgical and nonsurgical procedures in the United States (2005) and the percentage carried out for women. In the United States in 2005 more than 2.1 million cosmetic surgeries were done and nearly 9.4 million nonsurgical procedures (chemical peels, Botox injections, and so on), at a total cost of about $12.4 billion. From 1997 to 2005, the number of cosmetic procedures performed increased 444 percent.

SOURCE: American Society for Aesthetic Plastic Surgery, 2006.

found that women "were told by the media, plastic surgeons, women's magazines, other women, and the business world that they could enhance their lives by enhancing their bust lines . . . the social imperative for appearance was personalized, psychologized, and normalized." Social surveys indicate that, to the extent that women internalize the social imperative, they feel they are making the decision on their own.

Not surprisingly, women whose surgery resulted in medical complications often came to recognize the external processes of coercive persuasion that had led them to seek implants. In some ways, they resembled former cult members who had been deprogrammed: Their disillusionment caused them to question the system that had encouraged them to make the decision in the first place. The result was a gradual building of protest against the industry, expressed in networks, newsletters, support groups, workshops, and seminars. As have some former cult members, women have brought suit, testified before lawmakers,

and challenged in other ways some of the largest corporations and insurance companies in the land.

The choice of implants, they learn, is part of a matrix of controlling processes in which women are subjects. Given the right circumstances it could happen to anyone. In the Sudan, the young girl is told that FGM procedures are done for her and not to her. In the United States the mutilation of natural breasts is also done for the recreation of femininity. Although power is exercised differently in these two cases, Coco notes the similarity: "The operation on the female breast in [North] America holds much of the same social symbolism and expression of cultural mandate as does FGM in Sudan. Thus, the question of why women choose breast augmentation becomes moot."

Breast implantation is now spreading elsewhere, most notably to China. Will it become a functional equivalent to footbinding in China as part of the competition between patriarchies East and West? Whatever the answer, many social think-

ers agree that people are always more vulnerable to intense persuasion during periods of historical dislocation—a break with structures and symbols familiar to the life cycle—in which the media can bring us images and ideas originating in past, contemporary, or even imaginary worlds.

Feminist researchers have sought to crack controlling paradigms such as those that define women's capacities and those that construct a standardized body shape and determine what is beautiful in women. Some of their writings are attempts to free the mind from the beauty constructions of cosmetic industries and fashion magazines. Others relay how the one model of Western beauty is affecting members of ethnic groups who aspire to look the way advertisements say they should. Choice is an illusion, since the restructuring of taste is inextricably linked to shifts in the organization of consumption.

(Adapted from L. Nader (1997). Controlling processes: Tracing the dynamics of power. Current Anthropology 38, 715–717.) ■

STRUCTURAL POWER IN THE AGE OF GLOBALIZATION

All of the above makes it clear that a new form of expansive international capitalism has emerged since the mid-1900s. Operating under the banner of globalization, it builds on earlier cultural structures of worldwide trade networks, and it is the successor to a system of colonialism in which a handful of powerful, mainly European, capitalist states ruled and exploited foreign nations inhabiting distant territories.

Enormously complex and turbulent, globalization is a dynamically structured process in which individuals, business corporations, and political institutions are actively rearranging and restructuring the social field of force to their own competitive advantage, vying for increasingly scarce natural resources, cheap labor, new commercial markets, and ever-larger profits in a huge political arena spanning the entire globe. Doing this, of course, requires a great deal of power.

As discussed previously, power refers to the ability of individuals or groups to impose their will upon others and make them do things even against their own wants or wishes. Power plays a major role in coordinating and regulating collective behavior toward imposing or main-

taining law and order within—and beyond—a particular community or society.

There are different levels of power within societies, as well as among societies. The recently deceased Austrian-American anthropologist Eric Wolf pointed out the importance of understanding a macro level of power that he referred to as **structural power**—power that organizes and orchestrates the systemic interaction within and among societies, directing economic and political forces on the one hand and ideological forces that shape public ideas, values, and beliefs on the other.[12]

The concept of structural power applies not only to regional political organizations such as chiefdoms or states but also captures the complex new cultural formations currently emerging in the globalization process. It focuses attention on the systemic interaction between the global forces directing the world's changing econo-

---

[12]Wolf, E. (1999). *Envisioning power: Ideologies of dominance and crisis* (p. 5). Berkeley: University of California Press.

---

structural power Power that organizes and orchestrates the systemic interaction within and among societies, directing economic and political forces on the one hand and ideological forces that shape public ideas, values, and beliefs on the other.

mies and political institutions on the one hand and those that shape public ideas, values, and beliefs on the other.

Joseph Nye, a political scientist, international security specialist, and former Assistant Secretary of Defense in the U.S. government, refers to these two major interacting forces in the worldwide arena as "hard power" and "soft power."[13] **Hard power** is the kind of coercive power that is backed up by economic and military force. **Soft power** is co-optive rather than coercive, pressing others through attraction and persuasion to change their ideas, beliefs, values, and behaviors. Although propaganda is a form of soft power, the exercise of ideological influence (the global struggle for hearts and minds) also operates through more subtle means, such as foreign aid, international diplomacy, news media, sports, entertainment, museum exhibits, and academic exchanges.

In today's globalization process, the United States has more hard power at its disposal than any of its allies or rivals worldwide. It is the global leader in military expenditure, spending more than $420 billion in 2005, followed by China ($62 billion), Russia ($62 billion), Britain ($51 billion), Japan ($45 billion—despite its pacifist constitution), France ($41 billion), and Germany ($30 billion). In fact, as the world's dominant superpower, the United States spends more on its armed forces than the next fourteen leading countries combined and is responsible for 43 percent of the $1 trillion spent on arms worldwide.[14]

Moreover, although there are seven other nuclear weapons states (Britain, France, and China, as well as Israel, India, Pakistan, and now also North Korea, collectively possessing nearly 900 active nuclear warheads), Russia and the United States have by far the largest nuclear arsenals at their disposal—minimally 5,830 and 5,735 operational warheads, respectively. (There are also nearly 16,000 intact but nonoperational warheads, almost all in the hands of the United States and Russia.)[15]

In addition to military might, hard power involves the use of economic strength as a political instrument of coercion or intimidation in the global structuring process. Among other things, this means that economic size and productivity, technological capability, and finance capital may be brought to bear on the global market, forcing weaker states to break down trade barriers protecting their workers, natural resources, and local markets.

As the world's largest economy and leading exporter, the United States has long pushed for free trade for its corporations doing business on a global scale. Sometimes it uses military power to impose changes on a foreign political landscape by means of armed interventions or full-scale invasions. For instance, when the United Fruit Company, owner of enormous banana plantations in Guatemala, saw its economic interests threatened by that country's democratically elected government, the U.S. government engineered a military coup in 1954 that resulted in a dictatorship favorable to U.S.-based corporations.

Through history, the United States (like several other powerful countries, including Russia, Britain, and France) has engaged in such military interventions around the world. Because of this, many see the United States as an ever-present threat, apt to use overwhelming military force in order to benefit its corporate interests from fruit to fuel, from microchips to automobiles. The corporations, in turn, wield enormous political and financial power over governments and international organizations, including the World Trade Organization, headquartered in Geneva, and global banking institutions such as the International Monetary Fund (IMF) and World Bank, both based in Washington, D.C.

Specializing in short-term loans to assist poor or developing countries, the IMF's financial resources weigh in at about $300 billion. The five wealthiest countries in the world (United States, Japan, Germany, France, and Britain) control 40 percent of this global fund and dominate its executive board. The IMF's structural power is evident not only in which development projects and policies it chooses to give financial support, but also in its surveillance practices, which involve monitoring a borrower's economic and financial developments.

The World Bank makes long-term loans ($20 billion annually) for economic development projects such as roads, schools, and health systems to reduce poverty in about a hundred developing countries. Like the IMF, it is largely controlled by a handful of powerful capitalist states. Operating under geopolitical constraints, these global banking institutions strategically direct capital flows to projects in certain parts of the world, financially supporting some governments and withholding capital from others.

Both the IMF and the World Bank have been accused of being insensitive to the political and cultural consequences of the projects they support. For example, in the 1990s the World Bank provided loans to a hydropower project in southern Chile to build dams in the upper Bio-Bio River without any serious consideration for

---

[13]Nye, J. (2002). *The paradox of American power: Why the world's only superpower can't go it alone.* New York: Oxford University Press.

[14]www.globalissue.org.

[15]Norris, R. S., & Kristensen, H. M. (2006, July/August). Global nuclear stockpiles, 1945–2006. *Bulletin of the Atomic Scientists 62* (4), 64–66.

hard power Coercive power that is backed up by economic and military force.
soft power Co-optive power that presses others through attraction and persuasion to change their ideas, beliefs, values, and behaviors.

the human rights of local Pehuenche Indians. The dam flooded a large part of the Pehuenche's ancestral lands, forcing hundreds to be resettled against their own will. Likewise, the World Bank approved a $40 million loan to the Chinese government to relocate some of the country's poorest Han Chinese farmers to more fertile land in Qinghai, territory that Tibetans consider part of their homeland. Tibetans protested that the bank was supporting China's effort to dilute the Tibetan ethnic minority population in that region.

Globalization does more than create a worldwide field of force in which megacorporations reap megaprofits. It also wreaks havoc in many traditional cultures and disrupts long-established social organizations everywhere. By the early 21st century, the global trend of economic inequality is becoming clear: The poor are becoming poorer, and the rich are becoming richer. For the many thousands of big winners or have-lots, there are many millions of losers or have-nots.

As home base to more global corporations than any other country, the United States is endeavoring to protect its interests by investing in creating and controlling what it refers to as a *global security environment*. Numerous other countries, unable to afford expensive weapons systems (or blocked from developing or acquiring them), have invested in biological or chemical warfare technology. Still others, including relatively powerless political groups, have resorted to guerrilla tactics or terrorism as part of their local, regional, or even global warfare strategies.

In addition to reliance on military and economic hard power in the global quest for dominance and profit, competing states and corporations utilize the ideological persuasion of soft power as transmitted by means of electronic and digital media, communications satellites, and other forms of information and communication technology. One of the major tasks of soft power is to package and sell the general idea of globalization as something positive and progressive (as "freedom," "free" trade, "free" market) and to frame or brand anything that opposes capitalism in negative terms.

One outcome of this complex interaction between hard and soft power in structuring the global arena is the creation of a new collective awareness of worldwide connectivity, making peoples everywhere understand and possibly accept the new cultural order. Considering existing cultural differences, political divisions, and competing economic interests, combined with growing worldwide resistance against superpower domination, the emerging world system is inherently unstable, vulnerable, and unpredictable.

Structural power and its associated concepts of hard and soft power enable us to better understand the wider field of force in which local communities throughout the world are now compelled to operate. To comprehend it

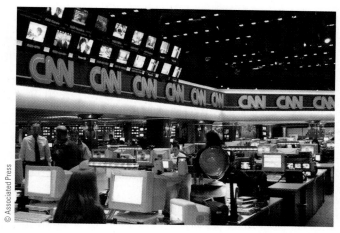

Global mass media corporations like Cable News Network (CNN) possess enormous "soft power." This U.S.-based private company produces and distributes news and other information through transnational cable and satellite networks, as well as websites. With bureaus in over thirty countries, its 24-hour news coverage is available to 1.5 billion people all over the world. Like even larger media giants, such as the British Broadcasting Corporation (BBC), CNN not only reports news, but also selects the visual imagery and determines what to stress or repress. By means of their awesome soft power, these corporations influence public perception and action ("hearts and minds").

is to realize how unequal the distribution of power is in today's global arena.

That said, no matter how effectively a dominant state or corporation combines its hard and soft power, globalization does run into opposition. Pockets of resistance exist within the wealthy industrial and postindustrial states as well as elsewhere in the world. This resistance may manifest itself in the rise of traditionalisms and revitalization movements—efforts to return to life as it was (or how people think it was) before the familiar order became unhinged and people became unsettled. Some of these reactionary movements may take the form of resurgent ethnonationalism or religious fundamentalist movements. Others may find expression in alternative grassroots movements from radical environmental groups to peace groups.

Increasingly, such movements use the Internet to further their causes. While it is true that states and big corporations have expanded their power and influence through electronic communication technologies, it is also true that these same technologies present opportunities to individuals and groups that have traditionally been powerless. They provide a means of distributing information and promoting activities that are distinct from or in opposition to those of dominant society.

The far-reaching capabilities of modern electronic and digital technologies have led to the creation of a new global media environment that plays a major role in how individuals and even societies view themselves and their place in the world. Together with radio and

Anthropologists of Note

Arjun Appadurai (b. 1949)

Arjun Appadurai is one of millions of transnational migrants in the world. Growing up in India, he studied at the University of Bombay before heading to the United States, where he continued his education and chose a life in academia. Living abroad, he became interested in the dispersion of ethnic groups around the globe and in the question of how widely scattered members of these groups maintain their sense of cultural identity. His research—including fieldwork in India, South Africa, and the Philippines—shows that migrants form part of strong social networks, which, thanks to modern technology, reach far beyond traditional geographic boundaries.

Appadurai has developed theoretical concepts that help us understand the complex and largely unpredictable processes that are currently rearranging human relations and restructuring cultural systems worldwide. Although most people in today's world still function within geographically defined communities, Appadurai points out that territorial borders have become increasingly irrelevant given the "cultural flows"

Courtesy of New School University

in our emerging global environment. He marks out five global spaces or dimensions in which transnational cultural flows occur, identifying them as "scapes" (meaning something crafted, configured, or transformed by humans):

- **Ethnoscapes:** the fluid and shifting landscape of migrants, refugees, exiles, tourists, and other moving groups and people
- **Technoscapes:** the global configuration of technologies moving at high speeds across previously restrictive borders

- **Financescapes:** the global crossroads of currency speculation and financial transfers
- **Mediascapes:** the distribution of electronic media capabilities to produce and spread information, plus the large complex repertoire of narratives and visual images generated by these media
- **Ideoscapes:** ideologies produced by the state and alternative ideologies developed by non-state and counter-hegemonic forces, around which societies organize their political cultures and collective cultural identities

Appadurai earned a doctorate from the University of Chicago in 1976 and has taught at the University of Pennsylvania, the University of Chicago, and Yale. Currently, he is provost at the New School University in New York City. Beyond university work, he has served as a consultant/advisor to a wide range of organizations, including the United Nations and the World Bank.

television, the Internet is now the dominant means of mass communication around the world. Today, the global flow of information made possible by fiber optic cables and communications satellites orbiting the earth is almost entirely digital-electronic and takes place in a new boundless cultural space that Indian anthropologist Arjun Appadurai refers to as a "global mediascape" (see Anthropologist of Note).

PROBLEMS OF STRUCTURAL VIOLENCE

Based on their capacity to harness, direct, and distribute global resources and energy flows, heavily armed states, megacorporations, and very wealthy elites are using their coercive and co-optive powers to structure or

structural violence Physical and/or psychological harm (including repression, environmental destruction, poverty, hunger, illness, and premature death) caused by impersonal, exploitative, and unjust social, political, and economic systems.

rearrange the emerging world system and direct global processes to their own competitive advantage. When such structural power undermines the well-being of others, we may speak of **structural violence**—physical and/or psychological harm (including repression, environmental destruction, poverty, hunger, illness, and premature death) caused by impersonal, exploitative, and unjust social, political, and economic systems.

Clearly, the current structures are positioned in a way that leads to more wealth, power, comfort, and glory for the happy few and little more than poverty, subservience, suffering, and death for multitudes. Every day millions of people around the world face famine, ecological disasters, health problems, political instability, and violence rooted in development programs or profit-making maneuvers directed by powerful states or global corporations.

A useful baseline for identifying structural violence is provided by the Universal Declaration of Human Rights, officially adopted by all members of the United Nations in 1948. Anthropologists played a key role in drafting this important document. The declaration's preamble begins with the statement that "recognition of the inherent dignity and of the equal and inalienable rights of all members of the human family is the foundation of freedom, justice, and peace in the world."[16] Generally speaking, structural violence concerns the impersonal systemic violation of the human rights of individuals and communities to a healthy, peaceful, and dignified life.

Although human rights abuses are nothing new, globalization has enormously expanded and intensified structural violence. For instance, it is leading to an ever-widening gap between the wealthiest and poorest peoples, the powerful and powerless. In 1960 the average income for the twenty wealthiest countries in the world was fifteen times that of the twenty poorest. Today it is thirty times higher.[17]

More remarkable is the fact that the world's 225 richest individuals have a combined wealth equal to the annual income of the poorest 47 percent of the entire world population. In fact, half of all people in the world get by on less than $2 per day, and more than 1.2 billion people live on just $1 a day. Measuring the gap in another way reveals that the poorest 80 percent of the human population make do with 14 percent of all goods and services in the world, the poorest 20 percent with a mere 1.3 percent. Meanwhile, the richest 20 percent enjoy 86 percent.[18]

Structural violence has countless manifestations in addition to widespread poverty. These range from the cultural destruction already indicated to hunger and obesity, environmental degradation, and emotional discontent, all discussed in the remaining pages of this chapter.

Overpopulation and Poverty

In 1750, 1 billion people lived on earth. Over the next two centuries our numbers climbed to nearly 2.5 billion. And between 1950 and 2000 the world population soared above 6 billion. Today, India and China alone have more than 1 billion inhabitants each. Such increases are highly significant because population growth increases the scale of hunger and pollution—and the many problems tied to these two big issues. Although controlling population growth does not by itself make the other problems go away, it is unlikely those other problems can be solved unless population growth is stopped or even reversed.

For a population to hold steady, there must be a balance between birthrates and death rates. In other words, people must produce only enough offspring to replace

themselves when they die. This is known as **replacement reproduction.** Prior to 1976, birthrates around the world generally exceeded death rates, with the exception of European and North American populations. Poor people, in particular, have tended to have large families because children have been their main resource. Children can provide a needed labor pool to work farms, and they are the only source of security for the elderly. Historically, people were apt to limit the size of their families only when they became wealthy enough that their money replaced children as their main resource; at that point, children actually *cost* them money. Given this, we can see why birthrates remained high for so long in the world's poorer countries. To those who live in poverty, children are seen as potentially valuable contributors to the household income.

Since the mid-1970s, birthrates have dropped below replacement level (which is about 2.1 children per woman) in virtually every industrialized country and also in nineteen developing countries—including China, the world's most populous country. Even in much of Africa, as well as South Asia and Central and South America (where most of the world's poorer nations are located), birthrates have also declined but far less dramatically.[19]

Despite progress in population control, the number of humans on earth continues to grow overall. Population projections are extremely tricky, given variables such as AIDS, but current projections suggest that global population will peak around 2050 at about 9.37 billion people.

The problem's severity becomes clear when it is realized that the present world population of more than 6 billion people can be sustained only by using up nonrenewable resources such as oil, which is like living off income-producing capital. It works for a time, but once the capital is gone, so is the possibility of even having an income to live on.

Hunger and Obesity

As frequently dramatized in media reports, hundreds of millions of people face hunger on a regular basis, leading to a variety of health problems, premature death, and other forms of suffering. Today, over a quarter of the world's countries do not produce enough food to feed their populations and cannot afford to import what

---

[16]www.ccnmtl.columbia.edu/projects/mmt/udhr.

[17]www.worldbank.org/poverty. (2003 statistics).

[18]Kurth, P. (1998, October 14). Capital crimes. *Seven Days, 7*; Swaminathan, M. S. (2000). Science in response to basic human needs. *Science 287*, 425. See also Human Development Report 2002, *Deepening democracy in a fragmented world,* United Nations Development Program.

[19]Bongaarts, J. (1998). Demographic consequences of declining fertility. *Science 282*, 419; Wattenberg, B. J. (1997, November 23). The population explosion is over. *New York Times Magazine*, 60.

---

replacement reproduction   The point at which birthrates and death rates are in equilibrium; people producing only enough offspring to replace themselves when they die.

Hunger afflicts much of the world. It is caused not only by drought and pests, but also by violent ethnic, religious, or political conflicts that uproot families and by global food production and a distribution system geared to satisfy the needs and demands of the world's most powerful countries. Without adequate nutrition, humans lose their ability to resist diseases. And without access to adequate health care, many of the poverty-stricken sick have little chance to survive. For the poor, especially in refugee camps, slums, and other places with miserable living conditions, suffering is a normal condition of life, and death looms everywhere. Here, an African woman carries empty containers to be filled with water at Abu Shouk camp, home to some 100,000 refugees facing hunger and thirst in Sudan's ethnic war-torn Darfur region.

is needed. The majority of these countries are in sub-Saharan Africa.

All told, about 1 billion people in the world are undernourished. Some 6 million children aged 5 and under die every year due to hunger, and those who survive often suffer from physical and mental impairment.[20] For the victims of this situation, the effect is violent, even though it was not caused by the deliberate hostile act of a specific individual. The source of the violence may have been the unplanned yet devastatingly real impact of structural power—for instance, through the collapse of local markets due to subsidized foreign imports—and this is what structural violence is all about.

Ironically, while many millions of people in some parts of the world are starving, many millions of others are overeating—quite literally eating themselves to death. In fact, the number of overfed people now exceeds those who are underfed. According to the World Watch Institute in Washington, D.C., more than 1.1 billion people worldwide are now overweight. And 300 million of these are obese (but still often malnourished in that their diets lack certain nutrients).

Seriously concerned about the sharp rise in associated health problems (including stroke, diabetes, cancer, and heart disease), the World Health Organization classifies obesity as a global epidemic. Overeating is particularly unhealthy for individuals living in societies where machines have eased the physical burdens of work and other human activities, which helps explain why more than half of the people in some industrial and post-industrial countries are overweight.

However, the obesity epidemic is not due solely to excessive eating and lack of physical activity. A key ingredient is the high sugar and fat content of mass-marketed foods. The problem is spreading and has become a serious concern even in some developing countries. In fact, the highest rates of obesity in the world now exist among Pacific Islanders living in places such as Samoa and Fiji. On the island of Nauru, up to 65 percent of the men and 70 percent of the women are now classified as obese. (That said, not all people who are overweight or obese are so because they eat too much junk food and do too little exercise. In addition to cultural factors, being overweight or obese can also have genetic or other biological causes.)

As for hunger cases, about 10 percent of them can be traced to specific events—droughts or floods, as well as various social, economic, and political disruptions, including warfare. During the 20th century, 44 million people died due to human-made famine.[21] For example, in several sub-Saharan African countries plagued by chronic civil strife, it has been almost impossible to raise and harvest crops, for hordes of hungry refugees, roaming militias, and underpaid soldiers constantly raid fields. Another problem is that millions of acres in Africa, Asia, and Latin America once devoted to subsistence farming have been given over to the raising of cash crops for export. This has enriched members of elite social classes in these parts of the world, while satisfying the appetites of people in the developed countries for coffee, tea, chocolate, bananas, and beef. Those who used to farm the land for their own food needs have been relocated—either to urban areas, where all too often there is no employment for them, or to areas ecologically unsuited for farming.

In Africa, such lands are often occupied seasonally by pastoral nomads, and turning them over to cultiva-

[20]Hunger Project 2003; Swaminathan, M. S. (2000). Science in response to basic human needs. *Science 287*, 425.

[21]Hunger Project 2003; White, M. (2001). *Historical atlas of the twentieth century*. http://users.erols.com/mwhite28/20century.htm.

tion has reduced pasture available for livestock and led to overgrazing. The increase in cleared land, coupled with overgrazing, has depleted both soil and water, with disastrous consequences to nomad and farmer alike. So it is that more than 250 million people can no longer grow crops on their farms, and 1 billion people in 100 countries are in danger of losing their ability to grow crops.[22]

One strategy urged upon so-called underdeveloped countries, especially by government officials and development advisors from Europe and the United States, has been to adopt practices that have made agriculture in industrialized societies incredibly productive. However, this strategy ignores the crucial fact that these large-scale, commercial farming practices require a financial investment that small farmers and poor countries cannot afford—a substantial outlay of cash for chemical fertilizers, pesticides, and herbicides, not to mention fossil fuels needed to run all the mechanized equipment.

U.S.-style farming has additional problems, including energy inefficiency. For every calorie produced, at least 8—some say as many as 20—calories go into its production and distribution.[23] By contrast, an Asian wet-rice farmer using traditional methods produces 300 calories for each 1 expended. North American agriculture is wasteful of other resources as well: About 30 pounds of fertile topsoil are ruined for every pound of food produced.[24] In the U.S. Midwest, about 50 percent of the topsoil has been lost over the past 100 years. Meanwhile, toxic substances from chemical nutrients and pesticides pile up in unexpected places, poisoning ground and surface waters; killing fish, birds, and other useful forms of life; upsetting natural ecological cycles; and causing major public health problems. Despite its spectacular short-term success, serious questions arise about whether such a profligate food production system can be sustained over the long run, even in North America.

Yet another problem with the idea of copying U.S. farming styles has to do with subsidies. Despite official rhetoric about free markets, governments of the wealthiest capitalist states in North America and western Europe spend between $100 billion and $300 billion annually on agriculture subsidies. In the United States, the world's largest agricultural exporter, 75 percent of these go to the wealthiest 10 percent of the farmers and large agricultural corporations.

Confronted with such economic forces in the global arena, small farmers in poor countries find themselves in

© Tony Freeman/PhotoEdit

Spraying chemicals on crops, as here in California's Central Valley, trades short-term benefits for long-term pollution and health problems.

serious trouble when trying to sell their products on markets open to subsidized agricultural corporations dumping mass-produced and often genetically engineered crops and other farm products. Unable to compete under those structural conditions, many are forced to quit farming, leave their villages, and seek other livelihoods in cities or as migrant workers abroad. Such is the fate of many Maya Indians today. Since the early 1980s, when so many fled Guatemala's violence and poverty, thousands have made their way to places like southeastern Florida and taken low-paying jobs as illegal immigrants. Because of endemic poverty in their homeland where they would face starvation, these victims of structural violence have no choice but to remain where they are, condemned to an uncertain life in exile as cheap laborers without civil rights, Social Security, or health insurance.

Pollution

The effects of big agribusiness practices are part of larger problems of environmental degradation in which pollution is tolerated for the sake of higher profits that benefit select individuals and societies. Industrial activities are producing highly toxic waste at unprecedented rates, and factory emissions are poisoning the air. For example, smokestack gases are clearly implicated in acid rain, which is damaging lakes and forests all over northeastern North America. Air containing water vapor with a high acid content is, of course, harmful to the lungs, but the health hazard is greater than this. As ground and surface water becomes more acidic, the solubility of lead, cadmium, mercury, and aluminum, all of them toxic, rises sharply. For instance, aluminum contamination is high

[22]Godfrey, T. (2000, December 27). Biotech threatening biodiversity. *Burlington Free Press*, 10A.

[23]Bodley, J. H. (1985). *Anthropology and contemporary human problems* (2nd ed., p. 128). Palo Alto, CA: Mayfield.

[24]Chasin, B. H., & Franke, R. W. (1983). US farming: A world model? *Global Reporter 1* (2), 10.

Figure 16.3

Global pollution. Almost all processes of physical geography begin and end with the flows of energy and matter among land, sea, and air. Because of the primacy of the atmosphere in this exchange system, air pollution is potentially one of the most dangerous human modifications in environmental systems. Pollutants such as various oxides of nitrogen or sulfur cause the development of acid precipitation, which damages soil, vegetation, and wildlife. Air pollution in the form of smog is often dangerous for human health. And most atmospheric scientists believe that the efficiency of the atmosphere in retaining heat—the so-called greenhouse effect—is being enhanced by increased carbon dioxide, methane, and other gases produced by industrial and agricultural activities. The result, a period of global warming, threatens to dramatically alter climates in all parts of the world.

SOURCE: From *Student Atlas of Anthropology*, by John Allen and Audrey Shalinksy, p. 132. Copyright © 2003 by the McGraw-Hill/Dushkin Publishing.

enough on 17 percent of the world's farmland to be toxic to plants—and has been linked to senile dementia, Alzheimer's, and Parkinson's diseases, three major health problems in industrial countries.

Finding their way into the world's oceans, toxic substances also create hazards for seafood consumers. For instance, Canadian Inuit face health problems related to eating fish and sea mammals that feed in waters contaminated by industrial chemical waste such as polychlorinated biphenyls (PCBs) (see Biocultural Connection).[25] Obviously, environmental poisoning affects peoples all across the globe (Figure 16.3).

Added to this is the problem of global warming—the greenhouse effect—caused primarily by the burning of fossil fuels (oil, gas, and coal). Although much is unknown about the extent of global warming, scientists now overwhelmingly agree it is real and poses a serious challenge. Experts predict that it will lead to an expansion of the geographic ranges of tropical diseases and increase the incidence of respiratory diseases due to additional smog caused by warmer temperatures. Also, they expect an increase in deaths due to heat waves, as witnessed in the 52,000 deaths attributed to the 2003 heat wave in Europe.[26]

[25]Inuit Tapiirit Kanatami. http://www.tapirisat.ca/english_text/itk/departments/enviro/ncp.

[26]Larsen, J. (2006, July 28). Setting the record straight. Earth Policy Institute, Eco-economy updates.

Biocultural Connection

Toxic Breast Milk Threatens Arctic Culture

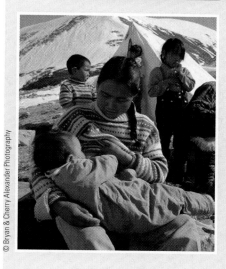

© Bryan & Cherry Alexander Photography

Asked to picture the Inuit people inhabiting the Arctic coasts of Canada, Greenland, and Labrador, you are likely to envision them dressed in fur parkas and moving across a pristine, snow-covered landscape on dogsleds—perhaps coming home from hunting seal, walrus, or whale.

Such imaginings are still true—except for the pristine part. Although Inuit live nearer to the North Pole than to any city, factory, or farm, they are not isolated from the pollutants of modern society. Chemicals originating in the cities and farms of North America, Europe, and Asia travel thousands of miles to Inuit territories via winds, rivers, and ocean currents. These toxins have a long life in the Arctic, breaking down very slowly due to icy temperatures and low sunlight. Ingested by zooplankton, the chemicals spread through the seafood chain as one species consumes another. The result is alarming levels of pesticides, mercury, and industrial chemicals in Arctic animals—and in

the Inuit people who rely on fishing and hunting for food.

Of particular note are toxic chemicals known as PCBs (polychlorinated biphenyls), used widely over several decades for numerous purposes, such as industrial lubricants, insulating materials, and paint stabilizers. Research shows a widespread presence of PCBs in the breast milk of women around the globe. But nowhere on earth is the concentration higher than among the Inuit—on average seven times that of nursing mothers in Canada's biggest cities![a]

PCBs have been linked to a wide range of health problems, from liver damage to weakened immune systems to cancer. Studies of children exposed to PCBs in the womb and through breast milk show impaired learning and memory functions. Beyond having a destructive impact on the health of humans (and other animal species), PCBs are impacting the economy, social organization, and psychological well-being of Arctic peoples. Nowhere is this more true than among the 450 Inuit living on Broughton Island, near Canada's Baffin Island. Here, word of skyrocketing PCB levels cost the community its valuable market for Arctic char fish. Other Inuits refer to them as "PCB people," and it is said that Inuit men now avoid marrying women from the island.[b]

The suggestion that the answer to these problems is a change of diet is soundly rejected by Inuit people, who have no real alternatives for afford-

able food. Abandoning the consumption of traditional seafood would destroy a 4,000-year-old culture based on hunting and fishing. Countless aspects of traditional Inuit culture—from worldview and social arrangements to vocabularies and myths—are linked to Arctic animals and the skills it takes to rely on them for food and so many other things. As one Inuit put it: "Our foods do more than nourish our bodies. They feed our souls. When I eat Inuit foods, I know who I am."[c]

The manufacture of PCBs is now banned in many western countries (including the United States), and PCB levels are gradually declining worldwide. However, because of their persistence (and widespread presence in remnant industrial goods such as fluorescent lighting fixtures and electrical appliances), they are still the highest-concentration toxins in breast milk, even among mothers born after the ban.

And even as PCBs decline, other commercial chemicals are finding their way northward. To date, about 200 hazardous compounds originating in industrialized regions have been detected in the bodies of Arctic peoples.[d] Global warming is fueling the problem, because as glaciers and snow melt, long-stored toxins are released.

---

[a]Colborn, T., et al. (1997). *Our stolen future* (pp. 107–108). New York: Plume (Penguin Books).
[b]AMAP. (2003). *AMAP assessment 2002: Human health in the Arctic* (pp. xii–xiii, 22–23). Oslo: Arctic Monitoring Assessment Project.

[c]Ingmar Egede, quoted in Cone, M. (2005) *Silent snow: The slow poisoning of the Arctic* (p. 1). New York: Grove Press.
[d]Additional sources: Johansen, B. E. (2002). The Inuit's struggle with dioxins and other organic pollutants. *The American Indian Quarterly 26* (3), 479–490; Natural Resources Defense Council. (2005, March 25). Healthy milk, healthy baby: Chemical pollution and mother's milk. www.NRDC.org; Williams, F. (2005, January 9). Toxic breast milk? *New York Times Magazine.*

Structural violence also manifests itself in the shifting of manufacturing and hazardous waste disposal from developed to developing countries. In the late 1980s, a tightening of environmental regulations in industrialized countries led to a dramatic rise in the cost of hazardous waste disposal. Seeking cheaper ways to get rid of the wastes, "toxic traders" began shipping hazard-

ous waste to Eastern Europe and especially to poor and underdeveloped countries in western Africa (see Globalscape). When news of this became public, international outrage led to the drafting and adoption of the Basel Convention to prohibit the export of hazardous wastes and minimize their generation. Today, the scope of the convention is severely limited by the fact that the United

GLOBALSCAPE

Probo Koala's Dirty Secrets One day in 2006, the *Probo Koala* unloaded a cargo of processed fuel in Nigeria, West Africa. Then the tanker sailed to Amsterdam where a Dutch treatment plant was to process its 400 tons of leftover toxic sludge. Navigating the oceans under the Panamanian flag, this ship's all-Russian crew serves under a Greek captain. Managed and operated by a Greek maritime company, the ship's registered owner is based in Norway. For this journey, it was chartered by a Dutch subsidiary of a multinational company headquartered in Switzerland and specialized in transporting oil and mineral products.

In Amsterdam, port authorities discovered that the *Probo Koala*'s captain had underreported the poison levels in his cargo, so the cost of treating the waste jumped to $600,000. Unwilling to pay the higher fee, the captain ordered his ship back to West Africa in search of a cheap place to dispose of the waste. Finding unscrupulous businessmen and corrupt officials in Ivory Coast, he negotiated a dumping fee of about $18,000. The sludge was deposited in open-air waste pits on the edge of Abidjan, home to 5 million Africans. In the weeks that followed, some 40,000 locals were poisoned and fell ill; ten died almost immediately.

The *Probo Koala* forms part of a profitable global business network capitalizing on the more than 350 million tons of hazardous waste generated annually, primarily by industrial societies. Although most of this waste is now properly disposed, some companies avoid environmental regulations and high treatment costs within Europe and North America, seeking cheaper (possibly illegal) alternatives—including dumping at sea. Many millions of tons of hazardous waste are transported across the oceans to distant poor countries. Remarkably, although over 150 states have signed treaties banning *import* of toxic and radioactive wastes (Ivory Coast is not among them), these agreements do not prohibit the *export* of waste.

Global Twister Although hazardous waste dumping by the *Probo Koala* resulted in the arrest of several African businessmen in Ivory Coast, should the other participants in this global crime be judged and punished? If so, under which laws?

States, the largest toxic residue producer in the world, has not ratified the agreement.[27] Moreover, the combination of unscrupulous entrepreneurs and corrupt government officials undermines people's health when it comes to circumventing international treaty obligations by dumping hazardous wastes and poisoning soil, air, and drinking water.

Given a general awareness of the causes and dangers of pollution, why is it that the human species as a whole is not committed to controlling practices that foul its own nest? At least part of the answer lies in philosophical and theological traditions. As we saw in the chapter

[27]Hazardous waste trafficking. www.Choike.org.

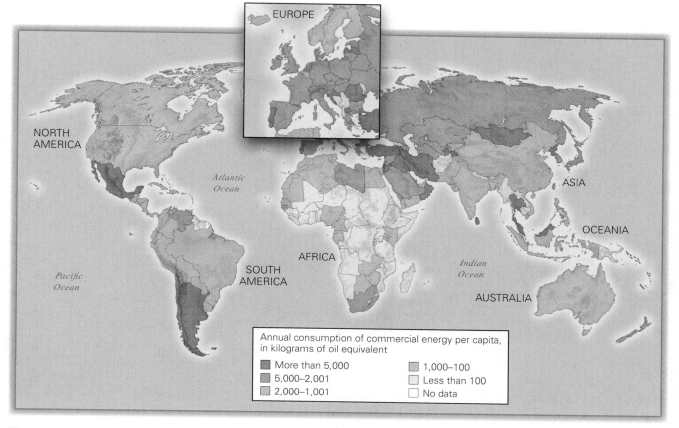

Figure 16.4

Global energy consumption. Most of the world's highest energy consumers are in North America and western Europe where at least 100 gigajoules of commercial energy per year are consumed by each person. (A gigajoule is the equivalent of about 3.5 metric tons of coal.) In some of these countries, such as the United States and Canada, the consumption rates are in the 300 gigajoule range (the equivalent of more than 10 metric tons of coal per person per year). At the other end of the scale are low-income countries, whose consumption rates are often less than 1 percent of those in the United States. (These figures do not include the consumption of noncommercial energy—the traditional fuels of firewood, animal dung, and other organic matter widely used in the less developed parts of the world.)

SOURCE: From *Student Atlas of Anthropology*, by Allen, J. L., & Shalinsky, A. C., p. 126. Copyright © 2004 McGraw-Hill/Dushkin Publishing.

on politics, Western industrialized societies accept the biblical assertion (found in the Koran as well) of human dominion over the earth, interpreting that it is their task to subdue and control the earth and all its inhabitants. These societies are the biggest contributors to global pollution. For example, on average, one North American consumes hundreds of times the resources of a single African, with all that implies with respect to waste disposal and environmental degradation (Figure 16.4). Moreover, each person in North America adds, on average, 20 tons of carbon dioxide (a greenhouse gas) a year to the atmosphere. In "underdeveloped" countries, less than 3 tons per person are emitted.[28] According to botanist Peter Raven, "if everyone lived like Americans, you'd need three planet earths . . . to sustain that level of consumption."[29]

The Culture of Discontent

For the past several decades, the world's poor countries have been sold on the idea they should and actually can enjoy a standard of living comparable to that of the rich countries. Yet, the resources necessary to maintain such a luxurious standard of living are not unlimited. This growing gap between expectations and realizations has led to the creation of a culture of discontent.

The problem involves not just population growth outstripping available natural resources, but also un-

[28]Broecker, W. S. (1992, April). Global warming on trial. *Natural History*, 14.

[29]Quoted in Becker, J. (2004, March). *National Geographic*, 90.

© Harald E. L. Prins

These Nambikwara children in southern Brazil are among the world's 300 million indigenous people to whom we have dedicated this book. With globalization now reaching even the most remote corners of the world, these Amazonian Indians are severely threatened, as are thousands of other small indigenous nations and ethnic minority groups that until now have survived the onslaught of colonialism, capitalist expansionism, and other forms of outside aggression. During the past five centuries, just a fraction of human existence, millions of indigenous peoples have perished due to foreign diseases, habitat destruction, warfare, and even genocide. Some 4,000 languages have disappeared due to acculturation, assimilation, or the physical extinction of their speakers. Yet, 6,000 languages remain, along with a still vast array of distinct peoples with unique cultures. Anthropologists study these different peoples for the sake of documenting their unique traditional cultures but also hope that information about their ways of life will lead to greater cross-cultural understanding, fostering tolerance and fundamental respect for human rights everywhere. Anthropologists have played and continue to play a valuable role in the long-term survival of indigenous groups—founding or helping to found organizations such as Cultural Survival, the Working Group on Indigenous Peoples, and Survival International.

equal access to decent jobs, housing, sanitation, health care, leisure, and adequate police and fire protection. It is one in which personal disappointments are echoed in a natural environment degraded by overcrowding, pollution, and soil erosion.

This culture of discontent is not limited to people living in poor and overpopulated countries. Because capitalism thrives on growing demands, powerful advertising strategies target people with financial means to purchase more and more luxury goods and services. In the process, even those whose needs are more than met will be made to feel the pinch of discontent and spend their money in pursuit of material dreams.

Some dramatic changes in cultural values and motivations, as well as in social institutions and the types of technologies we employ, are required if humans are going to realize a sustainable future for generations to come. The short-sighted emphasis on consumerism and individual self-interest so characteristic of the world's affluent countries needs to be abandoned in favor of a more balanced social and environmental ethic. This can be created from values still found in many of the world's non-Western cultures. Such values include a worldview that sees humanity as part of the natural world rather than superior to it. Included, too, is a sense of social responsibility that recognizes that no individual, people, or state has the right to expropriate resources at the expense of others. Finally, an awareness is needed of how important supportive ties are for individuals, such as seen in kinship or other associations in the world's traditional societies. Is humanity up to the challenge? And will anthropology play a role in meeting that challenge?

CONCLUDING REMARKS

As defined in this book's first chapter, anthropology is the comparative study of humankind everywhere and throughout time. It seeks to produce reliable knowledge about different peoples and cultures, their ideas and behaviors. Since the beginning of the discipline in the mid-1800s, generations of anthropologists have studied our species in all its cultural and biological varieties. In the process, they described in great detail an enormous number and range of different cultures and biological variations. They also collected a staggering volume of ethnographic artifacts and documented the sounds and sights of hundreds of different cultures with recording equipment and with still and motion cameras.

Today, many of the cultures studied by the earliest anthropologists more than a century ago have changed profoundly in response to powerful outside influences and internal dynamics. Others have disappeared as a result of deadly epidemics, violent conflicts, acculturation, ethnocide, or even genocide. All too often, the only detailed records we now possess of these altered and vanished cultures are those that some visiting anthropologist was able to document before it was too late.

But, anthropologists do much more than try to preserve precious information about distinctive peoples and cultures. As chronicled in the pages of this book, they also try to explain why cultures are similar or different, why and how they did or did not change. Moreover, they try to identify the particular knowledge and insights that each culture holds concerning the human condition—including contrasting views about humankind's place in the world, how natural resources are used and treated, and how one relates to fellow humans and other species.

Less apt than other scholarly specialists to see facts and activities as separate and unrelated, anthropologists are trained to understand and explain economic, social, political, ideological, and biological features and processes as parts of dynamic systems by means of theoretical concepts such as structural power and structural violence. Their cross-cultural and comparative historical perspective on local communities in the age of globalization enables them to make key contributions to our understanding of such troubling problems as overpopulation, food shortages, environmental destruction, and widespread strife and discontent in the world. This is evident, for instance, in hiring choices at the World Bank in the wake of a series of ill-conceived and mismanaged development projects that harmed more than helped local populations. Recognizing the value of anthropological knowledge and methods, the bank now employs and contracts dozens of professional anthropologists for projects all across the world. The same is true for other international organizations, as well as some global corporations and state government agencies.

Some anthropologists go beyond just studying different cultures and reach out to assist besieged groups that are struggling to survive in today's rapidly changing world. In so doing, they seek to put into practice their own knowledge about humankind—knowledge deepened through the comparative perspective of anthropology, which is cross-culturally, historically, and biologically informed.

The idea that anthropological research is fascinating in itself and also has the potential of helping solve practical problems on local and global levels has drawn and continues to draw a unique group of people into the discipline. Most of these individuals are inspired by the old but still valid idea that anthropology must aim to live up to its ideal as the most liberating of the sciences. As stated by noted anthropologist Margaret Mead, "Never doubt that a small group of committed people can change the world; indeed it is the only thing that ever has."

Questions for Reflection

1. No matter how divided peoples of the world are on economic, political, and ideological issues, all face the collective challenge of maintaining the long-term integrity of the planet we depend upon for survival. Do you think individuals like yourself can impact the current course toward environmental destruction that threatens all species, including our own? What steps do you think need to be taken individually and collectively to deal with this issue?

2. Most of the world's major global corporations are U.S. based, including Wal-Mart, which generates over $300 billion in an-

nual revenues. Measured in economic terms, this business is bigger than Turkey, inhabited by nearly 75 million people. In what ways might such a megacorporation use its enormous economic power? Could it influence the U.S. government in terms of world trade policies? If so, would the company benefit more from free trade or protectionism?

3. Considering the relationship between structural power and structural violence, does your own lifestyle in terms of buying clothes and food, driving cars, and so on reflect or have an effect on the globalization process?

4. In the global mediascape, television viewers and Internet users are not only consumers of news and entertainment but

are also exposed to soft power. Can you think of an example of soft power in your daily life? And at which point does such influence turn into propaganda or manipulation?

5. The World Health Organization, UNESCO, Oxfam, and Amnesty International are global institutions concerned with structural violence and human rights violations. Confronted with genocidal conflicts, famines, epidemics, and torture of political prisoners, people active in these organizations try to improve the human condition. Why do you think that an anthropological perspective on such worldwide problems might be of practical use? Can you think of an example?

Suggested Readings

Appadurai, A. (1996). *Modernity at large: Cultural dimensions of globalization*. Minneapolis: University of Minnesota Press.

In this fundamental contribution to how globalization works, a leading anthropologist discusses how forces such as migration and electronic mediation acquire shaping roles in the production of contemporary culture.

Bodley, J. H. (2000). *Anthropology and contemporary human problems* (4th ed.). Palo Alto, CA: Mayfield.

Anthropologist Bodley examines some of the most serious problems in the world today: overconsumption, resource depletion, hunger and starvation, overpopulation, violence and war.

Friedman, J. (Ed.). (2003). *Globalization, the state, and violence*. Walnut Creek, CA: Altamira Press.

A vibrant, insightful analysis of globalization and the "lethal explosiveness" that characterizes the current world order. Friedman leads a group of distinguished contributors in examining the global processes and political forces that determine transnational networks of crime, commerce, and terror, leading to economic, social, and cultural fragmentation.

Ginsburg, F. D., Abu-Lughod, L., & Larkin, B. (Eds.). (2002). *Media worlds: Anthropology on new terrain*. Berkeley: University of California Press.

Groundbreaking essays by pioneers of media studies in anthropology, discussing the place and function of film, video, radio, television, and cinema in different cultures and showing that contemporary peoples and cultures cannot be understood without the mediascapes they inhabit.

Lewellen, T. C. (2002). *The anthropology of globalization: Cultural anthropology enters the 21st century*. Westport, CT: Greenwood Publishing Group/Bergin & Garvey.

Readable introduction, summary, and critique of globalization with telling and timely ethnographic examples.

Ong, A. (1999). *Flexible citizenship: The cultural logics of transnationality*. Durham, NC: Duke University Press.

Ong demonstrates how the Chinese transnational community confounds notions of peripheral non-Westerners and argues that the contemporary world is creating the context for the rise of China.

Trouillot, M. R. (2003). *Global transformations: Anthropology and the modern world*. New York: Palgrave Macmillan.

Examining anthropology's history and discussing future possibilities for the discipline, the author challenges colleagues to question dominant narratives of globalization and to radically rethink key concepts of the discipline.

Thomson Audio Study Products

Enjoy the MP3-ready Audio Lecture Overviews for each chapter and a comprehensive audio glossary of key terms for quick study and review. Whether walking to class, doing laundry, or studying at your desk, you now have the freedom to choose when, where, and how you interact with your audio-based educational media. See the preface for information on how to access this on-the-go study and review tool.

The Anthropology Resource Center

www.thomsonedu.com/anthropology
The Anthropology Resource Center provides extended learning materials to reinforce your understanding of key concepts in the four fields of anthropology. For each of the four fields, the Resource Center includes dynamic exercises including video exercises, map exercises, simulations, and "Meet the Scientists" interviews, as well as critical thinking questions that can be assigned and e-mailed to instructors. The Resource Center also provides breaking news in anthropology and interesting material on applied anthropology to help you link what you are learning to the world around you.

The Student's Practical Guide:

Writing Term Papers for Anthropology

(and Related Subjects)

By

Steven M. Parish
Boston University

Department of Anthropology
Boston University
232 Bay State Road
Boston, MA 02215

Introduction

Imagine that it is now six weeks into the semester. You are taking a heavy course load: genetics, organic chemistry, math, and this anthropology class for which you are supposed to write a fifteen page term paper.

You have not even started the paper—somehow you have not managed to find the time for it. Other things always seemed more important or more fun. But you can't put it off any longer. You have to start right now. You have to get it done as quickly and efficiently as possible—and obviously you don't want to suffer any more than is necessary. Also, you don't want to take any chances with your GPA, so you want to write a good paper. But the whole project seems confusing, dreary, and a little overwhelming.

It doesn't have to be that bad. That is what this Guide is all about — making the writing of anthropology term papers easier.

There are ways to save time and effort. There are procedures and strategies that enable you to negotiate the necessary—but often tedious— process of finding the material you need in the library quickly and effectively. After finding the material you need, it is important to know the best way of organizing it in your paper. Learning these techniques and skills frees you to concentrate on the quality of the paper—or maybe on the beach.

This Guide is no substitute for your own effort and commitment. (Obviously we are not about to recommend that you wait six weeks to begin your paper.) Certainly there is no way to guarantee success or scholarly ecstasy; writing a term paper may never be as much fun as mountain climbing, or reading Russian novels, or whatever your idea of fun is. And there is no final or definitive answer to the question of what a professor wants in a paper. But this Guide will inform you of some of the basic features of an anthropology paper which you can be sure your professor will want you to know. And it shows you how to make your paper a more polished and expert product.

What is an anthropology term paper? It is a library research paper, written from an anthropological perspective, on a topic approved by your instructor. The anthropology paper has a distinctive citation format, also

1

used by several other social sciences, and requires that you use the anthropological "literature" in Mugar Library.[*]

You may already have taken a writing course. The skills learned there will be useful in writing papers for anthropology. The ability to organize ideas effectively and express them clearly is an important survival skill in the university environment. Mastering this skill early in your academic career can greatly increase your enjoyment of university life.[**] However, you probably did not learn the citation and bibliographic format used by anthropologists. One of the goals of the Guide is to introduce you to that format. A word of warning: you should set aside any ideas you have about using footnotes for documentation. (Documentation refers to methods of acknowledging the use of someone else's work.) You may also find that the writing style required for research papers is not the same as the style you learned in your writing classes. The style for research papers emphasizes the unambiguous, easily understood presentation of information and ideas, rather than the expressive use of evocative, complex, and richly ambiguous imagery and symbolism. In other words, research papers require an expository, not a literary, style.

---

[*] Literature as used here refers to the body of published material on some subject or topic—not to Russian novels. For example, there is a "literature" on medical anthropology, on African-American religions, on the kinship systems of Australian Aborigines, on witchcraft and magic and so forth.

[**] Writing skills are also useful in the world at large, of course. One of the practical aspects of anthropology courses is their frequent emphasis on writing. You will find the writing and research skills as taught in anthropology useful in the REAL WORLD—more useful than an ability to ace multiple choice exams. And research and writing are not really so hard, once you've had enough practice.

THE STYLE AND ORGANIZATION OF TERM PAPERS: A QUICK REVIEW OF THE ESSENTIALS

A term paper is not a "report" of the kind often assigned in high schools, which meekly repeats information found in one or two sources. Nor is a library research paper similar to a lab report, or a report on the results of an experiment. It is never merely the presentation of a set of data.[*] Writing a term paper requires a good deal more intellectual involvement and commitment than writing a report does.

Then what is a term paper? Like a report, a library research paper presents data and ideas (which are, however, typically drawn from several sources). Unlike a report, a research paper presents your *analysis* and *interpretation* of the data and ideas found in a survey of the anthropological literature relevant to the topic of your paper. *Analysis* is the process of organizing and summarizing the data and ideas in order to answer a question. *Interpretation* refers to a discussion of the meaning and implications of your answers for the issues, ideas, and problems that your paper addresses.

---

[*] Data are pieces of information that can be used in analysis. Technically, "data" is the plural of "datum," that is, of one piece of information. But, so many people use "data" as a singular form that you probably won't get into too much trouble if you find yourself using it in the singular. Other common singular /plural confusions: criteria (pl.)/criterion (sing.); phenomena (pl.) phenomenon (sing.)—if you mix these up someone may accuse you of illiteracy. So when in doubt, consult a dictionary or a writing handbook on word usage and words commonly misused.

Eight Magical and Wise Rules for Writing Term Papers

The style and organization of your paper have a single purpose: to help the reader understand what you have to say. So try to be as clear as possible. What you need to do in order to write clearly and coherently is to follow the eight magical rules listed here, and use them along with these books:

Kolb, Harold H.
> 1980   A Writer's Guide: The Essential Points. New York: Harcourt Brace Jovanovich.

Strunk, William, and E.B. White
> 1979   The Elements of Style. 3rd ed. New York: Macmillan.

Turabian, Kate
> 1976   Student's Guide for Writing College Papers. 3rd ed. Chicago: University of Chicago Press.

You should be able to find them all at the University Bookstore.

Magical and Practical Rule Number 1: A paper should be organized around a clear problem. The problem is formulated in the course of exploratory reading in the anthropological literature.

First, you should choose an appropriate topic and check it for feasibility by doing some preliminary research in the library and by consulting with your TA or professor. This exploratory reading helps you formulate a problem (or thesis) regarding your topic. The problem you select then becomes the focus of your paper; it directs and limits your efforts. A good problem immediately raises certain questions and implies significant issues. You use your library know-how to find the data that answer these questions and to find the ideas of the scholars who have discussed these issues.

You should use only the data needed to answer your questions. Otherwise your paper will lack coherence and unity, and you will have done more work than you needed to. And, worst of all, you may not get your paper in on time. The professor may then never get a chance to read it, because he has flown off to some delectable Pacific island, and you may be stuck with an Incomplete.

So subordinate your reading and note taking to a clear, well defined problem (or controlling idea), formulated in your exploratory reading.

Magical and Logical Rule Number 2: **After you have selected a problem and become acquainted with some of the literature on it, make a well thought out and fairly detailed *outline*.**

As you reading progresses, ask yourself what ideas and information are necessary for understanding your problem, and in what order they have to be presented, in order to have a logical and coherent presentation. Start out with a crude outline. Then revise and elaborate it as needed.

A good outline is indispensable; it helps you figure out what information you need as you carry out your research and in what order that information should be presented. A few superstars can juggle complex ideas and quantities of data in their heads, but for ordinary mortals the use of an outline makes sense. (It is wise to figure that you, like Socrates, are an ordinary mortal.)

Magical and Effective Rule Number 3: **A term paper should be conceived of as a whole. It should have thematic unity and an integrated structure.**

If you stick to your problem and your outline, you should have no trouble writing a unified paper; unity just means sticking to the central idea of your paper and your plan for discussing it.

Structure refers to the organization of the parts of your paper. A paper consists of three main parts: an opening or introduction, the body, and a conclusion. But these parts must be tied together, and subordinated to the main purpose of the paper, which is to tell someone about your analysis and interpretation of the problem you have formulated and researched. You want to make the paper as easy to understand as possible.

So first you tell them what you're going to say...

The introduction clarifies the nature of your topic; it states your research problem and your strategy for understanding this problem. Your opening ideally puts the reader in the mood for reading the paper; it serves to spark some interest. But mainly it prepares the reader intellectually for your main effort—the body of the paper. The best introductions are often written after the body of the paper is already drafted, so that they can lead to it as effectively as possible. Remember: one way to bomb on a paper is to promise one thing and deliver something else.

   ...and then you say it...

The body of the paper carries out your strategy or plan for analyzing and interpreting your material. This part of the paper goes into details: it lays out all the necessary information and ideas in a logical order (that is, in the sequence in which the reader needs to know them in order to understand you). The body is organized in terms of answers to questions, cause and effect, comparison and contrast; it supports generalizations with data, or derives generalizations from data.

   ...and then you tell them what you've said.

The conclusion wraps things up. It reminds the reader of the nature and significance of the problem you set out at the beginning, and sums up the meaning and implications of your analysis. It tells the reader what has actually been discovered and what it means. The conclusion concisely restates your intentions and plans, and tells the reader succinctly what happened when you carried out that plan. In other words, it summarizes and synthesizes the progression of your understanding from the opening statement of your problem through the detailed development of the problem in the body of the paper.

Magical and Essential Rule Number 4: Write with your readers in mind. Be clear and explicit so that they can follow your argument. Be concise and yet complete.

You are writing something that will be read and evaluated by someone. Keep in mind that all your readers can know of your thoughts is what you put down on paper. Telepathy is rare even among anthropologists. So be explicit. Don't refer or allude to ideas or information not contained in your argument, unless you can reasonable expect the readers to be familiar with that material. Make sure that the readers have all the information they need in order to follow you from point A to point B in your discussion. If your roommate doesn't understand how you argued your way from point A to point B, your TA or professor probably won't either.

And choose your words with care. You don't want to obscure your reasoning by putting it into the wrong words. A brilliant logical argument can be lost for want of precise words.*

Your outline will help you make the logical connections in your paper explicit. You may even want to use some subtitles in your paper (one or two per page) which serve up the points made on that page. These subtitles will correspond to your outline—or at least they will if you stick to it. Using subtitles can alert you when you start to stray from your plan. Subtitles also have the advantage of reminding the weary reader (who has just read 137 term papers before starting yours and has 79 yet to go) where he has got to in your argument. (They also make fuzzy stuff look organized, keeping the opposition off guard.) However, if you allude extensively to material not included in your paper, or ideas not explained in your paper, or do not choose your words with some care, then even subtitles won't save you.

You want to be clear, explicit and complete, but you don't want to bore your reader (or not *very* much anyway—not more than is necessary). So don't belabor the obvious. Put things in your paper because they're important in terms of your argument, not because you feel you should explain everything—twice. Be as concise as you can, while still being clear, explicit and complete.

So, it is important to be clear and complete, but on the other hand, it is important not to be boring or obvious. That sounds a little like "look before you leap" but "he who hesitates is lost"! And yet these points are not as contradictory as they may seem. It's a question of balance, which, in writing term papers, as in learning to ride a bicycle (and practically everything else), is only learned through practice—by doing it until you don't fall down. Too much explanation and qualification of your argument can distract the reader from the essential points you are trying to make. Too little explanation and elaboration makes a paper vague; the reader doesn't have enough information to judge the essential points of

---

* That may sound trite, but it is significant, and worth working on. A professor once remarked that he found some kind of wrongheadedness in the first sentence of almost every paper. If that's true (and who am I to argue with a professor?) then there is probably an awful lot of poor word choice going on. If *you* are careful to pick the best words for the ideas you want to express, you will probably be one of the few who do—that doesn't guarantee an A, but it comes closer to guaranteeing it than any other single writing habit I can think of.

your argument, or see how they are connected—or even, sometimes, see what they are.

When in doubt, it is better to bore than to be vague. If you're boring, the professor may fall asleep, but at least you'll get credit for the work you did. If you are vague, on the other hand, you leave the reader with no way of knowing what you meant. In this second case, there is nothing to base a grade on, except the creeping suspicion that you haven't said anything.

Vagueness is generally pretty boring anyway. It is better to work on being both clear and interesting; with practice and commitment, it is possible to be both.

Magical and Reasonable Rule Number 5: The paper should reflect the theme of the course.

You should be sensitive to the point of view the professor is trying to present and to the scope of the course. A good paper should reflect the theme of the course in some way, even if you do not agree with the professor's approach.* Consult your TA or professor before you invest a lot of time and energy investigating a topic that might not be appropriate.

For example, when you are writing for a class that focuses on some aspect of cultural symbolism, and you find yourself discussing astrology, King Tut, and holistic hang gliding, then you're stretching the boundaries of the course. You will probably find that you are stretching the boundaries of your GPA too.

More realistically, if your professor has been talking for weeks about political conflict, then a paper in which you marvel at the harmony and smooth integration of culture—and by implication deny the reality or significance of conflict—will probably raise some eyebrows, but not your grade. But a paper about the problems of political leadership in Arab villages in territory occupied by Israel, or about lineage feuding in classical China, would more appropriately reflect the theme of the course.

---

* If you are not belligerent and unreasonable, most professors have no objections to a little disagreement. (A lot of them are flattered anybody was paying attention!) You probably have a reason for disagreeing, after all, and if it is a good reason it might work into the basis of a good term paper.

Magical and Indispensable Rule Number 6: Revise, Rewrite and Proofread.

You should always plan on doing some revision and rewriting. But how much? And how do you know when it is necessary? Here again, if a friend (or enemy) has trouble understanding your paper or any part of it, you need to do something about it.

You need to rewrite the foggy and fuzzy sections. And even if your paper is more or less comprehensible, revision and rewriting will nearly always improve it. Basically, a sense of when and what to revise, what to throw out, and what to rewrite is developed through the practice of writing and through receiving feedback on your papers.

With your research problem, outline and the limitations of readers firmly in mind, go through your outline with a certain ruthlessness. Cut out any jumbles of excess or imprecise words. Don't be afraid to throw away sentences and whole passages which don't do the job of communicating your ideas. Clean up the grammar. Rewrite as necessary.

Now you can type or print your final draft. And then you should proofread it. You don't want to leave any little but distracting errors or typos uncorrected. (A typo can change the comment "Kroeber's theory is not considered adequate" into "Kroeber's theory is now considered adequate." But any type can eb distracting.*) Most word processing programs will check the spelling, and even simple grammar, automatically if you ask, so use these features. However, always read the paper yourself before you print the final copy—the Kroeber typo cited above is neither misspelled nor grammatically incorrect, but it is a mistake that will be noted.

Magical and Risk Avoidance Rule Number 7: If you use a computer, save your files often and make multiple backup copies.

Nothing is so debilitating as following the first six rules and then losing the whole work to a cyber-space demon. Saying you lost your work to the computer, or that it will not print out, now runs well ahead of dogs eating homework in the excuse category. It may be true, but it is very difficult to prove and, if the TA or professor is on a tight schedule to turn in final grades, you may not get the benefit of the doubt. Save your files regularly, especially after making extensive revisions, and when

---

* That's an on purpose typo.

you are finished be sure to copy your files onto a separate disk that can be stored in a drawer and moved to another machine if disaster strikes.

Magical and Unwritten Rule Number 8: Make a rule to fit in this space.

This is a freebie. Experience is the best teacher, so develop your own.

Sound like a lot of work? You're right. But in grade points per hour the magical rules are the best term paper bargain going.

THE CITATION FORMAT OF ANTHROPOLOGY PAPERS

The eight magical rules of term paper writing apply to all research papers. But anthropology term papers are different from papers you may have written for other courses, or for a writing class. Anthropology, like sociology and psychology, uses a distinctive citation format.

I think this format is easier to use than other formats. Once you are familiar with it, I think you'll agree.

Anthropologists document the use of other people's work—the sources of ideas or data used in a paper—by placing citations in the text of the paper. *Documentation,* for our purposes, means providing bibliographic references to sources. A *citation* is a bibliographic reference to a specific source—a book, an article, or other source of information. *In-text citation* simply means placing citations in the text of the paper, instead of in footnotes. In-text citation documents the use of sources of data and ideas, just as reference (bibliographic) footnotes do, but in-text citations are used instead of such footnotes in anthropology. You do not use reference footnotes or endnotes when you write a paper using the in-text citation format.

You were probably taught to use reference footnotes to document your use of sources, and the world is full of people who say "footnote" when they mean "citation." Hang in there; things will become clearer as we go along. For now, do the best you can to forget about using footnotes as a method of documentation.[*]

The important thing to understand, then, is that *in-text citation replaces reference footnotes.* Here's what in-text citation looks like:

```
The evidence for this hypothesis is suspect (Burns

1969:32).

Tonkinson (1978:27) notes that the Aborigines of

the Western Desert...
```

As you can see, the in-text citation supplies, in parentheses, the name of the author, the year of publication, and the page(s) on which the ma-

---

[*] You can still use *content* footnotes, if you like. Content footnotes discuss ideas, issues, or details that are pertinent (or, occasionally, important) but not a necessary or direct part of the exposition or argument of the paper. This type of footnote is for discussion and elaboration. Unlike reference footnotes, content footnotes do not (usually) provide bibliographic information.

terial cited can be found. Note the punctuation: this is exactly how it should appear in all your anthropology papers. Also note that when the name of the author is used as part of the text, as in the second example, only the year of publication and page numbers are placed within the parentheses.

Now, if I'm your inscrutable TA and I'm interested in finding out more about something I read in your paper (because it is just so bizarre or wonderful that I have to know more about it), then I turn from your citation to your reference list at the end of your paper. This list of all the works cited in your paper provides information needed to locate sources in the bookstore or library. The citations and the reference list make it possible for the reader to track down material that may be useful. As your TA, I can find interesting stuff simply by tracing your citation back to your source. In that source are more citations, leading me back to your source's sources (squared as it were). These in turn have citations and reference lists leading to their sources (sources cubed?). Your paper becomes a link in a *citation chain* when you cite from publications connected in this way. (TAs have funny ideas about how to spend their time.)

The citation format used in anthropology is less work than the footnote format because you only have to type out the complete bibliographic information for a source once—in the reference list. (Complete bibliographic information includes titles, publisher, place of publication, and so on. We'll get to that.) In a paper using reference footnotes, you have to type that information *twice*—once in the footnote itself, and then again in the reference list. This seems like extra work to me. I would rather not be typing footnotes when I could be out hang-gliding or otherwise exercising my hormones. I think in-text citations are quicker and easier than reference footnotes, and they do exactly the same thing in terms of documenting the use of a source and providing access to that source.

Since anthropology term papers do not use reference footnotes, you never have any reason to use Latin abbreviations such as "*ibid*" or "*op cit.*" In the footnote format, you use these expressions when you refer more than once to a single source. But when you use in-text citation, you give the same information every time that you refer to a source: the author's last name, year of publication of the work cited, and the page(s) on which the idea or data you use appears.

What if you refer to two different books or articles by the same author? How do you let the reader know that two different publications are being cited? You simply use the year of publication to distinguish them. They will be listed chronologically under the author's name in the reference list. What if they were published the same year? Then you can add lower case letters after the publication date.

(Stone 1979a)   (Stone 1979b)

What happens if two authors have the same last names? In that case, you use the initials of their first names, or their full names if they have the same first names, so that it is clear in your text which author you mean. So, if you cite both Karl Marx and Groucho Marx, you would use the initials of the first names in the citations, even though the years of publication are different.

(K. Marx 1853:334)   (G. Marx 1949:24)

If two sources have the same first and last names, then you may have to use middle initials, if available. The general rule is always to try to give enough information so that the reader will know exactly what individual or publication in the reference list you are referring to.

If there are two authors for a publication you wish to cite, you cite them this way:

(Stone & Burns 1956)

If there are more than two authors, then you can probably get away with using the name of the senior author—the one whose name appears first in an article, or under whose name a book is cataloged—followed by "*et al*" which means "and others."

Smith, Burns, Garcia, and Sullivan 1980:87 can be cited as (Smith *et al* 1980:87).

Smith is the senior author; do not use the alphabetical order of authors' names in deciding what names to use in a citation. (Note: *American Anthropologist*, a major journal, now prohibits the use of *et al* in the text, because it is undemocratic. I recommend the use of *et al* —not because I'm undemocratic, but because it seems to me that a citation with three or more names interferes with the ease of reading the text, and I do not believe many instructors would object to this use of *et al* in term papers. In your reference list, you must use the names of all the authors. Unless *you* are undemocratic.)

An Exception to the Ban on Footnote: Multiple Citations

There is an exception to the rule against using reference footnotes for citing your sources. If you have many citations for one sentence (in other words, many sources for one piece of information), then you may use a footnote to avoid cluttering the text and disrupting the reader's attention to your reasoning.

```
Beagles are fond of bagels (Collins 1967:67; Crenshaw
1934:98; Morton 1978:81-89 & 1979:97).  This means
that...
```

becomes

```
Beagles are fond of bagels.¹  This means that...
(rest of page)
```
_____
```
1. see Collins 1967:67; Crenshaw 1934:98; Morton
1978:81-89 & 1979:97.
```

Using the reference footnote makes this easier to read without losing the sense of the text. The idea is to avoid doing anything to distract the reader's attention from what you have to say.

Unless an idea is very complex or profound —like Beagle bagel-philia— or the data very technical or surprising, you rarely need to use many citations for one particular chunk of information. A single citation will generally do. Sometimes you may wish to use several citations in order to direct the reader to a particular literature or to important examples of something. A footnote is appropriate in such cases. For example, for the statement "Beagles are fond of bagels," you might use this footnote:

_____
```
1. The best references on Beagles and bagels are
Collins 1967, Crenshaw 1934, and Morton 1978 & 1979.
```

Footnotes should go at the bottom (foot) of the page. Some publishers put them at the end of the book. They claim this saves typesetting money (although with computerized typesetting that is no longer true). The real reason is that they hate readers. In any event, term paper footnotes should go at the bottom of the page. It not only keeps the professor from cursing your future posterity as he fumbles his way to the back in search of a note, it also improves the chances that he will actually pay attention to them. (Nothing is more infuriating, by the way, than to make one's way to the back of the book in search of footnote 73 from chapter fourteen only to find that it says *"op cit."* in reference to something last discussed six chapters earlier.)

Cite corporate authors (organizations or groups) by their corporate names.

```
(National Anthropological Institute 1989)
```

A very long corporate name may be abbreviated. The National Institute of Mental Health can be cited in the text as NIMH. However, the full corporate name must be used in the reference list. And you must be sure that you always provide enough information that a reader can find the source in the reference list without problems. If an individual can be identified as the author, the person rather than the organization should be cited.

Occasionally, you will run across a work that has neither a personal nor corporate author. In that case you can use a few identifying words from the title of the source, which are placed in the author position in the entry in the reference list.

```
There are as yet few employment opportunities
in the field of Martian anthropology ("Martian
Anthropology" 1986:569).
```

This citation corresponds to the following reference list entry:

```
Martian Anthropology: An Overview of a Non-field.
    1986    Encyclopedia of the Inner Planets.
    Abridged.   Space City L-5:L-5 Publishing Matrix.
```

What Needs To Be Cited?

You **must** document, by giving a citation, each and every case where you use someone else's ideas or information, except where it is reasonable to assume that the information or ideas are "common knowledge" in the field in which you are writing.

Quotations

Other people's exact words must be placed within quotation marks, or set off from the text by indentation and single spacing. A citation must be placed near the beginning or at the end of the quotation, so that it is clear who is being quoted. You could acknowledge a quotation from Clifford Geertz as follows:

```
"Culture is the fabric of meaning in terms of which
human beings interpret their experience and guide
their action; social structure is the form that ac-
tion takes, the actually existing network of social
relations" (Geertz 1957:533).
```

Here's another way to cite this quotation:

```
In an article critical of functional analysis,
Geertz (1957:533) distinguishes between culture and
social structure:
      Culture is the fabric of meanings in terms of
      which human beings interpret their experience
      and guide their action; social structure is
      the form that action takes, the actually ex-
      isting network of social relations.
```

Note that no citation is needed at the end of the quote. Finally you might choose to incorporate Geertz's works into your text in the following manner:

```
According to Geertz, culture is the "fabric of mean-
ing" by which people "interpret their experience and
guide their action" (1957:533).
```

Note: when you put somebody's words inside quotation marks, be sure to quote exactly—spelling, grammatical errors—everything must be just as it is in the original.

Paraphrase or Summary

Even when you put other people's ideas or information into your own words, you must cite the source of the idea and date.

For example, suppose that for a paper on socialization or cultural transmission I want to use T.R. Williams' idea that children take an active part in their own socialization into society. Williams (1972:224) calls this the "generative function of socialization." He defines this as,

comprising all of the ways children reflect upon, think about, and sort out the content of culture, in order to develop for themselves a cognitive map of adult culture.

16

I don't want to quote him, though, because I know using too many quotations is a cheap trick. It's *my* paper, after all, so I *paraphrase* him as follows:

```
Williams (1972:224) notes that children are active

agents in their own socialization.  They do not

merely absorb the norms and values of adult behavior

in a passive manner.  Rather, they think about their

experience of cultural behavior, and develop their

own theories about their position and roles in the

system of social interactions that surround them.
```

Data and Specialized Knowledge

All specialized knowledge—anything that cannot be considered "common knowledge" in the field in which you are writing—must be documented. Data from a source must be cited.

```
Naraun society is divided into three "status

classes."  The highest rank (temonibe) consists of

descendants from the eldest daughter of the woman

who founded the clan (Alkire 1972:44).
```

Data from an ethnography on a group is often specialized knowledge—anthropologists are "specialists" on the people they study.

Common Knowledge

How do you know if something is common knowledge?

There are fuzzy areas, of course. Generally, though, you can rely on common sense. You don't have to document the fact that the Plains Indians hunted buffalo on horseback in the nineteenth century. But if you describe the life of the Sioux before they got horses or moved onto the Great Plains, or describe a fight the Pawnee had with the Sioux while on a buffalo hunt in 1858, then you need to provide a citation referring the reader to the source of your information.

Common knowledge means common in the field in which you are writing. (That anthropologists are mostly geniuses is common knowledge—among anthropologists. Others may disagree—but they don't know the field.) Most anthropologists know what clans, lineages, cross cousin marriage, and classificatory kinship are, but only specialists can be expected to know the difference between Aluridja and Kariera type kinship systems, and so if you write a paper on how a particular group of Australian Aborigines combine features of both, a reference citation is called for, such as:

(Elkin 1954:49-79)

A pretty good rule of thumb is that if you knew it before you started your research, you probably don't need to provide a citation, unless you read about it recently. But if you learned it in the course of your research you'd better cite it. When in doubt, go ahead and cite.[*]

How Do You Use Citations?

How are citations related to sentences and passages in the text?

A citation must identify quotations. This can be done in several ways. Short quotations can be incorporated in a paragraph by using quotation marks and a citation. If you have more than a couple of lines, you can show that you are quoting by indenting and using single spacing. Here is an example of a longer quotation in a sample text:

Language requires and reinforces "shared understandings." There has to be some level of agreement concerning the meanings and use of words and sentences
in order for communication to be possible. So it is
reasonable to assume that language, in some sense,
standardizes the understandings of individuals.

However, language also differentiates individuals. In spite of the fact that language
acts as a socializing and uniformizing force,
it is at the same time the most potent single
factor for the growth of individuality (Sapir
1933:27).

---

[*] However, if you suspect that your audience will not be familiar with an idea or some body of information, then even if you have thought or known it for years, it is advisable to use a citation.

18

But you could quote Sapir in your text, if you wanted to. For example, you could do something like this:

```
Language requires and reinforces "shared understand-
ings." There has to be some level of agreement con-
cerning the meanings and use of words and sentences
in order for communication to be possible. So it is
reasonable to assume that language in some sense
standardizes the understandings of individuals.
However, Sapir, for one, notes in this context that
although language "acts as a socializing and unifor-
mizing force," it is, rather paradoxically, "at the
same time the most potent single factor for the
growth of individuality" (1933:27).
```

Remember, using citations is just like so many other things; it takes some practice. So don't worry if it doesn't feel right at first. You'll get the hang of it, and soon you will be doing it automatically.

Now what about paraphrases? A paraphrase is a rewording of someone's ideas or information. Suppose I want to use some information I find in *Tools for Thought* by C.H. Waddington, for a paper describing the impact of the "information explosion" on anthropological research. In a section of Waddington's book entitled "Complexity of Information in the Modern World," he discusses the number of scientific journals published as an index of complexity. Here is the passage I'm interested in.

The first two journals wholly devoted to science—*The Philosophical Transactions of the Royal Society of London* and the French *Journale des Savants*—were both started in 1665. A number more were started at regular intervals during the next century. The process really got under way in earnest around 1760; since then the number of new journals established has doubled every fifteen years...By now well over 100,000 scientific journals have been founded. Not all have persisted, and nobody knows quite how many journals are being published at the present time. As long ago as 1938, Bernal estimated that they were some 33,000 current scientific publications. Another estimate in the late 1960's put the number at 50,000, containing about 1 million separate scientific papers per year.

Citation Format

One attempt to handle this mass of material has been the foundation of secondary journals, whose function it is to summarize and abstract the papers published in the primary journals. The first of these appeared as long ago as 1714 in Germany. By the time there were enough of them to form a representative sample, they also started to multiply, at the same exponential rate as the primary journals, doubling in numbers every fifteen years, and reaching a total of 1,900 by the mid 1960's. By this time there had been developed a tertiary level of periodical publications, giving information about the abstracting journals (Waddington 1977:32-33).

I want to use some of these facts in a paper on how this flood of information affects anthropological research. First I make a point and then I paraphrase Waddington in support of that point. Then I go on to cite another source.

The library is a sophisticated information retrieval system. It is designed to give us access to the information we need. But we have to learn how to use it strategically, not haphazardly. This is especially true in anthropology, where the literatures used are both extensive and diverse. The general need for sophisticated library research strategies becomes apparent when we consider the volume of information that confronts us. Waddington reports that the first scientific journals were established in 1665. Since 1760 over 100,000 journals have been established; it was estimated in the 1960's that as many as half of that number were still being published. These 50,000 surviving journals publish something on the order of one million papers a year. Efforts to manage this flood of information include the use of secondary journals to condense and make accessible the contents of the primary journals. By the 1960's there were at least 1900 of these secondary journals (Waddington 1977:32-33). The situation in anthropology is the same. In 1875-76, the library of the Peabody Museum, perhaps the first specialized anthropological library in the United States, had less than 1000 publications in its collection; by 1975 it had 130,000 (Currier 1976:16). The third edition of Murdoch's *Ethnographic Bibliography of North America*, published in 1960, contained 17,3000 entries for books and articles; the fourth edition, published in 1976, contains an additional 28,000 entries for books and articles published between 1959 and 1972 (Currier 1976:27).

Note how the citations identify the source of the information. A citation is not needed for every sentence; a series of sentences (or passages) may only require a single citation, as in the paraphrase of Waddington above, if it is clear that the information contained in the entire passage is from a single source (and from only a few pages of the source). If you pull together information from different places in a book or long article (as I did from the article by Currier), then you need to use a citation within the paraphrase to indicate the different pages in the source where the material you used can be found. *Transitions* from one source to another obviously require you to position a citation in such a way that the reader can see that you have switched from one source to another. The crucial thing is that it must always be clear what ideas came from where. If it is not clear, then it is wrong.

When discussing a single book at length, you do not have to acknowledge the general concepts, concerns, or themes in it each time you mention one. But it must be clear to the readers that you are in fact discussing an idea or theme from that particular book. You must, of course, cite the pages where more specific data or concepts are found, when you use them, so that the reader can find them.

For example, you don't have to cite page numbers every time you state or imply that Frederik Barth, in his book *Political Leadership among Swat Pathans*, is interested in political leadership and authority, because that is the grand theme of the book. It runs all through it. Therefore, you don't have to cite specific pages when you say something non-specific about Barth's book.

> Barth shares this concern about the problem of po-
> litical leadership. His study of the Swat Pathans
> (1959) is a good early example of an approach to
> politics developed within social anthropology.

Once you have clearly established that you are discussing Barth's 1959 study of the Swat Pathans, you can drop the (1959) —as long as the reader knows you are referring to Barth's general theme or conceptualization. But as soon as you go on to discuss Barth's specific formulations, then you have to provide the reader with page numbers.

> Barth states that among the Swat Pathans, "Politi-
> cally corporate groups are created by the actions of
> leaders" (Barth 1959:72). These "corporate" groups
> are person-centered. The leader is the focus of the
> group; the group only exists in terms of and by vir-
> tue of his authority. The group includes anyone the
> leader can get to join him in collective action in
> response to threat, crisis, or conflict.

Note that since the quotation and paraphrase come from the same page, one citation is adequate to identity both. Compare the paraphrase with the original:

> Politically corporate groups are created by the actions of leaders.
> Any such group consists of all the persons whom a leader is able to
> mobilize in the event of conflict. Its limits are undefined except in
> relation to the leader, and its solidarity derives from the latter's
> authority (Barth 1959:72).

In theory, if you are not indebted to someone for an idea or date, you do not have to cite him or her, even if you come across their statement of that concept or information. However, in practice, it is usually better to go ahead and cite such a source, if the material is pertinent. If nothing else, you strengthen your argument by indicating that reputable scholars have made the same point. Besides, citing a source entitles you to list it in your bibliography and shows the professor how hard you worked.

Citation Format

You don't want the professor to think you have done a slap dash job of research because you have failed to use a significant source. Also, you don't want to risk an unfair suspicion of plagiarism—more on that in the next section.

PLAGIARISM: THE BIG "P"

Plagiarism is bad news. It is morally wrong. Thus it makes professors angry and gets students into trouble, even when it is done unintentionally. There are harsh but justifiable penalties for plagiarism. This section will tell you what is and how to avoid it.

Plagiarism is the use of someone's work without acknowledgment, as if it were your own. If in your term paper you were to use someone's dates, ideas, or words without documenting that use with a citation, then you would be guilty of plagiarism.

Plagiarism is cheating. The penalties for plagiarism include an "F" on a paper, failing the class, and probation or suspension from the university. It is your obligation to become familiar with the rules of academic conduct and not violate them.

To avoid plagiarism, you have to know how to document your use of other people's work. This is what we went over in the last section; in-text citation is the system of documentation used in anthropology. Documentation is more than a good thing to know—it is your responsibility to know how to document your use of sources, and to make sure that you do so in every paper that you write, whether you use in-text citation for an anthropology paper, or reference footnotes for a literature paper.

It is pretty easy to tell when a student has plagiarized. Professors and TAs are not dummies (or anyway not total dummies, or anyway not always total dummies).[*] They've had lots of experience in reading student papers, and they know what to expect. It is not always easy to tell whether a student *meant* to cheat (although some cases are so outrageous that there can be no doubt) but most professors and TAs can tell whether he *did* cheat. If you are ever tempted to download a paper from the internet, or borrow large chunks of text from an encyclopedia or magazine, be aware that the same search engines that allowed you to find the these things can also be used by professors to track you down. This is in fact quite easy and can be done from the professor's desk. In fact there are now whole websites devoted to uncovering plagiarism. Honesty is still the best policy even in an electronic age.

Read this section and the section on the use of citations with care, so that you never unintentionally fail to document the source of material you use in your papers. It is not all that hard to avoid plagiarism once

---

[*] You can get pretty dummy-like after reading 100 term papers in a row.

you know what is involved. I'll advise you on how to avoid unintentional plagiarism. The main thing is to know how to document any use of sources correctly.

A quotation, the use of someone's words, not only requires a citation, but must be set off from your writing by quotation marks or by indentation and single spacing. This is true of phrases as well as of whole sentences and passages. Consider the following example from *African Religions of Brazil* by Robert Bastide (1978:240). The original is:

> All religion is a tradition —a dual tradition of stereotyped actions and rites and of mental images and myths. It has often been claimed that the two elements are inseparable, myths being a definition or justification of the ceremonial action.

And here is the same passage plagiarized almost word for word in student paper. (The paper is hypothetical. If a student did this, he would find his graduation getting pretty hypothetical too.)

```
This religion is a dual tradition, like any other; a
tradition both of stereotyped actions and rites and
of psychological images and myths.  The two elements
are inseparable, with myth being the definition of
ceremonial action.
```

Only a few, very minor, changes have been made; essentially it consists of Bastide's words. Here is an example of how to use this passage properly:

```
According to Bastide, "all religion is a tradition"
and as such consists "of stereotyped actions and
rites and mental images and myths."  He notes that
it is possible to view ritual and myth as a unitary
phenomenon in which myth is a statement of the pur-
pose or meaning of ritual (Bastide 1978:240).
```

It is clear that Bastide is being quoted, so a single citation at the end of the passage does the trick. Remember: it is still plagiarism even if you put someone's thoughts or data into your own words (in a paraphrase or summary) and do not acknowledge that use with a citation.

Plagiarism

Plagiarism occurs whenever a citation is required, but is not given, whether for quotes or paraphrases, ideas or data.

Besides confusion about the purposes and methods of documentation, the major cause of unconscious plagiarism is probably lousy note taking. Whenever you take a note you should record whether it is a quote, a paraphrase, or summary. You should also immediately take down all the bibliographic information you will need, should you later decide to incorporate that material into your paper. If you don't do this, and you need to use that material, you'll have to haul yourself kicking and screaming back to the library to get this information. That will look pretty silly. (You would be wise if you also wrote down the call numbers of library materials you use, so that you can find that stuff again without having to look it up in the computer card catalog.) If you photocopy pages from something, you should immediately write down complete bibliographic information on the copy or, better yet, photocopy the title page. Otherwise in a couple of weeks you may want to use it, but have only a vague notion of where it came from. And so you won't be able to use it, until you go back to the library and get the information you need to document your use of it.[*]

---

[*] The best advice on taking notes —library notes or field notes— is to include everything necessary for someone *else* to be able to use them. Figure by the time you actually use them you'll be a lot older and wiser (or will have forgotten enough) that for all practical purposes you *will be* someone else. Making notes self explanatory is never a bad policy.

The Bibliographic Format of Anthropology Papers:
THE REFERENCE LIST

A reference list—sometimes known as a reference bibliography, or even just a bibliography—provides the information needed to find any source used in a paper. You must give this bibliographic information for every source you cite in your paper. But you should not include sources that you did not cite in the text of the paper.

A reference list is not a real "bibliography" in the sense of seeking either to cover a subject comprehensively, or to identify sources which share certain special qualities (as in a select bibliography). A reference list is less ambitious; it is an inventory of sources actually used rather than of all sources or selected sources. (Some people refer to reference lists as bibliographies, and others don't. Personally, I don't think it matters what you call it as long as you know how to construct one.)

A reference list gives the necessary bibliographic information in a particular format. The bibliographic format presented here is derived, for the most part, from the journal *American Anthropologist* and from the *International Encyclopedia of the Social Sciences*. The format may be somewhat different in other journals, and still more different in other disciplines.

The reference list follows the text of the paper. It can be headed at the top of the page "References Cited" or "Works Cited."

The entries in the list are organized alphabetically by the last names of the authors. Here is what an entry for a book looks like:

Geertz, Clifford
    1973 The Interpretation of Cultures. New York: Basic Books.

and for a journal article:

Keesing, Roger
    1979 Linguistic Knowledge and Cultural Knowledge: Some
        Doubts and Speculations. American Anthropologist 81:14-36.

The above examples give the general form for entering sources in a reference list. You should use the same layout and punctuation. Start typing from the regular margin.

Notice what bibliographic information is required:

1. Last name of author, then first name (and middle initial).

2. Date of publication.

3. Title.

4. Information about the publisher or periodical, or other information about the source of the publication.

> a. If a book, then the city of publication and name of the publisher.
>
> b. If an article, then the name of the periodical, volume number, and pages on which the article appears. (Note: if the journal or periodical does not number pages consecutively for the entire year, you also need to give the issue number. See point 7 below.)

The above form will work for most entries. But there are a variety of little details and special problems that you will encounter from time to time. Let's consider these one by one.

1. Book, single author.

Include complete subtitles.

Tonkinson, Robert
    1978   The Mardujara Aborigines: Living the Dream in
        Australia's Desert. New York: Holt, Rinehart, and Winston.

2. Book or article, more than one author.

Only the name of the first author is reversed

Berger, Peter, and Thomas Luckmann
    1966   The Social Construction of Reality. New York:
        Doubleday.

Harrison, G.A., J.S.Weiner, J.M.Tanner and N.A. Barnicot
    1977   Human Biology: An Introduction to Human Evolution,
        Variation, Growth, and Ecology. 2nd ed. Oxford: Oxford
        University Press.

Remember that it is (usually) acceptable, in a reference such as the one above, to use the principal author's name followed by *et al* in your in-text citation, but that you must give all of the authors' names in the reference list entry.

3. More than one publication by same author.

In this case, you list the works chronologically (by date of publication). The earliest work is cited first.

Bailey, F.G.
> 1963   Politics and Social Change. Berkeley: University of California Press.

> 1969   Stratagems and Spoils: A Social Anthropology of Politics. Oxford: Blackwell.

If more than one work was published in the same year, list them alphabetically and use lower case letters to distinguish them, as in the in-text citation (1963a, 1963b).

4. City and State of Publication.

If a book was published in some little known city or town—Tuba City, Arizona, or Weed, California, for example—then you should note the state, as well as the city, of publication.

Rosenberg, G. and D. Anspach
> 1973   Working Class Kinship. Lexington, Massachusetts: Lexington Books.

Place of publication is not required for periodicals, except to avoid confusion, as when journals with the same of similar names are published in different places.

5. Editor or compiler.

Use "ed." or "comp."

Hunt, Robert, ed.
> 1967   Personalities and Cultures: Readings in Psychological Anthropology. Austin: University of Texas Press.

6. Chapter or article in book.

Williams, T.R.
>1972   The Socialization Process: A Theoretical Perspective.
>In Primate Socialization. Frank E. Poirer, ed. Pp. 207-260.
>New York: Random House.

Notice that "in" is underlined (or italicized in print). This is to make sure that no one thinks it is part of the title of the book. Also, note that the name of an editor, when not in the author position, is not inverted.

7. Journal Articles.

If the periodical has continuous pagination, you omit the issue numbers.

Singer, M.
>1980   Signs of the Self: An Exploration in Semiotic
>Anthropology. American Anthropologist 82: 485-507.

Nowadays, most scholarly journals do not start off each issue with new pagination; rather, pagination is continuous throughout a volume, so providing an issue number would be superfluous. However, some periodicals start each issue with page one, in which case you must give the issue number in your entry. Whenever you are not sure whether pagination is continuous, provide the issue number, in parentheses, after the volume number.

Washburn, Sherwood L.
>1978   The Evolution of Man. Scientific American 239 (3):194-
>211.

8. Translator.

If you read Helen Sebba's translation of a book by Roger Bastide, the complete entry would be as follows:

Bastide, Roger
>1978   The African Religions of Brazil: Toward a Sociology of
>the Interpenetration of Civilizations. Helen Sebba, trans.
>Baltimore: Johns Hopkins University Press. (Original: Les
>Religions Afro-Brasiliennes: Contributions a une Sociologie
>des Interpenetrations de Civilisations, Paris, 1960).

Reference List

All of the above information is not always available, in which case you have to make do with what is available. There are also variations in what is done. For example, sometimes the language of the original is given: "Translated from the Nahuatl by...".

9. Corporate Author.

Laboratory of Comparative Human Cognition
    1978 Cognition as a Residual Category in Anthropology. *In* Annual Review of Anthropology 7:51-69.

10. Reprints of Older Works.

You should give the original publication date in brackets, if available, as well as the date of the reprint.

Smith, Arthur H.
    1971 [1899] Village Life in China. Boston: Little, Brown.

You probably should cite this in the text by both dates, at least on its first use, so the reader will be aware of the historical context of the source. Your page citation should be to the edition you used.

11. The Internet

Standards for citing references drawn from the Internet are still evolving. If you find a newspaper or magazine article on NEXIS-LEXIS, cite it using its print publication data the same as if you were using the printed version. If you are citing web pages or databases that exist only in electronic form, cite the web address and date you accessed it. For example, "Jakarta" *Encyclopædia Britannica Online*, http://www.eb.com:180/bol/topic?eu=109534&sctn=1 [Accessed 20 September 2001]. Note that web pages can disappear or change without notice, unlike a printed book. You might want to make a printed copy.

Reference List

A Sample Bibliography

Works Cited

Blom, Frans and Oliver LaFarge
    1926   Tribes and Temples. New Orleans: Tulane University
    Press.

Collier, Jane F.
    1973   Law and Social Change in Zinacantan. Stanford:
    Stanford University Press.

    1974   Women in Politics. *In* Women, Culture and Society. M.
    Rosaldo and L. Lamphere, eds. Pp. 89-96. Stanford:
    Stanford University Press.

    1977   Political Leadership and Legal Change in Zinacantan. Law
    and Society Review 11:131-163.

Emerson, Richard
    1962   Power-dependence Relations. American Sociological
    Review 27(1):31-40.

Levi-Strauss, Claude
    1975   La Voie Des Masgues. 2 vol. Geneva: Editions Albert
    Skira.

Strickmann, Michael
    1974   Taoism, history of. The New Encyclopedia Britannica.
    15th ed. Chicago: Encyclopedia Britannica. Vol. 17. Pp. 1044-
    1050.

The library can be a mystifying place. Well, okay—the library *is* a mystifying place. It's bad enough when you know how to use it. Not knowing how to use it is time consuming and frustrating.

Part of what makes a library confusing is the fact that it has to organize tons of different kinds of stuff—books, magazines and journals, government publications—from all over the world, about everything from the anthropology of art to zymurgy, in a way that can be used efficiently by everyone from anthropology students to zymurgists.

Anthropology uses an extremely wide range of library materials. If you go into the library "blind," you won't find most of them. To use the library effectively for anthropological research, you have to know the functional relationship between critical reference works (that is, various indexes and bibliographies) and the anthropological literature. And, of course, you have to know how to use each individual reference work, when you find it. Using a reference work, such as the *Social Sciences Citation Index*, is not simple. But with practice it becomes automatic. Librarians are not uniquely gifted superstars; they have simply taken the time to learn how the library works. If you take a little time, you can become "fluent" at using the library too (not as good as the librarians, but pretty good).* This Guide will get you started, and will, we hope, be something you can refer to as needed, whenever you do research in the University Library, for anthropology or allied disciplines.

Perhaps you are thinking you don't need to learn to use the library because you can get everything on the Internet. You would be wrong for two reasons. First, learning to use the library's resources gives you the skills you need to do the same thing on the Internet. Second, despite what you may have heard, the Internet does not have everything on it. It is a mile wide and an inch deep in most places. Most books, for example, cannot be found on the Internet. And there is a lot of bad information on the Internet, too. A good search engine will find something on any topic you choose, but cannot tell you if it is any good. Papers researched from information taken completely from the Internet rarely get 'A's. Indeed, they often end up embarrasing their writers when critical information is missing or they cite something as fact which is not.

---

* The reference librarians are always going to know more about the library than anyone else, so if you can't find what you need, don't assume the library does not have it until you have asked a librarian.

The Library: How to Get Started

So you walk into the library. What do you do first?

Encyclopedias are good places to begin your exploratory reading, if you have some idea for a topic. (But term papers are never based solely on encyclopedia articles.) I suggest you go either to the *Encyclopedia Britannica,* 15th ed., or to the *International Encyclopedia of the Social Sciences,* or to a specialized area or subject encyclopedia, if one is available for your topic. (See the next section for descriptions of individual reference works, including the ones mentioned here, plus directions on how to find them in the reference areas.) Encyclopedias and handbooks are the best way to get a quick introduction to a topic—to see if it really interests you and to check it for feasibility. And you can use their reference lists to identify good sources.

When you find a source in a reference work you then have to go to the computer "card catalog" (a now archaic reference to the time when you actually consulted the paper cards directly) and find its call number, so that you can locate it in "the stacks." The stacks are all those shelves of books that really make up a library. The reference area is a kind of map of the stacks. Using the reference works shelved in the reference area enables you to find that dingy brown book on the far end of the bottom shelf on the east side of the sixth floor which is just what you need for your paper. (It beats starting with the first book on the first floor and flipping through every book until you find the one you need.) After you have a call number, you can go find the book you want.[*] When you find it—or the place where it would be if it were on the shelf—take time to look at the books next to it on the shelf. Since they are in the same call number sequence, they may be relevant to your topic. This kind of browsing (by call number sequence) is often an effective way of finding useful sources. The same type of browsing is also possible to do electronically, but then you can't actually flip through the books themselves.

---

[*] Most libraries now use the Library of Congress classification system for book call numbers, so one number is good at most institutions. Sometimes these will be modified to show which are located in the reference section and which are in the stacks. (Mugar uses an 'X' before the call number to indicate reference.) However, some libraries with older collections retain their own idiosyncratic numbering system or use the old Dewey Decimal system.

Once you lay your hands on one good source, you can use its citations and reference list to identify additional sources. These sources will lead you on to their sources, and so on—this is the method of pursuing a citation chain, which was mentioned earlier, in the section on the use of citations. (Incidentally, many sources will use old fashioned reference footnotes instead of in-text citations, and may omit a reference list on the theory that the information was already given in footnotes. That is a pain, and we are inclined to think dark thoughts about their ancestry, but we're not so prejudiced that we'd pass up a good source on that account.)

Since each source can cite only earlier sources, a citation chain normally leads from recent to earlier and earlier publications. But it is also possible to pursue it in the opposite direction, i.e., from earlier to later citations. This is done by means of a remarkable set of reference tools called the *Social Sciences Citation Index.* We'll get to that.

Reference Works: Encyclopedias

Encyclopedias attempt to summarize the knowledge in an area. Here are two of the best encyclopedias for anthropological research. (Also see the section on more specialized handbooks.)

The New Encyclopedia Britannica (1990) 15th ed. 30 vols. Chicago: Encyclopedia Britannica, Inc. (AE5.N532.1990)

There are three parts to this encyclopedia. The first is a one volume "outline of knowledge" entitled the Propaedia. It is also a guide to the encyclopedia. Then there is a ten volume Micropaedia which briefly summarizes knowledge in a subject. It is intended to function as a ready reference, and as an index to the last nineteen volumes. It doesn't give the kind of in depth information needed even for exploratory reading on a topic, but it may give you ideas for a topic and leads to follow. The final nineteen volumes are the Macropaedia. They give what the editors (pretentiously) call "knowledge in depth." Often the articles in the Macropaedia are written by scholars famous in their fields. (The articles are initialed, and the initials are identified at the end of the Propaedia volume if you get curious.) These selections are the ones you are most likely to find useful. The reference lists are good. Note: one of the distinctive features of the 15th edition is its excellent cross indexing. The Micropaedia is a *splendid* index to the Macropaedia. It is *always* best to start there. The Propaedia also indexes the Macropaedia, though less obviously. Don't skip them.

Britannica Online provides in a web edition of the *Encyclopedia Britannica*. You can find it current connection through Boston University at http://www.bu.edu/library/indexes.html.

International Encyclopedia of the Social Sciences (17 vols.) edited by David Sills, New York: Macmillan, 1968-79. (H.40.F68)

Volume 17 is the index volume. USE IT! It is *much* better than relying on the broad subject headings used in the encyclopedia proper. The index volume lists specific topics—going to it first saves you time. Page 84 of the index gives a list of the articles on anthropology.

This encyclopedia has signed articles by heavyweights in their field. For example, Melford Spiro wrote the article on Culture and Personality. The reference lists are excellent.

Reference Works: Indexes and Bibliographies

Social Sciences Index (AI3.565m)

As you turn from the world of general encyclopedias, this is probably the index you will want to turn to first. It is selective about the material it covers, and so the sources you find by using it have a pretty good chance of being high quality.

It is easy to use. For example, suppose you are interested in Brazil. You look in the index for 1980 under the subject heading Brazil and find that it says, among other things:

Brazil

see also
Anthropological research--Brazil

You then turn to the anthropological research heading. There, under Brazil, a journal article is listed. The title, author, journal name, and volume and page numbers are given:

> Final report on the meeting of anthropologists and Indian experts. R. Cordoso de Oliveira. Cur Anthrop 20:451-4 Je' '79.

"Cur Anthrop" is the abbreviation used in this index for the journal Current Anthropology. (You can tell because there is a list of abbreviations used in the front of the index.) The volumes in which the article appears is 20, on pages 451-454, in June 1979. The article was written by R. Cordoso de Oliveira.

To get your hands on the article itself, look up the journal name in the *serials record*. This is a list of the journals and magazines in the library, and gives their call numbers. The serials record is found both in print and on computer at various locations—one is near the reference desk. The serials list also tells you what volumes the library has. Volumes that are bound are shelved in the stacks. Unbound periodicals may be located in the "Current Periodicals" room. Some unbound periodicals are also shelved in the stacks.

Armed with the call number for the journal and the volume and page number from the *Social Science Index* reference that you found, you may now march confidently into the stacks, walk right to the shelf, and pull out the volume you need, flip it open, and voilá: the desired article. (Remember, that if that article is useful, the sources it lists in its reference bibliography may also be useful.)

Essay and General Literature Index (AI3.F34)

This index identifies the contents of books (for example, essays in collections). The computerized card catalog does not do this.

In the index for 1970-74, under the heading "Brazil," you find nothing interesting. You turn to the anthropology heading. Again nothing seems useful. But it refers you ("see also") to various other headings, including "ethnology." Under "ethnology," you strike out. But it says "see also" kinship. Turning to the kinship heading, you find an article on kinship in Brazil. This is how it is listed in the index:

> Kinship
>> Levi-Strauss, C. Social Structures of Central
>> and Eastern Brazil.
>> *In* Gross, D.R., ed. Peoples and Cultures of Native South
>>> America.
>>> p. 263-74.

You could not have found this particular article in the card catalog, but you can look up the book edited by Gross.

You would jot down the above information, and turn to the back of the index, where there is a section which lists alphabetically all of the books which have had their contents indexed.

Under Gross, D.R., you find the following information.

> Gross, Daniel Russell (ed.) Peoples and Cultures of
> Native South America: An Anthropological Reader.

Ed. with introductions. Published by the American
Museum of Natural History Press 1973.

You use this information to look up the book.

The big advantage of this index is that it indexes the contents of
books. The fact that an article or essay has been selected for inclusion in
a collection means that there is a fair chance that the article is of high
quality.

Catalog of the Library of the Peabody Museum of Archeology and Ethnology, Harvard University (Z5119.F63)

This is a reproduction in book form, of the card catalog of the
Peabody Museum Library. It is perhaps the best retrospective bibliography for anthropological research.* It also indexes the contents of selected journals and books. It is divided into an author catalog and a subject catalog. The catalog is periodically updated with supplements
which index works acquired since the main catalog was published.

1. Subject Catalog

The subject catalog of the Peabody Museum Library is organized by
topical divisions (ethnology, technology), by human groups (political,
linguistic, and social) and by geographical areas. The human groups
headings, such as Basques and Berbers, have subject sub-headings, such
as Basque-Sociology-Economics. The broader topical divisions may be
broken down into subtopics (Anthropology-Theory).

Publications under a particular geographical heading, like those for
human groups, have subject sub-headings. So you can look first for the
geographical area that interests you, and then you look for the subject
headings that interest you. Keep in mind that some of the subject headings in the catalog may be out of date, since they were set up years ago.

Suppose I am interested in Bali, an island in Indonesia. Under Bali in
the fourth supplement to the catalog are reproduction of thirty-one cards
in the catalog of the Peabody Museum Library. Subject headings follow
the geographical headings; there are cards that say "Bali Island--Ethnol-
ogy," meaning that the publication listed on that card concerns the ethnology of Bali. Here are some of the subject headings that appear under
the geographic heading of Bali:

---

* Retrospective means covering older publications; looking back on past
works.

Ethnomusicology

Religion

Religion--Mythology

Religion--Possession

Sociology--Acculturation and Culture Change

The Peabody catalog indexes the contents of many books and journals. For example, on a card headed "Bali Island-Sociology-Authority and Leadership," we find a chapter in a book listed:

Hobart, Mark
Orators and Patrons: Two Types of Political Leaders in Balinese Village Society.

(In: Political Language and Oratory in Traditional Society. London: New York: Academic Press. c.1975, p. 65-92.)

Notice that this entry does not give you the name of the editor of the volume in which this work appears; it does give you page numbers.

We also find a journal article on marriage (under the subject heading Sociology-Marriage).

Boon, James A.
The Balinese Marriage Predicament: individual, strategical, cultural.

(In: American Ethnologist. 1976 v.3 no.2 p.191-214; diagrs.)

Both of the above appear in the fourth *supplement,* which updates the catalog. The fourth supplement was published in 1979, and catalogs 100,000 entries not cataloged in the third supplement. You should use *both the main catalog and each of the supplements* in your search of the literature. Otherwise you can miss valuable sources. For example, if I had not looked in the main catalog under Bali, I might have missed the following older, but classic, work:

Bali Island-Ethnography

Bateson, Gregory
Balinese Character: a photographic analysis; by Gregory Bateson and Margaret Mead. New York, 1942. xvi, 227 p.

100 illus. (Special Publications of the New York Academy of Sciences. Vol. II.)

Remember, this catalog is the best place to locate many older works; it is an excellent retrospective bibliography.

2. Author Catalog

Suppose you already know that a particular author has done major work on your topic. For example, maybe you are interested in some aspect of your topic. For example, maybe you are interested in some aspect of the work of Alfred Kroeber on California Indians. Under Kroeber, Alfred Louis, in the Peabody author catalog are listed 126 entries on works by Kroeber, covering the course of his career from 1900 through the 1950's. There are numerous articles on California Indians. After the publications *by* Kroeber are listed various works *about* Kroeber, which may also be useful.

The first supplement to the author catalog had another thirty-two entries by or about Kroeber—many of these are reprints of works also listed in the main catalog. These reprints may be more accessible to you than the original publications, so it may pay off to check the supplements even on older authors.

The Peabody Museum catalogue has also partly entered the electronic age. Information on anthropological articles and edited book chapters can be consulted on CD-ROM disks in the library itself, or through the Internet via restricted databases such as Eureka under the title *Anthropological Literature*. A similar periodical database that uses the resources of The Anthropology Library at the British Museum is called *Anthropological Index Online*. Both of these can be found through Mugar Library's website at http://www.bu.edu/library/indexes.html.

Social Sciences Citation Index (Z7161.S65)

The *Social Sciences Citation Index* (SSCI) is the versatile and sophisticated index we mentioned before. It consists of three different kinds of indexes, which are designed to be used together: the *Permuterm Subject Index,* the *Citation Index,* and the *Source Index.*

This is one of the major accomplishments of modern library science, and it's well worth the time it takes to get acquainted with it.

1. Subject and Source Index

If you have a topic, and want to find articles about it, you can use the SCCI *Permuterm Subject Index.* "Permuterm" means that the words in titles have been used to index articles; an article will be listed under various combinations of the words in the title, which are called terms and co-terms. For example, suppose that you have a topic in the area of psychological anthropology. You know that "culture and personality" studies are an important part of this field. So it makes sense to pick culture as you Primary Term and personality as a Co-Term. In the Permuterm Subject Index for 1980, under the primary term culture and the co-term personality the name Shweder is listed. Now you turn to the *Source Index* for 1980 and look up Shweder. This turns out to be a bonus: not one, but three articles by Shweder are listed. (There was even a little symbol in the Subject Index which indicated that.) The SSCI *Source Index* gives you the following information for the first of Shweder's articles:

Shweder, R.A.
   Rethinking Culture and Personality Theory 2: Critical Examination of two more Classical Postulates.

Ethos 7(4):279-311 79 77R

This is basically the same bibliographic information you find in a reference list: author, title, journal, volume and issue number, page numbers, and date of publication. Only the order is different from the format given earlier. The only mystery here is the "77R." That indicates the number of sources that Shweder cites. Seventy-seven sources is a lot. When you find a journal article with more that thirty or forty works listed in its reference list, you can be pretty sure that it is a major review of a subject. The article by Shweder is probably a review of some aspect of culture and personality theory, and so may be quite useful—for its reference list, if nothing else.

One beautiful thing about the SSCI is that in the *Source Index* it lists the reference sources of every article indexed. So you not only have a reference to Shweder's article in *Ethos*, you have a list of all the sources he cited, even before you go look at his article. His reference list is given right below the entry for his article. Let's look at one of Shweder's sources, as listed in the Source Index.

Bateson G. 67 AM Behavioral Sci 10 29

Bateson is the author. 67 means 1967. The name of the journal in which the article appears is American Behavioral Scientist. (The Index has a listing of all abbreviations used.) 10 refers to the volume number of the journal, 29 is the page number.

2. Citation Index

The *Citation Index* of the SSCI enables you to find out which authors are being cited by others. The authors who cite Shweder's articles on culture and personality, for example, are probably writing about the same or related issues. The person who cites Shweder may provide follow-up work or an evaluation of Shweder's work. So by using the *Citation Index*, you can "listen in" to the dialogues being carried on by various groups of scholars who are interested in the stuff that interests you.

When you find a good article on your topic, you can find other sources by finding out who has cited that article (or author) since its publication. The *Citation Index* lets you pursue citation chains in a new direction. Before, you could only trace sources cited in an article you had your hands on, which meant you could only find works published before the date of publication of the article you have. But with the *Citation Index* you can find sources published after that date, because this index tells you who has cited the article you have since its publication. So not only can you find a lot of potentially useful sources fast by using the SCCI, you can also keep up with the most recent developments and ideas in a field, and check to see how a work was later evaluated, a theory revised, or a conceptual framework expanded, modified or given up as worthless.

This kind of library research is likely to pay off a lot faster than paging through journals one by one.

Here's how you go about using the SSCI *Citation Index:* First you look up the author in the index. The titles of the author's articles are listed, by year of publication, under his or her name. Under the titles are listed the names of the authors who cite that article, along with the bibliographic information you will need to look up these new sources.

Again this reference also has an electronic counterpart through the restricted *Web of Science* database that includes the *Social Sciences Citation Index.* One advantage of this source is that you can also click to include the humanities or natural sciences citations as part of a single search. The Boston University link for this can be found at http://www.bu.edu/library/indexes.html.

Book Review Digest (Z7129.F06)

Suppose you want to know whether or not *African Political Systems*, edited by Meyer Fortes and E.E. Evans-Pritchard is worth using in your paper. You can use the *Book Review Digest* to find out. First, look up Fortes in the author/title index which is published in separate volumes (Author-Title Index 1905-74). This provides the title and year of publication of all books included in the *Digest*. You will find that *African Political Systems* was published in 1941. Turning to the volume for 1941, you will find digests (that is, summaries) from several reviews of this book which appeared in various periodicals, including *American Anthropologist* and *American Political Science Review*.

If a book is not reviewed by a major journal, it may not be worth using. There are a lot of pretty funny people writing pretty funny books, and it is embarrassing to base part of a term paper on a book which seems to be scholarly and rigorous, only to have the professor tell you that the results were considered impossible, or that fraud was involved, or that the author is famous for being an idiot. Therefore any book which seems to contain startling or controversial information or interpretation is worth checking out in the *Book Review Digest*. If you find no summaries there, be sure to check the *Book Review Index* (Z1035.A1.F65). Here you can find the citations to a much larger number of book reviews but without summaries. You will have to look them up yourself. Since academic journals are notoriously slow about reviewing books, you may find that a book published in 1990 has the bulk of its reviews appear in 1991 while others will straggle in over the next couple of years, so do not confine yourself just to the year the book was published.

Human Relations Area Files (HRAF)

The Human Relations Area Files (HRAF) are a microfiche collection of books, articles and unpublished papers on more than 300 ethnic, religious, cultural and national groups worldwide. They are particularly valuable if you want to do a cross-cultural comparison quickly since each piece of writing is intensively indexed by topic. Materials are arranged according to a classification system based on the following manuals:

Micro **Outline of Cultural Materials.** 5th ed. 1982.
Z   Subject index to the HRAF files. Assigns a numerical
5111   designation to more than 700 categories of human
M86   culture. It is used in conjunction with the *Outline of*
1982M *World Cultures* to locate information in the HRAF files.

Micro **Outline of World Cultures**. 6th ed. 1983.
Z   Classifies all known world cultures by geographic
5111   region. Assigns alpha-numeric designations to cultural
M87   groups.
1983

ADDITIONAL REFERENCE WORKS

No two bibliographies or indexes are exactly alike. So every time you use a new reference work, you will need to spend some time (fifteen minutes to a half hour), learning how to use it. That goes for the reference works that were discussed in more detail before—you can't learn how to use something like this entirely from someone's descriptions. You have to go and actually use these reference works in order to consolidate what you've learned. It takes some practice.

It is advisable to use several reference works when surveying the literature in preparation for a research paper. And remember that indexes and bibliographies organized by geographical areas index sources that focus on particular subjects (such as culture and personality or political systems), and the "subject" indexes will include sources that focus on ethnographic areas.

This is **not** an exhaustive list of reference works useful in anthropological research. I have tried here to list only the ones you will probably find most useful. There are many other useful reference sources. Try browsing in the reference area sometime to get a feel for the diversity of available reference works.* There is a list available in the reference area devoted just to reference works in anthropology, and there are similar lists for other subjects as well. Many reference works, including some of those cited above, are now becoming available on CD-ROM optical disks and through on-line computer services at a rapid pace. Check to find out what reference works are currently stocked by the library in this

---

* I think I already told you that TAs have funny ideas about how to spend their time.

format. It will allow you to run faster and more extensive computer searches.

Obviously, if you have any questions or problems, consult your librarian.

General

Z 5111 K53 1991	**Cultural Anthropology: A Guide to Reference and Information Sources.** 1991. Guide to reference literature in cultural anthropology, as well as libraries, publishers and organizations.
Z 5111 W94 1991	**Introduction to Library Research in Anthropology.** 1991. Guide to research tools, library services and the mechanics of term paper writing in anthropology.
Z 7161 S648 1989	**The Social Sciences: A Cross Disciplinary Guide to Selected Sources.** 1989. Consult the "Anthropology" chapter for an annotated list of recent reference sources in anthropology.
Z 7161 S666 1986	**Sources of Information in the Social Sciences.** 3rd ed. 1986. The "Anthropology" chapter contains an exhaustive annotated bibliography of the literature of this field. Available at the Reference Desk.
Z 5111 F58	**International Bibliography of the Social Sciences —Anthropology.** 1955-91+ This has an author-subject index at the back of each volume. It breaks the discipline into sub-areas in a "classification scheme"—for example, General Studies, Materials and Methods, Ethnographic Studies (by area), Social Organization (by area and by institution and type of behavior, e.g., sexual relations, inter-racial and inter-ethnic relations). The IBSS also includes bibliographies in political science, economics, and sociology. The anthropology part covers archeology and physical anthropology as well as cultural and social anthropology.

DICTIONARIES AND ENCYCLOPEDIAS

GN **Dictionary of Anthropology.** 1997.
307 Covers terms, theoretical concepts, and biographical
D485 profiles in social and cultural anthropology. Includes
1997 bibliography with more than 3000 references.

GN **Dictionary of Concepts in Cultural Anthropology.** 1991.
307 Contains definitions, historical origins and developments, and
W56 bibliographic references for 80 key concepts in cultural
1991 anthropology.

GN **Dictionary of Concepts in Physical Anthropology.** 1991.
50.3 Consists of brief definitions, historical origins and
S74 developments, and sources of additional information for 75+
1991 concepts in physical anthropology.

GN **Encyclopedia of Cultural and Social Anthropology**, 1996
307 This is more of a dictionary than an encyclopedia but has
E648 topical and geographical entries plus many short biographies.

GN **Companion Encyclopedia of Anthropology**. 1994
25 Series of long interelated essays on divided into three parts:
C65 Humanity, culture, and social life.

GN **Encyclopedia of Evolution: Humanity's Search for its**
281 **Origins.** 1990.
M53 Popular encyclopedia containing 600+ articles on evolution and
1990 its impact on society, from Bonzo to biogenetic law and from
"Planet of the Apes" to plate tectonics.

BP **Encyclopedia of Islam**, New Edition. vol. 1-4, 1960
40 Covers most major aspects of Islamic history and religion.
F65 More recent updates in Mugar Online.

GN **Encyclopedia of Human Evolution and Prehistory.** 2000
281 2nd edition covers 1200+ topics in human evolution. Contains
E53 photographs,drawings and charts and bibliographies..

GN **Encyclopedia of World Cultures.** 10 vols. 1991- .
307 Ten-volume encyclopedia, arranged by geographic region,
E53 provides descriptive summaries on world cultures.
1991

GN
20
I5
1991
International Dictionary of Anthropologists. 1991. Biographical dictionary of 725 anthropologists born prior to 1920. The scope is worldwide.

RC
334
I57
International Encyclopedia of Psychiatry, Psychology, Psychoanalysis, and Neurology, 1977 Volume 12 is the index volume. The articles are signed and have reference lists. The *International Encyclopedia of the Social Sciences* would also be useful in doing research in psychological anthropology.

GN
20
W63
1988
Women Anthropologists: A Biographical Dictionary. 1988. Biographical profiles of 58 women anthropologists born between 1836 and 1934. Profiles include a selected bibliography of works by or about each individual.

INDEXES AND ABSTRACTS

GN
1
F70
Abstracts in Anthropology. 1970 - . Abstracts are brief summaries of the contents of a publication and index journal articles in a subject arrangement. Abstracts, unlike book reviews, are non-evaluative. Most social sciences have their own abstracts. You may also find *Psychological Abstracts* and *Sociological Abstracts* useful. Divided into four sections: archaeology, physical anthropology, linguistics, and cultural anthropology. Does not index book reviews.

ASL
Z
3501
A32
Africa Bibliography. 1984 - . Index to articles, books and essays. Arranged by region and country, following a general section. Consult the social and cultural anthropology/sociology and anthropology/ archaeology/prehistory subject headings.

AI
3
F69
Alternative Press Index. 1970 - . Index to alternative and radical publications. Consult this index for articles on Australian aborigines, native Americans and other groups.

Index Table 3	**America: History and Life.** 1964 - . This work indexes and abstracts periodical articles in the field of North American history and culture. Includes articles on native American history, prehistory and culture. Includes book reviews.
Z 5111 R67	**Anthropological Index to Current Periodicals in the Museum of Mankind Library.** 1980 - . Indexes more than 600 periodicals in a geographical arrangement, subdivided by general, physical anthropology, archaeology, cultural anthropology, ethnography, and linguistics. No subject index. Annual author index published separately. Does not index book reviews. Now on-line, too, see http://www.bu.edu/library/indexes.html
GN 1 A65M	**Anthropological Literature: An Index to Periodical Articles and Essays.** 1979 - . Indexes over 1000 periodicals and 150 edited books from materials received at Harvard's Tozzer Library. Does not index book reviews. Now on-line, see http://www.bu.edu/library/indexes.html
Z 7163 A66	**Applied Social Sciences Index and Abstracts.** 1987 - . Index to journal articles in the applied social sciences. Includes social and cultural anthropology, archaeology, linguistics and physical anthropology.
Index Table 4	**Arts and Humanities Citation Index.** 1975 - . Provides author, subject and citation access to the literature in folklore, linguistics and archaeology. Includes book reviews. Now on-line, see http://www.bu.edu/library/indexes.html
ASL Z 3501 F625	**A Current Bibliography on African Affairs.** 1962 - . Quarterly index to books, articles, government documents and visual aids, arranged by general subject or geographical area.
Z 6001 G431	**Geographical Abstracts: Human Geography.** 1989 - . Index to 1000 geographical journals, books, proceedings, reports, theses and dissertations covering the literature of human geography. Classified subject arrangement.

HANDBOOKS

Z
1605
F36 — **Handbook of Latin American Studies,** 1935-
Publishes separate volumes on humanities and social sciences. Annotated.

F
1434
H3 — **Handbook of Middle American Indians.** 16 vols. 1964-1976.
Contains essays on the ethnography, archaeology, physical anthropology and social anthropology of the Indians of Middle America. Updated by recent supplements.

E
77
H25 — **Handbook of North American Indians.** 20 vols. [in progress] 1978 - .
When completed, this work will be the standard source of information on the prehistory, history and cultures of the native peoples of North America north of Mexico. Each volume contains essays on specific aspects of Native American life with an extensive bibliography and detailed index.

E
51
E87 — **Handbook of South American Indians.** 7 vols. 1946-1959.
Survey of tribes of South America, with emphasis on the European contact period.

GN
296
M423
1990 — **Medical Anthropology: A Handbook of Theory and Method.** 1990.
Presents the state of the art in medical anthropology, core theoretical issues, ethnomedicine, biomedicine, health issues in human populations, methodology and policy issues.

BIBLIOGRAPHIES

Z
5111
A57M — **Anthropological Bibliographies: A Selected Guide.** 1981.
Extensive list of bibliographies arranged geographically with a final section of topical bibliographies.

Z
5118
F44G7
1988 — **Anthropological Fieldwork: An Annotated Bibliography.** 1988.
Contains 700 entries on anthropological fieldwork from the early twentieth century to 1986. Includes geographical and subject indexes.

Z	**A Bibliography of Contemporary North American Indians:**
1209.2.	**Selected and Partially Annotated with Study Guide.** 1976
H67	Organized by topics—for example, the anthropology of
H6	development, culture and personality.

Z	**Cumulative Bibliography of African Studies.** 1973
7106	This is a reproduction of the author and subject catalog of
I5M	the IAI. Subject headings are organized under geographical
Folio	areas. It has a table of contents. The IAI has several other
	bibliographies which might be useful.

Z	**Cumulative Bibliography of Asian Studies.** 1941-
3001	These are two titles in the same continuous series. Broken down
C94	by topic and country, they cover an extraordinarily large range
	of publications and therefore runs four or five years behind (i.e.,
	volume covering 1986 was published in 1991).

Z	**Ecce Homo: An Annotated Bibliographic History of Physical**
5118	**Anthropology.** 1986.
S7S64	Contains 2340 references from ancient times to 1960 on the
1986	history of physical anthropology. Arranged chronologically.

Z	**Ethnographic Bibliography of North America.**
1209	4th edition, 1975 (supplement 1990)
F60	Organized by areas. It has 40,000 entries on articles and books,
	and covers the field through 1972, supplement takes it through
	the 1980s.

Z	**Ethnographic Bibliography of South America.** 1963
1209	Organized by area, then by tribe. Has tribal index.
F63	

Z	**The History of Anthropology: A Research Bibliography.**
5111	1977.
K44	Contains more than 2400 entries on the development of
	anthropology as a science and profession.

Z	**Index Islamicus: A Catalogue of Articles in Periodicals and**
7835	**Other Collective Publications.** 1958-85.
M6	Organized by subject and by area. Includes section on
F58	ethnology and anthropology (more current supplements issued
	periodically)

Z 3101 S63	**Modern Chinese Society: An Analytical Bibliography.** 1973 Good source for older work, but much new research has been conducted since it came out.
Z 1209.2 N67 P67 1988	**Native American Basketry: An Annotated Bibliography.** 1988. Comprehensive bibliography includes books, articles, theses, dissertations and newspaper articles. Organized by culture area. Contains author and subject indexes.
Z 4501 F51	**Pacific Bibliography: Printed Materials Relating to the Native Peoples of Polynesia, Melanesia, and Micronesia.** 1965. 2nd ed. This has author, subject, and group indexes.
Z 7165 I6 C5	**The Social System and Culture of Modern India: A Research Bibliography.** 1975 Organized by subjects—covers sociology and social and cultural anthropology, although all of the subject headings refer to "sociology."

YEARBOOKS AND REVIEW LITERATURE

GN 1 A623	**Annual Review of Anthropology.** 1972- This gives critical reviews of recent research in selected areas of anthropology, such as political and economic anthropology, symbolic studies, culture change, and area studies. The biblio- graphies for each article are generally quite extensive. Now on-line, see http://www.bu.edu/library/indexes.html
Z 5111 R47	**Reviews in Anthropology.** 1974 - . Quarterly journal which publishes long reviews on important new publications in anthropology.

ATLASES

G 1046 E1A8 1982	**Atlas of Mankind.** 1982. Contains general background information on peoples of the world, including issues such as migration, race, kinship, language, and environment.

G   **Atlas of World Cultures: A Geographical Guide to**
1046   **Ethnographic Literature.** 1989.
E1P7   Geographical guide to ethnographic books, articles, reports,
1989   archaeological materials, maps and atlases for 3500+ cultures.

DS   **Cultural Atlas of China.** 1983.
721   Visual representation of the culture history of China, with maps,
B59   photographs, tables and text. There are similar volumes on
1983M   Africa and Japan.

DIRECTORIES

GN   **AAA Guide.** Current year.
43   Describes anthropology departments in 485 institutions, lists
A2   American Anthropological Association members, recent Ph.D.
G84   dissertations in anthropology, and student statistics.

Z   **Biographical Directory of Anthropologists Born Before 1920.**
5111   1988
B56   Entries include biographical data, major contributions, and
1988   published sources of biographical information.

NOTES

NOTES

Glossary

acculturation: Massive culture change that occurs in a society when it experiences intensive firsthand contact with a more powerful society.

adaptation: A series of beneficial adjustments of organisms to their environment.

adjudication: Mediation with an unbiased third party making the ultimate decision.

advocacy anthropology: Research that is community-based and politically involved.

affinal kin: People related through marriage.

age grade: An organized category of people based on age; every individual passes through a series of such categories over his or her lifetime.

age set: A formally established group of people born during a certain time span who move through the series of age-grade categories together.

alphabet: A series of symbols representing the sounds of a language arranged in a traditional order.

ambilocal residence: A residence pattern in which a married couple may choose either matrilocal or patrilocal residence.

analogies: In biology, structures possessed by different organisms that are superficially similar due to similar function; without sharing a common developmental pathway or structure.

animatism: A belief that nature is enlivened or energized by an impersonal spiritual power or supernatural potency.

animism: A belief that nature is enlivened or energized by distinct personalized spirit beings separable from bodies.

applied anthropology: The use of anthropological knowledge and methods to solve practical problems, often for a specific client.

archaeology: The study of human cultures through the recovery and analysis of material remains and environmental data.

art: The creative use of the human imagination to aesthetically interpret, express, and engage life, modifying experienced reality in the process.

Australopithecus: The genus including several species of early bipeds from southern, eastern, and central Africa (Chad) living between about 1.1 and 4.3 million years ago, one of whom was directly ancestral to humans.

balanced reciprocity: A mode of exchange in which the giving and the receiving are specific as to the value of the goods and the time of their delivery.

band: A relatively small and loosely organized kin-ordered group that inhabits a specific territory and that may split periodically into smaller extended family groups that are politically independent.

biocultural: Focusing on the interaction of biology and culture.

bipedalism: A special form of locomotion in which an organism walks upright on two feet—characteristic of humans and their ancestors.

bride-price: Money or valuable goods paid by the groom or his family to the bride's family upon marriage. Also called bride wealth.

cargo cult: A spiritual movement (especially noted in Melanesia) in reaction to disruptive contact with Western capitalism, promising resurrection of deceased relatives, destruction or enslavement of white foreigners, and the magical arrival of utopian riches.

carrying capacity: The number of people that the available resources can support at a given level of food-getting techniques.

caste: A closed social class in a stratified society in which membership is determined by birth and fixed for life.

chiefdom: A regional polity in which two or more local groups are organized under a single chief, who is at the head of a ranked hierarchy of people.

clan: An extended unilineal kinship group, often consisting of several lineages, whose members claim common descent from a remote ancestor, usually legendary or mythological.

code switching: Changing from one mode of language to another as the situation demands, whether from one language to another or from one dialect of a language to another.

common-interest association: An association that results from the act of joining based on sharing particular activities, objectives, values, or beliefs.

conjugal family: A family established through marriage.

consanguineal family: A family of "blood relatives" consisting of related women, their brothers, and the women's offspring.

consanguineal kin: Biologically related relatives, commonly referred to as blood relatives.

conspicuous consumption: A showy display of wealth for social prestige.

contagious magic: Magic based on the principle that things once in contact can influence each other after the contact is broken.

core values: Those values especially promoted by a particular culture.

cross cousin: Child of a mother's brother or a father's sister.

cultural adaptation: A complex of ideas, activities, and technologies that enable people to survive and even thrive.

cultural anthropology: Also known as social or sociocultural anthropology. The study of customary patterns in human behavior, thought, and feelings. It focuses on humans as culture-producing and culture-reproducing creatures.

cultural control: Control through beliefs and values deeply internalized in the minds of individuals.

cultural evolution: Culture change over time (not to be confused with progress).

cultural loss: The abandonment of an existing practice or trait.

cultural relativism: The thesis that one must suspend judgment of other people's practices in order to understand them in their own cultural terms.

cultural resource management (CRM): A branch of archaeology tied to government policies for the protection of cultural resources and involving surveying and/or excavating archaeological and historical remains threatened by construction or development.

culture: A society's shared and socially transmitted ideas, values, and perceptions, which are used to make sense of experience and which generate behavior and are reflected in that behavior.

culture area: A geographic region in which a number of societies follow similar patterns of life.

culture core: Cultural features that are fundamental in the society's way of making its living—including food-producing techniques, knowledge of available resources, and the work arrangements involved in applying those techniques to the local environment.

density of social relations: The number and intensity of interactions among the members of a camp.

dependence training: Child-rearing practices that foster compliance in the performance of assigned tasks and dependence on the domestic group, rather than reliance on oneself.

descent group: Any kinship group with a membership lineally descending from a real (historical) or fictional common ancestor.

dialects: Varying forms of a language that reflect particular regions, occupations, or social classes and that are similar enough to be mutually intelligible.

diffusion: The spread of certain ideas, customs, or practices from one culture to another.

digital ethnography: The use of digital technologies (audio and visual) for the collection, analysis, and representation of ethnographic data.

displacement: Referring to things and events removed in time and space.

divination: A magical procedure or spiritual ritual designed to find out about what is not knowable by ordinary means, such as foretelling the future by interpreting omens.

doctrine: An assertion of opinion or belief formally handed down by an authority as true and indisputable. Also known as dogma.

dowry: Payment of a woman's inheritance at the time of her marriage, either to her or to her husband.

ecosystem: A system, or a functioning whole, composed of both the natural environment and all the organisms living within it.

egalitarian societies: Societies in which everyone has about equal rank, access to, and power over basic resources.

EGO: The central person from whom the degree of each relationship is traced.

eliciting device: An activity or object used to draw out individuals and encourage them to recall and share information.

empirical: Based on observations of the world rather than on intuition or faith.

enculturation: The process by which a society's culture is transmitted from one generation to the next and individuals become members of their society.

endogamy: Marriage within a particular group or category of individuals.

epic: A long dramatic narrative recounting the celebrated deeds of a historic or legendary hero—often sung or recited in poetic language.

Eskimo system: Kinship reckoning in which the nuclear family is emphasized by specifically identifying the mother, father, brother, and sister, while lumping together all other relatives into broad categories such as uncle, aunt, and cousin. Also referred to as lineal system.

ethnic group: People who collectively and publicly identify themselves as a distinct group based on various cultural features such as shared ancestry and common origin, language, customs, and traditional beliefs.

ethnicity: This term, rooted in the Greek word *ethnikos* ("nation") and related to *ethnos* ("custom"), is the expression of the set of cultural ideas held by an ethnic group.

ethnic psychosis: A mental disorder specific to a particular ethnic group.

ethnocentrism: The belief that the ways of one's own culture are the only proper ones.

ethnocide: The violent eradication of an ethnic group's collective cultural identity as a distinctive people; occurs when a dominant society deliberately sets out to destroy another society's cultural heritage.

ethnographic fieldwork: Extended on-location research to gather detailed and in-depth information on a society's customary ideas, values, and practices through participation in its collective social life.

ethnography: A detailed description of a particular culture primarily based on fieldwork.

ethnohistory: A study of cultures of the recent past through oral histories, accounts of explorers, missionaries, and traders, and through analysis of records such as land titles, birth and death records, and other archival materials.

ethnolinguistics: A branch of linguistics that studies the relationships between language and culture and how they mutually influence and inform each other.

ethnology: The study and analysis of different cultures from a comparative or historical point of view, utilizing ethnographic accounts and developing anthropological theories that help explain why certain important differences or similarities occur among groups.

ethnomusicology: The study of a society's music in terms of its cultural setting.

evolution: Changes in the genetic makeup of a population over generations.

exogamy: Marriage outside the group.

extended family: Two or more closely related nuclear families clustered together into a large domestic group.

fictive marriage: Marriage by proxy to the symbols of someone not physically present to establish the social status of a spouse and heirs.

fieldwork: The term anthropologists use for on-location research.

fission: The splitting of a descent group into two or more new descent groups.

folklore: A term coined by 19th-century scholars studying the unwritten stories and other artistic traditions of rural peoples to distinguish between "folk art" and the "fine art" of the literate elite.

food foraging: Hunting, fishing, and gathering wild plant foods.

forensic anthropology: Applied subfield of physical anthropology that specializes in the identification of human skeletal remains for legal purposes.

formal interview: A structured question/answer session carefully notated as it occurs and based on prepared questions.

gender: The cultural elaborations and meanings assigned to the biological differentiation between the sexes.

gendered speech: Distinct male and female speech patterns, which vary across social and cultural settings.

generalized reciprocity: A mode of exchange in which the value of what is given is not calculated, nor is the time of repayment specified.

genes: The basic physical units of heredity that specify the biological traits and characteristics of each organism.

genocide: The physical extermination of one people by another, either as a deliberate act or as the accidental outcome of activities carried out by one people with little regard for their impact on others.

gesture: Facial expressions and bodily postures and motions that convey intended as well as subconscious messages.

globalization: Worldwide interconnectedness, evidenced in global movements of natural resources, trade goods, human labor, finance capital, information, and infectious diseases.

glottochronology: In linguistics, a method for identifying the approximate time that languages branched off from a common ancestor. It is based on analyzing core vocabularies.

grammar: The entire formal structure of a language, including morphology and syntax.

group marriage: Marriage in which several men and women have sexual access to one another. Also called co-marriage.

hard power: Coercive power that is backed up by economic and military force.

Hawaiian system: Kinship reckoning in which all relatives of the same sex and generation are referred to by the same term.

holistic perspective: A fundamental principle of anthropology: that the various parts of human culture and biology must be viewed in the broadest possible context in order to understand their interconnections and interdependence.

hominoid: The broad-shouldered tailless group of primates that includes all living and extinct apes and humans.

Homo erectus: "Upright human." A species within the genus *Homo* first appearing just after 2 million years ago in Africa and ultimately spreading throughout the Old World.

Homo habilis: "Handy human." The first fossil members of the genus *Homo* appearing 2.5 million years ago, with larger brains and smaller faces than australopithecines.

household: The basic residential unit where economic production, consumption, inheritance, child rearing, and shelter are organized and carried out.

Human Relations Area Files (HRAF): A vast collection of cross-indexed ethnographic and archaeological data catalogued by cultural characteristics and geographic locations. Archived in about 300 libraries (on microfiche and/or online).

iconic images: Culturally specific people, animals, and monsters seen in the deepest stage of trance.

idealist perspective: A theoretical approach stressing the primacy of superstructure in cultural research and analysis.

imitative magic: Magic based on the principle that like produces like; sometimes called sympathetic magic.

incest taboo: The prohibition of sexual relations between specified individuals, usually parent and child and sibling relations at a minimum.

incorporation: In rites of passage, reincorporation of the individual into society in his or her new status.

independence training: Child-rearing practices that promote independence, self-reliance, and personal achievement on the part of the child.

informal economy: Network of producing and circulating marketable commodities, labor, and services that for various reasons escape government control.

informal interview: An unstructured, open-ended conversation in every-day life.

informed consent: Formal, recorded agreement to participate in research.

infrastructure: The economic foundation of a society, including its subsistence practices and the tools and other material equipment used to make a living.

intersexual: A person born with reproductive organs, genitalia, and/or sex chromosomes that are not exclusively male or female.

Iroquois system: Kinship reckoning in which a father and father's brother are referred to by a single term, as are a mother and mother's sister, but a father's sister and mother's brother are given separate terms. Parallel cousins are classified with brothers and sisters, while cross cousins are classified separately but not equated with relatives of some other generation.

key consultant: A member of the society being studied, who provides information that helps researchers understand the meaning of what they observe; early anthropologists referred to such individuals as informants.

kindred: An individual's close blood relatives on the maternal and paternal sides of his or her family.

kinesics: A system of notating and analyzing postures, facial expressions, and bodily motions that convey messages.

kinship: A network of relatives within which individuals possess certain mutual rights and obligations.

Kula ring: A form of balanced reciprocity that reinforces trade relations among the seafaring Trobriand people, who inhabit a large ring of islands in the southwestern Pacific Ocean off the eastern coast of Papua New Guinea, and other Melanesians.

language: A system of communication using sounds or gestures that are put together in meaningful ways according to a set of rules.

language family: A group of languages descended from a single ancestral language.

law: Formal rules of conduct that, when violated, effectuate negative sanctions.

law of independent assortment: The Mendelian principle that genes controlling different traits are inherited independently of one another.

legend: A story about a memorable event or figure handed down by tradition and told as true but without historical evidence.

legitimacy: The right of political leaders to govern—to hold, use, and allocate power—based on the values a particular society holds.

leveling mechanism: A cultural obligation compelling prosperous members of a community to give away goods, host public feasts, provide free service, or otherwise demonstrate generosity so that no one permanently accumulates significantly more wealth than anyone else.

lineage: A unilineal kinship group descended from a common ancestor or founder who lived four to six generations ago, and in which relationships among members can be exactly stated in genealogical terms.

linguistic anthropology: The study of human languages, looking at their structure, history, and/or relation to social and cultural contexts.

linguistic determinism: The idea that language to some extent shapes the way in which we view and think about the world around us;

sometimes called the Sapir-Whorf hypothesis after its originators Edward Sapir and his student Benjamin Lee Whorf.

linguistic divergence: The development of different languages from a single ancestral language.

linguistic nationalism: The attempt by ethnic minorities and even countries to proclaim independence by purging their language of foreign terms.

linguistic relativity: The idea that distinctions encoded in one language are unique to that language.

linguistics: The modern scientific study of all aspects of language.

Lower Paleolithic: The first part of the Old Stone Age spanning from about 200,000 or 250,000 to 2.6 million years ago.

market exchange: The buying and selling of goods and services, with prices set by rules of supply and demand.

marriage: A culturally sanctioned union between two or more people that establishes certain rights and obligations between the people, between them and their children, and between them and their in-laws. Such marriage rights and obligations most often include, but are not limited to, sex, labor, property, child rearing, exchange, and status.

materialist perspective: A theoretical approach stressing the primacy of infrastructure (material conditions) in cultural research and analysis.

matrilineal descent: Descent traced exclusively through the female line to establish group membership.

matrilocal residence: A residence pattern in which a married couple lives in the wife's mother's place of residence.

modal personality: The body of character traits that occur with the highest frequency in a culturally bounded population.

modernization: The process of political and socioeconomic change, whereby developing societies acquire some of the cultural characteristics of Western industrial societies.

moiety: Each group that results from a division of a society into two halves on the basis of descent.

molecular anthropology: A branch of biological anthropology that uses genetic and biochemical techniques to test hypotheses about human evolution, adaptation, and variation.

money: Something used to make payments for other goods and services as well as to measure their value.

monogamy: Marriage in which both partners have just one spouse.

morpheme: The smallest unit of sound that carries a meaning in language. It is distinct from a phoneme, which can alter meaning but has no meaning by itself.

morphology: The study of the patterns or rules of word formation in a language (including such things as rules concerning verb tense, pluralization, and compound words). In biology, morphology refers to the shape or form of a structure.

motif: A story situation in a tale.

Mousterian: The tool industry found among Neandertals in Europe and Southwest Asia, and their human contemporaries in northern Africa, during the Middle Paleolithic, generally dating from about 40,000 to 125,000 years ago.

multiculturalism: Public policy for managing cultural diversity in a multi-ethnic society, officially stressing mutual respect and tolerance for cultural differences within a country's borders.

multiregional hypothesis: The hypothesis that modern humans originated through a process of simultaneous local transition from *Homo erectus* to *Homo sapiens* throughout the inhabited world.

multi-sited ethnography: The investigation and documentation of peoples and cultures embedded in the larger structures of a globalizing world, utilizing a range of methods in various locations of time and space.

myth: A sacred narrative that explains the fundamentals of human existence—where we and everything in our world came from, why we are here, and where we are going.

naming ceremony: A special event or ritual to mark the naming of a child.

nation: A people who share a collective identity based on a common culture, language, territorial base, and history.

natural selection: The principle or mechanism by which individuals having biological characteristics best suited to a particular environment survive and reproduce with greater frequency than individuals without those characteristics.

Neandertals: A distinct group within the genus *Homo* inhabiting Europe and Southwest Asia from approximately 30,000 to 125,000 years ago.

negative reciprocity: A form of exchange in which the aim is to get something for as little as possible. Neither fair nor balanced, it may involve hard bargaining, manipulation, and outright cheating.

Neolithic transition: Sometimes referred to as Neolithic revolution. The profound culture change beginning about 10,000 years ago and associated with the early domestication of plants and animals and settlement in villages.

neolocal residence: A pattern in which a married couple establish their household in a location apart from either the husband's or the wife's relatives.

new reproductive technologies (NRTs): Alternative means of reproduction such as surrogate motherhood and in vitro fertilization.

nuclear family: A group consisting of one or more parents and dependent offspring, which may include a stepparent, stepsiblings, and adopted children. (Until recently this term referred only to the father–mother–child(ren) unit.)

Oldowan: The first stone tool industry, beginning between 2.5 and 2.6 million years ago at the start of the Lower Paleolithic.

opposable: Able to bring the thumb or big toe in contact with the tips of the other digits on the same hand or foot in order to grasp objects.

paleoanthropologist: An anthropologist specializing in the study of human evolutionary history.

paleoanthropology: The study of the origins and predecessors of the present human species.

pantheon: The several gods and goddesses of a people.

paralanguage: Voice effects that accompany language and convey meaning. These include vocalizations such as giggling, groaning, or sighing, as well as voice qualities such as pitch and tempo.

parallel cousin: Child of a father's brother or a mother's sister.

parallel evolution: In cultural evolution, the development of similar cultural adaptations to similar environmental conditions by peoples whose ancestral cultures were already somewhat alike.

participant observation: In ethnography, the technique of learning a people's culture through social participation and personal observation within the community being studied, as well as interviews and discussion with individual members of the group over an extended period of time.

patrilineal descent: Descent traced exclusively through the male line to establish group membership.

patrilocal residence: A residence pattern in which a married couple lives in the husband's father's place of residence.

peasant: A rural cultivator whose surpluses are transferred to a dominant group of rulers that uses the surpluses both to underwrite its own standard of living and to distribute the remainder to groups in society that do not farm but must be fed for their specific goods and services in turn.

personality: The distinctive way a person thinks, feels, and behaves.

phoneme: The smallest unit of sound that makes a difference in meaning in a language.

phonetics: The systematic identification and description of distinctive speech sounds in a language.

phonology: The study of language sounds.

phratry: A unilineal descent group composed of at least two clans that supposedly share a common ancestry, whether or not they really do.

physical anthropology: Also known as biological anthropology. The systematic study of humans as biological organisms.

pluralistic society: A society in which two or more ethnic groups or nationalities are politically organized into one territorial state but maintain their cultural differences.

political organization: The way power is distributed and embedded in society; the means through which a society creates and maintains social order and reduces social disorder.

polyandry: Marriage of a woman to two or more men at one time; a form of polygamy.

polygamy: One individual having multiple spouses at the same time; from the Greek words *poly* ("many") and *gamous* ("marriage").

polygyny: Marriage of a man to two or more women at the same time; a form of polygamy.

polytheism: Belief in several gods and/or goddesses (as contrasted with monotheism—belief in one god or goddess).

potlatch: On the northwest coast of North America, a ceremonial event in which a village chief publicly gives away stockpiled food and other goods that signify wealth.

power: The ability of individuals or groups to impose their will upon others and make them do things even against their own wants or wishes.

pressure flaking: A technique of stone tool manufacture in which a bone, antler, or wooden tool is used to press, rather than strike off, small flakes from a piece of flint or similar stone.

priest or priestess: A full-time religious specialist formally recognized for his or her role in guiding the religious practices of others and for contacting and influencing supernatural powers.

primary innovation: The creation, invention, or chance discovery of a completely new idea, method, or device.

primate: The subgroup of mammals that includes lemurs, lorises, tarsiers, monkeys, apes, and humans.

primatologist: A specialist in the behavior and biology of living primates and their evolutionary history.

primatology: The study of living and fossil primates.

progress: The notion that humans are moving forward to a better, more advanced stage in their cultural development toward perfection.

proxemics: The cross-cultural study of humankind's perception and use of space.

qualitative data: Nonstatistical information such as personal life stories and customary beliefs and practices.

quantitative data: Statistical or measurable information, such as demographic composition, the types and quantities of crops grown, or the ratio of spouses born and raised within or outside the community.

race: In biology, a subgroup within a species, not scientifically applicable to humans because there exist no subspecies within modern *Homo sapiens*.

racism: A doctrine of superiority by which one group justifies the dehumanization of others based on their distinctive physical characteristics.

rebellion: Organized armed resistance to an established government or authority in power.

recent African origins hypothesis: The hypothesis that all modern people are derived from one single population of archaic *H. sapiens* from Africa who migrated out of Africa after 100,000 years ago, replacing all other archaic forms due to their superior cultural capabilities. Also called the "Eve" or "Out of Africa" hypothesis.

reciprocity: The exchange of goods and services, of approximately equal value, between two parties.

redistribution: A form of exchange in which goods flow into a central place, where they are sorted, counted, and reallocated.

religion: An organized system of ideas about the spiritual sphere or the supernatural, along with associated ceremonial practices by which people try to interpret and/or influence aspects of the universe otherwise beyond their control.

replacement reproduction: The point at which birthrates and death rates are in equilibrium; people producing only enough offspring to replace themselves when they die.

revitalization movement: A movement for radical cultural reform in response to widespread social disruption and collective feelings of great stress and despair.

revolution: Radical change in a society or culture. In the political arena, it involves the forced overthrow of an old government and establishment of a completely new one.

rite of intensification: A ritual that takes place during a crisis in the life of the group and serves to bind individuals together.

rite of passage: A ritual that marks an important stage in an individual's life cycle, such as birth, marriage, and death.

sanction: An externalized social control designed to encourage conformity to social norms.

savannah: Grasslands with scattered trees and groves, as in East Africa.

secondary innovation: A new and deliberate application or modification of an existing idea, method, or device.

self-awareness: The ability to identify oneself as an individual, to reflect on oneself, and to evaluate oneself.

separation: In rites of passage, the ritual removal of the individual from society.

serial monogamy: A marriage form in which a man or a woman marries or lives with a series of partners in succession.

shaman: A person who enters an altered state of consciousness—at will—to contact and utilize an ordinarily hidden reality in order to acquire knowledge, power, and to help others.

signal: An instinctive sound or gesture that has a natural or self-evident meaning.

silent trade: A form of barter in which no verbal communication takes place.

slash-and-burn cultivation: Also known as swidden farming. An extensive form of horticulture in which the natural vegetation is cut, the slash is subsequently burned, and crops are then planted among the ashes.

social class: A category of individuals in a stratified society who enjoy equal or nearly equal prestige according to the system of evaluation.

social control: External control through open coercion.

social mobility: Upward or downward change in one's social class position in a stratified society.

social structure: The rule-governed relationships—with all their rights and obligations—that hold members of a society together. This includes households, families, associations, and power relations, including politics.

society: An organized group or groups of interdependent people who generally share a common territory, language, and culture and who act together for collective survival and well-being.

sociolinguistics: The study of the relationship between language and society through examining how social categories (such as age, gender, ethnicity, religion, occupation, and class) influence the use and interpretation of distinctive styles of speech.

soft power: Co-optive power that presses others through attraction and persuasion to change their ideas, beliefs, values, and behaviors.

species: A population or group of populations having common attributes and the ability to interbreed and produce live, fertile offspring. Different species are reproductively isolated from one another.

spirituality: Concern with the sacred, as distinguished from material matters. In contrast to religion, spirituality is often individual rather than collective and does not require a distinctive format or traditional organization.

state: In anthropology, a centralized polity involving large numbers of people within a defined territory who are divided into social classes and organized and directed by a formal government that has the capacity and authority to make laws, and use force to defend the social order.

stratified societies: Societies in which people are hierarchically divided and ranked into social strata, or layers, and do not share equally in basic resources that support survival, influence, and prestige.

structural power: Power that organizes and orchestrates the systemic interaction within and among societies, directing economic and political forces on the one hand and ideological forces that shape public ideas, values, and beliefs on the other.

subculture: A distinctive set of standards and behavior patterns by which a group within a larger society operates, while still sharing common standards with that larger society.

superstructure: A society's shared sense of identity and worldview. The collective body of ideas, beliefs, and values by which a group of people makes sense of the world—its shape, challenges, and opportunities—and their place in it. This includes religion and national ideology.

swidden farming: Also known as slash-and-burn. An extensive form of horticulture in which the natural vegetation is cut, the slash is subsequently burned, and crops are then planted among the ashes.

symbol: A sign, sound, emblem, or other thing that is arbitrarily linked to something else and represents it in a meaningful way.

syncretism: In acculturation, the creative blending of indigenous and foreign beliefs and practices into new cultural forms.

syntax: The patterns or rules by which morphemes are arranged into phrases and sentences.

tale: A creative narrative that is recognized as fiction for entertainment but may also draw a moral or teach a practical lesson.

technology: Tools and other material equipment, together with the knowledge of how to make and use them.

tonality: In music, scale systems and their modifications.

tonal language: A language in which the sound pitch of a spoken word is an essential part of its pronunciation and meaning.

totemism: The belief that people are related to particular animals, plants, or natural objects by virtue of descent from common ancestral spirits.

tradition: Customary ideas and practices passed on from generation to generation, which in a modernizing society may form an obstacle to new ways of doing things.

transgender: A person who crosses over or occupies a culturally accepted intermediate position in the binary male–female gender construction.

transition: In rites of passage, isolation of the individual following separation and prior to incorporation into society.

tribe: In anthropology, refers to a range of kin-ordered groups that are politically integrated by some unifying factor and whose members share a common ancestry, identity, culture, language, and territory.

unilineal descent: Descent that establishes group membership exclusively through either the male or female line.

Upper Paleolithic: The last part (10,000–40,000 years ago) of the Old Stone Age, featuring tool industries characterized by long slim blades and an explosion of creative symbolic forms.

urgent anthropology: Ethnographic research that documents endangered cultures; also known as salvage ethnography.

witchcraft: An explanation of events based on the belief that certain individuals possess an innate psychic power capable of causing harm, including sickness and death.

worldview: The collective body of ideas that members of a culture generally share concerning the ultimate shape and substance of their reality.

writing system: A set of visible or tactile signs used to represent units of language in a systematic way.

Bibliography

Abbot, E. (2001). *A history of celibacy.* Cambridge, MA: Da Capo Press.

Aberle, D. F., Bronfenbrenner, U., Hess, E. H., Miller, D. R., Schneider, D. H., & Spuhler, J. N. (1963). The incest taboo and the mating patterns of animals. *American Anthropologist 65,* 253–265.

Abu-Lughod, L. (1986). *Veiled sentiments: Honor and poetry in a Bedouin society.* Berkeley: University of California Press.

Adams, R. M. (1966). *The evolution of urban society.* Chicago: Aldine.

Adams, R. M. (2001). Scale and complexity in archaic states. *Latin American Antiquity 11,* 188.

Adbusters. www.adbusters.org.

Alemseged, Z., et al. (2006, September 21). *Nature 443,* 296–301.

Alland, A., Jr. (1970). *Adaptation in cultural evolution: An approach to medical anthropology.* New York: Columbia University Press.

Alland, A., Jr. (1971). *Human diversity.* New York: Columbia University Press. Allen, J. L., & Shalinsky, A. C. (2004). *Student atlas of anthropology.* New York: McGraw-Hill.

Amábile-Cuevas, C. F., & Chicurel, M. E. (1993). Horizontal gene transfer. *American Scientist 81,* 332–341.

AMAP. (2003). *AMAP assessment 2002: Human health in the Arctic.* Oslo: Arctic Monitoring Assessment Project.

American Anthropological Association. (1998). Statement on "race." www.ameranthassn.org.

Amiran, R. (1965). The beginnings of pottery-making in the Near East. In F. R. Matson (Ed.), *Ceramics and man* (pp. 240–247). Viking Fund Publications in Anthropology, 41.

Anderson, A. (2002). Faunal collapse, landscape change, and settlement history in Remote Oceania. *World Archaeology 33* (3), 375–390.

Andrews, L. B., & Nelkin, D. (1996). The Bell Curve: A statement. *Science 271,* 13.

Angrosino, M. V. (2004). *Projects in ethnographic research.* Long Grove, IL: Waveland Press.

Appadurai, A. (1996). *Modernity at large: Cultural dimensions of globalization.* Minneapolis: University of Minnesota Press.

Appenzeller, T. (1998). Art: Evolution or revolution? *Science 282,* 1,451–1,454.

Armstrong, D. F., Stokoe, W. C., & Wilcox, S. E. (1993). Signs of the origin of syntax. *Current Anthropology 34,* 349–368.

Ashmore, W. (Ed.). (1981). *Lowland Maya settlement patterns.* Albuquerque: University of New Mexico Press.

Aureli, F., & de Waal, F. B. M. (2000). *Natural conflict resolution.* Berkeley: University of California Press.

Avedon, J. F. (1997). *In exile from the land of snows: The definitive account of the Dalai Lama and Tibet since the Chinese conquest.* New York: Harper.

Babiker, M. A., Alumran, K., Alshahri, A., Almadan, M., & Islam, F. (1996). Unnecessary deprivation of common food items in glucose-6-phosphate dehydrogenase deficiency. *Annals of Saudi Arabia 16* (4), 462–463.

Bailey, R. C., & Aunger, R. (1989). Net hunters vs. archers: Variation in women's subsistence strategies in the Ituri Forest. *Human Ecology 17,* 273–297.

Baker, P. (Ed.) (1978). *The biology of high altitude peoples.* London: Cambridge University Press.

Balandier, G. (1971). *Political anthropology.* New York: Pantheon.

Balikci, A. (1970). *The Netsilik Eskimo.* Garden City, NY: Natural History Press.

Balter, M. (1998). On world AIDS day, a shadow looms over southern Africa. *Science 282,* 1,790.

Balter, M. (1998). Why settle down? The mystery of communities. *Science 282,* 1,442–1,444.

Balter, M. (1999). A long season puts Çatalhöyük in context. *Science 286,* 890–891.

Balter, M. (2001). In search of the first Europeans. *Science 291,* 1,724.

Banton, M. (1968). Voluntary association: Anthropological aspects. In *International encyclopedia of the social sciences* (Vol. 16, pp. 357–362). New York: Macmillan.

Barber, B. (1957). *Social stratification.* New York: Harcourt.

Barham, L. S. (1998). Possible early pigment use in South-Central Africa. *Current Anthropology 39,* 703–710.

Barnett, H. (1953). *Innovation: The basis of cultural change.* New York: McGraw-Hill.

Barnouw, V. (1985). *Culture and personality* (4th ed.). Homewood, IL: Dorsey Press.

Barr, R. G. (1997, October). The crying game. *Natural History,* 47.

Barth, F. (1961). *Nomads of South Persia: The Basseri tribe of the Khamseh confederacy.* Boston: Little, Brown (series in anthropology).

Barth, F. (1962). Nomadism in the mountain and plateau areas of Southwest Asia. *The problems of the arid zone* (pp. 341–355). Paris: UNESCO.

Bar-Yosef, O. (1986), The walls of Jericho: An alternative interpretation. *Current Anthropology 27,* 160.

Bar-Yosef, O., Vandermeersch, B., Arensburg, B., Belfer-Cohen, A., Goldberg, P., Laville, H., Meignen, L., Rak, Y., Speth, J. D., Tchernov, E., Tillier, A-M., & Weiner, S. (1992). The excavations in Kebara Cave, Mt. Carmel. *Current Anthropology 33,* 497–550.

Bascom, W. (1969). *The Yoruba of southwestern Nigeria.* New York: Holt, Rinehart & Winston.

Bates, D. G. (2001). *Human adaptive strategies: Ecology, culture, and politics* (2nd ed.). Boston: Allyn & Bacon.

Bates, D. G., & Plog, F. (1991). *Human adaptive strategies.* New York: McGraw-Hill.

Beeman, W. O. (2000). Introduction: Margaret Mead, cultural studies, and international understanding. In M. Mead & R. Métraux (Eds.), *The study of culture at a distance* (pp. xiv–xxxi). New York and Oxford: Berghahn Books.

Behrend, H., & Luig, U. (Eds.) (2000). *Spirit possession, modernity, and power in Africa.* Madison: University of Wisconsin Press.

Belshaw, C. S. (1958). The significance of modern cults in Melanesian development. In W. Lessa & E. Z. Vogt (Eds.), *Reader in comparative religion: An anthropological approach.* New York: Harper & Row.

Benedict, R. (1959). *Patterns of culture.* New York: New American Library.

Blackless, M., et al. (2000). How sexually dimorphic are we? Review and synthesis. *American Journal of Human Biology 12,* 151–166.

Blakey, M. (2003). *African Burial Ground Project.* Department of Anthropology, College of William & Mary.

Blok, A. (1974). *The mafia of a Sicilian village 1860–1960.* New York: Harper & Row.

Blok, A. (1981). Rams and billy-goats: A key to the Mediterranean code of honour. *Man, New Series 16* (3), 427–440.

Blumberg, R. L. (1991). *Gender, family, and the economy: The triple overlap.* Newbury Park, CA: Sage.

Blumer, M. A., & Byrne, R. (1991). The ecological genetics and domestication and the origins of agriculture. *Current Anthropology 32,* 30.

Boas, F. (1962). *Primitive art.* Gloucester, MA: Peter Smith.

Boas, F. (1966). *Race, language and culture.* New York: Free Press.

Bodley, J. H. (1985). *Anthropology and contemporary human problems* (2nd ed.). Palo Alto, CA: Mayfield.

Bodley, J. H. (1990). *Victims of progress* (3rd ed.). Mountain View, CA: Mayfield.

Boehm, C. (1984). *Blood revenge.* Lawrence: University of Kansas Press.

Boehm, C. (2000). The evolution of moral communities. *School of American Research, 2000 Annual Report,* 7.

Bogucki, P. (1999). *The origins of human society.* Oxford, England: Blackwell.

Bohannan, P. (Ed.) (1967). *Law and warfare: Studies in the anthropology of conflict.* Garden City, NY: Natural History Press.

Bohannan, P., & Middleton, J. (Eds.) (1968). *Kinship and social organization.* Garden City, NY: Natural History Press (American Museum Source Books in Anthropology).

Bohannan, P., & Middleton, J. (Eds.) (1968). *Marriage, family, and residence.* Garden City, NY: Natural History Press (American Museum Source Books in Anthropology).

Bolinger, D. (1968). *Aspects of language.* New York: Harcourt.

Bongaarts, J. (1998). Demographic consequences of declining fertility. *Science 182,* 419.

Bonvillain, N. (2000). *Language, culture, and communication: The meaning of messages* (3rd ed.). Upper Saddle River, NJ: Prentice-Hall.

Bordes, F. (1972). *A tale of two caves.* New York: Harper & Row.

Bornstein, M. H. (1975). The influence of visual perception on culture. *American Anthropologist 77* (4), 774–798.

Boshara, R. (2003, January/February). Wealth inequality: The $6,000 solution. *Atlantic Monthly.*

Bowen, J. R. (2004). *Religions in practice: An approach to the anthropology of religion* (3rd ed.). Boston: Allyn & Bacon.

Bowie, F. (2006). *The anthropology of religion: An introduction* (2nd ed.). Malden, MA: Blackwell.

Brace, C. L. (1981). Tales of the phylogenetic woods: The evolution and significance of phylogenetic trees. *American Journal of Physical Anthropology 56,* 411–429.

Bradfield, R. M. (1998). *A natural history of associations* (2nd ed.). New York: International Universities Press.

Bradford, P. V., & Blume, H. (1992). *Ota Benga: The pygmy in the zoo.* New York: St. Martin's Press.

Braidwood, R. J. (1960). The agricultural revolution. *Scientific American 203,* 130–141.

Brain, C. K. (1969). The contribution of Namib Desert Hottentots to an understanding of australopithecine bone accumulations. *Scientific Papers of the Namib Desert Research Station,* 13.

Branda, R. F., & Eatoil, J. W. (1978). Skin color and photolysis: An evolutionary hypothesis. *Science 201,* 625–626.

Brettell, C. B., & Sargent, C. F. (Eds.) (2000). *Gender in cross-cultural perspective* (3rd ed.). Upper Saddle River, NJ: Prentice-Hall.

Brew, J. O. (1968). *One hundred years of anthropology.* Cambridge, MA: Harvard University Press.

Brody, H. (1981). *Maps and dreams.* New York: Pantheon Books.

Broecker, W. S. (1992, April). Global warming on trial. *Natural History,* 14.

Brown, D. E. (1991). *Human universals.* New York: McGraw-Hill.

Brues, A. M. (1977). *People and races.* New York: Macmillan.

Buck, P. H. (1938). *Vikings of the Pacific.* Chicago: University Press of Chicago.

Burling, R. (1969). Linguistics and ethnographic description. *American Anthropologist 71,* 817–827.

Burling, R. (1970). *Man's many voices: Language in its cultural context.* New York: Holt, Rinehart & Winston.

Carneiro, R. L. (1970). A theory of the origin of the state. *Science 169,* 733–738.

Carneiro, R. L. (2003). *Evolutionism in cultural anthropology: A critical history.* Boulder, CO: Westview Press.

Caroulis, J. (1996). Food for thought. *Pennsylvania Gazette 95* (3),16.

Carsten, J. (Ed.) (2000). *Cultures of relatedness: New approaches to the study of kinship.* Cambridge, England: Cambridge University Press.

Cartmill, M. (1998). The gift of gab. *Discover 19* (11), 64.

Catford, J. C. (1988). *A practical introduction to phonetics.* Oxford, England: Clarendon Press.

Caton, S. C. (1999). *Lawrence of Arabia: A film's anthropology.* Berkeley: University of California Press.

Cavalli-Sforza, L. L. (1977). *Elements of human genetics.* Menlo Park, CA: W. A. Benjamin.

Chagnon, N. A. (1988). Life histories, blood revenge, and warfare in a tribal population. *Science 239,* 935–992.

Chambers, R. (1983). *Rural development: Putting the last first.* New York: Longman.

Chang, L. (2005, June 9). A migrant worker sees rural home in new light. *Wall Street Journal.*

Chapple, E. D. (1970). *Cultural and biological man: Explorations in behavioral anthropology.* New York: Holt, Rinehart & Winston.

Chase, C. (1998). Hermaphrodites with attitude. *Gay and Lesbian Quarterly 4* (2), 189–211.

Chasin, B. H., & Franke, R. W. (1983). US farming: A world model? *Global Reporter 1* (2), 10.

Chatty, D. (1996). *Mobile pastoralists: Development planning and social change in Oman.* New York: Columbia University Press.

Cheater, A. (2005). *The anthropology of power.* London: Routledge.

Chicurel, M. (2001). Can organisms speed their own evolution? *Science 292,* 1,824–1,827.

Childe, V. G. (1951). *Man makes himself.* New York: New American Library. (orig. 1936)

Childe, V. G. (1954). *What happened in history.* Baltimore: Penguin.

Clark, E. E. (1966). *Indian legends of the Pacific Northwest.* Berkeley: University of California Press.

Clark, W. E. L. (1960). *The antecedents of man.* Chicago: Quadrangle Books.

Clottes, J., & Bennett, G. (2002). *World rock art* (conservation and cultural heritage series). San Francisco: Getty Trust Publication.

Coe, S. D., & Coe, M. D. (1996). *The true history of chocolate.* New York: Thames and Hudson.

Cohen, J. (1997). Is an old virus up to new tricks? *Science 277,* 312–313.

Cohen, M. N. (1995). Anthropology and race: The Bell Curve phenomenon. *General Anthropology 2*(1), 1–4.

Cohen, M. N. (1998). *Culture of intolerance: Chauvinism, class, and racism in the United States.* New Haven, CT: Yale University Press.

Cohen, M. N., & Armelagos, G. J. (1984). *Paleopathology at the origins of agriculture.* Orlando: Academic Press.

Colborn, T., et al. (1997). *Our stolen future.* New York: Plume/Penguin Books.

Colburn, T., Dumanoski, D., & Myers, J. P. (1996). Hormonal sabotage. *Natural History 3,* 45–46.

Cole, J. W., & Wolf, E. R. (1999). *The hidden frontier: Ecology and ethnicity in an alpine valley* (with a new introduction). Berkeley: University of California Press.

Cole, S. (1975). *Leakey's luck: The life of Louis Seymour Bazett Leakey. 1903–1972.* New York: Harcourt Brace Jovanovich.

Collier, J., & Collier, M. (1986). *Visual anthropology: Photography as a research method.* Albuquerque: University of New Mexico Press.

Collier, J., Rosaldo, M. Z., & Yanagisako, S. (1982). Is there a family? New anthropological views. In B. Thorne & M. Yalom (Eds.), *Rethinking the family: Some feminist questions* (pp. 25–39). New York: Longman.

Collier, J. F., & Yanagisako, S. J. (Eds.) (1987). *Gender and kinship: Essays toward a unified analysis.* Stanford, CA: Stanford University Press.

Cone, M. (2005) *Silent snow: The slow poisoning of the Arctic.* New York: Grove Press.

Connelly, J. C. (1979). Hopi social organization. In A. Ortiz (Ed.), *Handbook of North American Indians, Vol. 9, Southwest* (pp. 539–553). Washington, DC: Smithsonian Institution.

Conner, M. (1996). The archaeology of contemporary mass graves. *SAA Bulletin 14* (4), 6, 31.

Coon, C. S. (Ed.) (1948). *A reader in general anthropology.* New York: Holt, Rinehart & Winston.

Coon, C. S. (1954). *The story of man.* New York: Knopf.

Coon, C. S. (1958). *Caravan: The story of the Middle East* (2nd ed.). New York: Holt, Rinehart & Winston.

Coontz, S. (2005). *Marriage, a history: From obedience to intimacy, or how love conquered marriage.* New York: Viking Adult.

Cornwell, T. (1995, November 10). Skeleton staff. *Times Higher Education,* 20.

Courlander, H. (1971). *The fourth world of the Hopis.* New York: Crown.

Court says same-sex marriage is a right. (2004, February 5). *San Francisco Chronicle.*

Cowgill, G. L. (1980). Letter, *Science 210,* 1,305.

Cowgill, G. L. (1997). State and society at Teotihuacan, Mexico. *Annual Review of Anthropology 26,* 129–161.

Crane, H. (2001). *Men in spirit: The masculinization of Taiwanese Buddhist nuns.* Doctoral dissertation, Brown University.

Crane, L. B., Yeager, E., & Whitman, R. L. (1981). *An introduction to linguistics.* Boston: Little, Brown.

Cretney, S. (2003). *Family law in the twentieth century: A history.* New York: Oxford University Press.

Crocker, W. H., & Crocker, J. G. (1994). *The Canela, bonding through kinship, ritual, and sex.* Fort Worth: Harcourt Brace.

Crocker, W. H., & Crocker, J. G. (2004). *The Canela: Kinship, ritual, and sex in an Amazonian tribe.* Belmont, CA: Wadsworth.

Culbert, T. P. (Ed.) (1973). *The Classic Maya collapse.* Albuquerque: University of New Mexico Press.

Culotta, E., & Koshland, D. E., Jr. (1994). DNA repair works its way to the top. *Science 266,* 1,926.

Cultural Survival Quarterly. (1991). *15* (4), 5.

Cultural Survival Quarterly. (1991). *15* (4), 38.

Current population survey. (2002). U.S. Census Bureau.

Dalton, G. (Ed.) (1967). *Tribal and peasant economics: Readings in economic anthropology.* Garden City, NY: Natural History Press.

Dalton, G. (1971). *Traditional tribal and peasant economics: An introductory survey of economic anthropology.* Reading, MA: Addison-Wesley.

Daniel, G. (1975). *A hundred and fifty years of archaeology* (2nd ed.). London: Duckworth.

Darwin, C. (1936). *The descent of man and selection in relation to sex.* New York: Random House (Modern Library). (orig. 1871)

Darwin, C. (1967). *On the origin of species.* New York: Atheneum. (orig. 1859).

Davenport, W. (1959). Linear descent and descent groups. *American Anthropologist 61,* 557–573.

Davies, G. (2005). *A history of money from the earliest times to present day* (3rd ed.). Cardiff: University of Wales Press.

Davis, S. H. (1982). *Victims of the miracle.* Cambridge, England: Cambridge University Press.

Deevy, E. S., Jr. (1960). The human population. *Scientific American 203,* 194–204.

de Laguna, F. (1977). *Voyage to Greenland: A personal initiation into anthropology.* New York: Norton.

del Carmen Rodríguez Martínez, M., et al. (2006). Oldest writing in the New World. *Science 313* (5793), 1,610–1,614.

del Castillo, B. D. (1963). *The conquest of New Spain* (translation and introduction by J. M. Cohen). New York: Penguin.

DeMello, M. (2000). *Bodies of inscription: A cultural history of the modern tattoo community.* Durham: Duke University Press.

d'Errico, F., Zilhão, J., Julien, M., Baffier, D., & Pelegrin, J. (1998). Neandertal acculturation in Western Europe? *Current Anthropology 39,* 521.

Desowitz, R. S. (1987). *New Guinea tapeworms and Jewish grandmothers.* New York: Norton.

Dettwyler, K. A. (1994). *Dancing skeletons: Life and death in West Africa.* Prospect Heights, IL: Waveland Press.

Dettwyler, K. A. (1997, October). When to wean. *Natural History*, 49.

de Waal, F. B. M. (1998). Comment. *Current Anthropology 39*, 407.

de Waal, F. B. M., Kano, T., & Parish, A. R. (1998). Comments. *Current Anthropology 39*, 408, 410, 413.

Diamond, J. (1996). Empire of uniformity. *Discover 17* (3), 83–84.

Diamond, J. (1997). The curse of QWERTY. *Discover 18* (4), 34–42.

Diamond, J. (1997). *Guns, germs, and steel.* New York: Norton.

Diamond, J. (1998). Ants, crops, and history. *Science 281*, 1,974–1,975.

Dicks, B., et al. (2005). *Qualitative research and hypermedia: Ethnography for the digital age (New technologies for social research).* Thousand Oaks, CA: Sage.

Dirie, W., & Miller, C. (1998). *Desert flower: The extraordinary journey of a desert nomad.* New York: William Morrow.

Dissanayake, E. (2000). Birth of the arts. *Natural History 109* (10), 89.

Dobyns, H. F., Doughty, P. L., & Lasswell, H. D. (Eds.). (1971). *Peasants, power, and applied social change.* London: Sage.

Doist, R. (1997). Molecular evolution and scientific inquiry, misperceived. *American Scientist 85*, 475.

Dozier, E. (1970). *The Pueblo Indians of North America.* New York: Holt, Rinehart & Winston.

Draper, P. (1975). !Kung women: Contrasts in sexual egalitarianism in foraging and sedentary contexts. In R. Reiter (Ed.), *Toward an anthropology of women* (pp. 77–109). New York: Monthly Review Press.

Driver, H. (1964). *Indians of North America.* Chicago: University of Chicago Press.

Dubos, R. (1968). *So human an animal.* New York: Scribner.

Dumurat-Dreger, A. (1998, May/June). "Ambiguous sex" or ambivalent medicine? *The Hastings Center Report 28* (3), 2,435 (posted on the Intersex Society of North America website: www.isna.org).

Duncan, A. S., Kappelman, J., & Shapiro, L. J. (1994). Metasophalangeal joint function and positional behavior in *Australopithecus afarensis. American Journal of Physical Anthropology 93*, 67–81.

Dundes, A. (1980). *Interpreting folklore.* Bloomington: Indiana University Press.

Durant, J. C. (2000, April 23). Everybody into the gene pool. *New York Times Book Review,* 11.

Duranti, A. (2001). Linguistic anthropology: History, ideas, and issues. In A. Duranti (Ed.), *Linguistic anthropology: A reader* (pp. 1–38). Oxford: Blackwell.

Durkheim, E. (1964). *The division of labor in society.* New York: Free Press. (orig. 1893)

Durkheim, E. (1965). *The elementary forms of the religious life.* New York: Free Press. (orig. 1912)

duToit, B. M. (1991). *Human sexuality: Cross cultural readings.* New York: McGraw-Hill.

Eastman, C. M. (1990). *Aspects of language and culture* (2nd ed.). Novato, CA: Chandler & Sharp.

Edwards, J. (Ed.) (1999). *Technologies of procreation: Kinship in the age of assisted conception.* New York: Routledge (distributed by St. Martin's Press).

Egan, T. (1999, February 28). The persistence of polygamy. *New York Times Magazine,* 52.

Eisenstadt, S. N. (1956). *From generation to generation: Age groups and social structure.* New York: Free Press.

El Guindi, F. (2004). *Visual anthropology: Essential method and theory.* Walnut Creek, CA: Altamira Press.

Elkin, A. P. (1964). *The Australian Aborigines.* Garden City, NY: Doubleday/Anchor Books.

Ellis, C. (2006). *A dancing people: Powwow culture on the southern plains.* Lawrence: University Press of Kansas.

Ellison, P. T. (1990). Human ovarian function and reproductive ecology: New hypotheses. *American Anthropologist 92*, 933–952.

Ember, C. R., & Ember, M. (1996). What have we learned from cross-cultural research? *General Anthropology 2* (2), 5.

Enard, W., et al. (2002). Molecular evolution of FOXP2, a gene involved in speech and language. *Nature 418*, 869–872.

Ervin-Tripp, S. (1973). *Language acquisition and communicative choice.* Stanford, CA: Stanford University Press.

Esber, G. S., Jr. (1987). Designing Apache houses with Apaches. In R. M. Wulff & S. J. Fiske (Eds.), *Anthropological praxis: Translating knowledge into action* (pp. 187–196). Boulder, CO: Westview Press.

Eugenides, J. (2002). *Middlesex: A novel.* New York: Farrar, Straus and Giroux.

Evans-Pritchard, E. E. (1951). *Kinship and marriage among the Nuer.* New York: Oxford University Press.

Evans-Pritchard, E. E. (1968). *The Nuer: A description of the modes of livelihood and political institutions of a Nilotic people.* London: Oxford University Press.

Fagan, B. M. (1995). *People of the earth* (8th ed.). New York: HarperCollins.

Fagan, B. M. (1999). *Archeology: A brief introduction* (7th ed.). New York: Longman.

Fagan, B. M., Beck, C., & Silberman, N. A. (1998). *The Oxford companion to archaeology.* New York: Oxford University Press.

Farmer, P. (1992). *AIDS and accusation: Haiti and the geography of blame.* Berkeley: University of California Press.

Farmer, P. (2001). *Infections and inequalities: The modern plagues* (updated edition with a new preface). Berkeley: University of California Press.

Farnell, B. (1995). *Do you see what I mean? Plains Indian sign talk and the embodiment of action.* Austin: University of Texas Press.

Fausto-Sterling, A. (1993, March/April). The five sexes: Why male and female are not enough. *The Sciences 33* (2), 20–24.

Fausto-Sterling, A. (2000, July/August). The five sexes revisited. *The Sciences 40* (4), 19–24.

Fausto-Sterling, A. (2003, August 2). Personal e-mail communication.

Feder, K. L. (1999). *Frauds, myths, and mysteries* (3rd ed.). Mountain View, CA: Mayfield.

Female genital mutilation. (2000). Fact sheet no. 241. World Health Organization.

Ferrie, H. (1997). An interview with C. Loring Brace. *Current Anthropology 38*, 851–869.

Field, L. W. (2004). Beyond "applied" anthropology. In T. Biolsi (Ed.), *A companion to the anthropology of American Indians* (pp. 472–489). Oxford: Blackwell Publishing.

Finkler, K. (2000). *Experiencing the new genetics: Family and kinship on the medical frontier.* Philadelphia: University of Pennsylvania Press.

The first Americans, ca. 20,000 B.C. (1998). *Discover 19* (6), 24.

Firth, R. (1946). *Malay fishermen: Their peasant economy.* London: Kegan Paul, Trench, Trubner & Co., Ltd.

Firth, R. (1952). *Elements of social organization.* London: Watts.

Firth, R. (1957). *Man and culture: An evaluation of Bronislaw Malinowski.* London: Routledge.

Firth, R. (Ed.) (1967). *Themes in economic anthropology.* London: Tavistock.

Fisher, R., & Ury, W. L. (1991). *Getting to yes: Negotiating agreement without giving in* (2nd ed.). Boston: Houghton Mifflin.

Flannery, K. V. (1973). The origins of agriculture. In B. J. Siegel, A. R. Beals, & S. A. Tyler (Eds.), *Annual Review of Anthropology* (Vol. 2, pp. 271–310). Palo Alto, CA: Annual Reviews.

Forbes, J. D. (1964). *The Indian in America's past.* Englewood Cliffs, NJ: Prentice-Hall.

Forbes International 500 List. (2003).

Forde, C. D. (1955). The Nupe. In D. Forde (Ed.), *Peoples of the Niger-Benue confluence.* London: International African Institute (Ethnographic Survey of Africa. Western Africa, part 10).

Forde, C. D. (1968). Double descent among the Yakö. In P. Bohannan & J. Middleton (Eds.), *Kinship and social organization* (pp. 179–191). Garden City, NY: Natural History Press.

Fortes, M. (1950). Kinship and marriage among the Ashanti. In A. R. Radcliffe-Brown & C. D. Forde (Eds.), *African systems of kinship and marriage.* London: Oxford University Press.

Fortes, M. (1969). *Kinship and the social order: The legacy of Lewis Henry Morgan.* Chicago: Aldine.

Fortes, M., & Evans-Prichard, E. E. (Eds.) (1962). *African political systems.* London: Oxford University Press. (orig. 1940)

Foster, G. M. (1955). Peasant society and the image of the limited good. *American Anthropologist 67*, 293–315.

Fountain, H. (2000, January 30). Now the ancient ways are less mysterious. *New York Times,* News of the Week, 5.

Fox, R. (1968). *Kinship and marriage in an anthropological perspective.* Baltimore: Penguin.

Fox, R. (1981, December 3). [Interview]. Coast Telecourses, Inc., Los Angeles.

Frake, C. (1961). The diagnosis of disease among the Subinam of Mindinao. *American Anthropologist 63*, 113–132.

Frazer, Sir J. G. (1961 reissue). *The new golden bough.* New York: Doubleday, Anchor Books.

Freeman, J. D. (1960). The Iban of western Borneo. In G. P. Murdock (Ed.), *Social structure in Southeast Asia.* Chicago: Quadrangle Books.

Freeman, L. G. (1992). *Ambrona and Torralba: New evidence and interpretation.* Paper presented at the 91st Annual Meeting, American Anthropological Association.

Fried, M. (1967). *The evolution of political society: An essay in political anthropology.* New York: Random House.

Fried, M., Harris, M., & Murphy, R. (1968). *War: The anthropology of armed conflict and aggression.* Garden City, NY: Natural History Press.

Friedl, E. (1975). *Women and men: An anthropologist's view.* New York: Holt, Rinehart & Winston.

Friedman, J. (Ed.) (2003). *Globalization, the state, and violence.* Walnut Creek, CA: Altamira Press.

Frisch, R. (2002). *Female fertility and the body fat connection.* Chicago: University of Chicago Press.

Fritz, G. J. (1994). Are the first American farmers getting younger? *Current Anthropology 35*, 305–309.

Frye, D. P. (2000). Conflict management in cross-cultural perspective. In F. Aureli & F. B. M. de Waal, *Natural conflict resolution* (pp. 334–351). Berkeley: University of California Press.

Furst, P. T. (1976). *Hallucinogens and culture* (p. 7). Novato, CA: Chandler & Sharp.

Gardner, R. A., Gardner, B. T., & Van Cantfort, T. E. (Eds.) (1989). *Teaching sign language to chimpanzees.* Albany: State University of New York Press.

Gamst, F. C., & Norbeck, E. (1976). *Ideas of culture: Sources and uses.* New York: Holt, Rinehart & Winston.

Garn, S. M. (1970). *Human races* (3rd ed.). Springfield, IL: Charles C Thomas.

Gates, H. (1996). Buying brides in China—again. *Anthropology Today 12* (4), 10.

Geertz, C. (1965). The impact of the concept of culture on the concept of man. In J. R. Platt (Ed.), *New views of man.* Chicago: University of Chicago Press.

Geertz, C. (1973). *The interpretation of culture.* London: Hutchinson.

Geertz, C. (1984). Distinguished lecture: Anti-relativism. *American Anthropologist 86*, 263–278.

Gell, A. (1988). Technology and magic. *Anthropology Today 4* (2), 6–9.

Gene study suggests Polynesians came from Taiwan. (2005, July 4). Reuters.

Gibbons, A. (1993). Where are new diseases born? *Science 261*, 680–681.

Gibbons, A. (2001). The riddle of coexistence. *Science 291*, 1,726.

Gibbons, A. (2001). Studying humans—and their cousins and parasites. *Science 292*, 627.

Gibbs, J. L., Jr. (1965). The Kpelle of Liberia. In J. L. Gibbs, Jr. (Ed.), *Peoples of Africa* (pp. 216–218). New York: Holt, Rinehart & Winston.

Gibbs, J. L., Jr. (1983). [Interview]. *Faces of culture: Program 18.* Fountain Valley, CA: Coast Telecourses.

Giddens, A. (1990). *The consequences of modernity.* Stanford, CA: Stanford University Press.

Ginsburg, F. D., Abu-Lughod, L., & Larkin, B. (Eds.) (2002). *Media worlds: Anthropology on new terrain.* Berkeley: University of California Press.

Gladdol, D. (2006). *English next.* London: British Council.

Gledhill, J. (2000). *Power and its disguises: Anthropological perspectives on politics* (2nd ed.). Boulder, CO: Pluto Press.

Godfrey, T. (2000, December 27). Biotech threatening biodiversity. *Burlington Free Press*, 10A.

Godlier, M. (1971). Salt currency and the circulation of commodities among the Baruya of New Guinea. In G. Dalton (Ed.), *Studies in economic anthropology.* Washington, DC: American Anthropological Association (Anthropological Studies No. 7).

Goodall, J. (2000). *Reason for hope: A spiritual journey.* New York: Warner Books.

Goodenough, W. (Ed.). (1964). *Explorations in cultural anthropology: Essays in honor of George Murdock.* New York: McGraw–Hill.

Goodenough, W. (1965). Rethinking status and role: Toward a general model of the cultural organization of social relationships. In M. Benton (Ed.), *The relevance of models for social anthropology.* New York: Praeger (ASA Monographs l).

Goodenough, W. (1970). *Description and comparison in cultural anthropology.* Chicago: Aldine.

Goodenough, W. H. (1990). Evolution of the human capacity for beliefs. *American Anthropologist 92*, 601.

Goodman, A., & Armelagos, G. J. (1985). Death and disease at Dr. Dickson's mounds. *Natural History 94* (9), 12–18.

Goody, J. (1969). *Comparative studies in kinship.* Stanford, CA: Stanford University Press.

Goody, J. (1976). *Production and reproduction: A comparative study of the domestic domain.* Cambridge: Cambridge University Press.

Goody, J. (1983). *The development of the family and marriage in Europe.* Cambridge, MA: Cambridge University Press.

Gordon, R. J. (1992). *The Bushman myth: The making of a Namibian underclass.* Boulder, CO: Westview Press.

Gordon, R. J., & Megitt, M. J. (1985). *Law and order in the New Guinea highlands.* Hanover, NH: University Press of New England.

Gould, S. J. (1983). *Hen's teeth and horses' toes.* New York: Norton.

Gould, S. J. (1985). *The flamingo's smile: Reflections in natural history.* New York: Norton.

Gould, S. J. (1989). *Wonderful life.* New York: Norton.

Gould, S. J. (1994). The geometer of race. *Discover 15* (11), 65–69.

Gould, S. J. (1996). *Full house: The spread of excellence from Plato to Darwin.* New York: Harmony Books.

Gould, S. J. (1996). *The mismeasure of man* (2nd ed.). New York: Norton.

Graburn, N. H. H. (1969). *Eskimos without igloos: Social and economic development in Sugluk.* Boston: Little, Brown.

Graburn, N. H. (1971). *Readings in kinship and social structure.* New York: Harper & Row.

Graves, J. L. (2001). *The emperor's new clothes: Biological theories of race at the millennium.* New Brunswick, NJ: Rutgers University Press.

Gray, P. M., Krause, B., Atema, J., Payne, R., Krumhansl, C., & Baptista, L. (2001). The music of nature and the nature of music. *Science 291*, 52.

Greenberg, J. H. (1968). *Anthropological linguistics: An introduction.* New York: Random House.

Grivetti, L. E. (2005). From aphrodisiac to health food: A cultural history of chocolate. *Karger Gazette*, 68.

Guillette, E. A., et al. (1998, June). An anthropological approach to the evaluation of preschool children exposed to pesticides in Mexico. *Environmental Health Perspectives 106*, 347.

Guthrie, S. (1993). *Faces in the clouds: A new theory of religions.* New York: Oxford University Press.

Gutin, J. A. (1995). Do Kenya tools root birth of modern thought in Africa? *Science 270*, 1,118–1,119.

Hafkin, N., & Bay, E. (Eds.) (1976). *Women in Africa.* Stanford, CA: Stanford University Press.

Hall, E. T. (1959). *The silent language.* Garden City, NY: Anchor Press/Doubleday.

Hall, E. T., & Hall, M. R. (1986). The sounds of silence. In E. Angeloni (Ed.), *Anthropology 86/87* (pp. 65–70). Guilford, CT: Dushkin.

Hallowell, A. I. (1955). *Culture and experience.* Philadelphia: University of Pennsylvania Press.

Halperin, R. H. (1994). *Cultural economies: Past and present.* Austin: University of Texas Press.

Halverson, J. (1989). Review of the book *Altimira Revisited and other essays on early art. American Antiquity 54*, 883.

Hannah, J. L. (1988). *Dance, sex and gender.* Chicago: University of Chicago Press.

Hanson, A. (1989). The making of the Maori: Culture invention and its logic. *American Anthropologist 91* (4), 890–902.

Harner, M. (1980). *The way of the shaman: A guide to power and healing.* San Francisco: Harper & Row.

Harpending, J. H., & Harpending, H. C. (1995). Ancient differences in population can mimic a recent African origin of modern humans. *Current Anthropology, 36*, 667–674.

Harris, M. (1965). The cultural ecology of India's sacred cattle. *Current Anthropology 7*, 51–66.

Harris, M. (1968). *The rise of anthropological theory: A history of theories of culture.* New York: Crowell.

Harris, M. (1979). *Cultural materialism: The struggle for a science of culture.* New York: Random House.

Harris, M. (1989). *Cows, pigs, wars, and witches: The riddles of culture.* New York: Vintage Books/Random House.

Harrison, G. G. (1975). Primary adult lactase deficiency: A problem in anthropological genetics. *American Anthropologist 77*, 815–819.

Hart, C. W., Pilling, A. R., & Goodale, J. (1988). *Tiwi of North Australia* (3rd ed.). New York: Holt, Rinehart & Winston.

Hart, D. (2006, April 21). Humans as prey. *Chronicle of Higher Education.*

Hatch, E. (1983). *Culture and morality: The relativity of values in anthropology.* New York: Columbia University Press.

Hatcher, E. P. (1985). *Art as culture, an introduction to the anthropology of art.* New York: University Press of America.

Haviland, W. A. (1967). Stature at Tikal, Guatemala: Implications for ancient Maya, demography, and social organization. *American Antiquity 32*, 316–325.

Haviland, W. A. (1970). Tikal, Guatemala and Mesoamerican urbanism. *World Archaeology 2*, 186–198.

Haviland, W. A. (1972). A new look at Classic Maya social organization at Tikal. *Ceramica de Cultura Maya 8*, 1–16.

Haviland, W. A. (1974). Farming, seafaring and bilocal residence on the coast of Maine. *Man in the Northeast 6*, 31–44.

Haviland, W. A. (1997). Cleansing young minds, or what should we be doing in introductory anthropology? In C. P. Kottak, J. J. White, R. H. Furlow, & P. C. Rice (Eds.), *The teaching of anthropology: Problems, issues, and decisions* (p. 35). Mountain View, CA: Mayfield.

Haviland, W. A. (1997). The rise and fall of sexual inequality: Death and gender at Tikal, Guatemala. *Ancient Mesoamerica 8*, 1–12.

Haviland, W. A. (2002). Settlement, society and demography at Tikal. In J. Sabloff (Ed.), *Tikal.* Santa Fe: School of American Research.

Haviland, W. A. (2003). *Tikal, Guatemala: A Maya way to urbanism.* Paper prepared for 3rd INAH/Penn State Conference on Mesoamerican Urbanism.

Haviland, W. A., et al. (1985). *Excavations in small residential groups of Tikal: Groups 4F-1 and 4F-2.* Philadelphia: University Museum.

Haviland, W. A., & Moholy-Nagy, H. (1992). Distinguishing the high and mighty from the hoi polloi at Tikal, Guatemala. In A. F. Chase & D. Z. Chase (Eds.), *Mesoamerican elites: An archaeological assessment.* Norman: Oklahoma University Press.

Haviland, W. A., & Power, M. W. (1994). *The original Vermonters: Native inhabitants, past and present* (2nd ed.). Hanover, NH: University Press of New England.

Hawkes, K., O'Connell, J. F., & Blurton Jones, N. G. (1997). Hadza women's time allocation, offspring, provisioning, and the evolution of long postmenopausal life spans. *Current Anthropology 38*, 551–577.

Hazardous waste trafficking. www.Choike.org.

Heita, K. (1999). Imanishi's world view. *Journal of Japanese Trade and Industry 18* (2), 15.

Heitzman, J., & R. L. Wordem, R. L. (Eds.). (2006). *India: A country study* (Sect. 2, 5th ed.). Washington, DC: Federal Research Division, Library of Congress.

Helm, J. (1962). The ecological approach in anthropology. *American Journal of Sociology 67*, 630–649.

Helman, C. B. (2003). *Culture, health, and illness: An introduction for health professionals.* New York: Butterworth Heinemann Medical.

Henry, J. (1965). *Culture against man.* New York: Vintage Books.

Henry, J. (1974). A theory for an anthropological analysis of American culture. In J. G. Jorgensen & M. Truzzi (Eds.), *Anthropology and American life.* Englewood Cliffs, NJ: Prentice-Hall.

Herdt, G. H. (1993). Semen transactions in Sambia culture. In D. N. Suggs & A. W. Mirade (Eds.), *Culture and human sexuality* (pp. 298–327). Pacific Grove, CA: Brooks/Cole.

Herskovits, M. J. (1952). *Economic anthropology: A study in comparative economics* (2nd ed.). New York: Knopf.

Hertz, N. (2001). *The silent takeover: Global capitalism and the death of democracy.* New York: Arrow Books.

Himmelfarb, E. J. (2000, January/February). First alphabet found in Egypt. Newsbrief. *Archaeology 53* (1).

Historical atlas of the twentieth century. http://users.erols.com/mwhite28/20centry.htm.

Hitchcock, R. K., & Enghoff, M. (2004). *Capacity-building of first people of the Kalahari, Botswana: An evaluation.* Copenhagen: International Work Group for Indigenous Affairs.

Hoebel, E. A. (1949). *Man in the primitive world: An introduction to anthropology.* New York: McGraw-Hill.

Hoebel, E. A. (1960). *The Cheyennes: Indians of the Great Plains.* New York: Holt, Rinehart & Winston.

Holmes, L. D. (2000). Paradise bent (film review). *American Anthropologist 102* (3), 604–605.

Holy, L. (1996). *Anthropological perspectives on kinship.* London: Pluto Press.

Hostetler, J., & Huntington, G. (1971). *Children in Amish society.* New York: Holt, Rinehart & Winston.

Hrdy, S. B. (1999). Body fat and birth control. *Natural History 108* (8), 88.

Hsiaotung, F. (1939). *Peasant life in China.* London: Kegan, Paul, Trench & Truber.

Hsu, F. L. (1961). *Psychological anthropology: Approaches to culture and personality.* Homewood, IL: Dorsey Press.

Hsu, F. L. K. (1979). The cultural problems of the cultural anthropologist. *American Anthropologist 81*, 517–532.

Hubert, H., & Mauss, M. (1964). *Sacrifice.* Chicago: University of Chicago Press.

Human development report. (2002). *Deepening democracy in a fragmented world.* United Nations Development Program.

Hunger Project. (2003). www.thp.org.

Hunt, R. C. (Ed.). (1967). *Personalities and cultures: Readings in psychological anthropology.* Garden City, NY: Natural History Press.

Hutter, M. (Ed.) (2003). *The family experience: A reader in cultural diversity* (4th ed.). Boston: Allyn & Bacon.

Hymes, D. (1964). *Language in culture and Society: A reader in linguistics and anthropology.* New York: Harper & Row.

Hymes, D. (Ed.) (1972). *Reinventing anthropology.* New York: Pantheon. icasualties.org.

Inda, J. X., & Rosaldo, R. (Eds.). (2001). *The anthropology of globalization: A reader.* Malden, MA, and Oxford: Blackwell.

Ingmanson, E. J. (1998). Comment. *Current Anthropology 39*, 409.

Inkeles, A., & Levinson, D. J. (1954). *National character: The study of modal personality and socio-cultural systems.* In G. Lindzey (Ed.), *Handbook of social psychology.* Reading, MA: Addison-Wesley.

International Union for Conservation of Nature and Natural Resources (IUCN). (2000).

Inuit Tapiirit Katami. http://www.taprisat.ca/english- text/itk/departments/enviro/ncp.

Irvine, M. (1999, November 24). Mom-and-pop houses grow rare. *Burlington Free Press.*

Italy-Germany verbal war hots up. (2003, July 9). *Deccan Herald.* (Bangalore, India).

It's the law: Child labor protection. (1997, November/December). *Peace and Justice News,* 11.

Jacobs, S. E. (1994). Native American two-spirits. *Anthropology Newsletter 35* (8), 7.

Jacoby, R., & Glauberman, N. (Eds.). (1995). *The Bell Curve debate.* New York: Random House.

Jennings, F. (1976). *The invasion of America.* New York: Norton.

Johansen, B. E. (2002). The Inuit's struggle with dioxins and other organic pollutants. *The American Indian Quarterly 26* (3), 479–490.

John, V. (1971). Whose is the failure? In C. L. Brace, G. R. Gamble, & J. T. Bond (Eds.), *Race and intelligence.* Washington, DC: American Anthropological Association (Anthropological Studies No. 8).

Johnson, A. (1989). Horticulturalists: Economic behavior in tribes. In S. Plattner (Ed.), *Economic anthropology* (pp. 49–77). Stanford, CA: Stanford University Press.

Johnson, D. (1996). Polygamists emerge from secrecy, seeking not just peace but respect. In W. A. Haviland & R. J. Gordon (Eds.), *Talking about people* (2nd ed., pp. 129–131). Mountain View, CA: Mayfield.

Johnson, N. B. (1984). Sex, color, and rites of passage in ethnographic research. *Human Organization 43* (2), 108–120.

Jones, S. (2005). Transhumance re-examined. *Journal of the Royal Anthropological Institute 11* (4), 841–842.

Jones, S., Martin, R., & Pilbeam, D. (1992). *Cambridge encyclopedia of human evolution.* New York: Cambridge University Press.

Jorgensen, J. (1972). *The sun dance religion.* Chicago: University of Chicago Press.

Kalwet, H. (1988). *Dreamtime and inner space: The world of the shaman.* New York: Random House.

Kaplan, D. (1972). *Culture theory.* Englewood Cliffs, NJ: Prentice-Hall (Foundations of Modern Anthropology).

Kaplan, D. (2000). The darker side of the original affluent society. *Journal of Anthropological Research 53*(3), 301–324.

Kedia, S., & Van Willigen, J. (2005). *Applied anthropology: Domains of application.* New York: Praeger.

Keen, B. (1971). *The Aztec image in western thought.* New Brunswick, NJ: Rutgers University Press.

Kehoe, A. (1989). *The ghost dance: Ethnohistory and revitalization.* Fort Worth: Holt, Rinehart & Winston.

Kehoe, A. (2000). *Shamans and religion: An anthropological exploration in critical thinking.* Prospect Heights, IL: Waveland Press.

Keiser, L. (1991). *Friend by day, enemy by night: Organized vengeance in a Kohistani community.* Fort Worth: Holt, Rinehart & Winston.

Kelly, T. L. (2006). Sadhus, the great renouncers. Photography exhibit, Indigo Gallery, Naxal, Kathmandu, Nepal. www.asianart.com/exhibitions/sadhus/index.html.

Kendall, L. (1990, October). In the company of witches. *Natural History,* 92.

Kennickell, A. B. (2003, November). *A rolling tide: Changes in the distribution of wealth in the U.S. 1989–2001.* Levy Economics Institute.

Kertzer, D. I. (1989). *Ritual, politics, and power.* New Haven, CT: Yale University Press.

Key, M. R. (1975). *Paralanguage and kinesics: Nonverbal communication.* Metuchen, NJ: Scarecrow Press.

Kirkpatrick, R. C. (2000). The evolution of human homosexual behavior. *Current Anthropology 41*, 384.

Klass, M. (1995). *Ordered universes: Approaches to the anthropology of religion.* Boulder, CO: Westview Press.

Klass, M., & Weisgrau, M. (Eds.). (1999). *Across the boundaries of belief: Contemporary issues in the anthropology of religion.* Boulder, CO: Westview Press.

Klein, R. G., & Edgar, B. (2002). *The dawn of human culture.* New York: Wiley.

Kleinman, A. (1976). Concepts and a model for the comparison of medical systems as cultural systems. *Social Science and Medicine 12* (2B), 85–95.

Kluckhohn, C. (1970). *Mirror for man.* Greenwich, CT: Fawcett.

Kluckhohn, C. (1994). Navajo witchcraft. *Papers of the Peabody Museum of American Archaeology and Ethnology 22* (2).

Knauft, B. M. (1991). Violence and sociality in human evolution. *Current Anthropology 32*, 391–409.

Koch, G. (1997). Songs, land rights, and archives in Australia. *Cultural Survival Quarterly 20* (4).

Konner, M., & Worthman, C. (1980). Nursing frequency, gonadal function, and birth spacing among !Kung hunter-gatherers. *Science 207*, 788–791.

Krader, L. (1968). *Formation of the state.* Englewood Cliffs, NJ: Prentice-Hall (Foundation of Modern Anthropology).

Krajick, K. (1998). Greenfarming by the Incas? *Science 281*, 323.

Kramer, P. A. (1998). The costs of human locomotion: Maternal investment in child transport. *American Journal of Physical Anthropology 107*, 71–85.

Kraybill, D. B. (2001). *The riddle of Amish culture.* Baltimore: Johns Hopkins University Press.

Kroeber, A. (1958). Totem and taboo: An ethnologic psycho-analysis. In W. Lessa & E. Z. Vogt (Eds.), *Reader in comparative religion: An anthropological approach.* New York: Harper & Row.

Kroeber, A. L. (1939). Cultural and natural areas of native North America. *American Archaeology and Ethnology* (Vol. 38). Berkeley: University of California Press.

Kroeber, A. L. (1963). *Anthropology: Cultural processes and patterns.* New York: Harcourt.

Kroeber, A. L., & Kluckhohn, C. (1952). *Culture: A critical review of concepts and definitions.* Cambridge, MA: Harvard University Press (*Papers of the Peabody Museum of American Archaeology and Ethnology, 47*).

Kruger, J., et al. (2005, December). Egocentrism over e-mail: Can people communicate as well as they think? *Journal of Personality and Social Psychology* 89 (6), 925–936.

Kunnie, J. (2003). Africa's fast growing indigenous churches. http://coh.arizona.edu/newandnotable/kunnie/kunnie.html. Kunzig, R. (1999). A tale of two obsessed archaeologists, one ancient city and nagging doubts about whether science can ever hope to reveal the past. *Discover* 20 (5), 84–92.

Kuper, H. (1965). The Swazi of Swaziland. In J. L. Gibbs (Ed.), *Peoples of Africa* (pp. 479–511). New York: Holt, Rinehart & Winston.

Kurth, P. (1998, October 14). Capital crimes. *Seven Days, 7.*

Kurtz, D. V. (2001). *Political anthropology: Paradigms and power.* Boulder, CO: Westview Press.

Kushner, G. (1969). *Anthropology of complex societies.* Stanford, CA: Stanford University Press.

LaFont, S. (Ed.). (2003). *Constructing sexualities: Readings in sexuality, gender, and culture.* Upper Saddle River, NJ: Prentice-Hall.

Lai, C. S. L., et al. (2001). A forkhead-domain gene is mutated in severe speech and language disorder. *Nature* 413, 519–523.

Lakoff, R. T. (2004). *Language and woman's place.* M. Bucholtz (Ed.). New York: Oxford University Press.

Lambek, M. (2002). *A reader in the anthropology of religion.* London: Blackwell.

Lampl, M., Velhuis, J. D., & Johnson, M. L. (1992). Saltation and stasis: A model of human growth. *Science* 258 (5083), 801–803.

Langan, P., & Harlow, C. (1994). *Child rape victims, 1992.* Washington, DC: Bureau of Justice Statistics, U.S. Department of Justice.

Lanning, E. P. (1967). *Peru before the Incas.* Englewood Cliffs, NJ: Prentice-Hall.

Larsen, J. (2006, July 28). Setting the record straight. Earth Policy Institute, Eco-economy updates.

Lawler, A. (2001). Writing gets a rewrite. *Science* 292, 2,419.

Layton, R. (1991). *The anthropology of art* (2nd ed.). Cambridge: Cambridge University Press.

Leach, E. (1961). *Rethinking anthropology.* London: Athlone Press.

Leach, E. (1962). The determinants of differential cross-cousin marriage. *Man* 62, 238.

Leach, E. (1962). On certain unconsidered aspects of double descent systems. *Man 214,* 13–34.

Leach, E. (1982). *Social anthropology.* Glasgow: Fontana Paperbacks.

Leacock, E. (1981). *Myths of male dominance: Collected articles on women cross culturally.* New York: Monthly Review Press.

Leacock, E. (1981). Women's status in egalitarian society: Implications for social evolution. In *Myths of male dominance: Collected articles on women cross culturally.* New York: Monthly Review Press.

Leap, W. L. (1987). Tribally controlled culture change: The Northern Ute language revival project. In R. M. Wulff & S. J. Fiske (Eds.), *Anthropological praxis: Translating knowledge into action* (pp. 197–211). Boulder, CO: Westview Press.

Leavitt, G. C. (1990). Sociobiological explanations of incest avoidance: A critical review of evidential claims. *American Anthropologist 92,* 982.

Leclerc-Madlala, S. (2002). Bodies and politics: Healing rituals in the democratic South Africa. In V. Faure (Ed.), *Les cahiers de l'IFAS,* No. 2. Johannesburg: The French Institute.

Lee, R. B. (1993). *The Dobe Ju/'hoansi.* Ft. Worth: Harcourt Brace.

Lee, R. B., & Daly, R. H. (1999). *The Cambridge encyclopedia of hunters and gatherers.* New York: Cambridge University Press.

Lee, R. B., & DeVore, I. (Eds.) (1968). *Man the hunter.* Chicago: Aldine.

Lees, R. (1953). The basis of glottochronology. *Language* 29, 113–127.

Lehman, E. C., Jr. (2002, Fall). Women's path into the ministry. *Pulpit & Pew Research Reports 1,* 4.

Lehmann, A. C., & Myers, J. E. (Eds.) (2000). *Magic, witchcraft, and religion: An anthropological study of the supernatural* (5th ed.). Mountain View, CA: Mayfield.

Leigh, S. R., & Park, P. B. (1998). Evolution of human growth prolongation. *American Journal of Physical Anthropology* 107, 331–350.

Leinhardt, G. (1964). *Social anthropology.* London: Oxford University Press.

LeMay, M. (1975). The language capability of Neanderthal man. *American Journal of Physical Anthropology* 43 (1), 9–14.

Lenski, G. (1966). *Power and privilege: A theory of social stratification.* New York: McGraw-Hill.

Levine, N. E., & Silk, J. B. (1997). Why polyandry fails. *Current Anthropology 38,* 375–398.

Lévi-Strauss, C. (1963). The sorcerer and his magic. In *Structural anthropology.* New York: Basic Books.

Lewellen, T. C. (2002). *The anthropology of globalization: Cultural anthropology enters the 21st century.* Westport, CT: Greenwood Publishing Group/Bergin & Garvey.

Lewin, R. (1987). Four legs bad, two legs good. *Science 235,* 969.

Lewis, I. M. (1976). *Social anthropology in perspective.* Harmondsworth, England: Penguin.

Lewis-Williams, J. D. (1990). *Discovering southern African rock art.* Cape Town and Johannesburg: David Philip.

Lewis-Williams, J. D. (1997). Agency, art, and altered consciousness: A motif in French (Quercy) Upper Paleolithic parietal art. *Antiquity 71,* 810–830.

Lewis-Williams, J. D., & Dowson, T. A. (1993). On vision and power in the Neolithic: Evidence from the decorated monuments. *Current Anthropology 34,* 55–65.

Lewis-Williams, J. D., Dowson, T. A., & Deacon, J. (1993). Rock art and changing perceptions of Southern Africa's past: Ezeljagdspoort reviewed. *Antiquity 67,* 273–291.

Lewontin, R. C. (1972). The apportionment of human diversity. In T. Dobzhansky et al. (Eds.), *Evolutionary biology* (pp. 381–398). New York: Plenum Press.

Lewontin, R. C., Rose, S., & Kamin, L. J. (1984). *Not in our genes.* New York: Pantheon.

Li, X., Harbottle, G., Zhang, J., & Wang, C. (2003). The earliest writing? Sign use in the seventh millennium BC at Jiahu, Henan Province, China. *Antiquity 77,* 31–44.

Lieberman, P. (2006). *Toward an evolutionary biology of language.* Cambridge, MA : Belknap Press.

Lindenbaum, S. (1978). *Kuru sorcery: Disease and danger in the New Guinea highlands.* New York: McGraw-Hill.

Lindstrom, L. (1993). *Cargo cult: Strange stories of desire from Melanesia and beyond.* Honolulu: University of Hawaii Press.

Littlewood, R. (1997). Military rape. *Anthropology Today* 13 (2), 14.

Livingstone, F. B. (1973). The distribution of abnormal hemoglobin genes and their significance for human evolution. In C. Loring Brace & J. Metress (Eds.), *Man in evolutionary perspective.* New York: Wiley.

Lloyd, C. B. (Ed.) (2005). *Growing up global: The changing transitions to adulthood in developing countries* (pp. 450–453). Washington, DC: National Academies Press, Committee on Population, National Research Council, and Institute of Medicine of the National Academies.

Lock, M. (2001). *Twice dead: Organ transplants and the reinvention of death.* Berkeley: University of California Press.

Louckey, J., & Carlsen, R. (1991). Massacre in Santiago Atitlán. *Cultural Survival Quarterly* 15 (3), 70.

Louie, A. (2004). *Chineseness across borders: Renegotiating Chinese identities in China and the United States.* Durham and London: Duke University Press.

Lounsbury, F. (1964). The structural analysis of kinship semantics. In H. G. Lunt (Ed.), *Proceedings of the Ninth International Congress of Linguists.* The Hague: Mouton.

Lowie, R. H. (1948). *Social organization.* New York: Holt, Rinehart & Winston.

Lowie, R. H. (1956). *Crow Indians.* New York: Holt, Rinehart & Winston. (orig. 1935)

Lucy, J. A. (1997). Linguistic relativity. *Annual Review of Anthropology 26,* 291–312.

Lurie, N. O. (1973). Action anthropology and the American Indian. In *Anthropology and the American Indian: A symposium.* San Francisco: Indian Historical Press.

MacCormack, C. P. (1977). Biological events and cultural control. *Signs 3,* 93–100.

MacLarnon, A. M., & Hewitt, G. P. (1999). The evolution of human speech: The role of enhanced breathing control. *American Journal of Physical Anthropology* 109, 341–363.

MacNeish, R. S. (1992). *The origins of agriculture and settled life.* Norman: University of Oklahoma Press.

Madison Avenue relevance. (1999). *Anthropology Newsletter* 40 (4), 32.

Mair, L. (1957). *An introduction to social anthropology.* London: Oxford University Press.

Mair, L. (1969). *Witchcraft.* New York: McGraw-Hill.

Mair, L. (1971). *Marriage.* Baltimore: Penguin.

Malefijt, A. de W. (1969). *Religion and culture: An introduction to anthropology of religion.* London: Macmillan.

Malinowski, B. (1922). *Argonauts of the western Pacific.* London: Routledge & Kegan Paul.

Malinowski, B. (1945). *The dynamics of culture change: An inquiry into race relations in Africa.* New Haven, CT: Yale University Press.

Malinowski, B. (1951). *Crime and custom in savage society.* London: Routledge.

Malinowski, B. (1954). *Magic, science, and religion.* Garden City, NY: Doubleday.

Mann, A., Lampl, M, & Monge, J. (1990). Patterns of ontogeny in human evolution: Evidence from dental development. *Yearbook of Physical Anthropology 33,* 111–150.

Mann, C. C. (2000). Misconduct alleged in Yanomamo studies. *Science 289,* 2, 253.

Mann, C. C. (2002).The real dirt on rainforest fertility. *Science 297,* 920–923.

Marcus, G. (1995). Ethnography in/of the world system: The emergence of multi-sited ethnography. *Annual Review of Anthropology 24,* 95–117.

Marcus, J., & Flannery, K. V. (1996). *Zapotec civilization: How urban society evolved in Mexico's Oaxaca Valley.* New York: Thames & Hudson.

Marks, J. (1995). *Human biodiversity: Genes, race and history.* Hawthorne, NY: Aldine.

Marshall, L. (1961). Sharing, talking and giving: Relief of social tensions among !Kung bushmen. *Africa 31,* 231–249.

Marshall, M. (1990). Two tales from the Trukese taproom. In P. R. DeVita (Ed.), *The humbled anthropologist* (pp. 12–17). Belmont, CA: Wadsworth.

Martin, E. (1994). *Flexible bodies: Tracking immunity in American culture—from the days of polio to the age of AIDS.* Boston: Beacon Press.

Martin, E. (1999). Flexible survivors. *Anthropology News 40* (6), 5–7.

Martorell, R. (1988). Body size, adaptation, and function. *GDP,* 335–347.

Mascia-Lees, F. E., & Black, N. J. (2000). *Gender and anthropology.* Prospect Heights, IL: Waveland Press.

Mason, J. A. (1957). *The ancient civilizations of Peru.* Baltimore: Penguin.

Maybury-Lewis, D. (1960). Parallel descent and the Apinaye anomaly. *Southwestern Journal of Anthropology 16,* 191–216.

Maybury-Lewis, D. (1984). The prospects for plural societies. *1982 Proceedings of the American Ethnological Society.*

Maybury-Lewis, D. (1993, fall). A new world dilemma: The Indian question in the Americas. *Symbols,* 17–23.

Maybury-Lewis, D. (2001). *Indigenous peoples, ethnic groups, and the state* (2nd ed.). Boston: Allyn & Bacon.

Maybury-Lewis, D. H. P. (1993). A special sort of pleading. In W. A. Haviland & R. J. Gordon (Eds.), *Talking about people* (2nd. ed., p. 17). Mountain View, CA: Mayfield.

McCorriston, J., & Hole, F. (1991). The ecology of seasonal stress and the origins of agriculture in the Near East. *American Anthropologist 93,* 46– 69.

McElroy, A., & Townsend, P. K. (2003). *Medical anthropology in ecological perspective.* Boulder, CO: Westview Press.

McFee, M. (1972). *Modern Blackfeet: Montanans on a reservation.* New York: Holt, Rinehart & Winston.

McGrew, W. C. (2000). Dental care in chimps. *Science 288,* 1,747.

McKenna, J. J. (1999). Co-sleeping and SIDS. In W. Trevathan, E. O. Smith, & J. J. McKenna (Eds.), *Evolutionary medicine.* London: Oxford University Press.

McKenna, J. J. (2002, September–October). Breastfeeding and bedsharing. *Mothering,* 28–37.

McKenna, J. J., & McDade, T. (2005, June). Why babies should never sleep alone: A review of the co-sleeping controversy in relation to SIDS, bedsharing, and breast feeding. *Pediatric Respiratory Reviews 6* (2), 134–152.

McNeill, W. (1992). *Plagues and people.* New York: Anchor Books.

Mead, A. T. P. (1996). Genealogy, sacredness, and the commodities market. *Cultural Survival Quarterly 20* (2).

Mead, M. (1928). *Coming of age in Samoa.* New York: Morrow.

Mead, M. (1960). Anthropology among the sciences. *American Anthropologist 63,* 475–482.

Mead, M. (1963). *Sex and temperament in three primitive societies* (3rd ed). New York: Morrow. (orig. 1935)

Mead, M., & Metraux, R. (Eds.) (1953). *The study of culture at a distance.* Chicago: University of Chicago Press.

Medicine, B. (1994). Gender. In M. B. Davis (Ed.), *Native America in the twentieth century.* New York: Garland.

Mellars, P. (1989). Major issues in the emergence of modern humans. *Current Anthropology 30,* 356–357.

Meltzer, D., Fowler, D., & Sabloff, J. (Eds.) (1986). *American archaeology: Past & future.* Washington, DC: Smithsonian Institution Press.

Merin, Y. (2002). *Equality for same-sex couples: The legal recognition of gay partnerships in Europe and the United States.* Chicago: University of Chicago Press.

Merriam, A. P. (1964). *The anthropology of music.* Chicago: Northwestern University Press.

Mesghinua, H. M. (1966). Salt mining in Enderta. *Journal of Ethiopian Studies 4* (2).

Miles, H. L. W. (1993). Language and the orangutan: The "old person" of the forest. In P. Cavalieri & P. Singer (Eds.), *The great ape project* (pp. 45– 50). New York: St. Martin's Press.

Millon, R. (1973). *Urbanization of Teotihuacán, Mexico: Vol. 1, Part 1. The Teotihuacán map.* Austin: University of Texas Press.

Mintz, S. (1996). A taste of history. In W. A. Haviland & R. J. Gordon (Eds.), *Talking about people* (2nd ed., pp. 81–82). Mountain View, CA: Mayfield.

Mitchell, W. E. (1973, December). A new weapon stirs up old ghosts. *Natural History,* 77–84.

Mitchell, W. E. (1978). *Mishpokhe: A study of New York City Jewish family clubs.* The Hague: Mouton.

Modell, J. (1994). *Kinship with strangers: Adoption and interpretations of kinship in American culture.* Berkeley: University of California Press.

Molnar, S. (1992). *Human variation: Races, types and ethnic groups* (3rd ed.). Englewood Cliffs, NJ: Prentice-Hall.

Monaghan, L., Hinton, L., & Kephart, R. (1997). Can't teach a dog to be a cat? The dialogue on ebonics. *Anthropology Newsletter 38* (3), 1, 8, 9.

Montagu, A. (1964). *The concept of race.* London: Macmillan.

Montagu, A. (1964). *Man's most dangerous myth: The fallacy of race* (4th ed.) New York: World Publishing.

Montagu, A. (1975). *Race and IQ.* New York: Oxford University Press.

Moore, J. (1998). Comment. *Current Anthropology 39,* 412.

Morgan, L. H. (1877). *Ancient society.* New York: World Publishing.

Morphy, H., & Perkins, M. (Eds.). (2006). *Anthropology of art: A reader.* Boston: Blackwell.

Morse, D., et al. (1979). *Gestures: Their origins and distribution.* New York: Stein & Day.

Murdock, G. P. (1960). Cognatic forms of social organization. In G. P. Murdock (Ed.), *Social structure in Southeast Asia* (pp. 1–14). Chicago: Quadrangle Books.

Murdock, G. P. (1965). *Social structure.* New York: Free Press.

Murphy, R. (1971). *The dialectics of social life: Alarms and excursions in anthropological theory.* New York: Basic Books.

Murphy, R., & Kasdan, L. (1959). The structure of parallel cousin marriage. *American Anthropologist 61,* 17–29.

Mydens, S. (2001, August 12). He's not hairy, he's my brother. *New York Times,* sec. 4, 5.

Myrdal, G. (1974). Challenge to affluence: The emergence of an "under-class." In J. G. Jorgensen & M. Truzzi (Eds.), *Anthropology and American life.* Englewood Cliffs, NJ: Prentice-Hall.

Nader, L. (Ed.) (1965). The ethnography of law, part II. *American Anthropologist 67* (6).

Nader, L. (Ed.) (1969). *Law in culture and society.* Chicago: Aldine.

Nader, L. (Ed.) (1996). *Naked science: Anthropological inquiry into boundaries, power, and knowledge.* New York: Routledge.

Nader, L. (1997). Controlling processes: Tracing the dynamics of power. *Current Anthropology 38,* 715–717.

Nader, L. (Ed.) (1997). *Law in culture and society.* Berkeley: University of California Press.

Nader, L. (2002). *The life of the law: Anthropological projects.* Berkeley: University of California Press.

Nader, L., & Todd, Jr., H. F. (1978). *The disputing process: Law in ten societies.* New York: Columbia University Press.

Nanda, S. (1990). *Neither man nor woman: The hijras of India.* Belmont, CA: Wadsworth.

Nanda, S. (1992). Arranging a marriage in India. In P. R. De Vita (Ed.), *The naked anthropologist* (pp. 139–143). Belmont, CA: Wadsworth.

Nash, J. (1976). Ethnology in a revolutionary setting. In M. A. Rynkiewich & J. P. Spradley (Eds.), *Ethics and anthropology: Dilemmas in fieldwork* (pp. 148–166). New York: Wiley.

Natural Resources Defense Council. (2005, March 25). Healthy milk, healthy baby: Chemical pollution and mother's milk. www.NRDC.org.

Needham, R. (Ed.) (1971). *Rethinking kinship and marriage.* London: Tavistock.

Needham, R. (1972). *Belief, language and experience.* Chicago: University of Chicago Press.

Neer, R. M. (1975). The evolutionary significance of vitamin D, skin pigment, and ultraviolet light. *American Journal of Physical Anthropology 43,* 409–416.

Nesbitt, L. M. (1935). *Hell-hole of creation.* New York: Knopf.

Nesse, R. M., & Williams, G. C. (1996). *Why we get sick.* New York: Vintage.

Netting, R. M., Wilk, R. R., & Arnould, E. J. (Eds.) (1984). *Households: Comparative and historical studies of the domestic group.* Berkeley: University of California Press.

Nietschmann, B. (1987). The third world war. *Cultural Survival Quarterly 11* (3), 1–16.

Norris, R. S., & Kristensen, H. M. (2006, July/August). Global nuclear stockpiles, 1945–2006. *Bulletin of the Atomic Scientists 62* (4), 64–66.

Nunney, L. (1998). Are we selfish, are we nice, or are we nice because we are selfish? *Science 281,* 1,619.

Nye, J. (2002). *The paradox of American power: Why the world's only superpower can't go it alone.* New York: Oxford University Press.

O'Barr, W. M., & Conley, J. M. (1993). When a juror watches a lawyer. In W. A. Haviland & R. J. Gordon (Eds.), *Talking about people* (2nd. ed., pp. 42–45). Mountain View, CA: Mayfield.

Obler, R. S. (1982). Is the female husband a man? Woman/woman marriage among the Nandi of Kenya. *Ethnology 19,* 69–88.

Offiong, D. (1985). Witchcraft among the Ibibio of Nigeria. In A. C. Lehmann & J. E. Myers (Eds.), *Magic, witchcraft, and religion* (pp. 152–165). Palo Alto, CA: Mayfield.

Okonjo, K. (1976). The dual-sex political system in operation: Igbo women and community politics in midwestern Nigeria. In N. Hafkin & E. Bay (Eds.), *Women in Africa.* Stanford, CA: Stanford University Press.

Olszewski, D. I. (1991). Comment. *Current Anthropology 32,* 43.

O'Mahoney, K. (1970). The salt trade. *Journal of Ethiopian Studies 8* (2).

Ong, A. (1999). *Flexible citizenship: The cultural logics of transnationality.* Durham, NC: Duke University Press.

Ortiz, A. (1969). *The Tewa world.* Chicago: The University of Chicago Press.

Oswalt, W. H. (1972). *Habitat and technology.* New York: Holt, Rinehart & Winston.

Otte, M. (2000). On the suggested bone flute from Slovenia. *Current Anthropology 41,* 271.

Otten, C. M. (1971). *Anthropology and art: Readings in cross-cultural aesthetics.* Garden City, NY: Natural History Press.

Ottenberg, P. (1965). The Afikpo Ibo of eastern Nigeria. In J. L. Gibbs (Ed.), *Peoples of Africa.* New York: Holt, Rinehart & Winston.

Ottenheimer, M. (1996). *Forbidden relatives: The American myth of cousin marriage.* Chicago: University of Illinois Press.

Otterbein, K. F. (1971). *The evolution of war.* New Haven, CT: HRAF Press.

Pandian, J. (1998). *Culture, religion, and the sacred self: A critical introduction to the anthropological study of religion.* Englewood Cliffs, NJ: Prentice-Hall.

Paredes, J. A., & Purdum, E. D. (1990). "Bye, bye Ted . . ." *Anthropology Today 6* (2), 9.

Parish, A. R. (1998). Comment. *Current Anthropology 39,* 414.

Parker, R. G. (1991). *Bodies, pleasures, and passions: Sexual culture in contemporary Brazil.* Boston: Beacon Press.

Parkin, R. (1997). *Kinship: An introduction to basic concepts.* Cambridge, MA: Blackwell.

Partridge, W. (Ed.) (1984). *Training manual in development anthropology.* Washington, DC: American Anthropological Association.

Peacock, J. L. (2002). *The anthropological lens: Harsh light, soft focus* (2nd ed.). New York: Cambridge University Press.

Pease, T. (2000, Spring). Taking the third side. *Andover Bulletin.*

Pelto, G. H., Goodman, A. H., & Dufour, D. L. (Eds.). (2000). *Nutritional anthropology: Biocultural perspectives on food and nutrition.* Mountain View, CA: Mayfield,

Pelto, P. J. (1973). *The snowmobile revolution: Technology and social change in the Arctic.* Menlo Park, CA: Cummings.

Pfeiffer, J. E. (1985). *The creative explosion.* Ithaca, NY: Cornell University Press.

Piddocke, S. (1965). The potlatch system of the southern Kwakiutl: A new perspective. *Southwestern Journal of Anthropology 21,* 244–264.

Piggott, S. (1965). *Ancient Europe.* Chicago: Aldine.

Pimentel, D. (1991). Response. *Science 252,* 358.

Pimentel, D., Hurd, L. E., Bellotti, A. C., Forster, M. J., Oka, I. N., Sholes, O. D., & Whitman, R. J. (1973). Food Production and the Energy Crisis. *Science,* 182.

Pink, S. (2001). *Doing visual ethnography: Images, media and representation in research.* Thousand Oaks, CA: Sage.

Piperno, D. R., & Fritz, G. J. (1994). On the emergence of agriculture in the new world. *Current Anthropology 35,* 637–643.

Pitt, D. (1977). Comment. *Current Anthropology 18,* 628.

Pitts, V. (2003). *In the flesh: The cultural politics of body modification.* New York: Palgrave Macmillan.

Plane, A. M. (1996). Putting a face on colonization: Factionalism and gender politics in the life history of Awashunkes, the "Squaw Sachem" of Saconnet. In R. S. Grumet (Ed.), *Northeastern Indian Lives, 1632–1816* (pp.140–175). Amherst: University of Massachusetts Press.

Plattner, S. (Ed.) (1989). *Economic anthropology.* Stanford, CA: Stanford University Press.

Plattner, S. (1989). Markets and marketplaces. In S. Plattner (Ed.), *Economic anthropology.* Stanford, CA: Stanford University Press.

Polanyi, K. (1968). The economy as instituted process. In E. E. LeClair, Jr., & H. K. Schneider (Eds.), *Economic anthropology: Readings in theory and analysis* (pp. 127–138). New York: Holt, Rinehart & Winston.

Pollan, M. (2001). *The botany of desire: A plant's-eye view of the world.* New York: Random House.

Pope Pius XII. (1954). *Sacra Virginitas.* encyclical on consecrated virginity. The Catholic Encyclopedia Online: www.newadvent.org.

Pospisil, L. (1963). *The Kapauku Papuans of west New Guinea.* New York: Holt, Rinehart & Winston.

Pospisil, L. (1971). *Anthropology of law: A comparative theory.* New York: Harper & Row.

Potts, R. (1997). *Humanity's descent: The consequences of ecological instability.* New York: Avon.

Powdermaker, H. (1939). *After freedom: A cultural study in the Deep South.* New York: Viking.

Powdermaker, H. (1976). *Stranger and friend: The way of an anthropologist.* London: Secker and Warburg.

Price, T. D., & Feinman, G. M. (Eds.) (1995). *Foundations of social inequality.* New York: Plenum.

Pringle, H. (1997). Ice Age communities may be earliest known net hunters. *Science 277,* 1,203–1,204.

Pringle, H. (1998). The slow birth of agriculture. *Science 282,* 1,449.

Prins, A. H. J. (1953). *East African class systems.* Groningen, the Netherlands: J. B. Wolters.

Prins, H. E. L. (1996). *The Mi'kmaq: Resistance, accommodation, and cultural survival* (p. 106). Orlando: Harcourt Brace.

Prins, H. E. L. (1998). Book review of Schuster, C., & Carpenter, E. *American Anthropologist 100* (3), 841.

Prins, H. E. L. (2002). Visual media and the primitivist perplex: Colonial fantasies, indigenous imagination, and advocacy in North America. In F. D. Ginsburg et al., *Media worlds: Anthropology on new terrain* (pp. 58–74). Berkeley: University of California Press.

Prins, H. E. L., & Carter, K. (1986). *Our lives in our hands.* Video and 16mm. Color. 50 min. Distributed by Watertown, MA: Documentary Educational Resources and Bucksport, ME: Northeast Historic Film

Prins, H. E. L., & Krebs, E. (2006). Toward a land without evil: Alfred Métraux as UNESCO anthropologist 1948–1962. In *60 years of UNESCO history. Proceedings of the international symposium in Paris, 16–18 November 2005.* Paris: UNESCO.

Profet, M. (1991). The function of allergy: Immunological defense against toxins. *Quarterly Review of Biology 66* (1), 23–62.

Profet, M. (1995). *Protecting your baby to be.* New York: Addison Wesley.

Puleston, D. E. (1983). *The settlement survey of Tikal.* Philadelphia: University Museum.

Radcliffe-Brown, A. R. (1931). Social organization of Australian tribes. *Oceana Monographs 1,* 29.

Radcliffe-Brown, A. R., & Forde, C. D. (Eds.) (1950). *African systems of kinship and marriage.* London: Oxford University Press.

Radin, P. (1923). The Winnebago tribe. In *37th annual report of the Bureau of American Ethnology, 1915–1916* (pp. 33–550). Washington, DC: Government Printing Office.

Rapp, R. (1999). *Testing the woman, testing the fetus: The social impact of amniocentesis in America.* New York: Routledge.

Rappaport, R. A. (1969). Ritual regulation of environmental relations among a New Guinea people. In A. P. Vayda (Ed.), *Environment and cultural behavior* (pp. 181–201). Garden City, NY. Natural History Press.

Rappaport, R. A. (1984). *Pigs for the ancestors* (Enl. ed.). New Haven, CT: Yale University Press.

Rappaport, R. A. (1999). *Holiness and humanity: Ritual in the making of religious life.* New York: Cambridge University Press.

Rathke, L. (1989). To Maine for apples. *Salt Magazine 9* (4), 24–47.

Rathje, W. L. (1974). The garbage project: A new way of looking at the problems of archaeology. *Archaeology 27,* 236–241.

Rathje, W. L. (1993). Rubbish! In W. A. Haviland & R. J. Gordon (Eds.), *Talking about people: Readings in contemporary cultural anthropology.* Mountain View, CA: Mayfield.

Recent demographic developments in Europe— 2000. Council of Europe.

Redman, C. L. (1978). *The rise of civilization: From early farmers to urban society in the ancient Near East.* San Francisco: Freeman.

Reid, J. J., Schiffer, M. B., & Rathje, W. L. (1975). Behavioral archaeology: Four strategies. *American Anthropologist 77,* 864–869.

Reina, R. E. (1966). *The law of the saints.* Indianapolis: Bobbs-Merrill.

Reynolds, V. (1994). Primates in the field, primates in the lab. *Anthropology Today 10* (2), 4.

Rindos, D. (1984). *The origins of agriculture: An evolutionary perspective.* Orlando: Academic Press.

Robben, A. C. G. M. (2007). Fieldwork identity: Introduction. In A. C. G. M. Robben & J. A. Sluka (Eds.), *Ethnographic fieldwork: An anthropological reader* (pp. 59–63). Malden, MA: Blackwell.

Robben, A. C. G. M. (2007). Reflexive ethnography: Introduction. In A. C. G. M. Robben & J. A. Sluka (Eds.), *Ethnographic fieldwork: An anthropological reader* (pp. 443–446). Malden, MA: Blackwell.

Robben, A. C. G. M., & Sluka, J. A. (Eds.) (2006). *Ethnographic fieldwork: An anthropological reader* (Part VII). Malden, MA: Blackwell.

Rogers, J. (1994). Levels of the genealogical hierarchy and the problem of hominid phylogeny. *American Journal of Physical Anthropology 94*, 81–88.

Romer, A. S. (1945). *Vertebrate paleontology*. Chicago: University of Chicago Press.

Roosevelt, A. C. (1984). Population, health, and the evolution of subsistence: Conclusions from the conference. In M. N. Cohen & G. J. Armelagos (Eds.), *Paleopathology at the origins of agriculture* (pp. 572–574). Orlando: Academic Press.

Rosas, A., & Bermdez de Castro, J. M. (1998). On the taxonomic affinities of the Dmanisi mandible (Georgia). *American Journal of Physical Anthropology 107*, 145–162.

Roscoe, P. B. (1995). The perils of "positivism" in cultural anthropology. *American Anthropologist 97*, 497.

Roscoe, W. (1991). *Zuni man-woman*. Albuquerque: University of New Mexico Press.

Ruhlen, M. (1994). *The origin of language: Tracing the evolution of the mother tongue*. New York: Wiley.

Rupert, J. L., & Hochachka, P. W. (2001). The evidence for hereditary factors contributing to high altitude adaptation in Andean natives: A review. *High Altitude Medicine & Biology 2* (2), 235–256.

Ruvdo, M. (1994). Molecular evolutionary processes and conflicting gene trees: The hominoid case. *American Journal of Physical Anthropology 94*, 89–113.

Sahlins, M. (1961). The segmentary lineage: An organization of predatory expansion. *American Anthropologist 63*, 322–343.

Sahlins, M. (1968). *Tribesmen*. Englewood Cliffs, NJ: Prentice-Hall (Foundations of Modern Anthropology).

Sahlins, M. (1972). *Stone age economics*. Chicago: Aldine.

Salzman, P. C. (1967). Political organization among nomadic peoples. *Proceedings of the American Philosophical Society 111*, 115–131.

Sanday, P. R. (1975). On the causes of IQ differences between groups and implications for social policy. In M. F. A. Montagu (Ed.), *Race and IQ* (pp. 232–238). New York: Oxford.

Sanday, P. R. (1981). *Female power and male dominance: On the origins of sexual inequality*. Cambridge, England: Cambridge University Press.

Sanday, P. R. (2002). *Women at the center: Life in a modern matriarchy*. Ithaca: Cornell University Press.

Sangree, W. H. (1965). The Bantu Tiriki of western Kenya. In J. L. Gibbs, Jr. (Ed.), *Peoples of Africa* (pp. 69–72). New York: Holt, Rinehart & Winston.

Sanjek, R. (1990). On ethnographic validity. In R. Sanjek (Ed.), *Field notes*. Ithaca, NY: Cornell University Press.

Sapir, E. (1921). *Language*. New York: Harcourt.

Savage-Rumbaugh, S., & Lewin, R. (1994). *Kanzi: The ape at the brink of the human mind*. New York: Wiley.

Scaglion, R. (1987). Contemporary law development in Papua New Guinea. In R. M. Wulff & S. J. Fiske (Eds.), *Anthropological praxis: Translating knowledge into action*. Boulder, CO: Westview Press.

Schaeffer, S. B., & Furst, P. T. (Eds.). (1996). *People of the peyote: Huichol Indian history,* religion, and survival. Albuquerque: University of New Mexico Press.

Scheflen, A. E. (1972). *Body language and the social order*. Englewood Cliffs, NJ: Prentice-Hall.

Schepartz, L.A. (1993). Language and human origins. *Yearbook of Physical Anthropology 36*, 91–126.

Scheper-Hughes, N., & Waquant, L. (2002). *Commodifying bodies*. London: Sage (Theory, Culture, and Society series).

Schlegel, A. (1977). Male and female in Hopi thought and action. In A. Schlegel (Ed.), *Sexual stratification* (pp. 245–269). New York: Columbia University Press.

Schoepfle, M. (2001). Ethnographic resource inventory and the National Park Service. *Cultural Resource Management 5*, 1–7.

Schrire, C. (Ed.). (1984). *Past and present in hunter-gatherer studies*. Orlando: Academic Press.

Schusky, E. L. (1983). *Manual for kinship analysis* (2nd ed.). Lanham, MD: University Press of America.

Schuster, C., & Carpenter, E. (1996). *Patterns that connect: Social symbolism in ancient and tribal art*. New York: Abrams.

Schwartz, J. H. (1984). Hominoid evolution: A review and a reassessment. *Current Anthropology 25* (5), 655–672.

Schwartz, M. (1997). *A history of dogs in the early Americas*. New Haven: Yale University Press.

Scupin, R. (Ed.) (2000). *Religion and culture: An anthropological focus*. Upper Saddle River, NJ: Prentice-Hall.

Seeger, A. (2004). *Why Suya sing: A musical anthropology*. Champaign: University of Illinois Press.

Sellen, D. W., & Mace, R. (1997). Fertility and mode of subsistence: A phylogenetic analysis. *Current Anthropology 38*, 886.

Seymour, D. Z. (1986). Black children, black speech. In P. Escholz, A. Rosa, & V. Clark (Eds.), *Language awareness* (4th ed.). New York: St. Martin's Press.

Shane, L., III. (2005). Happy couple both no-show wedding: Deployed troops make use of double-proxy ceremony. *Stars & Stripes 3* (17), 6.

Shapiro, H. (Ed.) (1971). *Man, culture and society* (2nd ed.). New York: Oxford University Press.

Shaw, D. G. (1984). A light at the end of the tunnel: Anthropological contributions toward global competence. *Anthropology Newsletter 25*, 16.

Shearer, R. R., & Gould, S. J. (1999). Of two minds and one nature. *Science 286*, 1093.

Shook, J. R., et al. (Eds.). (2004). *Dictionary of modern American philosophers, 1860–1960*. Bristol, England: Thoemmes Press.

Shore, B. (1996). *Culture in mind: Meaning, construction, and cultural cognition*. New York: Oxford University Press.

Shostak, M. (1983). *Nisa: The life and words of a !Kung woman*. New York: Vintage.

Shreeve, J. (1994). Terms of estrangement. *Discover 15* (11), 60.

Shuey, A. M. (1966). *The testing of Negro intelligence*. New York: Social Science Press.

Sillen, A., & Brain, C. K. (1990). Old flame. *Natural History 4*, 6–10.

Simpson, S. (1995, April). Whispers from the ice. *Alaska*, 23–28.

Sjoberg, G. (1960). *The preindustrial city*. New York: Free Press.

Sluka, J. A. (2007). Fieldwork relations and rapport: Introduction. In A. C. G. M. Robben & J. A. Sluka (Eds.), *Ethnographic fieldwork: An anthropological reader*. Malden, MA: Blackwell.

Small, M. F. (1997). Making connections. *American Scientist 85*, 503.

Small, M. F. (2000). Kinship envy. *Natural History 109* (2), 88.

Smedley, A. (1998). *Race in North America: Origin and evolution of a worldview*. Boulder, CO: Westview Press.

Smith, P. E. L. (1976). *Food production and its consequences* (2nd ed.). Menlo Park, CA: Cummings.

Snowden, C. T. (1990). Language capabilities of nonhuman animals. *Yearbook of Physical Anthropology 33*, 215–243.

Speck, F. G. (1920). Penobscot shamanism. *Memoirs of the American Anthropological Association 6*, 239–288.

Speck, F. G. (1970). *Penobscot man: The life history of a forest tribe in Maine*. New York: Octagon Books.

Spencer, H. (1896). *Principles of sociology*. New York: Appleton.

Spencer, R. F. (1984). North Alaska Coast Eskimo. In D. Damas (Ed.), *Arctic: Handbook of North American Indians* (Vol. 5, pp. 320–337). Washington, DC: Smithsonian Institution.

Spindler, G., & Stockard, J. E. (Eds.) (2006). *Globalization and change in fifteen cultures*. Belmont, CA: Wadsworth.

Spradley, J. P. (1979). *The ethnographic interview*. New York: Holt, Rinehart & Winston.

Spradley, J. P. (1980). *Participant observation*. New York: Holt, Rinehart & Winston.

Stacey, J. (1990). *Brave new families*. New York: Basic Books.

Stannard, D. E. (1992). *American holocaust*. Oxford: Oxford University Press.

Steady, F. C. (2001). *Women and the Amistad connection, Sierra Leone Krio Society*. Rochester, VT: Schenkman Books.

Steady, F. C. (2005). *Women and collective action in Africa*. New York: Palgrave Macmillan.

Stedman, H. H., et al. (2004). Myosin gene mutation correlates with anatomical changes in the human lineage. *Nature 428*, 415–418.

Stein, R. L., & Stein, P. L. (2004). *Anthropology of religion, magic, and witchcraft*. Boston: Allyn & Bacon.

Steward, J. H. (1972). *Theory of culture change: The methodology of multilinear evolution*. Urbana: University of Illinois Press.

Stiglitz, J.E. (2003). *Globalization and its discontents*. New York: Norton.

Stiles, D. (1979). Early Acheulean and developed Oldowan. *Current Anthropology 20* (l), 126–129.

Stockard, J. E. (2002). *Marriage in culture: Practice and meaning across diverse societies*. Ft. Worth: Harcourt College Publishers.

Stocking, G. W., Jr. (1968). *Race, culture and evolution: Essays in the history of anthropology*. New York: Free Press.

Stone, L. (1998). *Kinship and gender: An introduction*. Boulder, CO: Westview Press.

Stone, L. (2005). *Kinship and gender: An introduction* (3rd ed.). Boulder, CO: Westview Press.

Stone, R. (1995). If the mercury soars, so may health hazards. *Science 267*, 958.

Stuart-MacAdam, P., & Dettwyler, K. A. (Eds.) (1995). *Breastfeeding: Biocultural perspectives*. New York: Aldine.

Study estimates 250,000 active child soldiers. (2006, July 26). Associated Press.

Suarez-Orozoco, M. M., Spindler, G., & Spindler, L. (1994). *The making of psychological anthropology, II*. Fort Worth: Harcourt Brace.

Swadesh, M. (1959). Linguistics as an instrument of prehistory. *Southwestern Journal of Anthropology 15,* 20–35.

Swaminathan, M. S. (2000). Science in response to basic human needs. *Science 287,* 425.

Swartz, M. J., Turner, V. W., & Tuden, A. (1966). *Political anthropology.* Chicago: Aldine.

Tannen, D. (1990). *You just don't understand: Women and men in conversation.* New York: Morrow.

Tapper, M. (1999). *In the blood: Sickle-cell anemia and the politics of race.* Philadelphia: University of Pennsylvania Press.

Tax, S. (1953). *Penny capitalism: A Guatemalan Indian economy.* Washington, DC: Smithsonian Institution, Institute of Social Anthropology, Pub. No. 16.

Taylor, G. (2000). *Castration: Abbreviated history of western manhood.* New York: Routledge.

Tedlock, B. (2005). *The woman in the shaman's body: Reclaiming the feminine in religion and medicine.* New York: Random House.

Templeton, A. R. (1994). Eve: Hypothesis compatibility versus hypothesis testing. *American Anthropologist 96* (1), 141–147.

Templeton, A. R. (1995). The "Eve" hypothesis: A genetic critique and reanalysis. *American Anthropologist 95* (1), 51–72.

Terashima, H. (1983). Mota and other hunting activities of the Mbuti archers: A socio-ecological study of subsistence technology. *African Studies Monograph* (Kyoto), 71–85.

Thomas, E. M. (1994). *The tribe of the tiger: Cats and their culture* (pp. 109– 186). New York: Simon & Schuster.

Thorne, A. G., & Wolpoff, M. D. H. (1981). Regional continuity in Australasian Pleistocene hominid evolution. *American Journal of Physical Anthropology 55,* 337–349.

Thornhill, N. (1993). Quoted in W. A. Haviland & R. J. Gordon (Eds.), *Talking about people* (p. 127). Mountain View, CA: Mayfield.

Trouillot, M. R. (1996). Culture, color, and politics in Haiti. In S. Gregory & R. Sanjek (Eds.), *Race.* New Brunswick, NJ: Rutgers University Press.

Trouillot, M. R. (2003). *Global transformations: Anthropology and the modern world.* New York: Palgrave Macmillan.

Tumin, M. M. (1967). *Social stratification: The forms and functions of inequality.* Englewood Cliffs, NJ: Prentice-Hall (Foundations of Modern Sociology).

Turnbull, C. M. (1983). *Mbuti Pygmies: Change and adaptation.* New York: Holt, Rinehart & Winston.

Turnbull, C. M. (1961). *The forest people.* New York: Simon & Schuster.

Turnbull, C. M. (1983). *The human cycle.* New York: Simon & Schuster.

Turner, T. (1991). Major shift in Brazilian Yanomami policy. *Anthropology Newsletter 32* (5), 1, 46.

Turner, V. W. (1957). *Schism and continuity in an African society.* Manchester, England: University Press.

Turner, V. W. (1969). *The ritual process.* Chicago: Aldine.

Tylor, E. B. (1871). *Primitive culture: Researches into the development of mythology, philosophy, religion, language, art and customs.* London: Murray.

Tylor, Sir E. B. (1931). Animism. In V. F. Calverton (Ed.), *The making of man: An outline of anthropology.* New York: Modern Library.

UNESCO. www.unesco.org/webworld/babel.

Urban, G. (2001). *Metaculture: How cultures move through the modern world.* Westport, CT: Greenwood Press.

Ury, W. L. (1993). *Getting past no: Negotiating your way from confrontation.* New York: Bantam Books.

Ury, W. L. (1999). *Getting to peace: Transforming conflict at home, at work, and in the world.* New York: Viking.

Ury, W. (2002, Winter). A global immune system. *Andover Bulletin.*

U.S. Census 2000. www.adherents.com.

U.S. Census Bureau News. (2004, March 18).

Van Allen, J. (1997). Sitting on a man: Colonialism and the lost political institutions of Igbo women. In R. Grinker & C. Steiner (Eds.), *Perspectives on Africa* (p. 450). Boston: Blackwell.

Van den Berghe, P. (1992). The modern state: Nation builder or nation killer? *International Journal of Group Tensions 22* (3), 191–207.

Van Eck, C. (2003). *Purified by blood: Honour killings amongst Turks in the Netherlands.* Amsterdam University Press.

Van Gennep, A. (1960). *The rites of passage.* Chicago: University of Chicago Press.

Van Tilburg, J. A. (1994). *Easter Island: Archaeology, ecology, and culture.* London: British Museum Press.

Van Willigen, J. (1986). *Applied anthropology.* South Hadley, MA: Bergin & Garvey.

Venbrux, E., Rosi, P. S., & Welsch, R. L. (Eds.) (2006). *Exploring world art.* Longrove, IL: Waveland Press.

Vincent, J. (2002). *The anthropology of politics: A reader in ethnography, theory, and critique.* Boston: Blackwell.

Vogt, E. Z. (1990). *The Zinacantecos of Mexico: A modern Maya way of life* (2nd ed.). Fort Worth: Holt, Rine-hart & Winston.

Waldbaum, J. C. (2005, November/December). Tell it to the Marines: Teaching troops about cultural heritage. *Archaeology 58* (6).

Wallace, A. F. C. (1956). Revitalization movements. *American Anthropologist 58,* 264–281.

Wallace, A. F. C. (1966). *Religion: An anthropological view.* New York: Random House.

Wallace, A. F. C. (1970). *Culture and personality* (2nd ed.). New York: Random House.

Wallace, E., & Hoebel, E. A. (1952). *The Comanches.* Norman: University of Oklahoma Press.

Walrath, D. (2002). Decoding the discourses: Feminism and science, review essay. *American Anthropologist 104* (1), 327–330.

Walrath, D. (2003). Re-thinking pelvic typologies and the human birth mechanism. *Current Anthropology 44* (1), 5–31.

Walrath, D. (2006). Gender, genes, and the evolution of human birth. In P. L. Geller & M. K. Stockett (Eds.), *Feminist anthropology: Past, present, and future.* Philadelphia: University of Pennsylvania Press.

Wattenberg, B. J. (1997, November 23). The population explosion is over. *New York Times Magazine,* 60.

Weatherford, J. (1988). *Indian givers: How the Indians of the Americas transformed the world.* New York: Ballantine.

Weiner, A. B. (1977). Review of Trobriand cricket: An ingenious response to colonialism. *American Anthropologist 79,* 506.

Weiner, A. B. (1988). *The Trobrianders of Papua New Guinea.* New York: Holt, Rinehart & Winston.

Weiss, M. L., & Mann, A. E. (1990). *Human biology and behavior* (5th ed.). Boston: Little, Brown.

Wells, S. (2002). *The journey of man: A genetic odyssey.* Princeton, NJ: Princeton University Press.

Werner, D. (1990). *Amazon journey.* Englewood Cliffs, NJ: Prentice-Hall.

Wheeler, P. (1993). Human ancestors walked tall, stayed cool. *Natural History 102* (8), 65–66.

Whelehan, P. (1985). Review of incest, a biosocial view. *American Anthropologist 87,* 678.

White, D. R. (1988). Rethinking polygyny: Co-wives, codes, and cultural systems. *Current Anthropology 29,* 529–572.

White, L. (1949). *The science of culture: A study of man and civilization.* New York: Farrar, Straus.

White, L. (1959). *The evolution of culture: The development of civilization to the fall of Rome.* New York: McGraw-Hill.

White, M. (2001). *Historical atlas of the twentieth century.* http://users.erols.com/mwhite28/20century.htm.

White, R. (2003). *Prehistoric art: The symbolic journey of humankind.* New York: Abrams.

White, T., Asfaw, B., Degusta, D., Gilbert, H., Richards, G., & Suwa, G., Howell, F. C. (2003). Pleistocene *Homo sapiens* from the Middle Awash, Ethiopia. *Nature 423,* 742–747.

Whitehead, B. D. & Popenoe, D. (2004). *The state of our unions: The social health of marriage in America 2004.* Rutgers, NJ: Rutgers University National Marriage Project.

Whitehead, N. L., & Ferguson, R. B. (1993, November). Deceptive stereotypes about tribal warfare. *Chronicle of Higher Education,* A48.

Whiting, B. B. (Ed.) (1963). *Six cultures: Studies of child rearing.* New York: Wiley.

Whiting, J. W. M., & Child, I. L. (1953). *Child training and personality: A cross- cultural study.* New Haven, CT: Yale University Press.

Whiting, J. W. M., Sodergem, J. A., & Stigler, S. M. (1982). Winter temperature as a constraint to the migration of preindustrial peoples. *American Anthropologist 84,* 289.

Wiley, A. S. (2004). An ecology of high-altitude infancy: A biocultural perspective series. *Cambridge Studies in Medical Anthropology 12.*

Wilk, R. R. (1996). *Economics and cultures: An introduction to economic anthropology.* Boulder, CO: Westview Press.

Willey, G. R. (1966). *An introduction to American archaeology: Vol. 1. North America.* Englewood Cliffs, NJ: Prentice-Hall.

Willey, G. R. (1971). *An introduction to American archaeology, Vol. 2: South America.* Englewood Cliffs, NJ: Prentice-Hall.

Williams, F. (2005, January 9). Toxic breast milk? *New York Times Magazine.*

Williamson, R. K. (1995). The blessed curse: Spirituality and sexual difference as viewed by Euramerican and Native American cultures. *The College News 18* (4).

Willigan, J. V. (1986). *Applied anthropology.* South Hadley, MA: Bergin and Garvey.

Wills, C. (1994). The skin we're in. *Discover 15* (11), 79.

Wingert, P. (1965). *Primitive art: Its tradition and styles.* New York: World.

Winick, C. (Ed.). (1970). *Dictionary of anthropology.* Totowa, NJ: Littlefield, Adams.

Wirsing, R. L. (1985). The health of traditional societies and the effects of acculturation. *Current Anthropology 26* (3), 303–322.

Wittfogel, K. A. (1957). *Oriental despotism, a comparative study of total power.* New Haven, CT: Yale University Press.

Wolf, E. R. (1966). *Peasants.* Englewood Cliffs, NJ: Prentice-Hall.

Wolf, E. R. (1969). *Peasant wars of the twentieth century.* New York: Harper & Row.

Wolf, E. R. (1982). *Europe and the people without history.* Berkeley: University of California Press.

Wolf, E. R. (1999). *Envisioning power: Ideologies of dominance and crisis.* Berkeley: University of California Press.

Wolf, E. R., & Trager, G. L. (1971). Hortense Powdermaker 1900–1970. *American Anthropologist 73* (3), 784.

Wolf, M. (1985). *Revolution postponed: Women in contemporary China.* Stanford, CA: Stanford University Press.

Wolfson, H. (2000, January 22). Polygamists make the Christian connection. *Burlington Free Press,* 2c.

Wolpoff, M., & Caspari, R. (1997). *Race and human evolution: A fatal attraction.* New York: Simon & Schuster.

Woolfson, P. (1972). Language, thought, and culture. In V. P. Clark, P. A. Escholz, & A. F. Rosa (Eds.), *Language.* New York: St. Martin's Press.

World Almanac. (2004). New York: Press Publishing Co.

World Health Organization. http://www.who.int/about/definition/en.

World Meteorological Organization. (2003). Increasing heat waves and other health hazards. greenpeaceusa.org/climate/index.fpl/7096/article/907.html.

Worsley, P. (1957). *The trumpet shall sound: A study of "cargo" cults in Melanesia.* London: Macgibbon & Kee.

Worsley, P. (1959). Cargo cults. *Scientific American 200* (May), 117–128.

Wrangham, R., & Peterson, D. (1996). *Demonic males.* Boston: Houghton Mifflin.

Wulff, R. M., & Fiske, S. J. (1987). *Anthropological praxis: Translating knowledge into action.* Boulder, CO: Westview Press.

Yip, M. (2002). *Tone.* New York: Cambridge University Press.

Young, A. (1981). The creation of medical knowledge: Some problems in interpretation. *Social Science and Medicine 17,*1,205–1,211.

Young, W. (Ed.) (2000). Kimball award winner. *Anthropology News 41* (8), 29.

Zeder, M. A., & Hesse, B. (2000). The initial domestication of goats (*Capra hircus*) in the Zagros Mountains 10,000 years ago. *Science 287,* 2,254– 2,257.

Index